Introduction to the Old Testament

OTTO KAISER

Introduction to the Old Testament

A Presentation of its Results and Problems

Translated by John Sturdy

AUGSBURG PUBLISHING HOUSE
MINNEAPOLIS, MINNESOTA

United States Paperback Edition 1977
First United States Edition 1975

© in this translation Basil Blackwell, 1975

First published 1969 by Gütersloher Verlagshaus
Gerd Mohn, Gütersloh. Translated from the revised
second edition 1970, and incorporating further
revisions by the author to 1973

ISBN 0-8066-1575-3
Library of Congress Catalog Card No. 73-82220

Printed in the United States of America

Dedicated to Artur Weiser
on his 75th birthday
in gratitude

Contents

Preface

This book has grown out of University teaching, and is intended in the first instance for students, teachers and ministers in German-speaking countries, who require an introduction to the results and problems of Old Testament Introduction. This purpose comes out not only in the typography and presentation but also in the choice of books in bibliographies. The treatment is at greater length, and the bibliography fuller, when the author believes he can assume that the material treated will have been encountered by the reader either not at all or only marginally during his education. References to Introductions are indicated in the text by an asterisk placed after the name of the author (so e.g. Eissfeldt*). When Biblical references are being given however the asterisk indicates that the verse or section has in part been subject to secondary redaction. Material listed in the bibliography at the head of a section is generally referred to in the notes to that section only by the name of the author, or by this and *op. cit.* Variations from this will explain themselves from the context. The beginner is recommended when reading Section D to read § 23 and 24 after § 21, and then to return to § 22. I have thought it possible to dispense with yet another presentation of the history and problems of Old Testament textual tradition in view of the widespread use of Ernst Würthwein's handbook (*The Text of the Old Testament*, Oxford 1957). The bibliographies are intended to aid students in their own work on particular problems, not to set up a controlling standard. While for various reasons it was decided not to include an indication of those items which in my view should be read in any proper study of the Old Testament, the attentive reader will easily realize which of the books and articles referred to are of greater significance. Those who find the bibliographies given insufficient are reminded that fuller lists are found in almost all

commentaries, and that the *Zeitschriftenschau* (survey of period-
icals) of *ZAW*, and the surveys arranged by subjects of the
British Society for Old Testament Studies *Book List*, of the
Elenchus Bibliographicus of *Biblica*, and the *International Zeitschriftenschau für Bibelwissenschaft und Grenzgebiete* annually
give details of relevant new publications.

If the indications of recent years do not deceive me, Old
Testament scholarship, at least in Germany, is again in a period
of revolution, in which the great conceptions, worked out between the two world wars, of amphictyony and covenant, of law
and covenant, of covenant and prophecy, and perhaps also of
cult and prophecy, with their consequences which extend to
almost all areas of the subject, are being put in question. The
lively discussion of the names of literary types, and of the history
of the individual types, in many recent articles and books has
at least shown to what extent the problems connected with this
need further clarification. While Martin Noth, whose life as a
scholar, so suddenly ended, we thankfully commemorate, has
carried out the essential traditio-historical preparatory work
with an able examination of the literary-critical problems of
the Pentateuch, the tasks of a synoptic history of the law and of
investigation of the literary layers of the Deuteronomistic and
Chronicler's history works remain before us, in spite of much
preparatory work for which we can be grateful. So does the historical illumination of the growth of the books of the prophets.
It almost looks as if traditio-historical research, to which as a
whole we owe a deepened understanding of the growth of the
Old Testament and the growth of its religion, has absorbed
interest in this area of study too much, so that it needs to be
held in check by literary criticism. The attention of scholarship
on the prophets is thereby directed to the hitherto relatively
neglected area of the redaction-criticism of the individual books
and to a synoptic evaluation of them. The fact that there is no
agreement about even the names of the prophetic literary types
and their origins shows to what extent the religio-historical
picture of Israelite prophecy is disputed. It can be expected that
future work on the prophetic books will not only lead to a
solution of these problems, but also throw some light on perhaps
the most disputed area of current study, the history of the cult.
If in this book doubts are raised about the viability of both the

pillars which support the usual reconstruction of the history of the religion and literature of Israel and Judah, the connection of the reform of Josiah with Deuteronomy and the assumption of a reform of the Jewish community by Ezra, its author pays tribute gladly to the memory of a former holder of his chair, Gustav Hölscher, whose acuteness he has learned increasingly to value, but regards himself as indebted not to a name or to a *genius loci*, but to his writings.

In the present situation it is almost inevitable that an Introduction will bear a Janus face. Correctly understood however it has always been its task to work out what are the problems opening up for the present and subsequent generations, while looking back gratefully yet critically to the work of earlier scholars, and so to make these problems more conscious ones. To what extent the author has been able to carry out this aim it is not for him but for the reader to say. It will be clear to the initiated that he is more indebted to the giants of the discipline, especially to H. H. Rowley, Otto Eissfeldt, Artur Weiser, Leonhard Rost and Georg Fohrer, than the presentation in general shows. I express to them all the thanks I owe them when I dedicate this book to my revered Tübingen teacher Artur Weiser, with my warm respects, for his 75th birthday. In doing so I thank a scholar who was not only concerned for the cares and needs of a beginner, but who told his assistants when he first welcomed them not to feel bound by a single line of his in their own work, and in their future scholarly path to serve always the subject, not the person. It is in this spirit that German universities in the last more than one and a half centuries of their history have lived. May they recover it wherever it has been lost.

Preface to the English Edition

This translation incorporates alterations intended by the author for the third edition of this work in German, although these cannot be regarded as complete. Apart from the general incompleteness and deficiencies of this revision I greatly regret a number of serious gaps, particularly in the areas of Pentateuch study and of work on the redactional problems of the books of the prophets. Nevertheless I venture to hope that this edition too forms a not too inaccurate mirror of the present state of Old Testament studies. I must, I fear, ask for kindly understanding of the fact that in certain sections my own, no doubt partial, views have so pushed themselves to the fore that some readers may find disturbing my treatment of the problems of First Isaiah, and my evaluation of the prophetic tradition, which has grown more critical from edition to edition. I hope that the views more commonly held are still set out sufficiently clearly.

It remains a pleasant duty to thank those who have played their part in the production of this edition of the work, among them not least the publishers and the translator, who have generously met my wishes for alterations. If the book should prove more readable in translation than in the original, both I and the readers must be particularly grateful to the translator, the Revd. John Sturdy, of Gonville and Caius College, Cambridge. I would like to add a word of grateful commemoration of H. H. Rowley, which for me is much more than a mere gesture.

Cappel bei Marburg an der Lahn, April 1973   *Otto Kaiser*

Abbreviations

(a) Commentaries

A B–The Anchor Bible, Garden City, N.Y.
A T D–Das Alte Testament Deutsch, Göttingen
B A T–Die Botschaft des Alten Testaments, Stuttgart
 B C–Biblischer Commentar über das Alte Testament, Leipzig
 B K–Biblischer Kommentar, Altes Testament, Neukirchen
C A T–Commentaire de l'Ancien Testament, Neuchâtel
 C B–The Century Bible, London and Edinburgh
 E H–Exegetisches Handbuch zum Alten Testament, Münster
EtBi–Études Bibliques, Paris
H A T–Handbuch zum Alten Testament, Tübingen
 H K–Handkommentar zum Alten Testament, Göttingen
 H S–Die Heilige Schrift des Alten Testamentes, Bonn
H S A T–Die Heilige Schrift des Alten Testaments (ed. E. Kautzsch), ed. 4, Tübingen 1922–3
 I B–The Interpreter's Bible, New York and Nashville, Tennessee
 I C C–The International Critical Commentary, Edinburgh
K A T^1–Kommentar zum Alten Testament, Leipzig
K A T^2–Kommentar zum Alten Testament, Gütersloh
 KeH–Kurzgefasstes exegetisches Handbuch zum Alten Testament, Leipzig
K H C–Kurzer Hand-Commentar zum Alten Testament, Freiburg, Leipzig and Tübingen
O T L–The Old Testament Library, London
S A T–Die Schriften des Alten Testaments, Göttingen
 S C–Separate Commentaries (not in a series)
 Z B–Zürcher Bibelkommentare, Zurich and Stuttgart

(b) Periodicals and Series

AcOr(H)–Acta Orientalia, Copenhagen

AcOr(L)–Acta Orientalia, Leiden

AJSL–American Journal of Semitic Languages and Literatures

ALUOS–Annual of the Leeds University Oriental Society

AnBib–Analecta Biblica, Rome

ANET–Ancient Near Eastern Texts relating to the Old Testament, ed. J. B. Pritchard, Princeton, N.J., ed. 2 1955, ed. 3 1969

A N V A O–Avhandlingar utgitt av Det Norske Videnskaps-Akademi i Oslo, Oslo

AOT–Altorientalische Texte zum Alten Testament, ed. H. Gressmann, Berlin and Leipzig, ed. 2, 1926

ArOr–Archiv Orientální

A T A N T–Abhandlungen zur Theologie des Alten und Neuen Testaments, Zurich

A Th–Arbeiten zur Theologie, Stuttgart

BASOR–Bulletin of the American Schools of Oriental Research

B B B–Bonner Biblische Beiträge, Bonn

BFchTh–Beiträge zur Förderung christlicher Theologie, Gütersloh

BHHW–Biblisch-Historisches Handwörterbuch, ed. B. Reicke and L. Rost, Göttingen 1962–6

B H T–Beiträge zur Historischen Theologie, Tübingen

Bib–Biblica

BiLe–Bibel und Leben

B St–Biblische Studien, Neukirchen

B W A N T–Beiträge zur Wissenschaft vom Alten und Neuen Testament, Leipzig or Stuttgart

B W A T–Beiträge zur Wissenschaft vom Alten Testament, Leipzig

BZ–Biblische Zeitschrift

B Z A W–Beihefte zur Zeitschrift für die alttestamentliche Wissenschaft, Giessen, then Berlin

CBQ–Catholic Biblical Quarterly

C R B–Cahiers de la Revue Biblique, Paris

CTA–Corpus des tablettes en cunéiformes alphabétiques
découvertes à Ras Shamra—Ugarit de 1929 à
1939, par Andrée Herdner, Paris 1963
DJD–Discoveries in the Judaean Desert, Oxford 1955 ff.
DOTT–Documents from Old Testament Times, ed. D. W.
Thomas, London 1958
EvTh–Evangelische Theologie
FB–Fischer Bücherei, Frankfurt and Hamburg
FRLANT–Forschungen zur Religion und Literatur des Alten
und Neuen Testaments, Göttingen
FzB–Forschung zur Bibel, Würzburg
HO–Handbuch der Orientalistik, ed. B. Spuler, Leiden
and Cologne, 1952 ff.
HTR–Harvard Theological Review
HUCA–Hebrew Union College Annual
IEJ–Israel Exploration Journal
Interpr–Interpretation
JAOS–Journal of the American Oriental Society
JBL–Journal of Biblical Literature
JNES–Journal of Near Eastern Studies
JJS–Journal of Jewish Studies
JSS–Journal of Semitic Studies
Jud–Judaica
KS–Kleine Schriften
LUÅ–Lunds Universitets Årsskrift, Lund
MTS–Marburger Theologische Studien, Marburg
NZST–Neu Zeitschrift für Systematische Theologie und
Religionsphilosophie
OBL–Orientalia et Biblica Lovanensia, Louvain
OTL–Old Testament Library, London
OTMS–The Old Testament and Modern Study, ed. H. H.
Rowley, Oxford 1951
OTS–Oudtestamentische Studiën, Leiden
PEQ–Palestine Exploration Quarterly
RB–Revue Biblique
RGG–Die Religion in Geschichte und Gegenwart, Tübingen
RHPhR–Revue d'Histoire et de Philosophie Religieuses
RLA–Reallexicon der Assyriologie, ed. E. Ebeling and B.
Meissner, Berlin and Leipzig
RV–Religionsgeschichtliche Volksbücher, Tübingen

S A B–Sitzungsberichte der Deutschen (Preussischen) Akademie der Wissenschafte zu Berlin, Berlin

S A L–Sitzungsberichte der Sächsischen Akademie der Wissenschaften zu Leipzig, Leipzig

S A N T–Studien zum Alten und Neuen Testament, Munich

S B S–Stuttgarter Bibelstudien, Stuttgart

S B T Studies in Biblical Theology, London

SEÅ–Svensk Exegetisk Årsbok

S G–Sammlung Göschen

S G V–Sammlung gemeinverständlicher Vorträge und Schriften aus dem Gebiet der Theologie und Religionsgeschichte, Tübingen

S K H V L–Skrifter utgivna av kungliga Humanistiska Vetenskapssamfundet i Lund, Lund

S N V A O–Skrifter utgitt av Det Norske Videnskaps-Akademi i Oslo, Oslo

S S N–Studia Semitica Neerlandica, Assen

S V T–Supplements to Vetus Testamentum, Leiden

TDNT–Theological Dictionary of the New Testament, ed. G. Kittel and G. Friedrich, Grand Rapids, Michigan 1964 ff.

ThA–Theologische Arbeiten, Berlin

ThB–Theologische Bücherei, Munich

ThEx–Theologische Existenz heute, Munich

ThQ–Tübinger Theologische Quartalschrift

ThR–Theologische Rundschau

ThStKr–Theologische Studien und Kritiken, Hamburg, Gotha, Leipzig, Berlin

ThV–Theologia Viatorum. Jahrbuch der Kirchlichen Hochschule Berlin

ThZ–Theologische Zeitschrift

TLZ–Theologische Literaturzeitung

T O A–Theologische und Orientalistische Arbeiten, Herzberg

U U Å–Uppsala Universitets Årsskrift, Uppsala

VT–Vetus Testamentum

WA *DB*–Luther, M. *Werke*, Kritische Gesamtausgabe, *Die Deutsche Bibel*, Weimar 1906 ff.

WA *TR*–Luther, M. *Werke*, Kritische Gesamtausgabe, *Tischreden*, Weimar 1912 ff.

WMANT–Wissenschaftliche Monographien zum Alten und
Neuen Testament, Neukirchen

*WuD–Wort und Dienst, Jahrbuch der Theologischen Schule
Bethel*

WZ–Wissenschaftliche Zeitschrift

WZKM–Wiener Zeitschrift für die Kunde des Morgenlandes

*ZÄS–Zeitschrift für Ägyptische Sprache und Altertum-
skunde*

ZAW–Zeitschrift für die alttestamentliche Wissenschaft

*ZDMG–Zeitschrift der Deutschen Morgenländischen Gesell-
schaft*

ZDPV–Zeitschrift des Deutschen Palästine-Vereins

ZMH–Zeitschrift des Museums Hildesheim

ZTK–Zeitschrift für Theologie und Kirche

(c) Other abbreviations

ET–English translation

LXX–Septuagint

MT–Massoretic text (Hebrew)

NF–Neue Folge (new series)

A. Introduction

§ 1 The Task, History and Method of Old Testament Introduction

H. Gunkel, 'Die Grundprobleme der israelitischen Literaturgeschichte', *Reden und Aufsätze*, Göttingen 1913, pp. 29 ff.; J. Hempel, *Die althebräische Literatur und ihr hellenistisch-jüdisches Nachleben*, Potsdam 1930 (Berlin 1968²); W. Baumgartner, 'Alttestamentliche Einleitung und Literaturgeschichte', *ThR* NF 8 (1936), pp. 179 ff.; O. Eissfeldt, *The Old Testament. An Introduction*, Oxford 1965, pp. 1 ff.; K. Koch, *The Growth of the Biblical Tradition*, London 1969, pp. 102 ff.

1. The Task. The difficulty of the present-day reader of the Bible is of one of two kinds. He may believe that he knows exactly how and in what circumstances God revealed himself in the history of Israel and in the story of Jesus, because a book inspired by God gives him information about this which is free of contradiction and without any gaps. In this case he is all too often compelled, in the interests of his preconceived view, to ignore individual details, and if tensions and contradictions are pointed out to him, to seek with varying degrees of good conscience subterfuges which allow him to maintain this view. Or he may see in this book only an involved collection of documents of an old faith, whose childishness he believes, as a man of an age of enlightenment, he is above, without raising the question, or perhaps even suspecting, how deeply our western modes of thought have been influenced by this book, and how much greater this influence was up to the first quarter of this century than it is now. The apparent strangeness and remoteness prevent him from seeing that the claim made here to testify to God could have unsuspected strength and life even today. Both types of difficulty in our view result from the fact that we live in an age which thinks historically, and understands the course of history in its temporal and factual connections. Once we have grown out of childhood, we cannot now find honest access to a book which comes from earlier centuries, indeed millennia, which did not share these (to us obvious) presuppositions of thought, unless we are adequately informed about its historical origin and the world from which it comes. For this reason a knowledge of the formation of the Bible is an unavoidable prerequisite to our understanding of it. This is true for every reader of the Bible, in so far as historical and technical knowledge have become common property through the spread of education and of the means of mass communication, but is especially so for one who wishes to make intelligible to other men the claim of the Bible to bear witness to the word of God.

To hear and understand the witness of the Biblical books correctly, it is necessary to know at what times and in what circumstances they came into existence. This involves a knowledge of the history, religion and theology of Israel and of Judaism, as well as of the world from which they grew. It might be supposed that an 'Introduction to the Old Testament' would accordingly deal with everything needed for its full understanding. In the course of the development of scholarship this title has in fact come to cover a concentration on the treatment of the literary problems, of genres (or types) of literature, of the composition and formation of the individual books, and of the transmission of the text and origin of the canon. There are obvious practical reasons for this, in that it would be absurd to attempt to deal with all these subjects either in a single lecture, or in a single book in several volumes. Alongside Introductions to the Old Testament[1] there are works on the Hebrew and Aramaic languages[2], on the world of the Old Testament[3], biblical archae-

1. The basic reference work is O. Eissfeldt, *The Old Testament: an Introduction*, Oxford 1965; G. Fohrer, *Introduction to the Old Testament*, Nashville 1968, London 1970, and A. Weiser, *Introduction to the Old Testament*, London 1961, particularly deserve mention as textbooks for students.

2. Cf. e.g. R. Meyer, *Hebräische Grammatik*, Berlin I 1966[3], II 1969[3] and III 1972[3].

3. Cf. M. Noth, *The Old Testament World*, London 1966, and K.-H. Bernhardt, *Die Umwelt des Alten Testaments* I, Berlin and Gütersloh 1967.

ology[4] and geography[5], the history[6], religion and theology of Israel[7], the subsequent history of the Old Testament in the Christian Church[7a], and finally hermeneutics[8] as independent subjects. All of these disciplines depend to a greater or less extent upon the detailed exposition of individual verses, sections and books of the Old Testament, which in contemporary scholarly work, and no doubt also in future work, they advance almost as much as they are advanced by it. They create by reference to the results of exegesis a framework for the understanding of the individual passages. And they change to the extent that this understanding alters, and, it may be hoped, grows as well as alters.

2. *The History of Introduction.* Since the particular aims and methods of Old Testament Introduction are a result of its history, a brief survey of this history is appropriate. For clarity it is here divided into three sections, which correspond to its main periods. These are the pre-critical period of the early

4. W. F. Albright, *The Archaeology of Palestine*, Harmondsworth 1949; K. M. Kenyon, *Archaeology in the Holy Land*, London 1970[3]; D. W. Thomas (ed.), *Archaeology and Old Testament Study*, Oxford 1967; cf. also H. J. Franken and C. A. Franken-Battershill, *A Primer of Old Testament Archaeology*, Leiden 1963.

5. Apart from the standard works of Abel and Simons, D. Baly, *Geographical Companion to the Bible*, London 1963, and Y. Aharoni, *The Land of the Bible. A Historical Geography*, London 1967, are especially suitable for students; cf. also E. Orni and E. Efrat, *Geography of Israel*, Jerusalem 1966[2].

6. M. Noth, *History of Israel*, London 1960[2]; J. Bright, *A History of Israel*, London 1972[2]; M. Metzger, *Grundriss der Geschichte Israels*, Neukirchen 1967[2].

7. W. Eichrodt, *Theology of the Old Testament*, London I 1961, II 1967; G. von Rad, *Old Testament Theology*, Edinburgh I 1962, II 1965; L. Köhler, *Old Testament Theology*, London 1957; T. C. Vriezen, *An Outline of Old Testament Theology*, Oxford 1970[2]; G. Fohrer, *History of Israelite Religion*, Nashville 1972, London 1973.

7a. L. Diestel, *Geschichte des Alten Testaments in der christlichen Kirche*, Jena 1869; cf. also H. Donner, 'Das Problem des Alten Testaments in der christlichen Kirche. Überlegungen zu Begriff und Geschichte der alttestamentlichen Einleitung', in *Beiträge zur Theorie des neuzeitlichen Christentums*, Festschrift W. Trillhaas, Berlin 1968, pp. 37 ff.

8. Cf. e.g. C. Westermann (ed.), *Essays on Old Testament Interpretation*, London 1963, and J. Barr, *Old and New in Interpretation*, London 1965.

Church and of the Middle Ages, the philological period, lasting from the humanistic to the baroque period, and the critical period, beginning with the Age of the Enlightenment.

(a) *The Pre-Critical Period.* As long as the Church held to the belief that revelation was a firmly delimited, eternally valid event which took place in the inspiration of a book, it could not direct its attention primarily towards clarifying the history of revelation, but only towards demonstrating its freedom from contradiction, perspicuity, and intelligibility to the ordinary man. The nearest approaches to modern Old Testament Introduction were on the one hand explanations of unfamiliar objects and concepts from the past, and on the other hand demonstrations of the age and authenticity of the documents of revelation. For these latter reasons information was collected about the life of the Biblical authors as assigned by tradition to the individual books. Lastly the question had to be dealt with whether it was the Hebrew text or the Greek text or indeed that of a translation dependent on one of these that should be regarded as authoritative for the Church. These are in broad outline the features which go to form the first, pre-critical, stage of Old Testament Introduction, which dominated the period of the early and mediaeval church, but in its basic tendencies also remained dominant into the period of post-Reformation orthodoxy. The first work that used the title 'Introduction' in relation to the books of the Bible was written in A.D. 425 by a monk closely connected with the Antiochene tradition, Adrianus. It was called *eisagōgē eis tās theiās graphās*, *Introduction to the Divine Scriptures*, and in a modern reprint fills about thirty pages[9]. In content it is an attempt to introduce the pupil to the peculiarities of Hebrew style. It may be pointed out that the interest appearing here in the Hebrew Bible as such remained very much the exception in the early Church, as also in the mediaeval Church. In spite of the prodigious work of Origen in his Hexapla[10], and the no less great achievement of Jerome in the Vulgate[11], both of which go back to the Hebrew text, the view expressed by

9. Ed., transl. and comm. by F. Goessling, Berlin 1887.
10. Cf. E. Würthwein, *The Text of the Old Testament*, Oxford 1957, pp. 39 ff.
11. Cf. Würthwein, pp. 64 ff.

Augustine in *De civitate dei* XVIII, 43 of the relationship of the Hebrew and Greek Bible remained the accepted view: the first inspiration, which gave rise to the Hebrew text, was valid for the men of that age, but the second, which gave rise to the Greek translation, was valid for the Church, to which it bears witness of Christ. While Jerome could declare that 'ignoratio scripturarum ignoratio Christi est'[12], this meant something quite different from what it means for us today in scholarly work on the Bible. In his introductions to the Latin Bible, the Vulgate, he did collect a mass of traditional material about the origin of the individual Biblical books and their authors, but remarked in respect of the obvious confusion in the chronology of the Old Testament that to clarify this confusion was not a proper object of scholarly work, but was a task for the idle[13]. In the Middle Ages this position remained basically unaltered. It must be said, contrary to a widespread misapprehension, that at no time was the Bible so widely known as in the greatest days of this period[14]. It was believed that the inspired New Testament interpretation of Old Testament passages provided the key to the literal sense of the Old Testament (indeed the spirit which itself provided the exposition could not err), and at the same time that the many obscurities of the Old Testament could be solved by means of the hermeneutical principle of the fourfold sense of scripture[15], which distinguished as well as the literal sense an allegorical, a moral and an anagogic sense[16]. Thus it was not thought necessary to be concerned with what is in our view the

12. Migne, Patrologia Latina 24, p. 18.

13. Epist. 72, 5, in L. Diestel, op. cit., p. 98, n. 18.

14. Cf. B. Smalley, *The Study of the Bible in the Middle Ages*, Oxford 1952².

15. Cf. E. von Dobschütz, 'Vom vierfachen Schriftsinn', in *Harnack-Ehrung*, Leipzig 1921, pp. 1 ff., and G. Ebeling, *Evangelische Evangelienauslegung*, Munich 1942 (reprinted Darmstadt 1962), pp. 127 ff.

16. As an example of what was understood by the term 'literal sense' a quotation may be given from the *Glossa ordinaria* ascribed to Walafrid Strabo as given in Diestel, op. cit., p. 161, on Exod. 6.20: 'Amram interpretatur pater excelsus, qui significat Christum, Jochabed Dei gratia, quae significat Ecclesiam: ex Christo et Ecclesia nascitur Moses, id est lex spiritualis, et Aaron, scilicet verum sacerdotium.' ('Amram is translater by 'exalted father', which signifies Christ, Jochebed by 'grace of God', which signifies the Church: of Christ and the Church are born Moses, that is the spiritual law, and Aaron, that is the true priesthood.')

original historical sense of the Old Testament books, and the related questions of their origin. It was the contact between Christianity and Judaism in the fourteenth century which first provided the impetus for such work, an example of which is to be found in the *Postillae perpetuae* of Nicholas of Lyra. The Jewish exegesis of Ibn Ezra (d. 1167) and of Solomon Yiṣḥaqi (Rashi, d. 1170) was influential in this, and led to a stronger emphasis on the literal sense in the later Middle Ages. In spite of this apparently even at this date 'the Sentences of Lombard . . . were commented on a great deal more frequently than the Bible'[17].

(b) *The Philological Period.* Humanism and the Reformation created the freer atmosphere in which philological work proper could thrive. Johannes Reuchlin of Pforzheim published in 1506 his *Rudimenta linguae Hebraicae*, the first Hebrew grammar of the modern period. In his exposition of the seven penitential psalms he was the first exegete to start from a grammatical explanation of the forms of the words. Through Melanchthon Reuchlin influenced Luther and the whole Wittenberg circle. For Luther scripture moved to the central position, and the centre of scripture was the living Christ attested by it but not held prisoner in it; and as a result he achieved a freedom in historical evaluation which was remarkable for his period, a freedom attested particularly by his introductions to the individual books in his translation of the Bible. In Bornkamm's view he always discussed the problems of authenticity of particular books of the Bible with complete impartiality, and was prepared to deny authenticity whenever there seemed insufficient grounds to maintain it[18]. On the other hand it was the same man who declared that he would not believe the story of the prophet

17. Diestel, op. cit., p. 201.
18. *Luther and the Old Testament*, Philadelphia 1969, p. 194. On Luther's understanding of the Bible cf. especially Ebeling, op. cit.; also G. Krause, *Studien zu Luthers Auslegung der Kleinen Propheten*, BHT 33, Tübingen 1962. On Melanchthon cf. H. Sick, *Melanchthon als Ausleger des Alten Testaments*, Beiträge zur Geschichte der biblischen Hermeneutik 2, Tübingen 1959. On Calvin cf. H. H. Wolf, *Die Einheit des Bundes. Das Verhältnis von Altem und Neuem Testament bei Calvin*, Beiträge zur Geschichte und Lehre der Reformierten Kirche 10, Neukirchen 1958.

Jonah in the belly of the whale if it did not stand in scripture. What C. F. Meyer makes Ulrich von Hutten say about Luther:

> His spirit is the battlefield of two ages—
> I am not surprised that he sees devils,

is true also *mutatis mutandis* of his attitude to scripture: here too alongside a Reformation freedom we find a mediaeval constraint, for which the Bible was a metaphysical entity. His disciples and still more his later followers inherited from him not his freedom but his constraint. Nevertheless the significance of the Reformation for the theological and consequently also critical concentration on scripture should not be underestimated. Apart from the introductions by Luther already mentioned, we can recognize in Carlstadt's *De canonicis scripturis* at least the beginnings of a modern science of Old Testament introduction[19].

It is hardly too much to say that the revived predominance of dogmatic interests in the period of intensified orthodoxy, the seventeenth century, was not favourable to critical work in the strict sense. The work of this period on the body of scripture is dominated by a gentle philology devoted to the collection of material, the results of which were published in books with titles such as *Critica sacra, Isagoge,* or in Latin, *Introductio.* From a mass of titles we may single out the *Critica sacra* of Ludovicus Cappellus (1650), as a warning against looking down upon the work of this period. Here principles of textual criticism are developed which still remain valid today. It may indeed be claimed that later critical scholarship could not have advanced so quickly without the careful work of this century on the biblical text. A work such as the Walton Polyglot is unsurpassed even today[20].

The intensification of the Reformation principle of the centrality of scripture led to a rigorous version of the dogma of inspiration[21], and inevitably provoked the polemics of Roman

19. For its further development, cf. the accounts of E. G. Kraeling, *The Old Testament since the Reformation*, London 1955, and H.-J. Kraus, *Geschichte der historisch-kritischen Erforschung des Alten Testaments von der Reformation bis zur Gegenwart*, Neukirchen 1969[2].
20. *S.S. Biblia Polyglotta* ed. Brianus Waltonus I–VI, London 1657, reprinted as Brian Walton, *Biblia Sacra Polygotta* I–VI, Graz 1963–65.
21. Cf. e.g. what Flacius Illyricus says in his *Clavis scripturae* (1567)

Catholic theologians. These made use of the new philological
knowledge to refute the dogma. This in turn had the unintended
consequence that the more sceptical spirits in the ranks of the
Catholic theologians felt encouraged to publish their more
radical views under the pretext of the refutation of Protestant
heresy. This was done by the priest Richard Simon, in his
Histoire critique du Vieux Testament, printed in 1678, but confis-
cated before publication, a work which was of influence through
a reprint in the Netherlands, an English translation of 1682, and a
German edition of 1776 by Semler[22].

Strong attacks came in the first place not from the theologians
but from the philosophers. The view put forward by Simon, and
condemned by the Church, that the critic must concern himself
with nothing other than the literal sense of scripture, had been
anticipated thirty years before by the English philosopher
Thomas Hobbes in his *Leviathan*, III, 33. His principle that
views on the date of origin of the biblical books must be derived
from the evidence of the books themselves alone, and not
from tradition, has subsequently become the accepted view of
all commentators. We must also mention the great Jewish
philosopher Spinoza, who ably applied these newly developed
principles in his *Tractatus theologico-politicus* (1670), demonstrating the impossibility of Mosaic authorship of the Pentateuch
by a whole series of arguments which remain valid to this day.
In view of the struggles between confessions each making a
claim to unique possession of the saving truth, it was probably
inevitable that just the more open and conscientious minds
should become increasingly emancipated from the traditional
faith of the Church, and over against the claim of the state to
determine the religious allegiance of its citizens, should raise
the demand for tolerance, and over against church decisions
on doctrine should claim the competence of reason in the area
of religion too.

---

as given in E. Hirsch, *Hilfsbuch zum Studium der Dogmatik*, Berlin 1964[4],
p. 314: 'If the churches allow the devil to state this hypothesis [of the
subsequent addition of the vowel signs] will not the whole of scripture
become completely uncertain for us?'

22. Cf. on this R. Deville, 'Richard Simon, critique catholique du
pentateuque', *Nouvelle Revue Theologique* 73 (1951), pp. 723 ff. and
Kraus, op. cit., pp. 65 ff.

(c) *The Critical Period.* Finally even men from a pietistic background were caught by the spirit of the enlightenment in the eighteenth century. In this context we must mention first Johann Salomo Semler, whose *Abhandlung von freier Untersuchung des Canon* appeared in four volumes in 1771–1775[23]. Semler's epoch-making achievement consisted in demonstrating the historical conditioning of every form of canon, and the irrelevance of the canonicity of a book in answering the question of its truth. What Lessing maintained against Goeze, the Chief Pastor in Hamburg: 'The scriptural traditions must be explained from their own internal truth, and no scriptural traditions can give to it any internal truth if it have none', is here set out more fully, indeed sometimes rather longwindedly[24]. Semler was the real founder of historically oriented theology. Among other works he published one entitled in Latin *Institutio ad doctrinam christianam liberaliter discendam*, which was published in 1777 in German as *Versuch einer freiern theologischen Lehrart* (an attempt at a freer form of teaching in theology). Thereby he gave generations of theologians a catch-phrase, either for proud self-designation or for polemical attack, that of 'liberal theology'.

The time had come to move beyond a *Critica sacra, Isagoge* or *Introductio* to the modern critical introduction. In 1750 Johann David Michaelis of Göttingen had for the first time used the Latin *Introductio* in its German form in a book title, *Einleitung in die göttlichen Schriften des Neuen Bundes* (ET: *Introductory Lectures to the Sacred Books of the New Testament*, London 1761). This makes him godfather, so to speak, to the first Old Testament work which appeared under such a title, and which also initiated the modern study of introduction, Johann Gottfried Eichhorn's *Einleitung in das Alte Testament*,

---

23. Cf. the reprint of extracts in the series Texte zur Kirchen- und Theologiegeschichte, Heft 5, Gütersloh 1967; also G. Hornig, *Die Anfänge der historisch-kritischen Theologie. Johann Salomo Semlers Schriftverständnis und seine Stellung zu Luther*, Göttingen 1961 and H. Donner, 'Gesichtspunkte zur Auflösung des klassischen Kanonbegriffes bei Johann Salomo Semler', in *Fides et communicatio*, Festschrift M. Doerne, ed. D. Rössler, Göttingen 1970, pp. 56 ff.

24. 'Axiomata, wenn es deren in dergleichen Dingen gibt, wider den Herrn Pastor Goeze, in Hamburg', chap. 10, in *Gesammelte Werke*, ed. P. Rilla, VIII, Berlin 1956, p. 189; ET in M. M. Bernard, *Cambridge Free Thought and Letters on Bibliolatry*, London 1862, p. 47.

which appeared in 1780–1783 in three volumes, and later in five volumes[25]. The study of introduction is now a non-religious activity. Some sentences from the preface to the second edition of 1787 may serve to indicate the spirit of the work: 'The purely theological use which is usually made of the books of the Old Testament has up till now hindered the evaluation of these works of remote antiquity according to their deserts more than is usually realized. Only religious ideas have been sought in them, and the rest of their contents ignored; they have been read without any feeling for the past and its language, in much the same way as a work of recent date; and depending on men's different intellectual powers, extremely diverse results have come from this'[26].

This was the period in which Johann Gottfried Herder could discover *The Spirit of Hebrew Poetry* (Burlington, 1833: ET of *Der Geist der Ebräischen Poesie*, 1782). It was the period in which the movement towards a historical consciousness irresistibly, and so far as can be seen also irreversibly, broke new ground with the realization that every human utterance is linked to its situation, and is to be understood primarily from its situation. Already in Eichhorn we find the division of the material into a general and a special part, which is to become normative for the discipline. In the general introduction the transmission of the text and the origin of the canon are dealt with, and in the special introduction the composition and origin of the individual books.

It would take too long here to trace the history of the science of Introduction through the last two hundred years in detail. Since its various periods with their different methods can be seen reflected in the history of Pentateuchal scholarship, it is sufficient to refer to the outline of this in § 4, and to remark here that a first, literary-critical period was followed at the beginning of the century by a form-critical stage, and since the twenties by a traditio-historical stage in supplementation of it.

3. *The method.* Since work on form-criticism has produced a

25. On Eichhorn cf. E. Sehmsdorf, *Die Prophetenauslegung bei J. G. Eichhorn*, Göttingen 1971, and O. Kaiser, 'Eichhorn und Kant', in *Das Ferne und nahe Wort*, Festschrift L. Rost, BZAW 105, 1967, pp. 114 ff.
26. Quoted from the reprint at Reutlingen in 1790, p. V (translated).

programme for a history of the literature of Israel, which must be to some degree a rival of the Introduction, we must spend a moment on this question, which is not unimportant for our own presentation of the subject. Form-criticism starts from the fact that in normal human life specific simple forms of speech are bound to develop. In specific situations man makes use of specific forms of linguistic behaviour. At the beginning of a form-critical or 'genre-critical' analysis of a passage the question must consequently be raised who is speaking to whom, in what situation, and making use of what form. The starting point for scholarly work is then the undoubtedly correct assumption that at the beginning of the development there are simple, pure forms, which in the course of history and of the development into literature proper may be increasingly confused with one another. In the case of Israel it can be taken that we can demonstrate the existence on the one hand of simple forms which go back into its prehistory outside its later home in Palestine, and on the other hand of developed literary forms and mixed categories, which it has partly taken over from the old inhabitants of the land, partly taken over from the surrounding world, and partly no doubt also formed itself. Since in the pre-Greek and non-Greek world there is no real interest in the creative individual as such, works cannot as in modern literary scholarship, or can to a very much lesser extent, be explained from the personality and the life history of the author. They are generally anonymous or pseudonymous. And even when the name and life of the author are known to us, his individual personality cannot have an effect on what he writes in the way we know in modern times. What is written remains, to an extent that astonishes us, dependent on traditional literary and pre-literary forms. Accordingly a history of the literature of Israel can only properly be thought of as a history of its literary types, from their first pre-literary stage to their final elaboration and final literary fixation. Gunkel, who sketched out such a programme of work, himself also produced a first attempt at achieving it[27].

27. 'Die israelitische Literatur', in *Kultur der Gegenwart* I, 7, Leipzig 1925, reprinted separately Darmstadt 1963. A detailed evaluation of Gunkel has been published in W. Klatt, *Hermann Gunkel. Zu seiner Theologie der Religionsgeschichte und zur Entstehung der formgeschichtlichen Methode*, FRLANT 100, 1969.

Worthwhile though the goal here outlined is, there still remain some points in favour of the traditional analytical Introduction in the present state of scholarship. First it is obvious that a synthetic literary history stands upon the shoulders of an analytical introduction. Without this preliminary work it would soon degenerate into fiction. This preliminary work however, even in respect of the source analysis of the Pentateuch, is not as finally completed as it seemed to be in the first decades of this century. Moreover, an analytical introduction forms at the same time an indispensable source of knowledge for the history and religion of Israel. It is this that makes it necessary to give even the beginner the essentials of an analytical introduction. On the other hand an analysis which does not at the same time lead to a synthesis remains unsatisfying. For in the end the task of the introduction is not only source-criticism, but also to make the development of the Old Testament as a whole intelligible. It cannot attain this object without examining the process of tradition, and this means that it must itself take up the programme outlined by Gunkel. It should finally be said that it is precisely the present stage of development of scholarship, in which several results of form-criticism which appeared to be assured have proved to be disputable, which makes it a hazardous undertaking to present a history of the literature of Israel in the form outlined above.

From what has been said, it follows that our own presentation will take a middle course between the two extremes. It has first the task of providing basic knowledge about the results and problems of an analytical introduction, the general and special parts of which are expanded by material about form-critical, tradition-historical and redaction-critical scholarship. Secondly, it has the task of presenting some kind of coherent picture of the origin of the Old Testament and of the development of its literary forms. It attempts to achieve these aims by dividing the material up in a way that roughly corresponds to the three divisions of the Hebrew canon, dealing first with the historical narratives of Israel, then with the prophetic tradition and finally with the songs and wisdom material. It is intended consistently to omit points about the development of literary genres in a narrow sense in order not to make the whole work too overloaded. It is hoped to mention historical and theological points to the extent to which the material requires them[28].

A final reference to the theological significance of the discipline may be appropriate for the reader who approaches the Old Testament as a future minister, preacher or teacher of religious knowledge. It cannot be disputed that the Introduction to the Old Testament is an auxiliary discipline of theology. It could be said that in this activity we find ourselves working in the basement of theology. But just as a house needs its foundations and basement rooms, so theology needs historical foundations and accordingly the introduction to both Testaments. We have already said that there can be for us no scholarly access to the Bible without a knowledge of the circumstances of its formation. We are convinced that without this knowledge there will be no understanding of scripture and of its witness. It is just in this sense that Introduction, together with the other historical disciplines, prepares for an understanding of the scriptures which will lead to the word of God to which it bears witness being heard in our time. In that Introduction and exegesis constantly point to the historical limitation of scripture, they demand of theology as a whole that it should decide clearly how far the Bible is the word of God, or as I would prefer to put it, attests the word of God, although it is a book which has been formed in a checkable historical process. The reader who does not simply accept at a distance the results and problems of the science of Introduction, but at the same time asks what they mean for his faith, will no doubt discover that they constantly direct him to think about faith and history, about revelation and history, about revelation and the word of God, and about history and the word of God.

28. Cf. R. Rendtorff, 'Hermeneutik des Alten Testaments als Frage nach der Geschichte', *ZTK* 57 (1960), pp. 27 ff.

B. Underlying Factors

§ 2   Promised Land and Elect Nation

M. Noth, *The Old Testament World*, London 1966, pp. 2 ff.; D. Baly, *Geographical Companion to the Bible*, London 1963, pp. 13 ff.; Y. Aharoni, *The Land of the Bible*, London 1967, pp. 3 ff.; M. Noth, *History of Israel*, London 1960², pp. 53 ff.; W. Eichrodt, 'Bund und Gesetz', in *Gottes Wort und Gottes Land*, Festschrift H. W. Hertzberg, Göttingen 1965, pp. 30 ff.; G. Fohrer, ' "Amphiktyonie" und "Bund"?', *TLZ* 91 (1966), cols. 801 ff., 893 ff., and in *Studien zur alttestamentlichen Theologie und Geschichte*, BZAW 115, 1960, pp. 84 ff.; R. Smend, 'Zur Frage der altisraelitischen Amphiktyonie', *EvTh* 31 (1971), pp. 623 ff.

1. The Land. It is one of the commonplaces of modern historical study that the history and so also the literary history of a nation are decisively influenced by the geographical situation of its land. It does however need to be emphasized that this generalization is especially true of the course of Israelite history; for it applies both to the general position of Palestine as a part of the land-bridge between Asia and Africa, between Mesopotamia or Asia Minor and Egypt, and to its more specific position as a narrow strip of cultivated land between wilderness and sea. Its general position is also decisive for the fortunes of its inhabitants, since from very early times the cultural influences of Mesopotamia and Asia Minor, on the one hand, and of Egypt on the other, have met, and the claims of their empires to dominance have overlapped there. The position between sea and wilderness, together with the geologically developed form of the surface, determines the change in climate between day and night, rainy and dry season, but leads also to constant invasions of peoples from the wildernesses of flint stones and stunted bushes to the east and south.

An extremely sharply divided landscape is unfavourable to the formation of large kingdoms throughout the Syrian region, the southern part of which Palestine forms. The deep rift-valley which divides the land, running to the north between Lebanon and Antilebanon, to the south between Palestine and Transjordan, and continuing beyond the Dead Sea as the Araba and the Gulf of Akaba, is responsible for a sharp division of the land into an eastern and a western part. The Yarmuk and the Jabbok flow from the east into the Jordan as permanent streams, and the Arnon and Zered into the Dead Sea. From the west there is only the Wadi Galud to flow throughout the year into the Jordan. Finally the Yarkon is the only river that flows all the year into the Mediterranean, which offers rare natural harbours at Acco, Dor, Jaffa and Ashkelon. The coast is lined with dunes in the south as far north as Jaffa. Behind it there is a plain, which extends to the hill-country of the Shephelah. Then the Judaean hill-country rises to reach its highest point near Hebron at 1,090 metres. It merges with a hardly noticeable transition into the Samarian hill-country to the north. The highest point of this is to the north of Jerusalem, where it reaches about 1,000 metres. The plains of Shechem and Samaria provide it with some topographical differentiation. Towards the coast the promontory of Carmel juts out in the north, and on the far side of it the coastal plain of Acco, then, partly limited by the hills of Gilboa, the plain of Jezreel, and finally the plain of Beth-Shean make a clear incision in it. On the far side of the plains rise the low hills of southern Galilee, and then to the north of Lake Gennesaret the hills of northern Galilee, which reach 1,200 metres in height. To the north Lebanon, Hermon and Antilebanon provide natural barriers, but to the south and east where there are no natural frontiers the land lies open to enemy attack. The Transjordan, divided from the deeply carved valley of the Jordan by a range of mountains, is given its topographical differentiation by the river systems of the Yarmuk, Jabbok, Arnon and Zered. Between them lie fertile plateaux, one of which, between Yarmuk and Jabbok, still has a thin oak wood on it. To the north and north-east of the Yarmuk the cultivated land extends as far as the Jebel Druze, which at over 1,800 metres has the greatest elevation of the whole land. While this strip of land was part of the disputed area between the Israelites and

Aramaeans, the Ammonites were settled to the north of the Arnon, the Moabites between the Arnon and Zered, and the Edomites to the south of the Zered. The coastal plain was mostly settled by the Philistines and the Phoenicians, while the south, the Negeb, was occupied by nomadic tribes such as the Midianites and the Amalekites.

2. *The climate*. The early rains in the autumn, the main winter rains and the late rains of the late spring which come from the Mediterranean are intercepted in the south by the ridge of the Judaean hill-country, in the shadow of which the wilderness of Judah extends. The Samarian hill-country thanks to its lesser height enjoys the blessing of the rains across its whole breadth, while the Transjordan receives them only in its western parts, gradually changing towards the east into steppe and wilderness. The rains, unlike those of central Europe, are not soft persistent rains, but severe torrential downpours, rapidly followed by a blue sky. The development of the chalky hill-country into *Karst*, which has been going on progressively since prehistoric times, but especially since the end of the Byzantine period, hinders any real storage of the precipitation. The winter rainy period is followed by the summer dry period. Hot land winds can make the flowers fade in hours in the spring (cf. Isa. 40.7), and when they return in the autumn can make the temperature rise to 40 degrees centigrade even in Jerusalem, which is placed at a height. The alternation between warm land winds by day and cool sea winds by night brings with it in the summer high day temperatures and relatively cool evening and night temperatures. In the winter however the winds coming from the sea provide a measure of warmth in comparison with the east wind.

3. *Distances*. This land then is a land of contrasts, of hill-country and extremely deep incised valleys, of fertile plains and wildernesses, of high day temperatures and low night temperatures, of dry and rainy seasons. Those who do not know the Holy Land, the scene of the Biblical story, from personal inspection, are almost always inclined to form an exaggerated picture of its relative size because of the important role which it was called to play in the history of mankind. The reality is much more modest: the distance from furthest north to furthest south,

from Dan to Beersheba, is roughly 240 km. as the crow flies, and by road barely 320 km. From Jerusalem to Shechem is 67 km., to Hebron 37 km. and to Jaffa 75 km. by road. These are distances such as we can find in one English county. At the same time the great differences in height give the land a bizarre and sometimes sinister character: a man journeying from Jerusalem (ca. 790 m.) through the Jordan valley (Allenby Bridge, -373 m.; waterlevel of the Dead Sea, -390 m.) to Amman, the old Rabbath Ammon, will in vertical terms have traversed as much as 2,000 m. And yet what a land it is for one who looks at it with the eyes of nomads or seminomads seeking pastures. He does not think of the steppe and wilderness in the shadow cast by the mountains, but sees the fertile plains, the light woods, the ever-flowing springs and streams, the olives and fig-trees and the vines which climb beneath them, and the rich possibilities of pasture for his flocks starving outside in the wilderness in the summer heat.

4. *The conquest of the land.* In such a way did the ancestors of the later twelve tribes of Israel look longingly at the land as they appeared on its borders roughly from the fourteenth to the eleventh century, probably in two great waves. This land, which had been very largely uninhabited in the Late Bronze Age[1], divided up politically into a tangle of little city-states which were tributary to the Pharaoh until the collapse of the Egyptian Empire in the twelfth century, had room for both them and their flocks, especially in the hill-country. The tribes from the steppe and the wilderness, seeking pasture in the dry season of summer, will at first have come and in the winter gone again peacefully, until groups pressing in on them barred their way. So they continued, now tolerated, now brought by the old inhabitants of the land into a vassal relationship, now withdrawing into the wooded hill-country and so avoiding at first a collision with the Canaanites, who thanks to their war chariots had superior armaments, and then reduced their living space step by step until they won control over the hill-country and the smaller

1. The Early Bronze Age is roughly equivalent to the period of the Old Egyptian Kingdom, that of the Middle Bronze Age to the Middle Kingdom, and that of the Late Bronze Age to that of the New Kingdom.

plains, remaining a loose federation of tribes who were held together and protected from absorption into Canaanite life by their belief in the *one* Yahweh. It was the life and death struggle with the Philistines, who had invaded the coastlands to the south of the Phoenician cities and the plains below Galilee both from the north and over the sea in the course of the migrations of the sea peoples about 1200, which forced these tribes to form a state proper.

We have in passing replaced the traditional picture of the conquest of the land in this rough sketch by a different one which critical scholarship has developed in the first half of this century[2]. The picture, familiar to everyone from the Biblical narrative, of the Israel which starting from the twelve sons of Jacob miraculously became a numerous nation in Egypt, escaped from servitude under the leadership of Moses, was delivered at the Sea, taken into covenant with God at Sinai, and finally after forty years' wandering was led by Joshua into the promised land, is for us no longer part of history. We see in it the expression of a belief in a God who acts in history, and the result of the formation of a confession in an exceedingly complicated and slow process, which it will next be our concern to follow out. And yet this tradition is ultimately correct when it tells of patriarchs to whom the land was promised by God, when it places in the centre the concluding of the covenant at the mountain of God and sees in this, in the Exodus from Egypt and in the following deliverance at the Sea the basis of the whole further divine history. The difference is that this did not all happen to the same ancestors of the later Israel, but in a much more complicated way than our Biblical saga told it.

5. *The distinctive character of Israel.* From its beginnings Israel was and remained different from the nations. This was not only because it held fast to certain ideals of the nomadic life in the

2. Cf. especially A. Alt, 'The Settlement of the Israelites in Palestine' [1925] in *Essays on Old Testament History and Religion*, Oxford 1966, pp. 133 ff.; and 'Erwägungen über die Landnahme der Israeliten in Palästina' [1939], *KS* I, Munich 1953, pp. 126 ff., also in *Grundfragen der Geschichte des Volkes Israel*, ed. S. Herrmann, Munich 1970, pp. 136 ff.; and M. Weippert, *The Settlement of the Israelite Tribes in Palestine*, SBT[2] 21, 1971.

cultivated land[3], but also because its God made the unwavering claim to be the only God for Israel, and Israel could therefore only maintain its existence as Israel if it hearkened in trust to the witness of the fathers to the nature and activity of their God[4]. Because Yahweh, the God of Israel, was different from the gods, Israel too, as long as it remained Israel, was necessarily different from all other nations. Even if the formulations of the first commandment, and with it the collection of the whole Decalogue, may be no earlier than the Deuteronomistic period (cf. Exod. 20.2 ff., par. Deut 5.6 ff.), still without the presupposition of faith in the *one* God, who tolerates no other alongside himself, and must be worshipped without images, the whole history of Israel, and so the history of its literature too, remain unintelligible.

There is not the same unanimity now among scholars as there was a few years ago about the relations of the Israelite tribes, both within the tribe and between the tribes, in the premonarchical period. The question whether Israel understood its relationship with God from the very beginning basically as a covenant relationship is now disputed, as is also the question whether the individual tribes were united in a twelve tribe federation, an amphictyony, with quite specific structures. This discussion makes no difference to the fact that Israel was conscious that its earliest history was decisively formed by Yahweh, and that its salvation was dependent on its fidelity to its God. As long as Israel was what it was meant to be, it knew that its God was both the one who gives and the one who demands, and that a breach in the obligation of fidelity to him could set its own existence at risk. The relationship of religion and law herein contained, which in the course of the history of Israel and of Judaism led to ever new developments, just because of the claim of Yahweh to exclusivity prevented the absorption of Israel by the Canaanites, and the absorption of Judaism in Hellenistic syncretism. Instead of this the nation's historical experience, from the delivery at the sea through the conquest and the golden age of the Davidic and Solomonic period down to the loss of national independence in the sixth century B.C. and the crisis of the period of the

3. Cf. J. A. Soggin, *Das Königtum in Israel*, BZAW 104, 1967, pp. 159 ff.

4. F. Mildenberger, *Gottes Tat im Wort*, Gütersloh 1964, pp. 26 ff., in particular has pointed this out.

Maccabees, led to a deepening and broadening of Israel's understanding of God[5].

6. *The origin of the formation of the tradition.* If we look for a
specific starting point in the literature of Israel and of the Old
Testament, we must begin from the fact that Yahweh's claim to
lordship over Israel was expressed in the concrete demand for
an appearance of his people before his face, which means in his
sanctuary. Here God through the mouth of his chosen spokesman grounded his claim on Israel in his actions on behalf of
Israel. In this sense the utterance of God, the word of God,
stands at the beginning. Priestly instructions and prophetic
announcements readily find their places in this context in all
their complexity. The people respond to the word of their God
and the actions of their God, which they can only recognize as
such through the interpretative word, with praise, with hymns,
with songs of thanksgiving. They bow themselves before the
Holy One in confession of their guilt, and turn to him in lamentation and prayer. So from what they have learnt in the celebration
of the activity of God, grows the narrative of his actions towards
Israel. In this sketch it is not my wish to do violence to the rich
complexity of life, and so also of the origins of the literature of
Israel (one need only remember its wars with their victories and
defeats, and the life of the individual with its fortunes such as
illness and persecution, birth and death, to be conscious of this),
but to put at the centre that from which in my view the life and
confession of Israel, as of the Church which has an inner continuity with it, was and is renewed. This is the worship of God
in its narrower cultic sense, from and in relationship to which the
most varied utterances of the community about life can be most
readily understood. It must be remembered that cultic celebration is not something separated from normal life, but an explanation, which is binding upon the participants, of the whole of life
through the God who is revealed in the word and present in faith.

5. On this cf. e.g. the sketch of the history of the religion of Yahweh
in G. von Rad, *Old Testament Theology*, vol. 1, Edinburgh and London
1962, pp. 3 ff.; but also G. Kittel, *Erwählung und Gericht. Ein Vergleich
prophetischer und paulinischer Gotteserkenntnis*, Diss. theol. Marburg 1967,
pp. 114 ff.

§ 3   The Canaanite Inheritance

J. A. Knudtzon, *Die El-Amarna-Tafeln* I–II, Leipzig 1915, repr. Aalen 1963; J. Hempel, *Die althebräische Literatur und ihr hellenistisch-jüdisches Nachleben*, Potsdam 1930, Berlin 1968², pp. 10 ff.; W. F. Albright, *From the Stone Age to Christianity*, Garden City, New York, 1957²; C. H. Gordon, *The World of the Old Testament*, London 1960; A. Jirku, *Kanaanäische Mythen und Epen aus Ras Schamra-Ugarit*, Gütersloh 1962; id., *Der Mythus der Kanaanäer*, Bonn 1966; J. Aistleitner, *Die mythologischen und kultischen Texte aus Ras Schamra*, Budapest 1964²; J. Gray, *The Legacy of Canaan*, SVT 5, 1965²; A. S. Kapelrud, *The Ras Shamra Discoveries and the Old Testament*, Norman, Oklahoma 1963, Oxford 1965; H. Gese, 'Die Religionen Altsyriens', in *Die Religionen Altsyriens, Altarabiens und der Mandäer*, Religionen der Menschheit 10, 2, Stuttgart 1970.

In this chapter we are concerned with the underlying factors in Israelite culture, and primarily with the pre-literary and literary traditions and forms which the Israelites learned from the Canaanites in the course of or immediately after their transition to a sedentary life. It must be noted as a basic principle that the process of enriching their own traditions with foreign material continued until Judaism shut itself off from external influences. This stage is reached when the process of canonization of the books of the Old Testament is concluded, about the beginning of the second century A.D.

1. The script. We begin with an entirely external inheritance, but one which is vital for the growth of a literature, the script[1]. This was neither the awkward Akkadian cuneiform, nor the no less difficult Egyptian hieroglyphics, but a consonantal script with an alphabet of twenty-two signs, which was so simple and useful that it became the parent of a whole series of other scripts, among them by way of the Greeks and Romans our own.

The prehistory of this alphabet, which is called Canaanite, Old Phoenician or Old Hebrew, has not yet been completely clarified. The earliest antecedent of the Phoenician alphabet is a syllabic script

1. Cf. M. Noth, *The Old Testament World*, London 1966, pp. 202 ff., and E. Würthwein, *The Text of the Old Testament*, Oxford 1957, pp. 3 ff., and plates 1–5, 12 f. and 30.

appearing at Byblos about the beginning of the second millennium
B.C.[2] From about 1500 B.C. we know a script used in the Sinai peninsula,
which certainly has a long prehistory, and appears to be connected
with the hieroglyphic script. From the seventeenth to the fifteenth
centuries come some short inscriptions from southern and central
Palestine, whose signs are reminiscent of the Sinai script. While the
scripts mentioned are still strongly pictographic, i.e. pictorial, although
they are already consonantal signs, the Palestinian inscriptions coming
from the fourteenth to the twelfth centuries show direct anticipations of
the old Phoenician script, although the signs individually still vary.[3]
The Ugaritic cuneiform script with its thirty consonantal signs on the
other hand reflects a special development which has had no successors.
We must allow for the possibility that both our old Phoenician, south
Canaanite script and the Ugaritic, north Canaanite alphabet have a
common origin[4]. The south Canaanite writing system with its 22
consonants appears for the first time in its already fully developed form
in the two inscriptions on the tomb chamber and on the sarcophagus
of King Ahiram of Byblos, which are usually now placed in the tenth
century[5].

A direct line leads from these inscriptions to the texts discovered in Palestine of the first millennium B.C., whose number
is being constantly increased by new discoveries[6]. We must
mention at least the farming calendar of Gezer, the inscription
of King Mesha of Moab, the ostraca of Samaria, the Siloam
inscription, the Lachish ostraca, and the numerous inscriptions

2. Cf. J. Friedrich, *Geschichte der Schrift*, Heidelberg 1966, pp. 58 f.
3. On the chronology of the scripts discovered cf. W. F. Albright,
The Proto-Sinaitic Inscriptions and their Decipherment, Harvard Theological Studies 22, Cambridge, Mass. 1966, pp. 10 ff.
4. Cf. Albright, op. cit., p. 15, Friedrich, op. cit., pp. 96 ff., and R. R.
Stieglitz, 'The Ugaritic Cuneiform and Canaanite Alphabets', *JNES* 30
(1971), pp. 135 ff.
5. The recently discovered inscribed pieces of pottery from Tell Deir
'Alla on the eastern bank of the central Jordan valley from the late
thirteenth or early twelfth century may provide a transition to the early
Arabic writing systems, according to the first investigations, which are
however far from definitive. Cf. H. J. Franken, *VT* 14 (1964), pp. 377 ff.,
and Pl. V after p. 418, and most recently G. Sauer, *ZAW* 81 (1969),
pp. 145 ff.
6. The whole material apart from the inscriptions on jar handles and
seals is conveniently accessible down to the most recent discoveries in
H. Donner and W. Röllig, *Kanaanäische und aramäische Inschriften* I–III,
Wiesbaden, 1966[2].

on jar handles and on seals. When dealing with Old Testament literature, and especially with textual criticism, one must realize that the great majority of Old Testament books, with the probable exceptions only of Daniel and Esther, were originally written in this older script.

The transition to the Hebrew 'square script', which is still in use, took place between the fourth and the second centuries B.C. under the influence of Aramaic and its cursive script. The old Hebrew script however retained a special status until the bitter end of the Jewish state in the Bar Kochba rising (A.D. 132 to 135).

This is shown particularly by the fact that manuscripts found at Qumran in the wilderness of Judah written in the square script occasionally have the divine name Yahweh in the old Hebrew script. Even in a Greek roll of the Minor Prophets from Nahal Hever the tetragram has been inserted in this script. So we must remember that the old Hebrew script was still of importance in the copying of biblical texts when the 'square script' had long since become universal in daily life, an assumption which is supported by the existence of manuscripts of the Bible written in the ancient Hebrew script from the wilderness of Judaea. It should finally be remarked that Bar Kochba was still minting coins with a legend in the Old Hebrew script.

This script, like its successor, the 'square script', could be used on any material, apart from soft clay, which was unsuitable for its generally rounded letter forms. Ostraca, fragments of clay jars, for normal notices and announcements, papyrus for normal written transactions, leather for occasions requiring a durable material and frequent use, metal for writing down national treaties and other particularly important documents, and stones with or without a coating of chalk were equally suitable for this script, and were written with a reed cut to shape and an ink of organic material or with a stylus, depending upon the material.

The normal writing material will have been papyrus in Palestine as well as in Egypt. This is particularly liable to perish. This is why, until the recent discovery of a single sheet of papyrus written on twice in succession (a so-called palimpsest) in the caves of Murabba'at, inscribed first in the eighth century with a list and later with a letter, only some threads of papyrus attested to the use of this material in Israel. They were clinging to a seal which was discovered in the excavations at Lachish.

While it was an advantage for men of the time to be able to use a script which could easily be written in ink on a material which sometimes at least cost nothing, this is for us today a disadvantage. For since even the numerous discoveries of the last decades in the desert have so far only produced this single page of papyrus from the pre-exilic period, it can hardly be expected that further search in the land will lead to great surprises in this respect. We must be thankful that the number of ostraca has meanwhile increased, as is being shown now by Aharoni's excavations at Tell Arad, and must be content with the fact that the writings handed down to us in the Old Testament canon, from dates down to the beginning of the third century B.C., remain the only witnesses to an originally much richer Israelite and Judahite national literature.

The ability to read and write was basically confined in Israel to the king, his higher and lower officials, the wise, the priests and the staff of the temple, the higher ranks of landowners, craftsmen and tradesmen, and to a conjectured group of free scribes. It can be assumed to be absent among the small farmers, shepherds, ordinary craftsmen, day labourers and slaves, in fact among all the lower classes[6a].

2. *Language.* The most important gift of the Canaanites to the Israelites, which made possible all further borrowings, was their language. For a language is never a bare dead form, but much more like a house which with the floors, storeys, rooms and halls points to the life of its inhabitants. What language the Israelites had before they took Canaanite over from the ancient inhabitants of the land is a controversial question[7]. In the post-exilic period, when Aramaic had become the official language of the western half of the Persian empire, they took over Aramaic. Two biblical passages reflect this (second?) change of language, although their historical reliability is not above question: according to 2 Kgs. 18.26 the population of Jerusalem did not yet understand Aramaic in 701. According to Neh. 8.2 and 8, Ezra at a meeting of the congregation held in Jerusalem in about 400

6a. Cf. H.-J. Hermisson, *Studien zur israelitischen Spruchweisheit*, WMANT 28, 1968, pp. 97 ff., and on Judg. 8.14, p. 99.

7. Cf. C. Brockelmann, in HO I,III, Leiden 1954, p. 59; Noth, op. cit., p. 226, and R. Meyer, *Hebräische Grammatik* I[3], Berlin 1966, p. 11.

had to have the law which was being read out translated by interpreters[8]. But in spite of its displacement from everyday use, Hebrew persisted as the language of the cult. This is why apart from two words in Genesis (Gen. 31.47), one verse in Jeremiah (Jer. 10.11), and the documents in Ezra 4.(6) 8–6.18 and 7.(11) 12–26, only roughly two-thirds of Daniel (Dan. 2.4b–7.28) are in Aramaic[9].

3. Sagas. It is only natural that together with this language early Israel took over a multitude of fixed phrases, forms, and stylistic laws. It is no less natural that it altered and enriched its own sagas, which had to a large extent lost their point in changed conditions of living, under the influence of the stories which were told in the land[10]. It was a case not only of the taking over of local traditions, of aetiological sanctuary and nature sagas, as was natural with life in a new country, and with the taking over of Canaanite sanctuaries, but also of the entry into the area of major, in the strict sense international literature. The fact that there is a relationship extending to individual points between the biblical story of the flood and the flood saga preserved in tablet XI of the Gilgamesh epic, was established soon after the Akkadian texts became known, and has survived all attempts to disprove it. The epic, fragments of which have been found even in a Hittite translation, was obviously extremely popular in the ancient Near Eastern world[11]. It has recently been noticed that the Sumerian flood story (the Atraḥasis epic) which for a long time was only known in fragmentary form, begins with the creation of man and with the foundation of the oldest cities[11a]. Accordingly we may see in this Sumerian composition as a whole a pattern for the biblical primeval story of Gen. 1 ff.[12].

8. Cf. U. Kellermann, *Nehemia. Quellen, Überlieferung und Geschichte,* BZAW 102, 1967, p. 29, n. 128.

9. Cf. below, pp. 311 f.   10. Cf. below, pp. 70 ff.

11. On the Gilgamesh epic cf. A. Falkenstein, et al. in *RLA* III. 5, Berlin 1968, cols. 356 ff.

11a. Cf. M. Civil, 'The Sumerian Flood Story', in W. G. Lambert and A. Millard, *Atra-ḥasis. The Babylonian Story of the Flood,* Oxford 1969, pp. 138 ff.

12. Cf. H. Gese, *ZTK* 55 (1958), pp. 142 f., G. Fohrer, *ZAW* 73 (1961), p. 13 = *Studien zur alttestamentlichen Theologie und Geschichte,* BZAW 115, 1969, p. 66 and W. M. Clark, *ZAW* 83 (1971), pp. 184 ff.

While the intermediate stages between the Mesopotamian and the Israelite traditions have still not been clarified in detail sufficiently, there can no longer be any doubt, after the discovery of a cuneiform fragment of the Gilgamesh epic at Megiddo dating from the fourteenth century B.C., that here too the Canaanites were the intermediaries[13].

4. *Religion*. In the course of its adaptation or rejection of such religious traditions, and of genuinely Canaanite ones, Israel did not lose its belief in Yahweh, but expanded and deepened its own understanding of this. It is immediately clear that the cultivated land with its agriculture tied to the cycle of the year, which was given an interpretation in terms of myth, challenged this belief in Yahweh to determine the relationship of its own God, perhaps originally located in the wilderness and steppe areas to the south-east of Palestine, to the rhythm of agricultural life. For the Canaanites there were no areas of life not filled out by religion rather than at best by magical practices. On the evidence of the texts from Ugarit in northern Syria, they had a pantheon which for richness and complexity can stand alongside the most developed religions of antiquity. The Ugaritic texts belong to the fifteenth to the thirteenth centuries B.C., and are accordingly substantially older than the oldest sections of the Old Testament[14]. As well as the creator and father of the gods, El, and the mother of the gods, Asherah, we find in them the vegetation and weather god Baal, who is associated with Anath and Astarte as his partners. The myth of the fate of the weather-god in the course of the year, of his descent into the underworld, while Mot, the god of summer drought and of death, has dominion upon earth, his release from the underworld by Anath, and his victorious fight against the rebellious sea, i.e. the god Yam, who bestows on him the kingship, throws a striking light upon many passages of Old Testament mythology. It cannot however be simply assumed that the stories of the gods current in Palestine and the pantheon worshipped in the Palestinian cities were actually identical with those now known from Ugarit[15]. Further-

---

13. Cf. O. Kaiser, *Die mythische Bedeutung des Meeres in Ägypten, Ugarit und Israel*, BZAW 78, 1962², pp. 122 ff.

14. Cf. A. S. Kapelrud, op. cit., pp. 15 ff.

15. Cf. Kapelrud, op. cit., pp. 30 ff. On the problem of the identity of

more there are grounds for the assumption that the myth of the fortunes of Baal was connected with an autumn festival, and that Israel took over not only the feast, but also the idea of the victorious God from the Canaanites[16].

The important point is that the belief of the former inhabitants of the wilderness still preserved the distance from their unapproachable God, and was not distorted into a too familiar polytheism. El, the head of the Canaanite pantheon, was now identified with Yahweh, on the pattern of his identification with the gods of the fathers of the conquering tribes[17], while the relationship of Yahweh to Baal in the end took on polemical form. But the decisive point was that Israel transferred the characteristics of the gods of the land who ordered, gave and took away life, to their own *one* god, who was the Lord of all the powers of nature. Yahweh was the creator. He was the lord of clouds and winds. He commanded the rebellious sea. He gave growth and increase. The old pantheon was reduced in status to become his heavenly court (cf. Ps. 29.1; 82; 89.5–7 [Heb. 89.6–8]; 1 Kgs. 22.21 ff. and Gen. 28.12). The Canaanite agricultural feasts were taken over, but historicized, i.e. provided with a motivation from saving history. And when the old motifs from nature myths still clearly shine through, as is the case in the autumn festival with the idea of creation and struggle with chaos, here too historicization is to be seen; the hostile powers of the cosmos become the earthly enemies of Yahweh and of his people. It seems clear that when the cultic usages of the Canaanites were taken over some of the ritual appeared indispensable. The whole process sketched out here naturally did not take place without friction nor without internal conflict. This is shown especially by the Elijah stories and by the message of the prophet Hosea.

---

the gods mentioned in the Ugaritic texts and those mentioned in the Old Testament cf. K. H. Bernhardt, 'Aschera in Ugarit und im Alten Testament', *Mitteilungen des Instituts für Orientforschung* 13 (1967), pp. 163 ff.

16. Cf. Kapelrud, op. cit., pp. 65 ff., Gese, op. cit., p. 80 and J. C. de Moor, *New Year with Canaanites and Israelites* I–II, Kamper Cahiers 21/22, Kampen 1972.

17. Cf. also below, pp. 72 f. On Eissfeldt's assumption, *JSS* 1 (1956), pp. 25 ff. = *KS* III, Tübingen 1966, pp. 386 ff., that El was subordinated to Yahweh during a period of transition, cf. the criticism of G. Fohrer, *History of Israelite Religion*, Nashville 1972, London 1973, pp. 104 f.

5. *Cultic poetry.* The cultic poetry of the Canaanites is related to ancient Oriental and especially Mesopotamian poetry, and so to a store of forms and of formulas which was bound to tempt Israel to adopt it. It had already been concluded from the cuneiform texts found in the ruins of the capital of the Egyptian king Amenophis IV or Akhnaton, which are called the Amarna letters from the present name of the place, that the Canaanites had a literature of prayer in their own language[18]. There was bound to be a connection between their courtly style and their cultic poetry, and between both these and Old Testament psalm composition.

When we read the words addressed to the Pharaoh in Amarna letter 264:

> If we climb up to heaven,
> if we climb down to the earth,
> our head is in your hands!

we are bound to think of Psalm 139.8:

> If I ascend to heaven, thou art there!
> If I make my bed in Sheol, thou art there!

Nor is it difficult to discover a relationship between the confession in Amarna letter 195 and that in Psalm 123. In the letter we have:

> My lord is the sun in the heaven,
> and like the going up of the sun from the heaven,
> so do the servants wait for the going out of the words
> from the mouth of their lord.

In the psalm we have an echo of this:

> To thee I lift up my eyes,
>   O thou who art enthroned in the heavens!
> Behold, as the eyes of servants
>   look to the hands of their master,
> as the eyes of a maid
>   to the hand of her mistress,
> so our eyes look to the LORD our God.

18. Cf. F. M. T. de Liagre Böhl, *Opera Minora*, Leiden 1953, pp. 375 ff.

The Ugaritic discoveries have further strengthened the impression of the dependence of Israelite psalm composition upon Canaanite psalms, although until now no text of a prayer has been found which in form and content can really be put on a level with an Old Testament psalm.

The text understood by Aistleitner as a sacrificial song directed to El, *CTA* 30 (Gordon 53) is of disputed meaning. Aistleitner's translation of lines 6–9 in a form reminiscent of Pss. 10.12; 79.8 and 22.19 (Heb. 22.20) is in any case dubious.

So the contribution of Ugaritic material to the understanding of the psalms remains restricted on the one hand to the illumination of basic points in the history of religion, and on the other hand to phrases illuminated by these, and to individual formal points. With careful observation we could have already noticed in the quotations from the Amarna letters that the dependence is not restricted to the content, but is also formal. We could already have discovered here the basic law of Hebrew poetry, the so-called *parallelismus membrorum*, a duplication of the basic utterance[19]. The comparison of a Ugaritic verse coming from an epic text (*CTA* 2.IV.8 ff., Gordon 68.8 ff.) with a verse from Ps. 92 should make this clear[20]. The

> See, your enemy, O Baal,
> See, your enemy will you slay,
> See, your opponent will you destroy . . .

of the Ugaritic text corresponds in the graduated, climactic parallelism even more than in content to Ps. 92.9 (Heb. 92.10):

> For lo, thy enemies, O LORD,
> for, lo, thy enemies shall perish;
> all evildoers shall be scattered.

6. *Wisdom.* It would lead too far to pursue in detail all the connections between Canaanite and Israelite poetry. Instead the influence of Canaanite upon Israelite wisdom will be demonstrated from the example of the numerical proverb[21].

19. Cf. below, pp. 321 ff.
20. Cf. G. Sauer, *Die Sprüche Agurs*, BWANT 84, 1963, p. 21. On pp. 14 ff. references are found to further parallels.
21. Cf. Sauer, op. cit., pp. 64 ff. and 87 ff.

The Ugaritic text *CTA* 4.III.17 ff. (Gordon 51:III:17 ff.) runs:

> See, two banquets hates Baal, three
> the rider on the clouds: a banquet
> of humility and a banquet of bad behaviour
> of the maidens: for then truly shame appears,
> and then also the loathsome deeds of the maidens.

We can compare without comment Prov. 6.16–19:

> There are six things which the LORD hates,
> seven which are an abomination to him:
> haughty eyes, a lying tongue,
> and hands that shed innocent blood,
> a heart that devises wicked plans,
> feet that make haste to run to evil,
> a false witness who breathes out lies,
> and a man who sows discord among brothers.

Canaanite wisdom in its turn was subject to Egyptian and Mesopotamian influence. It is undisputed that Egyptian wisdom especially in the period of the monarchy had a direct influence upon Israelite wisdom[22].

7. *Law.* Mesopotamian influence was most significant in the area of Israelite law. The circumstances of their new life posed the immigrants a mass of legal problems, for the solution of which the old clan law from the wilderness and wandering period offered no basis. So it was natural that Israel should enter into the inheritance of the Canaanite legal pattern, which in its turn is to be regarded as an offshoot of the more comprehensive legal pattern of cuneiform law[23]. The fact that a whole series of legal

22. Cf. O. Kaiser, 'Israel und Ägypten', *ZMH* NF 14 (1963), pp. 15 ff. For the transmission of Babylonian wisdom in Syria and Canaan cf. now the Akkadian texts found at Ugarit, *Ugaritica* V, Paris 1968, pp. 265 ff.

23. Cf. A. Alt, *KS* III, Munich 1959, pp. 141 ff. and *KS* I, Munich 1953, pp. 278 ff., also in *Grundfragen der Geschichte des Volkes Israel*, Munich 1970, pp. 203 ff., and more generally R. Haase, *Einführung in das Studium keilschriftlicher Rechtsquellen*, Wiesbaden 1965; but also E. Seidl, 'Altägyptisches Recht', in *Orientalisches Recht*, HO I, Ergänzungsband III, Leiden 1964, pp. 4 f. The Mesopotamian and Hittite law codes can be found in translation in *ANET²⁻³*, pp. 159 ff. and in *ANET³*, pp. 523 f.

documents from the second millennium B.C. found in Palestine are written in Akkadian and in cuneiform is one argument for this. We can regard casuistic law as specific to the cultivated land with its complex social life. A look at the famous code of the Babylonian king Hammurabi (1792–1750 B.C.) will show how characteristic casuistic law is of cuneiform law[24]. When we consider that Israel understood its relationship with God as one of community, and so was able to describe it in legal categories, and when we further note that many scholars see in the Israelite covenant formulary a borrowing of the formulary of Ancient Near Eastern state treaties, it can be seen clearly[25] how deep the influence of the inheritance mediated by the Canaanites was upon early Israel, and how far from matter of course it is that Israel in the end went beyond what she had learnt from her instructors, and by penetrating it with its own faith in the one God Yahweh, created something new, and so proper to itself alone.

24. On casuistic law cf. below, pp. 56 f.
25. Cf. below, pp. 62 ff.

C. The Historical Narratives

§ 4   The History of Pentateuchal Research

H. Holzinger, *Einleitung in den Hexateuch*, Freiburg and Leipzig 1893, pp. 25 ff.; C. A. Simpson, *The Early Traditions of Israel*, Oxford 1948, pp. 19 ff.; O. Eissfeldt, 'Die neueste Phase in der Entwicklung der Pentateuchkritik', *ThR* NF 18 (1950), pp. 91 ff., 179 ff., and 267 ff.; C. R. North, 'Pentateuchal Criticism', *OTMS*, Oxford 1951, pp. 48 ff.; M. Noth, *A History of Pentateuchal Traditions* [1948], Englewood Cliffs, N.J., 1972, pp. 20 ff.; R. J. Thompson, *Moses and the Law in a Century of Criticism since Graf*, SVT 19, 1970.

Commentaries on the Pentateuch: Genesis: KeH Dillmann 1892[6]; KHC Holzinger 1898; HK Gunkel 1910[3] (= 1966[7]); SAT Gunkel 1921[2]; KAT[1] Procksch 1924[2-3]; HS Heinisch 1930; ICC Skinner 1930[2]; AB Speiser 1964; BK Westermann 1966 ff.; OTL von Rad 1972[3]; SC Delitzsch 1887; König 1925[2-3]; Cassuto I (Hebrew 1944) 1961, II (1949) 1964. Exodus: KeH Dillmann and Ryssel (Ex.-Lev.) 1897[3]; KHC Holzinger 1900; HK Baentsch (Ex.-Num.) 1903; SAT Gressmann (Ex.-Deut.) 1922[2]; HS Heinisch 1934; HAT Beer and Galling 1939; OTL Noth 1962; SC Cassuto (Hebrew 1951) 1967. Leviticus KHC Bertholet 1901; HS Heinisch 1935; OTL Noth 1965; HAT Elliger 1966; CB Snaith (Lev.-Num.) 1967. Numbers: KeH Dillmann 1886[2]; ICC Gray 1903; KHC Holzinger 1903; HS Heinisch 1936; OTL Noth 1968. Deuteronomy: KeH Dillmann 1886[2]; KHC Bertholet 1899; ICC Driver 1902[3]; KAT[1] König 1917; HK Steuernagel 1923[2]; HS Junker 1933; OTL von Rad 1966.

The statement made in § 1, that the reader of the Bible, as of every book in antiquity, needs the help of historical introduction and explanation[1], is especially true for the historical books and the prophets. The reader of the books of the prophets feels the lack of clear divisions and statements of situations, which would make it easier for him to understand them. Anyone who studies

1. Cf. pp. 1 f.

the books which are put together by Jewish tradition as 'Law'
(Torah) and 'Former Prophets' (*nᵉḇî'îm rî'šônîm*), the books of
the Pentateuch and the books from Joshua to 2 Kings, soon
discovers that the thread of the narrative does not break off with
the end of the individual books, that it is often interrupted by
longer or shorter insertions, and is made confused and obscure
by the presence of doublets. In respect of the names of authors
passed down by tradition too doubts arise at once. It is *a priori*
improbable that Moses (cf. Deut. 34.5 ff.) or Joshua (cf. Josh.
24.29 ff.) should have recounted their own deaths. It is strange
too that both, apart from inserted direct speech, should have
told of their own experiences in the third person. These and
other difficulties make a knowledge of the development of these
books indispensable to their understanding.

1. The pre-critical period. The tensions between the content and
the traditional authorship of the Pentateuch were observed at
an early date. But the power of tradition was for centuries so
strong that ways were sought to reconcile with it the difficulties
that were felt. Philo of Alexandria and Josephus thought they
could explain Mosaic authorship of Deut. 34.5 ff. by saying that
Moses had foretold his own death, including even the external
circumstances. In the Talmudic period the view prevailed that
Moses had written his own book, the Torah, but Joshua had
written his own book and also the last eight verses of the Torah
(cf. *b. Baba bathra* 14b). In the ancient and medieval Church
doubting voices were occasionally heard, but could not become
influential because the New Testament shared the traditional
Jewish view of the Mosaic authorship of the Pentateuch, and
was regarded as an incontestable authority in such questions as
in others. The struggle the historical viewpoint had to make its
way can be realized from the fact that Adolf Zahn, cousin of the
New Testament scholar, could still in the nineteenth century
regard the advance of Pentateuchal criticism as the cause of the
spread of the Social Democrats and of the Sisters of Mercy in
Stuttgart[2].

Among the men who very early suspected the true state of
affairs, the great Jewish medieval scholar Ibn Ezra deserves
special mention. In his commentaries on Genesis and Deutero-

2. According to H. Holzinger, *Einleitung in den Hexateuch*, p. 12.

nomy he gave very cautious expression to his doubts about Mosaic authorship. So he commented on Gen. 12.6, 'and the Canaanites were then in the land', 'it appears that Canaan, the grandson of Noah, took from another the land which bears his name; if this be not the true meaning, there lurks some mystery in the passage, and let him who understands it keep silence'[3]. He makes his view still clearer on Deut. 1.1. There he comments, 'if so be that thou understandest the mystery of the twelve . . . moreover Moses wrote the law. . . . The Canaanite was then in the land . . . it shall be revealed on the mount of God . . . then also behold his bed, his iron bed, then shalt thou know the truth'[4]. Ibn Ezra drew from Deut. 34, 31.9, Gen. 22.14 and Deut. 3.11 the conclusion that Moses cannot be the author of the Pentateuch, because the narrative obviously distinguishes between his time and the time of the narrator. But these remarks only became influential when Spinoza rescued them from oblivion in his *Tractatus theologico-politicus*, and supported them with further arguments.

2. *The philological period.* In the period which we have called philological, in contrast to the pre-critical stage of the discipline of Introduction[5], critical voices were not absent. Apart from Carlstadt in the sixteenth century, the Catholic jurist Andreas Masius also contested the Mosaic authorship of the Pentateuch, and declared that it had been put together by Ezra out of older documents. From the seventeenth century there may be mentioned, apart from Hobbes, Spinoza and Simon, the Protestant Jean le Clerc (Clericus). In 1685 he had ascribed the books of Moses to a priest returning from exile to Bethel (cf. 2 Kgs. 17.28), but found himself compelled a few years later to retreat behind what were for him in a literal sense the secure walls of the tradition. The time was clearly not yet ripe for such questions or for such results.

3. *The critical period.* It was only when the Enlightenment had gained ground in Europe, in the second half of the eighteenth

3. As quoted in B. de Spinoza, *Tractatus theologico-politicus*, tr. R. H. M. Elwes, London 1883, repr. New York 1951, *The Chief Works* I, p. 122.

4. Cf. Spinoza, op. cit., I, p. 121.   5. Cf. p. 6.

century, that the first properly historico-critical investigation of the sources, and hence also of the Pentateuch, could begin. It is here that the origins are to be found of our present views on the development of the five books of Moses (which are usually called the Pentateuch, the five-volume book, a name which probably developed in early Christian Alexandria). And depending on whether the first four books of the Pentateuch are connected together as an independent unit of tradition, or whether the stories of the books of Joshua, Judges, Samuel and Kings are regarded as originally a continuation of it, scholars speak of a Tetrateuch, Hexateuch, Heptateuch, Octateuch or even Enneateuch[6].

(a) THE OLDER DOCUMENTARY HYPOTHESIS. Modern Pentateuchal criticism took as its starting-point the alternation in the use of the term for God, Elohim, and the name of God, Yahweh. As early as 1711 the Hildesheim pastor Bernhard Witter in his book *Jura Israelitarum in Palestinam terram Chananeam commentatione in Genesin perpetua demonstrata* had referred to this, and drawn the conclusion that in Gen. 1.1–2.4 and 2.5–3.24 there are to be found two parallel narratives differing in the term used for God. His work was forgotten, and rediscovered only at the beginning of this century. More successful was the physician to the French king Louis XV, Jean Astruc, whom we may regard (in spite of his apologetic tendency, which was concerned to establish Mosaic authorship) as the real founder of the so-called older documentary hypothesis. In the year 1753 he wrote his book *Conjectures sur les mémoires originaux dont il paroit que Moyse s'est servi pour composer le livre de la Genèse* ('Conjectures about the original documents which Moses appears to have used in the composition of the book of Genesis'). Like Witter, on the basis of the variation between Elohim and (as the tetragram was then pronounced) Jehovah he assumed an Elohistic and a Yahwistic source of Genesis, alongside which he placed ten fragmentarily preserved sources. Moses had placed these sources in four columns alongside one another; then a later redactor had combined them in a single continuous narrative.

6. Tetrateuch = the fourfold, Hexateuch = the sixfold, Heptateuch = the sevenfold, Octateuch = the eightfold and Enneateuch = the ninefold (book).

It was probably through Jerusalem (the father of the unhappy original of Goethe's Werther), that Eichhorn became familiar with Astruc's views. It was before the publication in 1783 in Frankfurt of a German translation of Astruc's book that he independently took these views further in his Introduction of 1781[7], where assuming the compilation of both Genesis and Exodus from an Elohistic and a Jehovistic source he determined the style and content of both sources more precisely and so for the first time produced proper evidence of their existence. At first he thought of Moses as redactor, later he left the question of authorship open. It was still in the same century that Karl David Ilgen discovered that there were not one but two Elohistic sources.

(b) THE FRAGMENT HYPOTHESIS. But the fragment hypothesis was already in the field to dispel the influence of the documentary hypothesis; and in view of the more or less loose insertion of legal parts into the context of the narrative it seemed better suited to explain the growth of the Pentateuch. Its founder was the Scottish Roman Catholic priest and scholar Alexander Geddes. In two works, published in 1792 and 1800, he sought to show that in what were originally assumed to be two sources we had to deal in reality with a series of fragments, which belonged to two different circles of tradition, one of which had used the term Elohim, the other the name Yahweh for God. The leading representative of this view in Germany was Johann Severin Vater. His three volume work, which appeared between 1802 and 1805, has a title which can communicate to us an impression of the contemplative quiet of that (politically disturbed) period: 'Commentary on the Pentateuch . . . with introductions to the individual sections, an inserted translation of the more striking of Dr. Alexander Geddes' critical and exegetical observations, and a discussion of Moses and the authors of the Pentateuch'. Vater presents here the thesis of a development of the books of the Pentateuch over a period of time. He recognizes that the laws contained in it were occasioned by quite concrete and varied needs, and that they certainly did not come from a

---

7. Cf. his *Einleitung ins Alte Testament*, II, 1781, pp. 296 f. His dependence upon Astruc was demonstrated by M. Siemens, *ZAW* 28 (1908), pp. 221 ff.

single Mosaic lawgiving. He treats as the core of the Pentateuch a collection which was first made in the days of David and Solomon, preserved in Deuteronomy, and discovered at the time of Josiah, but from time to time thereafter enriched by further legislative and historical additions.

(c) THE SUPPLEMENTARY HYPOTHESIS. There is no simple answer to the question who the founder of the supplementary hypothesis was. As early as 1807 the Basel theologian Wilhelm Leberecht Martin de Wette, who can be regarded as a supporter of the fragment hypothesis, although his views constantly changed, published remarks which went in this direction[8]. In any case its scholarly elaboration, as well as later the impulse to its overthrow, is due to Heinrich Ewald, who as is well known was one of the 'Göttingen seven', and became the teacher of Julius Wellhausen. After originally rejecting the whole 'cat's cradle of hypotheses' he arrived at the view, published in an article in *Theologische Studien und Kritiken* in 1831, that at the basis of the Pentateuch, indeed of the Hexateuch, lay an old historical narrative, which extended from the beginning of the world to the conquest of Canaan by the Israelites. Into this writing, which could be recognized by the use of the divine name Elohim, and was characterized by a clear sequence of thought and simple style, a later hand inserted passages from a subsequent work running parallel with it, which used the divine name Yahweh, and preferred a saga style of narrative. Ewald's contribution lies especially in his examination of the composition of the Hexateuch. His view, which is here only very superficially sketched, seems in fact like a variant of the older documentary hypothesis, Ilgen's version of which he later took over and improved, recognizing two Elohistic sources. Bleek[8a] and Tuch held a supplementary hypothesis in the strict sense, since they identified the redactor with the Jehovist, and so denied the existence of an independent Jehovistic historical work.

8. Cf. for details R. Smend jr., *W. M. L. de Wettes Arbeit am Alten und am neuen Testament*, Basle 1958, pp. 11 ff.

8a. Cf. R. Smend, jr., 'Friedrich Bleek', in *Bonner Gelehrte. Beiträge zur Geschichte der Wissenschaften in Bonn. Evangelische Theologie*, Bonn 1968, pp. 37 f.

(d) THE NEWER DOCUMENTARY HYPOTHESIS. Our present understanding of the formation of the Pentateuch goes under the title
of the 'newer documentary hypothesis'. The appearance of
Hermann Hupfeld's *Quellen der Genesis und die Art ihrer Zusam-
mensetzung* in 1853 must be regarded as the first stage in its
development. He established the existence of three sources in
Genesis, an Elohistic basic writing, a further Elohistic source,
and an (as he believed) yet later Jehovistic source. These three
sources he distinguished sharply from the redactor who subsequently united them. This set things moving: one year later
Eduard Riehm won general recognition for the view de Wette
had arrived at of the original independence of Deuteronomy.
He dated it after the Jehovist.

In 1869 Theodor Nöldeke was able to determine the share of
the Priestly writing, the 'older Elohist' of earlier writers, for the
most part definitively. The main progress of these years however
was not in the area of literary criticism, of source division, but
in that of literary history, of the location in time of the individual
documents. This was achieved by Karl Heinrich Graf, Abraham
Kuenen and Julius Wellhausen, so that we speak of the Graf-
Kuenen-Wellhausen hypothesis. Graf recognized that the legal
parts of the books Leviticus and Numbers and the related chapters must be later than Deuteronomy. Kuenen went further
with a late dating of the whole Priestly writing (P). Wellhausen
in his collection of articles *Die Composition des Hexateuchs*
(1876 f., published in book form in 1885) and his *Geschichte
Israels* I, 1878 (published since 1883 under the title *Prolegomena
zur Geschichte Israels*, in ET *Prolegomena to the History of
Ancient Israel*, 1885) won almost universal acceptance for the
thesis that the Yahwistic (formerly called Jehovistic) source J
is to be regarded as the oldest, the second Elohistic source E as
the later, and the priestly writing P as the latest source. The
Prolegomena to the History of Israel is among the most sparkling
and attractive books which have been written in modern times in
the area of Old Testament study. It marked out a framework
for all later scholarly work on the Pentateuch and the Book of
Joshua. Apart from basic attacks on the four-source theory as
such and apart from further developments of it which now will
be described, the 'newer documentary hypothesis' has maintained a significant number of supporters up to the present

time, and in spite of continuing argument about details can still be regarded as the standard view on the composition of the Pentateuch.

(e) THE 'NEWEST DOCUMENTARY HYPOTHESIS'. Before we can deal with the most recent phase, that of form-critical and traditio-historical work, which began at about the turn of the century[9], we must look at the version of Wellhausen's theory sometimes known as the 'newest documentary hypothesis'. Budde in his *Biblische Urgeschichte* of 1883 proposed the theory that the Yahwistic thread in the primeval history of Gen. 1–11 had really been put together from two sources which were independent of one another, and Gunkel divided J in his commentary on Genesis of 1901 (1966[7]) into two subsidiary sources. R. Smend sr. went a stage further in his *Erzählung des Hexateuch auf ihre Quellen untersucht* of 1912, coming out in favour of a continuous division into two Yahwistic sources, an older J^1 and a later J^2. This hypothesis was taken up by Eissfeldt in his *Hexateuch-Synopse* of 1922, with one modification. He called J^1 the Lay source (L), and called J^2 J. He believes that J and E can be traced down to the Books of Samuel, indeed even further, at least to 1 Kgs. 12. C. A. Simpson made similar suggestions in 1948. The generation of scholars in Germany after Eissfeldt was silent about the 'newest documentary hypothesis', since it was believed that the tensions in J could be explained by means of the activity of the Yahwist as a collector, or from the previous history of the traditions adapted by him. Fohrer however has now declared his accession to it, but at the same time made important alterations in it. In his view we must distinguish between J and a 'nomadic source' N, and see in N a reaction against J^{10}. While it cannot be said that the question of the validity of the 'newest documentary hypothesis' in one or the other form is already settled, the investigations of Kilian[11] and Fritz[12], into the Abraham

9. Cf. pp. 66 ff.

10. Cf. G. Fohrer, *Überlieferung und Geschichte des Exodus*, BZAW 91, 1964, especially pp. 8 and 124, and his *Introduction to the Old Testament*, pp. 159 ff.

11. *Die vorpriesterlichen Abrahams-Überlieferungen*, BBB 24, Bonn 1966.

12. *Israel in der Wüste. Traditionsgeschichtliche Untersuchung der Wüstentraditionen des Jahwisten*, MTS 7, 1970.

traditions of Genesis, and the wilderness traditions of Exodus and Numbers, argue rather for the view that J already had one or more written documents before him which he reworked, supplemented from oral tradition and subordinated to a unitary theological viewpoint. If this were so, it would still show that the supporters of the 'newest documentary hypothesis' had pointed to a phenomenon which has been worth further investigation.

(f) FORM-CRITICAL AND TRADITIO-HISTORICAL INVESTIGATION. As has been indicated already, thanks to the work of Gunkel and Hugo Gressmann[13], form-critical work has come to take its place alongside literary-critical work in this century. Form-criticism starts by determining the literary type of the individual section of narrative[14]. We are justified in speaking of a literary type when a particular form is connected with a particular content, and both have a fixed point of reference, a fixed *Sitz im Leben*, or setting in life[15]. As we have already shown in § 1, the development and history of a form from the first, usually oral, stage to its final fixing in writing provides in itself a programme for a history of literature built around the development of forms and literary types. This work cannot from the point of view of the evidence available be separated from traditio-historical work. It asks especially what institution or what circle of persons took part in the transmission and further development of material handed down, how the individual traditions grew into union with others, and how finally the longer sources, collections and books preserved in the Old Testament, and indeed the Old Testament as such, originated. The nature of the questions means that sociological points also come into consideration.[16] While form-criticism led at first to an atomizing of the sources, since its

13. *Mose und seine Zeit*, FRLANT 18, 1913.
14. Cf. K. Koch, *The Growth of the Biblical Tradition*, London 1969, or K. H. Bernhardt, *Die gattungsgeschichtliche Forschung am Alten Testament als exegetische Methode*, Aufsätze und Vorträge zur Theologie und Religionswissenschaft 8, Berlin 1959. J. M. Schmidt, *EvTh* 27 (1967), pp. 200 ff., and E. Ruprecht, *ZAW* 84 (1972), pp. 293 ff., rightly point to some precursors of form-criticism.
15. Cf. also O. Kaiser, 'Old Testament Exegesis', in *Exegetical Method, a Student's Handbook*, by O. Kaiser and W. G. Kümmel, New York 1967, pp. 19 ff.
16. A survey of the first attempts at a sociological investigation of the

interests were directed primarily to the smallest narrative unit and to its development, tradition-history overcame this danger, since it led necessarily to the question of the origin of the various larger units. The latest works, especially, have shown that form-critical and traditio-historical method not only presuppose the results of literary criticism, but in their turn can contribute a clarification of the literary-critical evidence. Alt, von Rad and Noth, from what is now the older generation, deserve special mention as pioneers of the traditio-historical investigation of the historical traditions. At the same time it should be said that in their own and in the next generation all have learnt from them, both in dependence on them and in disagreement with them. In the last decade a growing reserve has begun to be felt about the literary-critical and redaction-critical method, which has now come to a head in Hannelis Schulte's *Entstehung der Geschichts-schreibung im Alten Israel*, a book which takes its starting-point from Gustav Hölscher's *Geschichtsschreibung in Israel*[17]. It may be hoped that a thoughtful combination of both types of question will lead to new agreement on the basic problems of Pentateuchal criticism.

(g) ATTACKS UPON THE DOCUMENTARY HYPOTHESIS. Discussion within the framework of the newer and newest documentary hypothesis still continues, and in particular there are those who like Volz, Rudolph, and Mowinckel reintroduce a supplementary hypothesis in respect of E[18], or like Kaufmann argue for an early date for P, or like F. M. Cross deny the independent existence of a separate source P, and instead regard it as a redaction of the Jehovistic history JE[19]. There are also a substantial number of scholars who fundamentally question the theory which Well-

---

Old Testament is given by J. van der Ploeg, 'The Social Study of the Old Testament', *CBQ* 10 (1948), pp. 72 ff.

17. Cf. Hölscher, SKHVL 50, 1952, and Schulte, BZAW 128, 1972.

18. Cf. also R. N. Whybray, 'The Joseph Story and Pentateuchal Criticism', *VT* 18 (1968), pp. 522 ff.

19. Cf. Y. Kaufmann, *The Religion of Israel from its Beginning to the Babylonian Exile*, Chicago 1960, pp. 175 ff., cf. also p. 156, and in comment Thompson, op. cit., pp. 120 ff.; and F. M. Cross, *Canaanite Myth and Hebrew Epic*, Cambridge, Mass. 1973, pp. 293 ff., cf. especially pp. 324 f.

hausen brought into a position of dominance. A contrary conception, worked out more fully in general outline than in detail, was produced in Scandinavia. There Engnell, as the most prominent representative of this school until now, rejected the whole of traditional literary criticism as a mistaken *interpretatio europaeica moderna*.[20] According to him the parallel narrative works assumed by the literary critics never existed (here we are reminded of the fragment hypothesis of Alexander Geddes), but only different circles of traditions, one of which preferred the name Yahweh, the other the term Elohim. The narratives now united in the Tetrateuch, the books from Genesis to Numbers, derive from a priestly circle of tradition working in Jerusalem, with its roots in Hebron, which had at its disposal a JE tradition partly still oral, partly already fixed in writing. Following Johannes Pedersen he argued that the narratives of the Tetrateuch had gathered successively around the Passover legend, which served as a core. A second circle of traditions, the Deuteronomistic circle, transmitted the historical narrative extending from Deuteronomy to 2 Kings, at first orally. It was only in the days of Ezra and Nehemiah that the P and D traditions reached their full form in writing, and were soon after united with one another. We will see that ultimately this picture differs from that formed by literary criticism only on the point that instead of the sources J, E and P corresponding circles of tradition are to be assumed, and that both types of scholarship agree that P forms the framework for JE. The views of the two schools are not very far apart on the existence of a Deuteronomistic history and its subsequent uniting with the Tetrateuch. The main difference lies in the answer given to the question whether we must allow for the narrative works being written down to any great extent in the pre-exilic period or not. The supporters of classical Pentateuchal criticism can in their own favour point to an over-estimation of the oral process of tradition even for oriental peoples of that date, to the numerous attestations of ancient oriental works of literature, and finally to the basic literary-critical criteria of the evidence of continuous doublets, to which differences of linguistic usage, style and *Tendenz* correspond.

Other objections to the newer documentary hypothesis have

20. Cf. I. Engnell, *Critical Essays on the Old Testament*, ed. J. T. Willis and H. Ringgren, London 1970, pp. 50 ff.

been made hitherto on too narrow a basis for it to be possible to see in them already a fully worked out alternative view. We will mention from among them only Redford's attempt to demonstrate from the example of the Joseph story that P is identical with the collector of the Genesis material, and at the same time to refute the assumption of written sources J and E[21]. It remains to be seen whether the tendency that can be observed both here and elsewhere to return to a form of supplementary hypothesis will win acceptance. It would be unwise overhastily to prophesy the end of the newer documentary hypothesis. At present it still fulfils, much better than all the hypotheses which are alternatives to it, the task of explaining the facts in the most comprehensive way possible; and this is the achievement that we must ask of a hypothesis. It should of course not be forgotten that it remains still a hypothesis.

If the beginner surveying Pentateuchal criticism feels forced to exclaim 'The Pentateuch is not Mosaic, but a mosaic!', we do have in this chapter in the history of scholarship nothing less than a cat's cradle of hypotheses. There is a measure of truth in each of the different attempts at an explanation: the documentary hypothesis, in spite of its numerous sub-varieties, many of which not even been mentioned here, has proved well suited to solve the problem of the involved narrative, and so performed not only a literary task, but one which is at the same time decisive for our knowledge of the sources for the history and theology of Israel. The sources have been by and large distinguished correctly, apart from the problems, which have not yet reached a final solution, of the compilation of J, of the nature of E as a written source or as a supplementary stratum, and the part played by the Jehovistic redaction and by a further Deuteronomistic redaction[22]. Furthermore they have been set, at least relatively correctly, in the context of the history of Israel, and so provide the framework for the history of its faith. The testimony of faith of each source is to be understood as the answer to a

21. D. B. Redford, *A Study of the Biblical Story of Joseph* (*Genesis 37–50*), SVT 20, 1970.

22. Cf. now W. Fuss, *Die deuteronomistische Pentateuchredaktion in Exodus 3,17*, BZAW 126, 1972, and in a somewhat clearer form in E. Zenger, *Die Sinaitheophanie. Untersuchungen zum jahwistischen und elohistischen Geschichtswerk*, FzB 3, 1971.

specific historical challenge. The fragment hypothesis has correctly recognized that single narratives and originally independent legislative sections are earlier than the continuous narrative. The supplementary hypothesis has correctly seen that one source, that is P, provides the framework for the Pentateuch. We can add in elaboration that within this framework J in turn takes the leading position, and E is incorporated into it. It is also correct in that the books of the sources even after their completion were expanded by individual sections. Form-criticism learnt to understand correctly the problems seen by the fragment hypothesis, in that it raised the question of the original setting in life of the individual narratives. Finally tradition-history has enlarged our view in that it has seen the question of the history of the individual narrative and of the Pentateuch as a whole as a problem. And together with form-criticism it has performed the inestimable service of recognizing and explaining the literature from life and as being in itself a piece of life[23].

If we look at the route traversed by scholarship since the age of orthodoxy, its divisions also mark the stages in method of all exegesis: it begins with textual criticism, passes through literary criticism and proceeds to form-critical and traditio-historical enquiry, and turns then to the explanation of the unit and of the whole. If we can once free ourselves from the wish that the human mind should always take the shortest and most direct route, we cannot deny the inner logic of the history of Pentateuchal scholarship which lies behind us.

§ 5 Literary Types of Israelite Narrative

H. Gunkel, *Genesis*, HK I, 1, Göttingen 1910³ (1966⁷), pp. vii ff.; ET of Introduction, *The Legends of Genesis*, New York 1901, reprinted 1964; id., 'Die israelitische Literatur', in Kultur den Gegenwart I, 7, Leipzig 1925, separate reprint Darmstadt 1963, pp. 15 ff.; A. Jolles, *Einfache Formen*, Halle 1930, Tübingen 1958²; W. Richter, *Traditionsgeschichtliche Untersuchungen zum Richterbuch*, BBB 18, 1963 (1966²), pp. 345 ff.; J. Hempel, *Geschichten und Geschichte im Alten Testament bis zur persischen Zeit*, Gütersloh 1964, pp. 60 ff.; C. Westermann, 'Arten der Erzählung in der Genesis', in *Forschung am Alten Testament*, ThB 24,

23. A. Weiser, *Introduction to the Old Testament*, pp. 81 f., in particular has pointed out the way the individual hypotheses add up together.

1964, pp. 9 ff.; K. Koch, *The Growth of the Biblical Tradition*, London 1969, pp. 148 ff.

History and the writing of history in general begin only when a people has developed into a state. Until then saga is the only form used to recollect a people's history. In accordance with this well established fact, in what Israel has to tell about its origins and down to the appearance of King David we have primarily sagas. Nothing is decided about the historicity or non-historicity of what is reported in assigning it to saga. This question needs to be examined in each case on the basis of the principles of method of the critical study of history[1].

1. Saga. Saga owes its immediacy and effectiveness primarily to the fact that stylistically, like all original popular composition, it is extremely reticent. It only tells what is important for the progress of the action, and makes no attempt to embellish subsidiary events. Correspondingly it restricts itself to a few characters, who are strongly and clearly characterized in their relationship to the main character. It is accordingly one-sided in the extreme, and paints its characters in black and white. The hero is contrasted to the coward, the crafty and clever to the fool or the less crafty. So the saga tells, and reveals, the ideals of the people. The few scenes it has are governed by the law that when there are in all three people or groups of people—only later can it be four or more—in every instance one vanishes from the stage, so that this is always occupied by only two. The course of action runs on simply. Its presentation is vivid, without getting lost in details. Its climax, marked by a speech or by a conversation, lies at the end. A clear beginning, a clear end and a sharply articulated structure give it its internal and external self-sufficiency. From what has been said it can already be deduced that it is the single saga that stands at the beginning of the development. It is only in the course of history that this grows together with other sagas to form a cycle of sagas. The old single sagas can be recognized by their brief style of narrative. Their interest lies in what they are recounting. Late sagas give themselves away by their more elaborate style. The centre of interest moves

1. Cf. e.g. Gunkel, *The Legends of Genesis*, pp. 1 ff.

from what they are narrating to the way in which they narrate it. The preliterary saga becomes a piece of real literature.

2. *Annals and historical narrative.* Finally saga dies out, as the interests of the state give rise to the forms of written historical tradition, which are simple at first, in the form of narrative annals and of historical narrative, which is related to the developed narrative art of the saga. Behind annals stand royal officials or scribes, behind historical narrative the individual author, behind saga a number of authors who are constantly adapting the material that has come down to them with slight variations to the needs of their own time. In respect of the Biblical sagas and historical narratives this process comes to an end in one way when they are fixed in writing, in another not until the last word of the religions dependent on the Old Testament, of Judaism, Christianity and Islam.

3. *Fairy tales and anecdotes.* The more history and the written transmission of the sagas become the dominant form for preserving the recollection of past events, the more popular imagination is restricted to the fairy tale and the anecdote. In order not to describe every folk narrative as a fairy tale, we follow Jolles, who has shown that the fairy tale is a creation of human sorrows and desires in a secular setting. It originates in the experience of the contradiction between naive desires for good fortune and the amorality of fate. It destroys the amoral world and creates a new one, in which men's desires and expectations of righteousness are fulfilled. It is sufficient to state that in the Old Testament not a single fairy tale proper has been preserved, but a whole series of fairy tale motifs, e.g. that of the young man who set out to look for his father's asses and found a kingdom (1 Sam. 9)[2]. The anecdote, unlike the saga and history writing, is no longer concerned to portray the large-scale fate of the nation, but individual significant traits of a great man. Thus it is no accident that anecdotes are found about David and his heroes (cf. 2 Sam. 23.8–23).

If the history of Israel and of Judaism is examined, it can be shown that written tradition then, as generally in antiquity and

2. Cf. Gunkel, *Das Märchen im Alten Testament*, RV II, 23–26, 1917 (1921).

down to the first centuries of the modern period, never played such an exclusive role as is taken for granted today at least in Western Europe. This means that even after the classical sagas of Israel were fixed in writing their life continued unbroken in the nation at the local sanctuaries, so that later writers could make fresh use of them.

4. *The types of saga.* Old Testament study of saga was dominated until the middle of this century by the work of Gunkel, whose commentary on Genesis broke new ground. It is only in these last years that objections have been raised to his nomenclature, although so far no general agreement has been reached among scholars. Accordingly it is best to set out first the classification given by Gunkel. In his work two systems of description overlap. One is based on the order of the Biblical narratives, and accordingly distinguishes between sagas of primeval history, sagas of the patriarchs, sagas of guidance and of heroes. The other is more formally based, and makes a roughly parallel division into myths, aetiologies and historical sagas. Gunkel has emphasized clearly that the basic types, which have here been given in an extremely simplified form, are rarely found in pure form, but mostly in connected series of motifs. It will be seen that recent scholarship has been particularly concerned to find more suitable names for the literary types of the sagas of the Old Testament.

Gunkel explains the myths as stories of the gods, and remarks at the same time that in the stories of the primeval period the Old Testament displays an 'unspoken aversion to mythology'[3]. Either God is the actor on his own, as in the story of creation in Gen. 1.1–2.4a, and then it is not a 'story' in the proper sense; or the story is acted out between God and men, and then the mythical element proper is yet further in the background.

Sagas which reflect historical events he called historical sagas, and those which record the situation of nations ethnographical. From Genesis he included among the first, for example, Gen. 34, and among the latter Gen. 4.1 ff.

The largest category in his work is that of the aetiology[4], a saga which is intended to explain something. The story answers the question 'Why?', by saying 'This is the reason'. Gunkel recognized that generally in the Old Testament sagas we do not

3. *The Legends of Genesis*, p. 16.   4. Cf. the Greek *aitia*, 'cause'.

have aetiological sagas in the full sense, but sagas with aetiological motifs. Here too there is a problem with which the most recent scholarly work has been concerned.

Gunkel distinguished between ethnological, etymological, cultic and geological motifs in aetiological sagas, and also between sagas explaining the fate of men and of animals. The ethnological saga or the ethnological motif enquires into the reasons for the relationships between the nations. The question why Canaan is the servant of his brothers is answered by the saga in Gen. 9.20 ff., the question why a Kenite is avenged sevenfold in Gen. 4.1 ff. The relationships between nations in the present are thus accounted for in terms of actions of the earliest men. Gunkel saw in this the beginning of a philosophy of history. Since, in accordance with the distinctive character of the Old Testament's self-understanding, God in these stories is always standing somewhere in the background, one could, in view of the final form of the sagas in which they are preserved to us, frequently speak also of the beginnings of a theology of history. For this is the specific quality of the Old Testament sagas, that in the end they are all drawn into the system of co-ordinates formed by God and nation, history as dialogue between God and man, God and Israel, God and the individual. The etymological themes look for an answer to the question why something has the name it does. Behind this stands not simply inquisitiveness, but a conviction that there is a secret natural connection between the name and the thing named[5]. The name is not explained philologically—there was at that time no philology in our sense, or only in the modest form of lexical lists—but by means of echoes from everyday language. The best example is probably the derivation of the name of the city of Babylon (Akkadian, 'Gate of God') from the Hebrew *bālal*, 'confuse', in Gen. 11.1 ff. Another large group is formed by the cultic sagas, which attempt to explain the holiness of a place, of a cult object or of a cultic usage. Gen. 1.1–2.4a answers the question of the holiness of the Sabbath; 28.10 ff. the question of the holiness of the stone of Bethel; Gen. 32.31 f. (Heb. 32.32 f.) the question why the Israelites do not eat a certain sinew in the area of the hollow of the thigh. Stories of this nature are now often called cultic

5. Cf. the proverb 'nomen est omen' ('the name has an effective significance').

legends. But this name is not without danger, because it encourages us to transfer the characteristic features of medieval
legends of the saints to these narratives. These medieval legends
were read on the anniversary of the saint during a service, to
encourage the Church to reverence and imitate the saint. It
must not be simply assumed that the Old Testament cultic sagas
really have their setting in life in the worship of the corresponding
sanctuaries. Even a conclusion from a saga back to a particular
institution responsible for its transmission should only be drawn
with the greatest caution. There are many aetiological sagas in
our own times which tell of the foundation of churches and yet
have not been read in a service of the church concerned[6]. It
should be sufficiently clear from these indications that the
interpretation and evaluation of the sagas of the Old Testament
is a difficult skill which requires wide-ranging knowledge. Like
every skill, it needs to be learnt.

The geological saga motifs, which Eissfeldt* more appropriately calls sagas of place and nature, attempt to explain the origin
of a locality, of a striking land form or of a single formation. The
best example here is the story of the destruction of Sodom in
Gen. 19. The strangely barren world of the Dead Sea, and
especially of the land surrounding it on the south-west, is explained as a consequence of a judgement on the immoral Sodom-
ites; a bizarre stone formation in the area is identified with Lot's
wife, who in spite of being forbidden to, turned round as she
fled, and was turned into a pillar of salt.

Finally the aetiological sagas and saga motifs also include
those which interpret the fate of man, and which attempt to
explain the form and fortune of animals. The Old Testament has
not preserved for us animal sagas proper, but it has motifs
coming from them like that of the explanation why the serpent
crawls on its belly, and why eternal hostility exists between man
and snake (Gen. 3.14 f.). The whole Yahwistic story of the
creation of woman and of the fall in Gen. 2 and 3 is a classic
example of a saga intended to explain the fate of man.

6. On the problem of aetiology see also M. Weippert, *The Settlement
of the Israelite Tribes in Palestine*, SBT² 21, 1971, pp. 136 ff., R. Smend,
jr., *Elemente alttestamentlichen Geschichtsdenkens*, Theologische Studien
95, Zurich 1968, pp. 10 ff., and B. O. Long, *The Problem of Etiological
Narrative in the Old Testament*, BZAW 108, 1968.

5. *The work of recent scholarship.* Jolles called at least part of the forms here called aetiologies myths. In his understanding of the concept myth is a narrative in which an object creates its own story in question and answer. The interpretation is taken not from objective investigation, but from the content the experience of the object has for the subject. We can learn from this at least that the mind of the narrators, unlike ours, was not aware of a subject-object division.

The real difficulties in the use of Gunkel's nomenclature result first from the fact that it is generally so formal that it makes an exact classification of the narrative more difficult; secondly from the fact that they also use criteria of historicity or non-historicity, which were not so consciously in the mind of the narrators. The first problem was perceived by Westermann, the second by Richter. In view of the misuse which has occasionally been made of the term aetiology in application to some sagas, Westermann has rightly emphasized that one should speak of an aetiology or of an aetiological saga only when the course of the narrative is coterminous with the course of the aetiology. In this sense the sagas of the primeval history of Gen. 1–11 are to be described as aetiologies (cf. e.g. 2.4b–3.24; 4.1–16 and 11.1–9, but also 19). In view of their content Westermann suggests for these sagas the name 'narratives of guilt and punishment'. The stories of the patriarchs he calls family narratives. This keeps in sight their limitation to life within the limits of the family and of the tribal unit. He divides them up by content into narratives of the fate of the mother of the tribe and of her child (e.g. 12.10–20; 16.1–16 and 18.1–16), those of strife about land (e.g. 13.5–13; 21.22–32 and 26.18–33), descriptions of success (e.g. 24), stories of promises (e.g. 15.7–21), and theological narratives (e.g. 22.1–19 and 18.17–33). Itineraries and genealogies provide the links between them. Genealogies serve first of all to provide compresible patterns in the world of the nations, e.g. in the form of the list of the nations in Gen. 10, and are accordingly close to the Ancient Oriental 'list wisdom' and represent an early form of scholarship[7]. Furthermore as genealogical trees of families and of tribes they are used for the evaluation and delimitation of social

7. Cf. below, pp. 371 f. On this subject cf. also A. Malamat, 'King Lists of the Old Babylonian Period and Biblical Genealogies', *JAOS* 88 (1968), pp. 163 ff.

claims, as can still be observed today among the Bedouin. Careful revisions of the lists in the historical period are more productive for the study of history than the beginner could imagine. It is certain that Westermann's encouragement of research into the development, consolidation and transmission of the narratives and motifs, together with their implicit references to the cultural level attained in them, will give fresh impulse to the study of the sagas.

Richter claims that the question of historicity played too great a part with Gunkel in his determination and delimitation of the literary types, since the stories themselves do not reveal what relationship they have to history. He starts therefore with an exact syntactical and stylistic analysis, and shows by the example of the Book of Judges that in this way more precise descriptions of the literary types can be obtained for the sections which until now have been loosely described as reworkings and redactions. Basically he distinguishes between genuine narratives, toned down historical reports based on narratives, and redactions. These he splits up into a series of sharply divided sub-types. But there remains the consideration that the literary type 'narrative' is very broad, so that if it is applied not to the relatively homogeneous material of the 'book of deliverers'[8] but to the sagas of Genesis, it will contain material that is very varied in content.

The discussion to date has shown that in determining the narrative types of the Old Testament we can dispense neither with formal criteria nor with criteria of content. It remains to be seen whether and in what way out of the different suggestions of recent years a new, unitary system which remains as faithful to the text as possible will develop. In looking back over what Gunkel's new ideas have signified for the scholarly work of this century, in spite of all our questions we cannot be sufficiently thankful for them.

§ 6 Literary Types of Israelite Law

L. Köhler, 'Justice in the Gate' [1931], in *Hebrew Man*, London 1956, pp. 149 ff.; A. Alt, 'The Origins of Israelite Law' [1934], in *Essays on Old Testament History and religion*, Oxford 1966, pp. 79 ff.; M. Noth, 'The

8. Cf. below, p. 146.

Laws in the Pentateuch' [1940], in *The Laws in the Pentateuch and Other Essays*, Edinburgh and London, 1966, pp. 1 ff.; D. Daube, *Studies in Biblical Law*, Cambridge 1947; id., *The Exodus Pattern in the Bible*, London 1963; J. J. Stamm and M. E. Andrew, *The Ten Commandments in Recent Research*, SBT²2, 1967; F. Horst, *Gottes Recht. Gesammelte Studien zum Recht im Alten Testament*, ThB 12, 1961; E. Gerstenberger, *Wesen und Herkunft des 'apodiktischen Rechts'*, WMANT 20, 1965; H. Graf Reventlow, 'Kultisches Recht im Alten Testament', *ZTK* 60 (1963), pp. 267 ff.; G. Fohrer, 'Das sogenannte apodiktisch formulierte Recht und der Dekalog' [1965], in *Studien zur alttestamentlichen Theologie und Geschichte*, BZAW 115, 1969, pp. 120 ff.; D. J. McCarthy, *Old Testament Covenant* [1966], Oxford 1972; H. Gese, 'Der Dekalog als Ganzheit betrachtet', *ZTK* 64 (1967), pp. 121 ff.; H. Schulz, *Das Todesrecht im Alten Testament*, BZAW 114, 1969; W. Schottroff, *Der altisraelitische Fluchspruch*, WMANT 30, 1969; L. Perlitt, *Bundestheologie im Alten Testament*, WMANT 36, 1969; G. Liedke, *Gestalt und Bezeichnung alttestamentlicher Rechtssätze*, WMANT 39, 1971; V. Wagner, *Rechtssätze in gebundener Sprache und Rechtssatzreihen im israelitischen Recht*, BZAW 127, 1972.

1. The Problem. The progress of the narrative in the Pentateuch is constantly interrupted by shorter or longer insertions. Series of laws, books of laws and cultic ordinances predominate among these both in length and in importance. Among the series of laws are the Decalogue (Exod. 20.2–17, par. Deut. 5.6–21); among books of laws the Book of the Covenant B (Exod. 20.22–23.19), the Code of Holiness H (Lev. 17–26)[1] and Deuteronomy (Deut. 4.44–30.20*)[2], and among priestly cultic ordinances the law of sacrifice (Lev. 1–7) and the law of purity (Lev. 11–15)[2a]. In view of the extent of the material and of the undeniably important connections between religion and law in Ancient Israel, the beginner must start with certain basic facts about the literary types of Israelite law. It should first be said that scholarship in this area, in spite of the existence of an extensive literature, has reached few assured results. If the signs of recent years do not deceive, there will be new work and argument in the immediate future not only on the question of the nature and extent of Israelite law, but also on the delimitation and setting in life of the individual legal forms, and on the dates of the series and books of laws. If Mosaic authorship is now only discussed in

1. Cf. below, pp. 113 ff.   2. Cf. below, pp. 115 ff.   2a. Cf. below, p. 107.

connection with the prehistory of the Decalogue, this is a result both of the general picture scholarship has formed of the growth of the Pentateuch[3], and of the realization that series of laws, books of laws and cultic ordinances generally arise out of concrete needs, and only in the rarest instances from an inspired Utopian purpose, whether prophetic or philosophical[4]. And since, even in the latter case, references are found to the state of affairs at the time of the formation of the material, we can regard it as a basic rule of the interpretation of legal texts that the social, economic and religious conditions presupposed by the legal maxims and instructions allow an inference to be made about their date[5]. In applying this rule we must of course realize that society in antiquity did not change as quickly and decisively as we are used to it changing in the twentieth century.

Generally rules which presuppose simpler conditions of society are to be regarded as older than those which presuppose a more developed form of society. So it is immediately obvious that in view of the historical course Israel took, rules which envisage nomadic conditions of society are to be regarded as older than those which can only be understood from the conditions of a settled society. The creation of a legal and of a social history of Israel accordingly go hand in hand. Alongside the criteria of content, we can set up as formal basic rules, which are only to be used together, that a short legal sentence is older than a longer one, one restricted to a concrete case older than a generalizing one, and a pure literary type older than a mixed literary type. Finally we must work from the understanding that, in this area too, the development proceeded from oral tradition to fixing in writing, from individual saying to a short series and from a short to a longer series, and from the formation of series to the compilation of a legal case-book. Before applying these rules schematically we must remind ourselves that the literary types of Israelite law can only be understood in the context of the history of ancient Oriental law. So e.g. the taking over of casuistic law from the Canaanites shows that conclusions cannot without qualifications be drawn from the legal form to the antiquity of a legal maxim[6].

3. Cf. above, pp. 40 ff.   4. Cf. e.g. Plato's *Laws*.
5. Cf. D. Daube, *The Exodus Pattern in the Bible*, pp. 16 ff. and 22 ff.
6. Cf. above, pp. 31 f., and below, pp. 56 f.

2. Example: the Book of the Covenant. An introduction to the literary types of Israelite law can best be made by the example of the Book of the Covenant (Exod. 20.22–23.19(33))[7]. This is a legal case-book, which has been secondarily inserted into the Sinai account in the Book of Exodus. It takes its name from the book mentioned in Exod. 24.7. To clarify the terminology we must say here that a legal case-book is distinguished from a law code by the fact that the latter derives from a unitary law-giving mind, and in general deals with legal problems systematically, and also, with respect to the needs of its period, completely. In a legal case-book on the other hand we have a collection of the laws that are actually in force. The legal material so gathered can be in origin of different dates and places, and may belong to different legal forms. In accordance with its origin, its contents are legal paradigms, i.e. examples, which however do not cover by any means all the situations which need a legal ruling. Consideration of the possibilities of conflict in an agricultural society would quickly show that in the Book of the Covenant we do not have a law code, but a legal case-book. The secondary character of the collection already appears in a list of the contents:

I 20.22–26		Rules about images of deities and the construction of altars
II 21.1		Superscription
	21.2–11	Laws about slaves
	21.12–17	Offences deserving the death penalty
	21.18–36	Physical injuries
	22.1–22.17	
	(Heb. 21.37–22.16)	Offences against property
III 22.18–31		
	(Heb. 22.17–30)	Religious and social rules
	23.1–9	Law court procedure
	23.10–19	Cultic regulations
IV 23.20–33		Speech of dismissal

20.22–26 and 23.20–33 are, in the opinion of most scholars, to be regarded as later additions[7a].

---

7. The reader is strongly urged to follow the passages quoted in a Bible. Otherwise he is like a blind man listening to a discussion of colours.

7a. Cf. however D. Conrad, *Studien zum Altargesetz Ex* 20.24–26, Marburg 1968, pp. 8 f.

(a) CASUISTIC LAW. The first real impulse to the investigation of the literary types of Israelite law was given by Alt's enquiry, 'The Origins of Israelite Law' (1934). Alt distinguished the two basic forms of 'apodictically' and 'casuistically' formulated law. The former he regarded as genuinely Israelite, the latter he saw as having been taken over from the Canaanites. The mark of the casuistic legal form is that, in the protasis of the sentence, the legal instance is introduced by a *kî*, 'if', and the treatment it is given is set out in the apodosis. Subsidiary instances are attached to the treatment of the main case with an *'im*, 'if'. This form is found in the Book of the Covenant in 21.2–22.17 (Heb. 22.16), apart from a few sentences in 21.12–17. The heading in 21.1 obviously applied originally only to the collection extending as far as 22.16. An examination of the contents makes it clear that the decisions on the law on slaves, physical injuries and offences against property were intended to regulate the common life of towns. Its setting in life must accordingly have been the place where the Israelite court met, the gate of the city[8].

Chapter 4 of the Book of Ruth gives us some idea of the procedure. Legal speeches in the historical books and in the prophetic books fill out the picture[9]. As soon as the city gate through which the farmers went out for their work in the fields was opened in the morning, the one seeking his rights sat down there, to await the coming of his opponent. He sought further to get a number of the elders of the place as judges, and in certain cases as witnesses as well. The passers by added themselves to the company, were called upon as witnesses and no doubt accompanied the whole proceedings with a commentary of oriental liveliness. And so the case went on with lively speeches and counter-speeches, with charges and attempts at reconciliation, appeals to the judges, speeches of accusation, appeals to witnesses and speeches of defence, until a confession was obtained, the defendant convicted by witnesses, or innocence proved, so that finally judgement could be passed (cf. also Jer. 26.10 ff.). The standard used for the verdict will no doubt as a rule have been the customary law in force, which as such was known especially to the elders, though it would not have been fixed in writing, nor would there be any need to refer to a written form of it.

8. Cf. Köhler, op. cit., pp. 149 ff.; A. L. Oppenheim, *Ancient Mesopotamia*, Chicago 1964, p. 128.

9. Cf. H. J. Boecker, *Redeformen des Rechtslebens im Alten Testament*, WMANT 14, 1964.

There is evidence that there were non-local appeal courts in the monarchical period in 2 Sam. 14.4 ff. and 1 Kgs. 3.16 ff. (cf. also Deut. 17.8 ff.).

Accordingly Liedke would derive the casuistically formulated legal sentences or *mišpāṭîm* (cf. Exod. 21.1) which are handed down in the Old Testament from verdicts which were reconciled with one another in the course of arbitration by the elders of the tribe[10].

(b) THE PROBLEM OF THE FIXING IN WRITING OF THE LEGAL MATERIAL. There is no consensus about when and in what concrete situation the collection of casuistic laws transmitted in the Book of the Covenant, and finally the whole of the material united here, was written down. Opinions vary between a dating in the period of the Judges and of the Kings. All that is agreed is that the Book of the Covenant represents an earlier stage of the formation of law than Deuteronomy. This however only gives a *terminus ad quem*. In its content the Book of the Covenant does indeed presuppose the situation in a cultivated land, but lacks allusions to a political state organization. For this reason it is possible to date it to the premonarchical period, but in view of what we have said about the practice of law in a local community, this is by no means necessary. Basically we have to consider the following three motives for fixing the legal material in writing: 1. the task of bringing unity to the law when there are divergent understandings of the law within one community; 2. the task of preserving legal usage in the face of collapse or of a break in tradition within a community, and 3. as an aid to the memory. It is obvious that the third possibility is particularly likely in the case of a developed and complicated legal tradition, but this does not exclude the earlier writing down of paradigmatic series of laws.

(c) APODICTIC LAW. Alt ascribed to the apodictic legal form prohibitives, commands, and death (*môṭ yûmaṭ*) and curse formulae. Prohibitives are found in Exod. 22.18–31* (Heb. 22.17–30*). In content they are religious and social prescriptions, which lack any casuistic qualification and also any statement of the punishment. They simply direct what may not take place.

10. Cf. Liedke, op. cit., pp. 53 ff.

Alongside the prohibitives, which are directed to a person in the second singular, there are positive commands, which state Yahweh's demands, in 22.29b, 30a (and 31a). There are also prohibitives reshaped in casuistic form in 22.23 f. and 26 f., which are evidence of a mixture of categories. If a single name for both commands and prohibitions were required, it would be possible to speak of 'prohibitive law'.

Further prohibitives are found in 23.1–9*. The content of all the prescriptions put together here has to do with the behaviour of the Israelites in a legal process. Like the social prescriptions in 22.18 ff. they are concerned to protect the poor and weak, over whose legal position Yahweh watches. In 23.10–19 follow cultic commands and prohibitions, among which we can also include 20.23–26. The material collected in 23.14–19 in particular states the cultic demands of Yahweh. Following a suggestion of Horst we may describe this section of the prohibitive law as the 'law of Yahweh's privileges'[11]. If it is correct that the demand for the exclusive worship of Yahweh was from its beginnings an intrinsic part of Israelite belief, we must postulate that lists of such demands, like those handed down in Exod. 34.14–26, go back to the premonarchical and even wilderness period. It must not of course be overlooked that the groups of laws we have now contain requirements which were only meaningful in the cultivated land of Israel.

Finally Alt, referring to the steles from N'gaous, well known from the discussion of sacrifice to Moloch, held that we could recognize in the use of the talion formula in Exod. 21.23–25, Lev. 24.18, 20 and Deut. 19.21 the result of a secondary expansion of the stylistic usage of a phrase which in the first instance regulated the exchange value of sacrifices[12].

(d) DISCUSSION. It is precisely the legal forms described by Alt as apodictic that have been subjects of lively discussion in recent years. His conclusions have been modified in the course of this. Gerstenberger has suggested that the origin of prohibitive law is to be sought in the clan ordinances of the premonarchical

---

11. Cf. Horst, op. cit., pp. 17 ff.

12. A. Alt, *KS* I, pp. 341 ff. For a discussion of the Punic sacrificial terminology cf. J. G. Février, 'Le vocabulaire sacrificiel punique', *Journal Asiatique* 243 (1955), pp. 49 ff., and J. Hoftijzer, *VT* 8 (1958), pp. 288 ff.

union of clans. The prohibitives would accordingly have been in the first instance authoritative commands of the elders of the clan or family. They would have received their esteem from the hallowed ordering of life which was represented by these natural authorities. The 'you' addressed would accordingly be male descendants. It may however be doubted whether at this cultural stage we should think in terms of a regular form of instruction. Kilian has attempted to show that apodictic law has non-Israelite (Egyptian) parallels, and so has questioned the hypothesis of apodictic law as a genuinely Israelite legal form[13]. Finally Weinfeld has referred to the Hittite instructions and to corresponding commands of the Assyrian kings which possessed the force of law, in which the situation of dialogue which is reflected in the second person address and the apodictic formulation recur.[14] The question whether in the case of the prohibitives we should not speak of rules for life and behaviour in apodictic formulation rather than of a legal form, as Fohrer has suggested, depends on the fundamental problem of defining what is law, which we cannot here go into.

(e) LAW RELATING TO DEATH. A further form claimed by Alt as apodictic is found in 21.12, 15–17 and 22.19 (Heb. 22.18). Its distinguishing feature is that the state of affairs given in a participial sentence is followed by a declaration of the death penalty. 21.15–17 show that the declaration of the penalty originally had the stereotyped form 'he shall be put to death' (*môṯ yûmaṯ*) (cf. also Exod. 31.12–17*; Lev. 20*; 24.10–23* and 27.29). Hermann Schulz has suggested the description 'law relating to death' (*Todesrecht*) for this legal form. Alt clearly felt the apodictic force of *môṯ yûmaṯ* and accordingly included these sentences, together with the series of curses in Deut. 27, within apodictic law. Others saw in them an apodictic reshaping of originally casuistic legal sentences. Schulz on the other hand assumes that the *môṯ yûmaṯ* is not a statement of legal consequences but a

13. Cf. R. Kilian, 'Apodiktisches und kasuistisches Recht im Licht ägyptischer Analogien', *BZ* NF 7 (1963), pp. 185 ff.; R. Hentschke, 'Erwägungen zur israelitischen Rechtsgeschichte', *ThV* 10 (1966), p. 108 ff.

14. Cf. M. Weinfeld, 'The Origin of the Apodictic Law', *VT* 23 (1973), pp. 63 ff.

declaration that the man has lost his right to life and is given over to death. He can at least show that the 'death' clauses have in every case a corresponding form in a prohibitive, cf. e.g. Exod. 21.12 with 20.13. Schulz conjectures as the setting in life a sacral legal procedure. The local legal community of citizens would accordingly have constituted itself a cultic legal community to pass and carry out a sentence of death. Wagner on the other hand remains nearer to Alt's view. He interprets the *môṭ yûmaṭ* formula as a technical term for the death sentence, and derives the material as we have it from a ten-element series of fixed form, which he regards as 'a collection of capital offences for the domestic tribal jurisdiction within nomadic law'[15].

(f) THE LAW OF TALION. The derivation of the formula for talion has also been disputed. So Wagner reverses the order proposed by Alt, and making reference to the context of the instances in the Old Testament, and to the preservation usual both in them and in non-Israelite lawbooks of an anatomical sequence in dealing with injuries to the body, claims the *ius talionis* as a legal form which has its setting in inter-tribal law, and treats it as part of the nomadic heritage of Israel.

3. Curse and law. Alt had, as has already been said, included the series of curses in Deut. 27.15–26 in apodictic law. Having in view the cultic situation presupposed in Deut. 27, he appealed to Deut. 31.10 ff., to postulate the existence of a feast of the renewal of the covenant, taking place every seven years on the occasion of the Feast of Tabernacles at Shechem. This festival would have been connected with the reading of apodictic series of laws such as the series of curses in Deut. 27.15 ff. or of the Decalogue (Exod. 20.2–17). While this hypothesis won widespread recognition in recent years, it has now also encountered much opposition. It is best to divide up the problems raised here into three groups of questions: 1. the question whether it is possible to include series of curses, and so also the liturgical single curse, among the legal forms; 2. the question of the date and earlier history of the Decalogue, and 3. the question of the connections between covenant and law, and between cult and law.

15. Wagner, op. cit., p. 30.

The Israelite curse formula is according to Schottroff a form of speech which originally grew up in the setting of the nomadic clan, and served for 'the solemn excommunication of an individual who is hostile to and damages the community', and which for this reason was, it is conjectured, used primarily as an exclusion formula by the head of the family or of the tribe (cf. Gen. 9.25; Josh. 9.23). It can therefore be attributed, with Wagner, to inter-tribal law. The curse further served the individual as a 'legal device to ensure and realize his legal claims' (cf. Judg. 17.2; Zech. 5.3 f. and Prov. 29.24)[16].

It was further used as an irrational form of providing proof in the priestly ordeal, if the normal requirements for a proper legal process were lacking (cf. 1 Kgs. 8.31 f. with Num. 5.11 ff.)[17].

The series of curses (Deut. 27.15 ff.) clearly goes back to legal clauses. In its present context it concludes Deuteronomy's paradigmatic instruction in the law. The curses are meant to be reinforced by the community, and so to serve to bind the partners in the covenant to keep the terms of the treaty[18].

4. The Decalogue (Exod. 20.2–17, par. Deut. 5.6–21). Of the questions to be dealt with here, that of the date and origin of the Decalogue (or Ten Commandments) continues to arouse especial interest[19]. The main problems in work on the Decalogue today are: 1, the question whether it belongs to one of the Pentateuch sources (E); 2, the reconstruction of its original form; 3, the question of the originality of its composition, and 4, of its setting in life. On the basis of Exod. 20.13–15 with its short prohibitives the idea has arisen of reconstructing a short original form of all ten commandments. At the same time it has been observed that our present composition goes back to older shorter series such as we have again in 20.13–15. A comparison

16. Cf. Schottroff, op. cit., pp. 205 ff., 216 f., and 231 f.

17. Schottroff, pp. 217 ff.

18. Cf. Schulz, op. cit., pp. 61 ff., but also Schottroff, pp. 220 ff.

19. For an introduction to the subject cf. J. J. Stamm and M. E. Andrews, *The Ten Commandments in Recent Research*, SBT[2] 2, 1967; also H. Graf Reventlow, *Gebot und Predigt im Dekalog*, Gütersloh 1962; E. Nielsen, *The Ten Commandments in New Perspective*, SBT[2] 7, 1968; A. Jepsen, 'Beiträge zur Auslegung und Geschichte des Dekalogs', *ZAW* 79 (1967), pp. 277 ff., and W. H. Schmidt, 'Die Komposition des Dekaloges', in *Uppsala Congress Volume*, SVT 22, 1972, pp. 201 ff.

with Ps. 50.8 or Hos. 4.2 shows that the formulation of these series had not yet become inflexible. In view of the conjectural nature of the prehistory of the Decalogue those scholars who regard Mosaic authorship as not worth discussing must surely be right.

Views differ over the question with what degree of certainty an original short form can be obtained from the present composition, which clearly shows Deuteronomistic, and in the case of the sabbath commandment secondarily P, influences. Since not one witness to the existence of the whole Decalogue can be found in the pre-Deuteronomistic period, and its formulations, by the criteria of date established above[20], must be regarded as late, I agree with those scholars who regard the Decalogue as Deuteronomistic. Its tendency towards generalizing and to broadening of meaning together with its formal lack of unity reveals it to be a latecomer, for which an original short form cannot be presupposed[21]. The possibility that other series did in fact have their setting in life in the cult is not thereby excluded. In accordance with the particular character of faith in Yahweh, it must be allowed that the beginnings of law connected with Yahweh reach back into the Mosaic period. Otherwise it would be impossible to understand why the tradition made Moses in particular be the mediator of divine law. Law was never regarded by the ancients as only a matter of human discretion, because the social and moral ordering of the world was regarded as an institution of God or of the gods. The protection of the law too was accordingly seen as a concern of the deity. For this reason it can be understood why the law was regarded as 'a gift of the gods; the power to issue laws is of divine origin'[22]. The fact that in Israel and in Judaism the fiction of Moses' mediation of the law in force or claiming validity was held to so persistently, shows that there was a desire to regard all later extensions of the law as in agreement with the Sinai covenant mediated by Moses in the earliest days of Israel[23].

5. *Covenant and Law.* If we turn our attention finally to the question of the relation between covenant and law, and be-

---

20. Cf. above, p. 54.   21. Cf. also W. H. Schmidt, op. cit., pp. 214 ff.
22. Fohrer, *Introduction*, p. 53.
23. On the Moses tradition cf. also the account of the present position of scholarship in H. Schmid, *Mose. Überlieferung und Geschichte*, BZAW 110, 1968, pp. 1 ff., and also V. Fritz, *Israel in der Wüste*, MTS 7, Marburg 1970, pp. 123 ff.; G. Widengren, 'What do we know about Moses?', in *Proclamation and Presence*, Festschrift G. H. Davies, London 1970, pp. 21 ff. and S. Schwertner, 'Erwägungen zu Moses Tod und Grab in Dtn 34, 5.6*', *ZAW* 84 (1972), pp. 25 ff.

tween cult and law, we touch upon one of the most difficult problems of Old Testament scholarship at the present. Without attempting even to set out the problems completely here, we will confine our remarks to some observations and to the sketching of a perspective. Von Rad in his 'Form-critical Problem of the Hexateuch' has pointed out that the structure of the Sinai pericope in the Book of Exodus and the structure of Deuteronomy have in common that in each case a paraenesis (i.e. exhortation) is followed by a recital of the law, commitment to covenant and conclusion of covenant, or blessings and curses[24]. Mendenhall, Beyerlin, Baltzer and McCarthy have attempted to show that this structure has its equivalent in the Ancient Near Eastern state treaties[25]. It is disputed how far this schema only goes back to Deuteronomy, or to (possibly Deuteronomistically influenced) redactions of the Pentateuch, or how far it was already determinative of the structure of the original Sinai narratives of J and E.

Perlitt is indeed right when he says that in the prophets of the eighth century there is no genuine evidence of any knowledge of the Sinai covenant, since Hos. 8.1b belongs to the Deuteronomistic redaction. In the Sinai pericope (Exod. 19–24 and 32–34) however J seems only to have told of theophany and sacrifice, E of theophany and a meal[26]. Neither Exod. 19.3b–8; 20.1–17; 20.22–23.19(33) nor 24.7 f. and 32–34 belong to the material in the ancient sources. On this view it was only when, following on from the Deuteronomist's understanding of *berît* as a solemn promise of land made to the fathers, law and covenant were identified in the work of the Deuteronomist or in the

24. *The Problem of the Hexateuch and Other Essays*, Edinburgh and London 1966, pp. 1 ff.

25. G. E. Mendenhall, *Law and Covenant in Israel and the Ancient Near East*, Pittsburgh 1955, W. Beyerlin, *Origins and History of the Oldest Sinaitic Traditions*, Oxford 1965, K. Baltzer, *The Covenant Formulary*, Oxford 1971, and D. J. McCarthy, *Old Testament Covenant*, Oxford 1972. In criticism cf. F. Nötscher, 'Bundesformular und "Amtsschimmel" ', *BZ* NF 9 (1965), pp. 181 ff., and E. Kutsch, 'Der Begriff *berît* in vordeuteronomischer Zeit', in *Das ferne und nahe Wort*, Festschrift L. Rost, BZAW 105, 1967, pp. 133 ff.; id., 'Sehen und Bestimmen. Die Etymologie von *berît*', in *Archäologie und Altes Testament*, Festschrift K. Galling, Tübingen 1970, pp. 165 ff.

26. Perlitt's results are in general corroborated by E. Zenger, *Die Sinaitheophanie*, FzB 3, 1971.

Deuteronomic and Deuteronomistic movement that the corresponding expansions of the Sinai pericope were made. Nor, according to Perlitt, does Josh. 24 offer a point of contact with an old, Shechemite covenant tradition, but is rather primarily to be understood as a summons to keep faith to Yahweh in view of the danger from Assyria in the seventh century. Since finally neither in the Sinai pericope nor in Deuteronomy is there reliable evidence for the existence of an ancient Israelite covenant formulary, and Deut. 31.9 ff. is not enough itself to carry the weight of the hypothesis of a proclamation of the law in the ancient Israelite Covenant Festival, things look bad for both of the hypotheses which have so much enriched Old Testament research in the last decades. It must be particularly emphasized that this has consequences for the hypothesis about the content of the pre-exilic Jerusalem autumn festival, presented in different forms by e.g. Mowinckel[27] and Weiser[28], and that psalms like 50 and 81 are perhaps again to be regarded as post-exilic.

It is however certain in my opinion that, as Psalms 15 and 24 show, there were entrance liturgies at the sanctuaries, in which the pilgrims were instructed in the conditions for admission to the sanctuary. They refer back in a clearly recognizable way to acknowledged legal demands of Yahweh[29].

It should finally be remarked that the narrative literature too can contribute to the clarification of legal ideas when interpreted by carefully thought out methods of legal analysis. Daube has worked out basic criteria for such a legal analysis of narrative literature. If 1. the sense of what is narrated only becomes clear in connection with a clarification of the legal position, 2. vocabulary and technical terms of the narrative are rooted in the legal and social area, and 3. the suggested legal ideas appear to be possible for ancient Oriental legal patterns, one can assume the dependence of the narrative on legal ideas, legal custom or legal sentences to be certain[30].

27. *Psalmenstudien* II, Kristiania 1922 (Amsterdam 1961).

28. On the question of the relationship of the psalms to the cult, 'Die Darstellung der Theophanie in den Psalmen und im Festkult', in *Festschrift A. Bertholet*, Tübingen 1950, pp. 513 ff., also in *Glaube und Geschichte im Alten Testament und andere ausgewählte Schriften*, Göttingen 1961, pp. 303 ff.

29. Cf. K. Koch, 'Tempeleinlassliturgien und Dekaloge', in *Studien zur Theologie der alttestamentlichen Überlieferungen*, Festschrift G. von Rad, Neukirchen 1961, pp. 45 ff.

30. On this cf. Daube, *Exodus Pattern*, pp. 22 f.

6. Blessing. Although it does not belong to the legal categories proper, a mention must be made of the nature of blessing. According to Schottroff in nomadic society it originally had the social function of giving a share in the salvation which was to be found within the common life of the clan, or of establishing this salvation. It is possible therefore to assume that it had its original setting in life in greetings on arrival (cf. Gen. 14.19 f., I Sam. 25.14, Ruth 2.4), and on departure (cf. Gen. 24.60, 28.1, 2 Sam. 13.25)[31]. With such an origin, the role of the blessing in the cult, as it appears in Num. 6.22 ff., in Deuteronomy (cf. e.g. Deut. 28.1 ff.), and especially in the psalms (cf. e.g. Ps. 24.5, 134.3) can readily be explained. In the cult the priest, as representative of Yahweh, promises to those who for their part maintain communion with God the salvation contained in such communion[32].

Retrospect. The demonstration of the distinctive character and of the original setting in life of the casuistic law may be regarded as an assured result of scholarship. The three forms claimed by Alt to be apodictic, the prohibitive, the death sentences and the legal curses, on the other hand, are to be regarded as each independent and separate literary categories. It cannot be said that these are genuinely Israelite forms. Form and content must be dealt with separately in this connection. Final judgements have not yet been passed on the relationship between covenant and law, and between cult and law. The aim of a coherent history of law in Israel has not yet been achieved by scholarship.

A final word may be added about the theological significance of law in the Old Testament, since the problem recurs in Christian theology in the form of the question of the relationship between law and gospel: 'Obedience . . . does not create communion with God . . . but is expected as the response of the people which has been counted worthy of communion with God and "chosen" '[33]. In other words, it is always the gift of God which stands first. But as the gift of *God*, it always contains in itself a task for man.

31. Cf. Schottroff, op. cit., pp. 188 ff.
32. Cf. on this also C. Westermann, *BHHW* III, cols. 1757 f.
33. E. Würthwein, 'Der Sinn des Gesetzes im Alten Testament', *ZTK* 55 (1958), pp. 266 ff., also in *Wort und Existenz. Studien zum Alten*

§7 The Growth of the Pentateuchal Narrative at the Pre-literary Stage

A. Alt, 'The God of the Fathers' [1929], in *Essays on Old Testament History and Religion*, Oxford 1966, pp. 1 ff.; G. von Rad, 'The Form-critical Problem of the Hexateuch' [1938], in *The Problem of the Hexateuch and other Essays*, Edinburgh and London 1966, pp. 1–78; M. Noth, *A History of Pentateuchal Traditions* [1948], Englewood Cliffs, N.J., 1972; A. Weiser, *Introduction to the Old Testament* [1949²], London 1961; A. Jepsen, 'Zur Überlieferungsgeschichte der Vätergestalten', *WZ Leipzig*, 3 (1953–54), pp. 139 ff.; C. Westermann, 'Arten der Erzählung in der Genesis', in *Forschung am Alten Testament*, ThB 24, 1964, pp. 9 ff.; S. Herrmann, *Die prophetischen Heilserwartungen im Alten Testament*, BWANT V, 5, 1965, pp. 64 ff.; H.-J. Zobel, *Stammesspruch und Geschichte*, BZAW 95, 1965; H. Seebass, *Der Erzvater Israel*, BZAW 98, 1966; H. Weidmann, *Die Patriarchen und ihre Religion im Licht der Forschung seit Julius Wellhausen*, FRLANT 94, 1968; H. Schulte, *Die Entstehung der Geschichtsschreibung im Alten Israel*, BZAW 128, 1972.

1. (a) THE STARTING-POINT. The Pentateuch as a completed literary unit is the only absolute datum at our disposal. The hypothesis that it originated basically in three redactions from a series of originally independent sources may be regarded as certain, however many questions still remain unsolved about the unity and extent of the sources. It is now part of the generally agreed picture of the origin of the Pentateuch in international Old Testament scholarship that first of all, perhaps even before the sixth-century exile, the Yahwistic and Elohistic works were united to form the so-called 'Jehovistic history'; that in the course of this the main thread of the narrative, with some exceptions, remained with J, and that E was used basically only to supplement J; that this 'Jehovistic history' was inserted into the priestly writing, which served as a framework, and that finally the resulting historical narrative was dovetailed with the Deuteronomistic history.[1]

Testament, Göttingen 1970, pp. 50 f., cf. also Noth, op. cit. On the basic significance of law in religion cf. C. H. Ratschow in *Die theologische Dimension der Frage nach dem Menschen*, ed. P. Görges and J. M. Meier, Donauwörth 1972, pp. 54 ff.

1. A thorough study of the theology of the redactor who combined JE

(b) METHOD. When we enquire into the formation of the Pentateuchal tradition at its pre-literary stage, and so at the same time
into the prehistory of the sources, we necessarily enter into an
entirely hypothetical area. While we cannot dispense completely
here with the formation of hypotheses, we must be aware of the
danger of building hypotheses uncritically one upon another.
The scholar should in every case consider what degree of hypo-
theticality attaches to the conclusions he draws. In each case
careful literary and redactional criticism, a precise determination
of the way the sources work, of the elements reworked by them
and of those newly formed by them, together with form-critical
considerations, must form the basis of the enquiry. It remains to
remark that there is a mutual interplay between form-critical and
traditio-historical considerations on the one hand, and the picture
of the prehistory and early history of Israel obtained by a particular method of source-criticism on the other. If one wished
fundamentally to put in question the traditio-historical method in
view of the circularity of the argument, the historian would be
left only with the criterion of historical probability, and so would
be exposed to the danger of regarding secondary groupings of
narrative as original, and tendentious compositions as reliable.

(c) THE PRESENT POSITION. In German Old Testament work we
now have basically two opposed attempts to explain the growth
of the Pentateuchal tradition. The first of them goes back to the
work of Albrecht Alt, and is predominantly traditio-historical in
orientation. It holds that the main themes of the Pentateuch had
already begun to grow together in a pre-literary form at the stage
of oral tradition. The original forms of this view which were
worked out by von Rad and Noth have subsequently been modified and corrected at many points. The other view, which has
so far only been worked out in very partial form by Hannelis
Schulte, and is based on the work of Hölscher, is very much more
literary-critical and based on source analysis. It ascribes at least
the uniting of the traditions of the individual patriarchs, the
composition of the Joseph story, the uniting of the traditions of
Midian and of Exodus, and finally the linking together of all this
material in Genesis and Exodus, to the Yahwist. This view still

and P remains to be carried out. Cf. as a specimen P. E. S. Thompson,
'The Yahwistic Creation Story', *VT* 21 (1971), pp. 197 ff.

leaves the history of the tradition of much of the material open. While on the first view the cult has a particularly important part to play in the formation of the tradition, the second view clearly returns to a stress on the history of saga.

2. No attempt will be made here to paint an even approximately complete and rounded picture of the prehistory and early history of Israel. The hypothesis can be regarded as certain that the Israelites entered the civilized territory of Palestine in at least two waves of invasion between the fourteenth and the eleventh centuries B.C., and carried out a conquest which was at first largely peaceful. Alt's argument in his articles 'The Settlement of the Israelites in Palestine'[1a], 'The God of the Fathers', 'Josua'[2] and 'Erwägungen über die Landnahme der Israeliten in Palästina'[3] has been so generally accepted by later scholars that we can assume it from the start as a basis in our traditio-historical work[4]. As regards the question whether in the period before the formation of the state there was an amphictyony, or federation of twelve tribes, or not, the views taken by scholars diverge more than ever now.

3. *The themes of the Pentateuch tradition.* It may be best to begin with a division of the Pentateuchal material by its great themes: we can separate out the primeval history told only by J and P (Gen. 1–11), the stories of the patriarchs (Gen. 12–36), the story of Joseph (Gen. 37–50), the story of the exodus (including the stories of the period in Egypt) (Exod. 1–15.21), the stories of the period in the wilderness (Exod. 15.22–ch. 18; Num. 10.11– ch. 21), and, to pass over the Balaam stories, the traditions of the entry (Num. 32–34*; Josh. 1–12 and Judg. 1). We keep till last the tradition of Sinai, or of the Mount of God (Exod. 19–24; 32–34), because its connection with the tradition of exodus and wilderness is one of the most discussed traditio-historical problems.

1a. *Essays on Old Testament History and Religion*, Oxford 1966, pp. 135 ff.

2. *KS* I, pp. 176 ff., *Grundfragen der Geschichte Israels*, Munich 1970, pp. 186 ff.

3. *KS* I, pp. 126 ff., *Grundfragen*, pp. 136 ff.

4. On the modifications of the hypothesis of 'the God of the Fathers' cf. below, pp. 69 f.

4. The story of the patriarchs and the tradition of exodus and entry.
For reasons both of the subject-matter and of the history of
scholarship we begin with the stories of the patriarchs. In the
present context they are tied in with the Pentateuchal tradition as
a whole by the theme of the promise of the land and of descendants, which like an arc spans the ground from the promises to the
patriarchs through the emergence of the nation in Egypt down
to the entry into the promised land. While at first sight this
connection seems organic, it appears more dubious on closer
examination.

Modern scholarship begins with Alt's work, *Der Gott der
Väter*, of 1929. Starting from the difference between pre-Mosaic
and Mosaic religion which appears in Exod. 3.6, 14 f., and which
is reflected in the worship of the gods of the fathers and of
Yahweh respectively, Alt drew attention to the parallels between
the references found in the stories of the patriarchs and exodus to
the God of Abraham, Isaac and Jacob, and the gods of the
fathers found in Nabataean and Palmyrene texts of the first
century B.C. to the third century A.D. (cf. e.g. Gen. 26.24, 28.13,
31.53, 46.1, 49.25 and Exod. 3.6, 15). He drew from this the
conclusion that there had once been a god of Abraham, a Pahad
(Fear) of Isaac and a mighty one of Jacob, gods who had obtained
their names in each case from the one who received the revelation.
These gods had promised to the patriarchs, or to the groups in
which memory of the patriarchs was particularly kept alive,
descendants and possession of the land. This would lead necessarily to difficulty in uniting the story of the patriarchs with those
of the exodus and entry, because now both of them recounted a
final taking of the land. This would then give rise to the reinterpretation of the taking of the land by the patriarchs as an
interlude between the primeval period and the period of the
exodus.

While this hypothesis has remained very popular to the present,
the problems which have subsequently been raised by scholars
cannot be overlooked. First must be mentioned the repeated
demonstration that reference to 'the God of my, your (etc.)
father' is older than reference to the God of Abraham, Isaac, and
Jacob[5]. Furthermore early Assyrian parallels raise doubts also

5. Cf. Seebass, op. cit., pp. 49 ff., and O. Kaiser, in *Theologie und
Religionswissenschaft*, ed. U. Mann, Darmstadt 1973, pp. 245 ff.

about the ensuing hypothesis that in the gods of the patriarchs we have originally nameless gods of tribes, and suggest rather their identification with the old Semitic high god El. This would explain yet more naturally the identification of the gods of the fathers with the local forms of El in the Canaanite local sanctuaries after the entry, which preceded their final identification with Yahweh. Equally dubious is the assumption that the gods of the fathers gave their worshippers a promise of the land and of descendants. While we must regard the promise of descendants, with Westermann, as being traditio-historically an expansion of the promise of a son, and, with Hannelis Schulte, as being probably in origin a redactional expansion of the promise of the land[6], the promise of the land itself cannot with certainty be traced back before J. Accordingly the possibility must be allowed for that it is in origin a part of the programme of the Yahwist, who by this device linked together the narratives of the patriarchs, which originally belonged only to individual groups, and the history of the exodus, which was already conceived of as being all-Israelite.

Alt's realization that we can derive from the points of anchorage of the narratives of the patriarchs indications of the areas of settlement of the groups which hand them down, remains untouched by these objections. Nor is it disputed that the traditions of exodus, Sinai, and entry originally do not belong together with the tradition of the patriarchs, connected as they are with different persons (Moses and Joshua) and points of anchorage (Midian, the mountain of God, Egypt, and the tribal territory of Benjamin). Furthermore there are particular problems of the history of religion connected with the tradition of the exodus and of Sinai.

The most immediate problem in the traditio-historical investigation of the stories of the patriarchs is the determination of (a) the original local points of anchorage, (b) the original state of the narrative and its subsequent enrichment with new material, (c) the interchange of traditions, and (d) the genealogical linking of the individual narratives of the patriarchs. It is clear that (b) and (c) and also (c) and (d) are traditio-historically linked. The enquiry has as its premiss the assumption that the traditions of

6. Cf. Westermann, op. cit., pp. 18 ff., and Hannelis Schulte, op. cit., pp. 48 f.

the different patriarchs also had different traditionists passing them on. It follows then that those sagas which serve to make a genealogical connection may be more recent at least in respect of this function than are those sagas connected with the figure of an individual patriarch, and indeed usually are. Conclusions can then be drawn from the points of anchorage of the patriarchal sagas about the areas of settlement of the groups passing down these traditions, and in certain circumstances even about the routes of their migrations, and about their secondary expansion.

The points of anchorage of the Abraham tradition are the sanctuaries of Beer-lahai-roi, Beersheba, and not least Mamre/ Hebron (cf. Gen. 16.13 ff., 21.22 ff.; 13.18; 18-19; 23). The few stories of Isaac are located in the area of Gerar and of Beersheba (cf. Gen. 26). The tradition of Jacob on the other hand belongs to the area of central Palestine, where it is localized in Shechem and Bethel, but partially also in the land east of the Jordan (cf. e.g. Gen. 28; 34-35 and 29-33). It is clear that the traditions of Abraham and Isaac overlap in the areas of Beer-lahai-roi, Beersheba and Gerar. We can further establish that the stories of Abraham are richer than the traditions about Isaac, in fact that, as Noth has shown, they have actually absorbed the Isaac traditions. For material which is preserved in Gen. 26 as an original Isaac story is found in parallel in Gen. 12, 20 and 21 in the tradition about Abraham. We can therefore picture a state of affairs in which the 'people of Abraham' in the area of Beer-lahai-roi, Beersheba and Gerar came into contact with the 'people of Isaac'. Finally their influence extended as far as Hebron. Clearly the figure of Abraham himself belongs in the prehistory of the southern tribes. Since the narratives of the patriarch Abraham from the period of the wilderness on the border of and finally fully in the civilized territory had lost their contemporaneity and relevance, the people of Abraham took over there the local traditions, that is, the stories of Isaac, and also sagas from the area of Hebron/Mamre and of the wilderness of Judah. There is a particular problem in the double localization of the figure of Jacob in central Palestine and in the area east of the Jordan. While Noth regards the Transjordan tradition as traditio-historically later, Seebass looks for a solution by means of a distinction between a central Palestinian patriarch Israel, and a Transjordan patriarch Jacob. In consequence the patriarch

Israel would be connected with the 'El God of Israel' mentioned in Gen. 33.20.

The belief in Yahweh had a yet stronger effect than the religion of the patriarchs on the formation of the tradition. In handling this problem the traditio-historical, historical and religio-historical aspects are so closely interwoven that one must proceed with extreme caution. The original connection of belief in Yahweh with the traditions of Midian[7] and of the Mount of God points to its originating in the area to the south-east of the civilized land of Palestine.

If the Jacob or Jacob and Israel tradition is connected with central Palestine, and the tradition of the entry in the Book of Joshua, as well as that of the assembly at Shechem, behind which could stand an event which was constitutive for the Yahweh group in the north, points to central Palestine, we may conjecture that the connection between the Yahweh tradition and the Jacob-Israel tradition took place in central Palestine. The distinguishing characteristic of the Yahweh tradition as it had effect in central Palestine, is the connection of the tradition of exodus and of entry. Only those groups which took part in the exodus, who were clearly the last entrants into central Palestine, are possible tradents of it[8]. Since the worship of Yahweh appears to be connected with Midian and the Mountain of God or Sinai, those who were saved out of Egypt either were already Yahweh worshippers, or became Yahweh worshippers subsequently in the area to the south of Palestine, or after their entry into central Palestine. In this latter case we would have to reckon with a 'Yahwizing' of the central Palestinian tribes taking place directly from the south-east. There are upholders of all the possibilities mentioned here. The decisive point was when those delivered from Egypt came into contact in central Palestine with the Jacob-Israel group: it was here according to Noth that the connection of the exodus and entry tradition with the Jacob-Israel tradition took place in the vicinity of the sanctuary at Shechem. Here the other patriarchs too will have received their present genealogical

7. Cf. on this A. H. J. Gunneweg, 'Mose in Midian', *ZTK* 61 (1964), pp. 1 ff.

8. Cf. O. Kaiser, 'Stammesgeschichtliche Hintergründe der Josephsgeschichte', *VT* 10 (1960), pp. 1 ff. and S. Herrmann, *Israel in Egypt*, SBT² 27, London 1973, p. 33.

arrangement, which reverses the process of growth: the Abraham tradition, the latest to be assimilated, moves in this way to stand first in order, on this view. When the Yahweh tradition of the exodus from Egypt and of the entry was united with the tradition of the patriarchs, the reinterpretation of the latter already mentioned took place, with the patriarchs represented as staying temporarily in the land as strangers; and at the same time the story of Joseph was inserted as a literary bridge. This shows how the descendants of the patriarchs came to Egypt: the story of the exodus could begin.

5. *The uniting of the Pentateuchal themes.* If the linking of the great themes of the Pentateuch is in this way taken back as far as the stage of oral tradition, the question of the *Sitz im Leben* of this process arises: is it to be found in the area of saga narration or of the cult, or do both have a share in it?

The decisive impetus towards answering this problem was given to traditio-historical study by von Rad's work 'The Form-critical Problem of the Hexateuch', of 1938. In this work he chose the so-called 'little historical credo' of Deut. 26.5–9[9] as his starting-point, regarding it in spite of its partially Deuteronomistic terminology as being substantially earlier in form and content than its context[10]. In this credo the Israelite, whose father had come to Egypt as a wandering Aramaean, was to acknowledge thankfully the God who had led Israel out of Egypt, and had brought it into its present land, when he offered the first fruits of his land. A striking point in this confession is that it proceeds from the period of the patriarchs to that of the entry, but omits the Sinai events. From a comparison with passages like Deut. 6.20–24 and Josh. 24.2–13, von Rad draws the conclusion that there must at an early stage have been a canonical form of the story of salvation of just this type: 'the solemn recital of the main parts of the redemption narrative must have been an invariable feature of the ancient Israelite cultus, either as a straightforward credal statement or as a hortatory address to the congregation'[11]. This deduction of a

9. On the 'little credo' cf. also L. Rost, *Das kleine Credo und andere Studien zum Alten Testament*, Heidelberg 1965, pp. 11 ff.; S. Herrmann, BWANT V, 5, pp. 67 ff.

10. *The Problem of the Hexateuch and Other Essays*, p. 4.

11. Op cit., p. 8.

cultic *Sitz im Leben* is illuminated in fact from the situation presupposed both in Deut. 26 and in Josh. 24. Von Rad finds grounds for his assumption of a pattern of the history of salvation in which the Sinai tradition was lacking, in the fact (as he regards it) that the Kadesh tradition in Exod. 17 and Num. 10–14 is interrupted by the series of Sinai sagas. In this the narratives of covenant and theophany predominate. It is clear that in both we are dealing with cultic events. The task remains therefore to determine the cultic *Sitz im Leben*, first for the tradition of the salvation history, and secondly for the Sinai tradition. Referring to Alt's hypothesis of a *Sitz im Leben* for the Decalogue in a feast of the renewal of the covenant at Shechem, and in a pattern of cultic origin which he assumes to lie at the basis both of the Sinai pericope and of Deuteronomy[12], von Rad draws the conclusion that in the Sinai tradition we have the content of the ancient covenant feast at Shechem[13]. Here he has in view also passages like Pss. 50 and 81, and Josh. 24. Since the tradition of the entry in the book of Joshua points to the sanctuary of Gilgal as its point of anchorage[14], and von Rad is further convinced that the offering of the first fruits took place at the Feast of Weeks (cf. Exod. 23.16; Lev. 23.15 f.; Deut. 16.9 f.), he concludes that the Feast of Weeks at Gilgal was the *Sitz im Leben* for the tradition of the salvation history. He ascribes to the Yahwist the development of the material in a literary form and the uniting of the Sinai tradition with the tradition of the history of salvation. The Yahwist 'gathered up the materials which were becoming detached from the cultus, and compacted them firmly together within a literary framework'[15]. Furthermore the Yahwist (and here von Rad is undoubtedly correct) placed the primeval history before the tradition of the history of salvation. The close argumentation of von Rad's reconstruction of the process of tradition has not failed to make an impression, but since the end of the forties it has been increasingly subjected to criticism, although so far no general agreement has been reached on the correct position.

Noth has attempted to support this hypothesis by the conjecture that the tradition of exodus and entry, according to the picture current when he wrote of the entry of the Israelites, could not belong to all the tribes, but only to a smaller group

12. Cf. above, p. 63, and below, pp. 120 f.
13. Op cit., p. 38.   14. Cf. below, p. 137.   15. Op. cit., p. 50.

which entered late into the civilized territory, and found there groups which had immigrated earlier, and which were already united by means of the Holy Mount traditions of covenant and election. The existence alongside one another of both circles of tradition would thus receive a historical justification. As the place for the incorporation of the Sinai theme in the tradition of the history of salvation he sees the area of the southern tribes as the most probable. The cautiousness of his argumentation makes it clear how difficult the explanation of the existence alongside one another at an early stage of the two great tradition complexes is[16]. Since, unlike von Rad, he disputes the assignment of the narratives of the entry in Joshua to one of the ancient Pentateuchal sources, he rejects the location of the traditions of the entry in the credo at the sanctuary of Gilgal.[17] Noth believed that he could conclude from his examination of the patriarchal narratives that the agreements between J and E, which appear especially in the framework of the narrative, are not to be attributed to E's having before him the text of J, so that he in effect brought out a new edition of the older work, but rather to a basic source (*Grundlage*, so G) which was common to both sources, whether it was orally transmitted or passed down in writing. It followed necessarily for him that the combination of the traditions of exodus and of the mountain of God or Sinai, which is common to both sources, was not made first by J, but went back as early as G.

Starting from other considerations, Weiser* has contested the hypothesis of an originally independent tradition of both the history of salvation and the Sinai tradition. First, he denies that the presentation of the first fruits in Deut. 26 is to be connected exclusively with the Feast of Weeks, and accordingly dismisses the first half of von Rad's theory. Then he points out that it is precisely in Josh. 24 that the survey of salvation history (as an announcement of the nature of God) and the commitment to the will of God (as an announcement of the will of God) traditio-historically stand alongside one another. Accordingly he fixes on the announcement of the nature and will of Yahweh as the content of the covenant festival at Shechem. It is from the cultic recitation of these traditions in the covenant festival that

16. *A History of Pentateuchal Traditions*, p. 62.
17. Op. cit., p. 52, n. 170.

the framework common to J and E can be explained. The expansion and alteration of the old material took place in the cultic setting itself. The actual achievement of the authors of the sources, or as Weiser more cautiously says of the source strata, consisted in 'the written development, transformation and combination of the material and the traditions handed down in the festival cult. For this at any given moment the determining factors were the particular cultic needs and intellectual trends of the historical situations.' To emphasize his point he says that the sources of the Pentateuch are to be understood 'as a kind of lectionary, i.e. as the written records of the tradition of salvation-history belonging to the union of the twelve tribes, and fostered by oral recital and transmission'[18]. It has however become questionable in the light of Perlitt's examination of the date of Israelite covenant theology whether it is permissible to connect the early formation of the tradition with a covenant feast or covenant cult[19].

Against the background of the questioning of the hypothesis that pre-monarchical Israel had the constitutional form of a kind of amphictyony or union of twelve tribes gathered round a central sanctuary, a hypothesis that has been more or less fundamental for traditio-historical reconstructions in the last decades, it can be seen why it is that Hannelis Schulte has re-examined the problem of the *Grundlage* (G), and after an examination of the Joseph story as a test-case has reached a negative decision, and also stated that the hypothesis of a cultic setting for the growth of the themes of the Pentateuch is unproven. On her view the linking of the traditions of the patriarchs and of the salvation history, which is already implied in the creation of a genealogy, is the work of the Yahwist, who not only inserted the Joseph story as a literary bridge, but also actually composed it out of one story of Egyptians, and another of brothers. So for Hannelis Schulte cultic tradition is replaced by the concern of the Yahwist to collect and give programmatic form to his material, a concern to which we owe even the pattern of the twelve brothers and of the twelve tribes.

If we attempt to give a preliminary summing up of the results of the latest discussion, it must be said first that in view of the

18. *Introduction to the Old Testament*, p. 97.
19. Cf. above, pp. 63 f.

historical continuity of the traditions of salvation history which extend from the exodus to the entry, a tendency can be seen to understand them again as determined by the actual course of history[20]. It remains to be seen whether the process of tradition lying behind this can be clarified without the assumption of an at least partially cultic *Sitz im Leben* at one of the central Palestinian sanctuaries, and in particular that of Shechem. Hannelis Schulte's study is particularly in need of supplementation at this point. It remains problematic whether the inclusion of the Abraham tradition in the story of Isaac, Jacob and Israel really took place at a central Palestinian stage of the tradition, and not in fact first in a southern Palestinian one. The detailed examination which still needs to be made of Noth's hypothesis of a common source G for J and E, and that of the hypothesis revived by Hannelis Schulte of a direct dependence of the Elohist upon J, will no doubt take us further in respect of this and other problems. Meanwhile we may well wonder how these slowly growing narratives came to be fixed in writing at all. Since in view of the distinctive nature of the stories united in the Pentateuch we cannot allow for a stimulus from Canaanite epics[21], we must remember that history writing, as the example of the Greeks shows, is called forth by events of the recent past. This was the case in Israel for the first time so far as we know with the story of the succession to David[22]. The existence of a historical narrative concerned with the most recent past may have created the wish to write down the remoter events in the history of the nation too. Accordingly, we must look for the first fixing in writing of the tradition of the history of salvation in the first eighty years after the division of the kingdom which took place upon the death of Solomon.

20. Cf. e.g. S. Herrmann, *Geschichte Israels in alttestamentlicher Zeit*, Munich 1973, pp. 110 f.

21. We have in any case no evidence at all for the writing down of these epics from Palestine, unlike the position at Ugarit. On the fragment found at Megiddo of the Gilgamesh epic cf. above, p. 27.

22. Cf. K. Budde, *Geschichte der althebräischen Litteratur*, Leipzig 1909[2], p. 43; for a similar process among the Romans cf. E. Kornemann, *Weltgeschichte des Mittelmeer-Raumes*, ed. H. Bengtson, Munich 1967, p. 230.

§ 8   The Yahwistic History

M. Noth, *Überlieferungsgeschichtliche Studien*, Halle 1943 = Tübingen (Darmstadt) 1967³, pp. 180 ff., 211 ff., id. *A History of Pentateuchal Traditions* [1948], Englewood Cliffs, New Jersey, 1972, pp. 20 ff., 236 ff.; G. Hölscher, *Geschichtsschreibung in Israel. Unterschungen zum Jahvisten und Elohisten*, SKHVL 50, 1952, pp. 20 ff.; O. Eissfeldt, *Die Genesis der Genesis*, Tübingen 1961² (expanded version of article 'Genesis' in *IDB*, vol. 2, New York and Nashville 1962, pp. 366 ff.); S. Mowinckel, *Tetrateuch, Pentateuch, Hexateuch. Die Berichte über die Landnahme in den drei altisraelitischen Geschichtswerken*, BZAW 90, 1964; id., *Erwägungen zur Pentateuch Quellenfrage*, Oslo 1964; G. Fohrer, *Introduction to the Old Testament*, New York and Nashville 1968, London 1970, pp. 146 ff., 159 ff.; R. Kilian, *Die vorpriesterlichen Abrahams-Überlieferungen*, BBB 24, 1966; V. Fritz, *Israel in der Wüste. Traditionsgeschichtliche Untersuchung der Wüstenüberlieferung des Jahwisten*, MTS 7, 1970; G. von Rad, 'The Beginnings of Historical Writing in Ancient Israel', *The Problem of the Hexateuch and other essays*, Edinburgh and London 1966, pp. 166 ff.; *Old Testament Theology*, vol. 1, [1957] Edinburgh and London 1962, pp. 48 ff.; M.-L. Henry, *Jahwist und Priesterschrift*, ATh 1, 3, 1960; H. W. Wolff, 'The Kerygma of the Yahwist' [1964], *Interpr* 20 (1966), pp. 131 ff.; F. J. Stendebach, *Theologische Anthropologie des Jahwisten*, diss. kath. theol. Bonn 1970; W. M. Clark, 'The Flood Story and the Structure of the Pre-patriarchal History', *ZAW* 83 (1971), pp. 184 ff.; H. Schulte, *Die Entstehung der Geschichtsschreibung im Alten Israel*, BZAW, 128, 1972.

The text can be found in German in O. Eissfeldt, *Hexateuch-Synopse*, Leipzig 1922, Darmstadt 1962², with the five-source theory presupposed, and in R. Smend jr., *Biblische Zeugnisse. Literatur des alten Israel*, FB 817, 1967, pp. 24 ff., with the four-source theory presupposed (only J and P).

1. Extent of the work. There is now very general agreement on where the Yahwistic history begins: in Gen. 2.4b, with the Paradise story. On the other hand there is disagreement about where both the original end and the present end of the narrative come. The different views can basically be reduced to two: 1. The work ended with the conquest of Canaan. 2. It continued at least to the period of David. Two varieties of the first of these views can be distinguished: (a) the Yahwistic account of the taking of the land was lost when the Yahwistic history was inserted into the framework of the Priestly writing (Noth); (b) apart from fragments in the book of Joshua (about which differing views are held) the account is preserved in Judg. 1 (von Rad, Pfeiffer*, Weiser*, Mowinckel, R. Smend jr.). The latter view is also necessarily shared by all those who believe they can show that the narrative was continued down to the time of David or even further. This brings us to the variations of the second view, which take the following forms: (a) the work ended with the Succession Narrative in 1 Kgs. 2 (Budde)[1]; (b) it concluded with the narrative of the division of the kingdoms in 1 Kgs. 12 (Hölscher, and also cautiously Hannelis Schulte); (c) it extended beyond 1 Kgs. 12 (Smend sr.[2] and Eissfeldt*)[3].

Internal indications show clearly that the Yahwistic narrative had as its goal at any rate the conquest of the land west of the Jordan: a clear thread leads from the promise of Gen. 12.1[3a] through the promises in Gen. 12.7 and Exod. 3.8 to Moses' declaration as the people leave Sinai in Num. 10.29: 'We are setting out for the place of which the LORD said, "I will give it to you".' The last verses in the Tetrateuch which can be assigned with some certainty to J, in Num. 32, tell of the conquest of the land east of the Jordan by the tribes of Reuben and Gad, and by the half-tribes of Manasseh, Machir and Jair. Accordingly there can be no argument whether the Yahwist narrated a conquest of the land to the west of the Jordan, but only whether his account is preserved. The basic form of the account of the conquest of the land in Josh. 1–11 does not come into consideration as a possibility, whether it is attributed to a later redaction of the Yahwist (Mowinckel), to the Elohist (Hölscher and many others), or to an originally independent source later edited by the Deuteronomist (Noth). Consideration is accordingly directed inevitably to Judg. 1, the so-called 'negative list of possessions', a historical and political survey of the results of the conquest enriched by

1. KHC 8, Tübingen and Leipzig 1902, pp. IX ff.; cf. however also his *Geschichte der althebräischen Litteratur*, Leipzig 1906, pp. 58 f.

2. *Die Erzählung des Hexateuch auf ihre Quellen untersucht*, Berlin 1912, pp. 351 f., esp. n. 3.

3. Pp. 297 ff.

3a. On the problem of Gen. 12.2 f. cf. H. Schulte, op. cit., pp. 48 f. Gen. 15.18 is also open to suspicion, and should in future be left out of the discussion of the date and interests of the Yahwist, in view of the very problematic question of the sources of the chapter.

anecdotes[4], which can be understood neither as a list nor as a semi-official document. It is therefore entirely possible that Judg. 1 forms the conclusion of the Yahwistic narrative. Its peculiar form would be explained either by the fact that the narrator had no further traditions about the conquest at his disposal or by the fact that for some reason only a selection is given as a summary of his originally fuller account. Since the statements in Josh. 15.13–19, 63; 16.10; 17.11–13, 14–18 and 19.47, which seem out of place in their present context, clearly display dependence on Judg. 1, they could be ascribed to J. The decision on both questions is however dependent on an analysis of the Books of Joshua and Judges and the resulting view taken of their prehistory. Since no one view of this has yet won general acceptance, the different opinions found in the literature on which source Judg. 1 belongs to is understandable[5].

Hannelis Schulte's attempt to give new grounds for Hölscher's hypothesis of a single historical work of the late tenth or early ninth century leading from creation to the division of the kingdom, must be regarded as open to question in view of the complex position in respect of the traditions, and in view of the number of questions left open even within the selective analyses which she presents. So e.g. her demonstration that Gen. 24 and 2 Sam. 25 link up different blocks of tradition in a similar way, and that there are relationships of motifs between Gen. 19 and Judg. 19, is not sufficient to establish that the author is identical. The reference in Judg. 18.29 probably takes us back only to Josh. 19.47, and not to Gen. 30.6 E, and that in Judg. 19.30 is so generally phrased that it will not allow us to conclude that a particular source is being referred to here. If we examine the deliverer formulae in Exod. 3.8, and then in Judg. 6.14, 13.5 and 1 Sam. 9.16, it remains at best dubious whether they are all written by the same author. The same is true of the passages stressing the unprecedented nature of a disaster in Exod. 9.18, 10.6 and Judg. 19.30.

In spite of the closeness of spirit between the Yahwistic work and the narratives of the rise of David and of the succession to him in 1 Sam. 16–2 Sam. 8 and 2 Sam. 9–20 with 1 Kgs. 1–2, which like the Yahwistic work are borne as if by an arc spanning the gap between promise and fulfilment, and which display a

4. Mowinckel, BZAW 90, 1964, pp. 27 ff.
5. Cf. inf., pp. 136 ff. and 144.

sharp eye for historical reality in its concrete context, there is
no compelling reason to suppose a direct literary connection with
the Yahwist. If the suggestion made above on p. 77 is correct,
that it was the existence of the Succession Narrative that caused
the Yahwist to write his work, such an assumption is in any case
excluded. Furthermore, the early history of the Books of Kings
appears to be too complicated to be done justice to by the source
hypothesis developed for the Pentateuch[6].

2. *The problem of the literary unity of the Yahwist.* We have
already pointed out in § 4 that the representatives of the 'newest
documentary hypothesis', R. Smend sr., Eissfeldt and Fohrer,
consider that in the Yahwistic source we have in reality a conjunction of two originally independent sources, which they call
J_1 and J_2 or L and J or J and N. R. H. Pfeiffer wished to separate
out a Southern or Seir source S, confined to Genesis[7]. The
present widespread hostility to this type of hypothesis is based
partly on the view that the older attempts led to a division of the
narrative into small or minute fragments, which seemed uncon-
vincing. It is now based increasingly on traditio-historical arguments. The Yahwist was, in a very great majority of instances,
not an author who disposed freely of his material in the manner
of modern narrators, but a collector, who gathered together
alongside larger narrative complexes, which were, as Kilian and
Fritz have shown to be probable, already collected in written
form, further traditions, and then connected these traditions
together. Furthermore, it is a result of form-critical study that
the larger narrative complexes too have regularly grown out of
or been composed from originally independent individual narratives. The tensions and contradictions in the narrative can be
explained from this prehistory of the material edited by the
Yahwist and from his activity as a collector, which cannot be
denied in spite of all the key ideas and developments of his own
which are clearly present. It must be admitted that the task of
investigating the sources at the disposal of J and his own activity
has been only in small part solved. Kilian has confined his work

6. Cf. below, pp. 165 ff.
7. 'A Non-Israelitic Source of the Book of Genesis', *ZAW* 48 (1930),
pp. 66 ff., and id., *Introduction to the Old Testament*, New York 1948[2],
London 1952, pp. 159 ff.

to the Abraham traditions, Hannelis Schulte to the narratives of the patriarchs, of Joseph and of the exodus, Fritz to the wilderness traditions. The results obtained by Kilian and by Hannelis Schulte are so divergent that we must wait for a new examination which will include the primeval history before we can regard the hypothesis of a continuous source underlying the work of the Yahwist, i.e. a proto-Yahwist, as in some measure assured in respect of Genesis. On the other hand in spite of Hannelis Schulte's reserve over the question whether the exodus tradition in a definite form, edited by J, which she has detected, existed already in writing, it can be noted that here she is supported by Fritz.

Since the 'newest documentary hypothesis' began with observations made on the primeval history in Genesis, at least some examples of the contradictions to be found in it should be given: there is a disagreement of fact between the genealogy of the Sethites in Gen. 4.25–26 and that of the Cainites in Gen. 4.17–24. The Yahwistic account of the flood in Gen. 6.5–8.22* is in conflict with an older narrative of Noah the wine-grower, which clearly did not know the story of the flood (cf. Gen. 5.29 with 9.20). Finally there is a disagreement between the list of the nations in Gen. 10* J and the story of the tower of Babel in Gen. 11.1–9. When we realize that Noth regarded the Yahwist as dependent for the outline of his narrative upon a basic source (G), while Hannelis Schulte regards this outline at least in respect of the narratives of the patriarchs and of Joseph as the work of the Yahwist, when we remember that Eissfeldt holds to the classical form of the 'newest documentary hypothesis' while at the same time Fohrer is concerned to reshape it and give it a stronger basis, and when finally we see that the problem of secondary expansions, including that of the extent of the Jehovistic redaction and of possible further Deuteronomistic redactions, has hitherto not finally been solved, we are forced to realize that Old Testament scholarship has still found no final solution to the problem of the Yahwist.

3. *Place and date of origin.* If what has been said so far is correct even only in the basic outlines, it shows that we must allow for a long prehistory of the material which is found in the Yahwistic book, or, if we look at it in its preserved state, in the Yahwistic part of the Pentateuch. We lack the necessary evidence to place it more precisely in time. Only the *terminus non ante* and the *terminus ad quem* can be fixed: since the work presupposes the period of David and Solomon, it cannot have been formed before

the tenth century B.C. And since no trace can be found anywhere in the whole work of the Assyrians endangering the Northern or Southern Kingdoms, it must have been formed before this happened. Solomon's accession took place in 965, the first clash between Israel and Assyria in the battle of Karkar in 853. Accordingly the Yahwistic work must have been formed between the middle of the tenth and the middle of the ninth century. The period of David and Solomon is pointed to by the all-Israelite concept expressed in the pattern of the twelve sons and of the twelve tribes, and also by the oracle of Balaam (Num. 24.17 f.) incorporated by J, which contains a *vaticinium ex eventu* of the subjection of the Moabites and Edomites by David. Further the motif so distinctively connected with the presentation of the wilderness period of murmuring in the wilderness could have as its background an attack upon Yahweh's protecting guidance of the nation in the establishment of the empire of David and Solomon[8], and might possibly already refer back to the division of the kingdom. Finally Gen. 33, which presupposes the independence of Edom, may point to the decades after the death of Solomon, and perhaps the struggle of Judah and Joseph for Benjamin in the Joseph story has as its background the rivalry of the two kingdoms in the struggle for the tribal area of Benjamin. If the 'negative list of possessions' in Judg. 1 can also be included in the Yahwistic work, Judg. 1.28, 30, 33 and 35 with their statement that the Canaanites or Amorites at last became obliged to do forced labour for the Israelites, would point to the reorganization of the empire under Solomon. If 1.29 can be subsumed under 1.28, the incorporation of Gezer by Solomon would also be presupposed (cf. 1 Kgs. 9.15 ff.). Fundamentally we must realize in any attempt to date this source that the final solution of this problem will only be possible after a full answer is available to the questions what sources J used and what redactions the book has subsequently undergone. If the hypothesis of a proto-Yahwist is established even only in respect of the salvation-history proper of exodus, wandering in the wilderness and entry, the problem of dating must be dealt with separately for each of these two works.

In spite of the scepticism expressed by Eissfeldt*[9], the question of the place of origin of the Yahwistic work can be answered

8. Cf. Fritz, op. cit., p. 136.   9. P. 203.

with certainty: the fact that J looks back in a positive sense to the founding of the Davidic empire, and the circumstance that the material peculiar to the source, such as the Abraham and Lot cycle of stories and the story of Judah and Tamar in Gen. 38, come from the south, point clearly to the answer. Only J is in a position to tell of Cain and the Kenites living in the south Judaean wilderness (Gen. 4); only J is interested in the dubious origins of Ammon and Moab (Gen. 19.30 ff.). And finally it is not unimportant for the place of origin of the source that in the Yahwistic version of the story of Joseph Judah takes over the role of leadership among the brothers, which traditio-historically belonged originally to Reuben. Accordingly we are justified in assuming that the Yahwistic history originated in the south.

4. Sources. While we have seen in the preceding chapter what varied significance is attached by scholars to oral tradition in the development of the narrative framework underlying J and E, it is at least certain that the Yahwist in portraying the period of the patriarchs could draw on at any rate individual sagas, collections of sagas and first stages in the formation of genealogies, while for the salvation-history proper extending from Exodus to entry he had necessarily at least a thematic outline, and in the views of Hannelis Schulte and of Fritz also traditions already in fixed form. In his own work he not only drew on further traditions. He also inserted novelistic compositions which are particularly characteristic of him, in order to link together unharmonized blocks of tradition, and so reworked the material that had come to him that it took its place as a whole in the total pattern of his theology of history. If the inclusion at the beginning of the primeval history is his own work, the understanding of world history as a salvation-history must go back to him. For the outline of this, with its sequence of creation, repeated sins of mankind, punishments by God and acts of mercy down to the Flood, and the new start in the history of man following upon this, the Yahwist is dependent upon the parallel Mesopotamian tradition which we have access to in the Atraḥasis epic[9a], and in his genealogy of primal man which is split up into a Cainite and a

9a. Cf. above, p. 26, and W. M. Clark, 'The Flood Story and the Structure of the Pre-Patriarchal History', *ZAW* 83 (1971), pp. 184 ff., who however does not trace back the genealogy to the Sumerian king-list.

Sethite family tree upon the tradition known to us from the Sumerian king-list.

It remains to mention that poetic material has often been incorporated into the narratives. How far it already belonged with the traditions that were taken over, and how far it was inserted by the Yahwist is something that must be decided from case to case. We will content ourselves with a list of the passages concerned: the joyful cry of the man when he first sees the woman (Gen. 2.23), the sayings of curse and destiny on the snake, the woman, the land and the man (Gen. 3.14 ff.), the song of Lamech (Gen. 4.23 f.), the sayings of Noah (Gen. 9.25–27), the oracles on the ancestors of Israel and of its neighbouring nations (Gen. 12.2 f.; 16.11 f.[10]; 24.60; 25.23; 27.27–29*) and the sayings on the tribes collected in Gen. 49[11]; the banner saying in Exod. 17.16, the ark sayings in Num. 10.35 f., and the oracles of Balaam in Num. 24.3–9, 15–19. Some scholars also include in the Yahwistic source the Song of Moses of Exod. 15.1–18, and most include the so-called 'cultic Decalogue' of Exod. 34.14–26.[11a]

5. The Yahwist's view of history and theology. Hölscher has characterized the intention of the Yahwist in these words: 'The leading idea which has shaped the view of history in J is the concept of the unity of the twelve-tribe nation. In reality this greater Israel is a creation of David . . .'[12]. Even those who assume that there was already in the premonarchical period a union of the Israelite tribes comparable to the Greek amphictyonies, and that the pattern of twelve tribes is older than the Davidic empire[13], will concede that the idea of greater Israel

10. On Gen. 12.2 f. cf. Kilian, op. cit., pp. 10 ff., with H. Schulte, op. cit., pp. 48 f.

11. Cf. also H.-J. Zobel, *Stammesspruch und Geschichte*, BZAW 95, 1965.

11a. On the various different attempts to reconstruct a decalogue cf. F.-E. Wilms, *Das jahwistische Bundesbuch in Exodus 34*, SANT 34, 1973, pp. 200 ff.

12. *Geschichtsschreibung in Israel*, p. 112.

13. The hypothesis enjoyed wide acceptance after the publication of M. Noth, *Das System der zwölf Stämme Israels*, BWANT IV, 1, 1930, repr. Darmstadt 1966. For the view taken of it at present cf. e.g. S. Herrmann, *Geschichte Israels in alttestamentlicher Zeit*, Munich 1973, p. 146.

first came to have a corresponding political reality as a result of David's formation of his empire, and to find its theological legitimation through the Yahwist. In this connection we need only recall once again the promise to Abraham in Gen. 12.7, the 'negative list of possessions', Judg. 1.27 ff., and the oracles of Balaam, especially Num. 24.17. But by isolating the political aspect we could easily misunderstand the concern of the Yahwist for the theology of history.

We can perhaps best grasp this if we follow the course of his narrative in broad outline: the creation of a world, of men and of animals united in happy peace is followed through the fault of man by the fall, which subjects him to the toil of work, to the hostility of the animals and to pain. Only the grace of God secures for mankind its future continued existence, admittedly one that cannot be compared with his original condition (Gen. 2.4b–3.24). Brother kills brother; but even the life of the murderer remains under God's protection (Gen. 4.1–16). Early mankind becomes so corrupt that Yahweh destroys it in the flood. But as Yahweh sees the men he has preserved from destruction, Noah and his descendants, after the flood has dispersed, he knows that nothing has changed in the basically evil nature of man, and voluntarily guarantees the continuation of the earth with its annual cycle[14]. Mankind at once justifies God's judgement by the hubristic work of the building of the tower, which compels Yahweh to scatter man over the earth and to confuse his language[15]. From the first pair of men the line of rejection and profligacy extends through Cain and Lamech to the giants. In Ham (Canaan) it continues after the flood. And with man's attempt to make a name for himself by the building of the tower, and to intrude into God's sphere, the theme reaches its climax (cf. Gen. 3.5, 22 with 11.4, 6). In this sense the whole primeval history, which on the Mesopotamian pattern is now sometimes regarded as ending in J not with the story of the Tower of Babel but with the story of the flood[16], stands under God's curse. And yet in God's punishments his grace always remains present, because the measure of punishment is always less than

14. J's share in the primeval history is: Gen. 2.4b–4.26; 5.28b, 29; 6.1–8; 7.1, 2, 3b–5, 10, 7*, 16b, 12, 17b, 22, 23*; 8.6a, 2b, 3a, 6b, 8, 9, 10*, 11–12, 13b, 20–22; 9.18–27; 10.8, 10–19, 21, 25–30; 11.1–9.

15. Gen. 11.1–9.

16. Cf. R. Rendtorff, 'Genesis 8.21 und die Urgeschichte des Jahwisten', *Kerygma und Dogma* 7 (1961), pp. 69 ff. and Clark, pp. 205 ff.; the opposite view is taken by O. H. Steck, 'Genesis 12, 1–3 und die Urgeschichte des Jahwisten', in *Probleme biblischer Theologie*, Festschrift G. von Rad, Munich 1971, pp. 525 ff.

the guilt[17]. By placing the primeval history before the old tradition of the history of salvation, the Yahwist has set the saving dealings of God with Israel in the framework of world history, and so ultimately interpreted world history as a history of salvation. World history as such is not for him the same as a history of salvation, but becomes this only through God's special saving action towards Israel. What there is to say about the world of the nations and about the men outside this saving action is said in the first eleven chapters of Genesis. But already here the saving action which begins fully with Abraham and reaches its objective in the empire of David stands out sharply: among the sons of Noah is Shem, the ancestor of the Semites and accordingly also of the children of Abraham. In the curse on Canaan and the blessing on Shem and Japhet the theme of Israel's lordship over the Canaanites can be seen (cf. Gen. 9.25–27 with Judg. 1).

Abraham, who in obedience to the call of Yahweh has left his country, his family and his father's house to journey into an unknown land, receives the promise that Yahweh will give this land to his offspring at the oracular shrine of Shechem (cf. Gen. 12.1 and 7)[18]. When the Israelites are groaning under the oppression of Pharaoh in Egypt, Yahweh appears to Moses in the burning bush to promise him that his people will be released from the oppression of the Egyptians and led into a good and broad land. Moses is to tell the Israelites that the God of the Fathers has promised this. So a restrained, but still perceptible, echo of the old promise of the land can be heard here (cf. Exod. 3.7, 16*). The hope of offspring, which cannot be achieved forcibly by Abraham's own action (Gen. 16.1b, 2, 4–8, 11–14), is realized against all human hope in the birth of Isaac (Gen. 18.1–16, 21.1a, 2a, 7). When the land which Abraham's nephew Lot has chosen (cf. Gen. 13.1–12) is subsequently destroyed by Yahweh with fire and brimstone because of the wickedness of its inhabitants (Gen. 19*) the readers' desire to see justice done is doubly satisfied, in that not only does Abraham's generosity lead to his preservation, but at the same time Lot's innocence leads to his deliverance. So our attention is drawn to the art of the Yahwist in preserving us from a one-sided partiality, and in making us sympathize with the disadvantaged. This can be seen particularly clearly in the story of Hagar (Gen. 16*), in the story of Leah (Gen.

17. This has been worked out especially by C. Westermann, 'Arten der Erzählung in der Genesis', in *Forschung am Alten Testament*, ThB 24, 1964, pp. 47 ff.

18. The cautious position here taken about the promise of offspring and of blessing, which is usually treated as a leading theological theme of the Yahwist, is based upon a fresh critical examination of the evidence of Genesis. Cf. also H. Schulte, op. cit., pp. 48 ff.

29.31 ff.) and in the Joseph narrative. The rejected maidservant is also a mother, whose tears God sees. The wife despised for her ugliness has a longing we can understand for a better fortune, which is satisfied by Yahweh. In the Joseph narrative the favourite son of Jacob is presented to us sympathetically with his moral uprightness in Potiphar's house, after he has already evoked our sympathy for having been sold into slavery by his brothers. The fact that in the further course of the story we learn to sympathize with the brothers too, and to feel that the pardon granted them is also just, serves to indicate to us how very different the justice of God is from that of men. We cannot fail to notice that in this only too human story Yahweh's special care for his people is there under the surface, and so be reminded of the hidden meaning of the story, which is under Yahweh's guidance and direction.

Once we have noticed this pattern we can discover the double theme of God's justice and of his guidance in history in the very human stories of Jacob and Esau, and of Jacob and Laban (Gen. 25.21–32.1*), and again in the story of the exodus, in which sympathy is at once evoked for the oppressed Israelites, and for Moses who intercedes for them. He must appear first before the elders of his people and then before Pharaoh, to proclaim to the elders the imminence of deliverance, and to make to Pharaoh the request that he should let the people journey into the wilderness to celebrate a feast of Yahweh. Apparently what he obtains is the direct opposite, the hardening of Pharaoh's heart, and an increase in the burden of forced labour laid upon the Israelites (cf. Exod. 5.22 f.; 6.1*). But Yahweh proves to be the stronger: his seven plagues break the will of Pharaoh, so that he lets the people go. When the mind of the King changes and he pursues the fleeing Israelites, Yahweh leads the Egyptians to their destruction at the sea. The rescued Israelites journey to the wilderness of Shur, where Moses makes the bitter water of Marah drinkable for the people and strikes water from the rock at Massah and Meribah, and where Joshua conquers the Amalekites. At Sinai Israel experiences the theophany of Yahweh, followed by a sacrificial meal, and then sets out for the land of the promise, now accompanied by Hobab (cf. Num. 10.29 ff.)[19]. In the course of their march through the wilderness, the people murmur in recollection of what they had to eat in Egypt. They are given water to drink by Yahweh from the rock, and fed with quails and manna, but they wish to choose a leader who will take them back to Egypt, because the entry into the promised land seems too dangerous when the returning spies tell them of its alluring fruits and its armed cities. For this reason Yahweh decides to punish the

19. Cf. Fritz, op. cit., pp. 35 ff.; L. Perlitt, *Bundestheologie im alten Testament*, WMANT 36, 1969, pp. 159 ff. and E. Zenger, *Die Sinaitheophanie*, FzB 3, 1971.

rebellious Israelites: only Caleb, because he has remained faithful, will be allowed to see the land which Yahweh had promised to give to the fathers. All attempts to enter the land by their own power are frustrated by the Amalekites and the Canaanites. As they wander round the area of Edom the people murmur again in longing for the land of their servitude. Fiery serpents attack them; only those who look on the bronze serpent are saved. We meet Balaam and his ass, we hear his blessing on Israel, the prophecy of the star from Jacob and the sceptre out of Israel; and yet at the same time are told that Israel fell away to Baal-Peor at the very borders of the land. We feel our way through the fragments of the Yahwistic narrative; in the last tangible fragments in Num. 32* Moses no longer appears. Clearly, just as in Deut. 34.2 ff., in the tradition available to the Yahwist too he died before the entry into the land. If we may include Judg. 1 in the work, it becomes clear how the arc of the promise curves up from the time of the patriarchs, over the time of the conquest, and down in the time of David, in which it found its fulfilment[20].

Yahweh is for the Yahwist truly a God of the universe. He dwells in heaven (Gen. 11.5). He created man and beast (Gen. 2.4 ff.). He sends wind and weather, sickness and plagues (Gen. 19.24; Exod. 7.14–14.31* J). He makes springs gush up (Exod. 17.6), and gives fertility to men and cattle (Gen. 21.1 f.; 25.21; 30.25 ff.). His name has been known to mankind from earliest times (Gen. 4.26). Kings are subordinate to his power (Exod. 3 ff.)[21], and yet it is revealed to Israel alone in the full sense, since the nations stand under his judgement. If we look back over the whole story told by the Yahwist, the emphasis on Yahweh's saving will which overcomes human wickedness and human unfaithfulness cannot be mistaken. And yet the other side as well must be seen and emphasized, the warning to the people to seek their salvation by their own efforts, even in difficult days to keep faithfulness to God, to whom belong both promise and judgement[22]. For Israel's God is, as is said in a probably postexilic addition to the story of the judgement of God upon Sodom,[23] the 'judge of the whole earth' (Gen. 18.25).

20. On J's share cf. the surveys in O. Eissfeldt, *Hexateuchsynopse*, M. Noth, *A History of Pentateuchal Traditions*, pp. 28 ff., and G. Hölscher, *Geschichtsschreibung in Israel*, pp. 20 ff.

21. Cf. Hölscher, op. cit., pp. 116 ff.

22. Cf. M.-L. Henry, *Jahwist und Priesterschrift*, ATh I, 3, 1960, pp. 15 ff.

23. On Gen. 18.22b–32a cf. also H. Schulte, op. cit., p. 47, n. 12.

Much of the material taken over has very primitive traits: Yahweh goes walking in the garden in the evening, he forms the woman from the rib of the man (Gen. 2.4b ff.). But where the Yahwist has himself formed the material, God remains hidden 'in the cloud'. The 'Then the LORD appeared to Abram and said . . .' in Gen. 12.7 is reserved. Where the Yahwist is himself the narrator, where older material places no restraints on him, God is recognized by his actions. This comes to pass very naturally: Abraham's servant recognizes by simple signs that he has found the right maiden, the one appointed for Isaac (Gen. 24.11 ff.). Yahweh hears prayer. Yahweh blesses the crops (Gen. 26.12 ff.), blesses Jacob's possessions in a foreign land (Gen. 35.25 ff.). He makes Joseph succeed in all that he does (Gen. 39.3), even uses sin to attain his aims. Where something miraculous occurs, as in the blinding of the men of Sodom (Gen. 19.11), we find again the presence of old material. The miraculous does not disturb him either, as the story of the thorn-bush which burnt and yet was not consumed shows (Exod. 3.2* ff.). But he himself prefers an interpretation which explains natural, immanent events as the action of God: his Egyptian plagues produce a much more natural effect in comparison with the accounts of E and P. Here we do not have water changed into blood, flies created out of dust, 'Egyptian darkness' conjured up: the pollution of the water by the death of fishes, frogs, dirt, the death of cattle, hail and locusts are quite 'natural' plagues. Even the death of the Egyptian first-born, which is significantly told in only a single verse (Exod. 12.29) he seems to have explained in his own way. In any case the motif was such a fixed one that he was not in a position to alter it. A similar pattern can be seen in his account of the deliverance at the Red Sea: it is not a passage through the sea, nor waves rising up to left and right and standing like a wall that dominate the scene, but an east wind drives the sea back during the night, and at dawn Yahweh drives the Egyptians into the returning waves[24]. Von Rad is certainly right to find in the Yahwist the spirit of the Davidic-Solomonic epoch, which formed his understanding for reality and for its relations to great historical events, and was connected with the international wisdom of experience, with its rational, if not rationalistic,

24. Cf. Noth, *Exodus*, pp. 113 ff.

tendencies[25]. This attitude to the world is still completely un-broken. Faith still believes that it is possible for it to recognize God's purposes in external events. The subsequent course of wisdom in Israel was to come to see that human knowledge in the end is confronted by the divine basis of the world as by an enigma[26].

§ 9   The Elohistic History

O. Procksch, *Das nordhebräische Sagenbuch. Die Elohimquelle*, Leipzig 1906; P. Volz and W. Rudolph, *Der Elohist als Erzähler—ein Irrweg der Pentateuchkritik?*, BZAW 63, 1933; W. Rudolph, *Der 'Elohist' von Exodus bis Josua*, BZAW 68, 1938; O. Eissfeldt, 'Die Komposition von Exodus 1–12. Eine Rettung des Elohisten' [1939], *KS* II, Tübingen 1963, pp. 160 ff.; M. Noth, *A History of Pentateuchal Tradition* [1948], Englewood Cliffs, New Jersey, 1972, pp. 38 ff., 228 ff.; G. Hölscher, *Geschichtsschreibung in Israel*, SKHVL 50, 1952, pp. 136 ff.; S. Mowinckel, *Erwägungen zur Pentateuch Quellenfrage*, Oslo 1964, pp. 59 ff.; R. Kilian, *Die Vorpriesterlichen Abrahams-Überlieferungen*, BBB 24, 1966; H. W. Wolff, 'Zur Thematik der elohistischen Fragmente im Pentateuch', *EvTh* 29 (1969), pp. 59 ff.; H. Schulte, *Die Entstehung der Geschichtsschreibung im Alten Israel*, BZAW 128, 1972.

1. E as an independent source. In view of the repeated attacks on the existence of an independent Elohistic work made in the last thirty years by scholars of the standing of Volz, Rudolph and Mowinckel, it may be as well to indicate the facts that do at any rate need to be made sense of. The one most basic criterion for a division into sources is the repeated occurrence of the same material in different versions, that is, doublets. The problem can be illustrated from the example of the Abraham tradition: the stories of Abraham and Lot, the narrative of the sacrifice of Isaac, and that of the death and burial of Sarah each occur in only one form. On the other hand the story of the ancestress of Israel in danger is transmitted in two forms: according to Gen. 12.10–20

25. *Old Testament Theology*, vol. 1, Edinburgh and London 1962, pp. 48 ff. On the possibility of the further transmission of J in wisdom circles, and perhaps even of its use in schools cf. H.-J. Hermisson, *Studien zur israelitischen Spruchweisheit*, WMANT 28, 1968, pp. 126 f.
26. Cf. below, pp. 393 f., and pp. 403 ff.

Sarah was taken into the harem of the Pharaoh, according to Gen. 20 into that of King Abimelech of Gerar[1]. The position is similar with the story of Hagar: according to Gen. 16.1–14* Hagar fled before the birth of Ishmael, according to Gen. 21.9–21 she was driven out long after his birth. The individual traditions can be assigned without difficulty to different sources: the Abraham–Lot series of sagas belongs to J, the story of the sacrifice of Isaac to E, and that of the death and burial of Sarah to P. In Gen. 12.10–20 and Gen. 20 on the one hand, and in Gen. 16.1–14* and Gen. 21.9–21 on the other hand, we have parallel narratives of J and E.

If we examine the position in more detail, we can see that J is the dominant source by comparison with E in the Abraham stories (and mostly also subsequently) and that the part played by E is accordingly a supplementary one. If we take into account the common spiritual outlook of the Elohistic passages, for which evidence will shortly be given, we will realize that we have a basically ambiguous position as regards the evidence. Within the context of the newer documentary hypothesis the evidence can be explained by the assumption that a redactor (R^JE) has inserted the parts which appear to him important of a continuous narrative Elohistic source into the Yahwistic source, which he has preferred presumably because of the earlier starting-point of its narrative. This redactor is then called the Jehovist, a name chosen to include the names of both sources. Or one can follow Volz, Rudolph, Mowinckel and now apparently Whybray[1a] in concluding that the Yahwistic source was supplemented by an Elohistic narrative stratum, but that there was never a continuous Elohistic narrative source. It must be granted that the evidence from the stories of the patriarchs is ambiguous, and that from the stories coming after the Sinai pericope problematic. Indications of longer alternative Elohistic narrative continuities in the Joseph and Exodus stories appear however to justify the assumption of the existence of a definite Elohistic work.

(a) LINGUISTIC AND THEOLOGICAL CHARACTERISTICS. The existence of continuous doublets can of course only be used as evidence in

1. Cf. also Gen. 26.1 ff.

1a. Cf. R. N. Whybray, 'The Joseph Story and Pentateuchal Criticism', *VT* 18 (1968), pp. 522 ff.

support of either theory if further distinctive criteria are found in connection with them. Different linguistic usages, styles, ideas of God and ethical levels are possible candidates. Since the time of Witter and Astruc the variation in the divine name has played an especially important part in the investigation of linguistic usage[2]. Most recently the objection has been made that the name Yahweh is always used when the reference is to the national God of Israel, while Elohim points to a more theological idea of God. For this reason, it is claimed, the change in the divine name cannot be used as an argument for source division. On the other hand the objection has been made that the Septuagint attests so variable a tradition in reproducing the name that for this reason it is impossible to have confidence in the reliability of this criterion. An examination of the position in the primeval history in Genesis however shows that the Septuagint or its Hebrew original has only attempted to cover over differences in the use of the divine name going back to the sources. If the variation in usage can be supported by the doublets, the old argument still deserves attention. So God is called Yahweh in the story of the stay of Sarah in the harem of Pharaoh (Gen. 12.10–20). He is also called Yahweh in the story of the flight of Hagar before the birth of Ishmael (Gen. 16.1–14*). This corresponds in fact to the conception of the Yahwist, according to which the name Yahweh has been known to men since the primeval period (cf. Gen. 4.26b). In the story of Sarah at the court of Abimelech in Gerar on the other hand, as in that of the banishment of Sarah after the birth of her son, it is Elohim who is mentioned (cf. Gen. 20 and 21.9–21). If we look further, we can show that this variation in the name corresponds to a particular theological idea: in the view of the Elohist the name of Yahweh is first revealed to Moses on the mountain of God (cf. Exod. 3.1*, 4b*, 6, 9–15). Up to Exod. 3 therefore he regularly uses the word for God, Elohim, instead of the name of God.

This characteristic is accompanied by other linguistic characteristics of the two sources[3]; the Yahwist calls the original inhabitants of Palestine Canaanites (cf. e.g. Gen. 12.6), while the Elohist speaks of Amorites (cf. e.g. Gen. 48.22). In the Yahwist

2. Cf. above, pp. 36 f.
3. On this cf. H. Holzinger, *Einleitung in den Hexateuch*, Freiburg and Leipzig 1893, pp. 181 ff., which is still the best treatment.

the father-in-law of Moses is simply described as a priest of Midian (cf. Exod. 2.16), in the Elohist he is called Jethro (cf. Exod. 3.1* and 4.18). The Yahwist calls the mountain where God is encountered Sinai (cf. Exod. 19.11); the Elohist on the other hand speaks of the mountain of God (cf. Exod. 3.1b and 18.5)[4].

If we return to our original example, the twofold tradition of Gen. 12.10–20 and Gen. 20, we can without difficulty find other criteria which can also be followed through a series of doublets. While Pharaoh learns the truth about Sarah in Gen. 12 from the plagues, God (Elohim) reveals the circumstances to Abimelech in Gen. 20 in a dream. The brief introduction to the narrative of the sacrifice of Isaac in Gen. 22.1–3 also presupposes a dream revelation. The dream motif can be followed further through the Elohistic narratives. The ladder up to heaven in Bethel appears to Jacob in a dream (Gen. 28.12). The angel of God appears to Jacob in a dream to demand that he should return home (Gen. 31.11 ff.). Similarly Laban is warned by God in a dream against speaking unkindly to Jacob (Gen. 31.24). The line continues in the story of Joseph: the dreams of Joseph start the story off in a mysterious half-light (Gen. 37.5 ff.). The dreams of the chief butler and the chief baker, the dreams of Pharaoh and their interpretation by Joseph (Gen. 40 f.), and finally the command given to Jacob in a vision of the night to set out for Egypt (Gen. 46.2), complete the picture: everywhere in the pre-Mosaic period the dream is the proper medium of revelation. In this a quite specific view of God is reflected, which is conscious of the distance between God and man, and wishes to preserve it.

Once we have become aware of the particular understanding of revelation in the Elohist, we will also easily notice the difference in moral sensitivity. In Gen. 12.10 ff. the Yahwist feels no hesitation in telling how Abraham pretends that his wife is his sister, so that things may go well with him and his life may be spared. Perhaps the narrator even takes delight in his crafty ancestor! It is quite different in the Elohistic parallel, Gen. 20. The material was clearly anchored so firmly in the tradition that the narrator could not pass it by. So he attempts at least to excuse his hero: Sarah was in fact, he says, the half-sister of

4. Cf. M. Noth, *Überlieferungsgeschichtliche Studien*, Halle 1943, Tübingen 1967[3], p. 29. n. 4.

Abraham! And while Abraham in Gen. 12 is let go by Pharaoh
with a bare 'take her, and be gone', the narrator of Gen. 20
makes him the deliverer of Abimelech. The prophet Abraham
has to heal the king of his illness by his intercession. The whole
story not only shows a refined moral feeling, it is also theologically more reflective than its predecessor: the Elohist turns the
story of the endangering of the ancestress of Israel into a contribution to the problem of the righteousness of God. Uncon-
sciously, and in this like the hero of a Greek tragedy, the foreign
king makes himself liable to punishment for sin. But God knows
that he is guiltless, and prevents him from actively sinning.
The theological and ethical permeation of the material from
tradition gives a quite different weight to the individual story in
the Elohist from that it has in the Yahwist.

It can be shown therefore that it is methodically correct for
literary criticism to start with the doublets, and that the other
arguments taken with this have not lost their evidential force.
It can accordingly be regarded as methodically reliable to apply
the criteria gained from clear examples to other less clear
passages.

(b) ILLUSTRATION FROM THE EXAMPLE OF THE NARRATIVES OF JOSEPH AND
OF THE PLAGUES. In the Yahwist the ancestor of the tribes, Israel, dwells
in Hebron (Gen. 37.14). The hatred of the brothers is aroused by the
preferential treatment for Joseph, which is expressed in the gift of the
'coat of many colours'. When he pays a visit to his brothers, who are
pasturing their flocks in the area of Shechem and Dothan, he is sold
by them to an Ishmaelite caravan. Judah acts as spokesman for the
brothers. The Ishmaelites in turn sell Joseph to a nameless Egyptian,
who makes him his steward. As the result of an attempt at seduction
by his wife and a subsequent false accusation Joseph is put in prison.
Here he rises to become the second in command. How Joseph there
got to know Pharaoh's butler and baker and through their help came to
be the counsellor of the king we can now only conjecture, since the
redactor (R^JE) has now given the lead in the narrative to E. In
the Elohist Jacob dwells in Beersheba (Gen. 46.1b–5a). Joseph incurs the
envy of his brothers through his dreams. Reuben, who here appears (in
a tradition which is clearly older compared with that of J) as the spokesman of the brothers, has him thrown into a pit, only to save him
secretly and send him back to his father. But his good intentions are
frustrated by the Midianites, who steal him from the pit, and sell him
to Potiphar the 'head butcher', i.e. the commandant of the fortress,

and commander of the royal bodyguard. So Joseph becomes his servant, and is appointed to serve the chief butler and the chief baker of the Egyptian king while they are held under arrest for investigation. Joseph interprets their dreams, and so, by recommendation of the chief butler, finally appears before the king, who is troubled by alarming dreams.

We find here quite clearly two independent self-contained narrative contexts, and can observe in the Elohistic strand the same characteristics as in the story of Abraham: the treatment is made more theological and more ethical[4a]. The father no longer appears as a weak and inadequate parent. The brothers are not ultimately responsible for the sale. Joseph too is not guilty, since his dreams come from God. All the decisive turning points in the story are brought about by dreams sent by God. God is the real moving power in the story. This is also expressed in the culminating words of the Elohistic narrative: 'You meant evil against me; but God meant it for good, to bring it about that many people should be kept alive' (Gen. 50.20).

In the story of the Egyptian plagues the differences appear in a similar way. It must first be pointed out that the Yahwist has seven plagues, but the Elohist only five[5]. He tells of a change of the water of the Nile into blood, of hail, of locusts and of a darkness by which only the Egyptians are affected. If we compare both series of plagues, we realise how a similar tendency towards rationalization also appears in the Yahwistic story of Joseph. Since the Elohistic narrative with its tendency towards ethicization seems to belong to a late period, it is doubtful whether the supposed older features in it are an instance of the effect upon it of an earlier stage in the history of tradition, or are not rather the consequence of a quite conscious and late tendency to archaize.

2. The limits of the work. We need here only refer to the attempts of Mowinckel and Hölscher to assign a share in the primeval

4a. The problem seen by Whybray, that the story of Joseph has to be viewed both as a *Novelle* stamped with the spirit of Wisdom, and at the same time as being dependent in both J and E on a basic source G, could be solved still within the framework of the newer documentary hypothesis if the Yahwistic story of Joseph were regarded (following H. Schulte, op. cit., pp. 9 ff., who appeals for support to H. Gressmann, 'Ursprung und Entstehung der Josefsage', in *Eucharisterion*, Festschrift H. Gunkel, FRLANT 19, 1, 1923, pp. 1 ff.) as a creation of J himself. For then E is not dependent upon the basic source, which can only be connected with difficulty with the Wisdom movement, but upon J. It can for now only be noted that D. B. Redford, *A Study of the Biblical Story of Joseph*, SVT 20, 1970 (cf. especially pp. 251 ff.) attempts to disprove the documentary hypothesis using precisely the example of the Joseph story.

5. Cf. above, p. 90.

story, Gen. 2–11, to the Elohist[6]. They have found no support among subsequent scholars. Furthermore Mowinckel has himself now abandoned this hypothesis[7]. Basically it can be said that the beginning of the Elohistic narrative was lost when it was inserted into J. It is disputed at what point E is now first heard. It is usually thought that the first Elohistic verses can be found in Gen. 15. Kaiser has argued against this, and found E first in Gen. 20[8]. In any case it can be conjectured that E also provided for a wandering of Abraham from north to south. If Josh. 24 contains an Elohistic core, vv. 2 f. would show that Abraham, in the view of the Elohist, was called from the farther side of the Euphrates. It is a distinctive mark of this source that all the patriarchs were resident at Beersheba (cf. Gen. 21.22–24, 27, 31, with 46.1b–5). We cannot here attempt to retell the whole of the Elohistic narrative[9]. We will proceed straightway therefore to the question where the narrative ends. It is regarded as certain by all scholars who allow for the existence of E that it ended like J with a story of the conquest. The only disputed question is whether it survives. It is only natural that Eissfeldt and Hölscher answer this question in a positive sense, since both believe that it is possible to follow through the old narrative sources on into the Books of Kings[10]. It is generally assumed that the stories of the conquest in Josh. 1–11* belong to E and that its end is to be found in Josh. 24. Procksch, Smend sr. and Weiser* for example

6. Cf. S. Mowinckel, *The two Sources of the Predeuteronomic Primeval History (JE) in Gen.* 1–11, ANVAO II, 1937, 2, 1937; Hölscher, op. cit., pp. 271, etc.

7. *Pentateuch Quellenfrage*, pp. 60 f. Meanwhile W. Fuss, *Die sogen-annte Paradieserzählung*, Gütersloh 1968, has attempted to show that E had a share in Gen. 2.4b–3.24.

8. *ZAW* 70 (1958), pp. 107 ff.; cf. also Mowinckel, op. cit., pp. 104 ff. A different view is taken most recently by R. Kilian, 'Der heilsgeschicht-liche Aspekt in der elohistischen Geschichtstradition', *Theologie und Glaube* 43 (1966), pp. 369 ff., and L. Perlitt, *Bundestheologie im Alten Testament*, WMANT 36, 1969, pp. 68 ff.

9. Cf. the surveys of the extent of E in Eissfeldt, *Hexateuchsynopse*, Noth, *A History of Pentateuchal Traditions*, pp. 35 ff., and Hölscher, *Geschichtsschreibung in Israel*, pp. 136 ff. It should be noted that V. Fritz, *Israel in der Wüste*, MTS 7, 1970, believes evidence cannot be found for the presence of E in Exod. 15–17 and Num. 10–21, cf. pp. 34 f. and in comment H. Cazelles, *VT* 21 (1971), pp. 506 ff.

10. Cf. above, p. 76, and below, pp. 165 f.

have taken this view. Noth on the other hand is convinced that the Jehovistic account of the conquest in JE was lost when the work was inserted in the Priestly Writing. The accounts of the conquest in Josh. 1–12 have, on his view, an independent history[11]. While all these views require critical examination in the future, the story of Balaam (Num. 23.1–26) must be regarded as the last undisputed Elohistic section.

3. Place and date of origin. While in the past there was widespread agreement that E was a North Israelite book of sagas (so Procksch) and that this work was later than J, present discussion shows striking uncertainty in regard to both points. The question of the date is answered by Noth with extreme caution, starting from the point that E was finished relatively late, but that there are no really convincing arguments for placing it later than J. He regards the possibility of fixing its place of origin with a similar reserve: E retells the narrative tradition as it was originally formed in the centre of Palestine and then filled out among the southern tribes. In view of Gen. 22 and Exod. 18 he favours a Judahite origin. The fact that E does not appear to know the Abraham and Lot cycle of stories, and that he has a preference for Beersheba as well as Shechem and Bethel (a sanctuary with which, according to Amos 5.5 and 8.14, the north still had connections in the eighth century) appears on the other hand to point to the Northern Kingdom. The negative argument that the Elohistic sayings of Balaam in Num. 23, unlike the Yahwistic ones, contain no allusions to the Davidic monarchy, acquires greater significance in connection with these facts. Accordingly Weiser*, Plöger[12] and Fohrer* preserve the traditional location, while Eissfeldt regards a decision between the two possible areas of origin as completely impossible in view of the complexity of the evidence. If Eissfeldt's view is not shared, before reaching a decision one must examine whether the reference to Reuben in the Joseph narrative, and the omission of the Davidic monarchy in the Balaam oracles in favour of the kingdom of God, are not to be understood as an attempt in a particular historical situation to renew the all-Israelite ideal as a counterblast to the particularistic restriction of it to Jerusalem. On the other hand the exclusion of

11. Cf. below, p. 137.
12. *RGG* II[3], cols. 436 f.

the sagas centred around Abraham in Hebron could only be occasioned by the sort of action they portray, which could not be harmonized with the religious and ethical ideas of the narrator. Here the religious outlook of Gen. 22 and Exod. 18 would be given expression.

The question of the date is still more difficult to answer. It is clear that it depends on the view we take of the extent of the work. If the end of the source is placed in 2 Kings 25 with Hölscher, E cannot be placed before the middle of the sixth century. There is general agreement only that E must have come into existence before the enforcement of the Deuteronomic demand for a single sanctuary (cf. Deut. 12). This would allow us on the generally held view to go down to the end of the seventh century, and on the view taken below down to the end of the sixth, if not the early fifth century[13]. The Elohistic Balaam oracles would then collectively be an expression of the expectation that the nation, living in separation from the Gentiles under its God and king, would see once again the hour of triumph over its enemies. Since a late date for the Elohist is probable in view of the level of reflection appearing in Gen. 20 and 22, we cannot in fact take it back before the last quarter of the eighth century, in order to ensure a Northern Israelite origin, but rather must come down as late as the exilic or early post-exilic period.

4. *Sources.* A decision on whether the general framework and the set of themes common to E and J is to be attributed, with Noth, to the dependence of both on an older basic source or *Grundlage* (G), whose ultimate setting is in the cult of premonarchical Israel, or, with Hölscher, Rost* and Hannelis Schulte, rather to a conscious dialogue of the Elohist with the work of his predecessor, depends on the view taken of the part played by the Yahwist himself, especially in the formation of the patriarchal and Joseph narratives, and on the date given to the archaisms of E. Hannelis Schulte has given us good reason to think that J bears a greater responsibility for the narrative complexes than Noth supposed. Since for Noth the archaisms of the Elohist were the decisive argument in the establishment of his hypothesis, the question must be raised whether these have to be seen as the consequence of direct dependence on a stage of tradition earlier than the

13. On the dating of Deuteronomy cf. below, pp. 124 ff.

Yahwist, or rather as the result of deliberate archaizing. The role
of Reuben in the Elohistic story of Joseph could be understood in
this way, and at the same time interpreted as indicating an anti-
Judahistic post-exilic bias. If E also has a fondness for revelations through dreams, and for the miraculous in the narrative of
the Egyptian plagues, we can be reminded of the popularity of
the former in apocalyptic, and of the latter in the late popular
traditions of the prophets. It can at least be said that the argument is by no means concluded in respect of this problem.

We are left then with the task of identifying the smaller and
larger source elements which E has incorporated in his narrative.
The words of blessing on Jacob and Esau in Gen. 27.28 f.* and
39 f. may come from oral tradition. It cannot be decided whether
a similar view should be taken of the Song of Miriam (Exod.
15.21), or whether, like Num. 21.14 f., it was taken over from the
Book of the Wars of Yahweh[14]. It seems clear that the Song of the
Well in Num. 21.17 f. and the taunt song over the King of
Heshbon in Num. 21.27–30 have an earlier history of their own.
The sayings of Balaam in Num. 23.7 ff. and 23.18 ff. are, at least
in their present form, an integral part of the narrative[15].

5. *The Elohist as narrator.* The Elohistic narratives of the patriarchs display a strange tendency to detach the patriarchs from
their old local points of anchorage and concentrate them in
Beersheba. Again it must remain open to question whether this
reflects a stage of tradition in which the sanctuary there played a

14. Cf. below, p. 329.
15. I cannot share the general optimism about whether we can know
if the so-called ethical Decalogue (Exod. 20.2–17) or the Book of the
Covenant as a whole (Exod. 20.22–23.19) belong to this source. Procksch,
like Holzinger before him, regarded B as the law proclaimed by Joshua
at the assembly at Shechem and then written down (Josh. 24.25). Rost*
takes the view that B originally stood before Deut. 27*, and was then
displaced by Deut. 12–26 from its old place. Moses, he claims, in E too
gave Israel a law shortly before the crossing of the Jordan, which was
then carved in Shechem on stone. Götz Schmitt in his *Der Landtag von
Sichem*, ATh I, 15, 1964, p. 101, allows for the possibility that the cultic
regulations of B could have stood in Josh. 24, but states at the same time
that the Book as a whole never had another setting than in the Sinai
pericope. Cf. now also E. Zenger, *Die Sinaitheophanie*, FzB 3, 1971, who
ascribes the insertion of the Decalogue to the Jehovist, and that of the
Book of the Covenant to a special redactional stratum.

particular part[16], or whether here too we do not find an archaizing
tendency concerned to reflect the exilic situation, which therefore
locates the patriarchs on the outermost edge of the cultivated
land. It is however also possible that with his undynastic version,
peculiar to himself, of the greater Israelite ideal, the Elohist had
roots in a tradition which derived from this sanctuary, with its
well-known links with the north (cf. Amos 5.5 and 8.14). The
process of detachment which can be seen in this concentration
of the patriarchs in one place itself serves to indicate that with E
we are dealing with a late stage of tradition, one of reflection.
This is supported by the tendencies to be seen generally in E
towards rounding off the individual narratives, and at the same
time towards linking them up by references forwards and backwards.

Abimelech reminds Abraham, at the conclusion of their treaty, of the
friendship which he has previously shown him (cf. Gen. 21.23 with
20.15). The Bethel saga in Gen. 28.10 ff.* presupposes the return of
Jacob from a foreign land (cf. Gen. 35.7 and 31.13 with 28.20 ff.). In
the salvation oracle by which God encourages Jacob in Beersheba to
travel to Egypt, his return is looked forward to (cf. Gen. 46.1b–5).
The dying Jacob prophesies to Joseph the return of his people to the
land of their fathers, and promises him in particular the hill of Shechem
as a possession. So the reader's view is prolonged beyond the exodus
from Egypt to the conquest (cf. Gen. 48.21 f.). Joseph as he is dying
requests his brothers to take his bones with them on their return
(Gen. 50.25). An arc extends from Gen. 50.25 to Exod. 13.19, and
whether primarily or secondarily to Josh. 24.32.

Stylistically E's preference for filling out scenes by duplication
is striking: Joseph has two dreams (Gen. 37.5 ff.); the head butler
and head baker both have two dreams (Gen. 40.5 ff.). Pharaoh
too has two dreams (Gen. 41.1 ff.). Twice messengers are sent
out, first to the king of Edom (Num. 20.14 ff.), then to the king of
Heshbon (Num. 21.21 ff.). A multiplication of characters, like the
doubling of scenes, serves to lengthen the narrative: while in J
there are rarely more than two or three, in E there can be as many
as seven. So in Gen. 21.9 ff. God, his messenger, Abraham, Sarah,
Isaac, Hagar and her son take part in the action. The introduction
of subsidiary characters also serves to fill out the story: Abraham
is accompanied on the route to the mountain in the land of

16. Cf. above, pp. 71 f.

Moriah by two servants (Gen. 22.3). The subsidiary characters
are freely given names, which give the impression of pure invention: the nameless Egyptian in Gen. 39.1* J corresponds to the
commander of the bodyguard Potiphar (Gen. 37.36 E)[17]. The
two devout midwives in Egypt are called Shiphrah and Puah
(Exod. 1.15). E shows a greater ability than J to paint characters
and situations. He employs speech more consciously as a means
towards this. A comparison between Gen. 12.10–20 (J) and
Gen. 20 (E) shows that J employs speech only so far as it is
necessary for the progress of the action. In E it serves also to
characterize the actors.

The deep seriousness of Gen. 22, the masterpiece of the
Elohist's narrative art, contrasts strikingly with the humour of
other passages: when Esau greedily asks for the pottage, which
he does not even recognize by name ('let me quickly taste of the
red, of that red stuff there; for I am weary!'), and so loses his
birthright (Gen. 25.29 ff.), humour can be recognized. And
when Rachel deceives her father when he is looking for his
household gods, the teraphim, we can surely hear good natured
mockery at dependence on such fetishes (Gen. 31.30 ff.)[18].

§ 10   The Priestly Writing

G. von Rad, *Die Priesterschrift im Hexateuch*, BWANT IV, 13, 1934;
P. Humbert, 'Die literarische Zweiheit des Priester-Codex in der
Genesis', *ZAW* 58 (1940/41), pp. 30 ff.; M. Noth, *Überlieferungs-
geschichtliche Studien*, Halle 1943, Tübingen 1967³, pp. 180 ff.; id.,
A History of Pentateuchal Traditions [1948], Englewood Cliffs, New
Jersey, 1972, pp. 8 ff., 239 ff.; K. Elliger, 'Sinn und Ursprung der
priesterlichen Geschichtserzählung [1952], *Kleine Schriften zum Alten
Testament*, ThB 32, 1966, pp. 174 ff.; R. Rendtorff, *Die Gesetze in der
Priesterschrift*, FRLANT 62, 1954, 1963²; K. Koch, 'Die Eigenart der
priesterschriftlichen Sinaigesetzgebung', *ZTK* 55 (1958), pp. 36 ff.;
G. von Rad, *Old Testament Theology*, vol. I [1957], Edinburgh and
London, 1962, pp. 232 ff.; K. Koch, *Die Priesterschrift von Exodus 25 bis
Leviticus 16*, FRLANT 71, 1959; M.-L. Henry, *Jahwist und Priester-
schrift*, ATh I, 3, 1960, pp. 20 ff.; W. Zimmerli, 'Sinaibund und

---

17. The mention of him in 39.1 is redactional.
18. On the style of E cf. Hölscher, op. cit., pp. 209 ff.

Abrahambund. Ein Beitrag zum Verständnis der Priesterschrift'
[1960], *Gottes Offenbarung*, ThB 19, 1963, pp. 205 ff.; S. Mowinckel,
Erwägungen zur Pentateuch Quellenfrage, Oslo 1964, pp. 9 ff.; S. R.
Külling, *Zur Datierung der 'Genesis-P-Stücke', namentlich des Kapitels
Genesis XVII*, Kampen 1964; P. R. Ackroyd, *Exile and Restoration*,
OTL, London 1968, pp. 84 ff.; S. E. McEvenue, *The Narrative Style
of the Priestly Writer*, AnBib 50, 1971; F. M. Cross, 'The Priestly
Work', in *Canaanite Myth and Hebrew Epic*, Cambridge, Mass. 1973,
pp. 293 ff.

The text is given in German in O. Eissfeldt, *Hexateuch-Synopse*,
Leipzig 1922, Darmstadt 1962[2] and in R. Smend jr., *Biblische Zeugnisse. Literatur des alten Israel*, FB 817, 1967, pp. 88 ff.

1. P as a historical narrative. Although the Priestly Writing is
later than Deuteronomy, we will deal with it first, because in it
we have the last of the three sources from which the Tetrateuch
has been composed. It owes its name to its ever-apparent interest
in the cultic and ritual rules of priestly observance. This interest
comes so much to the fore that its character as a historical narrative can be overlooked. The fact that P is no longer in its original
form is responsible for this. From the start it had contained
larger complexes of cultic and ritual laws, but it was expanded
by further rules of the same kind up to the final redaction of the
Pentateuch. We must accordingly distinguish between the basic
narrative proper (P[g]) and the secondarily inserted legislative
materials (P[s]) when establishing its original character.

The undisputed starting point of the priestly historical narrative (P[g]) is Gen. 1.1. Views differ about where its end comes.
While many scholars find a continuation of P in Joshua, others
like Noth and Elliger are convinced with Alt, whom they follow,
that Deut. 34.1a, 7–9 should be regarded as its conclusion[1].
While Löhr and Volz had previously contested the existence of
an independent source P, F. M. Cross has also recently argued
that we should understand the Priestly layer of the Pentateuch as
an exilic redaction of JE. Among other evidence he appeals to
the fact that on the one hand P presupposes the narratives of
J and E, while on the other hand it is improbable that (as would
otherwise have to be the case) he has deliberately left out the
making of the Sinai covenant[2].

1. Cf. pp. 107 and 136.
2. Cf. M. Löhr, *Untersuchungen zum Hexateuchproblem*, BZAW 38,

The original content of the priestly writing can be described, on the basis of a survey given by Hölscher[3], as consisting of the following material: in Genesis P deals with creation, the first men, the flood and covenant with Noah, the list of the nations, the family tree of the Semites, Abraham's emigration to Canaan, his separation from Lot, the birth of Ishmael, the covenant with Abraham, the birth of Isaac, the death and burial of Sarah, the death and burial of Abraham, the family tree of Ishmael, notices on Isaac, Jacob and Esau, the family tree of Esau, and notices on Joseph. In the book of Exodus it tells of the oppression of the Israelites in Egypt, the call of Moses, the miracles of Moses in Egypt, the passover and exodus, the crossing of the Sea of Reeds, the manna and quails, arrival at Sinai, instruction to build the dwelling place of God, its preparation and erection. In the book of Leviticus it tells of the priestly ordination and first sacrifice of Aaron, of Nadab and Abihu, of the priesthood of Eleazar and Ithamar, and of the great Day of Atonement. In the book of Numbers it tells of the mustering of the nation and of its order in the camp, the military inspection of the men from thirty to fifty years old and the departure from Sinai, the sending out of the spies, the rebellion of Korah, the murmuring of the people, the water from the rock, the death of Aaron, the installation of Joshua and in Deut. 34* of the death of Moses.

In this survey the sacrificial law of Lev. 1–7, the purification law of Lev. 11–15, and the law of holiness (Lev. 17–26), together with the rules about vows and tithes in Lev. 27 have been omitted. In Numbers we have retained of chapters 1–9 practically only chapters 1 and 2 as being original and, have further omitted chapters 15, 19, 28–30 as well as 32–35[4]. At least in respect of the book of Leviticus this procedure can be justified by means of an example: in Exod. 25–31 Moses seven days after his arrival at Sinai receives instructions from Yahweh for the initiation of the cult in the course of forty days and nights. Chapters 35–40

1924; P. Volz, in Volz and Rudolph, *Der Elohist als Erzähler—ein Irrweg der Pentateuchkritik?*, BZAW 63, 1933, and F. M. Cross, op. cit.

3. *Geschichte der israelitischen und jüdischen Religion*, Giessen 1922, pp. 142 f.

4. The complex Num. 32–35 seems to have reached its present position after the joining of the Deuteronomistic history work with the Tetrateuch. Cf. M. Noth, *Überlieferungsgeschichtliche Studien*, Halle 1943, Tübingen 1967[3], pp. 192 ff.

tell correspondingly of the erection and inauguration of Yahweh's dwelling in a tent, the tabernacle. The inauguration of the priesthood prescribed in Exod. 29 on the other hand is first told of in Lev. 8, while Lev. 9 tells of the first sacrificial action. We can tell that the sacrificial law of Lev. 1–7 breaks the narrative continuity, but also that the insertion has been made to form a preparation for Lev. 9. It can accordingly be understood why differing views are taken on whether the law on sacrifice (and on purity) is an original element in the priestly narrative.

The Priestly Writing is accordingly far from an accidental collection of cultic and legislative material; it is originally a planned account extending from the creation of the world to the death of Moses. The insertion of the cultic laws has its basis in a theological development. Language and style give it a stamp so distinctive that Theodor Nöldeke was able in 1869 to distinguish the Priestly Writing as a whole from the other narratives with almost complete finality. The breadth and sobriety of the style, with its preciseness of definition and its preference for chronology and for genealogy, allow even the beginner to recognize the priestly part of the Pentateuch with some certainty after a little practice.

2. Sources. Since the Priestly Writing follows the Jehovistic narrative (JE) in its general pattern, it seems clear that its author was familiar with this. In Genesis there is not one piece of narrative, apart from the death of Sarah and the purchase of the cave of Machpelah as a family burial ground (Gen. 23), which does not have a corresponding narrative in the Jehovistic work. Nevertheless P has not simply copied JE while introducing his own norms and biases, but has also reworked distinctive traditions of his own, as can be seen particularly clearly in the story of creation (Gen. 1.1–2.4a) and in the story of the flood. When it is seen that in the creation story a schema of eight works of creation and one of seven days have clearly been secondarily united with one another, and that a creation by deed and a creation by word compete with one another, it can be understood why von Rad in the thirties proposed to divide up not only the narrative of creation, but the whole priestly writing into an older source P^A and a later source P^B. He also suggested as a third element a so-called Book of Toledoth. This attempt has however not proved convincing[5]. Scholars prefer instead nowadays to explain the obvious internal inconsistencies, in so far as they are not due to subsequent redactions, by traditio-historical methods[6].

The assumption of an originally independent book of gene-alogies, or Book of Toledoth, is based on Gen. 5.1, where we read: 'this is the book of the generations (*tôlᵉḏôt*) of Adam'[7]. Since Adam in Gen. 5.1, unlike the story of creation, is under-stood as a proper name and not as a collective description, there is something to be said for the assumption that in this and similar headings we do not have a stylistic device of the priestly writing, but a characteristic of an old source. The fact that Gen. 5.2 had to provide a link between the two different under-standings of Adam of Gen. 1.1 ff. and Gen. 5.1 points in the same direction. Eissfeldt has correctly seen that the Toledoth formula always appears at a point when 'a narrowing down of the wider scene previously in view' is to be made[8], but that it is not necessary for this reason to regard these passages as in origin compositions of the priestly writer. P could have taken the narrowing down of the scene from world history to the history of salvation from such a book of genealogies, which in this way gave him a basis for his own narrative.

It is in any case certain that P could refer to a mass of priestly and cultic traditions, which in their turn had a long and com-plicated prehistory[9]. If no traces are found here of the ancient oracles of the priests obtained by technical methods (cf. e.g. 1 Sam. 14.36 ff. LXX and 30.6 ff.) such as may well have survived

---

5. Cf. the detailed criticism by P. Humbert, *ZAW* 58 (1940/41), pp. 30 ff.

6. Cf. e.g. the fine treatment of W. H. Schmidt, *Die Schöpfungs-geschichte der Priesterschrift*, WMANT 17, 1967², especially pp. 160 ff. and the analyses proposed by Elliger for Leviticus and by D. Kellermann for Num. 1–10.

7. Cf. further Gen. 6.9; 10.1; 11.10, 27; 25.12, 19; 36.1 (9); 37.2 and Num. 3.1.

8. 'Biblos geneseōs' [1958], *KS* III, Tübingen, 1966, p. 461. Cf. also Cross, op. cit., pp. 301 ff.

9. Cf. the monographs mentioned above of R. Rendtorff and K. Koch, the commentary on Leviticus by K. Elliger, HAT 1, 4, 1966, and most recently P. J. Bidd, 'Priestly Instruction in Pre-Exilic Israel', *VT* 23 (1973), pp. 1 ff.

in the priestly oracle of salvation after the rise of prophecy[10], it is
all the more clear that there are traces of the priestly *tôrôt* or directions in the form of instructions about the correct manner of
sacrifice as the sacrificial torah in Lev. 1–7, or about distinctions
between clean and unclean as purity torah in Lev. 11–15, cf.
Hag. 2.10 ff. It was inevitable that the cultic material, once
brought in, led to expansions and additions. The entrance
liturgies in Pss. 15 and 24 with their *tôrâ* of entry show a concrete
link between the priests and apodictic law[11], while Num. 5.11 ff.
demonstrates that the priestly ordeal was a means of effecting
justice.

3. P as the basis of the Pentateuch. Our short survey of the
original contents of the Priestly Writing has shown that Deuteronomy in its present form has been inserted between Num. 27
(or Num. 32* J) and Deut. 34. It appears from this that the old
narrative of the Pentateuch has been secondarily joined with
Deuteronomy, or more precisely with the Deuteronomistic
history[12]. It was only then that Num. 32–35 received their
present form, to link together the two historical works which
were originally separated from one another. This is the reason
why the description of the boundary of the tribe of Dan in Num.
34.7b–11 is absent in Josh. 13 ff.[13] The fact that in Deut. 34 it
is no longer the Deuteronomist but P who takes the lead is also an
indication of the secondary linking of the two history works.

For it can be demonstrated that within the Tetrateuch it is
basically P that provides the material. Only in places where this
source has passed over events too summarily, as in the story of
the patriarchs, or where it lacks visual quality, as in the primeval
history, or where it is silent about a tradition which is basic to
Israel's understanding of itself, as in the Sinai story, does the
Jehovistic history work come in to fill in the story in a supplementary way. It is certain that the insertion of E into J took place
before the resulting Jehovistic work was incorporated into P. It

10. Cf. J. Begrich, 'Das priesterliche Heilsorakel', *ZAW* 52 (1934),
pp. 81 ff., also in *Gesammelte Studien zum Alten Testament*, ThB 21, 1964,
pp. 217 ff.; Bidd, pp. 3 f., and below pp. 263 and 365.
11. Cf. above, p. 64 and below, p. 337.
12. Cf. Noth, op. cit., pp. 209 ff. and 211 ff.
13. Cf. Noth, op. cit., pp. 194 f.

is however doubtful whether the Jehovist can be identified with
the Deuteronomistic redactor who can be shown to have been at
work in the Tetrateuch[14]. The only *terminus ad quem* for the date
of the uniting of the Priestly Writing with the Jehovistic history
work, and of the uniting of the resulting historical narrative from
creation to the death of Moses, which is basically the Tetrateuch,
with the Deuteronomistic history work is the composition of the
work of the Chronicler, which already presupposes the existence
of the Pentateuch, and the beginning of the translation of the
Septuagint in the third century B.C.[15]. Speculations about a law
book brought by Ezra to Jerusalem (cf. Ezra 7) have in my view
no reliable historical basis, because in the Ezra narrative we have
a piece of edificatory 'church history'.[16]

4. Date and origin. In view of the literary analysis of the Pentateuch suggested above a distinction must be made between the
date of P^g and of the later expansions of it. The question of the
date of the traditions which have been redacted in P^g and P^s
is in each case a separate problem. The date of the priestly historical narrative can be fixed with certainty only relatively, while
the absolute dating is a matter for argument. Since P assumes one
single legitimate cultic centre as a matter of course, it is in any
case later than Deuteronomy[17]. But this provides only a relative

14. Cf. the analysis of W. Fuss, *Die deuteronomistische Pentateuchredaktion in Exodus 3–17*, BZAW 126, 1972, which gives a positive answer
to this question, with that of E. Zenger, *Die Sinaitheophanie*, FzB 3, 1971,
which indicates a definite distinction between them.

15. Cf. E. Würthwein, *The Text of the Old Testament*, Oxford 1957,
pp. 36 f., S. Jellicoe, *The Septuagint and Modern Study*, Oxford 1968,
pp. 55 ff., and below, p. 408.

16. Cf. G. Hölscher, in HSAT II[4], 1923, pp. 491 ff., and his *Geschichte
der israelitischen und jüdischen Religion*, pp. 140 f., and more recently
S. Mowinckel, *Studien zu dem Buche Ezra-Nehemia III. Die Ezrageschichte und das Gesetz Moses*, SNVAO II, 7, 1965, especially p. 136.
Cf. below, pp. 181 f. and 412.

17. On the attempt to argue for an early dating made by Y. Kaufmann,
The Religion of Israel from its Beginning to the Babylonian Exile, Chicago
1969, pp. 175 ff., cf. R. J. Thompson, *Moses and the Law in a Century of
Criticism since Graf*, SVT 19, 1970, pp. 120 ff. S. R. Külling, *Zur Datierung der 'Genesis—P—Stücke', namentlich des Kapitels Genesis 17*,
Kampen 1964, exaggerates the value of form-critical arguments for dating
in his argument for an early date.

terminus a quo, since the dating of Deuteronomy is itself controversial[18]. Accordingly the *terminus a quo* for the origin of P is
placed by most scholars at the end of the seventh century, but
by a minority only at the end of the sixth century. Elliger in
particular has argued for a date during the Babylonian exile.
He finds, especially in the strange end of the narrative, according
to which the generation of the exodus and wilderness was not
allowed to enter into the land of promise, a clear reference to
the situation of the nation in exile. Like them it possesses only
the promise and the graves of its fathers. P^g was therefore, he
argues, a book of exhortation and consolation to the exiles. But
this dating has some difficulties, the solution of which is connected with the view taken of other literary facts. The question
is particularly what view is to be taken of the relationship between
P^g and H (cf. p. 114 below), and between P^g and Ezekiel. It is
sufficient in this connection to mention some basic points: in P
the high priest has taken over the cultic position and apparel of
the king. But Zechariah's hopes show that at the end of the sixth
century men were still ready to make a distinction between the
priest and the king. The influence of the Priestly Writing can be
traced first in the history of the Chronicler. As scholarship now
stands the assumption that the Priestly Writing was composed at
the earliest in the fifth century provides the least difficulties.
This does not alter the fact that it had a lengthy prehistory.

Whether the place of origin was the Babylonian diaspora or
Jerusalem needs further examination. On the one hand it must
be taken into consideration that any extensive return of the
exiles in the sixth century clearly did not take place. Allowing
for the points made by Elliger, therefore, an exilic origin could
be argued for even in the fifth century. On the other hand it is
not ruled out that the priestly writing in its own way wished to
uphold the legitimacy of the post-exilic Jerusalem cult, the
original pattern for which it placed in the time of Moses.

5. *Theology.* The priestly writing is most strikingly distinguished
from its precursors J and E by the fact that its concern is no
longer with the concealed guidance and dispositions of Yahweh
in history, but with the growth of the eternally valid cultic
ordinances of God. They receive an astonishing emphasis very

18. Cf. below, pp. 124 ff.

early on in the fact that the story of creation reaches its climax in the God-given festival of the Sabbath (Gen. 2.3). While this is at first unknown to man, it is finally discovered by the Israelites in the non-appearance of the manna in the wilderness (Exod. 16.22 ff.), and then revealed at Sinai as an obligation (Exod. 31.12 ff.).

Wellhausen described the Priestly Writing as the Book of the Four Covenants (creation, Noah, Abraham, Sinai)[19]. But in fact it only speaks of the concluding of two covenants: neither in the case of creation (and as Zimmerli has pointed out this is strange) nor in that of the Sinai event is a covenant concluded. P tells only of the covenant with Noah (Gen. 9.1 ff.), which is valid for the whole of post-flood mankind, and of the covenant with Abraham in Gen. 17. The covenant with Noah takes in P the place of the sacrifice which is recounted in J: before the foundation of the Mosaic cult there could be for P no legitimate sacrifice, only non-religious slaughter of animals. Here we trace the effect of Deuteronomy (cf. Deut. 12.15 f.). On the basis of this covenant of preservation, which guarantees the continued existence of the world, and so finally rules out the imperilling of the world by chaos[20], God concludes an eternal covenant with Abraham and his offspring. If the rainbow was the sign of the covenant with Noah, circumcision is the sign of the covenant with Abraham. Since the Babylonians did not know circumcision it acquired for the exiles a confessional character, which subsequently came to hold good for the whole of Judaism. The content of the second covenant is the promise of numerous descendants, and of the eternal possession of the land of Canaan. While the priestly writer has hitherto only spoken of Elohim, now he makes God reveal himself as El Shaddai. He is described by this name at all particularly emphasized passages up to and including Exod. 6. At this point the name of Yahweh is revealed to Moses. So just as P bridges over the period between creation and flood by his genealogies, he covers the period between the covenants with Noah and with Abraham, and between the

19. Cf. e.g. *Die Composition des Hexateuchs und der historischen Bücher des Alten Testaments*, Berlin 1899³ (1963⁴), pp. 1 f.

20. Cf. E. Würthwein, 'Chaos und Schöpfung im mythischen Denken und in der Urgeschichte', in *Zeit und Geschichte*, Festschrift R. Bultmann, Tübingen 1964, pp. 317 ff.

covenant with Abraham and the story of the purchase of the cave
of Machpelah as a burial place for Sarah in Gen. 23 in the same
way. Of the rest of the stories of the patriarchs also only brief
remarks and genealogies remain. Accordingly each time when P
inserts a narrative we must enquire about its particular purpose.
The story of the purchase of the burial place in Gen. 23 is rather
to be understood, with von Rad, as a pledge of the fulfilment of
the promise of the land than with Mowinckel as a polemic
against a post-exilic cult connected with this cave. There must
have been some consolation for the diaspora in the emphasis of
this story. If our interpretation of the literary position is correct,
P remains silent about the revelation of the law on Sinai, which
in the usual understanding is already important for the older
narratives. Exod. 25.21, 31.18 and 34.29 show that P is familiar
with a lawgiving on Sinai. But he does not include it—unless
with Mowinckel we regard the insertion of the originally Deuteronomistic Decalogue in Exod. 20.2–17 as his work. Zimmerli
sees in the omission of the lawgiving on Sinai a conscious reaction
of the priest to Israel's failure to keep the law: P places the
period of Moses in the shadow of the period of the patriarchs.
What happened in the period of Moses is the redemption of the
promise given to Abraham: an arc extends from Gen. 17.7 over
Exod. 6.7 to Exod. 29.43 ff. and 40.34. In place of the proclamation of the divine law stands the foundation of the cult which
can effect atonement. The centre of the cult is the presence of
God in his sanctuary in the midst of his people. But the presence
of God is realized neither purely physically nor e.g. by means of
revelation in a dream, but in his *kābôd*. The point of the cult,
whose foundation P tells at such length, is atonement for human
guilt and unholiness, which themselves remain unexplained and
so appear almost like a fatal inevitability (Koch). Exod. 6 begins
a line of thought which can be followed through to the end of the
work: the people are not ready to accept from Moses the generous
promise of release, of his particular relationship to God, and of
his guidance into the land promised solemnly to the fathers.
After their deliverance from Egypt they murmur and wish for
death in Egypt rather than for a continuation of the journey
through the wilderness (Exod. 16.1–3). The returning spies give
such a bad impression of the land that a rebellion of the people
results, which God punishes with the death of all who are more

than twenty years old in the wilderness. Only Caleb and Joshua may enter the land of promise (Num. 14*). Even Moses and Aaron are forbidden to enter the land. Aaron dies on Mount Hor (Num. 20.28); Moses is allowed to lead the people to the border, but there dies in sight of the promised land (Deut. 34*). The promise however still remains open. In the community which murmurs in the face of the promise, we can see with Elliger a reflection of the exiles. But the greatness of the narrator is perhaps shown precisely in the point that the situations described by him for the community which lives in temptation under the promise, are not applicable to one single historical situation alone, but are capable of constant new applications: anyone who doubts the validity of the promise of God will not experience its fulfilment. But he who believes will experience that God's promises are not empty.

We may picture the priestly writer, or the circle of men who stand behind the Priestly Writing, as being experienced, clever but also somewhat detached. Mythical elements are repressed, as a comparison of Gen. 1.1–2.4a (P) with 2.4b–3.24 (J) shows particularly clearly. The stories of creation and of the flood are told factually and soberly. The rainbow in the covenant with Noah is almost the last mythological survival (Gen. 9.8 ff.), but otherwise all the magic of the primeval history has been lost. A quite obvious rationalism goes hand in hand with a deliberate archaism: the patriarchs, cleansed of all the blemishes, but also of all the colour, of the old traditions, remain wanderers in the land of promise. They only belong to the soil, as Holzinger correctly says, through the fact that they are buried in it[21]. The archaism is shown in the fact that the sanctuary in the wilderness, a strange mixture between an old tent shrine and the temple in Jerusalem, is so far assimilated to the situation presupposed that it is treated as transportable: the cherubim, which in 1 Kings 6.23 ff. are of considerable size, are reduced and placed as a decoration upon the flat top of the ark (Exod. 25.18 ff.; 37.7 ff.). The altar of burnt offerings becomes a wooden object covered with plates of metal. This rationalizing, archaizing and schematizing of material things is matched by P's schematization of history. The materials taken over are subordinated without exception to the theological bias. The whole is held together by

21. *Einleitung in den Hexateuch*, Freiburg and Leipzig 1893, p. 360.

a chronology according to which the exodus from Egypt takes place in the year 2666 (Samaritan text 2967, LXX 3446). The idea of a world epoch lasting 4000 years appears to underlie this. We can no longer discover what specific expectations formed the background of this dating of the exodus (in MT exactly two-thirds through the epoch)[22]. The details of size of the ark and the facts about the height of the flood give an equally rationalistic impression. The world of the priestly writer seems to contain only two real secrets: the one is the unfathomable decision of God to save, the other the unfathomable power of sin. But the cult, which makes atonement and purifies, relieves mankind of the necessity of reflecting on these secrets.

6. The Holiness Code. The Code of Holiness (H), Lev. 17–26, was first recognized by August Klostermann in 1877 as an independent unit. It is named after the demand which is found in 19.2, and in similar form in 20.7 and 26: 'You shall be holy; for I the LORD your God am holy.' We can follow Elliger in giving its structure as follows: Lev. 17 treatment of blood, 18 sexual intercourse, 19 relations with one's neighbour, 20 penalties, especially for sins of unchastity, 21.1–22.16 rules for the personal life of the priests, 22.17 ff. the quality of sacrifices, 23 feasts and festivals, 24.1–9 the care of the lamp and of the show-bread, 24.10 ff. blasphemy, 25 treatment of the land (the Year of Jubilee) and 26 blessings and curses.

The views taken of the origin of the Code of Holiness vary very widely, particularly at present. An extreme traditio-historical position is represented by Graf Reventlow[23]. According to him H had its original context in the ancient Israelite Covenant Festival and in this context, starting from a Decalogue in Lev. 19, underwent successive development to its present extent. The tradents of this development into the preaching of the law are appointed preachers and proclaimers of the law. The origin of the Code of Holiness accordingly reflects an 'unbroken transition from apodictic proclamation to parenetic preaching'[24]. As

22. Cf. P. R. Ackroyd, op. cit., pp. 91 f.
23. H. Graf Reventlow, *Das Heiligkeitsgesetz formgeschichtlich untersucht*, WMANT 6, 1961.
24. Id., *Wächter über Israel. Ezechiel und seine Tradition*, BZAW 82, 1962, p. 124.

for date, the process of its formation would fall within the long span of time between Sinai and the period after 725. On the other hand we have the primarily literary-critical attempt at a solution by Elliger[25]. He denies that H was ever an independent corpus, and argues that we have a collection which was prepared from the first for insertion into the priestly writing. It was intended to provide what was most clearly lacking in P, a non-cultic law-giving on Sinai. Elliger believes that the collection reached its final form in four stages which can be clearly distinguished, and accordingly divides off the four literary layers P^h1–P^h4. The post-Deuteronomic date of all the layers appears clearly from the assignment of 17.3 f. to P^h1, in spite of the fact, which Elliger of course realizes, that material which is traditio-historically in part very old has been reworked.

The relationship of the Code of Holiness to Deuteronomy and to Ezekiel has been evaluated in various ways in recent discussion. Feucht, who distinguished between an H_1 and an H_2, held that H_1 originated in the first half of the seventh century, and was circulated in the Southern Kingdom about the middle of the same century. Not until H_2 can direct or indirect influence by D be recognized[26]. In view of the similarities and differences that exist between H and Ezekiel, Fohrer assumes a '*Vorlage* common to both from the pre-Exilic period, whose laws Ezekiel quotes and assumes to be well known, but which are finally codified for the first time in H'[27]. Kilian, who places an early form of the Code of Holiness after Deuteronomy and before 586 and distinguishes it from an R^h, or redactor of the Holiness Code, who is to be placed at the earliest in the exilic period, sees Ezekiel as influenced by the early Code, and R^h by Ezekiel[28]. Kornfeld believed that Ezekiel had it in front of him as 'a text fixed in writing'[29]. For Reventlow on the other hand these connections can be explained from the identity of the office of 'proclaimer of the law' and that of prophet[30]. It will be seen that in recent

25. K. Elliger, *Leviticus*, HAT I, 4, 1966.

26. C. Feucht, *Untersuchungen zum Heiligkeitsgesetz*, ThA 20, 1964.

27. G. Fohrer, *Die Hauptprobleme des Buches Ezechiel*, BZAW 72, 1952, p. 147.

28. R. Kilian, *Literarkritische und formgeschichtliche Untersuchung des Heiligkeitsgesetzes*, BBB 19, 1963.

29. W. Kornfeld, *Studien zum Heiligkeitsgesetz*, Vienna 1952.

30. BZAW 82, pp. 123 ff.

scholarly work practically all varieties of view possible are represented. In the face of all these attempts however it still seems to me that we must ask whether they start from a correct literary-critical evaluation of Ezekiel. For according to the arguments of Schulz and Garscha the parts of Ezekiel adduced for comparison are in any case to be regarded as post-exilic[31]. In regard to Elliger's analysis of H, therefore, the features common to H and the Book of Ezekiel are either to be accounted for by derivation from traditions common to both, or by the assumption of a direct literary dependence of this stratum in Ezekiel upon H.

§ 11   Deuteronomy

P. Kleinert, *Das Deuteronomium und der Deuteronomiker*, Bielefeld 1872; J. Wellhausen, *Die Composition des Hexateuchs und der historischen Bücher des Alten Testaments*, Berlin 1885, 1963[4]; W. Staerk, *Das Deuteronomium. Sein Inhalt und seine literarische Form*, Leipzig 1894; id., *Das Problem des Deuteronomiums*, BFchTh 29, 2, 1924; C. Steuernagel, *Der Rahmen des Deuteronomiums*, Berlin 1894; id., *Die Entstehung des deuteronomischen Gesetzes*, Berlin 1895 (1901[2]); J. Cullen, *The Book of the Covenant in Moab. A Critical Inquiry into the Original Form of Deuteronomy*, Glasgow 1903; A. Klostermann, *Der Pentateuch. Beiträge zu seinem Verständnis und seiner Entstehungsgeschichte*, Neue Folge, Leipzig 1907; F. Puukko, *Das Deuteronomium. Eine literarkritische Untersuchung*, BWAT 5, 1910; J. Hempel, *Die Schichten des Deuteronomiums. Ein Beitrag zur israelitischen Literatur- und Rechtsgeschichte*, Leipzig 1914; G. Hölscher, 'Komposition und Ursprung des Deuteronomiums', *ZAW* 40 (1922), pp. 161 ff.; T. Oestreicher, *Das deuteronomische Grundgesetz*, BFchTh 27, 4, 1923; id., *Reichstempel und Ortsheiligtümer in Israel*, BFchTh 33, 3 1930; A. C. Welch, *The Code of Deuteronomy, A New Theory of its Origin*, London 1924; id., *Deuteronomy, The Framework to the Code*, London 1932; M. Löhr, *Das Deuteronomium*, Schriften der Königsberger Gelehrten Gesellschaft Gw. Kl.1, 6, Berlin 1925; A. Bentzen, *Die josianische Reform und ihre Voraussetzungen*, Copenhagen 1926; W. Baumgartner, 'Der Kampf um das Deuteronomium', *ThR* NF 1 (1929), pp. 7 ff.; G. von Rad, *Das*

---

31. *Das Todesrecht im Alten Testament*, BZAW 114, 1969, pp. 163 ff.; J. Garscha, *Studien zum Ezechielbuch*, Frankfurt and Berne 1974; cf. also Hölscher, *Geschichte der israelitischen und jüdischen Religion*, pp. 136 ff.

Gottesvolk im Deuteronomium, BWANT III, 11, 1929; id., 'The Form-critical Problem of the Hexateuch' [1938], in *The Problem of the Hexateuch and other Essays*, Edinburgh and London 1966, pp. 1 ff.; id., *Studies in Deuteronomy* [1949] SBT 9, London, 1953; F. Horst, *Das Privilegrecht Jahwes. Rechtsgeschichtliche Untersuchungen zum Deuteronomium*, FRLANT 45, 1930, and in *Gottes Recht*, ThB 12, 1961, pp. 17 ff.; H. Breit, *Die Predigt des Deuteronomisten*, Munich 1933; M. Noth, *Überlieferungsgeschichtliche Studien*, Halle 1943, Tübingen 1967³; J. H. Hospers, *De Numeruswisseling in het Boek Deuteronomium*, Utrecht 1947; A. Alt, 'Die Heimat des Deuteronomiums', *KS* II, Munich 1953, pp. 250 ff., and in *Grundfragen des Volkes Israel*, Munich 1970, pp. 392 ff.; B. Maarsingh, *Onderzoek naar de Ethiek van de Wetten in Deuteronomium (Inquiry into the Ethics of the Laws in Dt.)*, Winterswijk 1961; O. Bächli, *Israel und die Völker. Eine Studie zum Deuteronomium*, ATANT 41, 1962; G. Minette de Tillesse, 'Sections "tu" et sections "vous" dans le Deutéronome', *VT* 12 (1962), pp. 29 ff.; N. Lohfink, *Das Hauptgebot. Eine Untersuchung literarischer Einleitungsfragen zu Dtn 5–11*, AnBib 20, 1963; S. Loersch, *Das Deuteronomium und seine Deutungen*, SBS 22, 1967; J. G. Plöger, *Literarkritische, formgeschichtliche und stilkritische Untersuchungen zum Deuteronomium*, BBB 26, 1967; H. Schulz, *Das Todesrecht im Alten Testament*, Diss. theol. Marburg 1967; E. W. Nicholson, *Deuteronomy and Tradition*, Oxford 1967; R. P. Merendino, *Das deuteronomische Gesetz*, BBB 31, 1969; J. Lindblom, *Erwägungen zur Herkunft der josianischen Tempelurkunde*, SKHVL 1970/1, 3, 1971; G. Seitz, *Redaktionsgeschichtliche Studien zum Deuteronomium*, BWANT 93, 1971; M. Weinfeld, *Deuteronomy and the Deuteronomic School*, Oxford 1972.

Commentaries: cf. on § 4 and further Buis and Leclerq 1963.

1. The name. The name of this book of 34 chapters goes back to the mistranslation of *mišnê hattôrâ* in 17.18 by the Septuagint, which rendered 'the copy of the law' by 'the second law'. The lawgiving of Deuteronomy is in this way seen in contrast to the Sinaitic lawgiving as a second one which took place according to the narrative framework in the land of Moab, although in fact according to Deut. 4.13, 9.7–10.5 only the Decalogue was revealed on Horeb (as the Deuteronomist calls the mountain of God). In the Hebrew Bible the book, like the others in the Pentateuch, is named after its first words, 'and these are the words' (the others are Genesis: 'in the beginning'; Exodus: 'and these are the names'; Leviticus: 'and he called'; Numbers: 'in the wilderness').

2. Content. The book begins with a speech by Moses, delivered on the far side of the Jordan, extending from 1.6–4.40, and introduced by 1.1–5, in which he gives a hortatory retrospect of the events of the preceding forty years since the departure from Horeb. In 4.41–43 the account of the separation of the cities of asylum east of the Jordan follows. The main section, 4.44–30.20 (interrupted by 27), is occupied by the preaching of the law by Moses, at the centre of which stands the demand for the centralization of the cult. It is followed by the account of the writing down of the law by Moses and the installation of Joshua as his successor (31), the Song of Moses (32), the Blessing of Moses (33), and the account of the death of Moses (34). We can therefore treat 1.1–4.43 and 31–34 as a framework, in contrast to the central section 4.44–30.20. Within the preaching of the law in 4.44–30.20, a narrative introduction (4.44–49), the hortatory speech (5.1–11.32) and the final speeches (28–30) can be distinguished from the preaching of the law proper in 12.1–26.19, which is often called a corpus of law.

3. Character and problems. The distinctive nature of the preaching of the law in Deuteronomy over against the other legal collections of the Pentateuch lies in the fact that it is not presented as a speech of God to Moses, but as a speech of Moses to the people, or (as von Rad has appropriately described it) 'a divine charge' 'given to the lay community at second hand'[1]. The religio-historical and legal historical problems of Deuteronomy are connected with the problems of its date and origin. Apart from traditio-historical investigation and the question of possible reworking of sources, these problems are indissolubly connected with another problem, whether Deuteronomy, either in its present form or in some other form which has to be reconstructed, was the basis of the cultic reform carried through by Josiah king of Judah in 621 (cf. 2 Kgs. 22 f.). The literary-critical problem is raised by the at least in part conflicting headings 4.44, 45; 5.1; 6.1 and 12.1, by the change of number between second person singular and plural in addresses in 4.44–30.20, and finally by the conflicting concluding speeches 28.1–29.1, 29.2–29 (Heb. 28.1–69, 29.1–28); 30.1–14 and 30.15–20, not to mention ch. 27, the literary criticism of which is difficult. We

1. Von Rad, *Studies in Deuteronomy*, p. 13.

can best approach a solution of the problems raised by a survey of the history of scholarship, taken in order as its methods developed.[2]

4. Survey of the history of scholarship. The history of modern Deuteronomy scholarship begins with de Wette's *Dissertatio critica, qua a prioribus Deuteronomium Pentateuchi libris diversum, alius cuiusdam recentioris auctoris opus esse monstratur,* of 1805, in which he not only (as the title indicates) recognized the independence of Deuteronomy in relation to the preceding books, and its connection with the following books Joshua to Kings, but also the connections between Deuteronomy and the Reform of Josiah.

(a) THE LITERARY PROBLEM. After Graf in 1866 had demonstrated the greater antiquity of Deuteronomy than the Priestly Writing, and Wellhausen had brilliantly secured victory for the hypothesis in the next two decades[3], the identification of Deuteronomy with the Law Book of Josiah became the mainstay of the reconstruction of the history of Israelite religion and literature. Subsequent scholarship concentrated primarily on the questions of literary unity, date and prehistory of the book. After Kleinert had already in 1872 recognized the difference between the narrative framework (1–11) and the legal core (12–26), Wellhausen argued for the limitation of the Josianic law to 12–26 as an *Urdeuteronomium* (original form of Deuteronomy). At the same time he took the view that this had circulated in two separate editions which were subsequently united, one of which was introduced and concluded by chs. 1–4 + 27 and the other by chs. 5–11 + 28–30. A further advance, although one which is to this day contested, was the recognition in the same year 1894 by both Staerk and Steuernagel of the change in number as a criterion for source division. The method was however put at a disadvantage from the first by the fact that Puukko limited the content of *Urdeuteronomium* to the passages which are presupposed in the account of the reform in 2 Kgs. 22 f., and that finally Steuernagel connected it with Wellhausen's theory of different editions, a view which he developed further himself[4].

2. Cf. S. Loersch, op. cit.   3. Cf. above, pp. 39 f.
4. On this cf. also C. Steuernagel, HK I, 3.1, Göttingen 1923[2], pp. 4 ff.

It was Hölscher who first freed himself from both these pre-suppositions, and showed in 1923 that we must look for *Urdeuteronomium* in the singular sections from 4.44–29.1* (Heb. 4.44–28.69), though we must allow for expansions not only in the plural but also in the singular. Noth in particular came to support this hypothesis, and in 1943 he succeeded in showing that the Deuteronomistic history begins in 1.1[5], and that 1.1–4.40*[6]; 31.1–30* and 34.1*, 4, 5–6 are to be ascribed to its author, while in 34.1a, 7–9 P is the only Tetrateuchal source to be heard. Noth believed that the Deuteronomist already had before him 4.44–29.1 (Heb. 4.44–28.69) in basically its present form, but Minette de Tillesse was able to show in 1962 that the passages with an address in the plural in this block come from the Deuteronomist himself. He has thereby performed for literary-critical work on Deuteronomy, which has generally been regarded as finished, a service which has so far not been sufficiently acknowledged[7]. The task of extending the examination to the concluding speeches[8], and of connecting the layers that have been established with the redactions which can clearly be observed also within the Deuteronomistic history, the Deuteronomistic additions to the Pentateuch and the Deuteronomistically influenced parts of the Book of Jeremiah, still awaits a solution. Not until we have this can we expect a comprehensive knowledge of the working methods and of the diffusion of the Deuteronomistic school.

5. Cf. below, pp. 169 f.

6. On the analysis of 1.6–3.29 cf. N. Lohfink, 'Darstellungskunst und Theologie in Dt. 1,6–3.29', *Bib* 41 (1960), pp. 105 ff., and J. G. Plöger, op. cit., pp. 1 ff.

7. The approval of this view by Noth (cf. *VT* 12 (1962), p. 34, n. 3), Merendino (op. cit., pp. 407 f.) and G. Seitz (op. cit., p. 309), who however makes a distinction between Deuteronomy proper, which incorporates material formulated in the singular and also itself formulates it in this pattern, a Deuteronomistic redaction which formulates it in both singular and plural mixed, and the Deuteronomistic edition proper, contrasts with the rejection by Fohrer*, p. 171 and P. Diepold, *Israels Land*, BWANT 95, 1972, p. 19. Cf. further the cautious notice taken of his work in Lohfink, *Hauptgebot*, pp. vii f., von Rad, *Deuteronomy* (OTL), p. 12, and in the context of a statement of the problem, in J. G. Plöger, op. cit., p. 6, nn. 32 and 33.

8. On the analysis of chap. 28, cf. Plöger, op. cit., p. 130 ff.

(b) THE FORM-CRITICAL AND TRADITIO-HISTORICAL PROBLEM.
From the beginning of this century, the weight of the most
recent study of Deuteronomy has fallen on the form-critical and
traditio-historical problems. As a precursor of traditio-historical
study we must mention A. Klostermann, who in 1907 saw in
12–28 'the fully grown result of the living practice of the public
reading of the law[9], and who pointed to the religio-historical
parallels of the ancient Icelandic law book of the Grágás, which
grew out of the public oral recitation of the law.

It would take us too far to deal here with Hempel's division of the
sources of Josiah's Law into a Jerusalem temple rule coming from the
days of Solomon, a tô'ēbâ or Abominations law source from the time
of Manasseh, a source of social prescriptions, and the Book of the
Covenant, or with Steuernagel's distinction between the laws about the
centralization of the cult, the tô'ēbâ laws, the laws about elders, judges,
humanitarian principles and individuals, and Breit's understanding of
1.1–31.19 as a parenetic sermon on the basis of the Decalogue.

F. Horst's recognition that within the corpus a distinction is
to be made between the older legal clauses and the later legal
interpretations took scholarship further, though it was connected with the untenable hypothesis that a Decalogue of
privileges of Yahweh in law lay at the basis of 12–18. Finally
Alt's investigation of 'the Origins of Israelite Law' in 1934 (ET
in *Essays on Old Testament History and Religion*, Oxford 1966,
pp. 79 ff.) with its basic distinction between apodictically formulated and casuistically formulated law, and its connection of
recitation of the law and celebration of the covenant, has had a
decisive effect on scholarship[10]. First, he made available criteria
for an analysis of literary types and for a distinction between
older legal material and Deuteronomic interpretation, and
secondly he prepared the way for the question of the relationship of the whole to the covenant tradition. Von Rad, who had
already been concerned in his *Gottesvolk im Deuteronomium* of
1929 with the understanding of the theological nature of the
book, devoted himself to the solution of both tasks. His contribution, whose importance for the whole of subsequent Old
Testament scholarship cannot be too highly stated, consisted
primarily in the fact that in his 'The Form-critical Problem of

9. Op. cit., p. 347.   10. Cf. above, pp. 56 f. and 59 f.

the Hexateuch' of 1938 he succeeded in proving that the structure of Deuteronomy (which is certainly to be regarded as a literary product, with its sequence of historical presentation of the Sinai events and paraenesis in 1 and 6–11, recital of the law in 12.1–26.15, commitment to the covenant in 26.16–19 and blessings and curses in 27 ff.) corresponds to that of the Sinai pericope in the Book of Exodus, that this pattern can be traced even in the smallest liturgical units of Deuteronomy[11] and that in the background of the pattern the course of the ancient Shechem Covenant Festival can be recognized[12]. The principle of composition here postulated was followed out further by Lohfink in 5–12. He showed that the introductory speeches and the corpus of law are related as general and individual commandments to one another[13], and tried to demonstrate the influence of the covenant pattern in individual passages too. Finally Schulz has seen that the arrangement of sections within 12–25, in spite of some substantial disturbances, is basically influenced by the structure of the Decalogue.

So the cultic rules and rules concerned with privileges of Yahweh in 12–18 are followed by laws on murder, family, one's neighbour, and court procedure. The Decalogic principle of arrangement can also be demonstrated in the sequence of some individual sections, especially clearly in 21.1–22.4, where the ancient brief series *lō' tirṣaḥ lō' tin'ap lō' tignōḇ* ('You shall not kill. You shall not commit adultery. You shall not steal') is echoed in prescriptions on murder (21.1 ff.), on marriage and the family (21.10 ff.), and on the preservation of the property of one's neighbour (22.1 ff.)[14]. If the Decalogue (5.6–21) and the series of curses in 27.15–26* (excluding vv. 22 f.) are regarded as original elements of Deuteronomy, this frame to the preaching of the law would enable us to conclude the search for a corresponding principle of composition. A careful further investigation of the principle of composition underlying 12–26 using this approach remains a task for the future[15].

11. Cf. also Lohfink, *Hauptgebot*, pp. 107 ff.

12. Cf. above, pp. 74 ff., and from the extensive literature D. J. McCarthy, *Treaty and Covenant*, AnBib 21, 1963, and *Old Testament Covenant*, Oxford 1972. For criticism, cf. Perlitt, quoted on pp. 63 f. above.

13. Op. cit., p. 111.

14. Here we seem to have an interpretation of *lō' tignōḇ* which goes beyond the original connection with man-stealing.

15. The chapters of the Marburg dissertation of H. Schulz especially concerned with Deuteronomy will be published separately. Only the

In his *Studies in Deuteronomy* (1947, ET 1953) von Rad
worked out the distinctive nature of the Deuteronomic preaching
of the law[16], in which a distinction is to be made not only, with
Horst, between ancient legal clauses and legal interpretations
which are perhaps also old (cf. e.g. 15.1 f.), but also between
both of these and the parenetic presentation in contemporary
terms. In the course of this the distinction between legal forms,
introduced by Alt, was preserved in detail. This made it possible
to discover series formed by the Deuteronomist, such as an
'ideal for judges' (cf. 16.19), an apodictic series stressing cultic
duties (16.21–17.1), a similar series of incompatible actions
(22.9–11)[17], and one on membership of the *qāhāl*, the levy of
full citizens, 23.1–3, 7 (Heb. 23.2–4, 8). According to L'Hour we
should take with them the *bi'artā* laws, which are connected by
the formula 'and you shall purge the evil from the midst of you',
and by a concern for cultic purity, as well as the *tô'ēbâ* or abomination laws, prohibitions which have in common the justification
'for this is an abomination to Yahweh, your God'.[18] von Rad
recognizes that roughly fifty per cent of the prescriptions of the
Book of the Covenant have equivalents in Deuteronomy, and a

section on the curses of Deut. 27 has been included in BZAW 114, 1969,
pp. 61 ff.

16. While von Rad sees the world of law as having been left behind in
the preaching of the law, Schulz emphasizes that the parenesis too
remains within the field of jurisprudence, and that its purpose is to
give the legal clause the greatest obligatory force possible by making
it as vivid as possible. He suggests as a name for the literary type
of the parenesis beginning with a legal clause the expression 'legal paradigm'.

17. Against von Rad, 22.5 could possibly as L'Hour, *RB* 71 (1964),
p. 486, argues, belong to an abomination law source.

18. According to J. L'Hour, 'Une législation criminelle dans le
Deutéronome', *Bib* 44 (1963), pp. 1 ff., 13.1–5 (Heb. 13.2–6); 13.6–11
(Heb. 13.7–12); 13.12–18 (Heb. 13.13–19); 17.2–7; 19.11–13; 19.16–19;
21.1–9; 21.18–21; 22.13–21; 22.22; 22.23–27; 22.28–29; 24.1–4; 24.7 and
25.5–10 should be included in the *bi'artā* laws, and 17.1; 18.10–12;
22.5; 23.18 (Heb. 23.19) and 25.13–16 should be included in the *tô'ēbâ*
collection (cf. 'Les interdits to'eba dans le Deutéronome', *RB* 71 (1964),
pp. 481 ff., and now also Merendino, op. cit., pp. 326 ff.). It remains a
question in respect of the older legal materials not permeated with
homiletic commentary which appear from 21 in great mass, to what
extent these were first inserted in the course of the redactional process.
This is a problem which Hölscher and von Rad have seen.

comparison where one can be made shows clearly a later social situation in Deuteronomy[19]. He hesitates however, like Steuernagel before him, and like Merendino now, and with justification, to understand Deuteronomy with Eissfeldt* as a new edition of the Book of the Covenant, since it could have drawn on another source unknown to us[20]. He regarded the parenetic sections, which show no reference back to older legal clauses, such as 12.32–13.5 (Heb. 13.1–6); 13.6–18 (Heb. 13.7–19); 17.14–20; 18.9–22 and 19.1–13, as genuine Deuteronomic literary types. Finally he drew attention to the war laws coming on his view from the tradition of the Holy War (20.1–9; 20.10–18, 19–20; 21. 10–14; 23.9–13 (Heb. 23.10–14); 24.5 and 25.17–19) as well as the demands for war (cf. 20.1–9*; 7.16–26; 9.1–6; 31.3–6, 7–8, etc.)[21].

The work done so far has been brought by Merendino in 1969 to a measure of conclusion. On the basis of a new and more thorough analysis he demonstrates that the Deuteronomist, in addition to cultic and liturgical texts, made use of *bi'artā* and *tô'ēbâ* laws, of rules of civil law, of marital and humanitarian rules, and of independent apodictic series of laws, each of which groups had its own earlier history. He breaks up the *tô'ēbâ* laws to form separate strongpoints, but otherwise, retaining the material which he has before him, edits it in a style characterized by the language of sermon and parenesis. He makes the basis for a division of the material the assignment of 12–18 to the relationship of the people to Yahweh, of 19–25 to the relationship of man to man. The inclusion of Deuteronomy in the Deuteronomistic history work led to further redactional editing of 12–26. Meanwhile Seitz has published his studies made at about the same time, in which he makes a distinction between the law (12–28*) originating in a Deuteronomic collection, and a Deuteronomic redaction, which is responsible for the insertion at the head of it of 5–11*, the insertion of laws which are predominantly social (15.1–18, 21, 22 f., 22.1–12, 23.1–9, 16–24 (25–26), 24.17–22) and a revision of the original material, and

19. Cf. BWANT III, 11, p. 20, and *Deuteronomy* (OTL), p. 11, with the lists there given, as well as examples Exod. 21.2 ff. with Deut. 15.12 ff. and Exod. 23.10 f. with Deut. 15.1 ff.

20. Cf. Steuernagel, HK I, 3, 1², pp. 39 f., von Rad, *Deuteronomy*, p. 13, and now also Merendino, op. cit., pp. 401 f.

21. Cf. now F. Stolz, *Jahwes und Israels Kriege*, ATANT 60, 1972, pp. 17 ff.

which preceded the Deuteronomistic redaction[21a]. In view of the subsequent demonstration that the Deuteronomistic history is of several layers, both analyses require to be examined in reference to the question what influence its three (at least) redactions have had upon the Deuteronomic law[21b].

(c) THE PROBLEM OF ORIGIN AND DATE. It has already been mentioned that the identification of *Urdeuteronomium*, however delimited, with the lawbook of Josiah is to be regarded as the dominant view since the beginning of the nineteenth century. This working hypothesis is today generally connected with another one, that Deuteronomy originated between the middle of the eighth and the middle of the seventh century in the Northern Kingdom, after the fall of which it was deposited in the temple in Jerusalem, and there forgotten until the building works in the eighteenth year of King Josiah (639–609) (so Welch). In this way the disturbance at the court caused by the discovery of the book could be understood without the shadow of a pious fraud falling upon those who took part in it (cf. 2 Kgs. 22 f.), as would be more or less inevitable on the assumption of an authoritative participation of the Jerusalem priesthood or of the court in the origin of the book.

The hypothesis of the identification of the lawbook of Josiah with Deuteronomy is suggested by a series of parallels between the royal reforms and individual prescriptions of Deuteronomy: the demand for centralization of the cult in Deut. 12.13 ff. is matched by 2 Kgs. 23.8a, 9 and 19, that for abolition of star worship in Deut. 17.3 by 2 Kgs. 23.11 f. The male and female cult prostitutes too, in accordance with Deut. 23.17 (Heb. 23.18), were removed from the temple (cf. 2 Kgs. 23.7). Tophet, the place of child sacrifice in the valley of Hinnom, was in accordance with Deut. 18.10 defiled by Josiah (cf. 2 Kgs. 23.10). The much discussed point of difference, that the priests of the high

21a. Seitz (pp. 306 ff. and pp. 310 f.) in attempting to connect Deuteronomy, in view of the role ascribed to Moses, to circles in Gilgal going back to Elijah and Elisha (cf. 1 Kgs. 18 and 19, to which he appeals), and to date it to the time of Isaiah, overvalues the evidential value of the texts adduced for comparison, as he does also in adducing the connections between his Deuteronomic redaction of 2 Kgs. 23.4–14 and the Deuteronomic portions of the books of Jeremiah to date this redaction to the time of Josiah.

21b. Cf. below, p. 174.

places, against Deut. 18.6 ff., were not apparently accepted alongside the
Zadokides of Jerusalem as enjoying equal rights (cf. 2 Kgs. 23.9), seems
only to show that the law did not come in in a vacuum, but in a concrete
historical situation.[22]

Alt attempted to reinforce the North Israelite origin of
Deuteronomy by arguments from content. The limitation of
interest to the relationship between Yahweh and the nation
which Alt detects leaves the idea of his world dominion out of
consideration[23], and in view of the nature of the Jerusalem traditions as known to us is claimed to support a North Israelite
origin, as is the closeness of the law about the king in 17.14 ff.
to the charismatic form of kingship assumed by him for the
Northern Kingdom[24]. Finally, in the reserve towards kingship
expressed here, as well as in the Deuteronomic demand for love
for God, Alt saw an echo of the preaching of Hosea (cf. 6.5;
7.9; 10.12 with Hos. 11.1 ff.; 1.10 ff. [Heb. 2.1 ff.] and 3.1 ff.)[25].
Following a study made by Junge[26], von Rad would see in the
Judahite country Levites, who according to Neh. 8.1 ff. seem to
have been the tradents of the preaching of the law, the driving
element in the regeneration of the Judahite levy under Josiah,
and (like Bentzen before him) as the tradents of the Deuteronomic tradition. This does not exclude for him an origin of
Deuteronomy in the Northern Kingdom, where its place of
origin could be sought in the sanctuaries of Shechem or Bethel.
It is clear that the connection between the principle of composition of Deuteronomy as a whole and the supposed Shechem
covenant festival is on this view significant[27]. On the other hand

22. Cf. the detailed but not conclusive discussion in Lindblom, op. cit.,
pp. 45 ff.
23. Cf. against this O. Bächli, op. cit., p. 205.
24. For a criticism of this hypothesis cf. H. Wildberger, 'Samuel und
die Entstehung des israelitischen Königtums', *ThZ* 13 (1957), pp. 442 ff.;
G. Buccellati, 'Da Saul a David', *Bibbia e Oriente* 1 (1959), pp. 99 ff.,
and W. Beyerlin, 'Das Königscharisma bei Saul', *ZAW* 73 (1961), pp.
186 ff. For a criticism of the supposed Northern Israelite origin of the
Law concerning the king cf. Lindblom, op. cit., pp. 50 ff.
25. Cf. against this O. Bächli, op. cit., pp. 205 ff. and Lindblom,
pp. 66 ff.
26. E. Junge, *Der Wiederaufbau des Heerwesens des Reiches Juda unter
Josia*, BWANT IV, 23, 1937.
27. Cf. above, p. 74.

Weinfeld in tracing the origin of Deuteronomy to a circle of scribes at the court of Josiah[28], Nicholson to one of prophets come south from the Northern Kingdom[29] and Lindblom to one of Levites again come from the Northern Kingdom to Jerusalem, who were previously not linked to the cult, but are now taken up into the priesthood[30], all continue to maintain the identity of this lawbook with the document found in the temple under Josiah.

In spite of the impressively strong arguments adduced for it, it still needs to be asked whether the identification of the Law of Josiah with Deuteronomy is firmly enough based, or whether in the 'war over Deuteronomy' (Baumgartner's phrase) which raged especially in the decade after the end of the First World War, objections were not brought against it which still deserve consideration today. In the discussions at that time an early as well as a late date for Deuteronomy was suggested. Of the champions of an early dating only Oestreicher and Löhr need be noted here. Taking up a proposal of Kegel[31] Oestreicher sought to prove that Deuteronomy was in fact concerned not for cultic unity but for cultic purity. With the support of Staerk, he interpreted the demand for cultic centralization in 12.14 in a general sense in the light of 23.16 (Heb. 23.17): sacrifice could be offered at every place chosen by Yahweh. He connected with this hypothesis a very definite early dating, in which Löhr followed him. He believed he could find in 12–26* a priestly book of instruction, which belonged to the wilderness period of Israel. But it is understandable that the assumption of a Mosaic origin for Deuteronomy was no longer able to carry conviction. The distinctive character of the Deuteronomic preaching of the law in any case excludes an early date[32].

28. It is unfortunate that he has made no distinction in his argument for Wisdom influence between Deuteronomic and Deuteronomistic sections.

29. Cf. against this Lindblom, pp. 57 ff.

30. He seeks in this way to do justice to the clearly levitical interest, to the tensions with the Jerusalem ideology and to their redactional influence, e.g. in the substitution of the idea of the election of the people for the election of the king of the line of David.

31. M. Kegel, *Die Kultus-Reformation des Josia*, Leipzig 1919.

32. The contrary arguments of G. T. Manley, *The Book of the Law*, London 1957, and M. G. Kline, *Treaty of the Great King. The Covenant Structure of Deuteronomy: Studies and Commentary*, Grand Rapids, Michigan 1963, are not going to turn back the wheel of scholarship.

More serious are the attacks made in English speaking countries by Kennett and Berry, in Germany by Hölscher and Horst, upon the identification of Deuteronomy with the lawbook of Josiah, and the resultant late dating of Deuteronomy[33]. The fact that these were in part connected with idiosyncratic literary-critical or literary-historical hypotheses made it too simple for contemporary and subsequent generations of scholars to pass them over in favour of the established views[34]. Since Hölscher provided the most comprehensive justification for his thesis and thereby at least won the agreement of so great a scholar as Mowinckel,[35] we will confine ourselves mainly to a summary of his arguments. Hölscher starts from what is undoubtedly the only methodically reliable basis, that the date of Deuteronomy must first be established from its text alone without reference to 2 Kgs. 22 f. In reviewing the basic material of 12–26* phrased in the second person singular, which he assumes to be original, he underlines above all the ideological and unpractical character of the law, and its unsuitability to be made the basis of a reform by Josiah in particular.[36]

33. Of the sceptical voices of the nineteenth century M. L. Horst, 'Études sur le Deutéronome', *Revue de l'Histoire des Religions* 16 (1887), pp. 28 ff.; 17 (1888), pp. 1 ff.; 18 (1888), pp. 320 ff.; 23 (1891), pp. 184 ff. and 27 (1893), pp. 119 ff. still deserves mention. Apart from Hölscher's article listed above cf. R. H. Kennett, *Deuteronomy and the Decalogue*, Cambridge 1920; G. R. Berry, 'The Code Found in the Temple', *JBL* 39 (1920), pp. 44 ff.; id., 'The Date of Deuteronomy', *JBL* 59 (1940), pp. 133 ff.; F. Horst, 'Die Kultusreform des Josia', *ZDMG* 77 (1923), pp. 220 ff.

34. Cf. W. Eichrodt, 'Bahnt sich eine neue Lösung der deuteronomischen Frage an?', *Neue Kirchliche Zeitschrift* 32 (1921), pp. 41 ff.; H. Gressmann, 'Josia und das Deuteronomium', *ZAW* 42 (1924), pp. 313 ff.; K. Budde, 'Das Deuteronomium und die Reform König Josias', *ZAW* 44 (1926), pp. 177 ff.; Hans Schmidt, 'Das deuteronomische Problem', *Theologische Blätter* 6 (1927), cols. 40 ff.; J. A. Bewer, 'The Case for the Early Date of Deuteronomy', *JBL* 47 (1928), pp. 305 ff.; L. B. Paton, 'The Case for the Post-exilic Origin of Deuteronomy', ibid., pp. 322 ff.; G. Dahl, 'The Case for the Currently Accepted Date of Deuteronomy', ibid., pp. 358 ff., and in summary W. Baumgartner, 'Der Kampf um das Deuteronomium', *ThR* NF 1 (1929), pp. 7 ff.

35. *Erwägungen zur Pentateuch Quellenfrage*, Oslo 1964, p. 22.

36. Cf. also J. Pedersen, *Israel* III–IV, London and Copenhagen 1940 (1953), pp. 580 ff.

There can be disagreement about the value of his arguments in particular cases. It must however be granted that in the cases of 16.11, 14 and 15.1 ff. serious difficulties lie in the way of their realization. His view that neither 13.1 ff. nor 17.14 ff. are conceivable in the pre-Josianic or Josianic period can also be accepted. Similarly Berry has emphasized that the law of the king, with its requirement that no foreigner should be installed as king, would have been completely inappropriate during the existence of the monarchy[37]. If the provisions for the appointment of the judges in 16.18 are in fact to be understood against the background of the Judaean legal organization as it is reflected in 2 Chr. 19.8 ff.[38], the fact that the authority lies with the people can be regarded as further evidence that the monarchy has meanwhile disappeared[39]. Even Hölscher's point that 12.13 ff. does not give the impression of introducing the exclusive choice of Jerusalem as the legitimate cultic centre as a hitherto unheard of innovation, is, in spite of individual objections to the suppositions he there makes, worth examination.

The decisive proof of the correctness of the denial of Deuteronomy's identity with the law of Josiah, and of the consequent late dating, is the indirect negative evidence from the testimony of the prophets. While it may be better to leave Ezekiel out of consideration at present in view of the problems of the book, on which agreement has not yet been reached, it can be emphasized all the more strongly that the authentic Jeremiah in his prophecies of disaster directed against Jerusalem and Judah shows not the slightest knowledge of Deuteronomy[40]. This argument from silence is so strong that in my view the theory that Deuteronomy originated in the period of the gradual consolidation of the Jewish community in Palestine is definitely to be preferred to the prevailing hypothesis. It can indeed still be linked with the hypothesis of the origin of the book in Levitical circles, and the partial derivation of the material in the book from the area of the former Northern Kingdom[41]. If Deuteronomy is in this way

37. Cf. *ZAW* 40 (1922), pp. 192 f. and 199 f., and Berry, *JBL* 59 (1940), p. 137.

38. Cf. G. C. Macholz, 'Zur Geschichte der Justizorganisation in Juda', *ZAW* 84 (1972), pp. 333 ff.

39. Cf. P. Welten, *Geschichte und Geschichtsdarstellung in den Chronikbüchern*, WMANT 42, 1973, pp. 184 f.

40. Cf. below, pp. 239 ff. and 251 ff.

41. Cf. the objections made by Bächli, op. cit., pp. 184 ff., 203 ff., and

to be dated at a time close to that of P, this change of view could contribute to eliminating the dispute over whether Deuteronomy does in fact precede P, and whether Deuteronomy requires cultic unity or presupposes it. The question in what relationship the reform of Josiah, the account of the reform transmitted within the Deuteronomistic work in 2 Kgs. 22 ff., and Deuteronomy itself stand to one another belongs to another discussion, which is probably not yet closed[42].

5. *Urdeuteronomium.* The following survey is to be treated as a working hypothesis, not as a presentation of final results. It starts with the assumption that the address to Israel in the second person singular is characteristic of *Urdeuteronomium.* A decision is made difficult in individual cases by the fact that we have to allow both for successive filling out of the material, and for occasional assimilation of Deuteronomistic additions to the Deuteronomic style of address in the singular. The disturbance of the arrangement by subject matter which begins from chapter 19 further leaves open the question to what extent the insertion of further prescriptions led to transpositions in these chapters, and to what extent the present order goes back to associative links made by the first writer. For chs. 12–16 this survey uses with gratitude Merendino's analysis, but does not follow him in all points. Possible subsequent insertions are placed in square brackets, and Deuteronomistic additions in round brackets. A. Heading 4.45 (?); B. Introductory speech: 5.6–21 Decalogue; 6.4–9.7*; 10.12–14, 21–22; 11.1 the chief commandments (6* commands for life in the promised land; 7* commands for the conquest of the land; 8* commands for life in the land; 9.1–7a* further commands for the conquest of the land; 10.12–14, 21–22; 11.1 concluding emphasis of the main command to fear and love God)[43]; central section: (a) 12.13–18, 22* laws of Yahweh's

by H. Graf Reventlow, 'Gebotskern und Entfaltungsstufen in Deuteronomium 12', in *Gottes Wort und Gottes Land*, Festschrift H.-W. Hertzberg, Göttingen 1965, p. 185.

42. From the latest discussion cf. W. A. Irwin, 'An Objective Criterion for the Dating of Deuteronomy', *AJSL* 56 (1939), pp. 337 ff.; G. R. Berry, 'The Date of Deuteronomy', *JBL* 59 (1940), pp. 133 ff. (cf. also note 33); A. Jepsen, 'Die Reform des Josia', in *Festschrift F. Baumgärtel*, Erlanger Forschungen A 10, Erlangen 1959, pp. 97 ff.; R. Meyer, 'Stilistische Bemerkungen zu einem angeblichen Auszug aus der "Geschichte der Könige von Juda" ', ibid., pp. 114 ff.; as well as the cautiously weighed investigation of N. Lohfink, 'Die Bundesurkunde des Königs Josia. Eine Frage an die Deuteronomiumsforschung', *Bib* 44 (1963), pp. 261 ff. and 461 ff.   43. Cf. Lohfink, *Hauptgebot*, pp. 139 ff.

privileges*; 12.13–28* prohibition of sacrifice at a free choice of site (law of cultic centralization); 13.1–18, Heb. 13.2–19 (without 3b–4, 5aα*, 7, 16–17, Heb. 4b–5, 6aα*, 8, 17–18) against those who corrupt men into worship of foreign deities; 14.1–28 food regulations; 14.22–29* tithes; 15.1–18 (without 4–6 and [16–18]) the year of release, and the release of slaves from debt); 15.19–23 the sacrifice of the first-born of animals; 16.1–17 the three annual festivals; 16.18 the law of the judge; 16.19–17.1 regulations about trials and the cult (without 16.22b); 17.2–7 proceedings against adherents of foreign gods; 17.8–13 appeal to the central high court; 17.14–15 (16–20)? law of the king; 18.1–8 law of the priest; [18.9–14]? against soothsayers; [18.15–22]? law about prophets; (b) 19.1–25.19 rules about murder, the family, one's neighbour and court cases; 19.1–13 (without 8b, 9a, 13b) the law of asylum; [19.14] against moving boundaries; 19.15–21 law about witnesses; 20.1–20 (without 15–18) laws about war; 21.1–9 (without 5) atonement for a murder committed by an unknown hand; 21.10–14 marriage with a captive of war; 21.15–17 the rights of the first-born among the children of two wives; 21.18–21 punishment of a rebellious son; 21.22–23 burial of a man hanged; 22.1–4 actions in aid of a neighbour; 22.5 prohibition of transvestism; 22.6–7 protection of the mother bird; 22.8 about the parapet on the house roof; 22.9–11 mutually exclusive actions; [22.12] about the tassels on the cloak; 22.13–29 laws on unchastity; 22.30 (Heb. 23.1) prohibition of marriage with a wife of one's father; 23.1–3 (4–5) 6–8 [Heb. 23.2–4 (5–6) 7–9] commandments about admission to the community of Yahweh; 23.9–14 (Heb. 23.10–15) about the purity of the war-camp; 23.15–16 (Heb. 23.16–17) the treatment of a runaway foreign slave; [23.17 f. (Heb. 23.18 f.)] prohibition of cultic prostitution; 23.19–20 (Heb. 23.20–21) on interest; 23.21–23 (Heb. 23.22–24) on vows; 23.24–25 (Heb. 23.25–26) on picking grain; 24.1–4 a prohibition of remarriage with a wife who has been legally divorced and legally remarried; 24.5 about the freedom of the newly married; 24.6 prohibition on taking a millstone in pledge; 24.7 against man-stealing; (24.8–9)? behaviour in an attack of leprosy; 24.10–13 law on pledges; 24.14–15 the treatment of day-labourers; 24.16 limitation of death penalty to those guilty; 24.17–18 prohibition on perverting the justice due to persons not able to take part in a court case; 24.19–22 about gleaning; 25.1–3 moderation in the use of caning as a punishment; 25.4 prohibition on muzzling the mouth of an ox treading out the grain; 25.5–10 levirate marriage; 25.11–12 the punishment of a shameless wife; 25.13–16 correct weights and measures; [(25.17–19)?] command to exterminate the Amalekites; (c) 26.1–15 religious observances and creeds: 26.1–11 the offering of the first fruits (with the so-called small credo in 5, 6–7a,bα, 8aα and 9abα); 26.12–15 the offering of tithes; 26.16 concluding paraenesis; C 26.17–19 Commitment to the covenant; D 27.9–30.14* Blessing and curse; 27.9–10 transition; 27.15–26* [without 22–23] law curses:[44]; 28 [without 1b, 2b, 4b, 6b, 9aβ, bβ, 10b, 11b, 14, 18b, 20–21, 23–26, 32–34, 36–37, 42–44, 46–29.1 (Heb. 46–69)][45] blessings and curses; [30.1–14*] promise of Yahweh's renewed favour in response to repentance.

6. *Song and Blessing of Moses.* While there is no doubt that both the Song and the Blessing of Moses in chs. 32 and 33 were only subsequently added to Deuteronomy[46], their date and origin are disputed. The Song of Moses, 32.1–43, is placed by Eissfeldt in middle of the eleventh century, by Baumann in its basic form in the eight–seventh, by Budde in the sixth, and by Sellin in the fifth[47]. Since Budde seems to be correct in seeing that the Song expects no further judgement on the people of Yahweh, and looks back to very varied traditions and elements of literary types, a late post-exilic origin seems to be the most probable. In the Blessing of Moses, 33.2–29, a distinction must be made between the hymn (vv. 2–5, 26–29) and the sayings on the tribes (vv. 6–25). While the date of the hymn framework is hard to determine, a distinction must also be made between the question of the date of the individual sayings and that of the date of the composition. If the secular individual sayings belong to the premonarchical period, the new formations of theological character, as well as the connection of the individual sayings on a twelve tribe pattern may, as Zobel argues, have come about only in the monarchical period[48].

7. *The theology of Deuteronomy.* Deuteronomy's programme, which should probably be called an attempt at a reformation

44. Cf. above, pp. 59 ff.

45. Cf. Plöger, op. cit., pp. 130 ff.

46. Cf. Noth, *Überlieferungsgeschichtliche Studien*, p. 40.

47. Cf. K. Budde, *Das Lied Mose's, Deut. 32*, Tübingen 1920; E. Sellin, 'Wann wurde das Moselied Dtn 32 gedichtet?', *ZAW* 43 (1925), pp. 161 ff.; E. Baumann, 'Das Lied Mose's (Dt. XXXII 1–43) auf seine gedankliche Geschlossenheit untersucht', *VT* 6 (1956), pp. 414 ff.; O. Eissfeldt, *Das Lied Moses Deuteronomium 32,1-43 und das Lehrgedicht Asaphs Psalm 78 samt einer Analyse der Umgebung des Mose-Liedes*, SAL 104, 5, Berlin, 1958.

48. Cf. K. Budde, *Der Segen Mose's Deut. 33*, Tübingen 1922; F. M. Cross jr. and D. N. Freedman, 'The Blessing of Moses', *JBL* 67 (1948), pp. 191 ff., and H.-J. Zobel, *Stammesspruch und Geschichte*, BZAW 95, 1965.

rather than an attempt at a restoration, can be summarized in one sentence: one nation before the one God, who has chosen it for his property out of all nations; united in one cult at one place, which he has chosen for himself, to make his name dwell there; called to obedience in the love of God and in the fear of God, in the land which he has given them[49]. The basis of the relationship between Israel and its God is the election which began in Yahweh's love towards the fathers and in the covenant of promise sworn to them, a one-sided, solemn self-commitment of Yahweh to give the land to their descendants[50] (cf. 6.10; 10.15; 26.3, 15). This finds fulfilment in the exodus and in the gift of land—or rather as regards the land, is (in view of the supposed historical setting of Deuteronomy) in the future going to find fulfilment (cf. 6.12, 21 ff.; 7.6; 26.1 ff., 15). Facing the task of a spiritual refoundation of the community, the Deuteronomist, here related both to Deutero-Isaiah and his view of the release from Babylon as a second exodus, and to the Priestly theology of history, transposes his readers to the last days of the time of wandering under Moses in Transjordan, in order to impress on them that blessing and curse, possession of the land and life in the land depend entirely on their exclusive faithfulness to Yahweh, embracing all areas of life. By associating the cult with the one sanctuary he seeks both to avoid the danger of an infiltration of the worship of Yahweh by Canaanite practices and to overcome the conflict between partially outdated cultic practices and their own cultural situation[51]. The related secularization of slaughter, which only remained religious in its blood ritual, was bound to have as decisive an effect in the future on the relationship of Judaism to the Gentile world as the worship of God without images did (cf. 1 Cor. 8; Acts 15.20). The problems of belief connected with the loss of the ark, which was later to be treated by the Deuteronomist as a mere storage-vessel for the law (cf. 10.1 f.; 31.26), and with the destruction of the temple in 587, were solved by the *šēm* (name) theology, according to

49. It will not escape the notice of some readers that this summary is derived from Rudolph's description of the ideal of the Chronicler.
50. On the difference between Deuteronomic and Deuteronomistic covenant theology cf. G. Minette de Tillesse, *VT* 12 (1962), pp. 50 f.
51. Cf. V. Maag, 'Erwägungen zur deuteronomischen Kultzentralisation', *VT* 6 (1956), pp. 10 ff.

which it is not Yahweh himself, but, in preservation of the distance between God and world, only 'his name as the guarantee of his will to save' that is present at the shrine[52].

These changes demanded of the community a greater effort of conscious belief than did a totally cultic religion.[53] It now becomes much more clearly important that Israel understands itself from its history of revelation. This is why Deuteronomy commands that fathers should instruct their sons in the saving history (cf. 6.7, 20 ff.). This is why Deuteronomy in its preaching of the law keeps on returning to this history. This is why it is interested in the confessions to be uttered when gifts are offered (cf. 26.3 ff., 13 ff.). This is why it must also stress the continuing visible presence of his commandments in the form of phylacteries, and inscriptions on doorposts and gates (cf. 6.6 f.).

Deuteronomy must therefore be acquitted of a legalism which understands salvation as a deserved reward for Israel's own works, because election precedes all observation of the law, Israel is not given the land because of its own righteousness (cf. 9.4 ff.), and the obedience demanded is simply a straightforward response to God's preceding saving activity, and a consequence of the love and fear of God. For a nation which owes its existence and its land entirely to Yahweh, it follows as a consequence not only that because of its special position it must keep itself free of all alien cults, magical practices and all impurity, and be holy (cf. 7.6), but also that because of its own past it must pay respect to the socially weaker, to its widows and orphans, its resident aliens and slaves, indeed even to its cattle, in not oppressing them, not denying them their rights, making life possible for them and granting them festival days. If Israel is obedient it has the promise of a blessing which embraces equally nature and history, and which neither external enemies nor natural catastrophes, neither sickness nor infertility of man, of cattle or of fields can harm[54].

52. Von Rad, *Studies in Deuteronomy*, pp. 38 f. Cf. also F. Dumermuth, 'Zur deuteronomischen Kulttheologie und ihren Voraussetzungen', *ZAW* 70 (1958), pp. 59 ff.

53. It hardly needs to be emphasized that this description can only be used with qualifications of pre-exilic religion.

54. Of the most recent works on the theological character of Deuteronomy M. Weinfeld, *Deuteronomy and the Deuteronomic School*, Oxford 1972, deserves to be mentioned first, though with the reservations in n. 28

§ 12 The Book of Joshua

A. Alt, 'Judas Gaue unter Josia' [1925], *KS* II, pp. 276 ff.; id., 'Das System der Stammesgrenzen im Buche Josua' [1927], *KS* I, pp. 193 ff.; id., 'Josua', in *Werden und Wesen des Alten Testaments*, ed. P. Volz and F. Stummer, BZAW 66, 1936, pp. 13 ff. = *KS* I, pp. 176 ff. or *Grundfragen der Geschichte des Volkes Israel*, Munich 1970, pp. 186 ff.; W. Rudolph, *Der 'Elohist' von Exodus bis Josua*, BZAW 68, 1938; M. Noth, *Überlieferungsgeschichtliche Studien*, Halle 1943, Tübingen 1967³, pp. 40 ff.; S. Mowinckel, *Zur Frage nach Dokumentarischen Quellen in Josua 13–19*, ANVAO II, 1, 1946, 1946; C. A. Simpson, *The Early Traditions of Israel*, Oxford 1948; M. Noth, 'Überlieferungsgeschichtliches zur zweiten Hälfte des Josuabuches', in *Festschrift F. Nötscher*, BBB 1, 1950, pp. 152 ff.; G. Hölscher, *Geschichtsschreibung in Israel*, SKHVL 50, 1952; E. Jenni, 'Zwei Jahrzehnte Forschung an den Büchern Josua bis Könige. IV. Josuabuch', *ThR* NF 27 (1961), pp. 118 ff.; S. Mowinckel, *Tetrateuch-Pentateuch-Hexateuch*, BZAW 90, 1964; F. Langlamet, *Gilgal et les récits de la traversée du Jourdain*, CRB 11, 1969; id., 'Josué, II et les traditions de l'Hexateuque', *RB* 78 (1971), pp. 5 ff., 161 ff. and 321 ff.

Commentaries: KHC Holzinger 1901; HK Steuernagel 1923²; HS Schulz 1924; HAT Noth 1938; 1953²; ATD Hertzberg 1953 (1965³); CB Gray 1967; OTL Soggin 1972.

1. Name and author. The Book of Joshua owes its name to its main hero, who according to Rabbinic tradition is also author of the book down to 24.29 ff. These last verses, with the account of the death and burial of Joshua, were ascribed by tradition to Eleazar and Phineas. On the other hand Joshua is mentioned in 24.26 as the author of a book of the instruction of God, Joshua is referred to in the third person, and in a whole series of passages (e.g. 4.9, 5.9, 6.25 and 7.26) a considerable period of time is clearly envisaged between the date of the account and its content.

2. Content and division. The book tells of the combined conquest by the Israelites of the land west of the Jordan under the leadership of Joshua, as well as of the subsequent division of the land.

above. Cf. further H. H. Schmid, 'Das Verständnis der Geschichte im Deuteronomium', *ZTK* 64 (1967), pp. 1 ff., and S. Herrmann, 'Die konstruktive Restauration', in *Probleme biblischer Theologie*, Festschrift G. von Rad, ed. H. W. Wolff, Munich 1971, pp. 155 ff.

It begins after the death of Moses and ends with the death of Joshua. Two main sections and an appendix can clearly be distinguished:

I   1.1–12.24   The conquest of the land west of the Jordan by the Israelites.

II   13.1–21.45   The division of the land between the tribes west of the Jordan (13–19), and the designation of the cities of asylum and of the Levites (20 and 21).

III   22–24   (a) the erection of an altar by the Jordan by the tribes east of the Jordan (22).
                       (b) the farewell speech of Joshua (23).
                       (c) the meeting at Shechem, the death and burial of Joshua (24).

It will strike the reader at once that 23 and 24 conflict with one another.

3. *Origin.* In spite of the general recognition of the fact that the book of Joshua owes its present form to a Deuteronomistic redaction, scholars at present hold differing views on the pre-history of the book. A primarily literary-critical view and a literary-critical *cum* traditio-historical view stand opposed to one another without compromise. The first view follows on from the theory already advocated by Wellhausen, that the old sources of the Pentateuch continue in Joshua. This view is represented in recent years especially by Eissfeldt*, Rudolph, Pfeiffer*, Simpson, Weiser*, Hölscher, Mowinckel and Fohrer*. The views of the scholars mentioned vary in their specific assignment to sources, however, and the differences found in Penta-teuchal study between the representatives of the 'newer' (e.g. Weiser and Hölscher) and of the 'newest' source hypothesis (e.g. Eissfeldt, Simpson and Fohrer) appear again. Finally there are those who dispute the existence of an independent Elohistic source (Rudolph and Mowinckel). On the other side the explana-tion of the facts given by Noth, following suggestions by Alt, and his identification of the author of the book with that of the Deuteronomistic history, has also found support[1].

1. Cf. Jenni, op. cit., pp. 116 f.

I. Joshua 1–12. (a) Scholarship of a literary-critical type usually assigns only few verses in 1–12 to P, i.e. 4.19; 5.10–12; 9.15b and 9.17–21. Accordingly Rudolph, Eissfeldt and Noth see only a redactor working in the style of P here. Only Mowinckel and Fohrer have recently argued that ch. 12 too, either in whole or part, is to be regarded as a learned history of the conquest by P. It should be remembered that Noth and Elliger make P end with Deut. 34*. We can at least state that the existence of original P passages in Josh. 1–12 is very much open to question.

Apart from the Deuteronomistic redaction, which is to be sought according to Noth especially in 1.1–18; 8.30–35 and 11.16–12.24, the basic form of the narrative of 2–11 has since Wellhausen usually been ascribed to E. The basis for this assignment is the observation that we have here a picture of the entry which is in contrast to that of Judg. 1; while according to Judg. 1 it depends on the individual operations of the tribes, according to Josh. 1–12 it was a community operation by all Israel. The assignment to E is based therefore in the last resort on the assumption that it is J that is found in Judg. 1. Only a few fragments which are connected with Judg. 1 in content are then ascribed to J in Joshua (15.13–19, 63; 16.10; 17.11–13, 14–18 and 19.47).

Even if Judg. 1 can be ascribed to J, doubts arise about the identification of the conquest narratives in 2–11 with E. First the question must be asked whether E would have included such a story as that of the stay of the spies with the harlot Rahab in ch. 2 at all, since it goes against his ethicizing tendency which can be noticed elsewhere. It can further be established that the references to the miracle at the sea in 2.10 and 4.23 are not directly connected in their formulation with any narrative element in Exod. 14. Accordingly only a choice between the solutions proposed by Mowinckel and Noth seems to be left, if a decision is not to be postponed until a new analysis appears. It can be demonstrated that the fragments ascribed to J and listed above are redactional additions drawn from Judg. 1, rather than remains of a J narrative which has otherwise been lost. It is only in 17. (14–15) 16–18 that an independent narrative theme is present.

Mowinckel pointed out that the survey of the results of the entry in Judg. 1, with its geographical sequence central Palestine,

southern Palestine, and northern Palestine, could have provided
the pattern for the narrative of the conquest in 1–12. The narrator could have made out of the geographical sequence a chronological and historical one. On the basis of the assignment of
Judg. 1 to J he sees at work in the narrative of the conquest a
redactor of the Yahwist who is expanding his account, whom he
calls J^v, *Jahvista variatus*.

(b) Noth's solution is quite different. He starts from the
observation that in 2–9 we have a series of aetiological sagas from
the area of the sanctuary of Gilgal, which is to be looked for in
the neighbourhood of Jericho. These he claims to be Benjaminite
traditions. These sagas were already interpreted in Gilgal as all-
Israelite, and probably also fixed in writing. The connection
with the figure of Joshua the Ephraimite on the other hand took
place only at the next stage, when a Judahite collector active
about 900 connected the sagas with the war narratives from
chs. 10 and 11, and reshaped them into an account of the conquest of the land west of the Jordan. The figure of Joshua, however, does not have its primary location here, but is traditio-
historically at home in the subject-matter of chap. 24[2]. For the
dating of the collector it is decisive (1) that he did know that
Hazor was in ruins until its rebuilding by Solomon (cf. 11.10
ff.), (2) that he did not know of the Israelite settlement at Ai
which according to the archaeological evidence lasted into the
tenth century (cf. 8.29), while (3) the allusion to the refoundation
of Jericho under Ahab in 6.26 (cf. 1 Kgs. 16.34) is secondary.
Accordingly the collector is to be dated between Solomon and
Ahab. In relation to his place of origin Noth points out that in
11.2 and 11.16 the Judahite geographical terminology is transferred to other Palestinian areas, and that in chap. 10 a tradition
of Makkedah, which belongs in the Judaean Shephelah, is taken
over.

It must be the task of future scholarship to examine critically
the suggestions put forward since Rudolph. Against Mowinckel
it must be asked whether the account of the conquest has in fact
taken over the geographical sketch of Judg. 1, or just quite

2. On this problem see now also H. Schmid, 'Erwägungen zur Gestalt
Josuas in Überlieferung und Geschichte', *Jud* 24 (1968), pp. 44 ff., and
S. Herrmann, *Geschichte Israels in alttestamentlicher Zeit*, Munich 1973,
pp. 132 f.

simply made use of the normal orientation[3]. In respect of Noth's interpretation, which at first strikes one as impressive in its literary-critical and its traditio-historical grounding, it remains to be seen whether its literary-critical foundation will last, whether it is a compelling argument that the differences between the language of the accounts of the Entry and that of the older Pentateuchal sources count against the assumption of their continuation in Joshua[4], or whether traditio-historical arguments (the incorporation of material already formed) can be claimed to account for these differences, and above all whether the dating and the traditio-historical relationship proposed can be upheld.

In respect of the date proposed by Noth for the collector of about 900 B.C. the following counter-arguments deserve consideration: first, it is strange that a Judaean should not have known of the existence of an (admittedly small) Judahite locality from the preceding century, but on the other hand have been aware of the fact that a city lying far in the north, though admittedly a very much more important one, had lain in ruins until the days of Solomon. When scepticism is once aroused, the question has to be asked whether, at a time at which the tradition incorporated into Judg. I must have been known, the collector's fictional construction of an all-Israelite conquest could have been put forward in this way. Furthermore it must be considered dubious at best whether at that time the idea of a covenant of Yahweh with Israel already existed (cf. 7.11, 15)[5]. In addition the predilection for miracle, which is shared by the Elohist[6], such as is seen in the narrative of the passage through the Jordan in 3 and 4, and of the conquest of Jericho in 6, or in the themes of the outstretched spear of Joshua in 8.18, 26 and of the God who throws great stones upon the enemy from heaven in 10.11, should perhaps also be regarded as evidence of a relatively late date of origin for the collection[7]. Finally it is doubtful whether Gilgal really played the part assigned to it by Noth in the process of transmission lying behind the collection, and whether the choice of the site is not simply a fiction. The fact that 9.27 can (against Noth's view) hardly be

3. Cf. e.g. Gen. 15.18, and on the subject G. Morawe, *BHHW* II, col. 722.

4. Cf. now F. Langlamet, CRB 11, pp. 94 ff. and *RB* 78, pp. 5 ff., 161 ff. and 321 ff., and E. Zenger, *Die Sinaitheophanie*, FzB 3, 1971, pp. 137 ff., who argue in defence of the documentary hypothesis.

5. Cf. above p. 63 f. and 76.   6. Cf. above, p. 100.

7. Cf. also Langlamet, CRB 11, p. 144, who assigns the collection of the Gilgal traditions to a Deuteronomistic redactor to be distinguished from the Deuteronomist himself.

connected with Gilgal, but (with Hertzberg) perhaps first with Gibeon, and later with Jerusalem, may point in this direction.

II. Joshua 13–21. In explanations of the origin of the second half of the book we find a division of opinion similar to that in the first half. Scholars are generally convinced that P plays the leading part in these chapters. This view has most recently been put forward by Mowinckel, with the support of Fohrer. On the other hand Noth, following studies made by Alt, takes a different view: he sees as the basis of 13*–19* two documentary sources, a system of tribal boundaries from the period of the judges, and a list of the places in the Kingdom of Judah after its division into twelve administrative districts, coming from the period of King Josiah. Bächli understands the latter as the result of the activity of a land commission of this period, which was charged with the construction of a basic book of assessment of taxes and with the enumeration of the people, to establish the number of those liable for military service[8]. Both documents were first united to form a list of the possessions of the tribes, and then during the exile re-formed into an account of the conquest of the land under Joshua. 20 and 21 with their account of the separation of cities of asylum and Levitical cities are also to be regarded as post-Deuteronomic, although the former of these take the place religio-historically of the local sanctuaries spread out over the land, with which the cities of the Levites are in part identical. From the secondary anticipation of 23.1b in 13.1a Noth draws the conclusion that this whole section about the geography of the tribes was only added secondarily to the Deuteronomistic Book of Joshua by a second Deuteronomistic redactor. The insertion and redaction of 24.1–33 is also to be ascribed to the same redactor. He sees the formulaic headings and conclusions as being far too narrow a basis on which to build an assumption that the account of the division of the land has its origins in P.

Mowinckel has not ceased to examine this explanation critically since 1946, and in so doing to establish new support for the old assumption of a Priestly origin for 13–21.

Since he regards the whole system of the twelve tribes as a construction of the Davidic period, there being on his view only a federation of

8. O. Bächli, 'Von der Liste zur Beschreibung. Beobachtungen und Erwägungen zu Jos. 13–19', *ZDPV* 89 (1973), pp. 1 ff.

ten tribes in the period of the Judges[9], Mowinckel starts off by excluding the possibility of a list of the tribal frontiers from the period of the Judges. Furthermore he cannot see what point such a list could have had at that time. The drawing of the boundaries is in part (on this all sides are agreed) completely theoretical, as e.g. when individual tribes are assigned areas reaching as far as the sea which at no time belonged to Israel. The existence of literary sources for such a theory of religious entitlement, raising a claim to the possession of the whole of Canaan, could not, he argued, be demonstrated. Furthermore the traditions here edited by P reflect conditions from quite different periods. Mowinckel takes a different view of Josh. 15. He concedes to Alt that circumstances of the late Judahite monarchical period have in fact left a deposit here, and that we must allow for the existence of lists of this kind in the Jerusalem archives of the monarchical period. But he doubts whether such documents could have survived the catastrophe of 587. If it is taken into account that the memory of former boundaries could remain alive for a long period in the consciousness of the population, and that in any case certain administrative divisions from the late monarchical period did survive in the Persian province of Judah, the fixing of this tradition in the early post-exilic period makes sense even without the assumption of the existence of documentary sources.

On the other side it must be said first that the very fact that many literary documents from the pre-exilic period survived the fall of the Kingdom of Judah, and so entered into the Old Testament, must warn us against denying in principle that the lists in 13–19 could go back to old documents. The discussion of Alt's dating of the documents shows that there are no doubts in principle among scholars about such a hypothesis of sources. Thus Kallai-Kleinmann has attempted to show that the boundary system reflects the period of David and Solomon, and that behind the list of places in Judah a list from the period of King Hezekiah can be detected, and behind that of Benjamin a list from the time of Abijah[10]. Aharoni saw in the list of the Judahite cities a reflection of the administrative reform carried through by Jehoshaphat, and behind the lists of the cities of the Northern tribes, an Israelite list of provinces[11]. In any case scholars are agreed that the lists of the frontiers contain elements which can hardly go back to sheer imagination. A part of the variations objected to by Mowinckel can be explained by assuming secondary influence on the list material by the stories told in

9. Cf. his article 'Rahelstämme und Leastämme', in *Von Ugarit nach Qumran*, Festschrift O. Eissfeldt, BZAW 77, 1958, pp. 129 ff.

10. 'The Town Lists of Judah, Simeon, Benjamin and Dan', *VT* 8 (1958), pp. 134 ff.

11. 'The Province-List of Judah', *VT* 9 (1959), pp. 225ff.

Num. 32–34 and in Judg. 1 and 18. Noth finally supports his own position by his detailed literary criticism, according to which only very few verses of the post-Deuteronomistic redaction are formulated in the style of P, and make Joshua and Eleazar the leaders of a commission to divide up the land (cf. 14.1b; 19.51a and 18.1).

What has been said about the first half of Joshua is true also of the second: a decision on these disputed questions is only to be expected through a very careful examination, which weighs up all the facts, and is based on literary criticism as well as on traditio-historical method.

III. The general picture. With this reservation it can do no harm to summarize the picture developed by Noth of the origin of Joshua: a Judahite collection of accounts of the conquest, probably going back to a Benjaminite source, was provided with a Deuteronomistic framework, and then reworked, together with a composition about the division of the land by a second Deuteronomist from the time of the exile, into a complete narrative. Finally the work underwent limited priestly editing. Noth wished to assign Josh. 23 to the first Deuteronomist and Josh. 24 to the second Deuteronomist. Since then an increasing tendency can be observed among scholars to allow for a basic multiplicity of layers in the Deuteronomistic history, or even to think in terms only of corresponding redactions of the older narrative works; no generally agreed result however has yet been reached[12]. It is however worth mentioning that Smend assigns Josh. 24 to the history, but Josh. 23 only to a later legalistic redaction, traces of which he finds already in Josh. 1[13]. It should be mentioned for the sake of completeness that 24 is commonly assigned to E. If Joshua was originally a component of the Deuteronomistic history extending from Deut. 1 to 2 Kgs. 25, it was already separated from the Pentateuch, or from the Deuteronomistic history, at the latest in the third century B.C. For at the beginning of the work of translation of the Septuagint, which falls in this period, the Pentateuch

12. Cf. below, p. 174, and Fohrer*, pp. 202 f., together with the bibliography given there, F. Langlamet, CRB 11, p. 139, G. Schmitt, *Du sollst keinen Frieden schliessen mit dem Bewohnern des Landes*, BWANT 91, 1970, pp. 144 ff., and R. Smend, 'Das Gesetz und Die Völker. Ein Beitrag zur deuteronomistischen Redaktionsgeschichte', in *Probleme biblischer Theologie*, Festschrift G. von Rad, Munich 1971, pp. 494 ff.

13. Op. cit., pp. 501 ff.

was clearly treated already as a separate entity. At least the insertion of 24.29 ff., par. Judg. 2.6 ff., is to be ascribed to the division of the continuous narrative from Moses to the period of the Kings into separate books, while the original Deuteronomistic account placed Judg. 2.6 ff. immediately after Josh. 23.16.

§ 13   The Book of Judges

K. Budde, *Die Bücher Richter und Samuel, ihre Quellen und ihr Aufbau*, Giessen 1890; O. Eissfeldt, *Die Quellen des Richterbuches*, Leipzig 1925; M. Noth, *Überlieferungsgeschichtliche Studien*, Halle 1943, Tübingen 1967[3]; id., 'Das Amt des "Richters Israels"' [1950], *Gesammelte Studien zum Alten Testament* II, ThB 39, 1969, pp. 71 ff.; G. Hölscher *Geschichtsschreibung in Israel*, SKHVL 50, 1952; C. A. Simpson, *Composition of the Book of Judges*, Oxford 1957; E. Jenni, 'Zwei Jahrzehnte Forschung an den Büchern Josua bis Könige. V. Richterbuch', *ThR* NF 28 (1961), pp. 129 ff.; W. Beyerlin, 'Gattung und Herkunft des Rahmens im Richterbuch', in *Tradition und Situation*, Festschrift A. Weiser, Göttingen 1963, pp. 1 ff.; W. Richter, *Traditionsgeschichtliche Untersuchungen zum Richterbuch*, BBB 18, 1963, 1966[2]; id, *Die Bearbeitungen des 'Retterbuches' in der deuteronomischen Epoche*, BBB 21, 1964; id., 'Zu den "Richtern Israels",' *ZAW* 77 (1965), pp. 40 ff.; 'Die Überlieferungen um Jeptah Ri 10, 17–12, 6', *Bib* 47 (1966), pp. 485 ff.; H. Schulte, *Die Entstehung der Geschichtsschreibung im Alten Israel*, BZAW 128, 1972.

Commentaries: ICC Moore 1898[2]; KHC Budde 1897; HK Nowack 1900; EH Zapletal 1923; HS Schulz 1926; ATD Hertzberg 1963 (1965[3]); CB Gray 1967; SC Burney 1920[2].

1. Name and author. The Book of Judges takes its name from the heroes of whom it tells in its central part, who are described as judges. In Rabbinic tradition Samuel was regarded as its author. This attribution is no better founded than is that of the other historical books. Critical examination shows that Judges has a prehistory which extends over centuries.

2. Content and divisions. The Book of Judges covers in its central section, 2.6–16.31, the time from the death of Joshua to the death of Samson. The book as a whole divides up into three parts:

I   1.1–2.5a   Introduction
II   2.6–16.31   Central section
III 17–21   Appendix

In the introduction the entry into the land of the southern tribes and of the house of Joseph is narrated (1.1–26); there follows a list of the areas not conquered by the tribes, the so-called 'negative list of possessions' (1.27–36), and finally a basically redactional narrative of the journey from Gilgal to Bochim (2.1–5*).

The central section, extending from 2.6 to 16.31, contains the 'stories of the judges' proper. It begins in 2.6–3.6 with a new introduction, at the centre of which stands a treatment of the relation between God and the people in the period of the Judges in a 'theology of history' form (2.10–19*). 3.7–16.31 contains on the one hand narratives with theological frameworks which treat of individual tribal heroes, who are best regarded as deliverers from external enemies, on the other hand short notices in list form of judges of Israel. Corresponding to the length of the narratives, it is usual to distinguish between six major and six minor judges. The major ones are Othniel (3.7–11), Ehud (3.12–30), Deborah and Barak (4), together with the Song of Deborah (5), Gideon (6–8), which is connected with the narrative of the city-kingship of Abimelech (9), Jephthah (10.6–12.7) and Samson (13.1–16.31). The minor judges are Shamgar (3.31), Tola and Jair (10.1–5) and Ibzan, Elon and Abdon (12.8–15).

The third section, described as an appendix (17–21), consists of two narrative complexes. 17–18 tells how the sanctuary in Dan was founded; 19–21 tells of the shameful deed of the Benjaminites in Gibea, their punishment, and the saving of the remnant of them by providing them with wives. The introduction and the appendix stand outside the theological framework characteristic of the central section, and thereby direct our attention to the problem of the origin of the book.

3. Origin. The only point on which scholarship is agreed is that the central section 2.6–16.31 is preserved in a Deuteronomistic redaction. Apart from this there are at the moment three rival attempts to explain the prehistory of the book. They can be described as literary-critical, traditio-historical, and literary-critical *cum* traditio-historical.

(a) The traditional literary-critical explanations follow on from the results of work on the Pentateuch or Hexateuch, and seek to show that the old sources, apart from P, continue in Judges too. In support of this documentary hypothesis it is more arguments of fact than linguistic arguments that are adduced. Reference is made both to internal contradictions in the narratives, and also to their varied theological positions. In attempts at a solution the differences between the representatives of the 'newer' and of the 'newest' documentary hypothesis are again to be seen. An analysis along the lines of the 'newer documentary hypothesis' has most recently been made by Pfeiffer* and Hölscher (J and E). Eissfeldt (with L, J and E) and Simpson (J_1, J_2 and E) have attempted to solve the literary problem of the pre-Deuteronomistic Book of Judges along the lines of the 'newest documentary hypothesis'. Finally Hannelis Schulte has been concerned to demonstrate that the basic content of the book belongs to J. About the turn of the century Budde had attempted to make J and E the basis of his analysis, but emphasized that in his view both J and E were schools, whose activity was not confined to one generation. All that was certain in his view was that the parts of Judges and Samuel assigned by him to these two schools were ultimately parts of the larger works J and E. Since such analyses led very largely to a dissolution of the narratives, and since also the 'theology of history' ideas most characteristic of J could not be shown to be present, it is understandable that scholars have now mostly turned to other types of solution. A large number of scholars argue however that Judg. 1 contains J's account of the entry into the land, and that here we have the end of this source[1].

(b) As with the Book of Joshua, the new direction in the study of Judges was introduced by Noth. In his *Überlieferungsgeschichtliche Studien* he attempted to show that Judges too is an original part of the Deuteronomistic history, and that the author of Judges is the same as the author of the whole work[2]. The two characteristic signs of this extensive work are found in Judges too. Its chronological details are directly related to the

---

1. Cf. above, pp. 79 f.   2. Cf. below, § 16.

chronology which extends from Deut. 1.3 to 1 Kgs. 6.1, which allows 480 years from the Exodus from Egypt to the beginning of the construction of the temple[3]. And as in the other books belonging to the work, here too historical turning points are especially emphasized (cf. 2.10 ff.*). Furthermore Noth argued that 2.6 follows directly on from Josh. 23.16. The period of the judges beginning in 2.6 ff. does not end until 1 Sam. 12. As sources the Deuteronomist had for this period two originally independent traditions, the list of judges preserved in 10.1–5 and 12.7–15, and a collection of narratives about tribal heroes and their victorious deeds, which extended from Ehud to Jephthah. The narratives about Samson, as well as the introduction and appendix, are to be regarded as later additions. The fact that the figure of Jephthah is found in both traditions not only led to the placing of the list of judges before and after the story of Jephthah, but also provided the opportunity to supply the framework for the history of the period of the Judges from the list of judges, and to interpret the tribal heroes as judges. This argument is tied up with the view that the so-called minor judges were holders of an all-Israelite office of judge. Alt, starting with a comparison with the ancient Icelandic proclaimers of the law, and taking up suggestions of Klostermann, had seen in the judges of Israel the transmitters and preservers of casuistic law. Noth ascribed to them more broadly the preservation of the divine law as a whole. The hypothesis can be summarized (with Elliger) as meaning that the judges were the proclaimers of an amphictyonic law which is valid for all Israelites, and the men responsible for the decision of unusual cases and for the development of the common legal material[4]. It is clearly dependent on the amphictyonic hypothesis, and must necessarily stand or fall with it.

(c) Beyerlin and Richter have independently demonstrated that there is a difference between the 'theology of history' introduction in 2 and the framework of the stories of the heroes, which leads to an assumption of different authors. Since Richter has dealt with the problem in detail, we will only give his results. Characteristic of his method is a combination of literary criticism, form-criticism, and a criticism of style depending on

3. On the details cf. Noth, op. cit., pp. 18 ff.
4. *RGG* V[3], col. 1095. Cf. however below, p. 148.

syntactical observations[5]. In his view the basis of the whole narrative, which was later incorporated into the Deuteronomistic history, was a North Israelite 'book of deliverers', which we have in 3.12 to 9.55[*].

The field of vision of the author, who is to be regarded as a collector and redactor, is limited by Benjamin in the south (3.15), Naphthali, Zebulun and Asher in the north (4.10, 7.23), and Manasseh and Ephraim in the centre (6.11, 8.2 and 7.23 ff.). Issachar and the Israelites of the Transjordan on the other hand are not mentioned. In any case he gives us no example of a deliverer for these areas. From this it can be concluded that the book of deliverers was written at a time when Gilead no longer belonged to Israel, i.e. in the second half of the ninth century. The collector reworked his traditions when it seemed necessary to him. He took over the story of Ehud unaltered. He changed the story of Deborah and Barak. The story of Gideon, including the identification of the hero with Jerubbaal, the father of Abimelech, is his own work. He has formed it out of traditions which have come down to him in such a way that the rejection of the monarchy by Gideon in 8.22 f. stands in effective contrast to the story of Abimelech. Abimelech is thus made into a horrifying example of monarchy as such, an intention which is emphasized by the inclusion of the fable of Jotham. The positive interest of the collector and redactor is in the war of Yahweh, with its deliverers called by Yahweh, and his negative interest in the monarchy, which naturally could no longer make use of the old war of Yahweh. So his bias can be characterized as antimonarchical, and directed towards old Israelite ideals. Since the prophetess Deborah is set alongside the deliverer Barak, Richter thinks it is possible that the author of the book of deliverers should be sought among prophetic circles in the Northern Kingdom.

This old book of deliverers was then twice edited in the spirit of Deuteronomy, and finally re-edited on its insertion into the Deuteronomistic history. The framework of the narratives from 3.12 to 9.57 goes back to the first Deuteronomic editing.

The restriction of the framework to these narratives is for Richter the proof that the book of deliverers did not go beyond the story of Gideon and Abimelech in its subject matter. The mark of this redaction is the pattern of sin, oppression, the cry of the people to Yahweh with subsequent deliverance, and the statement that the land had rest[6]. The

---

5. Cf. now Richter, *Exegese als Literaturwissenschaft. Entwurf einer alttestamentlichen Literaturtheorie und Methodologie*, Göttingen 1971.

6. To this redaction (Rdt[1]) Richter ascribes 3.12abα, 14 (without the

reinterpretation of the local deeds of the heroes as the delivery of all
Israel leading to the attainment of rest in the land would therefore be
ascribed to this redaction. A connection with Deuteronomy could be
indicated by the closeness of the 'sin' formula to Deut. 17.2. Richter
conjectures that this redaction aimed to create a book of examples,
which on the occasion of the restoration of the Judahite levy under King
Josiah was intended to stress that the help of Yahweh can give rest to
the sinful nation that cries to God.

A second Deuteronomic redactor would then have added the
'example section', 3.7–11*. The choice of heroes for examples
suggests an origin in the Southern Kingdom. The concrete
mention of the sin as the worship of idols would allow us to
recognize that this redactor was active after the publication of
Deuteronomy.

It would then be the Deuteronomistic redaction which took
place after the catastrophe of 587 that set the book of deliverers
with its framework into the larger context of the Deuteronomistic
history work. The dates were now inserted in the interests of the
predominant chronology, the 'judge' formulas and the notices of
death inserted together with other material, and the introductions
(2.7–19* and 10.6–16) added. By means of the incorporation
of the list of judges, of the story of Jephthah and, if I understand Richter aright, also of the Samson story, the line was
drawn out which stretched from the deliverers through the
judges Jephthah, Samson and Eli to Samuel and his sons[7]. On
the view of the Deuteronomist the degeneration in character of
the judges led to the choice of the deliverer Saul as king. The
theological concern was to show the connection between the
falling away of the nation to other gods, and the ever recurring
disasters to Israel.

It is immediately clear that the correctness of this complicated
picture depends on the validity of the literary analyses. It can

number?), 15 aα, 30; 4.1a, 2, 3a, 23 f.; 5.31b (without the number), 6.1
(without the number), 2a; 8.28 (without the number) and 9.16b–19a, 22
and 55.

7. The separation of the Jephthah tradition from the book of deliverers
is justified by Richter, *Bib* 47 (1966), p. 555, with the argument that it is
only in the last redaction of it, which was responsible for the complex
10.17–12.6, that it was connected with the edition of the book of deliverers
as already expanded by 3.7–11. On incorporation into the Deuteronomistic history, apart from 10.1–5, 6–16, 12.7–15 was also added to it.

be stated as a result of this discussion that we must allow for the existence of a pre-Deuteronomistic collection of stories of deliverers. Further Richter's study has directed attention again to the problem of the different redactions under Deuteronomic influence. Smend has meanwhile turned his attention to this problem. He regards 1.1–2.5 as an insertion by a post-Deuteronomistic redactor, who was using older material for it. 2.17, 20 f., 23, and possibly also 3.5 f., are to be ascribed to him, while 3.1–4 are to be regarded as yet later[8]. It remains however to be tested whether the pre-Deuteronomic or pre-Deuteronomistic collection as Noth or Richter sees it can be clearly delimited, and whether differences in the framework are not in part determined by the material of the sections. It should be noted that Richter sees in the judges of the list in 10.1 ff. and 12.7 ff. not representatives of an amphictyonic office, but 'representatives of an order in transition from tribal to state administration, coming from city or tribes, appointed by the (tribal) elders for civil administration and dispensation of justice over a city or a corresponding country area'[9]. The drawing up of the list with its systematic arrangement as 'judges of Israel' only took place in the early monarchical period under the influence of the royal annals.

(d) Unfortunately there are no really thorough recent treatments of the literary problem of the Samson narrative of 13–16 and of the *chronique scandaleuse* of the tribes of Dan and Benjamin in 17–21, which is best treated as an appendix to it. It cannot be deduced with certainty from the fact that the concluding Deuteronomistic notice about Samson is already found in 15.20 (cf. 16.31) that 16 was passed over by the Deuteronomist and only inserted again, or for the first time, by a later hand; for the notice comes in its appropriate position, before the hero passes to Philistine territory for the rest of his life[10].

In the Samson narrative we have what are originally Danite sagas of

---

8. Cf. R. Smend, 'Das Gesetz und die Völker. Ein Beitrag zur deuteronomistischen Redaktionsgeschichte', in *Probleme biblischer Theologie*, Festschrift G. von Rad, Munich 1971, pp. 494, cf. especially pp. 504 ff.

9. *ZAW* 77 (1965), p. 71. Cf. now also S. Herrmann, *Geschichte Israels in alttestamentlicher Zeit*, Munich 1973, pp. 148 ff.

10. Since 16.1–3 said nothing of an encounter of Samson with his own countrymen, the Deuteronomist may for this reason have preferred to insert his notice after 15.19.

the child of nature Samson, who made trouble for the Philistines by his cunning and his strength. The disagreements between the birth narrative and the theme of his parents taken over from it into the saga cycle (13.25–15.19) in 14.5–7, and between the theme of his call as a Nazirite and his behaviour as a hero, which pays no regard to this call apart from his long hair, and not least the repetition of the motif of the deception of Samson by his wife in 14.1 ff. and 16.4 ff. (cf. also 16.1 ff.) indicate a complicated prehistory to the material as we now have it, which in its present form links the mighty deeds of Samson with the coming deliverance of Israel from the hand of the Philistines by King Saul in 13.5b (cf. 1 Sam. 9.16). The definitive explanation of the literary development of the Samson narrative must therefore be expected to emerge in connection with that of the Book of Samuel. The individual stories which can be classified according to their material as stories of Samson the cunning and of Samson the strong were certainly transmitted orally for a relatively long period, before they attained their definitive form in the cycle of sagas of 13.25–15.19* and in 16. Since the story of Delilah ended with the death of the hero it was necessarily placed at the end when the two narratives were united in literary form[11].

Nor can it be expected that the stories of the foundation of the sanctuary in Dan in 17–18 and of the misdeed of the Benjaminites in 19–21, which form a negative background for the positively understood monarchy (cf. 17.6, 18.1, 19.1 and 21.25) should have needed a Deuteronomistic redaction, in the sense of a divergent evaluation of the facts or of a chronological placing of the events. The literary problem of these chapters, like that of the Samson narative, is to be solved in connection with that of the Book of Samuel.

The narrative of the foundation of the sanctuary in Dan (17–18) is regarded by Noth as of Israelite origin, and to be attributed to the ninth century B.C. If its attitude to monarchy in 17.6 and 18.1 is original and its attribution to the Northern Kingdom certain, we would have here a further part of a Northern Israelite history leading up to the reign of Saul. It has frequently been conjectured that there are two threads combined in the narrative, which has been skilfully composed from a story of the private sanctuary of an Ephraimite called Micah and a story of spying from the period of the migration of the Danites from their original settlement in north-western Judah into the north. If this is the

---

11. Cf. H. Gunkel, 'Simson', in *Reden und Aufsätze*, Göttingen 1913 pp. 38 ff.; H. Gese, article 'Simson', *RGG*³ VI, cols. 41 ff., and H. Schulte, op. cit., pp. 83 ff., who finds J here again.

case the second strand, which is throughout closely related to the first, only comes in in supplementation[12].

The story of the misdeed at Gibeah and of the punishment of the Benjaminites in 19–21 reminds us by its beginning of 17, and by its continuation in 19 of Gen. 19 and 1 Sam. 11. It is obvious that the all-Israelite action in 20 is out of proportion to the occasion given for it, and that 21 is linked with the preceding material rather artificially and only externally. This odd composition, which probably has a complicated prehistory, should be regarded with Gressmann as a literary, late production. Its tendency to be expanded to deal with all Israel to support the view of 19.1 and 21.25 has led to the enlargement of a narrative which originally probably dealt with a local quarrel between Gibeah and the neighbouring Ephraimites. It is not legitimate to draw from the present story conclusions about the functions and the Holy War of an Israelite amphictyony. What underlies 21 is perhaps primarily a cultic usage of Shiloh[13].

While it can be stated in conclusion that the most recent work has tended to explain the origin of the Book of Judges by means of a traditio-historical explanation rather than by means of a documentary hypothesis, it must be said that the last word has not yet been spoken on the prehistory of the book.

4. Fable, similitude, parable, and allegory. The fable of Jotham transmitted in 9.8–15 provides an opportunity to add a few words on the literary types of fable, similitude, parable and allegory. The fable is found here, as in 2 Kgs. 14.9, in the form of a plant parable. The characteristic of the literary type as such is that human relationships are portrayed as an occurrence between animals (animal fable) or plants (plant fable) or as both together, and in this way a symbol is provided. The underlying sense, the moral, is not expressed, but is to be discovered by the listeners. While this suggests the idea that it had primarily a

12. Cf. M. Noth, 'The Background of Judges 17–18', in *Israel's Prophetic Heritage*, Festschrift J. Muilenburg, London and New York 1962, pp. 68 ff. For evidence of different strata, cf. e.g. 17.4 with 5, and 6 with 12; 18.17 with 18 and 30 with 31.

13. Cf. H. Gressmann, *Die Anfänge Israels*, SAT I, 2, Göttingen 1922², pp. 255 ff. O. Eissfeldt, 'Der Geschichtliche Hintergrund von Gibeas Schandtat', *KS* II, Tübingen 1963, pp. 64 ff. and most recently H. Schulte, pp. 96 ff. For a criticism of the treatment by M. Noth in *Das System der zwölf Stämme Israels*, Stuttgart 1930, pp. 162 ff. cf. Eissfeldt, op. cit., pp. 77 ff.

socially critical function in enabling those who were socially subordinate to make critical utterances which were not liable to punishment[14], the opposite seems from the history of the literary type to be the case: it assumed the present social and moral order, and appealing to the play instinct of man, it had not least the upholders of the current ordering of society in view as its addressees[15]. The similitude is different from a simple comparison, a metaphor, only in its elaboration. It represents a typical constantly recurring occasion. The parable proper on the other hand has in mind a specific once only occasion. In this sense the song of the vineyard (Isa. 5.1–7), and (if it should not rather be called a legal paradigm) 2 Sam. 12.1–4 too can be claimed as parables. In the parable as in the similitude the point of comparison lies in the course of the story as a whole, not in the individual features. If the individual features too demand an interpretation, the story is then an allegory, a mysteriously allusive way of expressing a situation (cf. e.g. Ezek. 17.1 ff.).

§ 14   The Books of Samuel

K. Budde, *Die Bücher Richter und Samuel, ihre Quellen und ihr Aufbau*, Giessen 1890, pp. 167 ff.; L. Rost, *Die Überlieferung von der Thronnachfolge Davids*, BWANT III, 6, 1926, also in *Das kleine Credo und andere Studien zum Alten Testament*, Heidelberg 1965, pp. 199 ff.; O. Eissfeldt, *Die Komposition der Samuelisbücher*, Leipzig 1931; M. Noth, *Überlieferungsgeschichtliche Studien*, Halle 1943, Tübingen 1967³, pp. 54 ff.; H.-U. Nübel, *Davids Aufstieg in der Frühe israelitischer Geschichtsschreibung*, Diss. ev. theol., Bonn 1959; E. Jenni, 'Zwei Jahrzehnte Forschung an den Büchern Josua bis Könige. VI. Samuelbuch', *ThR* NF 27 (1961), pp. 136 ff.; F. Mildenberger, *Die vordeuteronomistische Saul-David-Überlieferung*, Diss. ev. theol. Tübingen 1962; A. Weiser, *Samuel. Seine geschichtliche Aufgabe und religiöse Bedeutung*, FRLANT 81, 1962; id., 'Die Legitimation des Königs David. Zur Eigenart und Entstehung der sogen. Geschichte von Davids Aufstieg', *VT* 16 (1966), pp. 325 ff.; R. A. Carlson, *David—The Chosen King. A Traditio-historical Approach to the Second Book of Samuel*, Stockholm 1964;

14. Cf. Richter, BBB 18, 1963, p. 299.
15. Cf. W. Schottroff, *ZAW* 82 (1970), pp. 86 f., who appeals to E. Leibfried, *Fabel*, Stuttgart 1967 (1973²), pp. 1 ff. and J. J. A. van Dijk, *La sagesse suméro-accadienne*, Leiden 1953, pp. 31 ff. Cf. however also van Dijk, pp. 12 f. and 38 f.

L. Delekat, 'Tendenz und Theologie der David-Salomo-Erzählung', in *Das ferne und nahe Wort*, Festschrift L. Rost, BZAW 105, 1967, pp. 26 ff.; H. J. Boecker, *Die Beurteilung der Anfänge des Königtums in den deuteronomistischen Abschnitten des I. Samuelbuches*, WMANT 31, 1969; J. H. Grønbaek, *Die Geschichte vom Aufstieg Davids (1 Sam. 15–2 Sam. 5). Tradition und Komposition*, Acta Theologica Danica 10, Copenhagen 1971; H. Schulte, *Die Entstehung der Geschichtsschreibung im Alten Israel*, BZAW 128, 1972; E. Würthwein, *Die Erzählung von der Thronfolge Davids—theologische oder politische Geschichtsschreibung?*, Theologische Studien, Zurich 1974.

Commentaries: HK Nowack 1902; KHC Budde 1902; ICC Smith 1912; EH A. Schulz 1919/20; KAT Caspari 1925; HS Leimbach 1936; OTL Hertzberg 1964; KAT² I Stoebe 1973.

1. Name, authorship and division of the book. Until the fifteenth century the Book of Samuel formed a unity in the Hebrew manuscripts. The present division into two goes back to the Septuagint, from which the Vulgate took it. The Septuagint counts our books of Samuel and Kings as *basileiōn* a–d, the Vulgate as *libri regnorum* I–IV. The Hebrew name of the book, which has been taken over into the more recent translations of the Bible, is connected with the rabbinic tradition which regarded Samuel as the author of the Books of Judges and of Samuel. Since however the greater part of the Book of Samuel treats of events after the death of Samuel, which is reported in 1 Sam. 25.1 and 28.3, tradition regarded the seer Gad and the prophet Nathan as the authors of the narratives going beyond the death of Samuel (cf. 1 Chr. 29.29 f.). In the narratives themselves no support at all can be found for such an ascription. What is certain is that the narrative of the succession of David which begins in 2 Sam. 9, omitting 2 Sam. 21–24, comes to an end only in 1 Kgs. 1 f. The present abrupt separation of the Books of Samuel from the Books of Kings may, if we follow a conjecture of Budde, have been made easier by the additions in 2 Sam. 21–24. The first book ends appropriately with the account of the death of Saul in 1 Sam. 31, the second awkwardly with the account of David's census in 2 Sam. 24. The title Samuel is to some extent appropriate for the first book, but not at all for the second. As far as subject matter goes the names in the Septuagint and in the Vulgate are preferable.

2. *Content.* The Books of Samuel tell of the end of the period of the judges, and the beginnings of the Israelite and the Judahite kingdoms under Saul and David. For purposes of memorizing the content can be divided as follows:

I	1 Sam. 1–7	Eli and Samuel
II	1 Sam. 8–15	Samuel and Saul
III	1 Sam. 16–2 Sam. 1	Saul and David
IV	2 Sam. 2–12	David and his kingdom
V	2 Sam. 13–20	(+ 1 Kgs. 1–2) David and the succession
VI	2 Sam. 21–24	Additions to the story of David

3. *Origin.* The discussion of the prehistory of the Book of Samuel is not yet concluded. Wellhausen had already noted the twofold character of the narrative, and contrasted to the pro-monarchical account of the origin of the monarchy of Saul (a), an anti-monarchical account (b)[1]. Usually the two strands are now defined as follows: (a) 1 Sam. 9.1–10.16 + 10.27b–11.15 and (b) 1 Sam. 7.2–8.22 + 10.17–27a + 12.1–25. In the second series it is thought that the hand of the Deuteronomist can be recognized, although traces of his redactional work are strikingly less evident in Samuel in comparison with the Books of Joshua and of Judges. Duplications and disagreements in content can also be shown elsewhere in the narrative: so e.g. there are in 1 Sam. 13.7b ff. and ch. 15 two rival accounts of the rejection of Saul, in 16.14 ff. and 17.55 ff. two accounts of the way in which David came to Saul's court, in 21.1 ff. and 27.1 ff. two accounts of David's stay at the court of the Philistine king Achish of Gath, and in 24 and 26 two accounts of the sparing of Saul by David.

(a) Accordingly it can be understood why under the influence of the results of Pentateuchal scholarship an attempt was made in the case of Samuel as in those of Joshua and Judges to solve the literary problem by means of the source hypotheses established for the Pentateuch. Along these lines Budde at the turn of the century believed he could find in the pre-Deutero-nomistic Book of Samuel the work of the Yahwistic and of the

1. *Die Composition des Hexateuchs und der historischen Bücher des Alten Testaments,* Berlin 1899[3], 1963[4], pp. 240 ff.

Elohistic school. Hölscher is the most recent scholar to attempt a solution along the lines of the 'newer documentary hypothesis', seeing here J and E at work. On the other hand Eissfeldt has attempted here too a source division using the 'newest documentary hypothesis', and has assumed the existence of L, J and E.

(b) With Rost's *Überlieferung von der Thronnachfolge Davids* of 1926 the literary-critical attempts to solve the problems of the Book of Samuel receded into the background before the question of the sources incorporated in it, and of the oral and written traditions used by these. Even when the question is raised again now of the relationship with the Pentateuchal sources, and in particular of the significance of the Yahwist for the development of the pre-Deuteronomistic Book of Samuel, as most recently by Hannelis Schulte, the continued effect of the form of posing the problem introduced by Rost is inescapable. Building upon earlier observations (e.g. by Klostermann) he established the existence of a history of the succession to David consisting of 2 Sam. (6) 9–20 + 1 Kgs. 1–2. Its author had already before him a history of the fate of the ark, preserved in 1 Sam. 4.1b–7.1* and 2 Sam. 6.1–20*, an early form of 2 Sam. 7, and an account of the war against the Ammonites, preserved in 2 Sam. 10.6–11 + 12.26–31. He dovetailed his own work into these sources.

The account of the ark, 1 Sam. 4.1b–7.1* and 2 Sam. 6*, through its vocabulary, style, theme and bias, stands apart from its surroundings as a unity. It tells of the fate of the ark from its removal from Shiloh to its establishment in Jerusalem[2].

The narrative flows on uninterrupted, alternating between briefer and fuller presentation. The brief account of the defeat of the army and of the loss of the ark at Ebenezer and Aphek is followed by the fuller account of the death of Eli and of the birth of Ichabod. The effects of the ark in Ashdod and Ekron are told of fully, the terror evoked by its arrival in Gath in between these two briefly. The preparations for the recovery of the ark are told fully, its transfer to Kiriath-Jearim briefly, and its removal by David to Jerusalem again fully. The story has a straightforward course, and jumps from the one side to the other, and so creates a lively change of scene. The unimportance of a historical

2. On the ark cf. J. Maier, *Das altisraelitische Ladeheiligtum*, BZAW 93, 1965, but also G. Fohrer, *History of Israelite Religion*, London 1973, pp. 106 ff.

interest proper is shown in the complete omission of the reign of Saul, and in the lack of any chronological information. The dominant position of the ark and the miraculous accounts of it place the account in the realm of legend. It cannot as a whole lay claim to historicity.

Its author is to be looked for in the circle of the priests of the ark in Jerusalem. Since the narrative supports the dwelling of the ark in a tent, it must have originated before the erection of the temple of Solomon. Rost indeed believes that the narrative served as a *hieros logos* (festival legend) for the shrine of the ark in Jerusalem, and had the intention of representing the significance of the ark to the pilgrims at the festival. Whether the account of the ark can be called a *hieros logos* in the strict sense must remain open to question. It seems rather to pursue the aim of defending the arbitrary transfer of the ancient Israelite sanctuary to Jerusalem by David as having taken place in accordance with the will of Yahweh[3].

In the story of the succession to David (2 Sam. (6) 9–20 + 1 Kgs. 1–2) Rost would see the narrative of a man who had been an eyewitness from afar of the events recounted in it, and who is shown by his feeling for the real connections between events to be (as von Rad later put it) a child of the Davidic-Solomonic enlightenment. The story attempted to answer the question put by the prophet Nathan to David, 'Who shall reign on the throne of my Lord, the king, after him?' (1 Kgs. 1.27). The answer 'Solomon, the son of Bathsheba' was in spite of its basis in historical fact far from a matter of course for contemporaries, since the Queen Mother had been formerly the wife of Uriah the Hittite, whom David had had killed, and a whole chain of internal dynastic disturbance lay between the birth of her second child, the later king Solomon, and his accession. So the narrator went right back to the sterility of Michal, daughter of Saul and wife of David (2 Sam. 6.16, 20b–23), and therefore included the story of the ark. Nor could he omit the prophecy of Nathan in 2 Sam. 7*, in order to demonstrate the legitimacy of David, nor in view of the circumstances of Solomon's birth the account of the Ammonite war. Then he let his readers see how the legitimate heirs Amnon, Absalom and Adonijah were in succession murdered,

3. On its later significance cf. H. Timm, 'Die Ladeerzählung und das Kerygma des deuteronomistischen Geschichtswerks', *EvTh* 26 (1966), pp. 509 ff.

after they had previously disqualified themselves for the succession. With a few allusions the narrator allowed it to be seen that Yahweh himself stands behind this so dark (humanly regarded) chapter of history, and that its final result corresponded to his will (cf. 11.27, 12.1, 15, 24 and 17.14). The closeness of this theology of history, tracing the workings of God not in unusual events, but in the course of history itself, to that of the Yahwist, can hardly be overlooked[4]. Rost, in agreement with scholars from the beginning of this century, looked to find the author of the narrative among the eyewitnesses of the story in the circle of the court in Jerusalem. Both older Israelite and wisdom tendencies are united in his work[5].

While there need be no disagreement with the general location of the narrative in the history of thought by Rost, it remains to be asked whether he has correctly stated the bias and delimitation of the story. First Delekat protested against the assumed pro-Solomonic tendency, because this could not explain the selection of material, which was unfavourable to the image of both David and Solomon. Then Würthwein found in the story (whose limits he restricted to 1 Sam. 10–20 + 1 Kgs. 1–2) alongside an anti-Davidic and anti-Solomonic bias a contrary one serving to justify Solomon. This made the literary unity of the story, which had already been doubted before Rost, once again a problem. Würthwein found that the whole stratum arguing the theological and political justification of the kingship of Solomon in 11.27b, 12.1–15a, 24b, 14.2–22, 15.16b (17a), 24–26, 29, 31; 16.5–13, 21–23; 17.5–14; 18.2b–4a, 10–14; 20.3, 4, 5, 8–13 and 1 Kgs. 2.5–9 was added only secondarily to the Succession Narrative, in order to reverse its originally anti-monarchical intention. The fact that more than half of the original material of the narrative consists in speeches or conversations, that for many scenes there are no witnesses, and that the choice of material is consistently

---

4. Rost, op. cit., p. 129 = 235. Cf. also G. von Rad, 'The Beginnings of Historical Writing in Ancient Israel', *The Problem of the Hexateuch and other Essays*, Edinburgh and London 1966, pp. 166 ff.

5. The connections of the succession narrative with wisdom are examined in detail in R. N. Whybray, *The Succession Narrative*, SBT[2] 9, 1968. The possibility of its having been further transmitted in wisdom circles, and even having been used in schools, is discussed by H.-J. Hermisson, *Studien zur israelitischen Spruchweisheit*, WMANT 28, 1968, pp. 126 f.

partisan, makes Würthwein warn us to exhibit caution in respect of emphasizing the eyewitness character of the author, and so too in our historical evaluation of the narrative. With Duhm he looks to find the author in the circle of Abiathar, the priest of the ark who was deposed by Solomon from his office and banished to Anathoth[6]. In the interests of clarifying the still unsolved problems of Samuel, which undoubtedly even after the removal of the Deuteronomistic redaction consists of several strata, it should be examined whether the tendencies and strata found by Würthwein are not also to be found outside the Succession Narrative in the story of the rise of David. This would also lead to consideration of the problem of the degree of stratification in the Deuteronomistic redaction of the book (indicated by Dietrich's assignment of 2 Sam. 12.1–14 to a second redactor (Dtr P) who stands for a specific prophetic theology)[7], and also of the question whether the Succession Narrative with its strongly antimonarchical tendency was in circulation at all in Judah under the monarchy and so re-edited in a promonarchical sense.

The narrator has followed the events with an almost epic breadth. He writes a rhythmic prose, which makes rich use of accumulations of verbs and adjectives, of connecting words and subordinate clauses. Pictorial comparisons, partly influenced by wisdom, enliven and deepen his presentation (cf. 9.8; 14.14 and 17.8 and 10). His narrative art is shown especially in the rich forms and frequent use of speeches. As well as the question, the demand, varying from the bare imperative to the artistic speed of exhortation, the messenger speech in the form of the conveying of a commission or of a report, there are accounts and disputations. Particularly characteristic is the use of the *plokè*. In this the end of the speech returns to its beginning, so that there is a pattern a-b-a (cf. e.g. 15.19 f.; 19.12 f. or 11.20–22). The speech can be broken up into a whole series of exchanges. It thus loses its subordinate position and becomes a means of the building up of a scene. The link between scenes separated in space is made by the journey of the messenger, which is divided into departure and arrival scenes (cf. e.g. 18.19 ff.). The speeches and conversations show the author's skill in characterization (cf. e.g. 16.16 ff. and 17.7 ff.).

The reserve in theological emphasis is striking. It is limited to a few remarks (cf. 11.27; 12.1, 15, 24 and 17.14). We hear

6. KHC XI, Tübingen and Leipzig 1901, p. 3.

7. *Prophetie und Geschichte*, FRLANT 108, 1972, pp. 127 ff. Cf. below, pp. 167 f. and 174.

neither of dreams sent by God nor of oracles or miracles. Here 'the activity of God in history is a greater miracle than individual miracle stories'. God's activity is not for the narrator something that is added to secular events, but something that is accomplished in these events themselves. The same confidence is found here as in the latest layers of the Yahwistic historical narrative, that it is possible for men to recognize God's hand in the course of the history of the world. For one who surveys it as a theologian, the question is posed how long it will be before belief in the perceptibility of God's action in history turns into scepticism, and how Israel will then preserve its faith.

(c) The differences of theological position observable in the narratives of the Book of Samuel, which previously led to the division of the material between the sources J and E, have also led to other literary-critical investigations in the last fifteen years.

Nübel has produced an examination limited to 1 Sam. 16–2 Sam. 12, and attempted to show that in the story found here of the rise of David an older basic story from the first half of the reign of David is present, which was worked over in the Northern Kingdom about the turn of the ninth to the eighth centuries. The redaction is to be attributed to the forerunners of the Deuteronomic movement. Mildenberger has examined 1 Sam. 9–1 Kgs. 2, and found a historical narrative extending from the beginning of the reign of Saul to the climax of the reign of David, which with the incorporation of the narrative of the ark was then joined up with the annals of 2 Sam. 8, the story of the birth of Solomon in 2 Sam. 10–12, the story of Tamar (2 Sam. 13 f.) and the story of the succession proper to form a whole. The basic story was concerned with the legitimation of the claim of the Davidic dynasty to the kingship over all Israel. It underwent a prophetic redaction about 700 B.C. This redaction contrasted a Saul rejected by God with a David chosen by him, and brought in the role of the prophets in the designation of the king by Yahweh.

Both Nübel's attempt and the more immediately convincing theory of Mildenberger allow for a basic narrative and redactions, of which the last is the Deuteronomistic.

(d) The most coherent picture of the formation of the Book of Samuel has been drawn by Weiser*.

In various different articles he has attempted to show that the stories of the anti-monarchical source, 1 Sam. 7.2–8.22; 10.17–27a and 12, do not form a unity, but go back to very varied traditions, of which a common fixing in writing by the Deuteronomist must remain open to question[8]. He has further suggested that in 1 Sam. 16–2 Sam. 8 we should see an originally independent story of the rise of David. Its author is to be regarded as the collector of circulating independent traditions, which were of varying historical and artistic value, and which he did not regard himself as entitled to smooth out completely and to harmonize with one another. It can be seen from e.g. 1 Sam. 22.8 and 19 that he was selecting from a broader range of tradition. In connection with the lament of David over Saul and Jonathan which he incorporates in 2 Sam. 1.19–27, he mentions in 1.18 the 'Book of the Valiant'[9] as a source. He may have taken over from other sources the lament for Abner (2 Sam. 3.33 f.), the song of victory in 1 Sam. 18.7 (cf. 21.11 [Heb. 21.12] and 29.5), and the list in 30.27–31 as well. He had the intention of defending David's rise to the kingship in succession to Saul against possible and actual suspicions.[10] The author is to be looked for in the circle of the cult of Yahweh in Jerusalem. His aim was to present 'the divine legitimation of King David and of his dynasty over Israel as the sacral tribal confederacy. . . .'[11]

At the beginning then was the formation of both popular and court individual traditions. At a second stage they were collected into continuous accounts in a story of the rise of Saul, 1 Sam. 9–11 and 13–14, a story of the rise of David, 1 Sam. 16 to 2 Sam. 7(8), and a succession narrative, 2 Sam. 9–20 and 1 Kgs. 1–2. At a third stage these accounts were joined up to one another with the accretion of further traditions. At a fourth stage, to which 1 Sam. 1–3; 7–8; 10.17 ff. and 15 in particular belong, the continuous narrative so produced was expanded

8. Cf. also H. Seebass, 'Traditionsgeschichte von 1 Sam. 8; 10.17 ff. und 12', *ZAW* 77 (1965), pp. 286 ff., and id., '1 Sam. 15 als Schlüssel für das Verständnis der sogenannten königsfreundlichen Reihe 1 Sam. 9.1–10.16; 11.1–15 und 13.2–14.52', *ZAW* 78 (1966), pp. 148 ff. For criticism of Weiser cf. Boecker, op. cit.

9. Cf. below, pp. 329 f.

10. Cf. 1 Sam. 16.1 ff.; 18.8; 20.15, 32; 21.11 (Heb. 21.12) (par. 29.5); 23.15 ff.; 24.21; 25.28, 30; 26.25; and 2 Sam. 3.9 ff., 18; 5.2 f., 12; 6.21 and 7.8–11.

11. *VT* 16 (1966), p. 354. On the other hand J. Conrad in his 'Zum geschichtlichen Hintergrund der Darstellung von Davids Aufstieg', *TLZ* 97 (1972), cols. 321 ff., has suggested, in view of points which seem to him to be intended to reveal the relationship of David to Saul and Jonathan, a dating of the narrative in the ninth century. It is then seen as directed against the usurpation of the Israelite throne by Jehu, and places before the dynasty of David the image of their energetic ancestor.

under prophetic influence and altered to a complete history with a theological interpretation. The fifth stage, that of the Deuteronomistic redaction, has significantly smaller importance for Weiser than for Noth[12]. Finally in a sixth, post-Deuteronomistic, stage the poetic, cultic sections, 1 Sam. 2.1–10; 2 Sam. 22 and 23.1–7, were added[13].

The appendix consisting of chapters 2 Sam. 21–24, whose symmetrical structure with its correspondence between 21.1 ff. and 24.1 ff., 21.15 ff. and 23.8 ff., and 22.1 ff. and 23.1 ff. was already recognized by Wellhausen[14], has according to Cazelles the intention of portraying David as both king and prophet in the manner of Deut. 18. A conscious contrast between the high-place of Gibeon and the site of the Jerusalem temple is, he claims, intended.[15]

Summary. It is now undisputed that we have the Book of Samuel in a Deuteronomistic redaction. It is also undisputed that disagreements in content, doublets and divergent purposes can be found in the story of the rise of Saul as in that of the rise of David. It looks as if, in contrast to the older attempts at a literary-critical solution along the lines of the documentary hypothesis, the way opened up by Rost of looking for older, originally independent single works, is winning the day. Attention to the problem of the layers of Deuteronomistic and pre-Deuteronomistic redactions, which today is again strongly to the fore, is likely to be especially fruitful for future scholarship.

12. Cf. below, § 16.

13. A consistently traditio-historical interpretation of 2 Samuel on the basis of the hypothesis, upheld especially by Engnell, of the growth of Old Testament traditions in a primarily oral process, has recently been published by R. A. Carlson, in *David—the Chosen King. A Traditio-historical Approach to the Second Book of Samuel*, Stockholm 1964. According to him the material of the book is based on an epic of David, which has been edited by the Deuteronomistic group, and which presents David (a) as under the blessing, 2 Sam. 2–7, and (b) as under the curse, 2 Sam. 9–24. He rejects any independent narrative of the succession.

14. Op. cit., pp. 260 ff.

15. 'David's Monarchy and the Gibeonite Claim', *PEQ* 87 (1955), pp. 165 ff. and especially p. 175.

§ 15   The Books of Kings

I. Benzinger, *Jahvist und Elohist in den Königsbüchern*, BWAT NF 2, 1921; G. Hölscher, 'Das Buch der Könige, seine Quellen und seine Redaktion', in *Eucharisterion*, Festschrift H. Gunkel, FRLANT 36, 1, 1923, pp. 158 ff.; J. Begrich, *Die Chronologie der Könige von Israel und Juda und die Quellen des Rahmens der Königsbücher*, BHT 3, Tübingen 1929; M. Noth, *Überlieferungsgeschichtliche Studien*, Halle 1943, 1967³, pp. 66 ff.; G. von Rad, 'The Deuteronomistic Theology of History in the Book of Kings', *Studies in Deuteronomy* [1948], SBT 9, 1953, pp. 74 ff.; G. Hölscher, *Geschichtsschreibung in Israel*, SKHVL 50, 1952; A. Jepsen, *Die Quellen des Königsbuches*, Halle, 1953, 1956²; E. Janssen, *Juda in der Exilszeit*, FRLANT 69, 1956, pp. 12 ff.; G. Fohrer, *Elia*, ATANT (31) 53, (1957) 1968²; E. Jenni, 'Zwei Jahrzehnte Forschung an den Büchern Josua bis Könige. VII. Königsbücher', *ThR* NF 27 (1961), pp. 142 ff.; A. Jepsen and R. Hanhart, *Untersuchungen zur israelitisch-jüdischen Chronologie*, BZAW 88, 1964; J. Debus, *Die Sünde Jerobeams. Studien zur Darstellung Jerobeams und der Geschichte des Nordreichs in der deuteronomistischen Geschichtsschreibung*, FRLANT 93, 1967; O. H. Steck, *Überlieferung und Zeitgeschichte in den Elia-Erzählungen*, WMANT 26, 1968; W. Dietrich, *Prophetie und Geschichte. Eine redaktionsgeschichtliche Untersuchung zum deuteronomistischen Geschichtswerk*, FRLANT 108, 1972; H.-C. Schmitt, *Elisa. Traditionsgeschichtliche Untersuchungen zur vorklassischen nordisraelitischen Prophetie*, Gütersloh 1972.

Commentaries: KHC Benzinger 1899; HK Kittel 1902; EH Šanda 1911–12; HS Landersdorfer 1927; ICC Montgomery and Gehman 1951; BK Noth I, 1 1968; OTL J. Gray 1970².

1. Division into two books and author. Like the Book of Samuel, the Book of Kings, which in the Hebrew manuscripts formed a unity, was also divided into two books in the fifteenth century under the influence of the Septuagint and the Vulgate. The division is not very well made, since it splits up the story of Ahaziah. The first two chapters of the first book belong in subject to the story of the succession to David, which begins in 2 Sam. 9[1]. Rabbinical tradition regards Jeremiah as the author of the book. This conjecture is untenable in the light of the content and genesis of the book.

1. On this see above, pp. 154 ff.

2. Content. The Books of Kings cover the time from the accession of Solomon to the release of Jehoiachin from Babylonian imprisonment. They can be naturally divided up as follows:

I	1 Kgs. 1–11	The story of Solomon
II	1 Kgs. 12–2 Kgs. 17	The history of the kings of Israel and Judah to the fall of the Kingdom of Israel (722 B.C.)
III	2 Kgs. 18–25	The history of the kings of Judah to the destruction of Jerusalem in 587, together with the epilogue about the governorship of Gedaliah and the release of Jehoiachin (561 B.C.)

3. Framework. The book acquires its distinctive character from the framework which holds together the material from tradition. It consists of introductory and concluding notices. The introductions contain at most five elements (this only with the kings of Judah), the concluding notices four elements. The five elements of the introduction are:

1. A synchronistic dating of the accession of the king of one kingdom by the regnal year of the contemporary king of the other kingdom. So the accession of a king of Judah is dated by the regnal year of the king of Israel at the time, and *vice versa*.

The synchronisms are only possible as long as both kingdoms exist side by side. So the first synchronism is for King Abijah of Judah in 1 Kgs. 15.1, and the last for King Hezekiah in 2 Kgs. 18.1. In the absence of an absolute chronology such as we have now in the Christian era, such a relative chronology represents the only possibility for an objective fixing of the dates of the reigns. It should be noted that these synchronisms, together with certain dates in Ancient Near Eastern history which can be calculated by astronomy, form the real basis for placing the history of the period of the kings in terms of our era, and so in world history. Addition of the figures obtained from the synchronisms, and of the absolute figures for the length of the reigns of individual kings, leads to different results. However, neither set of figures should be regarded as being basically erroneous. We must allow for mistakes in the transmission of individual figures, and occasionally for different dating systems. Begrich and after him Jepsen in Germany have striven with especial success towards clarification of the chronology[2].

The synchronisms determine the distinctive structure of the book: because of them the history of the king of one kingdom is followed each time by that of all the kings of the other who came to the throne during his lifetime. So e.g. after the concluding notice on Jeroboam I of Israel an account is given of the Judahite kings Rehoboam, Abijah and Asa. Only then does the narrative go on to the successors of Jeroboam, Nadab and Baasha, who reigned at the same time as Asa. So there is an alternation in the narrative between Northern and Southern Kingdoms, until there is only the latter to tell of.

2. For the kings of Judah only a statement of their age on accession to the throne.

3. Generally a statement of the length of the reign. Here it should be noted that any years of co-regency are included in the total.

4. For the kings of Judah only the name of the king's mother, and

5. again generally a verdict on the piety of the king, which is obviously the heart of the whole presentation.

The concluding notices begin

1. with a reference to fuller sources. Especially interesting events or achievements are occasionally mentioned here. There follow

2. an account of the death,

3. for the kings of Judah only a report of the burial with their fathers and

4. again generally a mention of the successor as king. For practical reasons this scheme is frequently broken. There is no

---

2. The chronology proposed by W. F. Albright in *BASOR* 100 (1945), pp. 16 ff.; 130 (1953), pp. 4 ff. and 143 (1956), pp. 28 ff., has also achieved widespread recognition. Cf. on the subject also J. Finegan, *Handbook of Biblical Chronology*, Princeton 1964. The problems of method have been set out clearly even for beginners in A. Jepsen, 'Noch einmal zur israelitisch-jüdischen Chronologie', *VT* 18 (1968), pp. 31 ff. E. R. Thiele, *The Mysterious Numbers of the Hebrew Kings*, Exeter 1966², V. Pavlovsky and E. Vogt, 'Die Jahre der Könige von Juda und Israel', *Bib* 45 (1964), pp. 321 ff., and K. T. Andersen, 'Die chronologie der Könige von Israel und Juda', *StTh* 23 (1969), pp. 69 ff., have proposed chronologies which diverge from that of Jepsen down to the reign of Manasseh.

introduction for Jeroboam I or for Jehu, since for both kings a more detailed account of their road to the throne was included. With the Judahite usurper Queen Athaliah the whole framework is lacking. This is to indicate that she was not included in the official enumeration of the kings of Judah. Finally the concluding remarks are lacking when kings are deported or if a more detailed account of their end is given.

4. *Sources*. Kings itself mentions as sources 1, the 'book of the history of Solomon'; 2, the 'chronicle of the kings of Israel'; and 3, the 'chronicle of the kings of Judah'. So 1 Kgs. 11.41 says: 'Now the rest of the acts of Solomon and all that he did, and his wisdom, are they not written in the book of the acts of Solomon?'. If the story of Solomon contained in 1 Kgs. 3–11 is examined, the question arises whether it has only drawn on this source or on others too. For apart from the accounts of Solomon's buildings, the mining and forced labour needed for them, the dedication of the buildings, and of trade, treasures and trade voyages, we are told here of his wisdom (cf. 3 and 4.29–34 [Heb. 5.9–14]). It is hard to decide whether the author (or circle of authors) in addition to the work mentioned by him had access also to special lists of Solomon's officials and of his kingdom (cf. 4.1–28 [Heb. 4.1–5.8]), because the source mentioned is clearly a generally available work, which is not identical with the official annals kept at the royal court, but must have been formed with the use of them and possibly of further traditions.

The Chronicle of the Kings of Israel is first mentioned under Jeroboam I in 1 Kgs. 14.19, and last under Pekah in 2 Kgs. 15.31. It seems therefore that the editing of the annals was not continued in the nine years of the reign of the last Israelite king Hoshea. It must be assumed either that the work was written in Judah or that after the fall of the Northern Kingdom it was brought to safety in the south.

The Chronicle of the Kings of Judah is first mentioned under Rehoboam in 1 Kgs. 14.29, and last under Jehoiakim in 2 Kgs. 24.5. As in the north, the work was clearly not completed in the south after the final catastrophe. It is a reasonable assumption that the author of the Book of Kings took his synchronisms, the facts about the lengths of reigns of the Judahite kings, and the remaining dates from this source. The question of the origin of the prophetic narratives incorporated into the book, and of the date of their incorporation, on the other hand, is a separate problem.

5. *Purpose.* The choice of material and the evaluation of the kings of both kingdoms, which is made entirely from a religious viewpoint, are in themselves sufficient to indicate that the book is not the kind of portrayal of the monarchical period down to its catastrophic end that requires to be evaluated by the standard of Greek or modern history writing. The central idea of faithfulness to Yahweh, which is manifested in faithfulness to the Temple of Jerusalem[3], led to a special interest in everything that was connected with this temple. Everything that provided material for accounts of works of renovation in the temple, of its fitting out and of its plundering, of its defilement and of cultic reforms leading to its purification, was included in the book. We are generally given information about the strictly political activities of the kings only when and to the extent that they had an effect on the temple cult. After what has been said it is clear that the Northern Kingdom, because of its 'apostasy' from the Jerusalem sanctuary, is viewed primarily under the negative category of holding fast to 'the sin of Jeroboam'[4].

6. *Origin.* According to the dominant view the Book of Kings is a constituent element of the Deuteronomistic history which extends from Deut. 1.1 to 2 Kgs. 25.30. Views differ on whether this history is a unitary composition including all the books or only a thorough redaction of the already existing books.

(a) There are scholars who find in the Books of Kings the Pentateuch sources J and E, or J_1 or L, J_2 or J and E. Along the lines of the 'newer documentary hypothesis' Benzinger and Hölscher have attempted to demonstrate the existence of two pre-Deuteronomic sources. Benzinger believes he can trace J down to the beginning of the reign of Hezekiah, and E down to the reign of Josiah, seen as a climax to the story. For Hölscher J ends with the so-called division of the kingdoms in 1 Kgs. 12, and E with the end of the whole narrative, the release of Jehoiachin, in 2 Kgs. 25. Further he believes that here, as in the other

3. This tendency can readily be understood in the post-exilic period.
4. Cf. J. Debus, op. cit.

books from Genesis on, he can establish the existence of supplements from an E₂. Smend, whose views can only be gathered from fragmentary notes in the material he left when he died, tried tentatively to demonstrate the occurrence of J_1, J_2 and E beyond the destruction of Samaria[5]. Eissfeldt expresses himself confidently on the basic question: he is convinced that the Deuteronomistic author or editor of the book had before him L, J and E for the period of the kings too. The sources cannot of course go on beyond the date of their formation, L between 950 and 850, J between the end of the tenth and the last quarter of the eighth, and E between the middle of the ninth and the second half of the eighth century. Eissfeldt regards a reconstruction of the pre-Deuteronomic book of Kings and its division into individual strands as impossible. It is no accident that an increasing reserve towards such attempts can be observed in the last few decades.

(b) Jepsen has made a different sort of attempt to demonstrate the existence of a pre-Deuteronomistic Book of Kings. He sees a synchronistic Chronicle of the Kings as the basis. To this the framework belonged, except element 5 of the introduction, the verdict on the piety of the kings. This chronicle covered the time from David to Hezekiah[6]. Jepsen bases his hypothesis on the fact that with Hezekiah the brief reports, usually only of one sentence, about buildings, wars and the like disappear. This chronicle had pursued the aim of 'contrasting the constant change of the Israelite dynasties with the permanence of the Davidic dynasty. It was by this that both the fall of Samaria and the continued existence of Judah were to be explained.'[7] Then after the catastrophe of 587 priestly circles expanded this synchronistic chronicle by adding the verdicts on the attitude of the kings to the cult (element 5 of the introduction) and also annalistic material, and at the same time continued the book down to 587. Soon afterwards the book underwent a prophetic redaction. To this we owe the incorporation of the prophetic legends, the stories about Ahijah of Shiloh, Elijah and Elisha, the

5. Cf. R. Smend, 'J E in den geschichtlichen Büchern des AT', ed. H. Holzinger, *ZAW* 39 (1921), pp. 181 ff.

6. Cf. the continuous translation of the assumed source in Jepsen, *Quellen*, pp. 30 ff.

7. Op. cit., p. 38.

stories about prophets of 1 Kgs. 20 and 22, the traditions about the extermination of Baal worship in Samaria (2 Kgs. 8.28–10.27), and the Isaiah legends. At the same time the Solomon tradition was expanded in this redaction and the end of the succession narrative incorporated into the book. This prophetic redaction like the priestly one extended backwards to the Book of Judges. The prophetic redactor is in effect identical with the Deuteronomist[8]. Finally the book was again edited by Levitical circles and expanded yet again later. No comprehensive discussion or refutation of Jepsen, who supports his arguments with linguistic statistics, has as yet appeared.

(c) In comparison with this complicated picture of the origin of the Book of Kings, Noth's view appears simple: the author of the book is for him identical with the author of the whole Deuteronomistic history. Apart from the succession narrative, the book of the history of Solomon, the Chronicles of the kings of Israel and of the kings of Judah, and also some minor sources, he was able to use the prophetic traditions already mentioned. On this view, apart from the choice of material and the concise schematic presentation of it, his contributions are the verdicts on the piety of the kings, and the parts of the prayer at the consecration of the temple related to them (1 Kgs. 8.14–53*), the 'theology of history' discussion appended to the account of the fall of the Northern Kingdom (2 Kgs. 17.7–23*) and the certainly strangely brief reports of the final catastrophe of the Southern Kingdom (2 Kgs. 22.16 f. and 24.3 f.)[9]. Dietrich after an examination of the prophetic traditions in the Book of Kings reached the result that we must distinguish between the author of the Deuteronomistic history, Dtr G, a deuteronomistically oriented redactor interested in prophecy, Dtr P, and finally the legalistic redactor Dtr N. Future scholarly work will have to take notice of his findings[10].

Future Developments. The most recent discussion indicates that the solution suggested by Noth was too simple, and that the Book of Kings owes its present form to at least several Deuteronomistic redactions[11]. The studies published simultaneously by Dietrich

8. Cf. below, p. 173. 9. Cf. below, pp. 169 ff.
10. Cf. above, pp. 141 and 148, and below, p. 174 f.
11. Cf. Debus, op. cit., pp. 109 ff. and Dietrich, op. cit.

and Schmitt start from different problems, and in part also use different parts of the book for their material; but just for this reason the similarity of their results is striking. Both come to the conclusion that a distinction must be made between the Deuteronomistic author of the Book of Kings and two further redactions. Dietrich finds as well as the author of the Deuteronomistic history Dtr G, whom he regards as the author of the book, and dates between 587 and 580, a prophetic redactor Dtr P, who not only inserted newly composed prophetic speeches and statements of their fulfilment into older contexts, but was also responsible for the inclusion of 1 Kgs. 13*, 14*, 16.34, 17*, 20*, 22*, 2 Kgs. 1*, 14.25 and 19.17–20.19*. He is followed by the legalistic redactor Dtr N (the N is from 'nomistic', i.e. legalistic), who about 560 made of the prophets preachers of Deuteronomy. Schmitt in his study of the Elisha tradition reaches the conclusion that not only 1 Kgs. 20* and 22*, but also 2 Kgs. 3.4–27* and 6.24–7.16* belong to a second layer in the Book of Kings. Further study will show whether his assumption that the prophetic redaction of this section had already taken place when it was assembled to form a collection of war stories before its inclusion in the Book of Kings is tenable, or whether it must be amended in the direction of a view more like that of Dietrich. Again it remains as yet unclear whether a connection can be established between the editor who inserted into the Book of Kings the collection of miracle stories placed by Schmitt in the middle of the eighth century (2 Kgs. 4.1–44*; 6.1–23* and 8.1–6*), the succession stories (1 Kgs. 19.19–21* and 2 Kgs. 2*) assigned to the seventh century, and the stories of the Aramaeans (2 Kgs. 5.1–14*; 8.7–15* and 13.14–17*) which developed between the end of the ninth and the middle of the eighth centuries, at the same time interpreting Elisha as a Man of God, and Dietrich's Dtr N, or whether the position will in the end turn out to be yet more complicated than this.[12]

12. For an example cf. E. Würthwein, 'Zur Komposition von I Reg 22, 1–38', in *Das Ferne und nahe Wort*. Festschrift L. Rost, BZAW 105, 1967, pp. 245 ff.; A. Jepsen, 'Ahabs Busse', in *Archäologie und Altes Testament*, Festschrift K. Galling, Tübingen 1970, pp. 145 ff.

§ 16 The Problem of the Deuteronomistic History

M. Noth, *Überlieferungsgeschichtliche Studien*, Halle 1943, Tübingen 1967³; O. Eissfeldt, *Geschichtsschreibung im Alten Testament*, Berlin 1948; A. Jepsen, *Die Quellen des Königsbuches*, Halle 1953, 1956²; E. Janssen, *Juda in der Exilszeit*, FRLANT 69, 1956, pp. 12 ff. and 73 ff.; H. W. Wolff, 'Das Kerygma des deuteronomistischen Geschichtswerks', *ZAW* 73 (1961), pp. 171 ff. and in *Gesammelte Studien zum Alten Testament*, ThB 22, 1964, pp. 308 ff.; E. Jenni, 'Zwei Jahrzehnte Forschung an den Büchern Josua bis Könige. III. Das deuteronomistische Geschichtswerk', *ThR* NF 27 (1961), pp. 97 ff.; P. R. Ackroyd, *Exile and Restoration*, OTL, 1968, pp. 62 ff.; E. W. Nicholson, *Preaching to the Exiles*, Oxford 1970; R. Smend, 'Das Gesetz und die Völker', in *Probleme biblischer Theologie*, Festschrift G. von Rad, Munich 1971, pp. 494 ff.; W. Dietrich, *Prophetie und Geschichte*, FRLANT 108, 1972. Cf. also the lists for §§ 11–15.

Two works which are independent of one another, but because of the circumstances of the time were published ten years apart, have attempted to demonstrate the existence of a Deuteronomistic history extending from Deut. 1 to 2 Kgs. 25: Noth's *Überlieferungsgeschichtliche Studien* and Jepsen's *Quellen des Königsbuches*.

(a) NOTH. For Noth the Deuteronomist is not a simple redactor who collects and edits his sources, but the author of a work formed on the basis of a uniform view of the theology of history.

1. Sources. He had at his disposal, apart from lists and subsidiary sources, Deuteronomy, for Joshua a collection of accounts of the conquest, for Judges a collection of stories of deliverers, for Samuel the traditions of Saul and David, which had already been combined, and for Kings apart from the sources expressly mentioned there, in particular stories of the prophets.

2. The work. The Deuteronomist wanted to show that Israel owed its catastrophic fall not to the impotence of its God, but to its own guilt.

Accordingly he began his presentation immediately before the conquest.[1] Against the background of the conquest, which demonstrated

1. He could omit an account of the primeval history of the nation since it existed already in the form of JE.

the faithfulness of God, the following story of disaster was bound to appear all the more striking. So the Deuteronomist began his narrative with a farewell speech of Moses in the Transjordan, into which he inserted the whole of Deuteronomy (Deut. 4.44–30.20)[2]. In Deut. 1–3 he makes Moses give a retrospect of the events from the departure from Mount Horeb up to the division of the Transjordan. He ends with the announcement of his future death, and with the charge to install Joshua as his successor[3]. The whole speech is concluded in 31 with the farewell sermon of Moses. It is followed by the account of the installation of Joshua and of the writing down of the law. Omitting the Song of Moses in 32 and the Blessing of Moses in 33 the story continues in 34 with the account of the death of Moses. A positive basis is thus laid for the ensuing historical narrative[4].

In Joshua the Deuteronomist is able to show how the faithfulness of the people is rewarded by the faithfulness of God[5]. As long as Joshua leads the nation in the spirit of Moses and of his instructions, God's promises are fulfilled. After his death and that of his fellow warriors, the situation alters. The period of the judges consists of an alternation of backsliding and repentance, foreign domination and deliverance (cf. Judg. 2.11–18), until the people wantonly demand a king.

At all the turning points in the story the Deuteronomist inserts speeches put in the mouths of the leaders, which indicate 'the course of affairs in prospect and in retrospect' and draw 'the practical consequences for men's behaviour from this'[6].

So after the farewell speech of Moses which concludes Deuteronomy, there appear the speeches which Yahweh directs to Joshua (Josh. 1.2–9), and Joshua to the tribes east of the Jordan (Josh. 22.1–8). The transition from the period of the conquest to that of the judges is marked by the farewell speech of Joshua (Josh. 23). The period of the judges, introduced with a general survey in Judg. 2.6 ff. and 2.11 ff., ends with the withdrawal of Samuel and with his farewell speech (1 Sam. 12). This makes clear that the fate of the nation is dependent not on its

2. Cf. above, p. 119.

3. On Deut. 1–3 see now J. G. Plöger, *Literarkritische, formgeschichtliche und stilkritische Untersuchungen zum Deuteronomium*, BBB 26, 1967.

4. The connections within the work are shown e.g. by Deut. 1.35 ff. and Josh. 14.6 ff.; Deut. 3.28; 31.7 f. and Josh 1.6.

5. On the process of development of Joshua assumed by Noth cf. above, pp. 137 f. and 141 ff.

6. *Überlieferungsgeschichtliche Studien*, p. 5. Cf. also O. Plöger, 'Reden und Gebet im deuteronomistischen und chronistischen Geschichtswerk', in *Festschrift G. Dehn*, Neukirchen 1957, pp. 35 ff., or in *Aus der Spätzeit des Alten Testaments*, Göttingen 1971, pp. 50 ff.

constitution, but on the fulfilment or rejection of God's demand for obedience[7]. While he simply allows his sources to speak for themselves for the period of Saul and David, the dedication of the temple in Jerusalem by Solomon gives him a new occasion for a programmatic declaration that he sees in the temple the place intended in the law, which Yahweh will choose to make his name dwell there. So he follows the speech at the dedication of the temple by Solomon, which is a piece of older tradition (1 Kgs. 8.12 f.), with an introductory speech put in the mouth of Solomon (1 Kgs. 8.14–21), and with the prayer for the dedication of the temple (8.22–53*).

The next speech would have been due on the occasion of the fall of the Northern Kingdom. But here the Deuteronomist, as in Judg. 2, used a 'theology of history' treatment. In 2 Kgs. 17.7–23* the fall of the state of Israel is presented as a consistent consequence of the 'sin of Jeroboam' (cf. 1 Kgs. 12.26 ff.). The interpretation of the final catastrophe of the Southern Kingdom in 2 Kgs. 22.16 f., 23.26 f. and 24.3 f. is surprisingly brief.

The uniform theological thread of the whole narrative can be shown to be the connection between the correct worship of God, obedience to the commandment given by Moses in the form of Deuteronomy, and obedience to the words of the prophet[8]. In this way the Deuteronomist answered the question of his contemporaries about the causes of the complete collapse: God has answered the ever renewed backsliding of his people with warnings, punishments and finally with destruction.

Apart from the main theological ideas emphasized by means of the inserted speeches and 'theology of history' discussions a further factor which links together the elements from tradition is the chronology, according to which a period of 480 years elapsed from the Exodus from Egypt to the beginning of the building of the temple of Solomon (cf. Deut. 1.3 and 1 Kgs. 6.1)[9].

Noth assumed that the period of composition was the middle of the sixth century, and the place of composition Palestine.

7. Noth ascribes to the Deuteronomist the whole so-called anti-monarchical sequence, 1 Sam. 7.2–8.22 + 10.17–27a + 12.1–25.

8. On the Deuteronomistic theology of the prophets cf. K.-H. Bernhardt, *Prophetie und Geschichte*, SVT 22, 1972, pp. 20 ff.

9. Cf. now W. Richter, BBB 21, 1964, pp. 132 ff., and G. Sauer, 'Die chronologischen Angaben in den Büchern Deut. bis 2. Kön.', *ThZ* 24 (1968), pp. 1 ff.

2 Kgs. 25.27 ff. gave him a *terminus a quo* for this (561), while he took it as an argument for his location of the book that the sources used would have been most readily available to the Deuteronomist in the old homeland. Such a hypothesis would most readily explain his familiarity with traditions anchored in the region of Bethel and Mizpah, and not least the supposed absence of a future hope[10]. Janssen has produced further arguments in support of the localization proposed by Noth. He sees indications of the origin of the work in Palestine in the warnings against apostasy to the worship of Canaanite gods, in the understanding of the temple as a place of prayer (cf. 1 Kgs. 8.33 f.) and in the lack of any marked interest in the exiles[11]. On the other hand Soggin and Nicholson appeal to Josh. 23.13 ff. and Deut. 4.29 ff., 30.1 ff. and 1 Kgs. 8.46 ff. in support of an origin of the work among the exiles[12]. Ackroyd regards it as impossible to settle the question of the place of origin, while deducing from the absence of any direct reference to the rebuilding of the temple and to the existence of the Persian empire that the *terminus ante quem* for the work is 520[13].

3. *Purpose*. Noth astonishingly enough assumed that the purpose of this great undertaking was a purely negative one. The Deuteronomist regarded the divine judgement portrayed by him as final and conclusive, and gave no expression even in the most modest form to the expectation of a future gathering together of scattered Israel. Noth found here no programme for the future. On the other hand the question was raised already by the literary assumptions he made whether this was to be expected at all apart from the basic pattern found in Deuteronomy. Following this approach Janssen has interpreted Deut. 29.28 as the hermeneutic rule of the Deuteronomistic school: obedience in respect of the law brings also the possibility of restoration and recovery[14]. Further it must not be overlooked that the prayer at the temple dedication (1 Kgs. 8.46 ff.) envisages the prayer of those in exile being heard (cf. Deut. 30.1 ff.), and finally it is not ruled out that 2 Kgs. 25.27 ff. is in fact to be regarded as indicating the abandonment of the hopes placed on the line of David or

10. Noth, op. cit., pp. 12 and 110, n. 1.
11. Janssen, op. cit., pp. 17 f.
12. Cf. J. A. Soggin, OTL, pp. 218 f., and Nicholson, op. cit., pp. 117 ff.
13. Ackroyd, op. cit., pp. 68 and 64 f.
14. Janssen, op. cit., p. 74, and Nicholson, pp. 75 ff.

as a simple statement of the last known fact in the history of the kings[15].

(b) JEPSEN. The differences in Jepsen's conception from that of Noth result from the prehistory assumed by him for the Book of Kings, whose core he considers to be a synchronistic chronicle of the kings[16]. When it was expanded after 587 by a priest, a continuous story was formed extending from the story of the rise of David, perhaps even from a historical narrative beginning with Judg. 1 + 17–21, down to the end of the period of the Kings. This work was then expanded by the Deuteronomist with the whole of Deuteronomy, the Benjaminite narratives of the conquest in the Book of Joshua, the stories of the Judges, the traditions of Samuel, the narrative of the succession to the throne and traditions of prophets.

4. The position of the debate. It is undisputed that the books Deuteronomy–2 Kings in the form in which they have been transmitted give a continuous historical account, which owes its inner unity to Deuteronomistic editing. Studies made in the last decade show however that the solution suggested by Noth was too simple, and that the problem cannot be regarded as having reached an agreed conclusion. The hypothesis which has again been put forward of a Yahwistic history extending from the Creation down to the division of the kingdom[17] must be regarded as open to question at least in the form in which it has been put forward. Both its ending at 1 Kgs. 12 and the assumed incorporation of the Succession Narrative, which as Würthwein has seen has a strongly anti-Davidic tendency[18], would lead to the assumption of a quite lengthy period of transmission in northern Israel[19]. So for the present the basic conception held by both Noth and Jepsen of a continuous historical narrative first put together in the sixth century, and extending from Deuteronomy to 2 Kings, remains unshaken.

15. Cf. Wolff, op. cit., p. 323; Ackroyd, pp. 78 ff.; Nicholson, pp. 78 ff., and now also Dietrich, op. cit., p. 142.

16. Cf. above, pp. 166 f.

17. Cf. H. Schulte, *Die Entstehung der Geschichtsschreibung im Alten Israel*, BZAW 128, 1972, pp. 201 ff.

18. Cf. above, pp. 156 f.

19. Cf. above, p. 157.

The proof produced by Smend and Dietrich on the basis of a limited group of passages that at least three different hands can be distinguished within the Deuteronomistic history, that of the author of the history proper, Dtr G, that of a Dtr P found in the prophetic narratives, and standing for a prophetic theology of history, and that of a legalist who gauges the course of history by the Deuteronomic law, Dtr N[20], makes a redaction-critical examination of the whole book essential. When this is made it will indicate to what extent the newer analyses of Deuteronomy which have meanwhile been published are tenable[21]; how the clearly complicated position of the sources in Joshua can be explained[22]; what modifications the picture drawn by Richter of the redactions of the Book of Judges must undergo[23]; how the presence of several strata in the so-called anti-monarchical portion of the Book of Samuel, which has been demonstrated by Weiser, can be related to the various Deuteronomistic redactions[24], and whether as well as the syntactically striking glossing of the Book of Kings[25] there is also found a further redaction, which incorporates the stories of the prophets into the book[26].

We can also not least expect from these studies a clarification of the problem of the original location of the Deuteronomist. It remains to be seen whether there is a variation between the areas of activity of the different redactions, and whether this will explain the differences of view among scholars hitherto. Now that Smend has claimed Josh. 23 for Dtr N[27], an exilic origin at least for this redaction is probable. If the inclusion of 2 Kgs. 25.21b in the work of Dtr G suggested by Dietrich can be upheld, this work can also be considered as originating among the exiles. In that case the date proposed for it by Dietrich of between 587 and 580 cannot be maintained, because we already have here a picture of the emptying of the land of its inhabitants, which corresponds

20. Cf. above, pp. 141, 148 and 167.
21. Cf. R. P. Merendino, *Das deuteronomische Gesetz*, BBB 31, 1969, and G. Seitz, *Redaktionsgeschichtliche Studien zum Deuteronomium*, BWANT 93, 1971.
22. Cf. above, pp. 136 ff.   23. Cf. above, pp. 145 ff.
24. Cf. above, pp. 158 ff.
25. Cf. e.g. 2 Kgs. 21.6, 23.8b, 10, 14a.
26. This is the 'man of God' redaction proposed by H.-C. Schmitt, *Elisa*, Gütersloh 1972, pp. 127 ff. and 131 ff. Cf. above, p. 168.
27. Cf. above, p. 141.

with the theory, which is ascribed to Dtr N, of the departure of the remainder of the population to Egypt (2 Kgs. 25.26). This theoretical construction cannot be reconciled with the dating of Dtr N in about 560, because at that date the actual facts must still have been known quite well. It does however make sense if it is seen as a part of the debate between the exiles, Palestinian Jewry and the Egyptian diaspora. The prayer at the dedication of the temple (1 Kgs. 8.22 ff.), the analysis of which into strata has not yet been carried through, probably presupposes the existence of the second temple in 8.33 f. It is quite clear that 8.46 ff. has the exiles in mind.

§ 17   The History of the Chronicler
The Books of Chronicles, Ezra and Nehemiah

Literature on Chronicles: G. von Rad, *Das Geschichtsbild des chronistischen Werkes*, BWANT IV, 3, 1930; id., 'The Levitical Sermon in I and II Chronicles' [1934], *The Problem of the Hexateuch and Other Essays*, Edinburgh and London, 1966, pp. 267 ff.; A. C. Welch, *The Work of the Chronicler. Its Purpose and its Date*, London 1939; M. Noth, *Überlieferungsgeschichtliche Studien*, Halle 1943, Tübingen 1967³, pp. 110 ff.; J. G. Botterweck, 'Zur Eigenart der chronistischen Davidgeschichte', *ThQ* 136 (1956), pp. 402 ff.; T. Willi, *Die Chronik als Auslegung*, FRLANT 106, 1972; P. Welten, *Geschichte und Geschichtsdarstellung in den Chronikbüchern*, WMANT 42, 1973.

Commentaries: KHC Benzinger 1901; HK Kittel 1902; ICC Curtis and Madsen 1910; KAT¹ Rothstein and Hänel I, 1927; HS Goettsberger 1939; ATD Galling 1954; HAT Rudolph 1955; AB Myers I–II 1965; CAT Michaeli 1967.

Literature on Ezra and Nehemiah: E. Meyer, *Die Entstehung des Judenthums*, Halle 1896, Hildesheim 1965; C. C. Torrey, *Ezra Studies*, Chicago 1910; G. Hölscher, 'Die Bücher Esra und Nehemia', in *HSAT* II, Tübingen 1923⁴, pp. 491 ff.; H. H. Schaeder, *Esra der Schreiber*, BHT 5, Tübingen 1930; A. S. Kapelrud, *The Question of Authorship in the Ezra-Narrative*, SNVAO II, 1944, 1, 1944; H. H. Rowley, 'The Chronological Order of Ezra and Nehemiah' [1948], *The Servant of the Lord*, Oxford 1965², pp. 135 ff.; S. Mowinckel, 'Erwägungen zum chronistischen Geschichtswerk', *TLZ* 85 (1960), cols. 1 ff.; id. *Studien zu dem Buche Ezra-Nehemia*. I. Die nachchronische Redaktion der Buches. Die Listen, SNVAO II. NS 3, 1964; II. Die Nehemia-Denkschrift, SNVAO II. NS 5, 1964; III. Die Ezrageschichte und das

Gesetz Moses, SNVAO II. NS 7, 1965; G. von Rad, 'Die Nehemia-Denkschrift', *ZAW* 76 (1964), pp. 176 ff. and *Gesammelte Studien zum Alten Testament*, ThB 8, 1965³, pp. 297 ff.; U. Kellermann, *Nehemia. Quellen, Überlieferung und Geschichte*, BZAW 102, 1967; K. Pohlmann, *Studien zum 3. Esra. Ein Beitrag zur Frage nach der Gestalt und der Theologie des chronistischen Geschichtswerkes*, FRLANT 104, 1970; W. T. In der Smitten, *Esra. Quellen, Überlieferung und Geschichte*, SSN 15, 1973.

Commentaries: HK Siegfried 1901; KHC Bertholet 1902; ICC Batten 1913; HAT Rudolph 1949; ATD Galling 1954; HS Schneider 1959⁴; CAT Michaeli 1967; CB Brockington 1969.

1. The book. The history of the Chronicler in its final form includes the books of 1 and 2 Chronicles, Ezra and Nehemiah. The identity of 2 Chr. 36.22 f. and Ezra 1.1–3aα shows that the separation of the books of Ezra and Nehemiah is secondary, probably connected with their canonization. Because Chronicles overlaps in content with the other Old Testament historical books, especially with those collected in the Deuteronomistic history, Ezra and Nehemiah attained canonical status before Chronicles. This is why both are placed before Chronicles in the Hebrew Bible[1]. Their position in the third part of the Hebrew canon, the *ketûbîm* or writings, itself points to a relatively late origin for the books, which meant that it was not possible to incorporate them into the 'Former Prophets'[1a]. It was in the Alexandrian community that the books were first placed in the position which their subject-matter suggested, after the Books of Kings. In the Hebrew Bible 1 and 2 Chr. had the title 'events of the days', i.e. 'annals', and were regarded as a single book, as were Ezra and Nehemiah. The division only appeared in Hebrew manuscripts in the fifteenth century under the influence of the Septuagint and Vulgate, and from them passed into later printed editions. But in the Septuagint too the division of Chronicles appeared only relatively late, and is not attested before the third century.

1. T. Willi, op. cit., pp. 180 ff. and P. Welten, op. cit., p. 4, n. 15, argue for the completion of Ezra-Nehemiah before that of Chronicles, while assuming that both have the same author. On the other hand S. Japhet, 'The Supposed Authorship of Chronicles and Ezra-Nehemia Investigated Anew', *VT* 18 (1968), pp. 330 ff. argues for different authors. Cf. on this Welten, ibid.

1a. Cf. below, pp. 406 f.

In the Septuagint the Books of Chronicles have the title *paraleipomena*, a title which Jerome retained in the Vulgate. The name shows that Chronicles was regarded as a supplementation of the information given in the Books of Samuel and of Kings[2]. The name Chronicles, which is usual in English and German Bibles, goes back to a description which was used by Jerome in his *prologus galeatus* and was taken up by Luther. In using the Septuagint and Vulgate the different titles for Ezra and Nehemiah must be observed. The relationship is:

LXX	V	MT
Esdras a	liber tertius Esdrae	–
Esdras b	⌈liber primus Esdrae	Ezra
	⌊liber secundus Esdrae	Nehemiah
–	liber quartus Esdrae	–

The Greek *Esdras a*, called 3 Ezra after the Vulgate (in English bibles 1 Esdras), is a historical narrative containing 2 Chr. 35.1 to Ezra 10 + Neh. 7.72–8.13a, and as extra material the story of the three pages. It is a disputed question whether 3 Ezra, apart from the story of the pages, is a fragment of an older and later rejected translation of the oldest form of the history of the Chronicler, or whether it is a later redaction of it. Although a majority of contemporary scholars incline to the second assumption, Mowinckel, Hölscher and Pohlmann produce strong arguments for the first hypothesis. The so-called 4 Ezra (or 2 Esdras) is a Jewish apocalypse of the last decade of the first century A.D.

2. Content. The history work of the Chronicler covers the time from Adam to Ezra and Nehemiah, although in a very ill-proportioned way. In the genealogical introduction, 1 Chr. 1–9, the period from Adam down to and including Saul is summarized genealogically. In 1 Chr. 10–29 on the other hand the reign of David is narrated extremely fully and with particular mention of his measures taken in preparation for the building of the temple. Characteristic of the presentation of the Chronicler is that he omits all the darker aspects of the tradition about David. Accordingly he includes neither the story of the rise of David nor that of his succession. In similar detail the Chronicler tells of Solomon in 2 Chr. 1–9, and then deals with the remaining

2. Greek *paraleipomenon* = 'what is passed by, or left out'.

kings of Judah in 2 Chr. 10–36. This outline will already show that the especial interest of the Chronicler is in the foundation of the Jerusalem cultus.

A survey of the contents of the books of Ezra and Nehemiah shows that the structure has been disturbed. The Book of Ezra forms a continuous narrative. Ezra 1–6 tells of a return of the exiles brought about by the decree of Cyrus, and their building of the temple, Ezra 7–10 of Ezra's journey to Jerusalem and the dissolution of mixed marriages which he carries out there. Then the story jumps ahead in Neh. 1 to the activity of Nehemiah. In Neh. 7.73b–10.39 (Heb. 7.72b–10.40) however the main subject of the narrative is again Ezra, while Neh. 11–13 returns to Nehemiah. Accordingly it is clear that Neh. 7.73b–10.39 (Heb. 7.72b–10.40) break up the story of Nehemiah. Any explanation of this situation is indissolubly bound up with the question of the original form of the work of the Chronicler.

3. Sources. The question of the sources used by the Chronicler, of the unity and original extent of his work can only be treated in context. It is more appropriate in view of the position to deal with Chronicles and with Ezra-Nehemiah separately.

(a) THE BOOK OF CHRONICLES. Particularly in Chronicles we are apparently in a better position in the matter of sources than in the other Old Testament books, because the Chronicler has been generous with details about his sources. In the course of the narrative there are mentioned:

(1 Chr. 9.1) 2 Chr. 20.34 a Book of the Kings of Israel
2 Chr. 33.18 a History of the Kings of Israel
2 Chr. 16.11 a Book of the Kings of Judah and Israel
2 Chr. 27.7　a Book of the Kings of Israel and Judah
2 Chr. 24.27 a Midrash (Commentary) on the Book of the Kings

There are also the following prophetic sources:

1 Chr. 29.29 a history of Samuel the seer
　　　　　　a history of Nathan the prophet
　　　　　　a history of Gad the seer
2 Chr. 9.29　a history of Nathan the prophet
　　　　　　a prophecy of Ahijah the Shilonite
　　　　　　a vision of Iddo the seer

2 Chr. 12.15 a history of Shemaiah the prophet
and of Iddo the seer
2 Chr. 13.22 a midrash of Iddo the prophet
2 Chr. 20.34 a history of Jehu son of Hanani
2 Chr. 26.22 a history of Uzziah, which Isaiah the prophet the son
of Amoz wrote
2 Chr. 32.32 a vision of the prophet Isaiah
2 Chr. 33.19 a history of his (Manasseh's) seers

In 2 Chr. 20.34 and 32.32 it is expressly stated that the documents mentioned are found in the Book of the Kings of Israel, or in the Book of the Kings of Judah and Israel. Two questions are settled by this: 1. We do not need to allow for the existence of prophetic sources for the period of the monarchy not preserved to us, and used by the Chronicler. 2. The five different historical sources that are quoted are in fact identical, and are varied ways of referring to the canonical Books of Kings. The Chronicler had available for the genealogical introduction in 1 Chr. 1–9 the Pentateuch, for the story of David the Books of Samuel, and for the story of the period of the monarchy the Books of Kings. When he repeatedly refers to prophetic sources, he is sharing the view of the authorship of the historical books which is known to us in Rabbinic tradition, that the writing down and transmission of the sacred history goes back to the prophets and to men of similar stature[3].

In the light of the existence of a whole series of notices about the defences, weapons and wars of the Kings of Judah of the post-Solomonic period, for which there is no equivalent in the canonical Book of Kings, it remains to be tested whether we have here a 'creation' of the Chronicler (Wellhausen) or accounts drawn from one or several different sources[4], whether the Chronicler had available a further source for the period of the kings, for instance in the form of an unofficial excerpt from the annals of the kings (Noth) or an expanded new edition of the Book of Kings (Budde, Klostermann, Rudolph). Mowinckel on the other hand raised the same objection to this as to the assumption of the reworking of documentary sources in Josh. 13–19[5]. He assumed that the Chronicler had drawn his special material from

3. Cf. Rudolph, HAT I, 21, p. XI.
4. Cf. 2 Chr. 11.5b–10a; 13.3 ff.; 25.5; 26.6–8a, 9, 15a; 27.3; 33.14a; 28.18; 32.30; 35.20–24* and 33.10 ff.   5. Cf. above, pp. 139 f.

oral tradition. Welten's examination of the evidence basically supports Wellhausen's view, in that he demonstrates that the accounts of the buildings and wars of the kings are used to serve the paradigmatic characterization and evaluation of the reigns of the individual kings, and that the wars successfully waged in succession against enemies in north, south, east and west by Abijah, Asa, Jehoshaphat and Uzziah reflect the oppressed situation of the post-exilic and early Hellenistic Jewish communities in Palestine, while only 2 Chr. 11.5–10*, 26.6, 10; 31.30a remain as coming from sources, and 11.22 f. and 21.1 ff. as drawn from oral tradition. Lastly reference must be made to the fact that in 1 Chr. 2–9 we have secondary accretion rather than the original work of the Chronicler, and that apart from other smaller insertions we have a later addition in 1 Chr. 23–27 in particular.

(b) THE BOOK OF EZRA. Nowadays it is relatively undisputed that we can identify the author of Ezra 1–6 with the Chronicler. The list of temple vessels allegedly given back by Cyrus to the Jerusalem community in Ezra 1.9–11a, the list of the returning exiles in Ezra 2.2–67 (69) and the collection of Aramaic documents in Ezra 4.6–6.18 are regarded as coming from sources. We do not need here to decide whether the list in Ezra 1.9–11a depends on a return of the temple vessels at a later date, e.g. under Darius I, on a later inventory of the temple vessels, or on free invention by the Chronicler. It does not in any case belong to the period of Cyrus. There is disagreement whether the list of returning exiles in Ezra 2.2–67 was a source available to the Chronicler or not. Mowinckel regards it as a census list of the community of Judah from the period about 400. The Aramaic collection of letters in Ezra 4.6–6.18 has been regarded as genuine by the majority of scholars since Eduard Meyer. The scarcely heeded objections of Hölscher, who sees the letters as a clumsy forgery, deserve to be considered seriously. It may prove that the so-called temple building decree of Cyrus (Ezra 6.3–5) is as fictitious as the decree permitting the return (Ezra 1.2–4). Apart from the sources mentioned above the Chronicler built his presentation of the return of the exiles and of the building of the temple upon facts in the books of Haggai and Zechariah.

The views of scholars differ on the story of Ezra (Ezra 7.1–
10.44+Neh. 8.1–18). While Torrey, Hölscher, Noth and
Kellermann regard it as a composition of the Chronicler going
back to an either fabricated or authentic Aramaic document
about the installation of Ezra (Ezra 7.12–26), Meyer, Schaeder
and Rudolph assume memoirs of Ezra or a report of Ezra as a
source. On Schaeder's and Rudolph's views Ezra, whom they
regard as a sort of state commissar for Jewish religious affairs,
prepared in this report a statement of account for the Persian
government on his fulfilment of the task assigned to him. While
Kapelrud considers distinguishing an older Ezra tradition serving
the Chronicler as a source and transmitted in sources related to
him impossible, Mowinckel believes that it is still possible to
establish the distinction between Chronistic redaction and the
underlying narrative. Since individual details of the story seem to
him such that they could not have been invented, he sees in it a
sort of edificatory Church history, which is supposed to have
originated about 370 B.C.

The change between an account in the first person, Ezra
7.27–9.15, and one in the third person, Ezra 7.1–26, 10.1–44
and Neh. 8.1–18, has been supposed to be evidence for the
existence of a book going back to Ezra himself. The change does
not however indicate the difference between a quoted source
and the redaction. Rather we are dealing, as Mowinckel has
shown, with a deliberately chosen stylistic form found in both
Jewish and ancient Oriental literature, cf. e.g. the Aramaic
Ahikar Story[6] and the Book of Tobit. It is above all however
the content that gives rise to suspicions of the authenticity of the
tradition. These concern in my view in particular not only the
document of appointment of Ezra in Ezra 7.12–26 and the list
of treasure in Ezra 8.26 f. but also the legendary attempt to
outdo Neh. 2.9 in Ezra 8.22 f., which seems also to indicate the
familiarity of the Ezra narrative with the memoirs of Nehemiah.
The lists in 8.1–14 and 10.18, 20–44a too are not authentic
documents. Accordingly the only alternatives which can be
considered seriously as solutions of the problem of the Ezra
narrative are the identity of the author (that is, inventor) of the
story of Ezra with the Chronicler, or an adaptation of an

6. Cf. *AOT*[2], pp. 454 ff. and *ANET*[2], pp. 427 ff.

edificatory Ezra narrative, whether circulating orally or already fixed in written form, by the Chronicler[7].

4. The original end of the work. The answer given to the question how the dovetailing of the story of Ezra with the memoirs of Nehemiah is to be explained also affects a decision on the original end of the work of the Chronicler. Noth, Rudolph and Kellermann regard the position of Neh. 8–10 as original. Correspondingly they are convinced that the Chronicler incorporated the memoirs of Nehemiah too into his work. Mowinckel, Hölscher and Pohlmann on the other hand point out, as several scholars in the nineteenth century had already done, that in 1 Esdras (3 Ezra) Neh. 8 follows immediately on from Ezra 10, and that Josephus in his *Antiquities* uses the text of 1 Esdras, and makes Ezra die before the arrival of Nehemiah in Jerusalem. Furthermore he rightly emphasizes that Sirach in his praise of the fathers mentions Nehemiah, but omits Ezra (cf. Sir. 49.13). It can be concluded from this that Josephus used an edition of Chronicles from which the Memoirs of Nehemiah were lacking. Pohlmann further points out that Neh. 8 is a possible end for the work of the Chronicler, but Neh. 13.23 ff. is not. While the end if it were Neh. 8 would take place at a climax, always indicated by the Chronicler by a festival—the purified community receives the law and celebrates the Feast of Tabernacles—the Chronicler would in Neh. 13.26, in contrast to his tendency which can be observed in the whole of the story of Solomon, not have removed the blemishes from his declared favourite. The Chronicler who dealt so freely with the Books of Samuel and Kings, would hardly have tied himself in this way to the Memoirs of Nehemiah. Accordingly Neh. 8 must be regarded as the original end of the history of the Chronicler.

The prayer of repentance in Neh. 9, and chapter 10, which draws on two different sources, do not belong to the Chronicler's story of Ezra, but like the whole complex Neh. 7.5b–10.39 (Heb. 10.40) were first inserted into the work of the Chronicler in connection with the incorporation of the Memoirs of Nehemiah. It is difficult to decide whether the original introduction to

7. A different view is accordingly taken in the two alternative solutions of whether the lists in Ezra. 8.1–14 and 10.18, 20–44a belong to the narrative of the Chronicler.

the Memoirs of Nehemiah (1.1–2.6) was only now or already earlier given a novelistic form, to make clear that his mission was an instance of the guidance of God. 1.1–4, 11b, 2.1–6abα can in any case only be regarded as part of the basic text of the book with this reservation, and it has also been further expanded, especially by means of material taken from lists of the fifth to second centuries B.C. On a generous view the original elements of the Memoirs of Nehemiah are to be found in 1.1–4, 11b; 2.1–6abα, 9b, 11–20; 3.33–7.5a; 12.31 f., 37–40 and 13.4–5, 8–28, 31b[8]. It is clear from this to how great an extent the work of the Chronicler has been subjected to subsequent editing. On the one hand it has been filled out especially by material of a list-like nature, on the other hand by the incorporation of the Memoirs of Nehemiah. Whether Galling's hypothesis, that the work of the Chronicler in its final form is the result of one comprehensive redaction, will be generally accepted remains to be seen.

5. *Date.* In dating the work of the Chronicler in its original form, extending from 1 Chr. to Ezra 10 + Neh. 8, we must naturally start from the latest event recorded in it, the activity of Ezra in Jerusalem.

Excursus: in what order did Nehemiah and Ezra appear? Since the question of the relative order of Nehemiah and Ezra is disputed in contemporary scholarship, a brief discussion of this problem cannot be avoided. The reader of the narrative in its present form necessarily receives the impression that Ezra arrived in Jerusalem before Nehemiah, that both were active for a period together, and that finally the activity of Nehemiah went on beyond that of Ezra. Quite independently of one's views on the original form of the work of the Chronicler, this picture requires critical examination.

It cannot be excluded *a priori* either that the redactor (or the Chronicler) had at his disposal a reliable tradition, or that he had theological reasons for the sequence he chose. It appears from Neh. 1.1 and 2.1

---

8. On a detailed analysis only the following verses remain as original after the heavily altered introduction: 2.9b, 11–13a, 14–15, 16*, 17–20; 3.33–34abα, β*, 35–38; 4.1–10a, 12b, 13–15a, bβ, 16a, 17aα*, βb; 5.1–9, 10aα*βb, 11–13abα*, 14aα*γb, 15–19; 6.1aα*βb, 2–10a, bα*β, 11aαb, 12abαβ*, 13aβ*b*, 14a*b, 15, 16aαγb, 17–19; 7.1a, 2a*, b, 3a*, 4, 5a; 12.31, (32?), (37abα?), 37bβ, 38a(b, 39aα?), 39aβ(b?), 40; 13.4a*, b, 5aα*, 8–10a, b*, 11–13aα, b, 14, 15aα*, 16bα*, 17, 18aαb, 19abα, 20–21, 22b, 23a, 24a, 25–28, 31b.

that Nehemiah was called in the twentieth year of King Artaxerxes. For chronological reasons this must be the Persian king Artaxerxes I (464–424). Accordingly the commissioning of Nehemiah took place in the year 444, or if one follows Josephus, who speaks of the 25th year, in the year 439. According to 5.14 his governorship of Judah lasted twelve years. It is to be placed therefore in the years 444–433 or 439–428. Since 13.6 is redactional, the assumption of a temporary absence and of a second governorship following is unnecessary. Ezra 10.6 is the starting point for the dating of Ezra. According to this verse Ezra stayed in the room of Johanan son of Eliashib in the temple. From the list of the Jewish high priests in Neh. 12.10 f., 22 we have the sequence Jeshua, Joiakim, Eliashib, Joiada and (with a correction on the basis of 12.22) Johanan and Jaddua. From the list inserted later of those who took part in the building of the wall in 3.1 ff. it can be deduced that Eliashib was High Priest at the time of Nehemiah. Josephus on the other hand can state that the Johanan already mentioned acted as High Priest under the governor Bagoas, a contemporary of Artaxerxes II (404–359). Accordingly it can be assumed that the Johanan mentioned in Ezra 10.6 was the grandson of Eliashib, and that Ezra, in so far as we are dealing with a historical person at all, was active under Artaxerxes II. If however for one reason or another it is not desired to give so much weight to Ezra 10.6[9], it can be established that the Chronicler was working with the sequence of Persian kings Cyrus (Ezra 1.1), Xerxes (4.6), Artaxerxes (4.7), Darius (4.24) and Artaxerxes (7.1), while it should be noted that Neh. 13.13 knows nothing of Ezra 8.33, and Neh. 13.23 ff. nothing of Ezra 9–10. The dating given in Ezra 7.8 should therefore be regarded as being August 398.

The arrangement chosen by the editor of the story of Ezra and of the Memoirs of Nehemiah accordingly depends on a confusion of Artaxerxes I and Artaxerxes II, and is supported by the theological intention of placing before Nehemiah's secular mission of building the wall the spiritual activity of Ezra, which alone could ensure the prosperity of the Jewish religious community and the functioning of the theocracy. Since the Ezra narrative itself shows that the Chronicler had no authentic historical memory of this period, we must place the work of the Chronicler substantially later than the last event recounted by him. The professedly authentic Aramaic source, at least in its edited form, shows no basic knowledge of the history of the sixth and fifth centuries. It places the corres-

9. Cf. In der Smitten, p. 98.

pondence between Persian officials of the province of Samaria and King Artaxerxes I in Ezra 4.7–22 before that between the officials of the province Beyond the River and King Darius I (521–486) in 5.6–6.12, and expressly emphasizes in 4.24 that in this arrangement the correct sequence is being followed. Probably the author has confused Darius I with the Darius II (424–405) who reigned between the two Artaxerxes. This could hardly have been possible before the end of the Persian empire. The work of the Chronicler then is to be placed not before the year 300. Since Ezra 6.22 ascribes the assistance during the building of the temple to the Assyrian (i.e. Syrian) king, 2 Chr. 26.15 antedates the catapult, which was first invented in Syracuse about 400 B.C., to the eighth century, and Chronicles no less anachronistically presupposes for the period of the monarchy in Judah the Hellenistic Greek organization of the army, with its distinction of light and heavy armed troops, and its large numbers of troops, we must come down as late as the Seleucid period. Not the least argument for a late date is the literary character of the work of the Chronicler, which is a distinctive combination of both interpretation of the sources and free composition[10]. The work of the Chronicler must accordingly be placed between 300 and 200, its concluding redaction probably in the first half of the second century B.C. It should be noted that Rudolph and others oppose this late dating with an early date at the beginning of the fourth century.

6. *Purpose.* The concern of the book has been judged in different ways. While von Rad sees in it primarily a legitimation of cultic offices, and understands it at the same time as a transmitter of Messianic hopes[11], Noth has laid emphasis on the anti-Samaritan bias. Fundamentally one must agree with Rudolph, who ascribes to the Chronicler the intention of portraying the realization of the theocracy upon the territory of Israel, a realization based upon the separation off of Israel and the election of Jerusalem and Judah. With an eye to the stories of Ezra and Nehemiah, both of which he includes in the work of the Chronicler, he has formulated its purpose concisely as follows: '. . . a community gathered in zealous worship around its temple, devoted behind

10. Cf. Welten, pp. 98 ff. and 196 ff.
11. *Theology of the Old Testament* I, Edinburgh and London 1962, p. 352.

its secure walls to the performance of the law of God and inwardly separated from all external influences'[12]. In the paradigmatic representation of the period of the monarchy with its patterns of obedience to God, salvation and peace, and of sin, disaster, defeat and ruin, a theme with a future reference is contained[13]. If in the light of his representation of the period of the monarchy the question is put whether the Chronicler saw the theocracy as fully realized in his own time, the answer must in view of Ezra 9.7 be a negative one. When the community gathered around the temple paid full obedience to God, he would grant it also independent statehood, which for the Chronicler means also the restoration of the monarchy. Since the brief summary of the pre-Davidic period in the genealogical preface can be understood with this purpose in view, it is not necessary with Noth to understand this brevity from the fact that the Pentateuchal tradition was common to the Jerusalem and Samaritan communities, and accordingly was not controversial. An element of religious polemic cannot be excluded, even if 2 Chr. 13 and 30 are regarded as primarily interpretation of their Deuteronomistic original, in view of Ezra 4.1–3 with its possible reference to 2 Kgs. 17.24 ff., since such polemic is a necessary consequence of the exclusive Jerusalem outlook[14]. A measure of caution is necessary in respect of von Rad's hypothesis of the Levitical origin of the work, since with Willi we must allow for the possibility of a secondary expansion of the role of the Levites[15]. The prominence given to the Levites (cf. e.g. 2 Chr. 29) appears especially in the fact that for the Chronicler the Aaronite priesthood was included among the Levites. The belief in retribution, which has often been observed, and which has even been active as a hermeneutical principle in the editing of the tradition (cf. e.g. 2 Chr. 16.12 with 1 Kgs. 15.23; 2 Chr. 26.16–21 with 2 Kgs. 15.5; 2 Chr. 33.1–20 with 2 Kgs. 21.1–18 and 2 Chr. 35.20–25 with 2 Kgs. 23.29 f.) has its place as part of the theocratic ideal, as does the emphasis on the help to be expected exclusively from Yahweh, and dependent on no human assistance (cf. 2 Chr. 16.12 and 20.1–30).

12. HAT I, 20, p. xxiii; cf. HAT I, 21, p. xxiii.
13. Cf. also Willi, pp. 10 f. and 111 f.
14. Cf. Willi, pp. 190 ff. and Welten, pp. 172 f.
15. Cf. Willi, pp. 194 ff.

7. *The memoirs of Nehemiah.* The original extent of the memoirs of Nehemiah is given above[16]. In the definition of its literary character Mowinckel has at any rate eliminated one dead end. While before him scholars spoke readily of the memoirs of Nehemiah, he has kept it in mind that the fact of an account being in the first person is not on its own sufficient for such a description. Memoirs proper form a literary genre which can only arise against the background of biography and autobiography, and like these presupposes an interest in the individual personality which appeared in the Greek *polis*, and was lacking in the world of the Ancient Near East. What we find on comparable ancient Near Eastern royal inscriptions and on Egyptian tomb inscriptions is primarily intended not for the human reader but for the divine reader. If with these facts in mind we inquire into the literary genre of Nehemiah's work, we must start from 4.4 f. (Heb. 3.36 f.); 5.19; 6.14; 13.22 and 13.31, passages in which Nehemiah addresses himself directly to God. The verses 'Remember this also in my favour, O my God, and spare me according to the greatness of thy steadfast love' (13.22) and 'Remember me, O my God, for good' (13.31) are accordingly decisive for our understanding of the book. The book then is addressed to God. Mowinckel drew from these facts the conclusion that it is intended to bear witness for all time to Nehemiah's piety towards God, so that God will remember him while he is alive (and secure for him when dead a good repute and an eternal name). In regard to the specific ancestry of the book, von Rad has reminded us of its greater closeness to the biographical inscriptions from Egypt than to the ancient Near Eastern royal inscriptions. Kellermann, carrying the discussion further, observed that the book shared the appeal formula, the presentation of the material in the first person singular and the reference to enemies as well as the prayer for their punishment with the psalms of lamentation, and more particularly with the 'prayer of the man accused'. This literary type is found here in a specific variation adapted to the situation. The opposition of the clergy had compelled the governor upon his recall by the Persian king, which took place under pressure from his enemies, to put in writing his prayer, which had hitherto been uttered personally in the temple, and then to deposit it in the temple or to entrust it to friends. In any case the double character

16. Cf. p. 150.

of the book as intended for political self-justification and as a prayer for God's help is unmistakable. The intention of self-justification is sufficiently prominent for it to be necessary to regard the book as intended definitely for human readers too. If the attempt is made to find a name for its type, this must be broad enough to include both addressees. So the name proposed by Mowinckel of a *Denkschrift* is perhaps best suited in view of its neutrality to do justice to the ambivalence of the book. This is not to settle the question whether Mowinckel was wrong in attributing to Nehemiah at the same time the intention of erecting a monument to himself.

He also pointed to the possibility that the 'memorial book' was written by a scribe under the directions of Nehemiah, on the analogy of the ancient Near Eastern and Egyptian inscriptions (cf. Neh. 13.13). But the example of the statement of accounts deposited by Hannibal before his departure from Italy in the sanctuary of Hera on Cape Lacinium should warn us against overhasty conclusions[17].

The 'memorial book' is clearly divided into three main sections. The editing undertaken in the course of its incorporation into the work of the Chronicler has led to various disturbances of the original wording, which apart from the introduction are found especially in the third part.

I. Introduction: Nehemiah's appointment as governor and journey to Jerusalem, 1.1–4, 11b; 2.1b–11a*.
II. The main work of Nehemiah: the re-erection of the walls of Jerusalem, 2.11b–7.3*; 12.31 f., 37–40*.
III. Brief account of his other good works: 7.1–5a*; 13.4–31*.

The original introduction has been so altered by the novelistic embellishments of its redactors that the original text can no longer be established with certainty. The redactions wish to stress that God has directed the course of affairs in a miraculous manner. Thus they connect the book secondarily with the tradition of the stories of guidance as we encounter them e.g. in the stories of the patriarchs and of Joseph, of the rise of David and of the succession to him, and from the late period in the Book of Ruth, as well as in the books of Esther and Judith in their own par-

17. Cf. Polybius iii, 33, 18; 56, 4; Livy xxviii, 46, 16 and E. Groag, *Hannibal als Politiker*, Vienna 1929, p. 107.

ticular forms. When Nehemiah speaks, he recounts what he did and what difficulties he had to overcome in the course of this. By passing over the surrounding circumstances the story produces a deliberate concentration on the hero, who always stands at the centre of the action. All other characters appear either as receivers of a command or as followers, or else as obstacles or enemies to be overcome. Only when the good works are intended to be emphasized to produce an effect do we have a more detailed account of the difficulties which Nehemiah saw himself as facing. So in the last resort it is not the event with its internal connections but the single hero in his lonely greatness and in his pleasingness to God that stands at the centre of the story. It is this which gives the whole the monumental character of a memorial.

§ 18   The Book of Ruth

H. Gunkel, 'Ruth' [1905] in *Reden und Aufsätze*, Göttingen 1913, pp. 65 ff.; W. E. Staples, 'The Book of Ruth', *AJSL* 53 (1936–7), pp. 145 ff.; P. Humbert, 'Art et leçon de l'histoire de Ruth', *Revue de Théologie et Philosophie* 26 (1938), pp. 257 ff.; H. H. Rowley, 'The Marriage of Ruth', *HTR* 40 (1947), pp. 77 ff., and in *The Servant of the Lord*, Oxford 1965², pp. 169 ff.; J. M. Myers, *The Linguistic and Literary Form of the Book of Ruth*, Leiden 1955; S. Bertman, 'Symmetrical Design in the Book of Ruth', *JBL* 84 (1965), pp. 165 ff.; O. Eissfeldt, *Wahrheit und Dichtung in der Ruth-Erzählung*, SAL 110, 4, 1965, pp. 23 ff.
   Commentaries: KHC Bertholet 1898; KAT¹ Rudolph 1939; HAT Haller 1940; ATD Hertzberg 1953 (1965³); BK Gerleman 1960; KAT² Rudolph 1962; CB Gray 1967; HAT Würthwein 1969.

1. The Book. The Book of Ruth, consisting of only four chapters, is one of the masterpieces of Old Testament narrative art. Related to the old family sagas, and it may be conjectured growing from a popular narrative which was originally orally transmitted, its symmetrical structure, its elaborate style and speeches which serve to characterize the persons and bring out the significance of what is happening, indicate that it is artistic prose. The description of the legal process in the gate in 4.1–12 is unique within the Old Testament, and accordingly of the greatest importance for the history of ancient Israelite law[1].
   1. Cf. L. Köhler, 'Justice in the Gate', in *Hebrew Man*, London 1956,

The book is named after its main heroine. In Rabbinic tradition Samuel was regarded as its author, a hypothesis which because of its content can be regarded as untenable. The position of the book in the third part of the Hebrew canon, the *kᵉṯûḇîm* or writings, varied until it was placed among the five Megilloth or festival rolls[2]. Depending on whether the arrangement was made from the point of view of the supposed antiquity, or of the order of the feast assigned to the book, it was put either in the first place in the Megilloth or, as in the Codex Leningradensis, in second place. The connection of the book with the Feast of Weeks, which was the feast of wheat harvest and the forerunner of the Christian feast of Pentecost (cf. Exod. 23.16 and Acts 2.1), took place only in the post-Rabbinic period. The position of the book in Luther's Bible (and the English versions) and in other translations following the Book of Judges goes back to the Septuagint and the Vulgate, and depends on the date given in 1.1.

2. *Content.* The following division attempts to indicate the symmetrical structure demonstrated by Bertman:

1.1–5	The early history of Ruth.
1.6–18	Orpah's separation from Naomi when she returns home.
1.19–22	Ruth's decision to go with Naomi.
2	The encounter of Ruth and Boaz in the course of gleaning in the field.
3	Naomi's plan and the encounter at night between Ruth and Boaz on the threshing-floor.
4.1–12	The renunciation of Ruth by her 'redeemer'.
4.13–17a	Boaz's decision to take Ruth.
4.17b–22	The subsequent history of Ruth's family.

The narrative clearly takes its readers to times in the remote past: 'In the days when the judges ruled there was a famine in the land' (1.1). The theme of hunger, rooted in the Israelite saga tradition, in which it compels the patriarchs to emigrate (cf. Gen.

pp. 149 ff. I have unfortunately not been able to include a consideration of the study by T. and D. Thompson, 'Some Legal Problems in the Book of Ruth', *VT* 18 (1968), pp. 79 ff.

2. Cf. below, p. 406.

12, 20, 26 and 41 ff.), is given a new use and development: because of a famine which befalls Judah, the Bethlehemite Elimelech with his wife Naomi ('charm') and his two sons Mahlon ('sickness') and Chilion ('consumption') set out to go to Moab. After his death the two sons, already condemned to death by their names, take Moabite wives, Orpah ('rebellious') and Ruth ('companion'). The description of the relationship between Naomi and Ruth is perhaps intended as an example as is that of the behaviour of Boaz. The gleaning throws a significant light on the legal position of Ruth as a foreigner. The subtlety of the solicitous mother-in-law, which almost gives the effect of intrigue, is also intended as an example.

3. Purpose. Scholars differ about the purpose, background and dating of this narrative, which in type is to be classified as an idyllic tale. Starting from 4.17b ff. Budde thought that it was concerned to explain how it came about that David took his parents to Moab in flight from Saul[3]. Gerleman on the other hand assumes that the narrative is intended to explain the fact of the Moabite ancestry of Ruth. But it can be demonstrated that the connection of the narrative of Ruth with the genealogy of the family of David is secondary, and depends on a later identification of the name Boaz, which occurs in both traditions. In the background could stand the intention of providing the otherwise missing legend of the birth of David[4]. The genealogy in 4.18–22 comes from 1 Chron. 2.9–15 (cf. Matt. 1.3–6 and Luke 3.31–33). Further 4.17b is to be regarded as a secondary connection of the story of Ruth to the genealogy: after 4.17a one would have expected that a name would have been given to the child in 17b which connected up with a preceding mention of a name, e.g. Ben Noam (cf. e.g. 1 Sam. 4.21). The genealogical list in 4.18b begins with Perez. It conflicts therefore

3. K. Budde, *ZAW* 12 (1892), p. 43; cf. 1 Sam. 22.3.

4. Cf. J. Hempel, *Geschichten und Geschichte im Alten Testament*, Gütersloh 1964, p. 130; but cf. already Goethe, 'Noten und Abhandlungen zu besserem Verständnis des West-östlichen Divans', Gedenkenausgabe ed. E. Beutler, III, Zurich and Stuttgart 1959[2], p. 415: 'for example let us consider the Book of Ruth, which with its high purpose of providing respectable, interesting ancestors for a king of Israel, can also be treated as the most attractive little complete work which has been handed down to us in the epic and idyllic tradition'.

with the wish expressed in 4.12 that the house of Boaz should become as that of Perez. Finally it appears strange that Obed is regarded as the son of Boaz, and not, as the preceding narrative demands, as the son of Chilion. The historical problem is not eased if the conflict is ascribed to a difference between the intentions of the oral narrative and those of the author of the book.

More common is the view of e.g. Bertholet, Rost* and Weiser*; they find in the book an anti-rigorist bias directed against the dissolution of mixed marriages practised by Ezra and Nehemiah. To this it must be objected that undertones of this sort are contained neither in 1.4 nor in 4.6. The narrator does not indicate that he sees anything unusual in the marriage of the sons of Elimelech with the Moabite women, nor does he make the anonymous 'redeemer' retreat from the purchase of the field and from the marriage because of Ruth's Moabite origins.

Gunkel came nearer to the true position, although his view that the narrative is intended to celebrate the heroism of Ruth's fidelity and its reward by God does not satisfy. Rudolph, Haller, Hertzberg and Gerleman have in different ways emphasized the character of the story as a narrative of divine guidance. Here Rudolph has correctly pointed to 2.12 as the key. Perhaps one may with Würthwein say still more correctly, doing justice better too to the multiplicity of links within the narrative, that *hesed*, fidelity, stands at the centre of the story. From fidelity to the family of her dead husband Ruth travels with Naomi to Bethlehem, and connects herself with their people, God and land. Boaz rewards her fidelity to her family by keeping fidelity for his part. And Naomi, who because of her age can no longer play an active part, shows herself useful at least through her wise counsel. In the background stands God, who arranges all things so that human fidelity is given its reward. The didactic purpose, and therefore an origin in wisdom circles, are accordingly clear. The symbolic names of the sons and of the daughters-in-law of Naomi indicate to the reader the paradigmatic character of the narrative. The choice of a Moabite woman may also have been made deliberately in connection with the legal problem of Levirate marriage treated especially in 4.1 ff., in order to offer a solution of the problem of the special case of marriage with a non-Israelite. The place of origin of the story, in view of its setting in Bethlehem, is to be sought in Judah.

Staples, with whom Haller is in agreement, has sought the ultimate background of the story in a Bethlehemite vegetation cult, in which Elimelech and Naomi play the role of Tammuz and Ishtar, and Boaz/Baal that of the returning consort of the Goddess. He found in the background of the encounter of Ruth and Boaz on the threshing floor a fertility rite. Haller himself states that nothing of this can be seen now in the story itself. This being so, such conjectures can fairly be left out of consideration.

4. Date. The dating is not simple, as the divergent views about it show. It is clear in view of 1.1 and 4.7 that one cannot approach too near to the period of the judges. Scholars who look for a historical core behind the connection of the story of Ruth with the genealogy of David are inclined to a dating in the later part of the period of the kings, to provide time for the development of David into an ideal figure for the nation, and so to avoid a clash with the Deuteronomic, anti-Moabite tendency (cf. Deut. 23.3 ff. [Heb. 23.4 ff.]). The legal procedure in 4.1 ff., which is assumed to be older than that in Deut. 25.5 ff., is also claimed in support of a pre-exilic dating of the book[5]. On the other hand it is thought that a later post-exilic period must be excluded in view of the reforms of Ezra and Nehemiah. Since the account of Ezra is to be regarded as a very late fiction, one can only really rely on Neh. 13.23 ff. in support of this argument. When it is considered that in late Judaism there was a tendency to evade Deut. 23.3 ff. (Heb. 23.4 ff.), there are no insuperable objections to assuming the origin of the book in the fourth century B.C., nor to the connection of it with the genealogy of David being still later[6]. The late phrases, the clear references in the story to motifs from the Pentateuch, and the picture of a 'period of the judges' which is undoubtedly not pre-Deuteronomistic, can be claimed positively in favour of a late date[7].

5. Cf. e.g. M. Burrows, 'The Marriage of Boaz and Ruth', *JBL* 59 (1940), pp. 445 ff.
6. On the Ezra narrative cf. above, p. 181, on the Memoirs of Nehemiah, pp. 187 ff.; further J. Jeremias, *Jerusalem in the time of Jesus*, London 1969, pp. 235 and 320 ff.
7. Cf. the surveys in the commentaries. On the problem of a 'period of the judges' cf. above, p. 148.

Hans Schmidt, *Jona. Eine Untersuchung zur vergleichenden Religions-geschichte*, FRLANT 9, 1907; O. Loretz, 'Herkunft und Sinn der Jonaerzählung', *BZ* NF 5 (1961), pp. 18 ff.; N. Lohfink, 'Jona ging zur Stadt hinaus (Jona 4, 5)', *BZ* NF 5 (1961), pp. 185 ff.; U. Steffen, *Das Mysterium von Tod und Auferstehung. Formen und Wandlungen des Jona-Motivs*, Göttingen 1963; E. J. Bickerman, 'Les deux erreurs du prophète Jonas', *RHPhR* 45 (1965), pp. 232 ff.; H. W. Wolff, *Studien zum Jonabuch*, BSt 47, 1965; G. H. Cohn, *Das Buch Jona im Licht der biblischen Erzählkunst*, SSN 12, 1969; W. Rudolph, 'Jona', in *Arch-äologie und Altes Testament*, Festschrift K. Galling, Tübingen 1970, pp. 233 ff.; A. Jepsen, 'Anmerkungen zum Buche Jona', in *Wort–Gebot–Glaube*, Festschrift W. Eichrodt, ATANT 59, 1971, pp. 297 ff.; O. Kaiser, 'Wirklichkeit, Möglichkeit und Vorurteil. Ein Beitrag zum Verständnis des Buches Jona', *EvTh* 33 (1973), pp. 91 ff.

Commentaries: KHC Marti 1904; ICC Bewer 1912; HK Nowack 1922[3]; KAT[1] Sellin 1929[2–3]; HS Lippl 1937; HAT Robinson 1954[2] (1964[3]); CAT Keller 1965; ATD Weiser 1967[5].

1. The book. In the corpus of Old Testament prophets Jonah, which is part of the book of the twelve prophets, occupies a distinctive position, since it contains not a collection of prophetic sayings, but a narrative about a prophet.

2. Content. 1–2 tell of the flight of Jonah, who instead of obeying Yahweh's command and going to Nineveh, takes ship from Joppa to Tarshish, runs into a storm at sea on the way, and after his guilt has been recognized is thrown by the sailors into the sea, where a great fish swallows him at Yahweh's command, and after three days and nights spews him out again. The individual song of thanksgiving inserted in 2.2–9 (Heb. 2.3–10)[1] is intended to be appropriate to the specific situation of Jonah (cf. 2.3 and 5, Heb. 2.4 and 6).

In 3–4 we are told how Jonah obeyed the command of Yahweh which was now repeated, and went to Nineveh to announce to the city its destruction within forty (in the Septuagint, three) days. Then he leaves the city. But since Jonah's preaching brings all Nineveh to repentance, God decides not to destroy the city. In his wrath at this Jonah prays for death for himself. Yahweh

1. On the literary type cf. below, pp. 267 f.

however makes a castor oil plant grow up to give shade and consolation to Jonah, but makes a worm attack it next morning so that it withers. In his wrath at this the prophet again prays for death. With Yahweh's question whether his distress over Nineveh, that great city, is not more justified than that of Jonah over the castor oil plant, the story reaches both its goal and its end in 4.10 f.

3. *Intention and distinctive character.* The connection between 1–2 and 3–4 is loosely achieved by 4.2, where the flight of the prophet receives an explanation subsequently from his knowledge of God's mercy. While it is clear that the materials used have a previous history, it remains to be asked what factors were decisive for the author in his composition. Here it is better not to start from individual features such as the heathen sailors' fear of God, but to understand the *Novelle*, which moves forward purposefully from scene to scene towards its end, from its climax in 4.10 f. (as the story of Joseph is to be understood from Gen. 50.20). It is clearly directed against a temptation which had arisen in the Jewish community through the non-fulfilment of prophetic sayings directed against foreign nations, and been nourished by the juxtaposition of their own weakness and conscience of election with the superior strength of the Gentile nations, reminding them that the Gentiles too are God's creation and possibly more God-fearing than the Jews who profess to fear God (cf. 1.9 with 1.10–15, and 1.3 with 3.5–9). In this context the first two chapters (and in part the castor oil plant motif in 4) have the task of presenting Yahweh as the almighty Lord of his creation, and so of excluding doubt about his power. They also give the opportunity of contrasting the flight of the prophet from God with the devoutness of the Gentiles, in this case the sailors. It is clear that in this story we have a didactic composition which moves close to the question of theodicy. As such it did not have to avoid miraculous and comical traits, since its purpose and character could not be mistaken by contemporary readers or hearers. It does not deal with a conversion of Jonah. His last word is his wish for death: Yahweh's answer in 4.10 f., like Matt. 20.15, is left an open question to the reader.

4. The style is characterized not only by his liking for Biblical

phrases[2], but also by a preference for repetitions, whether of introductions to scenes (cf. 1.1–3 with 3.1–3), of phrases (cf. 1.10a with 16a; 1.11b with 13b; 1.6b with 3.9b; 4.4 with 9; 4.3b with 8bβ, cf. also 1.14 aα) or of particular words, like '*āmar*, 'say' (cf. 1.1, 6, 7, 9, 10, 11, 12, 14; 2.2, 4, 10 (Heb. 2.3, 5, 11); 3.4, 7; 4.2, 9 and 10), *qārā*', 'cry' (1.2, 6, 14; 2.2 (Heb. 2.3); 3.1, 4, 5, 8), *qûm*, 'arise' (1.2, 3, 6; 3.2, 3, 5), *mānâ*, 'appoint' (1.17 (Heb. 2.1); 4.6, 7, 8), *yārē*', 'be afraid' (1.5, 10, 16) *hēṭîl*, 'throw' (1.4, 5, 12, 15), *gāḏôl*, 'great' (1.2; 3.2; 4.11; 1.4, 12; 1.10, 16; 3.1; 3.5, 7; 4.1, 6) and for the creation of etymological plays on words (2.1, Heb. 2.2; 4.1 and 6). The clear flow of the narrative is increased by the fact that the captain of the ship used for the flight to Tarshish is left unnamed, as is the King of Nineveh, and that the scenes comprise at most two persons or groups. With its choice of words, its repetitions, Biblical allusions and repetitive style (cf. 1.5b, 10b; 4.2, 5) it must be regarded as a very consciously artistic prose.

5. *Literary-critical problems.* It is not certain, as is usually held, that 1.13 should be placed after 1.6, 4.5 after 3.4, and 4.5b deleted. On the other hand after the first question of Yahweh in 4.4 the missing answer of the prophet should perhaps be supplied from 4.9b as it stands. The change from Yahweh to Elohim which takes place in 4.6 and is maintained up to 4.9 (in 1.6, 3.5–10 Elohim (God) is found on the lips of Gentiles or in a narrative about them quite naturally, alongside Yahweh in 1.10 and 14) does not permit the deduction of a Yahweh and an Elohim recension (a hypothesis put forward most recently by Robinson), but is either to be regarded with Nowack as original, in an allusion to the creation narratives, or with Rudolph as a gloss made to emphasize the distance of man from the God who acts here so incomprehensibly. The psalm of 2.2–9 (Heb. 2.3–10) can be shown to be, for the most part, if not simply a compilation, at least a composition making use of fixed phrases from the psalter[3]; so that it may be doubted whether it ever existed independently. This may warn us to be cautious about the usual hypothesis of a subsequent insertion of the psalm into the book.

2. Cf. the instances in Kaiser, op. cit., p. 92, n. 7.
3. Cf. the instances in Kaiser, op. cit., p. 97, n. 22.

6. Motifs. The narrator chose a prophet of salvation mentioned in 2 Kgs. 14.25, but otherwise unknown, Jonah son of Amittai, as the hero of his *Novelle*. The fact that at the time of Jeroboam II Nineveh was not yet the capital of the Assyrian empire, but only obtained this position under Sennacherib, will not have been known to him, nor would it have worried him if it were. The motif of the swallowing up of the hero by a sea monster and of his release he may have taken from a story current in Joppa. It is not possible to decide whether it was already known to him as a miraculous sailors' story, or still in its earlier mythical form, in which it was connected with the fight of the rebellious sea against Baal.[4] The motif of the rapidly growing plant may have been taken from a fairy-tale. The reference back to Biblical motifs is not limited to the choice of the hero and of the subject of his message, the 'great city' of Nineveh (cf. Gen. 10.12).[5] The prophet's refusal and prayer for death (cf. 1 Kgs. 19.4) have been taken from scripture, as have some individual phrases. It is all the more striking that the author has succeeded in creating out of traditional material something completely new.

7. Date. Not only the author's manner of working, but also the language, which is full of Aramaisms, show that the book belongs to the late period. Sirach (cf. 49.10) and Tobit (cf. 14.4, 8), two writing which go back to the beginning of the second century B.C., presuppose a knowledge of it. The book comes from scribal wisdom circles, and can hardly have been written before the end of the fourth century, and more probably in the third, in view of its literary traditionalism and its description of Yahweh as the God of Heaven, which would fit the Persian period. On the other hand it is doubtful whether we can with Jepsen deduce from Jonah's refusal as a Hebrew to be God's envoy among the gentiles an origin in the eastern diaspora, and assume an argument against readiness for self-sacrifice.

8. Subsequent history. While Jesus meant by the sign of Jonah the faith which his preaching found (cf. Matt. 12.39, 41), the post-Easter Church saw in the fate of the prophet a prefiguring of the stay of the Son of Man in the underworld and of his

4. Cf. the discussion in Kaiser, op. cit., p. 96, n. 19.
5. Cf. above, n. 2.

release (cf. Matt. 12.40) and saw in this the sign that calls to repentance. In the Early Church Jonah became the symbol of the Christian hope of resurrection.

§ 20   The Book of Esther

H. Gunkel, *Esther*, RV II 19/20, 1916; J. Hoschander, *The Book of Esther in the Light of History*, Philadelphia 1923; H. Striedel, 'Untersuchungen zur Syntax und Stilistik des hebräischen Buches Esther', *ZAW* 55 (1937), pp. 73 ff.; H. Ringgren, 'Esther and Purim', *SEÅ* 20 (1955), pp. 5 ff.; R. Stiehl, 'Das Buch Esther', *Wiener Zeitschrift für die Kunde des Morgenlandes* 53 (1956), pp. 4 ff.; S. Talmon, ' "Wisdom" in the Book of Esther', *VT* 13 (1963), pp. 419 ff.; G. J. Botterweck, 'Die Gattung des Buches Esther im Spektrum neuerer Publikationen', *BiLe* 5 (1964), pp. 274 ff.; G. Gerleman, *Studien zu Esther*, BSt 48, 1966; J. C. H. Lebram, 'Purimfest und Estherbuch', *VT* 22 (1972), pp. 208 ff.

Commentaries: KHC Wildeboer 1898; HK Siegfried 1901; ICC Paton 1908; HAT Haller 1940; HS Schildenberger 1941; ATD Ringgren 1962²; KAT² Bardtke 1963; HAT Würthwein 1969; BK Gerleman 1973.

1. Evaluation and position in the Canon, Name and Author. While it is highly valued in Judaism, the Book of Esther with its ten chapters is one of the least known books of the whole Old Testament in the Christian Church. Within Protestantism this certainly does not depend solely on the well-known negative verdict of Luther, which he passed in the course of his work on 2 Macc.: 'I am so great an enemy to the second book of the Maccabees, and to Esther, that I wish they had not come to us at all, for they Judaize so much, and have too many heathen unnaturalities'[1]. It depends also on its subject matter as the *hieros logos* of the feast of Purim, and especially on its apparently completely secular attitude. Whatever view is taken of its value for the Christian reader, such judgements do not alter the fact that in this romance we have a noteworthy instance of Jewish literature in the age of Hellenism. Esther is one of those literary treasures of the Bible which are revealed to the reader on an

1. WA *TR* 1, p. 208, 30 f. A more complex picture is painted by H. Bardtke, *Luther und das Buch Esther*, SGV 240/1, 1964.

unprejudiced reading. However much the course of events in the book reads like a fairy-tale, on closer examination the narrator passes a sober judgement on both pogrom and counter-pogrom.

Like Ruth the Book of Esther is passed down in the Hebrew canon among the *keṯûḇîm*, the writings, and within them again among the *Megilloth*, the festival rolls². The first point is connected with the late origin of the book, the other with its appointment as a reading for the feast of Purim. The Septuagint places the book after *Esdras b* (Ezra-Nehemiah) and before Judith among the historical books³. In the Lutheran Bible and the versions which agree with it, Esther comes at the end of the historical books, in consequence of the omission of the so-called Apocrypha. The book is named after its heroine. From late antiquity until recently Mordecai was regarded as its author in the western parts of the Church, an assumption that rests on a misunderstanding suggested by 9.20.

2. Division and content. The book divides into three parts:

I	1.1–2.23	Exposition
II	3.1–9.32	Central section
III	10.1–3	Conclusion

The exposition begins in 1 with the narrative of the repudiation of the Persian queen Vashti by her husband Ahasuerus, in order to make clear how the beautiful Jewess Esther or Hadassah, the cousin and ward of Mordecai, a man from the family of King Saul who was active in the king's gate in the court city of Susa, was able to rise to be queen (2.1–18). To provide the setting for the later change in fortunes of Mordecai and of the Jews in the whole empire, we are next told of his discovery of a plot directed against the life of the king (2.19–23). In 3.1–15 the dramatic plot at once thickens: the second man in the kingdom, Haman, had obtained a decree from Ahasuerus according to which he too was entitled to obeisance. Mordecai's refusal to obey led

2. Cf. below, pp. 406 f.

3. It should be noticed that the Greek versions contain important variations, and an addition now usually placed in the Apocrypha, compared with the Hebrew text. C. C. Torrey, *HTR* 37 (1944), pp. 1 ff., attempts to explain the differences by the assumption that an Aramaic original underlies both forms of the text.

to a royal decree which exposed all Jews to plunder and murder. The 13th of Adar was decided upon by lot (*pûr*) for carrying out the decree. Mordecai meanwhile succeeded in persuading Esther to risk her life on an intervention with the king (4.1–17). Appearing before Ahasuerus unsummoned, she obtained his favour, and a promise that he would accept her invitation to come to a feast together with Haman (5.1–8). So Haman fancied himself at the high point of his favour, and urged on by his supporters had the gallows erected in advance for Mordecai (5.9–14). But the king could not sleep, and was reminded by the reading of his chronicles of the unrewarded service of Mordecai. Accordingly he had Haman called, to question him in general terms about the circumstances of royal honouring. Assuming that the question concerned himself, he suggested clothing in the royal garments, and presentation upon one of the king's horses in the city, advice which he himself then had to carry out for Mordecai (6.1–14). At the following banquet, at which the king appeared together with Haman according to Esther's invitation, Esther revealed the plot of Haman against the Jews. When the king after rushing out in anger returned into the hall, and found Haman weeping for his life upon the queen's couch, he misinterpreted the scene, and ordered Haman's execution upon the gallows erected for Mordecai (7.1–10). A further intervention of Esther with the king obtained authorization for Mordecai, who meanwhile had been admitted to the king's presence, to carry out a new decree which made possible for the Jews the destruction of their enemies in the whole kingdom (8.1–17). So on the previously appointed day of the 13th of Adar, and in Susa also on the following 14th, the enemies of the Jews in the whole kingdom were destroyed (9.1–19). In accordance with a decree of Mordecai and a command of Esther the feast celebrated by the Jews after the massacre became a regular institution of the Jews in the whole kingdom (9.20–32). The conclusion in 10.1–3, apart from v. 1, which must be considered separately, attempts to underline the impression of the historicity of the narrative by a reference to a 'chronicle of the Kings of Media and Persia'.

3. The problem of historicity. The book attempts to give an impression of historicity elsewhere too through an appearance of exactness in its narrative, in which there are numerous dates[4], and even very subsidiary figures are given a name[5]. Facts about the kingdom and its provinces[6], distinction made among the

4. Cf. 1.3; 2.16; 3.7, 12; 4.11; 5.1, 9; 6.1; 8.1, 9, 12; 9.1, 15, 17–19 and 21.
5. Cf. 1.10, 14; 2, 3, 14, 21; 4.5; 5.10; 7.9 and 9.7–9.
6. Cf. 1.1 and 9.30.

royal officials and servants[7] and a whole series of facts about the royal palace in Susa[8] have the same purpose.

Nevertheless it can be demonstrated without difficulty that Esther is not a factual account, but a historical romance. Ahasuerus, the Greek Xerxes I, reigned from 486–465/4 B.C. He had neither a wife called Vashti nor one called Esther. She was in fact called Hutaosa, or in Greek Atossa. In his seventh year (cf. 2.16) Xerxes had other things on his mind than choosing a new wife: the battle at Salamis fell in the year 480. Finally Mordecai, who according to 2.6 was deported together with Jeconiah or Jehoiachin under Nebuchadnezzar (597 B.C.), would now be about 120 years old, and his cousin an ageing matron rather than an attractive girl.

4. Previous history. When this has been established, the real puzzle begins with the search for the antecedents of the materials taken over. In spite of the compositional skill of the author, it can still be seen that the stories of Vashti, of Haman and Mordecai, and of Esther, each had their own prehistory. The story of Vashti is not indispensable for what follows. The independence of the story of Haman and Mordecai still appears e.g. in the name Hadassa given to Esther in 2.7. Lebram has deduced from the strange fact that according to 9.18 f. a distinction is made between the feast celebrated by the Jews in the provinces on Adar 14, and that celebrated by the Jews in Susa on Adar 15, that we must distinguish between a Palestinian Mordecai tradition (cf. 2.21–23; 3.1–6; 5.9–14; 6.1–13 and 7.7–10) and an Esther tradition located in the eastern diaspora, which have been skilfully united by the author of the book, though not without inconsistencies (cf. 2.22 with 6.1f.; 3.7 ff. with 9.24, and 9.25 with 8.2, 3 ff. and especially 8 ff.). The names of the heroes and of their opponents too are noteworthy: in the names of Mordecai and of Esther we can hear those of the Babylonian gods Marduk and Ishtar, in the names of Haman and Zeresh (cf. 5.14) those of the Elamite gods Human and Kiri-Risha. It should not however be overlooked that Mordecai is listed among the returning exiles in Ezra 2.2, par. Neh. 7.7. It has also been thought that in Vashti the Elamite goddess Mashti could be recognized, but her name

7. Cf. 1.3, 10, 13 f.; 2.3, 14, 21; 3.12, 13, 2 and 2.9.
8. Cf. 1.5; 2.11; 4.11; 5.1 f.; 6.4 f.; 2.19; 4.6 and 2.3.

is now read as Parti. The fact that the story correctly connects the Jewish feast of Purim with the non-Hebrew word *pûr* (lot), which is found in Akkadian in this sense, and with determining in the first month a day in the following twelfth month (cf. 3.7) must encourage the search for non-Jewish antecedents of the feast.

Winckler and Zimmern thought in terms of a Babylonian nature myth, in which the Babylonian gods of light conquer the Elamite gods (of darkness). Since no evidence has so far been found for this hypothesis, we may think rather more generally of the Babylonian New Year Festival, to which a determining of fates for the following year belonged[9]. It must however be noticed that the feast of Purim does not fall on the day of the casting of lots at the beginning of the year, but on the day at the end of the year which was chosen by lot. Finally a reference to the feast of the Magophonia attested by Herodotus, III, 68 ff., which the Persians are supposed to have celebrated in remembrance of the murder of Pseudo-Smerdes and his Magi, finds a place in the discussion. Ringgren sees in it the autumn form of the Persian New Year Festival. Lagarde at the end of the last century thought of a Persian feast of the dead. If one is thinking of a non-Palestinian centre for the formation of the legend it can be understood well especially in the Hellenistic period that it should be Susa, the old capital of the Elamites, which was well suited to be a crucible for very different traditions[10].

It may be cautiously conjectured that the Jewish feast of Purim originated in a Persian New Year Festival, and was first taken over by the Jews in the Eastern diaspora[11]. Experiences of persecution of Jews must have played a part in this. Since the Book of Esther wishes to commend the feast among the Jews and give it a Jewish basis, it can be understood why it has carefully avoided more precise indications of the antecedents of the feast.

5. *Date and place of origin*. It is already apparent that the Book of Esther is a relatively late book from the fact that the author has no more precise information about the Persian period. If in view of the numerous details about the royal court in Susa one allows for local knowledge (Gunkel), one must go down to the Seleucid

9. Cf. A. O. Haldar in *RLA* III, 1, Berlin 1957, pp. 42 f.

10. Cf. also R. de Vaux, *Ancient Israel*, London 1961, pp. 515 ff.

11. H. Ringgren, *SEÅ* 20 (1955), pp. 5 ff., cf. pp. 23 f., refers to a series of parallel motifs which form a pattern, some of which the book of Esther has taken up in a new pattern.

period, in which the court was first moved to the citadel, cf. 1.2 (Ruth Stiehl). Bardkte has seen correctly that nothing compels us to attribute to the author more than current ideas about life at a royal court in his days. Linguistic studies have shown that the book cannot be dated before 300 B.C. The *terminus ad quem* is given by the colophon, or concluding formula, of the Greek translation, which Bickerman has dated to the year 78/77 B.C.[12]. The book originated therefore between 300 and 100 B.C. From the relationship of certain features in the Book of Esther to features in the books of Daniel and of Judith we can probably more exactly infer a date in the first half of the second century B.C.

As the colophon to the Greek translation shows, the book did not in any case originate in Egypt. In spite of Bardtke, it cannot be demonstrated that the author had available a written source for the situation at the Persian court. In spite of the closeness emphasized by Stiehl to the Hellenistic novel, from which the erotic role of the woman has been taken over into Jewish literature, and of the subject matter of the pogrom, the author is not necessarily to be placed in diaspora Judaism; for if it is right that we must follow Lebram in distinguishing between a Palestinian Mordecai tradition and an Esther tradition belonging to the eastern diaspora, we must look for the author who united the two traditions in Palestine rather than in the east.

6. *Purpose.* In spite of the stress placed on the aim of commending the feast of Purim, it is not possible to bring the purpose of the book under a single heading.

Gerleman's attempt to show that the narrative is written in conscious antithesis to the Exodus story, and in view of its strikingly secular character means to speak as it were in code of a saving act of God, must be regarded as dubious. It is better to assume, with Lebram, that in its present form it is designed to interpret political events as the fulfilment of eschatological expectations, in the spirit of the Maccabaean period (cf. 9.22 with Deut. 12.10, 25.19 and Jer. 31.13).

The belief in a special divine protection of the Jews does indeed appear clearly enough in 4.14 and 6.13 (with the actual word God avoided) for the Jewish reader. Against the background of this faith the novel is concerned with what Jews

12. *JBL* 63 (1944), p. 347.

themselves can do to save themselves in a time of persecution. In Mordecai the image of a man is held up to them who holds fast faithfully to his Judaism, and does not deny it even at risk of his life. Esther is the Jewess who obtains rank and respect in a strange world and marriage but is saved by her fellow-believers from complete assimilation, and then nevertheless risks her life for the deliverance of her people. In this paradigmatic picture Talmon correctly recognizes the influence of wisdom and of its didactic tendencies, as well as the linking up of wisdom and fairy tale motifs[13]. Lebram has underlined that the traditions which are re-worked here have their roots in Jewish wisdom, pointing out that certain traits from the Story of Ahikar[14] live on in the figure of Mordecai, that cross-connections seem to exist in the figure of Haman himself with the Book of Tobit (cf. Tob. 14.10 G[pl MSS]), the hero of which is in turn said by Tob. 1.21 to be Ahikar's uncle, and that a relationship to Dan. 1–6 cannot be overlooked.[15] Equally correctly Daube sees that the narrator has not only Jewish but also Gentile readers in view. He intends to suggest to them the view that the state will improve its finances not by a pogrom but by taxation. He assures them that the Jews, unlike their enemies, do not aim to seize the property of their enemies[16]. The fairy-tale motifs appear e.g. in the rise of a young girl who is one of an oppressed group to be queen, in the granting of a petition up to half the kingdom (cf. 5.6; 7.2) and in the victory of the innocent persecuted man over his persecutor. The characters are strongly stylized. The rejected Vashti is contrasted with the wise and fortunate Esther, the overbearing, self-seeking and cruel Haman is contrasted with

13. *VT* 13 (1963), pp. 419 ff.

14. The Story of Ahikar was discovered in an Aramaic version of the fifth century B.C. in the ruins of the Jewish military colony of Elephantine. A narrative framework about the fate of Ahikar, chancellor of the Assyrian kings Sennacherib and Esarhaddon, stylized as a first-person account, has inserted into it sayings of the wise, in which repeated mentions of Shamash, the sun-god and upholder of righteousness, also argue for a Mesopotamian origin for the story. So the Story of Ahikar gives us evidence for the connections between Jewish and Mesopotamian wisdom. Cf. the translations in *AOT²*, pp. 454 ff., *ANET³*, pp. 427 ff. and *DOTT*, pp. 270 ff., where the Syriac version is translated.

15. Op. cit., pp. 213 ff.

16. Cf. 10.1 and 9.10, 15, and Daube, 'The Last Chapter of Esther', *Jewish Quarterly Review* 37 (1946/7), pp. 139 ff.

the faithful and successful Mordecai. The role of the mighty man is portrayed only inconsistently in the figure of the king, who in the last resort appears as the irresolute tool of his surroundings. The fairy-tale expresses an expectation of how things should properly be in the world. In the story a positive solution is given to the real conflict between a naïve desire for good fortune, the expectation of righteousness, and the amoral reality. It should not be overlooked that Judaism in a time of uncertainty and persecutions could express in this story the fulfilment of the wishes which history withheld from it, the fulfilment of the wish for recognition and righteousness, and for the visible confirmation of the faith that God is hiddenly but nevertheless miraculously at work in history.

D. Israel's Prophetic Tradition

§ 21 Prophecy in Israel

G. Hölscher, *Die Propheten*, Leipzig 1914; B. Duhm, *Israels Propheten*, Tübingen 1922²; A. Jepsen, *Nabi*, Munich 1934; A. R. Johnson, *The Cultic Prophet in Ancient Israel*, Cardiff 1944, 1962²; G. von Rad, *Old Testament Theology*, vol. 2 [1960], Edinburgh and London 1965; J. Lindblom, *Prophecy in Ancient Israel*, Oxford 1962; J. Scharbert, *Die Propheten Israels bis 700 v. Chr.*, Cologne 1965; id., *Die Propheten Israels um 600 v. Chr.*, Cologne 1967; P. R. Ackroyd, *Exile and Restoration*, OTL, London 1968.

H. H. Rowley, 'The Nature of Old Testament Prophecy in the Light of Recent Study' [1945], in *The Servant of the Lord*, Oxford 1965², pp. 95 ff.; G. Fohrer, 'Neuere Literatur zur alttestamentlichen Prophetie', *ThR* NF 19 (1951), pp. 277 ff.; NF 20 (1952), pp. 193 ff., 295 ff.; O. Eissfeldt, 'The Prophetic Literature', in *OTMS*, Oxford 1951, pp. 115 ff.; H. Krämer, R. Rendtorff, R. Meyer and G. Friedrich, '*prophētēs*', *TDNT* VI, Grand Rapids, Michigan 1968, pp. 781 ff.; *Tradition und Situation. Studien zur alttestamentlichen Prophetie*, Festschrift A. Weiser, ed. E. Würthwein and O. Kaiser, Göttingen 1963; F. Nötscher, 'Prophetie im Umkreis des alten Israel', *BZ* NF 10 (1966), pp. 161 ff.; G. Fohrer, *Studien zur alttestamentlichen Prophetie*, BZAW 99, 1967; I. Engnell, 'Prophets and Prophetism' [1962], in *Critical Essays on the Old Testament*, ed. J. T. Willis and H. Ringgren, London 1970, pp. 122 ff.; K.-H. Bernhardt, *Prophetie und Geschichte*, SVT 22, 1972, pp. 20 ff.

Name. The word prophet goes back to the Greek *prophētēs*, which originally 'denotes the one who speaks in the name of a god, declaring the divine will and counsel in the oracle'[1]. The Septuagint uses *prophētēs* to render the Hebrew word *nabî'*, which is related to the Akkadian *nabû*, 'cry, announce', and the

---

1. H. Krämer, *TDNT* VI, p. 795.

Arabic *naba'a*, 'inform'. Depending on whether the Hebrew noun form is understood as an active or a passive, the translation 'speaker', or else 'one called', is obtained. At present the passive interpretation is preferred, with the support of the Akkadian *nabium*, 'one who is called'[1a].

1. The Problem. A history of Israelite prophecy which solves satisfactorily all the problems that arise cannot yet be written. In view of the position about sources, it must be assumed that many problems can only be solved conjecturally for all time. The prehistory of Old Testament prophecy is obscure to us. We have to rely on religio-historical and ethnological comparative material to illuminate it. The beginnings of Israelite prophecy are in semi-darkness; we have available as sources for it only accounts by non-prophets, often in the form of scattered reports, which until their fixing in writing have undergone a lengthy process of oral transmission, during which they have been exposed to the most varied influences. We have a large number of collections of sayings of the classical prophets of the eighth–sixth centuries, and also of the exilic and post-exilic prophets, but not clear reports of the circumstances of their activity. The prophetic books themselves have undergone a history often lasting centuries until their final completion, in the course of which the prophetic sayings originally contained in them have been frequently worked over, expanded, rearranged, supplemented by sayings of different origin, and linked up with whole blocks of tradition with a separate provenance. The history of the redaction of the books has up till now been only inadequately investigated. In answering the question who their transmitters and redactors were we are dependent on conjectures. Establishing which individual sayings are to be ascribed to each particular prophet depends on a careful delimitation of the units with application of strict criteria about literary types, a comparative investigation of vocabulary, style and ideas, and not least of the general historical picture of the period. In view of the situation just sketched, it is methodologically justified to work with the

1a. An examination of the instances of the noun in the Old Testament shows that the description of individual prophets as *nābî'* is essentially due to the Deuteronomistic movement. Cf. K.-H. Bernhardt, op. cit., pp. 26 ff.

postulate that it is not the inauthenticity but the authenticity of the sayings ascribed to the prophets that needs to be proved.

2. *The phenomenon of prophecy.* Although there has occasionally been a one-sided derivation of Old Testament prophecy from the ecstatic prophecy of the Canaanites, it is probable that it had a double origin. One origin, in accordance with the sociological origin of the later Israelite tribes, is to be found in nomadic seers, the other in Ancient Oriental ecstatic prophecy, which is not confined to the Canaanites. While it cannot be excluded that the Israelites had already come into contact with it in the pre-historic period, they must in any case have encountered it after their entry into the land. What is determinative for Israelite prophecy however is not its prehistory, but its connection with Yahweh, whose claim to lordship it asserted.

The self-understanding of the prophets as messengers of Yahweh appears clearly in the messenger formula *kô 'āmar yahwê*, 'Thus says Yahweh . . .' at the beginning of a saying, and in the quotation formula *nᵉ'um yahwê*, 'utterance of Yahweh' at the end of a saying. If we see in the prophet the proclaimer of the will of God, who with exhortation, invective, threats and consolation announces to the nation the future determined for it by God, we must nevertheless remain conscious that the prophets understood their word not as a bare announcement, but at the same time as an active power, itself bringing about the thing announced (cf. Isa. 9.8 [Heb. 9.7]; Hos. 6.5; Jer. 23.29; Isa. 55.10 f. and Ps. 107.20). Similarly the symbolic actions of the prophets are not only understood as pedagogical and propagandist means of emphasizing their sayings, but as effective actions which bring about that which has been portrayed (cf. e.g. 2 Kgs. 13.14 ff.; Isa. 8.1 ff.; 20.1 ff.; Hos. 1.2 ff.; 3.1 ff.; Jer. 13.1 ff.; 32.1 ff.; Ezek. 4, 5 and 12)[2]. In both cases there is a clear link between prophecy and a magical understanding of the world. In contrast to magic as such, however, the effect of word and action depends not on the proper performance of them by

---

2. Cf. G. Fohrer, *Die symbolischen Handlungen der Propheten*, ATANT, 54, 1968[2]; id., 'Prophetie und Magie', *ZAW* 78 (1966), pp. 25 ff., also in *Studien*, BZAW 99, 1967, pp. 242 ff.; and K. Goldammer, 'Elemente des Schamanismus im Alten Testament', in *Ex orbe religionum*, Festschrift G. Widengren II, Leiden 1972, pp. 266 ff.

a particularly gifted and instructed personality, but on commissioning by God.

The reception of the word, the audition is the principal means of revelation, and is part of the primary function of the prophets. The word of Yahweh was experienced not as a result of a man's own wishes or dreams, but as something external, which pressed in on the prophet even against his will and peremptorily demanded to be proclaimed (cf. Jer. 20.7 ff.)[3]. The prophets also tell of their visions, not because of the abnormal experience, but either to legitimate their commissioning (cf. Isa. 6; Jer. 1.4 ff.; Amos 7.1 ff.), or to communicate the word revealed in the course of the vision (cf. Amos 9.1 ff.; Jer. 24.1 ff.; Zech. 1.7–6.8). The visions are consequently subordinated to the auditions[4].

The dream was regarded as of lesser quality in comparison with the revelation by word, as is shown by Num. 12.6 ff. and Jer. 23.25 ff. (cf. also Sir. 31.1 ff.; Aristeas 213 ff.), although it was regarded as a means of revelation down to the late period (cf. Job 33.15 f.; 4.12 ff.). The prophetic receipt of revelation is like every inner experience open to the possibility of a causal explanation. There is a limit to the possibilities of psychological analysis imposed by the nature of the sources. For the prophets were concerned not to describe their extraordinary situations and experiences, but to carry out the commission given to them. For this reason any psychological inquiry is dependent largely on analogical deductions and circumstantial evidence, in which the comparative material must be taken from our own period. This assumes that the mental experiences of men have remained identical at least within limits down the ages. But we must also allow for the possibility, if not the fact, that in the course of the history of mankind a change in the nature of consciousness has taken place, which is matched by a change in the view generally taken of unusual states of consciousness. Otherwise the general opinion would treat prophetic auditions and visions out of hand as psychopathological phenomena, since the material for com-

---

3. Cf. F. Haeussermann, *Wortempfang und Symbol in der alttestamentlichen Prophetie*, BZAW 58, 1932; S. Mowinckel, *Die Erkenntnis Gottes bei den alttestamentlichen Profeten*, Oslo 1941; I. P. Seierstad, *Die Offenbarungserlebnisse der Propheten Amos, Jesaja und Jeremia*, SNVAO II, 1946, 2, 1946 (1965[2]).

4. Cf. F. Horst, 'Die Visionsschilderungen der alttestamentlichen Propheten', *EvTh* 20 (1960), pp. 193 ff.

parison from our own time within the orbit of European civilization is primarily clinical[5].

As a starting point for examination and more exact description of the phenomena attested in the texts only the following points of differentiation need be mentioned here: in acoustic occurrences a distinction must be made between internal and external auditions; in internal auditions voices are heard without any connection with the external world in the imagination, in external auditions the origin of that which is heard is located in the external world. The case is similar with internal and external visions: in internal visions (*visio interna*) the place where the experience takes place is completely blotted out, and both the place seen and the objects come from the imagination. In external visions (*visio externa et corporalis*) the object seen is projected into the world of experience. Symbolic visual perceptions are to be distinguished from visions in the strict sense. Their subject is objectively given in external experience, but obtains the quality of revelation for the observer by its symbolic content.

In respect of content, following Horst we can distinguish between symbolic visions, assonance or word-play visions, and event visions[6]. A symbolic vision is to be found e.g. in Jer. 1.13 f., an assonance or word-play vision in Jer. 1.11 f. and an event vision in Isa. 6.

In giving a psychological explanation of all these phenomena it is best to start from the dream, which as an experience known to all men allows us to recognize that many of the problems which concern man by day are worked out at a subconscious level of the mind. So too in the auditions and visions of the prophets the life of the mind and its normal conscious content are not abrogated. If the prophet is particularly concerned with a problem, it is worked out in his subconscious. To the extent that it is emotionally charged for him, a mental and sometimes physical tension can take hold of him, which can be expressed in a way that either releases or binds up energy. Meanwhile an answer to the problem is being prepared in the subconscious, to break at last violently into his consciousness. An abrogation of normal consciousness does not have to take place in the course

5. Cf. K. Jaspers, *General Psychopathology*, Manchester 1963, pp. 733 and 738 ff. 6. Op. cit.

of this eruption from the depths of the mind[7]. On the basis of this attempt at an explanation, which is based on that of Haeussermann, it is understandable that attempts were made to induce a prophetic situation by means of musical and rhythmical inspiration, or by inspiration through concentration (cf. 2 Kgs. 3.14 ff.; Hab. 2.1 and Isa. 21.8), although such attempts are not characteristic of the writing prophets. In analysing the sayings of the prophets a distinction must be made at least in theory between the secret experience of the prophet (as Gunkel puts it) and its rational and artistic interpretation and formation. If it cannot be excluded on the analogy of poetic inspiration that sayings came to the prophet in poetic form, we must at least ask whether and how far we have in them the result of a process of reflection and a conscious choice of form. Traces of rationalizing editing can be found especially in the grounds given for divine judgements[8], and the artistic choice of form in the use of literary types which do not necessarily belong to prophetic speech. The fact that prophetic utterance as being divine utterance had to be made in exalted language assists in distinguishing between sayings of the prophets that were really uttered, and literary additions in the prophetic books.

3. Prophecy and cult. It is a disputed question whether and to what extent the prophets were institutionally connected with a sanctuary. The fact that in the prophets we are dealing with charismatic figures suggests that at best we could have a unity of charisma and cultically ordered function which was full of tension. Talk of a prophetic office introduces the picture of an institution that does not fit the facts, and is therefore better avoided[9].

In this connection a brief retrospect of the early history of Old Testament prophecy is inevitable. As well as the *rō'eh*, the seer, we encounter the *ḥōzeh*, the viewer (cf. 1 Sam. 9.9; 2 Sam. 24.11). It can be seen from 1 Sam. 9 that a man would have

7. For a discussion of prophetic ecstasy cf. Rowley, op. cit., pp. 97 ff.

8. On the phenomenon of an incongruence between judgement and its grounds, guilt and punishment, cf. H. W. Schmidt, *EvTh* 31 (1971), pp. 630 ff.

9. Cf. O. Plöger, 'Priester und Prophet', *ZAW* 63 (1951), also in *Aus der Spätzeit des Alten Testaments*, Göttingen 1971, p. 29.

recourse to the seer, from whom the 'viewer' cannot be functionally distinguished, if he wanted to uncover a state of affairs
which was hidden to him. This does indeed presuppose that the
seer had a certain measure of control over his abilities. Since his
presence is expected on a *bāmâ*, a cultic mound, his power of
divination was no doubt explained by inspiration by the deity.
As well as the seer we find in the story of Saul the band of the
prophets, *ḥebel nᵉbî'îm* (1 Sam. 10.5 ff.). These seem to have
reached an ecstatic state by means of music and dancing (cf.
also 1 Sam. 19.18 ff. and Jer. 29.26). We meet groups of prophets
among the Canaanite prophets of Baal (1 Kgs. 18.21 ff.), in the
Samarian court prophets (1 Kgs. 22.6 ff.) and also in the *bᵉnê
hannᵉbî'îm*, the (sons of) the prophets (1 Kgs. 20.35 ff., 2 Kgs. 2–9),
in the circle of Elisha[10]. It can be deduced from 1 Kgs. 22.6 ff.
that the court prophets had the task of ensuring *šālôm*, prosperity,
for the community. The (sons of the) prophets appear to have
been connected particularly with the sanctuaries of Gilgal and of
Bethel. A connection with a wandering individual prophet, such
as we find as a type first in Elijah and Elisha, is also implied.
But such men too, like the seer earlier, were asked about private
problems in a holy place at a holy season, according to 2 Kgs.
4.23. It cannot be denied that some at least of the so-called
writing prophets appeared at a sanctuary too (cf. e.g. Amos 7.10
ff.; Isa. 6; Jer. 7.1 ff.; 26.1 ff.; 19.1 ff.; 20.1 ff.; Lam. 2.20)[11].
It is also certain that they were not the only prophets in their
time (cf. Isa. 28.7 ff.; Mic. 3.5 ff.; Jer. 23.9 ff. and 28.1 ff.), and
that a priest was appointed in the temple at Jerusalem to exercise
oversight of the prophets (Jer. 20.1 f. and 29.26 ff.). On the basis
of a whole series of psalms the assumption has further been
made that there were prophets within the cult who were active
as intercessors and as givers of oracles (cf. e.g. Ps. 2.7 ff.; 50.7 ff.;
60.6 ff. [Heb. 60.8 ff.] par. 108, 7 ff. [Heb. 108.8 ff.] and 89.19
ff. [Heb. 89.20 ff.]; also 2 Chr. 20.14 ff.). The more the position
of the prophet in the cult was a liturgical one the more inevitably

10. Cf. H.-C. Schmitt, *Elisa*, Gütersloh 1972, pp. 162 ff. and 189 f.
11. The intercession practised by the prophets may also point to their
cultic function (cf. e.g. Gen. 20.7; Amos 7.2, 5; Jer. 14.1 ff., 11; 14.19–15.4
and F. Hesse, *Die Fürbitte im Alten Testament*, 1951, but also H. W.
Hertzberg, 'Sind die Propheten Fürbitter?', in *Tradition und Situation*,
pp. 63 ff.).

the question is posed to what extent they gave their oracles on the basis of genuine inspiration. The controversial central problem however is the further question whether the writing prophets too are in whole or part to be put on the same level as the cultic prophets in principle or not[12]. Even if it must be allowed that most of the prophetic sayings preserved to us from the time of the first temple were uttered in the temple, two possible ways of understanding the prophets remain open. The writing prophets could have made external use of the image of the cultic prophet. The difference would then lie less in their function than in the content of their message. Or it could be assumed that these prophets had nothing at all in common with the activities of the cultic prophets, but only appeared in the sanctuary if they were driven to it by a specific divine commission. Even if it is remembered that such an alternative may be artificial, because all prophets as charismatics claimed at least to speak only under the influence of inspiration, so that the difference between the cultic prophets and the writing prophets would again rest only in the content of their message, it must be realized that Yahweh could make use of a cultic or guild prophet, of another cultic person, or even of a layman as a recipient of revelation, just as was the case with the prophets of Mari[13]. As charismatics the prophets remained essentially unpredictable (cf. Amos 7.10 ff.; Jer. 29.26 ff.) and their utterance uncontrollable (Lam. 2.9)[14].

4. Prophecy and tradition. The prophets, like everyone else, were as children of their own time dependent on their own presuppositions of thought, and on religious and general ideas which they regarded as obvious. For this reason traditio-historical investigation of the sayings of the prophets forms a legitimate branch of scholarship. But more decisive for the understanding of their message than the demonstration of links with past and present is noticing what they have to say in respect of the tension between tradition and their own situation. A traditio-historical investigation accordingly is only worthwhile when it contributes

12. It is almost universally agreed now that Nahum, Habakkuk, Obadiah and Haggai, and to a certain extent also Zechariah and Joel, were cultic prophets of salvation.

13. Cf. F. Ellermeier, *Prophetie in Mari und Israel*, TOA 1, 1968, p. 83.

14. Jer. 23.30 refers to abuses (the stealing of sayings).

to our understanding of the texts. It can be demonstrated that the dependence of the prophets on tradition increases as the living force of prophecy flags, and finally gives way to scribalism and apocalyptic speculation, or falls into contempt (cf. Zech. 13.1 ff.).

5. *Content of the preaching.* With regard to the content of the prophetic message it can first be stated that it consists not of prophecy as a neutral prediction of an unalterably fixed future, but of the announcement of the future of the nation or of the individual as God's future. Accordingly a 'near expectation' is typical for it, independent of its content. The usual distinction between prophets of salvation and of disaster is to this extent correct, that the pre-exilic prophets in fact primarily announced the impending judgement of God[15], but the exilic and post-exilic prophets announced the coming salvation. It must be decided in each individual case how far the prophet of judgement saw the disaster as unavoidable, allowed for the repentance of the nation and for the corresponding withdrawal of the punishment declared by God, or regarded the judgement as a necessary step on the way to salvation. A warning must in any case be given against a schematic judgement. If the question arises, in relation to a dynamic understanding of 'the word', whether there was room at all for a repentance of the people and for a corresponding withdrawal of the disaster announced, it must be observed that Yahweh remained for the prophets the Lord of his word and the Lord of his people, who stood in a relationship of dialogue with him.

§ 22   The Writing Prophets of the Old Testament and their Books

(a) Amos

B. Duhm, *Anmerkungen zu den zwölf Propheten*, Giessen 1911, pp. 1 ff. = *ZAW* 31 (1911), pp. 1 ff.; E. Balla, *Die Droh- und Scheltworte des Amos*, Leipziger Reformationsprogramm 1926; F. Horst, 'Die Doxologien im Amosbuch', *ZAW* 47 (1929), pp. 45 ff., also in *Gottes Recht*,

15. A clear exception is Nahum. Zephaniah appears to take an intermediate position.

ThB 12, 1961, pp. 155 ff.; A. Weiser, *Die Prophetie des Amos*, BZAW
53, 1929; E. Würthwein, 'Amos-Studien', *ZAW* 62 (1950), pp. 10 ff.,
also in *Wort und Existenz*, Göttingen 1970, pp. 68 ff.; V. Maag, *Text,
Wortschatz, und Begriffswelt des Buches Amos*, Leiden 1951; A. S.
Kapelrud, *Central Ideas in Amos*, SNVAO II, 1956, 4, 1956 (1961[2]); id.,
'New Ideas in Amos', SVT 15, 1966, pp. 193 ff.; H. Graf Reventlow,
Das Amt des Propheten bei Amos, FRLANT 80, 1962; R. Smend, 'Das
Nein des Amos', *EvTh* 23 (1963), pp. 404 ff.; H. W. Wolff, *Amos'
geistige Heimat*, WMANT 18, 1964; W. H. Schmidt, 'Die deuterono-
mische Redaktion des Amosbuches', *ZAW* 77 (1965), pp. 168 ff.

Commentaries: KHC Marti 1904; ICC Harper 1905; HK Nowack
1922[3]; KAT[1] Sellin 1929[2-3]; HS Thiess 1937; HAT Robinson 1964[3];
CAT Amsler 1965; ATD Weiser 1967[5]; BK Wolff 1969; KAT[2]
Rudolph 1971; SC Wellhausen 1898[3] (1963[4]).

1. The prophet. Amos is the earliest of the writing prophets. He
comes from the little town of Tekoa on the edge of the wilderness
of Judah, and before his call was probably a herdsman and
dresser of sycamore trees (Amos 1.1 and 7.14). His ministry falls
in the period of Kings Uzziah of Judah (787–736) and Jeroboam
II of Israel (787–747), since his message presupposes the last
period of prosperity of the Northern Kingdom, and probably in
the decade between 760 and 750 B.C. It has been deduced from
3.9 ff.; 4.1 ff. and 6.1 ff. that he was active at the capital of Israel,
Samaria. 7.10–17, one of the most discussed passages in the
prophetic literature[1], attests that before his expulsion from the

1. On the debated problem whether the noun clause in Amos 7.14 is
to be translated as a present ('I am no prophet . . .') or as a preterite
('I was no prophet . . .') a position is taken up in almost every publication
to appear about the prophets. From the extensive literature directly on
the passage mention will be made only of H. H. Rowley, 'Was Amos a
Nabi?', in *Festschrift O. Eissfeldt zum 60. Geburtstag*, Halle 1947, pp.
191 ff.; S. Lehming, 'Erwägungen zu Amos,' *ZTK* 55 (1958), pp. 145 ff.;
A. H. J. Gunneweg, 'Erwägungen zu Amos 7.14', *ZTK* 57 (1960), pp.
1 ff.; H. N. Richardson, 'A critical Note on Amos 7.14', *JBL* 85 (1966),
p. 89, and H. Schmid, ' "Nicht Prophet bin ich, noch bin ich Propheten-
sohn". Zur Erklärung von Amos 7.14a', *Judaica* 23 (1967), pp. 68 ff.
On the discussion of Amos' original profession cf. also M. Bič, 'Der
Prophet Amos—ein Haepatoskopos', *VT* 1 (1951), pp. 293 ff.; A. Mur-
tonen, 'The Prophet Amos—a Hepatoscoper?', *VT* 2 (1952), pp. 170 f.;
H. J. Stoebe, 'Der Prophet Amos und sein bürgerlicher Beruf', *WuD* 5
(1957), pp. 160 ff., and S. Segert, 'Zur Bedeutung des Wortes nōqēd', in
Hebräische Wortforschung, Festschrift W. Baumgartner, SVT 16, 1967,
pp. 279 ff.

Northern Kingdom by Amaziah the priest he had appeared at the royal sanctuary of Bethel. The whole of his prophetic activity can hardly have exceeded a few months. It is a particularly disputed question whether Amos regarded himself according to 7.14 as a *nābî'* or not.

The question remains open whether his judgements on the lawless behaviour of the nation, and particularly of its upper classes, are to be traced back to the sacral law, and especially to the apodictically formulated laws[2], to the influence of clan wisdom[3] or of school wisdom[4] or to the conscience of the prophet[5] himself who keeps watch in his own time, is experienced and wise about life, and reactivates the traditional standards of his people.

Amos attacks breaches of the law, the oppression of the poor, the luxurious living of the upper classes, and self-confidence against the background of a falsely understood faith in election, and announces future disaster to the king and people.

2. *The book.* The Book of Amos is a constituent element of the book of the twelve prophets, or Dodekapropheton, in which it stands in third place (second in LXX). It contains nine chapters, and in its present form, even apart from obviously later additions, can hardly go back to the prophet himself. We should probably regard a small book of visions found in 7.1–8, 8.1–2 and 9.1–4 and at least one collection of sayings, passed down in 1–6, as originally

2. Cf. Würthwein, op. cit., pp. 40 ff. = 98 ff.; R. Bach, 'Gottesrecht und weltliches Recht in der Verkündigung des Amos', in *Festschrift G. Dehn*, Neukirchen 1957, pp. 23 ff.; Reventlow, op. cit., pp. 73 ff.; O. Kaiser, in *Tradition und Situation*, Festschrift A. Weiser, Göttingen 1962, pp. 79 ff.; W. Zimmerli, *The Law and the Prophets*, Oxford 1965, pp. 67 f., and finally also Kapelrud, op. cit., pp. 59 ff. and especially p. 68.

3. Cf. Wolff, WMANT 18, pp. 60 ff. and BK 14, 2, pp. 120 and 201.

4. Cf. the cautious remarks of H.-J. Hermisson, *Studien zur israelitischen Spruchweisheit*, WMANT 28, 1968, pp. 88 ff. and 128.

5. Cf. J. Wellhausen, *Prolegomena to the History of Ancient Israel*, Edinburgh 1885, pp. 470 ff.; id., *Israelitische und jüdische Geschichte*, Berlin 1958⁹, pp. 122 ff.; B. Duhm, *Israels Propheten*, Tübingen 1922², p. 128; R. Smend, op. cit., pp. 404 ff.; H. H. Schmid, 'Amos. Zur Frage nach der "geistigen Heimat" des Propheten', *WuD* NF 10 (1969), pp. 85 ff.; O. Kaiser, *NZST* 11 (1969), p. 320, and Rudolph, KAT² 13, 2, pp. 98 f.

independent collections. The collection of sayings in its turn
seems to go back to smaller originally independent series of
sayings. The report in the third person in 7.10–14 must be a
relatively late accretion. If we follow Wolff, we must see in the
book a basic core going back to Amos himself in the book of
visions and perhaps in two collections of sayings (1.3–2.16* and
3.1–6, 14*), and then the additions of an ancient 'School of
Amos' (1.1*; 6.2; 7.9; 7.10–17; 8.3, 4–7, 8, 9–14 and 9.7, 8a,
9–10), which was active in Judah between 760 and 730 with a
floruit about 735; a 'Bethel interpretation' from the time of Josiah
which understood the destruction of the sanctuary at Bethel
which occurred at that time as a fulfilment of corresponding
threats of the prophet (1.2; 3.14; 4.6–12; 5.6), and is also responsible for the doxologies, which really form a three-strophe
hymn (4.13; 5.8 f. and 9.5 f.); a Deuteronomistic redaction (1.1*;
the sayings against Tyre, Edom and Judah, 1.9–12; 2.4 f.; and
also 2.10–12; 3.1b, 7 and 5.25 f.), and finally a post-exilic
salvation-eschatology redaction (9.8b, 11–15). It should be noted
that the late dating proposed for Deuteronomy above, pp. 128 f.,
places doubts against his dating for the 'Bethel interpretation'.
Amos is first attested by quotation in later tradition with the
reference to 8.10 in Tobit 2.6.

(b) Hosea

B. Duhm, *Anmerkungen zu den zwölf Propheten*, Giessen 1911, pp.
18 ff., also in *ZAW* 31 (1911), pp. 18 ff.; W. Baumgartner, *Kennen
Amos und Hosea eine Heils-Eschatologie?*, Diss. phil. Zurich 1913;
P. Humbert, 'Osée le prophète bedouin', *RHPhR* 1 (1921), pp. 97 ff.;
A. Allwohn, *Die Ehe des Propheten Hosea in psychoanalytischer Beleuch-
tung*, BZAW 44, 1926; H. S. Nyberg, *Studien zum Hoseabuch*, UUÅ
1935, 6, 1935; N. H. Snaith, *Mercy and Sacrifice. A Study on the Book
of Hosea*, London 1953; G. Fohrer, 'Umkehr und Erlösung beim
Propheten Hosea' [1955], in *Studien zur alttestamentlichen Prophetie*,
BZAW 99, 1967, pp. 222 ff.; G. Östborn, *Jahwe und Baal*, LUÅ NF 1,
51, 6, 1956; H. H. Rowley, 'The Marriage of Hosea' [1956], *Men of
God*, London 1963, pp. 66 ff.; H. W. Wolff, 'Hoseas geistige Heimat',
TLZ 81 (1956), pp. 83 ff., and in *Gesammelte Studien zum Alten Testa-
ment*, ThB 22, 1964, pp. 232 ff.; H. Frey, 'Der Aufbau der Gedichte
Hoseas', *WuD* NF 5 (1957), pp. 9 ff.; A Caquot, 'Osée et la royauté',

RHPhR 41 (1962), pp. 123 ff.; W. Rudolph, 'Präparierte Jungfrauen?', *ZAW* 75 (1963), pp. 65 ff.; id., 'Eigentümlichkeiten der Sprache Hoseas', in *Studia Biblica et semitica Th. Ch. Vriezen dedicata*, Wageningen 1966, pp. 313 ff.; H. Donner, *Israel unter die Völkern*, SVT 11, 1964; E. Jacob, 'Der Prophet Hosea und die Geschichte', *EvTh* 24 (1964), pp. 281 ff.; M. J. Buss, *The Prophetic Word of Hosea*, BZAW 111, 1969.

Commentaries: KHC Marti 1904; ICC Harper 1905; HK Nowack 1922³; KAT¹ Sellin 1929²⁻³; HS Lippl 1937; HAT Robinson 1964³; BK Wolff 1965²; CAT Jacob 1965; KAT² Rudolph 1966; ATD Weiser 1967⁵; SC Wellhausen 1898³ (1963⁴).

1. The prophet. With Hosea we meet the only writing prophet who not only was active in the Northern Kingdom, but probably also came from there. According to 1.1 he appeared during the reign of Jeroboam II of Israel (787–747), and of the Judahite kings from Uzziah (787–736) to Hezekiah (728–700 or 725–697). Since 1.4 presupposes that the dynasty of Jehu has not yet been overthrown, and 7.11 f. and 12.2 refer to the anti-Assyrian policies of the last king of the Northern Kingdom, Hoshea (731–723), who relied upon Egyptian help, but no allusions to the final stage of the history of the Kingdom of Israel are to be found, his activity must have taken place in the years between 750 and 725 B.C. His appearances may have occurred at the sanctuaries of Bethel and Gilgal, as well as at the capital Samaria. Apart from the name of his father Beeri, nothing is told us of his origins. The most discussed problem in the study of Hosea is that of his marriage, told of in ch. 1 in the third person, and in ch. 3 in the first person.

Now that the older view that these reports are not of a real marriage, but are an allegory, has, it may be hoped, finally been ruled out of the discussion, the questions remain (a) whether 1 and 3 deal with the same marriage, and (b) whether the wife was a prostitute already before her marriage, or whether she was only unfaithful during the marriage, so that the accounts themselves reflect the experience of the prophet. To explain how the prophet could have married a prostitute, it is assumed either that we are dealing with a temple prostitute, or that Israelite girls were subjected to an initiation rite. It should be assumed with Rudolph that the description of Gomer as a whore in 1.2 is secondary. The symbolic action in ch. 1 lies not in the marriage as such, but in the naming of the children as Jezreel, Not pitied, and Not my people.

In Ch. 3 on the other hand we have an event whose symbolic character lies in the manner in which it was carried out.

Hosea thought of the relationship between God and people as one of love from God, to which the love of the people should respond (cf. 3.1; 9.15; 11.1 ff.; 14.3 (Heb. 14.4) with 4.1 and 6.6). The prophet was expecting a judgement of destruction as a punishment especially for the apostasy of Israel to the Canaanite fertility cult. Later he came to expect that after the loss of the land the people would meet their God anew in the wilderness, obtain their land again, and then experience a time of salvation. The ascription of a hope of salvation to Hosea is however dependent on the literary-critical view taken especially of chapter 2.

2. The book. Hosea stands at the head of the Book of the Twelve Prophets, and contains 14 chapters. The heading in 1.1 shows that it reached its final form in Judah. Clearly the Hosea tradition was transmitted there after the fall of Samaria in 722. The book is perhaps based on two originally independent smaller collections, (1) a collection of narratives and sayings centred on symbolic actions in chs. 1–3, and (2) the collection of sayings in chs. 4–14, consisting primarily of invectives and threats. While Marti wished to deny to the prophet all the salvation sayings, and, with Nowack, also the mentions of Judah, a more cautious treatment is found in more recent commentaries. Mentions of Judah must certainly be allowed for at the time of the Syro-Ephraimite war (cf. e.g. 5.8–14). On the authenticity of the salvation sayings in the Book of Hosea, the last word has probably not been spoken. With Fohrer we must regard as secondary, besides 1.7, at least 1.10–2.1 (Heb. 2.1–3), 2.4–8, 10, 12 (Heb. 2.6–10, 12, 14); 4.15; 5.5; 7.13b f.; 11.11; 11.12 (Heb. 12.1) and 14.9 (Heb. 14.10). It should be mentioned that the text of 4–14 is in parts one of the most poorly preserved in the whole of the Old Testament.

(c) Isaiah (1–39)

F. Giesebrecht, *Beiträge zur Jesajakritik*, Göttingen 1890; T. K. Cheyne, *Introduction to the Book of Isaiah*, London 1895; H. Cornill, 'Die Komposition des Buches Jesaja', *ZAW* 4 (1884), pp. 83 ff.; S. Mowinckel, 'Die Komposition des Jesajabuches Kap. 1–39', *AcOr(L)* 11 (1933), pp. 267 ff.; R. B. Y. Scott, 'The Literary Structure of Isaiah's Oracles', in *Studies in Old Testament Prophecy*. Festschrift T. H. Robinson, Edinburgh 1950, pp. 175 ff.; S. H. Blank, *Prophetic Faith in Isaiah*, London 1958; G. Fohrer, 'Entstehung, Komposition und Überlieferung von Jesaja 1–39', *ALUOS* 3 (1961–2), pp. 3 ff. = *Studien zur alttestamentlichen Prophetie*, BZAW 99, 1967, pp. 113 ff.; R. Fey, *Amos und Jesaja*, WMANT 12, 1963; H. Donner, *Israel unter den Völkern*, SVT 11, 1964; B. S. Childs, *Isaiah and the Assyrian Crisis*, SBT² 3, 1967; J. Vermeylen, *La composition littéraire du livre d'Isaïe, I–XXXIX*, Louvain 1970 (typescript).

Commentaries: BC Delitzsch 1889⁴; HK Duhm 1892, 1922⁴ (1967⁵); KeH Dillmann and Kittel 1898⁶; KHC Marti 1900; ICC Gray 1912; EH Feldmann 1925; KAT¹ Procksch 1930; HS Fischer 1937; ATD Herntrich 1950 (1954); ZB Fohrer I 1960, 1966²; II 1962, 1967²; BAT Eichrodt I 1960, II 1967; BK Wildberger I 1972, II 1973–; OTL Kaiser (1–12) 1972, (13–39) 1974; SC König 1926; Kissane I 1941 (1960); Bentzen 1944.

1. The prophet. Isaiah, the son of Amoz (1.1), was called to be a prophet, according to the tradition, in the year of the death of King Uzziah of Judah (6.1), a date which in absolute terms is disputed in modern scholarship (between 747–6 and 736–5). His ministry, which was confined to Jerusalem, ended in any case in the year 701. The legend of his death as a martyr under Manasseh probably comes from the period of the Maccabees, and is worthless for the biography of the prophet. It cannot be decided on the basis of the text whether Isaiah came from a family of farmers in the city (Seierstad), or from the family of an official (Fohrer). Since ch. 6 may well be a post-exilic narrative, it can neither be proved that the prophet received his call as early as the year of the death of Uzziah, nor that he received his call in the temple, nor yet as Kaiser earlier suggested, that he was destined for temple service. It may however be allowed that he went to a school for scribes (cf. 30.8). According to what is likewise later tradition, he was married to a prophetess (cf. 8.3). The names of his sons Shear-Jashub ('a remnant will return') and Maher-shalal-hash-baz ('the spoil speeds, the prey hastes') have been handed down because of their symbolic content (cf. 7.3, 8.1 ff. and 8.18). A number of scholars regard the Immanuel mentioned in 7.14 ff. as another son of the prophet.

If the more or less traditional picture of the message of the prophet is followed, Yahweh's intention to destroy the nation was already revealed to him at his call, and the task of further hardening the nation's heart was assigned to his own ministry (cf. 6.1 ff.). Five periods are usually distinguished within his prophetic activity. The first ('the early period') includes the years from his call down to the outbreak of the Syro-Ephraimite war. Usually 6.1–11; 1.2–3; 1.10–17; 1.18–20; 1.21–26; 2.6–22*; 3.1–9; 3.12–15; 3.25–4.1; 5.1–7; 5.8–24 + 10.1–4* are assigned to this. In this period, in spite of occasional exhortations, the preaching of judgement is already predominant. The second period covers the years of the Syro-Ephraimite war (734–733), and reached written form in the so-called *Denkschrift* or memorial of the prophet from the period of the Syro-Ephraimite war (Budde)[1]. This opened with ch. 6, and contained 7.1–9; 7.10–17; 7.18–25*; 8.1–4; 8.5–8; 8.16–18 and (9.1) 9.2–7 [Heb. (8.23) 9.1–6]. 17.1–3 is usually assigned to this period too. The sayings of the prophet from the time before the fall of the Northern Kingdom, in which he foretold the fall of Israel, are treated as forming the third period (9.8–21, Heb. 9.7–20 + 5.25–30* and 28.1–4). In his fourth period, the decade of the Philistine movement of revolt against Assyria from 721 to 711, Isaiah foretold the fruitlessness of the revolts and accordingly warned his nation against taking part in them (cf. 14.28–32*; 20.1–6* and perhaps also 18.1–4*). Finally in the fifth and last period before, during and immediately after the Syro-Palestinian revolt of the years 703(5)–701 Isaiah quite certainly raised his voice to announce uncompromisingly its end to the blinded and rebellious nation (cf. 28.7–13*; 29.9–10a; 29.13–14; 29.15–16; 30.1–5*; 30.6–7, 8; 31.1–3 and 22.1–4, 12–14). On the other hand there is no reason to treat 10.27b–34* and 32.9–14 as Isaianic. The saying against Shebna the steward (22.15–18) stands in a special position, if it really derives from the prophet. 7.10–17, the Immanuel prophecy, probably occupies the front rank in scholarly discussion. It is generally not borne in mind (any more than it is in the case of 7.1–9 with its saying about faith) that we do not have here a first-person account, but a third-person account from a later date. It is disputed whether the Messianic prophecies of 9.2–7 (Heb. 9.1–6) and 11.1–9 can be assigned to the prophet or not, and

1. Cf. note 5 below.

whether before 701 Isaiah allowed for the possibility of the deliverance of Jerusalem or not (cf. 28.16–17a; 29.1–8; 30.27–33 and 31.4–9*). In our view all these last-mentioned passages, and also 2.2–5, are to be treated as redactional. The historical prophet Isaiah was neither a preacher of repentance nor a man who one day proclaimed the deliverance and the next day the ruin of his nation, but consistently announced the coming disaster as an unalterable act of punishment by Yahweh (cf. e.g. 5.1 ff. with 22.1–4, 12–14). The picture of the preacher of repentance and exhorter goes back only to an editor of the words of the prophet at work in the exilic or early post-exilic period, to whom we owe at least 1.2–9 in its present form as an introduction and 30.(8), 9–17 as the original closing saying[2]. It is scarcely possible to establish whether he had before him an Isaiah tradition fixed in writing, or whether he drew on oral tradition. The 'hardening of heart' theology of chap. 6 derives from post-exilic reflection, which presupposed the image of the prophet in the Isaiah tradition that has already been sketched out, and attempted to answer the question why the hortatory preaching of the prophet did not find faith, and why the nation rushed on into disaster.

2. *The book.* Of the 66 chapters of Isaiah chs. 40–55 (Deutero-Isaiah) and 56–66 (Trito-Isaiah) must in any case be separated off[3]. It is only in chapters 1–39 that utterances of the prophet Isaiah are contained; but here too there is more material not by him to be found than authentic material. The process of redaction is extremely complex, and only reached its conclusion at the earliest in the last decades of the third century B.C., probably in the Maccabaean period. It has been said with some justification that our present book of Isaiah contains a whole prophetic library. In 1–39 a three-element eschatological scheme can be seen, though not without a few difficulties in the material: so 1–12 contains predominantly sayings against Isaiah's own nation, 13–23* sayings against other nations and 24–35* prophecies of salvation. 36–39 can in this context be described as a biographical appendix. If the reader keeps in his mind's eye the conception followed out by the eschatological and proto-apocalyptic editors and redactors, he witnesses a powerful drama,

2. Cf. O. Kaiser, *Isaiah 13–39*, London 1974, pp. 234 f.
3. Cf. below, pp. 263 ff. and 268 ff.

which leads through a renewed threat to Jerusalem in the revolt
of the nations to its eternal liberation and glorification. The
picture of the threat to and the deliverance of Jerusalem in 701
formed by tradition in the Isaiah legends in chs. 36 and 37 is
thus made the antitype of the events of 587, and at the same time
the model for the eschatological event.

The three headings in 1.1, 2.1 and 13.1 already show that the
book 1–39 is not all from a single source. 1.1 serves as a heading
for the whole book, but at the same time also for what is now at
any rate an independent and thematically ordered collection,
chap. 1[4]. There is a fundamental disagreement over whether a
single collection of utterances of Isaiah gradually expanded by
further sayings of the prophet forms the basis of the book (e.g.
Mowinckel), or whether we have a successive joining up of
originally independent collections of sayings of Isaiah (so most
recently Fohrer). The redactions to serve liturgical needs, which
placed after a series of prophecies of disaster an oracle of salvation (two-element eschatological pattern) can be understood as
intrusions upon one or more original collections, or as conclusions of individual collections. 2–4 and 5 + 9–11 are usually
regarded as the two originally independent collections from the
early period (period 1) of the prophet. With the insertion of
6.1–9.7 (Heb. 9.6), the so-called 'memoirs of the prophet Isaiah
from the period of the Syro-Ephraimite war' (Budde)[5] the
collection 5 + 9–11 was torn apart and partially rearranged.
But according to the examination recently carried out by Kaiser
from redaction-critical and *Tendenz*-critical viewpoints (on this
cf. his commentary in OTL) 6.1–9.7 (Heb. 9.6) do not contain
any genuine Isaianic material. Even the poem of the outstretched
hand of Yahweh in 9.8–21 (Heb. 7–20) and 5.25–30 turns out in
this examination to be a later compilation. In the light of our
discussion it is doubtful now whether scholarship can get back at
all behind the exilic or early post-exilic edition of the sayings of
Isaiah to the earlier collections. There follow in 13–23, secondarily introduced by the independent heading 13.1, predominantly
oracles against foreign nations, not by Isaiah apart from a core in

4. Cf. G. Fohrer, 'Jesaja 1 als Zusammenfassung der Verkündigung
Jesajas', *ZAW* 74 (1962), pp. 251 ff. and in BZAW 99, 1967, pp. 148 ff.
5. K. Budde, *Jesaja's Erleben. Eine gemeinverständliche Auslegung der
Denkschrift des Propheten (Kap. 6,1–9,6)*, Gotha 1928.

ch. 22. The so-called apocalypse of Isaiah of 24–27 is certainly post-exilic. Its dating varies between the early post-exilic[6], Hellenistic[7] and Maccabean period[8]. Even later datings are now excluded by the textual discoveries at Qumran. Kaiser's analysis shows that the 'city songs' (24.7 ff.; 25.1 ff. and 26.1 ff.) have never had any other setting than the Book of Isaiah. The core is 24.1–13, 16aβ–20 and 26.1–18, 20–21; into this first the songs of thanksgiving (24.14–16aα and 25.1–5), then the more strongly apocalyptically influenced prophecies (24.21–23 and 25.6–8*) with 25.9–10a as a reflection of thanksgiving, and finally the promises of the abolition of death, and of the resurrection, in 25.8aα and 26.19 were inserted. 27.1, 12, 13 may be accretions which are earlier than 25.8aα and 26.19. While the resurrection stratum because of its closeness to Dan. 12.2a belongs at the latest to the years 167–4, 24.21 ff. and 25.6 ff. can be dated to the first third of the same century. For the rest the period from the middle of the fourth to the end of the third century is available, but the date cannot be fixed more exactly. 28–32 are usually described as the 'Assyrian cycle', since here the sayings from the fifth period of the prophet have been collected. 33–35 can perhaps again be described as a little apocalypse, which in its language is to some

6. M.-L. Henry, *Glaubenskrise und Glaubensbewährung in den Dichtungen der Jesaja-apokalypse*, BWANT V, 6, 1967, connects the poems about the city with the fall of Babylon in 539; J. Lindblom, *Die Jesaja-Apokalypse, Jes 24–27*, LUÅ NF I, 34,3, 1938, with the capture of Babylon by Xerxes in 485. G. W. Anderson, 'Isaiah xxiv–xxvii reconsidered', SVT 9, 1963, pp. 118 ff. also argues for an early post-exilic dating.

7. W. Rudolph, *Jesaja 24–27*, BWANT IV, 10, 1933, connects the 'city songs' with the fall of Babylon in 331 B.C.; S. E. Mulder, *Die Teologie van die Jesaja-Apokalipse, Jesaja 24–27*, Groningen and Djakarta 1954, with the conquest of Dibon in Moab about 270 B.C.; similarly Eissfeldt*. O. Plöger, *Theocracy and Eschatology*, Oxford 1968, allows for the redaction of older material in 24–26 in the Ptolemaic period, with a tendency towards a late dating, while he places 27 in the period after Ezra and Nehemiah.

8. O. Ludwig, *Die Stadt in der Jesaja-Apokalypse. Zur Datierung von Jes. 24–27*, Diss. ev. theol. Bonn 1961, dates the individual parts between 167 (desecration of the temple in Jerusalem by Antiochus IV Epiphanes) and 141 B.C. (conquest of the Syrian Akra of Jerusalem by Simon the Younger), and the completion of the composition between 145 and 140 B.C. There is a detailed survey of other attempted solutions since Ewald ibid., pp. 51 ff.

extent reminiscent of Deutero-Isaiah, shows at least partial kinship in ideas with 24–27, and whose content prophesies final judgement on the nations, especially Edom, and then the inbreaking of the time of salvation. Here too we have at least postexilic, if not even late post-exilic, material. Finally there follow the so-called legends of Isaiah, 36–39[9], a block of tradition which is found in almost exactly the same wording in 2 Kgs. 18.13, 17–20.19 (cf. also 2 Chr. 32.1, 9–26). Since 2 Kgs. 18.13, par. Isa. 36.1 clearly belongs to 2 Kgs. 18.14–16, there can be no doubt that the narratives have been taken over from the Book of Kings into Isaiah. Since they reached their present form at the earliest in the post-exilic period, they can have been taken into the Book of Isaiah no earlier than the fourth century. Ch. 39 now forms a transition in theme to Deutero-Isaiah. The insertion of 38.9–20, the so-called Psalm of Hezekiah[10], took place when the material was added to Isaiah, and it was at the same time that the material taken over from 2 Kgs. 20.1–11 was rearranged.

(d) Micah

B. Stade, 'Bemerkungen über das Buch Micha', *ZAW* 1 (1881), pp. 161 ff.; B. Duhm, *Anmerkungen zu den zwölf Propheten*, Giessen 1911, pp. 43 ff. = *ZAW* 31 (1911), pp. 81 ff.; H. Gunkel, 'The Close of Micah' [1924], in *What Remains of the Old Testament*, 1928, pp. 115 ff.; J. Lindblom, *Micha literarisch untersucht*, Acta Academiae Aboensis Humaniora VI, 2, Åbo 1929; K. Elliger, 'Die Heimat des Propheten Micha' [1934], *Kleine Schriften zum Alten Testament*, ThB 32, 1966, pp. 9 ff.; A. Jepsen, 'Kleine Beiträge zum Zwölfprophetenbuch 2', *ZAW* 56 (1938), pp. 96 ff.; W. Beyerlin, *Die Kulttraditionen Israels in der Verkündigung des Propheten Micha*, FRLANT 72, 1959; E. Hammershaimb, 'Some Leading Ideas in the Book of Micah' [1961], in *Some Aspects of Old Testament Prophecy from Isaiah to Malachi*, Publications de la Société des Sciences et des Lettres d'Aarhus, Série de Théologie 4, Copenhagen 1966, pp. 29 ff.; A. S. Kapelrud, 'Eschatology in the Book of Micah', *VT* 11 (1961), pp. 392 ff.; B. Renaud, *Structure et attaches litteraires de Michée IV–V*, Cahiers de la Revue Biblique 2, Paris 1964; T. Lescow, *Micha 6.6–8. Studien zu Sprache*,

9. Cf. J. Meinhold, *Die Jesajaerzählungen Jesaja 36–39*, Göttingen 1898, and B.S. Childs, *Isaiah and the Assyrian Crisis*, SBT[2] 3, 1967, pp. 69 ff.

10. J. Begrich, *Der Psalm des Hiskia*, FRLANT 42, 1926.

Form und Auslegung, ATh I, 25, 1966; id., 'Redaktionsgeschichtliche Analyse von Micha 1–5', *ZAW* 84 (1972), pp. 46 ff.; J. T. Willis, 'The Structure of Micah 3–5 and the Function of Micah 5.9–14 in the Book', *ZAW* 81 (1969), pp. 191 ff.; J. Jeremias, 'Die Deutung der Gerichtsworte Michas in der Exilszeit', *ZAW* 83 (1971), pp. 330 ff.

Commentaries: KHC Marti 1904; ICC Smith 1911; HK Nowack 1922[3]; KAT[1] Sellin 1929[2–3]; HS Lippl 1937; HAT Robinson 1964[3]; ATD Weiser 1967[5]; CAT Vuilleumier 1971–; SC Ryssel 1887; Wellhausen 1898[3] (1964[4]).

1. The prophet. The activity of Micah falls according to 1.1 in the period of the Judahite kings Jotham, Ahaz and Hezekiah. None of the sayings transmitted under his name however goes back with certainty earlier than the last years of Ahaz or the first years of Hezekiah (728–700 or 725–697). The prophecy of disaster directed against Samaria in 1.2–7* comes of necessity from the time before the fall of Samaria, probably from the years before the beginning of the siege by Shalmaneser V in 725. The lament over Judah in 1.8–16* comes probably from the year 701 (Elliger and Weiser), but according to others from an earlier period. Jer. 26.17 ff. also mentions the appearance of the prophet under Hezekiah. In any case the prophet must have been active in the last quarter of the eighth century B.C. as a contemporary of Isaiah. At least 3.1 ff. and 3.9 ff. show that like Isaiah he was active in Jerusalem. All we know about his life is (from 1.1, cf. 1.14) that he came from Moresheth-Gath (*tell ed-judēde*), a country town situated about 35 km south-west of Jerusalem.

Micah proclaimed complete destruction to Samaria because of the Canaanite cult dominant there, unless as Jepsen and Lescow hold the Samaritan schism is presupposed by 1.6 f. and it is therefore to be regarded as a later addition. The breaches of the law by the upper classes (3.1 ff., 3.9 ff.), the acquisitiveness of the rich (2.1 ff., 2.6 ff.), and the venality of the prophets and priests (3.5 ff., 3.9 ff.) invited the judgement of Yahweh upon Jerusalem and Judah too in his view. His prophecy of disaster reaches its climax in the announcement of the destruction of Jerusalem and of the temple in 3.12. The answer to the question whether a proclamation of salvation, in particular a Messianic expectation, can be ascribed to Micah (cf. 5.2–4[6], Heb. 5.1–3[5]) is dependent on the view taken of the literary problem, especially in 4–7. On the same grounds it is disputed whether

6.1–7.6 can be used to fill out the picture of his preaching of judgement.

2. *The book*. The Book of Micah, with its seven chapters, stands sixth in the Book of the Twelve Prophets. Its construction displays a double two-element eschatological schema. The announcements of judgement against Samaria and the Southern Kingdom in 1–3 are followed by prophecies of salvation in 4–5, and further sayings of judgement in 6.1–7.7 are followed by the prophecy of salvation in 7.8–20. It is only 1–3 that contain material which undisputedly goes back to the prophet Micah. Here, apart from smaller additions, only 2.12–13 are to be regarded as a probably post-exilic addition. For 4–5 Renaud has attempted to demonstrate an origin in the fifth century. Here 4.1–5, par. Isa. 2.2–5; 4.6–8; 4.9–13 and 5.7–9 (Heb. 6–8) can be excluded without further discussion as not by Micah, while 4.14 and 5.10–15 (Heb. 9–14) are disputed, but are probably also to be regarded as post-exilic[1]. While Micah's authorship of the Messianic prophecy in 5.2–4(6), Heb. 5.1–3(5) still finds defenders today in Weiser, Beyerlin[2] and S. Herrmann[3] it must with Lindblom[4], Robinson, Mowinckel[5], Eissfeldt*, Fohrer and Lescow be regarded as exilic or rather post-exilic. Lescow has painted a detailed picture of the redactional growth of the book. According to him the original threat sayings of Micah handed down in 1–3* were used liturgically in Jerusalem after the catastrophe of 587 in solemn lamentations round the destroyed sanctuary, and at the time expanded by 1.16; 4.10, 13, 14 and 4.8. Apart from a Deuteronomistic redaction, which is also to be dated in the exilic period, and which can be seen particularly clearly in 1.1a and 3.9, but which also affected 1.5a, 14; 3.5, 6 and 12, further expansion is to be explained especially by liturgical use in the post-exilic feast of the dedication of the temple, apart from the

---

1. J. T. Willis, 'The Authenticity and Meaning of Micah 5.9–14', *ZAW* 81 (1969), pp. 353 ff., is the most recent scholar to argue for Micah's authorship of 5.10–15 (Heb. 9–14).

2. Op. cit., pp. 78 ff.

3. *Die prophetischen Heilserwartungen im Alten Testament*, BWANT V, 5, 1965, pp. 146 ff.

4. Op. cit., pp. 95 ff.; cf. also Lindblom, *Prophecy in Ancient Israel*, Oxford 1962, p. 285.

5. *He That Cometh*, Oxford 1956, p. 19.

anti-Samaritan additions in 1.6 f. and the apocalyptic saying against Assyria inserted in ch. 5. If his results are compared with those of Jeremias, it will be seen that scholarship still requires some time to reach a new consensus. On the post-exilic character of 7.8–20 there can today be no serious difference of opinion. Gunkel has very appositely determined the character of the section as a prophetic liturgy composed from different literary types. While 6.1–7.7 are generally ascribed to Micah, the doubts about this expressed by scholars from Ewald down to Pfeiffer* and Fohrer* have not been stilled. The reference back to the Exodus traditions, the individualization in wisdom style and the disputative and liturgical character do give rise to doubts about the authenticity of 6.1–8. Unless 6.9–16 are connected with Samaria, this passage can hardly be claimed for Micah. The internal dissolution of the community presupposed in 7.1–7 provides no point of reference for the dating, but could naturally be understood as coming from the late exilic or post-exilic period. Accordingly the possibility must be allowed for that 6–7 are to be denied in their entirety to Micah. This assumption emphatically reminds us in respect of 6.1–8 that literary-critical judgements are not theological ones.

(e) Zephaniah

B. Duhm, *Anmerkungen zu den zwölf Propheten*, Giessen 1911, pp. 55 ff. = *ZAW* 31 (1911), pp. 93 ff.; G. Gerleman, *Zephanja textkritisch und literarisch untersucht*, Lund 1942; J. P. Hyatt, 'The Date and Background of Zephaniah', *JNES* 7 (1948), pp. 25 ff.; L. P. Smith and E. L. Lacheman, 'the Authorship of the Book of Zephaniah', *JNES* 9 (1950), pp. 137 ff.; D. L. Williams, 'The Date of Zephaniah', *JBL* 82 (1963), pp. 77 ff.

Commentaries: KHC Marti 1904; ICC Smith 1911; HK Nowack 1922³; KAT¹ Sellin 1930²⁻³; HS Junker 1938; HAT Horst 1964³; ATD Elliger 1967⁶; CAT Keller 1971; SC Wellhausen 1898³ (1963⁴).

I. The prophet. The heading in 1.1 sees Zephaniah as a contemporary of the Judaean King Josiah (639–609). Since the religious syncretism presupposed in 1.4 f. and the indictment levelled in 1.8 against the king's sons (instead of against the king) fit well the beginning of Josiah's reign when he was still a minor, there is no sufficient reason to doubt the correctness of this information[1]. The prophet appeared then about 630 B.C. in Jerusalem. The striking fact that in 1.1. the genealogy of the prophet goes back through four generations from one Cushi ('Ethiopian') to a Hezekiah has its basis either in a desire to document a royal origin for Zephaniah, or in the intention to quieten doubts about his Judaean origin provoked by the name of his father. His message places the prophet, in spite of the small extent of the material which has survived, in a class with the prophets Amos and Isaiah. He shares with both of them an expectation of a day of the Lord which will be directed against his own people (cf. 1.14 ff.[2]; 2.1 ff. with Amos 5.18 ff. and Isa. 2.12 ff.). Alongside the exhortation to strive after righteousness there appears in a way that is characteristic of Zephaniah a summons to humility (2.3b). Whether the theological idea of the remnant is to be ascribed to him depends on the literary evaluation of 3.9–13. The expectation of a judgement of purification can certainly not be denied *a priori* to the prophet. Whether the expectation of the day of the Lord and the sayings directed against the Philistines and Assyrians can be connected with a Scythian attack reported by Herodotus in I, 103 ff. remains at best obscure.

2. *The book.* This little book, consisting of three chapters, stands ninth in the Book of the Twelve Prophets. In its present form it is the result of an undoubtedly compound process of redaction. To this it owes its structure on the three-element eschatological pattern: the announcements of judgement upon Judah and Jerusalem in 1.2–2.3 are followed by oracles against foreign nations, which end with a saying against Jerusalem (2.4–3.8), and finally by oracles of salvation in 3.9–20. The announcements of judgement in 1.4–5, 7, 8–9, 10–11, 12–13a, 14–16, the word of exhortation in 2.1–3* and the oracles against foreign nations in 2.4(5–6*?), 12(?), 13–15 can with some certainty be ascribed to Zephaniah. It is disputed whether and how

1. Accordingly the attempt of Hyatt and Williams to transfer the appearance of the prophet to the time of Jehoiakim or of Zedekiah is not convincing. Smith and Lacheman's view of the book as a pseudepigraph to be dated about 200 B.C. ignores the weight of the literary-critical argument.

2. The *Dies irae* of the Latin church goes back to this text.

far genuine material can be traced in 3.1–13. Redactional activity is in any case responsible for: 1, the expansions of the saying against the Philistines and the incorporation of a saying directed against Ammon and Moab; 2, the addition of the predictions of salvation (3.14–20) and 3, the expansion of the judgement announced into a world judgement, an expansion which is clearly post-exilic. Special emphasis should be laid on the universalism found in 2.11 and 3.9b–10 of a redactor, who, probably under the influence of Deutero-Isaiah, expected as a result of the judgement on the nations a conversion of the Gentiles. A similar dependence on Deutero-Isaiah is shown also by 3.14–20.

(f) Nahum

H. Gunkel, 'Nahum 1', *ZAW* 13 (1893), pp. 223 ff.; P. Kleinert, 'Nahum und der Fall Ninives', *ThStKr* 83 (1910), pp. 501 ff.; B. Duhm, *Anmerkungen zu den zwölf Propheten*, Giessen 1911, pp. 62 ff. = *ZAW* 31 (1911), pp. 100 ff.; P. Humbert, 'Le problème du livre de Nahoum', *RHPhR* 12 (1932), pp. 1 ff.; A. Haldar, *Studies in the Book of Nahum*, UUÅ 1946, 7, 1947; J. L. Mihelic, 'The Concept of God in the Book of Nahum', *Interpr* 2 (1948), pp. 199 ff.; S. J. de Vries, 'The Acrostic of Nahum in the Jerusalem Liturgy', *VT* 16 (1966), pp. 476 ff.; J. Jeremias, *Kultprophetie und Gerichtsverkündigung in der späten Königszeit Israels*, WMANT 35, 1970; H. Schulz, *Das Buch Nahum*, BZAW 129, Berlin 1973.

Commentaries: KHC Marti 1904; ICC Smith 1911; HK Nowack 1922[3]; KAT[1] Sellin 1930[2–3]; HS Junker 1938; HAT Horst 1964[3]; ATD Elliger 1967[6]; CAT Keller 1971; SC Wellhausen 1898[3] (1963[4]).

This little book of three chapters has been handed down in the seventh place within the Book of the Twelve Prophets. According to 1.1 it is by a prophet Nahum of Elkosh, a place which has not so far been identified. Haldar suggests the possibility that the name of the prophet has been derived secondarily from 3.7. In that case we would have an originally anonymous cultic prophecy. On a hypothesis proposed by Humbert and repeated with variations by Sellin and Lods[1] the book is a liturgy for the New Year

1. Cf. A. Lods, 'Trois études sur la littérature prophétique', *RHPhR* 11 (1931), pp. 211 ff.

Festival next after the destruction of Nineveh in 612. The possibility that the prophecies were collected and read after they had been fulfilled is allowed for by Horst, Weiser* and Fohrer*, who describes the artificially composed series of passages of different literary types as a 'cantata' intended for cultic reading. It is disputed whether the supposed hymn in 1.2–8(10) is an original part of the preaching (Haldar), a hymn prefixed by the prophet himself when he was writing the book (Horst) or an addition of the exilic or post-exilic period (Gunkel and Elliger).

Apart from the hymn in 1.2 ff. and a prophecy of salvation for Judah in 1.15, 2.2 (Heb. 2.1, 3) the prophecy of Nahum concentrates on the expected destruction of the capital of the Assyrian empire Nineveh. If the original part of the book is regarded as a prophecy contemporary with the historical events dealt with in it the *terminus post quem* is the conquest of Thebes in Upper Egypt by the Assyrians in 663, which is presupposed in 3.8 ff., and the *terminus ad quem* is the destruction of Nineveh by the Babylonians and Medes in 612. The time of origin must be within the one and a half decades of the decline of Assyrian power between the death of Ashurbanipal in 628(?) and its collapse in 612.

Hermann Schulz gives a different explanation of the origin of the book, deriving it from the worship of the second temple, of which it gave a literary portrayal, and for reading in which it was intended. The author, who came from circles responsible for the handing down of prophetic material, linked together a song on the battle of Nineveh (3.1; 1.11, 14; 2.1, 5aα, 4b, 3, 4a [Heb. 2.2, 6aα, 5b, 4, 5a]; 3.2–3bα; 2.5aβbα, 8bβ, 7aα¹, 5bβ, 3aβ², 7aα²bα¹, 6, 8abα, 9 [Heb. 2.6aβbα, 9bβ, 8aα¹, 6bβ, 4aβ², 8aα² bα¹, 7, 9abα, 10]) and a mocking lamentation on Nineveh (3.7aβ–13a, 15aβ, 13b, 18) with a saying of salvation for Judah (1.12aαb, 13; 1.15 [Heb. 2.1]) and a theophany hymn (1.2a, 3b–6) to form the present composition. The two poems connected with Nineveh are regarded as post-exilic. The reinterpretation of them as a fulfilled prophecy from the period before 612 fits in with the eschatological purpose of the book as a whole, and is intended to underline the finality of the radical change which came in with the exile, and which has likewise been announced in the judgement on the nations already realized in the case of Assyria. 1.2–2.10 (Heb. 2.11) makes a contrast between universal judgement on the nations and salvation for Judah in an eschatological setting. 2.11 (Heb. 2.12)–3.6 contains an eschatological cycle of judgement, which in turn leads on to 3.7–19.

(g) Habakkuk

F. Giesebrecht, *Beiträge zur Jesajakritik*, Göttingen 1890, pp. 196 ff.; K. Budde, 'Die Bücher Habakuk und Zephanja', *ThStKr* 66 (1893), pp. 383 ff.; id., 'Habakuk', *ZDMG* 84 (1930), pp. 139 ff.; J. W. Rothstein, 'Über Habakkuk, Kap. 1 u. 2', *ThStKr* 67 (1894), pp. 51 ff.; B. Duhm, *Anmerkungen zu den zwölf Propheten*, Giessen 1911, pp. 100 ff. = *ZAW* 31 (1911), pp. 188 f.; W. W. Cannon, 'The Integrity of Habakkuk cc. 1.2', *ZAW* 43 (1925), pp. 62 ff.; C. C. Torrey, 'Alexander the Great in the Old Testament Prophecies', in *Vom Alten Testament*, Festschrift K. Marti, BZAW 41, 1925, pp. 281 ff.; M. J. Gruenthaner, 'Chaldeans or Macedonians? A Recent Theory on the Prophecy of Habakkuk', *Bib* 8 (1927), pp. 129 ff., 257 ff.; W. Staerk, 'Zu Habakuk 1, 5–11. Geschichte oder Mythos?', *ZAW* 51 (1933), pp. 1 ff.; P. Humbert, *Problèmes du livre d'Habacuc*, Mémoires de l'Université de Neuchâtel 18, Neuchâtel 1944; H. Schmidt, 'Ein Psalm im Buche Habakuk', *ZAW* 62 (1950), pp. 52 ff.; E. Nielsen, 'The Righteous and the Wicked in Habaqquq', *StTh* 6 (1953), pp. 54 ff.; W. Vischer, *Der Prophet Habakuk*, BSt 19, 1958; J. H. Eaton, 'The Origin and Meaning of Habakkuk 3', *ZAW* 76 (1964), pp. 144 ff.; A. S. van der Woude, 'Der Gerechte wird durch seine Treue leben. Erwägungen zu Habakuk 2:4–5', in *Studia biblica et semitica Th.Ch. Vriezen dedicata*, Wageningen 1966, pp. 367 ff.; J. Jeremias, *Kultprophetie und Gerichtsverkündigung in der späten Königszeit Israels*, WMANT 35, 1970.

Commentaries: KHC Marti 1904; ICC Ward 1911; HK Nowack 1922[3]; KAT[1] Sellin 1930[2-3]; HS Junker 1938; HAT Horst 1964[3]; ATD Elliger 1967[6]; CAT Keller 1971; SC Wellhausen 1898[3] (1963[4]); Duhm 1906.

The little Book of Habakkuk, which with its three chapters has come down to us in the eighth place in the Book of the Twelve Prophets, is one of the most puzzling parts of the Old Testament. It can be divided up, apart from the headings in 1.1 and 3.1, into 1.2–4, a lament of the prophet over oppression and violence, 1.5–11, an oracle of Yahweh over the victorious advance of troops stirred up by Yahweh, 1.12–17, a lament of the prophet over Yahweh's inactivity in the face of the superior power of the enemy, 2.1–4(5?), an answer of Yahweh put in the stylistic form of a report of an experience of the prophet, 2.(5?)6–20, five (six?) cries of woe, and 3.2–19, a hymn describing a theophany. 2.6a, 8b, 13a, 14, 18–20; 3.2b, 4b, 6b, 7a, 8a, (14b?), 17–19 can be regarded as secondary expansions.

The main problems are (1) the question of the correct arrangement of the sections, (2) the original unity of the book, (3) the identification of the oppressors presupposed in 1.2–4; 1.12–17 and 2.(5?), 6–17, and (4) the correctness of the identification made in 1.6 of God's punishing power with the Chaldaeans. With this last problem both those of the dating and that mentioned under (3) are connected.

On (1), Giesebrecht and Wellhausen separated off 1.5–11 as an older oracle, which announced an attack by the nations on the pattern of the Scythian attack. In 1.2–4 and 12–17 they saw a connected lament. Budde also linked 1.12–17 with 1.2–4, but gave up the deletion of 1.(5)6–11 from the context, and instead placed the passage after 2.4, since 2.3 f. were not sufficient in his view as an answer.

On (2), alerted by Balla[1] to the possibility of the presence of a prophetic liturgy, scholars now abandon transpositions of this sort, but attempt either to understand the book as being a liturgy (e.g. Sellin and Humbert), or maintain its present arrangement (e.g. Horst and Elliger). It cannot be disputed that the laments in 1.2–4 and 1.12–17 are in each case related to the answers of Yahweh in 1.5–11 and 2.1–4(5?) (cf. e.g. Jer. 14.1–15.4; Mic. 6.1–8 and Isa. 33). The woes follow on appropriately as a consequence from 2.2–4(5?). The hymnic description of a theophany is to be understood as an expression of the certainty of the victory of Yahweh over his enemies. It gives the book a harmonious conclusion, and there are no compelling grounds to deny it, as does Hans Schmidt, to the author of the book. The planned arrangement of the book undoubtedly allows us to conclude that it was used for worship. In view of 2.1 f. however it must remain dubious whether we have here a prophetic liturgy in the strict sense, or whether we should not rather think that 1.2–11 and 1.12–2.4(5) originally had their own setting in life. The same question applies to 2.(5?), 6–17. The linking of the units can be ascribed to the prophet himself. The expansions show that the book has undergone later editing.

1. *RGG* II[2], Tübingen 1928, cols. 1556 f.

On (3), in view of the identification of Yahweh's tool of vengeance with the Chaldaeans, i.e. the neo-Babylonians, in 1.6 it seems reasonable to connect the oppressors of 1.2–4 with the Assyrians (Budde). But if the prophet is to be placed in the last third of the seventh century the political situation of the Assyrian empire argues against this. The connection with internal Judahite factors, argued for in various forms by Rothstein, Junker and Humbert[2] leads either to the giving up of a uniform interpretation of the prophecies, since 2.13, 17 and 3.13 stand in the way of an identification of the oppressor with the Judahite King Jehoiakim, or to an exegesis of these verses which must be described at the least as daring (Humbert). Since it is improbable that a fairly large interval of time comes between 1.2 ff. and 2.1 ff. and 2.(5?), 6 ff., a division into a message of judgement against Jehoiakim and a proclamation of judgement against the Babylonians is improbable. The reasons given above argue against a complete identification with Jehoiakim. In any case if the factual correctness of 1.6 is upheld, the oppressors must be seen continuously as the Babylonians, while 2.1–4 can be seen as a lament bound up simply with cultic language, and quite generally having the internal circumstances of Judah in mind. This seems to be Nielsen's view.

On (4), the originality of the mention of the Chaldaeans in 1.6 has been repeatedly contested, though with different consequences. Some see no need for a dating in the period of the rise of the neo-Babylonian empire if this is not original, while others nevertheless continue to hold it. The most effective attack on the dating at the end of the seventh century is probably that made by Duhm (and Torrey[3]), who were supported by Nowack and for a time by Sellin. Duhm regarded the reading *hakkasdîm* (the Chaldaeans) as a secondary corruption of an original *kittiyîm* (the Kittim). He saw in the whole prophecy a reflection of the campaign of Alexander the Great after the Battle of Issus in 333

2. Cf. also Nielsen, op. cit., who emphasizes more strongly the significance of cultic language. W. Staerk, op. cit., had already referred to the cultic and mythical connections.

3. Torrey, op. cit. p. 283, gives the justification which many have missed for the secondary insertion of the Chaldaeans in 1.6: the retention of the original *kittîm* would have pointed to the late origin of the book, and so stood in the way of its inclusion among the prophets. I have unfortunately not been able to see his article on 'The Prophecy of

and before the battle of Gaugamela or Arbela in 331 B.C. In favour of his hypothesis he referred to the movement of attackers from west or north-west to east presupposed in 1.9, the unsuspected appearance of the power in 1.5, corresponding to the attack of Alexander, and the apocalyptic note of 2.3. More important than the historical objections raised by for instance Budde is the change which has taken place in our picture of religious history and tradition history, as this bears on the late dating of the psalms presupposed by Duhm[4], and the discovery of the phenomenon of cultic prophecy[5]. Finally most recently the discovery of the fact that 1QpHab also has the reading Chaldaeans in 1.6, although this is explicitly interpreted as Kittim[6], has contributed to a strengthening of support for a dating in the last third of the seventh century. It is interesting that Elliger, in spite of his assumption, based on the Septuagint, that the Chaldaeans were only subsequently added in 1.6, ascribes the addition to the prophet himself, and keeps to a dating between 609 and 598[7], which is the only one seriously considered by present day scholarship. Habakkuk is today seen therefore as a salvation and cultic prophet[8] from the time of Jeremiah. Whether he remains there, or whether there will be anyone to follow in the footsteps of Duhm with a new late dating (for which Sirach, with his mention of the twelve prophets, is the lower limit), remains to be seen.

Nothing is known about the personality of Habakkuk. The story of him as Daniel's helper in the lions' den in the apocryphal addition to Daniel, Bel and the dragon, is part of the later growth of legend. The name of the prophet, which is probably borrowed from Akkadian, means a garden plant. Habakkuk sees in the

---

Habakkuk' in the Kohut memorial volume, *Jewish Studies in Memory of G. A. Kohut 1874–1933*, ed. S. W. Baron and A. Marx, New York, 1935, pp. 565 ff.

4. Cf. below, pp. 342 ff.

5. The linguistic analysis of Humbert, op. cit., is not satisfactory from a literary-critical point of view.

6. Cf. K. Elliger, *Studien zum Habakuk-Kommentar vom Toten Meer*, BHT 15, 1953, p. 173.

7. G[WApc] insert after 'the Chaldaeans', 'the warriors'. Sellin sees in this a gloss on the basis of Jer. 5.16.

8. A different view is of course taken by Junker and Humbert. Humbert regards Habakkuk as simply a prophet of judgement.

invading world-power the tool of God, and in view of its violent
deeds raises the question of his righteousness in history. His
answer is derived from the expectation of the destruction of the
enemies of Yahweh which is part of the Jerusalem cultic traditions. 2.1 gives a rare insight into the prophetic reception of the
word as it was actively sought after at least in the circle of the
cultic prophets.

(h) Jeremiah

F. Schwally, 'Die Reden des Buches Jeremiah gegen die Heiden. xxv.
xlvi-li', *ZAW* 8 (1888), pp. 177 ff.; B. Stade, 'Bemerkungen zum Buche
Jeremia', *ZAW* 12 (1892), pp. 276 ff.; W. Erbt, *Jeremia und seine Zeit*,
Göttingen 1902; G. Jacoby, 'Zur Komposition des Buches Jeremia',
ThStKr 79 (1906), pp. 1 ff.; S. Mowinckel, *Zur Komposition des Buches
Jeremia*, Videnskapsselskapets Skrifter II, 1913, 5, Kristiania 1914;
W. Baumgartner, *Die Klagegedichte des Jeremia*, BZAW 32, 1917;
P. Volz, *Studien zum Text des Jeremia*, BWAT 25, 1920; H. W. Hertz-
berg, *Prophet und Gott*, BFchTh 28, 3, 1923; F. Horst, 'Die Anfänge
des Propheten Jeremia', *ZAW* 41 (1923), pp. 94 ff.; T. H. Robinson,
'Baruch's Roll', *ZAW* 42 (1924), pp. 209 ff.; A. C. Welch, *Jeremiah.
His Time and His Work*, London 1928; J. Skinner, *Prophecy and
Religion. Studies in the Life of Jeremiah*, Cambridge 1930[3]; H. Bardtke,
'Jeremia der Fremdvölkerprophet', *ZAW* 53 (1935), pp. 209 ff.; 54
(1936), pp. 240 ff.; C. C. Torrey, 'The Background of Jeremiah 1–10',
JBL 56 (1937), pp. 193 ff.; J. P. Hyatt, 'Jeremiah and Deuteronomy',
JNES 1 (1942), pp. 156 ff.; id., 'The Beginnings of Jeremiah's Proph-
ecy', *ZAW* 78 (1966), pp. 204 ff.; H. G. May, 'Towards an Objective
Approach to the Book of Jeremiah: The Biographer', *JBL* 61 (1942),
pp. 139 ff.; id., 'The Chronology of Jeremiah's Oracles', *JNES* 4
(1945), pp. 217 ff.; H. Wildberger, *Jahwewort und prophetische Rede
bei Jeremia*, Diss. theol. Zurich 1942; H. H. Rowley, 'The Prophet
Jeremiah and the Book of Deuteronomy', in *Studies in Old Testament
Prophecy*, Festschrift T. H. Robinson, Edinburgh 1950, pp. 157 ff.,
and in *From Moses to Qumran*, London 1963, pp. 187 ff.; id., 'The
Early Prophecies of Jeremiah in their Setting', *Men of God*, London
1963, pp. 133 ff.; J. Bright, 'The Date of the Prose Sermons of Jere-
miah', *JBL* 70 (1951), pp. 15 ff.; id., 'Jeremiah's Complaints: Liturgy or
Expressions of Personal Distress?', in *Proclamation and Presence*,
Festschrift G. H. Davies, London 1970, pp. 189 ff.; L. Rost, 'Zur
Problematik der Jeremiabiographie Baruchs', in *Viva vox evangelii*,
Festschrift Landesbischof Meiser, Munich 1951, pp. 241 ff.; H.
Kremers, 'Leidensgemeinschaft mit Gott im AT. Eine Untersuchung

der "biographischen" Berichte im Jeremiabuch', *EvTh* 13 (1953), pp.
122 ff.; R. Rendtorff, 'Zum Gebrauch der Formel *nᵉ'um jahwe* im
Jeremiabuch', *ZAW* 66 (1954), pp. 27 ff.; E. Vogt, 'Jeremias-Literatur',
Bib 35 (1954), pp. 357 ff.; W. Holladay, 'Prototype and Copies: A
New Approach to the Poetry-Prose Problem in the Book of Jeremiah',
JBL 79 (1960), pp. 351 ff.; id., 'Style, Irony and Authenticity in the
Book of Jeremiah', *JBL* 81 (1962), pp. 44 ff.; A. Neher, *Jérémie*, Paris
1960; S. H. Blank, *Jeremiah, Man and Prophet*, Cincinnati 1961; E.
Gerstenberger, 'Jeremiah's Complaints. Observations on Jer. 15, 10–21',
JBL 82 (1963), pp. 393 ff.; H. Graf Reventlow, *Liturgie und prophet-
isches Ich bei Jeremia*, Gütersloh 1963; id., 'Gattung und Überlieferung
in der "Tempelrede Jeremias" ', *ZAW* 81 (1969), pp. 315 ff.; H. J.
Stoebe, 'Jeremia, Prophet und Seelsorger', *ThZ* 20 (1964), pp. 385 ff.;
C. F. Whitley, 'The Date of Jeremiah's Call', *VT* 14 (1964), pp. 467 ff.;
S. Herrmann, *Die prophetischen Heilserwartungen im Alten Testament*,
BWANT V, 5, 1965, pp. 159 ff.; C. Rietzschel, *Das Problem der Urrolle*,
Gütersloh 1966; M. Kessler, 'Jeremiah Chapters 26–45 Reconsidered',
JNES 27 (1968), pp. 81 ff.; A. H. J. Gunneweg, 'Konfession oder
Interpretation im Jeremiabuch', *ZTK* 67 (1970), pp. 395 ff.; E. W.
Nicholson, *Preaching to the Exiles. A Study of the Prose Tradition in the
Book of Jeremiah*, Oxford 1970; G. Wanke, *Untersuchungen zur sogen-
annten Baruchschrift*, BZAW 122, 1971; W. Thiel, *Die deuteronomistische
Redaktion von Jeremia 1–25*, WMANT 41, 1972.

Commentaries: KHC Duhm 1901; HK Giesebrecht 1907²; KAT¹
Volz 1922; HS Nötscher 1934; IB Hyatt 1956; AB Bright 1965; ATD
Weiser 1966⁵; HAT Rudolph 1968³; SC Graf 1862; Cornill 1905;
Leslie 1954.

1. The book. The Book of Jeremiah, which consists of 52
chapters, comes in Masoretic Bibles between Isaiah and Ezekiel,
after which the Book of the Twelve Prophets follows. In the
Septuagint it is again placed between Isaiah and Ezekiel, together
with the apocryphal Book of Baruch, Lamentations and the
apocryphal Letter of Jeremiah, but here Isaiah is preceded by
the Book of the Twelve Prophets, while Ezekiel is followed by
Susanna and Daniel. The text of the Septuagint is roughly an
eighth shorter than the Masoretic text. In spite of some obvious
abbreviations, as a whole it may well preserve an older stage of
the tradition than the Masoretic text. Among the fragments of
the text of the book that have been found in the Qumran Caves
are some which come close to the textual form of the assumed
Hebrew original of the Septuagint.

The arrangement within the book in the Septuagint also seems to be more original than that in the Hebrew Bible, which is followed by the Vulgate and by modern translations. Here the prophecies of disaster against Judah and Jerusalem of 1–25.13 are followed by 25.14–32.38 (= 46–51 + 25.25–38 in MT), the oracles against the foreign nations[1] and by the predominantly narrative tradition, which is here understood as a prediction of salvation, of 33–51 (26–45 in MT), while 52 (= 52 in MT) contains a historical supplement, which has been taken from 2 Kgs. 24.18–25.30 with the omission of 25.22–26 and the insertion of the special tradition of vv. 28–30. The Septuagint accordingly attests the original structure of a three-element eschatological pattern, in which oracles of disaster against the author's own nation are followed by oracles of disaster against foreign nations and by prophecies of salvation. The pattern is found again less clearly in the Book of Isaiah, and clearly in the Book of Ezekiel. As in Isaiah a biographical supplement is attached as a fourth division[2].

2. The literary problem. The prehistory of the book is much more complicated than its structure indicates. The basic literary problem of the book results from the fact that apparently four different forms of tradition can be distinguished in it: 1, prophetic sayings; 2, prose sermons; 3, first person narratives, and 4, third person narratives. Further individual problems are the question of the extent of Jeremianic material within 1–25, together with the question posed by 36 of an *Urrolle* or original roll coming from the year 605, the problem posed especially by 31–33 of the salvation preaching of Jeremiah, and finally that of Jeremiah's share in the oracles against foreign nations, 46–51.

The hypothesis which has had most influence towards a solution of the main problem is that proposed by Mowinckel on the basis of observations of Duhm. He ascribed the Jeremianic sayings and first person accounts in 1–25 to a source A, which

---

1. The oracles against the foreign nations are probably in the original order in MT, as Egypt, Philistia, Moab, Ammon, Edom, Damascus, Kedar, Elam and Babylon. The LXX order is Elam, Egypt, Babylon, Philistia, Edom, Ammon, Kedar, Damascus and Moab. Cf. C. Rietzschel, *Das Problem der Urrolle*, p. 45.

2. Cf. below, pp. 301 f.

was simply intended to present as full a collection as possible of the sayings of the prophet. He saw in the third person accounts 19.2–20.6*; 26; 28 f.* and 36–44* a source B, whose historical narratives told of the occasions of individual sayings and of their consequences for Jeremiah. These sections are often called by scholars the *Leidensgeschichte*, or passion narrative, of Jeremiah, and ascribed to his supposed secretary and pupil Baruch ben Neriah (cf. 36 and 45). Mowinckel further ascribed the Deuteronomically influenced sermons in 7.1–8.3*; 11*; 18*; 21*; 25*; 32*; 34 f.* and 44* to a source C, which is not primarily Jeremianic. Finally he saw in the prophecies of salvation in 30 f., and also in the oracles against the foreign nations 46–51, an originally independent anonymous collection (D). In the joining of A and B and also of AB with C both thematic and more often chronological principles had been followed.

Of recent commentators Rudolph and Hyatt have taken over Mowinckel's hypothesis of the sources A–C each in their own way, though both, with Volz, see genuine Jeremianic sayings in 30 f. and, unlike Mowinckel and Volz, also in 46–51. Volz believed that the problem could be solved by the assumption that Baruch not only was the author of the narratives, but also had expanded the Jeremianic sayings in the sermons. Weiser attempts to solve the basic problem in a different way. Like Volz, Rudolph and Hyatt he assumes a Jeremianic core within 46–51. But at the same time, following Volz, he contests the existence of a separate source C. It should rather be assumed, he argues, that Jeremiah and Baruch had made use of a liturgical form of speech, which traditio-historically relates to the prehistory of the Deuteronomic movement. It cannot however be decided in individual cases how far the original Jeremianic language had been expanded by any later liturgical adaptation that took place[3].

If the literary-critical solution of Mowinckel and the traditio-historical solution of Weiser are examined, it appears that on any theory the problem of oral tradition is raised by the material ascribed to Block C. The question arises whether in respect of Block B, the so-called notes of Baruch, it is possible to confine the chain of tradition to Jeremiah and Baruch, or whether here too the position is more complicated. In respect of the Deutero-

---

3. On the various attempts to solve the problem of the Deuteronomistically influenced sermons, cf. Nicholson, op. cit., pp. 21 ff.

nomistically coloured sermons and narratives containing a sermon, the point must be made against deriving them from Jeremiah or Baruch that the undisputedly Jeremianic prophetic sayings show no influence at all of Deuteronomy. Whether this is to be connected, with Rietzschel, simply with diverging chains of tradition, one of country Levites, the other of prophets, or rather with a later origin or development of Deuteronomy, is a question which can be left unexamined[4]. The objection must be made, with S. Herrmann, that the Jeremiah of these passages does not appear as a prophet representing God's inescapable demands, but as one posing alternatives which are of a Deuteronomistic conception. The conclusion can hardly be avoided that the Deuteronomistically coloured narratives and sermons have undergone a lengthy period of oral transmission, which goes back to Jeremiah, but cannot now be disentangled in its individual stages. Whether these passages were originally collected separately and codified, or successively added in to the original Jeremianic collection, cannot be decided with certainty in view of the obscure nature of the history of the tradition. But similar doubts arise about the derivation of the 'stories of suffering' (it would be better to call them stories of the proclamation by Jeremiah and rejection by Judah of the word of Yahweh) from Baruch, however probable this may at first appear in view of the many historical details. Rietzschel has in my view convincingly shown from the example of ch. 36 that its ascription to and derivation from Baruch is improbable, since in this chapter we have to deal with a literary product formed on the basis of dramatic viewpoints. Reventlow has demonstrated this also for 26.1–19, and emphasized the parenetic intention of this edificatory narrative[5]. This could easily be demonstrated for 27* and 28 too. M. Kessler has expressed doubts in respect of 45, the so-called Consolation of Baruch. It may be conjectured that Baruch was of exceptional significance in the handing on of the Jeremiah traditions. The generally sober presentation, interested in the fulfilment of the prophetic word, also makes it impossible to allow for too long a chain of tradition, as does the

4. Cf. above, pp. 124 ff.

5. Cf. Rietzschel, op. cit., pp. 105 ff., M. Kessler, 'Form-critical Suggestions on Jer. 36', *CBQ* 28 (1966), pp. 389 ff., and Reventlow, *ZAW* 81 (1969), pp. 341 ff.

number of concrete details. In spite of 42–44 the traditions must
have been preserved and fixed in Palestine or Babylonia. Nicholson has seen that Deuteronomistic preaching among the exiles
is the tradition circle common to the prose sermons and the
narratives, and has pointed to the connections existing between
the prophet theology of Deut. 18.9 ff., the prophetic declaration
(Steck's phrase) in 2 Kgs. 17.13 ff., and the narratives in 26–29
and 36. On the other hand Wanke has found in 19.1–20.6; 26–29
and 36, in 37–44 and finally in 45 and 51.59–64 originally separate
tradition complexes which show different redactions. When it is
noticed that Thiel has demonstrated the existence of a thorough-
going Deuteronomistic redaction of Jeremiah, the different
redactions shown by Smend and Dietrich to exist within the
Deuteronomistic history are inevitably recalled, and the question
is whether a final solution cannot be outlined which will see
here too several Deuteronomistic redactions. It will not be right
in doing this to take a single step backwards from the basic
insight attained by Nicholson. When it is remembered that the
prose narratives of Jeremiah themselves form the main source for
the preaching of the prophet in the last phase of the history of
Judah, and also the main source for our picture of this period, the
urgent need will be realized for a comprehensive treatment which
will take into consideration all the points of view which have
emerged in the latest discussion. [6]

Whether we can go further along these lines and with Rietzschel assume that the origin of the book lies in blocks of tradition
comprising different materials and corresponding to the main
divisions of the book, blocks which in their turn have been
formed from originally independent tradition complexes, seems
to me doubtful, since the insertion of the Deuteronomistic
sections in 1–24 can be explained as redactional, while the
ascription of salvation sayings to Jeremiah remains dubious[7].
So the next problem is the question of the *Urrolle*, or of the
extent of the collection of genuine sayings of Jeremiah.

Scholars take differing views on the possibility of recovering
the *Urrolle* mentioned in 36 as having been destroyed by King

6. I have unfortunately not had access to the Brandeis dissertation of
M. Kessler, *A Form-critical Study of Jer. 26–29, 32–45.*

7. Cf. Rietzschel, op. cit., pp. 122 ff. and p. 127; but also S. Herrmann,
op. cit., pp. 159 ff.

Jehoiakim and dictated again by Jeremiah to Baruch, and later expanded.

While Cornill found the *Urrolle* in the basic form of 1–10 + 25, including the prose passages, scholars now take one of two views in respect of the problem of form[8]. The view taken by Robinson, Eissfeldt* and Miller, not very probable in itself, that the *Urrolle* consisted precisely of the first person narratives and sermons in 1–25, is no longer of importance in view of the probable prehistory of the greater part of these very passages. So it is understandable that most scholars take the opposite course and look for prophetic sayings from before 605. The fact that neither the confessions nor the (traditio-historically problematic) accounts of symbolic actions were suitable for reading out before the people so limits the possible passages that within 1.4–23.40* only 1.4–9.6* (Heb. 9.5*), and perhaps from the collection of sayings against kings and prophets, 21.11–23.40*, just 21.11–22.19*, are possible candidates, though it remains unclear whether the last-mentioned complex had a separate existence right from the beginning. Finally the original form of the oracles against foreign nations (46.1–49.13*) must also be taken into consideration, since it could come from this period. This represents Rudolph's position, apart from minor variations. Hyatt and Rietzschel narrow down the extent of the roll yet further to 1.4–9.6 (Heb. 9.5)* or 1.4–6.30*, and are clearly led to this by traditio-historical considerations.

Since however it is not certain to what extent the present collections of authentic sayings of Jeremiah are original, it may be better, with Duhm, Mowinckel and Weiser, to give up the attempt to discover the exact limits of the roll, if we do not simply regard it as a bogus problem.

There is disagreement to this day among scholars about the authenticity of the sayings of salvation contained in the Book of Jeremiah. While Mowinckel simply denied the whole collection of oracles of salvation in 30–31 to the prophet, and Duhm, Giesebrecht and Cornill in different ways looked for a Jeremianic core in these chapters, a more favourable view of the tradition can be found in Volz, and reaches its peak in Rudolph and Weiser. Weiser sees in 30.1–4 an introduction which goes back

8. Fohrer* takes an individual position on this question, since in spite of his basic scepticism about the possibility of a reconstruction of the *Urrolle*, the problem takes a different form for him because of his assumption of a 'short verse' form.

to Baruch, and later additions only in 30.23 f. and 31.38–40. The decision on the point at issue depends on the view taken of the relation between the preaching of Jeremiah and the Deuteronomistic movement, especially in respect of the promise of the covenant in 31.31–34, but also upon the literary and traditio-historical view taken of the individual passages. According to Herrmann's careful investigation only the sayings about Israel, Rachel and Ephraim in 3.12aβ–13a and 31.15–17, 18–20 remain as a possible Jeremianic core, which must then be ascribed to the period of Josiah's occupation of the territory of the former Northern Kingdom. Rudolph has not altered his view in the latest, third edition of his commentary.

Scholars also take very different views on the authenticity of the sayings about the nations (46–51). While Duhm, Mowinckel and Volz denied the whole collection to the prophet, it is at least agreed today that the oracle on Babylon 50.1–51.58 certainly does not go back to Jeremiah, and that the sayings against Egypt in 46.3–12 certainly do. The saying on Damascus in 49.23–27 also finds no defender of authenticity.

On the other hand Rudolph and Weiser, although they differ in detail, regard the second oracle against Egypt (46.13–18), the oracle against the Philistines in 47, the oracle on Moab in 48 (but in any case without vv. 21–27, 29–39), the oracle on Ammon (49.1–6*), a minimal original section of the saying on Edom (49.7–22**), the saying against the Arabian tribes (49.28–33*) and the saying on Elam (49.34–39) as genuine too. Bardtke holds a special position among views on the Jeremianic core of 46–49 in that he dates it to a first period of oracles of salvation of the prophet in 617–6, taking the view that he first became a prophet of disaster in 615. Against this ingenious hypothesis we must however ask, as Weiser does, why there is not then an oracle directed specifically against Assyria. It should be noted that the third person account in 51.59–64 is generally ascribed to the Baruch narrative or to source B.

Although Stade and Hölscher had already raised the question of the authenticity of the so-called Confessions of Jeremiah (cf. 11.18 ff.; 12.1 ff.; 15.10 ff.; 17.12 ff.; 18.19 ff. and 20.7 ff.) it was until very recently generally given a positive answer, following Baumgartner, because the use of the already existing literary type of the individual lament by the prophet in his situation seemed in itself to contain no problem. While Graf Reventlow, in view of the difficulty of connecting the poems with the prophetic commission, wanted to understand them as part of a liturgical formula, within which the prophet stood before God lamenting as representative of the nation before God, and answering as the representative of God before the nation, Gunneweg now explains them as later interpretations of the preaching and person of Jeremiah, which were intended to interpret his life as that of the righteous man who suffers and prays in an exemplary way, and to look back to the disaster as the fulfilment of the words of the prophet[9].

The following passages in 1–25 should be excluded as a primary source for the message of Jeremiah, as being in great probability passages which were not written by him, but which in various ways contain an echo of his message and of his fate, as well as later editing of the collection of sayings, sermons and narratives ascribed to him: 1.1–3, 10, 15–16; 2.1–3; 3.6–12aα, 13b–18; 3.21–4.4; 4.9–12, 14, 18, 22–28; 5.18–20; 7.1–8.3; 8.10–12; 9.12–16 (Heb. 11–15); 10.1–16, 22, 23–25; 11.1–14; 12.14–17; 15.12–14; 16.1–13, 14–15, 19–21; 17.12–13, 19–27; 18.1–12; 19.1–20.6; 20.12; 21.1–10; 22.1–5, 8–9, 11, 25–27; 23.1–8, 18, 33–40; 25.1–14, 18–29, 30–31, 33. I would add as doubtful 1.4–9, 11–14, 17–19; 2.4–13, 14–19, 28; 3.12aβ–13a; 11.18–12.6; 13.1–14; 14.11–16; 14.19–15.4, 15–21; 17.5–11, 14–18; 18.18; 20.7–11, 13–18; 23.16–32; 24.1–10 and 25.32, 34–38.

3. The prophet. Thanks to the rich narrative tradition we are ostensibly better informed about the life of Jeremiah than about that of any other Old Testament prophet. Jeremiah, son of Hilkiah, came according to 1.1 (cf. 32.7, 37.11) from a priestly family whose home was Anathoth in Benjamin, north of Jerusalem. From such a place of origin it would be understandable that the prophet was concerned about the fate of the diaspora of the Northern Kingdom (cf. 3.12a–13a and 31.15–20). It is possible, but not capable of proof, that he was a descendant of Abiathar, of the family of Eli (cf. 1 Kgs. 2.26). According to 1.2 he was called in the thirteenth year of Josiah (639–609), i.e. 627–6, and so must have been born about 650[10]. According to 16.1 f. he gave up marriage and children as a sign of the catastrophe

9. Cf. also E. Gerstenberger, 'Jeremiah's Complaints. Observations on Jer. 15,10–21', *JBL* 82 (1963), pp. 393 ff.

10. Doubts about a call in the thirteenth year of Josiah have not been quietened since the article by Horst in *ZAW* 41 (1923), pp. 94 ff. H. G. May (*JNES* 4 (1945), pp. 217 ff.) and J. P. Hyatt, *ZAW* 78 (1966), pp. 204 ff., have supported a redating to 609/8. Whitley in *VT* 14 (1964),

which would soon overtake parents and children. The 'Confessions of Jeremiah' in 11.18 ff.; 12.1 ff.; 15.10 ff.; 17.12 ff.; 18.19 ff. and 20.7 ff. appear to show that Jeremiah suffered sorely from the rejection of his message and the persecution which came even from the ranks of his own family (cf. 12.6). 20.1–6; 26; 28; 29.25 ff.; 32.1 ff.; 36–44 tell of the hostility, accusations and persecutions to which the prophet was subjected from 605 to the time of his deportation to Egypt, after which he disappears from sight. 36; 45; 32 and 43.3 presuppose a special connection of Jeremiah with the scribe Baruch, the son of Neriah and brother of the court official Seraiah. If Baruch was not, as is generally assumed, the author of at least a part of the stories about Jeremiah, he must at least represent an important link in the chain of tradition, especially since he also, we are told, survived the fall of Jerusalem in 587.

If we accept the year of the call given in 1.2 as correct, Jeremiah's preaching covered four decades, and took place in Jerusalem from the beginning and probably right down to his deportation to Egypt, apart from the brief interval under Gedaliah at Mizpah. The sayings against apostasy to the Canaanite fertility cults in 2–3 are generally dated[11] in the early years of the prophet before Josiah's reform of 621. The announcements of a foe from the north (cf. 1.14; 4.6 and 6.22) are generally dated in the same period, and an echo is often seen in them of a Scythian attack mentioned in Herodotus I, 103 ff. but which is on this large scale historically very dubious. More probably this is a pure prophecy which does not know who the enemy is. Rietzschel on the other hand already connects 1.11 ff. and the scattered announcements of an enemy's attacks in 4.5–6.35 with the Babylonians, and accordingly dates them to 605. The first saying whose date can be firmly fixed from its content is 22.10, par. 22.11, the demand to mourn not the dead King Josiah, but Shallum (Jehoahaz), who was being deported at the time. The date of this saying is 609–8 (cf. 2 Kgs. 22.33 f.).

The material preserved in 7–20 is ascribed to the time of Jehoiakim. From this period 22.13–19, a saying directed against

pp. 467 ff., would go as late as 605, but this can hardly be upheld in view of 22.10, par. 22.11.

11. With the exception of course of all those who argue for a late date for the call of Jeremiah.

Jehoiakim (608–598), and so not fulfilled, certainly comes. Already in the first months of his reign Jeremiah in his temple speech, reported in 7.1 ff. and in 26, opposed a false trust in the temple of Jerusalem, and like Micah before him prophesied its destruction, thus incurring legal proceedings, which ended however with his release. The preaching of disaster against Jerusalem and Judah led to his punishment by Pashhur the priest and overseer of the temple district, and perhaps also to a prohibition on entering the temple (cf. 19.1–20.6*; 36.5). In the same year the prophet dictated the sayings of judgement he had so far uttered to Baruch, who read them in the temple, an act which led to the destruction of the roll by Jehoiakim and to its writing again (cf. 36). The Jeremianic core of the sayings against the foreign nations may also have originated in this year. Finally the story of the faithfulness of the Rechabites in 35 also takes us to the time of the reign of Jehoiakim.

To the brief reign of Jehoiachin (December 598–March 597) belong apart from 13.15–27 and 22.20–23 only the royal sayings 22.24 par. 22.25–27 and 22.28–30. For the final phase of Judahite history under Zedekiah (597–587) we depend primarily on the third person accounts. Of these 27–29 take place during the period of a Phoenician and Palestinian revolt planned in 594, while 21.1–10; 32–34 and 37–40.6 all belong to the final phase of the reign of Zedekiah, the period of the Babylonian siege of Jerusalem which lasted from January 588 to 29 July 587. It is unnecessary to repeat the content of the narratives of Zedekiah's vacillations, of the sufferings of Jeremiah, and his release from the cistern by the Cushite Ebedmelech, since we can assume that the reader is familiar with these stories[12]. Apart from the

12. Instead an account of the principle of composition pointed out in M. Kessler, 'Jeremiah Chapters 26–45 Reconsidered', *JNES* 27 (1968), pp. 81 ff., may be of use. While 26 gives the legitimation of Jeremiah as a true prophet, 27–29 give an outline of the content of his message. In this the aspect of the contrast between true and false prophets must not be ignored. 28 serves at the same time according to Kessler as a catalyst for Jeremiah's oracles of salvation in 29–32. Chapters 34–36 return to the motif of 26, the hoped-for obedience which would avert the threatening disaster. The greater historical interest in 37–45 serves to emphasize the fulfilment of the word of the prophet after it had been rejected. 37–39 brings us to the time before the fall of Jerusalem, and with an hortatory purpose underline Jeremiah's faithfulness even under the most adverse

problematic description of a vision in 24 and perhaps also the sayings against false prophets in 23.9 ff. only 15.5–9, a saying which
others place in the year 598–7, could be a genuine saying of
Jeremiah preserved from this decade. Finally for the activity and
suffering of the prophet after the fall of Jerusalem and in Egypt
we depend entirely on the third person accounts in 40.6–44.30.
It is understandable that the fearsome validation of the message
of disaster uttered by Jeremiah from the time of his call made a
deep impression on those who survived the catastrophe, that
men told of his activity and worked over his words to fit the
needs of a new hour.

(i) Ezekiel

J. Herrmann, *Ezechielstudien*, BWAT 2, 1908; L. Dürr, *Die Stellung
des Propheten Ezechiel in der israelitisch-jüdischen Apokalyptik*, Alttestamentliche Abhandlungen IX, 1, Münster 1923; G. Hölscher,
Hesekiel, der Dichter und das Buch, BZAW 39, 1924; M. Burrows, *The
Literary Relations of Ezekiel*, Diss. Philadelphia, New Haven 1925;
W. Kessler, *Die innere Einheitlichkeit des Buches Ezechiel*, Herrnhut
1926; S. Sprank, *Studien zu Ezechiel*, BWANT III, 4, 1926; C. C.
Torrey, *Pseudo-Ezekiel and the Original Prophecy*, Yale Oriental Studies
18, New Haven 1930; id., 'Certainly Pseudo-Ezekiel', *JBL* 53 (1934),
pp. 291 ff.; S. Spiegel, 'Ezekiel or Pseudo-Ezekiel?', *HTR* 24 (1931),
pp. 245 ff.; J. Smith, *The Book of the Prophet Ezekiel*, London 1931;
V. Herntrich, *Ezechielprobleme*, BZAW 61, 1932; C. Kuhl, 'Zur
Geschichte der Hesekiel-Forschung', *ThR* NF 5 (1933), pp. 92 ff.; id.,
'Neuere Hesekiel-Literatur', *ThR* NF 20 (1952), pp. 1 ff.; W. A. Irwin,
The Problem of Ezekiel, Chicago 1943; id., 'Ezekiel Research since
1943', *VT* 3 (1953), pp. 54 ff.; N. Messel, *Ezechielfragen*, SNVAO II 1,
1945; K. Jaspers, 'Der Prophet Ezechiel. Eine pathographische Studie',
in *Arbeiten zur Psychiatrie, Neurologie, und ihren Grenzgebieten*.

conditions. 40–44 tell of the fate of the 'remnant' after the catastrophe,
44 consisting of a genuine warning against the worship of idols, which
was a real problem in the exilic and post-exilic period. The 'Consolation
of Baruch' (45) which with the meagre content of its promise gives an insight into the gloomy background of this literature, underlines his role as
the next stage in the Jeremiah tradition, but does not make certain his
authorship of these chapters. Kessler conjectures as the setting in life or
in the cult of these narratives the repeated reading of them before the exilic
and post-exilic Jews with the aim of encouraging them by this example.

Festschrift K. Schneider, Heidelberg 1947, pp. 77 f.; H. W. Robinson, *Two Hebrew Prophets: Studies in Hosea and Ezekiel*, London 1948; C. G. Howie, *The Date and Composition of Ezekiel*, *JBL* Monograph Series 4, Philadelphia 1950; J. G. Aalders, *Gog en Magog in Ezechiël*, Diss. theol. Amsterdam, Kampen 1951; G. Fohrer, 'Die Glossen im Buche Ezechiel', *ZAW* 63 (1951), pp. 33 ff. = *Studien zur alttestamentlichen Prophetie*, BZAW 99, 1967, pp. 204 ff.; id., *Die Hauptprobleme des Buches Ezechiel*, BZAW 72, 1952; id., 'Das Symptomatische der Ezechielforschung', *TLZ* 83 (1958), cols. 241 ff.; W. Zimmerli, *Erkenntnis Gottes nach dem Buche Ezechiel*, ATANT 27, 1954 = *Gottes Offenbarung*, ThB 19, 1963, pp. 41 ff.; id., 'Das Gotteswort des Ezechiel', *ZTK* 48 (1951), pp. 249 ff. and in ThB 19, pp. 133 ff.; id., 'Die Eigenart der prophetischen Rede des Ezechiel', *ZAW* 66 (1954), pp. 1 ff., and in ThB 19, pp. 148 ff.; id., ' "Leben" und "Tod" im Buche des Propheten Ezechiel', *ThZ* 13 (1957), pp. 494 ff. and in ThB 19, pp. 178 ff.; id., 'Der "neue Exodus" in der Verkündigung der beiden grossen Exilspropheten', in *Festschrift W. Vischer*, Montpellier 1960, pp. 216 ff. = ThB 19, pp. 192 ff.; id., 'Der Wahrheitserweis Jahwes nach der Botschaft der beiden Exilspropheten', in *Tradition und Situation*, Festschrift A. Weiser, Göttingen 1963, pp. 133 ff.; id., *Ezechiel. Gestalt und Botschaft*, BSt 62, 1972; id., 'Deutero-Ezechiel?', *ZAW* 84 (1972), pp. 501 ff.; H. H. Rowley, 'The Book of Ezekiel in Modern Study' [1953], in *Men of God*, London 1963, pp. 169 ff.; K. von Rabenau, 'Die Entstehung des Buches Ezechiel in formgeschichtlicher Sicht', *WZ Halle* 5 (1955/6), pp. 659 ff.; id., 'Die Form des Rätsels im Buche Hesekiel', *WZ Halle* 7 (1957/8), pp. 1055 ff.; id., 'Das prophetische Zukunftswort im Buch Hesekiel', in *Festschrift G. von Rad*, Neukirchen 1961, pp. 61 ff.; H. Gese, *Der Verfassungsentwurf des Ezechiel (Kap. 40–48) traditionsgeschichtlich untersucht*, BHT 25, 1957; H. Graf Reventlow, 'Die Völker als Jahwes Zeugen bei Ezechiel', *ZAW* 71 (1959), pp. 33 ff.; id., *Wächter über Israel. Ezechiel und seine Tradition*, BZAW 82, 1962; S. Herrmann, *Die prophetischen Heilserwartungen im Alten Testament*, BWANT V, 5, 1965, pp. 241 ff.; W. Eichrodt, 'Der neue Tempel in der Heilshoffnung Hesekiels', in *Das ferne und nahe Wort*, Festschrift L. Rost, BZAW 105, 1967, pp. 37 ff.; H. Schulz, *Das Todesrecht im Alten Testament*, BZAW 114, 1969; D. Baltzer, *Ezechiel und Deuterojesaja*, BZAW 121, 1971; J. Garscha, *Studien zum Ezechielbuch*, Berne and Frankfurt 1974.

Commentaries: KeH Smend 1880²; KHC Bertholet 1897; HK Kraetzschmar 1900; HS Heinisch 1923; KAT¹ Herrmann 1924; HAT Bertholet and Galling 1936; ICC Cooke 1936; HAT Fohrer and Galling 1955; IB May 1956; CB Wevers 1969; BK Zimmerli 1969; OTL Eichrodt 1970; SC Cornill 1886; Jahn 1905; Matthews 1939.

1. The book. The Book of Ezekiel, consisting of 48 chapters, is placed in the Hebrew Bible between Jeremiah and the twelve Minor Prophets, in the Greek between the Epistle of Jeremy and Susanna or Daniel. The shorter form of the text found in the Septuagint goes back to an older Hebrew original, which is in general to be preferred to the Masoretic text. Ezekiel also is constructed, more clearly than Isaiah and the Hebrew form of Jeremiah, on the three-element eschatological scheme of prophecies of woe against his own nation, prophecies of woe against other nations, and prophecies of salvation for his own nation. So we find in

1–24 announcements of judgement upon Judah and Jerusalem

25–32 the same against foreign nations and

33–48 promises of salvation.

Within 1–24, 1.1–3.27 contains the story of Ezekiel's call and sending by God; 4–5; 12.1–20; 21.6 f., 18–24 (Heb. 21.11 f., 23–29) and 24.1–24 (cf. also 37.15–28) contain accounts of the symbolic actions of the prophet, which have as their subject the judgement on Jerusalem, 8–11 the temple vision, 13.1–14.11 sayings against false prophets. The rest of the section is prophecies of disaster against Judah, Jerusalem and the royal family, among which the allegories of the prostitute Jerusalem in 16, and of the two sisters Oholah (Samaria) and Oholibah (Jerusalem) in 23, the allegory of the eagle, the cedar branch and the vine in 17, the prophetic dirge for Zedekiah, and finally the discussion of the justification of the deportation and exile with its principle of individual divine recompense in 18, deserve special mention.

The oracles against foreign nations follow in 25–32: against Ammon, Moab, Edom and the Philistines in 25, against Tyre and Sidon in 26–28, and against Egypt in 29–32; cf. also the saying against Edom in 35 and the prophecy against Gog from Magog in 38–39.

Within 34–48, 34–39 deal with the approach of salvation and 40–48 with the time of salvation. In 34–39 we find the speech on the shepherds in 34, the saying against the mountains of Seir in 35, the promise to the mountains of Israel and the collection and renewal of the people of God in 36, the vision of the field of the dead and the report of a symbolic action signifying the reunion of the Northern and Southern Kingdoms in 37, and the announcement of the attack and the fall of Gog from Magog in 38–39. 40–48, described as Ezekiel's reconstruction programme consist in the vision of the new temple in 40–42, the entry of Yahweh into the sanctuary in 43, the laws of the sanctuary in 44–46, the temple spring and the river of paradise in 47.1–12, and the specifications of the frontiers and the division of the land in 47.13–48.35.

2. *The literary problem.* Earlier scholars were persuaded by the planned structure and generally uniform linguistic form of the book to regard chapters 1–48 as a literary whole which had no problems. Its prolixity was dealt with partly by having recourse to the shorter and better Septuagint text, partly by understanding Ezekiel as a late prophet who actually wrote his oracles down[1]. Kraetzschmar with his commentary which appeared in 1900 brought new life into the discussion. He believed he could discern a difference between two parallel recensions, distinguished by having accounts in the first and third persons, from which a redactor had formed the present whole. While the basis in the text for this hypothesis appears to be too weak, the idea of different versions of the book which were subsequently joined together found many adherents, until J. Herrmann in 1908 abandoned formal unity in favour of a unity of content, and so opened up the way to the recognition of Ezekiel as a real prophet.

The problem of authenticity first became a live issue in 1924 with the work of Hölscher, although he had some predecessors. Stimulated by Duhm's commentary on Jeremiah, he made his basic criterion of authenticity the distinction between poetry and prose, only admitting the narrative of the call and the accounts of the symbolic actions and visions as genuine prophetic prose texts. Using a number of additional objective and even aesthetic criteria he reduced the basic part of the book going back to Ezekiel from 1273 to 170 verses in chapters 1–32, treating the whole proclamation of salvation in 33–48 as secondary. Everything that was reminiscent of Deuteronomy, of the late date of which Hölscher was convinced[2], and of the Code of Holiness, was denied to the prophet by the use of the theory of a redactor and of several later writers who supplemented Ezekiel, while the work of the redactor was regarded as a polemical writing of the Zadokite priesthood in Jerusalem from the early fifth century[3].

1. Cf. the surveys of the development of scholarship in C. Kuhl, op. cit.; G. Fohrer, *Hauptprobleme*, pp. 27 ff.; W. A. Irwin, *VT* 3 (1953), pp. 54 ff.; H. H. Rowley, op. cit., and H. G. May, *IB* 6, 1956, pp. 41 ff.
2. Cf. above, pp. 127 f.
3. Hölscher left to the prophet Ezekiel 1.4, 28*; 2.8–3.2, 10–11?,

Torrey went yet further (indeed certainly went too far) in regarding the book as a pseudepigraph, the core of which had originated about 230 B.C., and which purported to be a prophecy from the thirtieth year of Manasseh (cf. 1.1, with 2 Kgs. 21.1 ff. in the background). Subsequently the book was attributed to an exilic prophet Ezekiel, and re-edited, the dates being then altered to the era of the deportation of Jehoiachin. While Burrows supported Torrey, J. Smith argued that the prophet did in fact appear under Manasseh in the Northern Kingdom, and Messel that he appeared about 400; these hypotheses found no supporters.

In view of the sections which undoubtedly presupposed the exile Smith distinguished between a northern Israelite and a later exilic book. The question of a Palestinian ministry of the prophet, raised by 8–11, was brought into prominence however by Herntrich. He believed that in the basic form of 1–39 he could find the work of an Ezekiel active in Jerusalem before 587, and in the rest of the book, including the plan for a constitution, a redactor active in exile, according to 40.1 about 573. While this hypothesis found support especially among English-speaking scholars, it was modified by Bertholet in 1936 to the claim that within the activity of the prophet himself a distinction must be made between a Jerusalem period extending from 593 to 586, introduced by the vision of the scrolls, and an exilic period beginning in 585 with the vision of the chariot, a view which found support from H. W. Robinson, Kuhl and Steinmann into the fifties. Pfeiffer's* thesis of a return of the prophet to Jerusalem after his deportation in 598 and a second journey to Babylonia in 588 or 587 is a distinctive variant of this. On the other hand Cooke, in his commentary which appeared at the same time as Bertholet's, strongly rejected Herntrich's view and upheld an exclusive activity of the prophet in exile, regarding the temple vision in 8–11 as ecstatic, as do all the more recent defenders of this view. If the temple vision is not to be excluded

14b–15; 3.16a, 24b; 4.1–2, 9a, 10–11; 5.1–2; 8.1–3*, 5–7a, 9–12*, 13–17; 9.1a, 2, 3b, 4–5a, 6*, 7b; 11.24*, 25; 15.1–2*, 3, 4b, 5; 16.3–4*, 6–12*, 15*, 24–25*?; 17, 3–9*; 19.2–6, 7b, 9*; 21.9, 11a, 14b*, 15b, 16 (Heb. 21.14, 16a, 19b*, 20b, 21); 23.3, 4a, 5–6*, 11a, 14b*, 15*, 16, 17*, 19–20*, 22a*, 23a*, 24, 25a*, 27; 24.3b–5*, 16–17*; 27.3–9*, 26–36*; 28.12–19*; 29.3–5*; 30.21*; 31.3–8*; 32.18–19*, 22–24*, 26–27*.

as secondary, the assumption of a double or still more a purely Palestinian ministry creates more problems than it solves.

Among German-speaking scholars at least Fohrer gave this view its death blow in 1952. Because of his acceptance of the hypothesis proposed by Balla and to this day disputed, of the 'short verse', i.e. a metrical unit without parallelism, consisting of two or three beats, several of which can be joined together to form a strophe[4], for Fohrer the justification of the basic literary-critical argument used by Hölscher disappears. Apart from the numerous glosses, with which he like every expositor of the book has to struggle, the relationship between the original and the redactional material is precisely the opposite for him of what it is on Hölscher's view. He considers that he is only compelled to exclude 210 verses as larger redactional additions[5]. In his view Ezekiel wrote down his sayings, which were originally orally uttered, individually, and left them without arrangement either by date or subject matter. The basic form of the book was built up, on a partly chronological and partly subject-matter basis, out of individual collections themselves in part formed on considerations of subject-matter, in part just on association by catchword. The transposition of the sayings against the nations to follow the sayings of disaster directed against Judah and Jerusalem, expansions, glosses, links and transpositions are also redactional.

Eichrodt on the other hand works in terms of two documents written by Ezekiel, one containing the oracles about the nations in 26–32, and another whose *leitmotif* is derived from the first-person reports of the prophet. Apart from this a whole series of individual writings of the prophet are to be allowed for, which were joined up with the rest of the material when the two collections were linked together by a redactor. Apart from this he takes a similar view of redactional activity to that of Fohrer. Zimmerli represents the development of the book as taking place

4. Cf. Fohrer, *Hauptprobleme*, pp. 60 ff.; id., 'Über den Kurzvers', *ZAW* 66 (1954), pp. 199 ff. = BZAW 99, 1967, pp. 59 ff., cf. S. Mowinckel, *ZAW* 65 (1953), pp. 167 ff.; *ZAW* 68 (1956), pp. 97 ff.

5. Fohrer brackets as additions, apart from the glosses, 6.8–10; 12.16; 16.30–34, 44–58, 59–63; 17.22–24; 21.28–32 (Heb. 21.33–37); 22.6–13, 15–16, 23–31; 23.36–49; 27.9b, 11–24; 28.20–26; 30.13–19; 32.9–16; 33.7–9; 40.38–43; 41.15b–26; 43.10–27; 45.18–20; 45.21–46.15; 46.16–18, 19–24; 48.1–29, 30–35.

essentially in three stages. The oral delivery by the prophet, still reflected in the rhythmically formed passages, is followed by a fixing in writing carried out by Ezekiel himself. This is followed by a continuous development in several stages, which goes back partly to the prophet, partly to further redaction of the work by the school of Ezekiel, although the additions of the prophet cannot always be distinguished clearly from those of his school. While the problem of the successive layers of the book has been brought into sight again, and the way pointed for future literary-critical work on the book, it remains to be seen whether the relatively conservative approach to traditio-historical criticism to be seen in his work as well as in Eichrodt's and most recently in Fohrer's will stand the test of criticism.

May ascribes the present largely unitary linguistic form of the book to an editor who was active also as an author, and is to be placed, with Hölscher, in the early fifth century. His editing of the Ezekiel material that was passed down to him was so intensive that the genuine core can often hardly be separated out[6]. Of the material preserved he ascribes roughly 40 per cent to Ezekiel's pen. Among the passages to be regarded as late in their entirety he includes 3.17–21; 6; 10; 14; 18; 20; 25; 33.1–20, 23–29; 34; 35.1–15; 36 and 38–39, while in 22 and 37 he allows for the possibility of redaction of sayings of Ezekiel. As well as upholding the genuineness of the chariot vision he leaves Ezekiel the temple vision (apart from 10) and a core of the plan for the constitution[7].

May's observations find further support from H. Schultz in his debate with Zimmerli, H. Graf Reventlow and von Rabenau, in that he has succeeded in proving that a single sacral law tradition is to be found in 3.17–21; 14.1–11, 12–20; 18.1–20; 22.1–16 and 33.1–20, while this is completely lacking in the chapters with concrete allusions to the historical situation, which must serve as the basis for the reconstruction of the message of Ezekiel, 4–7*; 9*; 12*; 13*; 15–16*; 19*; 21* and 23–24*. He calls the passages listed first the deutero-Ezekielic basic stratum. Partly following Schulz, but going far beyond his results, Garscha has put forward a full analysis of chs. 1–39, according to which

---

6. Cf. also S. Herrmann, op. cit., pp. 281 f.: 'Ezekiel is as near and as far from us in his book as is the historical Jesus in the Gospel of John.'

7. On the plan for the constitution cf. H. Gese, op. cit.

only 17.1–10* and 23.2–25* go back to Ezekiel, while the basic core of the book is a prophetic book which originated in the first quarter of the fifth century, and which had available a not very extensive stock of material composed in the early post-exilic period. This prophetic book already distinguished between a first period lasting until the fall of Jerusalem, and a following period of public preaching of salvation, in its concern to commend its eschatological preaching, and looked forward beyond the sayings on the foreign nations to the destruction of Gog from Magog. The redaction in the first half of the fifth century includes for Garscha a large part of what Schulz had called 'school' tradition, and which he calls the deutero-Ezekielic stratum. The insertion of the vision of the throne-chariot and of the temple vision (8–11), and probably also that of the basic core of 40–48, is characteristic of this source. The parts claimed by Schulz to form the deutero-Ezekielic basic stratum on the other hand are ascribed to a sacral law stratum which was inserted about 300 B.C. We must then ascribe the picture of the prophet at work among the exiles, and the striking polemic of the book against Palestinian Judaism in favour of the exiles, as well as the view of history as a process leading men to Yahweh, to the unknown redactor of the deutero-Ezekielic stratum. He also inserted the dating pattern, which therefore has no independent value as evidence. It remains to be seen whether this critical position will be supported by form-critical and linguistic evidence in studies still to be made. Zimmerli now ascribes the didactic language of 18, 33.10–20 and 33.1–9 (3.17–21) to a school which attached itself to the prophet, handed on his preaching and edited it. In my view this is in effect in the last resort to recognize the validity of Schulz's arguments[7a], although no consensus seems to be on the way this early about the conclusions to be drawn from them.

3. *The prophet.* In spite of the critical discussion just reported the traditional picture of the prophet will still be given here. The prophet Ezekiel son of Buzi received his call according to 1.1–3; 3.15 on 31 July 593 on the Kebar by the exiles' settlement of Tell Abib. The Kebar is probably the present-day *šaṭṭ en-nîl*, a canal which leaves the Euphrates near Babylon and comes out into it again at Uruk or Warka, and cuts through the ancient Nippur,

7a. ZAW 84, p. 515.

in the neighbourhood of which Tell Abib is to be looked for. Ezekiel, described as a priest, belonged accordingly to the *Golah* (exiles) deported to the south of Babylonia by Nebuchadnezzar in 597, and was probably fully adult at the time of his call[8]. According to Jer. 27–29 (cf. 28.1), in the previous year there had been an anti-Babylonian movement or revolt in Phoenicia and Palestine, which, as the prophetic activity of Ahab ben Kolaiah and Zedekiah ben Maaseiah shows, had also aroused the hopes of the exiles. In contrast to these men, and in agreement with Jeremiah, Ezekiel regarded the days of the kingdom of Judah and of its capital Jerusalem as numbered. His prophetic activity, according to the dates which are scattered through the book, but are in part problematic, lasted at least down to 26 April 571 (cf. 29.17)[9]. According to 3.24 and 8.1 (cf. also 12.1 ff.) the prophet possessed a house of his own, in which according to 8.1 the elders of the exiles occasionally gathered to obtain from him messages from God. According to 24.15 ff. he was married, but his wife died at the beginning of the siege of Jerusalem, in January 588[10]. It is especially the temple vision of 8–11 that has given the prophet the reputation of being an ecstatic and telepathic, while a cataleptic condition has been deduced from 4.4 ff., a puzzling account of a symbolic action. On the basis of 1.1–3.27; 8–11; 37 and 40 ff. Ezekiel has come to be regarded as a visionary. Scholars take different views over how far it is only secondary tradition that is responsible for the features in the picture of the prophet which are felt by us to be paranormal. Even if the chariot vision in 1.1 ff. and the temple vision in 8–11 are in whole or part denied to him, his prophetic dirge over the King of Tyre in 28.12 ff., his threats and his dirge

8. The 'thirtieth year' of 1.1 may be an addition made on the basis of the Jewish view according to which the study of 1.1–28 is only allowed from the age of thirty on, cf. Fohrer, HAT, ad loc.

9. On the dates in 1.1 f.; 8.1; 20.1; 24.1; 26.1; 29.1, 17; 30.20; 31.1; 32.1, 17; 33.21 and 40.1, which count by the year of the deportation of Jehoiachin in 597, cf. the commentaries, the discussion in G. Hölscher, *Hesekiel*, pp. 11 ff., and Fohrer, *Hauptprobleme*, pp. 105 ff., and now also A. Malamat, *IEJ* 18 (1968), pp. 144 ff. The conversion of the dates into our calendar is made on the basis of R. A. Parker and W. H. Dubberstein, *Babylonian Chronology 626 B.C.–A.D. 75*, Brown University Studies 19, Providence 1956.

10. On this problematic narrative cf. Hölscher, op. cit., pp. 128 ff.

over Pharaoh in 29.3 ff.; 31.3 ff. and 32.2 ff. show how strongly
the prophet was influenced by mythical ideas. His taste for
allegories (cf. 16, 17 and 23), pictorial metaphors (cf. 15.2 ff.;
19; 29.3 ff. and 31.3 ff.), and vivid descriptions (cf. 21.9 ff.
[Heb. 21.14 ff.]; 27.3 ff. and 32.17 ff.) show a poet rich in fantasy,
able to use strong colours, who expected Yahweh's judgement
not only on sinful Jerusalem and Judah with their faithless king,
but also on arrogant Egypt and its Pharaoh, wrongly regarded
by the Judaeans as a saviour. His symbolic actions were drastic,
but hardly in as bad taste as later re-editing made them appear.
His reputation as a watcher and exhorter, at home in priestly
circles of ideas, as well as that of being the father of apocalyptic,
has come to him as a result of a failure to recognize the many
redactional expansions of the book. Usually a distinction is made,
if Hölscher's radical literary criticism is rejected, between a first
period of prophecy of judgement lasting down to 587, and a
second period following on from this of prophecy of salvation[11].
This would include the expectations of a second David (cf.
34.23 f. and 37.24 ff.), of the gathering and return of the exiles
and the dispersed of the Southern and the Northern Kingdoms
(cf. 36 and 37), of the giving of a new heart and spirit (cf. 36.24
ff.), in the period of the new covenant (cf. 37.26 ff.), in which
Yahweh's *kāḇôḏ* (glory) is present in the temple (cf. 43.4 ff.),
and a stream flows from the foundations of the temple, whose
life-giving waters swell into a river and flow into the sea, which
is no longer salt, but swarming with fishes (cf. 47.1 ff.).

(j) Obadiah

A. Condamin, 'L'unité d'Abdias', *RB* 9 (1900), pp. 261 ff.; H. Bekel,
'Ein vorexilisches Orakel über Edom in der Klageliederstrophe—die
gemeinsame Quelle von Obadja, 1–9 und Jeremia 49, 7–22', *ThStKr*
80 (1907), pp. 315 ff.; B. Duhm, *Anmerkungen zu den zwölf Propheten*,
Giessen 1911, pp. 87 ff. = *ZAW* 31 (1911), pp. 175 ff.; T. H. Robinson,
'The Structure of the Book of Obadiah', *Journal of Theological Studies*

11. I may state here my own basic agreement with S. Herrmann's
traditio-historically based view that 'it is highly probable that in the
present book of Ezekiel nothing has been preserved which can be regarded
as an expectation of salvation on the part of the exiled prophet', op. cit.,
p. 290.

17 (1916), pp. 402 ff.; W. W. Cannon, 'Israel and Edom: The Oracle of Obadiah', *Theology* 15 (1927), pp. 129 ff., 191 ff.; W. Rudolph, 'Obadja', *ZAW* 49 (1931), pp. 222 ff.; M. Bič, 'Ein verkanntes Thronbesteigungsfestorakel im Alten Testament', *ArOr* 19 (1951), pp. 568 ff.; id., 'Zur Problematik des Buches Obadjah', SVT 1, 1953, pp. 11 ff.; J. Gray, 'The Diaspora of Israel and Judah in Obadiah v. 20', *ZAW* 65 (1953), pp. 53 ff.; G. Fohrer, 'Die Sprüche Obadjas', in *Studia biblica et semitica Th. Ch. Vriezen dedicata*, Wageningen 1966, pp. 81 ff.

Commentaries: KHC Marti 1904; ICC Bewer 1911; HK Nowack 1922[3]; KAT[1] Sellin 1929[2–3]; HS Theis 1937; HAT Robinson 1964[3]; CAT Keller 1965; ATD Weiser 1967[5]; KAT[2] Rudolph 1971.

In spite of, or perhaps because of, its mere twenty-one verses the little book of Obadiah, which comes fourth in the Dodekapropheton, is one of the literary-critical and exegetical cruces of the Old Testament. Apart from the problem of the dating of the oracle of destruction against Edom, which ends with an allusion to the restoration of Israel and to the Kingdom of God, there is disagreement about the unity and subdivisions of the book, and about its relationship to Jer. 49.7 ff.

When an early date after the revolt of Edom against Judah about the middle of the ninth century is maintained for the whole book (e.g. Theis) or for part of it (1*, 2–10, Sellin), the genuineness of all or part of Jer. 49.7 ff. is assumed, and the dependence is seen as lying with Jeremiah. Bič's attempt to see in Obadiah a cult drama, or more exactly a liturgically expanded Enthronement Festival oracle, which was topically reused by Jeremiah after the fall of Jerusalem, is original, but thoroughly improbable. In view of the obvious connection of vv. 11–14, 15b with the participation of the Edomites in the plundering of Jerusalem in 587 (cf. also Lam. 4.21) the problem necessarily changes as soon as one maintains the unity even only of 1–14. If Jer. 49.7 ff. is ascribed to the prophet, our passage has to be explained as dependent on it. If on the other hand 49.7 ff. is regarded as only partially or not at all from Jeremiah, the opposite position becomes inevitable, so e.g. Rudolph,[1] Weiser and Keller. If the unity of the book is abandoned, as it is by Robinson, it is possible to see in 1–4 (par. Jer. 49.14–16) and 5 (par. 49.7–9) an excerpt from the prophecies transmitted in the book of Jeremiah. Finally Bekel presents a quite different possibility, that Obadiah and Jeremiah go back to a common original which has not

1. Cf. now also Rudolph, *Jeremia*, HAT, Tübingen 1968[3], on Jer. 47.7 ff., where he takes a different view of Jeremiah's share in authorship from that in *ZAW* 49 (1931), p. 228.

been preserved, probably to an oracle against Edom by Jeremiah from the period about 605 B.C. The Book of Obadiah would then derive solely from the wish to adapt it to the exilic and post-exilic embitterment against Edom, while the text of Jeremiah is the result of a still later post-exilic redaction.

The general view is that the parallel verses in Jer. 49.7 ff. are dependent on the Book of Obadiah, and that at least 1–14 are to be placed shortly before the fall of Jerusalem in 587, cf. Rudolph, Weiser, Eissfeldt*, Fohrer* and Keller[2]. More allowance will have to be made in the future for Ackroyd's justified remark that on the one hand in view of our relatively limited knowledge of the historical relationships between Judah and Edom we have no certain basis for an exilic dating, and that on the other hand we must bear in mind the possibility of a later stylizing of Edom to be a 'type' of the enemy nation[3].

It is not possible here to examine the numerous different attempts to subdivide the book.[4] Apart from unity (Condamin, Theis and Bič), a division into two, 1–14, 15b after the fall of Jerusalem, 15a, 16–21 a supplement from the late exilic or Maccabaean period (Wellhausen, Marti, Duhm and Nowack), a division into three, 1–14, 15b; 16–18 and 19–21 with all three regarded as originating soon after 587 (Weiser and Rudolph, although the latter regards 21 as the original ending, and 19 f. as an addition which cannot be more exactly dated), a division into six units, of which the first five are to be dated after 587, while 19–21 are to be regarded as a post-exilic addition, the units being 1b*–4, 5–7; 8–11; 12–14; 15b; 15a; 16–18 and 19–21 (Fohrer), Sellin and Robinson have provided yet more detailed analyses. Sellin finds in 1.2–10 an oracle from the ninth century, in 11–14, 15b a saying from the period after 587, in 15a, 16, 17a and 21 an announcement of the Day of the Lord from the period about 400, and in 17b, 19 and 20 a yet later announcement of the restoration of Israel. Robinson divides the book into eight fragments, which he places between the sixth and the fourth centuries.

If the different attempts at a solution are examined, it will be seen that the main problem rests in 16–21 or 19–21, and that at least 19–21 are to be regarded as post-exilic; while the mention

2. Cf. the survey in M. Bič, *ArOr* 19 (1951), pp. 568 ff.
3. *Exile and Restoration*, OTL, 1968, p. 224.
4. Cf. the survey in G. Fohrer, 'Sprüche Obadjas', op. cit., pp. 81 ff.

of the Day of the Lord in 16–18 does not provide a compelling reason to abandon a dating in around 587.

It is hardly possible to decide whether the book is pseudonymous and the name Obadiah (meaning 'servant of the Lord') taken from 1 Kgs. 18.1 ff., or whether the old prophecies brought together here really go back to a prophet called Obadiah; but this is of no importance for the understanding of the book. While its core may go back to a cultic prophet, v. 15b shows us that it is not only his feelings of neighbourliness and national honour, which have been injured, but also the belief in the justice of God ruling in history, that provide the basis for the proclamation of judgement upon Edom. The belief found in 15a, 16–21 in the Day of the Lord, which is connected with the judgement on the nations, in the significance of Zion as a place of refuge in the world struggle and the conviction of the future restoration of Israel under the rule of Yahweh suffice to give these verses, whether or not they are wholly or partly redactional, a significance in the history of Jewish religion.

(k) Deutero-Isaiah (Isaiah 40–55)

H. Gressmann, 'Die literarische Analyse Deuterojesajas', *ZAW* 34 (1914), pp. 254 ff.; L. Köhler, *Deuterojesaja (Jesaja 40–55) stilkritisch untersucht*, BZAW 37, 1923; J. Hempel, 'Vom irrenden Glauben' [1930], *Apoxysmata*, BZAW 81, Berlin 1961, pp. 174 ff.; S. Mowinckel, 'Die Komposition des deuterojesajanischen Buches', *ZAW* 49 (1931), pp. 87 ff., 142 ff.; id., 'Neuere Forschungen zu Deuterojesaja, Tritojesaja und dem Äbäd-Jahwä-Problem', *AcOr(L)* 16 (1938), pp. 1 ff.; K. Elliger, *Deuterojesaja in seinem Verhältnis zu Tritojesaja*, BWANT IV, 11, 1933; W. Caspari, *Lieder und Gottessprüche der Rückwanderer (Jes 40–55)*, BZAW 65, 1934; L. Glahn, 'Die Einheit von Kap. 40–66 des Buches Jesaja', in L. Glahn and L. Köhler, *Der Prophet der Heimkehr (Jesaja 40–66)*, Copenhagen and Giessen 1934; J. Begrich, *Studien zu Deuterojesaja*, BWANT IV, 25, 1938 = ThB 20, 1963; S. Smith, *Isaiah Chapters XL–LV. Literary Criticism and History*, London 1944; C. R. North, 'The "Former Things" and the "New Things" in Deutero-Isaiah', in *Studies in Old Testament Prophecy*, Festschrift T. H. Robinson, Edinburgh 1950, pp. 111 ff.; K. Elliger, 'Der Begriff "Geschichte" bei Deuterojesaja' [1953], *Kleine Schriften zum Alten Testament*, ThB 32, 1966, pp. 199 ff.; H. E. von Waldow, *Anlass und Hintergrund der Verkündigung des Deuterojesaja*, Diss. ev. theol. Bonn 1953; R. Rendtorff, 'Die theologische Stellung des Schöpfungsglaubens bei Deuterojesaja', *ZTK* 51 (1954), pp. 3 ff.; E. Jenni, 'Die Rolle des Kyros bei Deuterojesaja', *ThZ* 10 (1954), pp. 241 ff.; B. J. van der Merwe, *Pentateuchtradisies in die prediking van Deuterojesaja*, Groningen and Djakarta 1955; P. A. H. de Boer, *Second-Isaiah's Message*, OTS 11, 1956; L. G. Rignell, *A Study of Isaiah Ch. 40–55*, LUÅ NF 1, 52, 5, 1956; J. Morgenstern, 'The Message of Deutero-Isaiah in its Sequential Unfolding', *HUCA* 29 (1958), pp. 1 ff., 30 ff.; 30 (1959), pp. 1 ff.; id., 'Isaiah 49–55', *HUCA* 36 (1965), pp. 1 ff.; A. S. Kapelrud, 'Levde Deuterojesaja i Judaea?', *Norsk Teologisk Tidsskrift* 61 (1960), pp. 23 ff.; W. Zimmerli, 'Der "neue Exodus" in der Verkündigung der beiden grossen Exilspropheten' [1960], *Gottes Offenbarung*, ThB 19, 1963, pp. 192 ff.; id., 'Der Wahrheitserweis Jahwes nach der Botschaft der beiden Exilspropheten', in *Tradition und Situation*, Festschrift A. Weiser, Göttingen 1963, pp. 133 ff.; B. W. Anderson, 'Exodus Typology in Second Isaiah', in *Israel's Prophetic Heritage*, Festschrift J. Muilenburg, ed. B. W. Anderson and W. Harrelson, 1962, pp. 177 ff.; O. Eissfeldt, 'The Promises of Grace to David in Isaiah 55, 1–5', ibid., pp. 196 ff.; M. Haran, 'The Literary Structure and Chronological Framework of the Prophecies in Is. xl–xlviii', SVT 9, 1963, pp. 127 ff.; J. C. Kim, *Jahwe und die Götter bei Deutero-jesaja*, Diss. theol. Heidelberg 1964; C. Westermann, 'Das Heilswort bei Deuterojesaja', *EvTh* 24 (1964), pp. 355 ff.; id., 'Sprache und Struktur der Prophetie Deuterojesajas', in *Forschung am Alten Testament*, ThB 24, 1964, pp. 92 ff.; id., 'Jesaja 48 und die "Bezeugung gegen Israel"', in *Studia biblica et semitica Th. Ch. Vriezen dedicata*, Wageningen 1966, pp. 356 ff.; E. Hessler, 'Die Struktur der Bilder bei Deuterojesaja', *EvTh* 25 (1965), pp. 349 ff.; H. M. Orlinsky and N. H. Snaith, *Studies on the Second Part of the Book of Isaiah*, SVT 14, 1967; L. J. Schüppenhaus, 'Stellung und Funktion der sogenannten Heilsankündigung bei Deuterojesaja', *ThZ* 27 (1971), pp. 161 ff.; R. F. Melugin, 'Deutero-Isaiah and Form Criticism', *VT* 21 (1971), pp. 326 ff.

Commentaries: BC Delitzsch 1889[4]; KeH Dillmann, rev. Kittel 1898[6]; KHC Marti 1900; HK Duhm 1892, 1922[4] (=1968[5]); HSAT[4] Budde 1922; EH Feldmann 1926; KAT[1] Volz 1932; HS Fischer 1939; IB Muilenburg 1956; Zürcher Bibelkommentare (Zurich and Stuttgart) Fohrer 1967[2]; AB McKenzie 1968; OTL Westermann 1969; BK Elliger 1970 ff.; SC König 1926; Kissane 1943; Bentzen 1943; North 1964; Knight 1965; Smart 1965 (1967).

1. The book. The sixteen chapters of Isaiah 40–55 form a distinct unit, as has been generally recognized since Duhm's commentary on Isaiah of 1892[1]. Eichhorn a full hundred years earlier had already observed that 40–66 could not possibly come from the Isaiah active as a prophet in the eighth century. But it was Duhm who first taught us to distinguish between 40–55 and 56–66, and thus between Deutero- and Trito-Isaiah. In the anonymous prophecies collected in 40–55 the unity of language, style, message and situation show that we have the work of one man, whom we call Second Isaiah or Deutero-Isaiah because his words were handed down in the Book of Isaiah.

The prologue (40.1–11) and the epilogue (55.6–11) give the collection its relatively self-contained appearance. 41–48 are related to the expectation of Cyrus, 49–55 centre on the coming salvation for Zion and for the people of God. While Mowinckel attempted to explain the structure on the basis of an association by catchwords, Elliger has underlined the connection in content between the individual passages, and sees in Trito-Isaiah the actual collector and redactor of the book. Westermann also sees a planned structure in the book. Larger connected groups of passages are rounded off by hymns. The placing of the controversy sayings or disputations in 40.12–31 and 49.14–26 each at the beginning of one of the two parts of the collection, the contrasting to be seen in 40.12–31 and elsewhere of sections which are concerned with the question of Yahweh's power to redeem, with those which hold out the prospect of this redemption[2], and the separate place given to 54 f., which refer not to deliverance but to the coming period of salvation, show that in 40–55 we have a conscious composition. On the question whether the songs of the Servant of Yahweh (the servant songs) 42.1–4(9); 49.1–6; 50.4–9(11) and 52.13–53.12 are in whole or part to be denied

---

1. Other views such as that of J. Morgenstern, who limits Deutero-Isaiah to 40–48, of M. Haran, who ascribes all of 40–66 to the same prophet, but distinguishes between an exilic and a Palestinian period of his activity in 40–48 and 49–66, and of C. C. Torrey and J. D. Smart, who regard (34–)35 and 40–66 as a unity, are gathered together in F. Maass, 'Tritojesaja?', in: *Das ferne und nahe Wort*, Festschrift L. Rost, BZAW 105, 1967, pp. 153 ff. In view of the arguments in D. Michel, 'Zur Eigenart Tritojesajas', *ThV* 10 (1965–66), pp. 213 ff., the assignment of 56–66 to Deutero-Isaiah remains improbable. Cf. also the survey in N. H. Snaith, SVT 14, pp. 218 ff. Snaith himself assigns 60–62 to Deutero-Isaiah.

2. Cf. R. F. Melugin, op. cit., pp. 336 f.

to the prophet, the views taken by scholars differ both on literary-critical grounds and on grounds of content[3]. The polemics against the making of idols and the cult of idols in 40.19–20; 41.6–7; 42.17; 44.9–20; 45.16–17, 20b; 46.5–8 and 48.22 are in any case to be regarded as later additions.

We must also allow for the insertion of smaller additions in 40.7a?, b, 14bα, 16; 41.8b, 19a?, 20?; 42.16bβ, 21, 24bβγ; 43.5a, 7b*, 8?, 12b. 14bβ, 21?, 28a; 44.5, 28b; 45.5b?, 9–10?, 14?, 18aα*, b?; 46.9bβ; 47.3a, 14b; 48.1bβ, 4, 5b, 8–10, 16aα*, b, 19b?, 22; 49.18bα*?, 21bα*; 50.3?, 11?; 51.1–2, 4–8?, 11 and 52.4–6[4].

This survey shows that the book is in general preserved in its original form.

2. *Literary types.* An examination of the main literary types and elements of types used by Deutero-Isaiah, such as promise of salvation, announcement of salvation, discussion saying or disputation, lawsuit oracle, formula of self-predication and hymn, already introduces us to the message of the prophet.

The promises of salvation, which according to Begrich are derived from priestly oracles of salvation, 'announce the coming of salvation as a fact' (Westermann). They go back to the cultic practice of the communication of oracles by priests or prophets (von Waldow and Kaiser), which answered an individual lament. They consist of a direct address, a declaration of salvation ('fear not'), and the grounds for and consequences of it (cf. e.g. 41.8–13; 41.14–16; 43.1–4; 43.5–7; 44.1–5 and 54.4–6). With Westermann a distinction must be made between the oracle of salvation or promise of salvation and the announcement of salvation, which holds out the prospect of future salvation, and is found either in connection with the promise of salvation (cf. 41.8–13), or independently. It lacks the address and declaration of salvation; instead it first harks back to the communal lament, in order then to give assurance of God's attention and intervention in the announcement, and finally to declare the purpose of these (cf. 41.17–20; 42.14–17; 43.16–21; 45.1, 14–17 and 49.7–12). Elements of the announcement of salvation are found also within other literary types, all of which are at the service of the prophet's announcement of salvation[5].

3. Cf. below, pp. 266 ff.
4. Cf. Fohrer and Westermann on these passages.
5. J. Schüppenhaus, op. cit., has expressed doubts about classing all form-elements set in the future as a special literary type to be called an

The discussion saying (disputation saying) or contestation serves to refute objections made against the message of salvation. It may or may not begin by taking up the objection, and consists of the basis of the disputation, and the inference. The basis serves to establish a basic agreement with the partner in the discussion, the inference to take up his objection and lead him to give it up. The objection can often only be deduced from the questions put, which at the same time provide the basis of the disputation. The intention of the contestations is parenetic (cf. 40.12–31 and 49.14–26). Functionally the frequently occurring lawsuit oracle is related to the discussion saying. It is found in two forms. In one Yahweh stands over against the nations or their gods, in the other over against Israel. As the basic form we may, with Westermann, assume a construction from summons, hearing, divided up into speeches of the parties and hearing of witnesses, and decision[6]. In the speeches in which Yahweh stands over against the nations, the question at issue is the decision made on his claim to be the true and only God (cf. 41.1–5; 41.21–29; 43.8–13(15); 44.6–8 and 45.20–25). In these proceedings Yahweh represents himself as the first and last and only God (cf. 41.4; 43.10–13, 15; 44.6, 8; 45.21–23, and also 44.24–28; 45.5, 18f.; 46.9–11; 48.12 f.). When Yahweh and Israel are opposed, the question at issue is the refutation of the charges made by Israel against Yahweh, and therefore also Israel's guilt in the past (cf. 43.22–28; 50.1–2(3) and 42.18–25*). Here the reference back by the prophet to the communal lament again appears clearly. As well as the hymnic participial style, and the recurring self-predications of God as the first and last, the creator and redeemer, there are found small hymns which respond to the message of salvation with anticipatory joy (cf. 42.10–13; 44.23; 45.8; 48.20 f. and 52.9 f.).

3. The prophet. Whether we can learn more about the person of Deutero-Isaiah than can be deduced from 40.1–11, a kerygmatically re-formed call narrative, is a contested point, and depends on the interpretation of the servant songs. If the Servant of Yahweh is identified with the prophet, as e.g. by Elliger and

---

announcement of salvation, and instead describes them as 'comforting promises, and asseverations which refuse to entertain doubt, directed into the future'. In doing so he is undoubtedly right in directing attention to the function of these form-elements.

6. Cf. also L. Köhler, *Deuterojesaja stilkritisch untersucht*, pp. 110 ff.; J. Begrich, *Studien zu Deuterojesaja*, pp. 19 ff. = 26 ff.; H. J. Boecker, *Redeformen des Rechtslebens im Alten Testament*, WMANT 14, 1964, and C. Westermann, 'Sprache und Struktur der Prophetie Deuterojesajas', op. cit., pp. 134 ff.

Weiser*, we find here statements about the call, commission, suffering and death of the prophet. On other interpretations too at least 50.4–9(11) must be connected with the experience of the prophet. We are on firm ground with the question of the date. In 44.28 and 45.1 the Persian king Cyrus (559–529) is mentioned by name. 41.2 f., 25 speak of his surprising victorious advance; according to 48.14 f. he is to perform Yahweh's will on Babylon and the Chaldaeans, according to 44.26 and 45.13 to build again Jerusalem and its temple[7]. The situation of the exile is everywhere presupposed (cf. 40.10; 52.8; 49.17; 44.26; 52.11 f.; 42.14 and 47.1). Deutero-Isaiah is accordingly a contemporary of Cyrus. Since his activity seems to cover quite a long period, his work should not be restricted to the period immediately before the conquest of Babylon by Cyrus in 539. It cannot be decided with certainty whether his activity began as early as the capture of the capital of Media, Ecbatana, in 553 or, as is more probable, only after the conquest of the capital of Lydia, Sardis, in 546 by Cyrus, or some time later still; but this is unimportant for the understanding of his message. Begrich's attempt to distinguish between an early stage of his message, purely eschatological in character, and a later stage which placed its hope in Cyrus, has found no supporters. It depends on a failure to recognize the intimate connection of divine and historical event, and leads to an unjustified atomization of the book. While it is now generally assumed that Deutero-Isaiah was one of the exiles, it must be emphasized that his place of ministry too cannot be established with certainty. The prophet can hardly be localized, with Duhm, in Lebanon because of his knowledge of cedars and other woodland trees (cf. 41.19), nor, with Hölscher, in Egypt because of 45.14 and 49.12. Only Babylonia and Palestine are seriously in question. In favour of the first possibility the familiarity of the prophet with Babylonian religion (Volz), and in favour of the second 48.20 and 52.11 (Mowinckel) are especially adduced. There has even been an attempt to distinguish between a Babylonian (40–48) and a Palestinian period (49–55) (Kittel). While the prophet is widely regarded, following Duhm, as purely a writer, it is now more and more recognized as a result of the study of the Servant Songs (Volz)

7. Cf. also O. Kaiser, *Der königliche Knecht*, FRLANT 70, 1962[2], pp. 128 f.

and of the literary types used by the prophet (von Waldow, Kaiser, Westermann) that Deutero-Isaiah too spoke directly to the community gathered for a service of the word, including lament for what had been lost, and prayer for its restoration. Westermann allows for the possibility that parts especially of 49–55 were intended from the first to be written down. Baltzer connects the anonymity of the prophecy with the transmission of the prophetic commission to Israel as a whole which is undertaken by Deutero-Isaiah in the Servant Songs: the individual recedes behind Israel, of which he is a part and to which he belongs.[8]

4. The servant songs. The never ending scholarly discussion of the servant songs (42.1–4(9); 49.1–6; 50.4–9(11) and 52.13–53.12) shows that the bewilderment which the treasurer of the Ethiopian queen is stated to have felt about who the servant was in Acts 8.34 has still not been dispelled. Recent scholarship received its decisive impetus from Duhm, who saw in them compositions about a teacher of the law who had become a martyr, dating from the first half of the fifth century. While there has been no lack of identifications of the servant with pre-exilic and post-exilic figures, especially in the first thirty years of this century, in the individual interpretation the dominant position is still the identification of the servant with the prophet Deutero-Isaiah, a view held for a while by Mowinckel, in which case the fourth song is understood either as prophetic or as the composition of a pupil (e.g. Trito-Isaiah), cf. e.g. Sellin*, Volz, Elliger, Begrich, Weiser*, Zimmerli, Lindblom, Fohrer and Orlinsky. The traditional messianic interpretation of the Church has recently found a successor, adapted of course to the changed understanding of scripture, through the discovery of motifs coming from the royal cult. The fact that royal and prophetic motifs and others taken from the language of the psalms are linked with one another in a distinctive manner, and that individual and corporate traits intersect, has led a whole series of scholars to see in the servant the coming Messiah, or some other future mediator figure (cf. Engnell, Rowley, Mowinckel, North,

8. K. Baltzer, 'Zur formgeschichtlichen Bestimmung der Texte vom Gottes-Knecht im Deuterojesaja-Buch', in *Probleme biblischer Theologie*, Festschrift G. von Rad, Munich 1971, p. 43.

von Rad and Westermann). But there continue to be many representatives of the collective interpretation, which can appeal to 49.3, where the servant in the text as it stands is identified with Israel, as well to mentions of the servant in context, when he is clearly identified with Israel. This view was defended by Budde, Giesebrecht, and Marti, and has found supporters in Robinson, Eissfeldt, de Boer, Rignell, Kaiser, Snaith, Baltzer and Kapelrud.[9] Of these Robinson and Eissfeldt in particular make use of the Hebrew idea of corporate personality, the understanding of a community as an individual, to explain the individual features of the portrait of the servant. The decision for or against Deutero-Isaiah's authorship, and the view held of the songs, lead to different presentations of the message of the prophet[10].

5. *Message.* In the face of the temptation of the continuing exile, of the collapse of the chosen kingdom of David, of the destruction of the temple, devastation of the land and deportation of its upper classes to Babylonia, the prophet promises to men who doubt Yahweh's power and his will to save the continuation of election, the release of the captives in a second Exodus which will surpass the first, the return of Yahweh to Zion, the coming of his reign over the nations, and the arrival of the time of salvation. The emphasis on the belief in creation, the reference back to the fulfilled prophetic announcements, the repeated emphasis on the activity of Yahweh alone, are all put at the service of the proclamation of salvation, of the opening up of the listeners to the message of the activity of Yahweh now beginning, an activity spanning the world of nature and of the nations, at the centre of which stands Israel, because Yahweh wishes to reveal himself before the nations as he leads Israel out of distress into glory. Israel is in a double sense the servant of Yahweh, both

9. A. S. Kapelrud, 'Second Isaiah and the Suffering Servant', in *Hommages à A. Dupont-Sommer*, Paris 1971, pp. 297 ff.

10. On the history of the interpretation of the servant songs cf. C. R. North, *The Suffering Servant in Deutero-Isaiah*, Oxford 1956[2]; H. H. Rowley, 'The Servant of the Lord in the Light of Three Decades of Criticism', in *The Servant of the Lord*, Oxford 1965[2], pp. 1 ff., and E. Ruprecht, *Die Auslegungsgeschichte zu den sgn. Gottesknechtsliedern im Buch Deuterojesaja unter methodischen Gesichtspunkten bis zu Bernhard Duhm*, diss. Heidelberg 1972. For the literature cf. also Kaiser, op. cit.

standing in his special protection, and being specially witnessed to by him[11].

(*l*) The Trito-Isaianic Collection (*Isa. 56–66*)

Cf. above under (k), and further H. Gressmann, *Über die in Jes. c. 56–66 vorausgesetzten zeitgeschichtlichen Verhältnisse*, Preisschrift phil. Fak. Göttingen, Göttingen 1898; E. Littmann, *Über die Abfassungszeit des Tritojesaja*, Freiburg, Leipzig and Tübingen 1899; K. Cramer, *Der geschichtliche Hintergrund der Kap. 56–66 im Buche Jesaja*, Dorpat 1905; A. Zillesen, ' "Tritojesaja" und Deuterojesaja', *ZAW* 26 (1906), pp. 231 ff.; R. Abramowski, 'Zum literarischen Problem des Tritojesaja', *ThStKr* 96/97 (1925), pp. 90 ff.; K. Elliger, *Die Einheit des Tritojesaja (Jesaja 56–66)*, BWANT III, 9, 1928; id., 'Der Prophet Tritojesaja', *ZAW* 49 (1931), pp. 112 ff.; H. Odeberg, *Trito-Isaiah (Isaiah 56–66). A Literary and Linguistic Analysis*, UUÅ 1931, Teologi 1, Uppsala 1931; W. S. McCullough, 'A Re-Examination of Isaiah 56–66', *JBL* 67 (1948), pp. 27 ff.; W. Zimmerli, 'Zur Sprache Trito-Jesajas' [1950], *Gottes Offenbarung*, ThB 19, 1963, pp. 217 ff.; W. Kessler, 'Studien zur religiösen Situation im ersten nachexilischen Jahrhundert und zur Auslegung von Jes 56–66', *WZHalle* 6 (1956–7), pp. 41 ff.; D. Michel, 'Zur Eigenart Tritojesajas', *ThV* 10 (1965–6), Berlin 1966, pp. 213 ff.; F. Maass, 'Tritojesaja?', in *Das ferne und nahe Wort*, Festschrift L. Rost, BZAW 105, 1967, pp. 153 ff.; N. Pauritsch, *Die neue Gemeinde. Die Botschaft des Tritojesaia-Buches literar-, form-, gattungskritisch und redaktionsgeschichtlich untersucht*, AnBib 47, 1971; E. Sehmsdorf, 'Studien zur Redaktionsgeschichte von Jesaja 56–66 I' and 'II', *ZAW* 84 (1972), pp. 517 ff. and 562 ff.

Commentaries: see under (k), and further BAT Kessler 1960.

1. The history of research. Among the problems of the prophetic tradition which have not yet been satisfactorily solved is the question of the literary unity, distinctive character and date of Isa. 56–66. The decisive turning point in recent scholarship was the view proposed by Duhm in 1892 that these chapters were independent of the preceding Deutero-Isaianic collection. With the support of Marti, Littmann and Zillesen he believed he could see in 56–66 the work of an author active as a contemporary of Ezra in Jerusalem, whom he called Trito-Isaiah. In the last forty years the unity of the book has been upheld especially by

11. Cf. also Kaiser, *RGG* III[3], cols. 606 ff.

Elliger and Kessler. Building upon style-critical and historical arguments Elliger, who was supported by Meinhold* and Sellin, took the view that Trito-Isaiah was a pupil of Deutero-Isaiah, and was active in Jerusalem between 538 and a time shortly after 515 in Jerusalem. Kessler on the other hand thinks of a longer period of activity between 520 and 445, but in any case before Malachi. The separation of the Trito-Isaianic prophecies from those of Deutero-Isaiah has been so well established through the investigations of Zillesen, Elliger, Odeberg, Zimmerli and Michel, who have demonstrated differences of style, form and content between the two collections, although chaps. 56–66 are dependent on 40–55, that (in spite of repeated counter-arguments down to the present day) it can be regarded as proved[1]. At the same time it must be said that there have always been some, and are now an increasing number, who doubt the original unity of the Trito-Isaianic collection. So scholars such as Kittel, Budde*, Abramowski, Volz, Eissfeldt*, Weiser*, Anderson*, Fohrer and Westermann divide up the sayings collected here in different ways over the period between the seventh and the third century.

2. *Literary-critical problem.* The literary problem lies in the fact that the passages collected in 56–66 neither consistently presuppose the same external and internal situation for the community, nor are dependent in the same way on the Deutero-Isaianic and other traditions. It is also a matter for question whether the same eschatological ideas are to be found everywhere.

The analysis is best begun from the passages for which an exilic or even pre-exilic origin has often been suggested. The lament of the people (63.15–64.12, Heb. 64.11) belongs with greatest certainty to the period of the exile, since 63.18 and 64.10 f. (Heb. 64.9 ff.) presuppose the destruction of Jerusalem, but not the developments after 538. It must remain doubtful, in spite of Volz, Fohrer and Westermann, whether it is right to place the communal lament 63.7–14, which is dominated by traits of the historical psalm, in the same period. It is noteworthy that both songs show no trace of influence by Deutero-Isaiah. Accordingly a special position is appropriate for both sections. The course of discussion shows how uncertain the theory of a pre-exilic origin for 56.9–57.13 is. If, with Westermann, we were to place

1. On this cf. F. Maass, 'Tritojesaja?', op. cit.

56.9–12 and 57.3–6 so early, while allowing the post-exilic composition of 57.1 f. and 57.7–13*, we would still have to refute the arguments produced by Fohrer for dependence on sayings in Jeremiah and Ezekiel. Abramowski abandoned the attempt to date this section and to solve its problems definitively, and this remains a last resort. At the head of the numerous passages to which, in spite of their poetic power, an atmosphere of scriptural learning attaches, are 60–62. They centre on the themes of the future glorification of Jerusalem, its temple, the return of the people of Yahweh and the subservient status of the nations. Here it must be noticed that words in sentences and phrases taken over from Deutero-Isaiah sometimes alter in sense (cf. 58.8; 60.4, 9, 16 and 62.11). The alteration of Deutero-Isaianic sayings appears especially clearly in 57.14–20 (21), where 40.4 ff. has been taken over figuratively to be an 'element of a general pious exhortation' (Zimmerli). 58.1–12, the exhortation about proper fasting, appears according to Michel to have three layers: a prophetic answer to a communal lament, a midrashic exposition and a subsequent qualification of this. Since the prophetic answer contains quotations from Deutero-Isaiah, Hosea and Micah, at least the first two strata appear to be preaching based on scripture. The distinctive recasting of Deutero-Isaianic ideas is found again in 65.16b–24(25). The idea that Yahweh's new action will make men forget his former one, which in Deutero-Isaiah is connected with the expectation of the second exodus, is now transferred to the tangible salvation which is imminent for Jerusalem (cf. 43.18 ff.). A similar position can be observed with 66.6–16. 59.1–20(21), a quite distinctive sermon imitating a prophetic liturgy, which announces Yahweh's intervention on behalf of his repentant people, also has numerous echoes of Deutero-Isaiah. Compared with these passages, 63.1–6, a powerful description of God returning from the judgement of the nations, 65.1–16a, the announcement of salvation for the pious and of disaster for the worshippers of idols, 66.1–4, a polemic against sacrifices perhaps expanded by a Deuteronomistic addition, and 56.1–8, a prophetic Torah on membership of the community which serves as a prologue, as well as some smaller passages, have a separate position and are more independent.

A survey will show that 63.7–64.12 (Heb. 64.11) are in a separate position, as are 65.1–16a, 66.1–4, 56.1–8 and 56.9–57.13. Here we seem to have sayings which, apart from 63.15–64.12 (Heb. 64.11), may all come from the post-exilic period, without any influence of Deutero-Isaiah being traceable. This leaves only 60–62; 65.16b–24(25); 66.6–16 and 57.14–21 as proclamations of salvation, and 58.1–12 and 59.1–20(21) in a position separate from the first complex, as Trito-Isaianic in the strict sense. The first problem is whether in the central block of Isaiah 60.19–20; 65.17a, 25 and 66.6, 15–16 are with Westermann to be regarded as apocalyptic additions to be taken together with 66.20, 22–24. The second problem is whether with Sehmsdorf we can regard 56.1–8; 58.13 f.; 60.18a; 62.8 f.; 65.1–16   19b–24* and 66.1–4* as belonging to redactions in several stages from a viewpoint close to the Deuteronomistic theology, and what part they played in the history of the Trito-Isaianic collection if we regard the case for this as proved. The third is whether it is conceivable, in view of what we know about early post-exilic prophecy from Haggai and Zechariah, to ascribe even just this central block to a Trito-Isaiah active between 538 and 515. While the possibility of an apocalyptic redaction must be held open because of 66.20, 22–24, it appears to me that the assumption that the material in Trito-Isaiah originated at the end of the sixth century is laden with difficulties, because it must be agreed with Michel that the period of scriptural exposition begins with this material. It is questionable whether they can even be dated as early as the period before Nehemiah.

3. Structure. The origin of the collection 56–66 and its attachment to the book of Isaiah as enlarged by 40–55 is best understood if we take as coming first the addition of the texts above called the Trito-Isaianic central block, 57.14–20; 60–62*; 65.16b–19a and 66.7–14. Next, 58.1–12 and 59.1–20 will have been added. The subsequent development can only be conjectured. It looks as if the present structure of the book is based on the two-element eschatological scheme. The sections reflecting the tensions within the community, 56.9–57.13; 65.1–16a and 66.1–4, in so far as they have not been successively added, could have been inserted as a group together with 63.7–64.12 (Heb. 64.11), so that a pattern resulted of 56–59 judgement and 60–62 salvation, 63–65.16a judgement and 65.16b + 66.7–14 salvation. 63.7 is in any case responsible for the addition of 63.1–6. When this pattern was being formed 56.1–8 may have been prefixed as a prologue. It can hardly be decided whether the passage stressing the keeping of the sabbath (58.13–14) and the consolation saying for the pious (66.5), were added at the same time or later. 57.13b, 20, 21; 59.21; 60.12 and 65.25 are secondary additions.

The last full redaction is that of the apocalyptic additions, which must, with Westermann, be reckoned to include not only 66.20, 22–24, but also 60.19–20, 65.17a, 25 and (earlier in date) 66.6, 15–16.

4. Significance. It will be clear that a collection including passages from very different centuries is of exceptional interest for the history of religion and literature, because with correct analysis and arrangement it can extend our knowledge of an obscure period in Jewish history. The communal lament 63.15–64.12 (Heb. 64.11) is added to the exilic documents as a companion piece to Lamentations. The Trito-Isaianic compositions on the one hand bear witness to the influence of Deutero-Isaiah, and the hopes of salvation of Judaism, which did not die out with him. They give us on the other hand an important insight into a familiarity with tradition, and a preaching of scripture, which at least stand on the border between prophecy and exegesis. From a comparison of the redactions of and additions to the prophetic books it will be possible to paint a more exact picture of the history of Jewish expectations of salvation than we possess today. The sections which deal with the internal problems of the community are also of immediate interest. Perhaps in part older than the Trito-Isaianic compositions, they make possible for us an insight into the social and religious dangers to which Judaism in Palestine was exposed, and at the same time into a piety not narrowly bound by the cult, which was uneasy about the significance of fasts and sacrifices, was consciously separated from all idolatry, and at least in part took a far from narrow view of the possibility of membership of its community (it must be noted that 56.1 ff. set aside taboos of all kinds) and yet could regard the observance of the sabbath and abstention from all evil as forming a unity, and indeed had to[2].

(m) Haggai

K. Budde, 'Zum Text der drei kleinen Propheten', *ZAW* 26 (1906), pp. 1 ff.; J. W. Rothstein, *Juden und Samaritaner*, BWAT 3, 1908; B.

2. Cf., though with different literary critical presuppositions, also O. Kaiser, *RGG* III³, col. 610.

Duhm, *Anmerkungen zu den zwölf Propheten*, Giessen 1911, pp. 69 ff.
= *ZAW* 31 (1911), pp. 107 ff.; F. James, 'Thoughts on Haggai and
Zechariah', *JBL* 53 (1934), pp. 229 ff.; P. R. Ackroyd, 'Studies in the
Book of Haggai', *JJS* 2 (1951), pp. 163 ff.; 3 (1952), pp. 1 ff.; id., 'The
Book of Haggai and Zechariah 1–8', *JJS* 3 (1952), pp. 151 ff.; H. W.
Wolff, *Haggai*, BSt 1, 1951; F. S. North, 'Critical Analysis of the Book of
Haggai', *ZAW* 68 (1956), pp. 25 ff.; R. T. Siebeneck, 'The Messianism
of Aggeus and Proto-Zacharias', *CBQ* 19 (1957), pp. 312 ff.; F. Hesse,
'Haggai', in *Verbannung und Heimkehr*, Festschrift W. Rudolph,
Tübingen 1961, pp. 109 ff.; K. Galling, 'Serubbabel und der Hohe-
priester beim Wiederaufbau des Tempels in Jerusalem', in *Studien zur
Geschichte Israels im persischen Zeitalter*, Tübingen 1964, pp. 127 ff.;
K. Koch, 'Haggais unreines Volk', *ZAW* 79 (1967), pp. 52 ff.; W. A. M.
Beuken, *Haggai-Sacharja 1–8. Studien zur Überlieferungsgeschichte der
frühnachexilischen Prophetie*, SSN 10, 1967.

Commentaries: KHC Marti 1904; ICC Mitchell 1912; HK Nowack
1922[3]; KAT[1] Sellin 1930[2–3]; HS Junker 1938; HAT Horst 1964[3];
ATD Elliger 1967[6]; SC Wellhausen 1898[3] (1963[4]).

I. The book. The Book of Haggai with its two chapters, handed
down tenth in the Book of the Twelve Prophets, takes us to the
time before and after the beginning of the rebuilding of the
temple in the year 520 B.C.

Chapter 1 contains a report of the beginning of the work of rebuilding the temple in Jerusalem which was set off by Haggai's
preaching. Two discussion sayings, 1.2–5 and 9–11, as well as a conditional promise, 1.7 f., are set in a narrative framework. The two discussion sayings are meant to show the listeners that their present economic
distress is a consequence of the fact that the temple is still in ruins.
The conditional promise links the demand to proceed to rebuilding
with the announcement of the revelation of the glory of Yahweh. The
speech of the prophet which is composed out of these units is dated to
the first day of the sixth month of the second year of the Persian king
Darius, i.e. to 29 Aug. 520 B.C. (cf. 1.1), the beginning of the work of
reconstruction to the twenty-fourth day of the sixth month, i.e. to
21 Sept. 520. Chapter 2 is divided into three sections. In 2.1–9 the
narrative introduction in 1–2 is followed in 3–5 by an exhortation and
promise introduced by three questions, so that we can speak here of a
conditional word of exhortation, as in 6–9 of a further unconditional
promise. In the present context 6–9 are to be understood as in effect the
grounds for the promise of 4 f. The questions demand a comparison
of the former glory of the temple with its present ruined state, the

exhortation summons men to work on the temple, while the promise holds out the prospect of God's assistance. The concluding promise looks to the imminent coming of a new era in which the glory of the first temple will be surpassed by that of the second. This second speech of the prophet is dated to the twenty-first day of the seventh month, the last day of the Feast of Tabernacles, i.e. 18 Oct. 520. In 2.10–19 follows a section consisting of an account of a discussion with a concluding prophetic Torah in 11–14, and a salvation saying introduced by a discussion saying. The discussion of clean and unclean ends with a declaration of the uncleanness of 'this people', the discussion in 15 ff. reminds men of present distress, to which a promise of future blessing is contrasted. This third speech is dated to the 24th day of the ninth month, i.e. 18 Dec. 520. Finally the Messianic prophecy addressed to Zerubbabel is also dated to the same day (2.20–23).

This survey already shows that a distinction must be made between the sayings of the prophet proper and the narrative (or sometimes only dating) framework. 1.1–3, 12–15; 2.1–2, 10 and 20 belong to the framework. This poses the difficult traditio-historical problem whether the actual sayings of the prophet were originally transmitted either orally or in writing without the framework, or whether from the start they were written down within it. Eissfeldt's* view, that the narratives are writings of the prophet, which he himself put in the third person for stylistic reasons, has rightly found no supporters. The fact that 1.14 and 2.2 speak in a technical sense of the remnant of the people, while Haggai himself speaks of the '*am hā'āreṣ*, the people of the land, is enough to show the untenable nature of this hypothesis. It cannot be deduced from the dates that the complete composition was finished shortly after 520, as is usually assumed. While they may rest on good tradition, they may, as Ackroyd's careful discussion shows[1], be a late invention, for which all that was needed was a recollection that the work on the temple was begun in the second year of Darius. The secondary character of the dates cannot of course be proved. In the light of the present arrangement of the sayings of the prophet it must be allowed that they could also have been deduced by a redactor from the content[2]. It deserves consideration, as Ackroyd

1. Cf. *JJS* 2 (1951), pp. 172 ff. But cf. now also W. A. M. Beuken, op. cit., pp. 21 ff.

2. The reconstruction of a basic narrative and of a supposed original

suggests, whether the structure shows the two-element eschato-logical scheme, although, because of the particular nature of the material, not so clearly as elsewhere (1 represents the preaching of judgement, 2.1–9 the preaching of salvation, 2.10–19 again the preaching of judgement, and 2.20–23 the preaching of salvation). For the reasons given the book can hardly be dated before the beginning of the fourth century. The possibility must be allowed for that it did not reach its present form until a century later still[3].

The tension between 1.1 and 1.3 is not insuperable. The exclusion of 1.13 is connected with what are, as we shall see, at best dubious literary-critical attacks on 2. Whether 2.17 (cf. Amos 4.9) goes back to the compiler of the book, or to a later redactional insertion, is a question which must be left open. Rothstein has won strong support for his suggestion that 2.15–19 should follow on from 1.15a, a move which results from his connection of 2.10–14 with the exclusion of the Samaritans from the building of the temple. This interpretation depends entirely upon the Chronicler's presentation of the tensions already beginning then between the Jews and the Samaritans (cf. Ezra 4.1 ff.). Whatever view is taken of the historical value of Ezra[4], it must be said that the text provides no support for this inter-pretation. If the question of the specific basis of the cultic disqualification of 'this people' in 2.14 is not to be left open, it can only be connected in the context, with Koch, with the cultic uncleanness of the people resulting from the non-existence of the atoning temple cult. It is in any case Haggai's own people that is to be understood by 'this people'[5]. Then the grounds for the transposition of 2.15–19 and the deletion of 1.13 and 2.18b also disappear.

2. The prophet. We do not know anything about Haggai's place of origin, and nothing compels us to include him among the returning exiles. According to the tradition he was active in

form of the book by F. S. North, op. cit., is ingenious but methodically undisciplined.

3. According to Beuken the redactor of Haggai is identical with the redactor of Zechariah 1–8. Cf. below, pp. 277 f.

4. Cf. above, pp. 181 f.

5. Cf. K. Koch, op. cit., pp. 61 ff.

Jerusalem from 29 August to 18 December 520 B.C. It cannot be decided whether he was really only active in these few months as a prophet, since the sayings collected in the book represent only a selection made from the viewpoint of his contribution to the restoration of the temple in Jerusalem. The Persian disturbances over the succession which began after the death of Cambyses, and lasted from March 522 to November 521, are sometimes supposed to have given rise to Haggai's prophetic activity, but if it is assumed that the dates given in the book are correct, this can only have been to the extent that they may have shattered the feeling of the permanence of the existing political position. Haggai's preaching centres upon the necessity for the rebuilding of the temple, because for him the creation of cultic purity is the precondition of the coming of the time of salvation, of the victory of Yahweh over the nations and of the glorification of Zion. In Zerubbabel, the Persian governor of Judah[6], who was of the Davidic royal line, he saw the king of the time of salvation[7].

(n) *Zechariah* (1–8)

J. W. Rothstein, *Die Nachtgesichte des Sacharja*, BWAT 8, 1910; B. Duhm, *Anmerkungen zu den zwölf Propheten*, Giessen 1911, pp. 73 ff. = *ZAW* 31 (1911), pp. 161 ff.; K. Marti, 'Die Zweifel an der prophetischen Sendung Sacharjas', in *Studien zur Semitischen Philogie und Religionsgeschichte*, Festschrift J. Wellhausen, ed. K. Marti, BZAW 27, 1914, pp. 281 ff.; H. G. May, 'A Key to the Interpretation of Zechariah's Visions', *JBL* 57 (1938), pp. 173 ff.; A. Jepsen, 'Kleine Beiträge zum Zwölfprophetenbuch III', *ZAW* 61 (1945–8), pp. 95 ff.; L. G. Rignell, *Die Nachtgesichte des Sacharja*, Lund 1950; K. Galling, 'Die Exilswende in der Sicht des Propheten Sacharja', in *Studien zur Geschichte Israels im persischen Zeitalter*, Tübingen 1964, pp. 109 ff.; M. Bič, *Die Nachtgesichte des Sacharja*, BSt 42, 1964; W. A. M.

6. Whether he is really to be regarded as governor, or whether he was in Jerusalem with a more limited mandate, can no longer be decided in view of the inadequacy of the sources.

7. On the view given above, the following chronological framework for work on the temple rebuilding results from the dates given in the book: beginning of work on clearing the temple ruins, 21 Sept. 520, interrupted by the Feast of Tabernacles, specific encouragement to further work after the end of the feast, 18 Oct. 520, and laying of the foundation stone, 18 Dec. 520.

Beuken, *Haggai-Sacharja 1–8. Studien zur Überlieferungsgeschichte der frühnachexilischen Prophetie*, SSN 10, 1967; A. Petitjean, *Les oracles du Proto-Zacharie*, Études Bibliques, Paris and Louvain 1969.

Commentaries: KHC Marti 1904; ICC Mitchell 1912; HK Nowack 1922³; KAT¹ Sellin 1930²⁻³; HS Junker 1938; HAT Horst 1964³; ATD Elliger 1967⁶; SC Wellhausen 1898³ (1963⁴); Bič 1962.

1. The book. The Book of Zechariah, handed down in eleventh position in the Book of the Twelve Prophets, consists of fourteen chapters. Of these only 1–8 contain sayings going back to a prophet of this name active in Jerusalem in the last quarter of the sixth century (Proto-Zechariah). 9–14 (Deutero-Zechariah, or on another theory Deutero- and Trito-Zechariah) are a separate problem[1]. The material that can be distinguished as due to Zechariah in 1–8 is:

1. The seven night visions in the first person, 1.7–15* (the rider); 1.18–21 (Heb. 2.1–4)* (the horns and the smiths); 2.1–5 (Heb. 2.5–9) (the measuring line); 4.1–6a, 10b–14* (the lampstand); 5.1–4 (the scroll); 5.5–11 (the woman in the ephah and the winged women) and 6.1–8 (the chariots).

2. The vision of the investiture of the high priest Joshua, 3.1–7*; the stone and its inscription before the high priest, 3.8–10*; the symbolic action of the making of a crown for Zerubbabel, 6.9–14* and the discourse on fasting, 7.1–6* + 8.19.

3. The individual sayings, 1.16; 2.6–9 (Heb. 2.10–13)*; 4.6a–7; 4.8–10a; 8.2, 3, 4–5 and 6.

1.(2)3–6; 1.9b and the resulting corrections in 1.2–15; 1.17; 1.21b (Heb. 2.4b)*; 2.6b, 9b, 10–12 (Heb. 2.10b, 13b, 14–16); 3.2a*; 3b, 5b, 8a, b; 4.9b, 12; 5.3b; 6.10b, 11b, 12b, 13–14*, 15; 7.7–14; 8.7–8, 9–17 and 20–22 are to be regarded as secondary expansions.

(a) The composition of the night-visions, which probably goes back to Zechariah himself, 1.7–6.8*, formed the starting point. The sections listed under 2 were incorporated or added, probably at a later date, and these may come from a collection (b). Whether the individual sayings belonged to a collection (c), or were attached as an appendix to (a) or (b), can no longer be decided. The formation of 1–8 as we have them as a composition may be the work of a Levitical redaction, which is related to the Deuteronomistic work and to the work of the Chronicler. 1.(2),

1. Cf. below, pp. 286 ff.

3–6; 7.7–14 and 8.9–17 at least are to be ascribed to this redaction[2]. 8.9–17 shows that the Levitical redaction probably goes back to the same hand as the narrative framework of the Book of Haggai. How far the revisions in 3, 4 and 6 are also to be ascribed to it must be left an open question. Finally the eschatological additions in 1, 2, 6 and 8 may belong to a last redaction.

2. *The prophet.* Zechariah is described in 1.1 and 1.7 as the son of Berechiah and grandson of Iddo. Since he appears as son of Iddo in Ezra 5.1 and 6.14 (cf. also Neh. 12.16), the name Berechiah may have got in as a consequence of a confusion with the Zechariah son of Berechiah mentioned in Isa. 8.2. Neh. 12.16 suggests the assumption of priestly descent. According to 1.1 and 7.1 Zechariah appeared between October/November 520 and 7 December 518 B.C.[3] 1.7 dates (?the announcement of) the night visions to the 15 February 519. Whether it is a no longer distinguishable core of 1.(2), 3–6 or other parts of the book (b or c) that are to be connected with 1.1, can no longer be decided. The latest dated passage in any case is the discourse on fasting. Ezra 5.1 and 6.14 correctly see the prophet as a contemporary of Haggai[4]. As with Haggai it must remain an open question whether the dates in the tradition mark the end of his prophetic activity, or whether we have only a selection of his sayings chosen thematically.

The seven night-visions[5] 1.7–6.8* are our primary source for his message: the first (the four horsemen) and the second (the four horns and the four smiths) announce the judgement of Yahweh on the nations which have laid waste Jerusalem and destroyed Judah. The third (the measuring line) prophesies the future expansion of a Jerusalem which is only protected by Yahweh's wall of fire. The fourth (the lampstand and the two olive trees) presents the Messiah and the High Priest united in the service of Yahweh. The fifth (the flying scroll)

2. W. M. A. Beuken would also ascribe 3.6 f., 4.11–14 and 6.13 to this redaction.

3. Calculation according to R. A. Parker and W. H. Dubberstein, *Babylonian Chronology 626 B.C.–A.D. 75*, Brown University Studies 19, Providence, Rhode Island 1956.

4. Cf. above, pp. 275 f.

5. Jepsen and Elliger exclude 3.1–7*, in my view correctly, as a secondary insertion. 3 has been drawn in by 4, and destroys the symmetrical construction of the composition.

announces the purification of the land from thieves and perjurers, the sixth (the woman in the ephah and the two winged women) the transfer of all iniquity to Babylonia. The seventh (the four chariots) has some activity of the spirit, which can no longer be defined, in view. The vision and symbolic activity in ch. 3 centre on the installation of the High Priest Joshua, who can carry out the cult which atones for sin. The appearance of a Satan, an accuser, in 3.1–7* (cf. Job 1.6–12, 2.1–7; 1 Chr. 21.1 and Ps. 109.6)[6] is significant in the history of the religion of Judah. 6.9–14* originally tells of the making of a crown for Zerubbabel, of the line of David, who according to Hag. 1.1 was governor of Judah. The account was subsequently applied to Joshua, and the crown then reinterpreted as a wreath intended as a dedicatory gift for the temple. 4.6b–7 and 8–10 are two sayings also directed to Zerubbabel, which promise the successful completion of building work on the temple[7].

The work on the rebuilding of the temple in Jerusalem awoke in Zechariah hopes of the coming of the time of salvation, of the casting down of the world powers, of the return of Yahweh to Zion and the enthronement of Zerubbabel as king. He ascribed no less significance than Haggai to the atoning cult, as both 3 and 5.5–11 show, although he did not develop the theme in terms of the salvation of nature expected by Haggai.

(o) Joel

A. Merx, *Die Prophetie des Joel und ihre Ausleger von den ältesten Zeiten bis zu den Reformatoren*, Halle 1879; H. Holzinger, 'Sprachcharakter und Abfassungszeit des Buches Joel', *ZAW* 9 (1889), pp. 89 ff.; B. Duhm, *Anmerkungen zu den zwölf Propheten*, Giessen 1911, pp. 96 ff. = *ZAW* 31 (1911), pp. 184 ff.; W. Baumgartner, 'Joel 1 und 2', in *Festschrift K. Budde*, BZAW 34, 1920, pp. 10 ff.; L. Dennefeld, *Les problèmes du livre de Joel*, Paris 1926; A. Jepsen, 'Kleine Beiträge zum

6. Cf. also A. Lods, 'Les origines de la figure de Satan. Ses fonctions a la cour céleste', in *Mélanges Syriens offerts à René Dussaud* II, Paris 1939, pp. 649 ff.

7. No convincing interpretation has yet been found for 4.6b. K. Galling, 'Serubbabel und der Hohepriester beim Wiederaufbau des Tempels in Jerusalem', in *Studien*, pp. 141 f., thinks of a miraculous removal of the heap of ruins by Yahweh's storm wind. Whether this is correct cannot here be discussed. On 4.7 cf. E. Sellin, 'Der Stein des Sacharja', *JBL* 50 (1931), pp. 242 ff.; id., 'Noch einmal der Stein des Sacharja', *ZAW* 59 (1942/3), pp. 59 ff. and Galling, op. cit., p. 143.

Zwölfprophetenbuch', *ZAW* 56 (1938), pp. 85 ff.; A. S. Kapelrud, *Joel Studies*, UUÅ 1948, 4, Uppsala and Leipzig, 1948; M. Treves, 'The Date of Joel', *VT* 7 (1957), pp. 149 ff.; E. Kutsch, 'Heuschrecken-plage und Tag Jahwes in Joel 1 und 2', *ThZ* 18 (1962), pp. 81 ff.; J. M. Myers, 'Some Considerations Bearing on the Date of Joel', *ZAW* 74 (1962), pp. 177 ff.; O. Plöger, *Theocracy and Eschatology* [1962], Oxford 1968; H. W. Wolff, *Die Botschaft des Buches Joel*, ThEx NF 109, Munich 1963; W. Rudolph, 'Wann wirkte Joel?', in *Das ferne und nahe Wort*, Festschrift L. Rost, BZAW 105, 1967, pp. 193 ff.; G. W. Ahlström, *Joel and the Temple Cult of Jerusalem*, SVT 21, 1971 (not taken into consideration here).

Commentaries: KHC Marti 1904; ICC Bewer 1911; HK Nowack 1922[3]; KAT[1] Sellin 1929[2-3]; HS Theis 1937; HAT Robinson 1964[3]; CAT Keller 1965; ATD Weiser 1967[5]; BK Wolff 1969; KAT[2] Rudolph 1971; SC Wellhausen 1898[3] (1963[4]); Bič 1960.

1. The book. The little Book of Joel, which contains only four chap-ters, stands in second place among the Minor Prophets. Despite its small size the questions of its unity and date have been repeatedly discussed for the last hundred years, and at present one can see a loosening of positions rather than a general agree-ment.

At first sight the book gives the impression of a planned, but complicated composition. The thoughts of the reader are led on from an actual plague of locusts and drought, interpreted as a sign of the coming day of the Lord, to the distress of the end-time, which the community in possession of the spirit, the com-munity that repents, will escape. The proclamation of the final judgement, with its double aspect of the destruction of the enemy and the delivery of Israel, forms a rounded conclusion to the book.

But it is completely in dispute whether we have here a composition going back to the prophet Joel mentioned in 1.1, or only a tradition. It must be noted that in 1 and 2 we must, with Jepsen, distinguish between passages which speak of a plague of locusts (1.(1–4)5–7; 2.2a–5,7–9, 15–20 and 25–27) and those which speak of a drought (1.8–14, 16–20; 2.12–14 and 21–24)[1]. It must also be noticed that within the book both self-quotations and quotations from elsewhere are found. 2.15a, 1.14a, 2.21bβ, 2.27b, 2.10b, 2.10a and 2.27 are as Jepsen has correctly seen picked up in 2.1aα; 2.15b; 2.20bβ; 2.26b; 3.15 (Heb.

1. It should particularly be noted that H. W. Wolff sees in 2.1–17 only an announcement of future distress.

4.15); 3.16aβ (Heb. 4.16aβ) and 3.17a (Heb. 4.17a). Further, 1.15 quotes Ezek. 30.2 f. and Isa. 13.6; 2.1b, 2.aα Zeph. 1.14 f.; 2.31b (Heb. 3.4b) Mal. 3.23; 2.32 (Heb. 3.5) Obad. 17; 3.1a (Heb. 4.1a) Jer. 33.15 and 50.4, 20; 3.16aα (Heb. 4.16aα) Amos 1.2 and 3.18a (Heb. 4.18a) Amos 9.13b. Finally there is also the great divergence in content between 1–2.27 (Heb. 1–2) with their concrete references, and 2.28–3 (Heb. 3–4) with their eschatological pictures.

In spite of these features, the number of scholars who think that unity either of composition or of tradition is to be ascribed to Joel is surprisingly large. It is supported by Wellhausen, Nowack, Marti, Theis, Kapelrud, Weiser*, Bič, Wolff, Fohrer*, Keller and Rudolph. Doubts based on the quotations and self-quotations are excluded for Kapelrud and Bič because they think in terms of a cultic prophecy with its roots in the liturgy. If one begins from other presuppositions, one must, with Weiser, assume that the prophet added 2.28–3 (Heb. 3–4) when he came to write down 1–2.27 (Heb. 1–2) and when appropriate carried through a reinterpretation of 1–2.27 at the same time. Bewer, Jepsen and Eissfeldt* take an intermediate position in that they allow for a basic core coming from Joel in both parts of the book, which was later apocalyptically re-edited. A consistent division into two elements has been supported first by M. Vernes (1872), and then by Rothstein, Duhm, for a while but in the end un-decidedly by Sellin, by Robinson and finally by Plöger. Since Duhm's fragmentation of the book has no doubt rightly found no support, we will here only summarize Plöger's analysis. On his view the allusions to the Day of Yahweh in 1.15; 2.1b, 2 and 11 are an imaginative interpretation of an actual drought and an actual plague of locusts. In 2.21–27 follows the promise of salvation which concludes both distresses. The traditional theme of the Day of Yahweh was accordingly 'de-eschatologized' by Joel. The end of the original collection is to be found in 2.27. At the next stage of development 3 (Heb. 4) (without 3.4–8, Heb. 4.4–8) was added to underline the eschatological interpre-tation, with a conscious repetition of 2.10 in 3.15 (Heb. 4.15). Finally 2.28–31 (Heb. 3.1–4) was added as a warning against an etiolated hope of a remnant, while 2.32 (Heb. 3.5) is to be regarded as a reinterpretation. The origin of the whole book, apart from 3.4–8 (Heb. 4.4–8), is on this view to be placed between 400 and 330.

If a survey of the attempts at a literary-critical solution shows that a new inquiry examining all the arguments brought forward in past discussion is needed, a look at the arguments produced about dating shows a similar picture. It hardly needs to be said that the literary-critical position employed is of decisive importance in this. Present datings vary between the ninth and the third centuries B.C.[2] If the unity of 1–3 (Heb. 1–4) is assumed, a date about 400 is undoubtedly correct, with only 3.4–8 (Heb. 4.4–8) excluded. Apart from traditio-historical and religio-historical grounds, the existence of a diaspora, which is assumed in 3.2 ff. (Heb. 4.2 ff.), provides a *terminus non ante* of the exile, and the date is further depressed by the fact that the integrity of the temple (515) and wall (Nehemiah) are presupposed in 1.14; 2.7 ff., 16 f. (cf. also 2.32, Heb. 3.5). If the book is divided into a basic section coming from Joel and one or more eschatological redactions, the picture becomes more complicated. If the allusions to the Day of Yahweh in 1–2.27 (Heb. 1–2) are to be excluded as secondary, the prophet could indeed have appeared in the pre-exilic period. But if this is not so, we can hardly avoid the dates suggested by Plöger[3].

2. *Significance.* While our picture of the prophet Joel son of

2. Those who argue for unity or for a basic form of the book including 2.28–3 (Heb. 3–4) date it as follows: Theis, between 843 and 765; Bič, end of the ninth century; Keller, between 630 and 600; Kapelrud, about 600; Rudolph, between 597 and 587; Jepsen, during the exile; Myers, about 520; Marti and Nowack, about 400; Bewer, after Nehemiah but before the middle of the fourth century; Weiser, at the earliest about 400; Wolff, between 445 and 343; Fohrer, in the first half of the fourth century; Treves, between 323 and 285; Eissfeldt, in the fourth to third century. Those who divide up the book give the following dates: Duhm, a = 1.2–2.17 after Haggai and Zechariah but before Malachi, b = 2.18–3.21 (Heb. 4.21) in the period of the Maccabees; Sellin, a = 1–2.27 (Heb. 1–2) about 500, b = 2.28–3 (Heb. 3–4) between 400 and 300; Robinson, a = 1–2.27 (Heb. 1–2) not before the fourth century, compilation of b = 2.28–3 (Heb. 3–4) not before the third century. Plöger places Joel after Nehemiah, the formation of the book, without 3.4–8 (Heb. 4.4–8) and the additions at the end, between 400 and 330.

3. M. Treves has made the dating of 3.4–8 (Heb. 4.4–8) between 323 and 285, so in the time of Ptolemy I, at least probable. It seems to me doubtful whether the argument produced by J. M. Myers about the loss of control of the trading routes by the Sabaeans from the sixth century on, cf. 3.8 (Heb. 4.8), is compelling for an early dating.

Pethuel continues to change, there is no reason to doubt his actual existence. On the occasion of a plague of locusts and a drought he called the people in Jerusalem together for a service of lamentation and repentance, announced to the people an end to the disasters, and then experienced the confirmation of his words (cf. 2.19). It may be to this circumstance in the first instance that we owe the preservation of his words (cf. Deut. 18.21 f.). If he did not himself speak of the Day of Yahweh, it is understandable that later followers saw in his lively description of the plague of locusts a prefiguring of the attack of the nations in the final battle on the Day of Yahweh, and correspondingly altered and expanded his literary remains in several different stages. However this may be the book is an important witness to the eschatological expectations of the Jewish Community in the fourth century.

(p) Malachi

C. C. Torrey, 'The Prophecy of "Malachi" ', *JBL* 17 (1898), pp. 1 ff.; L. Levy, 'Der Prophet Maleachi', in *Festschrift zum 75 jährigen Bestehen des jüdisch-theologischen Seminars Fraenkelscher Stiftung* II, Breslau 1929, pp. 273 ff.; O. Holtzmann, 'Der Prophet Maleachi und der Ursprung des Pharisäerbundes', *Archiv für Religionswissenschaft* 29 (1931), pp. 1 ff.; D. Cameron, 'A Study of Malachi', *Transactions of the Glasgow University Oriental Society* 8 (1936–7), Glasgow 1938, pp. 9 ff.; E. Pfeiffer, 'Die Disputationsworte im Buche Maleachi', *EvTh* 19 (1959), pp. 546 ff.; H. J. Boecker, 'Bemerkungen zur formgeschichtlichen Terminologie des Buches Maleachi', *ZAW* 78 (1966), pp. 78 ff.; G. Wallis, 'Wesen und Struktur der Botschaft Maleachi', in *Das ferne und nahe Wort*, Festschrift L. Rost, BZAW 105, 1967, pp. 229 ff.

Commentaries: KHC Marti 1904; ICC Smith 1912; HK Nowack 1922[3]; KAT[1] Sellin 1930[2–3]; HS Junker 1938; HAT Horst 1964[3]; ATD Elliger 1967[6]; SC Wellhausen 1898[3] (1963[4]); von Bulmerincq, I 1921–1926 II 1929–1932, *Acta et Commentationes Universitatis Dorpatensis* B, I, 2, Dorpat 1921; B III, 1, 1922; B, IV, 2, 1923; B VII, 1, 1926; B XV, 1, 1929; B, XIX, 1, 1930; B, XXIII, 2, 1931; B XXVI, 1, 1932 and B, XXVII, 2, 1932; J. G. Botterweck (parts only), *BiLe* 1 (1960), pp. 28 ff.; 100 ff.; 179 ff. and 253 ff.

The Book of Malachi contains three chapters and stands last in the Book of the Twelve Prophets. Its heading, probably from the same hand as Zech. 9.1 and 12.1, ascribes it to an otherwise unknown Malachi. But there can be no doubt that the name (= my messenger) goes back to 3.1[1]. The book is therefore originally anonymous, or if it owes its book form to the author of the heading, at least contains anonymous prophecies, which however certainly go back to a single prophet.

The book displays a planned structure. The heading 1.1 leads on to a promise for Israel connected with a threat against Edom in 1.2–5. The love of God, which has been questioned, shows itself precisely in the differential treatment of Jacob and Esau, Israel and Edom. 1.6–2.9* contains an invective and threat speech against the priests, a proclamation of judgement with reasons given. The priests are attacked for the offering of defective sacrificial animals. In 2.10–16 follows an invective and hortatory speech against divorce directed to the people. 2.17–3.5* contains an invective and threat speech directed against doubt of God's righteous judgement, which underlines especially the certainty of judgement on the men of property who oppress the poor and those with no rights. In 3.1 the prophet is identified with God's messenger who is sent before the judgement. 3.6–12 consists of invective, hortatory speech and promise, and contains a conditional promise of future fertility of the land, if only tithes and offerings are brought to the temple in full measure. 3.13–4.6 (Heb. 3.24)* inveighs against doubt of God's judgement of the godless, and promises that the pious will be spared on the future day of judgement. 3.16 tells how those who fear God are listed in a book of remembrance. 4.4 (Heb. 3.22) stresses the keeping of the law given by Moses on Horeb. 4.5 (Heb. 3.23 f.) announces the coming of Elijah before the day of the Lord. Formally we have discussion sayings in all six instances; but the descriptions of literary types chosen above can be justified as corresponding to their different functional construction.

From a literary-critical viewpoint the book offers hardly any problems. Following Sellin, Weiser suggests the transposition of 3.6–12 and 2.10–16 to after 1.2–5, so that the order is: preaching of repentance to the people, preaching of repentance to the priests, and preaching of repentance to the doubters. Since however no reasons can be found for conjecturing a subsequent disturbance in the present arrangement, and 1.2–5 must be

1. Cf. however G. Wallis, op. cit., pp. 229 f.

understood as an independent saying, it is better to keep the existing order. Finally Wallis wishes to distinguish between a series addressed to the laity and one addressed to the priests, in 1.2–5; 2.10–16; 2.17 + 3.5; 3.6–12; 3.13–4.3 (Heb. 3.21), and 1.6–2.9 and 3.1–4, without drawing literary-critical conclusions from this. Apart from smaller additions, it is at most 1.11–14; 2.2, 7, 11b–12, 15abα, 16b; 3.3–4 and 4.4–6 (Heb. 3.22–24) that are to be regarded, with Elliger, as redactional additions. The additions inside 2.10–16* reinterpret the prophet's words to apply them to mixed marriages. In 4.4 (Heb. 3.22) we have an exhortation, and in 4.5–6 (Heb. 3.23–24) a proclamation which is clearly caused by a conflict of the generations, and comes from the hand of the last redactor.

To date the prophecies we must start from the existence of the temple, which is presupposed in 1.10, 3.1 and 10. The mention of a governor in 1.8 show that it is the second temple that is in question.

The predominance of the disputation, which is stronger than in any other prophet, suggests that it is advisable to place the prophet in any case after Haggai and Zechariah. Since we have insufficient knowledge of the fate of the Edomites in the fifth and fourth centuries, and only know that the Nabataeans controlled Edom at least at the end of the fourth century, 1.2–5 does not help further with the dating. It is disputed whether 3.13–4.3 (Heb. 3.21) have in mind the contrast between Jerusalemites and Samaritans, as von Bulmerincq and Elliger assume, and this takes us no further, since we have only inadequate information about the development of the Samaritan schism. It is in any case impossible to draw conclusions from the internal conditions of the community presupposed to an activity of the prophet before Ezra and Nehemiah[2] if the Ezra narrative is regarded as a piece of edificatory church history, and the introduction of a new law under Ezra as faulty exegesis.[3] No conclusions for the dating of Malachi can be drawn from the fact that Nehemiah had to plead for the payment of tithes (cf. Neh. 13.10 ff.). This sort of thing can be repeated! What is said about the payment of tithes and of the offering in 3.6–12 does not agree with Deut. 14.22 ff., but does with Num. 18.21 ff. (P). It has been thought that the conclusion can be drawn from 3.4,8 that the prophet, in accordance with the Deuteronomic ideal, did not yet differentiate

2. Von Bulmerincq's detailed ordering of the passages between 485 and 445 has justifiably found no following.
3. Cf. above, pp. 181 f. and 108 f.

between priests and Levites, and so must have worked before the introduction of P. Since however the priests were regarded not only by D,
but also by P and Chr., as belonging to the tribe of Levi[4], no more far-
reaching conclusions can be drawn, in spite of the mention of a covenant
with Levi, behind which Deut. 33.8 ff. stands. It must then at least be
granted that the usual dating of the prophet before (Ezra and) Nehemiah is not as well-founded as the almost universal consensus would
suggest. The only *terminus a quo* is the completion of the second temple
in 515, the *terminus ad quem* the familiarity of Jesus Sirach with our
book (cf. Sir. 49.10 and 48.10). The predominance of argumentative
discussion sayings argues for a relatively late date, while the eschatology,
which apart from 1.2–5 is unpolitical, argues against too late a date.
We can hardly therefore go below the Persian period. Whether in view
of the drought and plague of locusts presupposed in 3.10 f. the book
should be ascribed to a contemporary of Joel, must be left a completely
open question, in view of our complete lack of knowledge of the
frequency of such events[5].

A date for the prophet between 400 and 350 would in any case
fit naturally into the historical and religio-historical picture of
this period.

With his stress upon cultic righteousness the prophet is a
man of his time. The observance of the cultic and ritual commandments is for him undoubtedly also a precondition of salvation, but not the only one. The activity of neither the priests nor
the laity is measured only by their fulfilment of cultic demands,
but in both cases also by their righteousness in respect of
relations between men. Failure in this area makes sacrifice worthless for Malachi too, as 2.10–16* shows. In the face of increasing
objections to the faith inherited from tradition he holds fast to
the belief that God remains the righteous judge, that present
distress is the consequence of human disobedience, and that
God's imminent judgement on the day prepared by him will
reveal the difference between the fate of the righteous and that
of the godless.

(q) *Deutero- and Trito-Zechariah* (*Zech. 9–14*)

B. Stade, 'Deuterozacharja. Eine kritische Studie', *ZAW* 1 (1881), pp.
1 ff.; 2 (1882), pp. 151 ff., 275 ff.; B. Duhm, *Anmerkungen zu den zwölf*

4. Cf. A. H. J. Gunneweg, *Leviten und Priester*, FRLANT 89, 1965,
pp. 185 ff. and 208 f.   5. Cf. above, p. 283.

Propheten, Giessen 1911, pp. 101 ff. = *ZAW* 31 (1911), pp. 189 ff.;
A. Jepsen, 'Kleine Beiträge zum Zwölfprophetenbuch II', *ZAW* 57
(1939), pp. 242 ff.; P. Lamarche, *Zacharie IX–XIV. Structure littéraire
et messianisme*, Études bibliques, Paris 1961; D. R. Jones, 'A Fresh
Interpretation of Zechariah ix–xi', *VT* 12 (1962), pp. 241 ff.; B. Otzen,
Studien über Deuterosacharja, Acta Theologica Danica 6, Copenhagen
1964; H.-M. Lutz, *Jahwe, Jerusalem und die Völker. Zur Vorgeschichte
von Sach 12,1–8 und 14,1–5*, WMANT 27, 1968; O. Plöger, *Theocracy
and Eschatology*, Oxford 1968; M. Saebø, 'Die deuterosacharjanische
Frage. Eine forschungsgeschichtliche Studie', *StTh* 23 (1969), pp.
115 ff.; id., *Sacharja 9–14*, WMANT 34, 1969.
Commentaries: cf. on § 22(n).

1. The history of scholarship[1]. Three phases can be distinguished
in the more recent history of the exposition of Zech. 9–14, 1, a
precritical English stage (ca. 1620 to 1785), 2, a German stage
(1784–1880), and 3. the critical stage introduced by Stade in
1881, which lasts to the present.

The precritical discussion was begun by Mede's observation that
Zech. 11.12 f. is quoted in Matt. 27.9 f. as a saying of Jeremiah. The
antedating of 9–11 (Mede) or 9–14 (Kidder) to the period of Jeremiah,
or even of 9–11 to the pre-Jeremianic period (Newcome) seemed therefore justified. When the debate was introduced to Germany by Flügge,
a dominant position was at once won by the views of Bertholdt, who
ascribed 9–11 to the Zechariah ben Berechiah mentioned in Isa. 8.2,
and in the rest saw pre-exilic additions to this. Although a late date for
9–14 was suggested by Eichhorn, and argued for first by Corrodi, the
early dating was predominant until 1880. It was Stade who made
possible a breakthrough for the late date in 1881 by assigning 9–14 to an
eschatological writer, Deutero-Zechariah, active between 306 and 278.
In Wellhausen we find already the division of the chapters into six
independent units from the Hellenistic period, though he dated 12.1–
13.6 to the Maccabaean era. Duhm distinguished between Deutero-
Zechariah in 9–11 + 13.7–9, and Trito-Zechariah in 12.1–13.6 + 14,
whom he assigned to about 135 B.C.

Today there is still no unanimity over dating. Otzen can be
regarded as an exponent of pre-exilic dating. He ascribes 9–13
to the late pre-exilic period, but 14 to the late post-exilic period.
Lamarche places 9–14 between 500 and 480. Horst allows for

1. On this cf. in detail Otzen, op. cit., pp. 11 ff.; also Lutz, op. cit.,
pp. 1 ff.

pre-exilic elements in 9.1–11.3, while he dates the rest of the material cautiously to between the middle and end of the fourth century. Elliger, who is followed generally by Eissfeldt and Fohrer, separates out a basic layer from the early Hellenistic period (9.1–8; 9.11–17; 10.3b–12; 11.4–17), which was later reinterpreted in a general eschatological sense. He regards 9.9 f., 10.1 f., 11.1–3 and 11.17 as possibly later insertions of undetermined origin. 12–14 were subsequently added to the collection 9–11, and 14 is to be regarded as independent and late, but certainly not Maccabaean. His analysis accordingly upholds a distinction between a Deutero- and Trito-Zechariah collection. While a fundamental disagreement with Otzen remains, and fragments of older tradition must in principle be allowed for (cf. 9.9 f. and 10.1 f.), a dating of 9–11 in the early Hellenistic period, and of 12.1–13.6 and 14 (between which 13.7–9 has been inserted as a redactional bridge) in the third century may well be the correct answer.

2. *Deutero-Zechariah* (*Zech. 9–11*). 9.1–8* takes us to the period after the conquest of Syria and Phoenicia by Alexander the Great in 332 B.C. The unknown prophet announces doom to the Philistines, excepting the Jewish mixed population in Ashdod and Ekron, but divine protection to Jerusalem[2]. 9.11–13* prophesies the return of the captives taken by the Macedonians, and the revenge of the worshippers of Yahweh in south and north upon their enemies under divine protection. 10.3–12* expects the release of the worshippers of Yahweh in south and north, and the subjection of the Egyptians and Assyrians, i.e. of the kingdoms of the Ptolemies and of the Seleucids. 11.4–16* tells of a symbolic action, the shepherding of sheep doomed to slaughter by means of the staffs Grace and Union, the breaking of the first staff, the sale of the sheep, the payment and rejection of the wages of the shepherd, and the breaking of the second staff. Its meaning is the ending of fellowship between Jews and Samaritans.

It cannot be decided whether these four prophecies come from one author or from several. The passages appear in chronologically correct order, and reflect not only the eschatological expectations of the beginning of the Hellenistic period, but the growing estrangement between the Jerusalem community and the Samaritans in the last third of the fourth century.

2. Cf. K. Elliger, 'Ein Zeugnis aus der jüdischen Gemeinde im Alexanderjahr 332 v. Chr.', *ZAW* 62 (1950), pp. 63 ff.

9.9 f. contains a messianic prediction in the form of a herald's cry. We must allow for the reworking of older traditions at least in 9.9. 10.1 f. summons men to pray for spring rain. In the present context this means the dawning of the time of salvation. 11.1–3 contains a satirical song which announces the fall of Lebanon, of Bashan and of the Jordan valley. While it arises perhaps out of a specific situation, the saying in its present position should be interpreted, with Wellhausen and others, as an announcement of the fall of a world power. The threat saying in 11.17 against the wicked shepherds is written with 11.16 in mind, and must therefore be redactional.

The following verses are secondary: 9.8a in part; 9.11*, 12a*, 12b*, 13aβ*, 16b*; 10.3a, 6b, 8a*, 11aβ*, as well as 11.6, 8a, 15–16. The expansions in 11.4–16 are certainly used for an eschatological elaboration, and perhaps even a messianic interpretation of the passage[3].

3. The prophecies of Trito-Zechariah (Zech. 12–14).

Within 12–14 two complexes, primarily reflecting different eschatological expectations, 12.2–13.6, and 14, can be distinguished. While in 12.2–13.6 the nations come to grief upon an invulnerable Jerusalem, in 14 they are only destroyed after a conquest of the city by Yahweh, in connection with a nature theophany.

Within 12.2–13.6 some passages appear to be relatively independent: so 12.1–8*, an announcement of the delivery of Jerusalem in the attack of the nations. We must with Lutz, following Elliger, separate 12.5,6b and 8 as pro-Jerusalem and pro-dynastic, and 2b,4bα,6a,7 as pro-Judah redactional material. 3b and 4bβ may also belong to the second group. In 12.9–14 there follows a summons to lamentation for one 'whom they have pierced'. While earlier attempts were made to identify him with Josiah, Zedekiah or Zerubbabel, Marti and Sellin saw in him the High Priest Onias III (d. 170 B.C.), and Duhm Simon Maccabaeus (d. 134) (cf. 2 Macc. 4.32 ff. and 1 Macc. 16.11 ff.). Wellhausen suggested a martyr of the Maccabaean period, whose name has been subsequently deleted, and who was not to be identified with one of the Maccabees. Mitchell suggested the possibility that the summons was to lament for the Servant of Isa. 52.13 ff., historicized and understood as a precursor of the Messiah. Junker, Elliger and Plöger leave the identification open for want of sufficient knowledge of the historical background; Plöger thinks the possibility of a reworking of the theme of the Suffering Servant worth considering. Otzen attempts to prove a connection with the ritual of the suffering king, and places the passage after 587. With the group of scholars just mentioned, it is best to assume that we have to

3. In my analysis of Zech. 9–14 I follow K. Elliger, ATD 25.

deal with a figure of history whom we can no longer identify, and who is most probably to be placed in the third century. 13.1 looks forward to an eschatological fountain of purification for Jerusalem. The theme of purification is continued in 13.2–6, where the destruction of idols and of the prophets is announced. Here a striking devaluation of prophecy can be felt, which no doubt has its roots in disappointments which prophetic predictions of the same century had occasioned.

From 13.1 ff. it seems reasonable with Plöger and Lutz to ascribe 12.2–13.6 to theocratic circles in Jerusalem. 13.7–9, the announcement of the slaying of the shepherd and the reduction of the herds to a third of their former size, is to be regarded with Junker, Plöger and Lutz as a redactional transition between the tradition complexes 12.2–13.6 and 14.

14.1–5 looks to the conquest of the city of Jerusalem by the nations, followed by a theophany of Yahweh on the Mount of Olives, and his entry into Jerusalem accompanied by the court of heaven. 14.2bβγ,4b and 5a are to be distinguished as secondary. 14.6–11 announces the beginning of the reign of Yahweh and the transformation of the earth (Jerusalem). Here 14.7a*,10–11aα are to be excluded as secondary expansions. 14.12–21 (secondarily expanded in 14.12,14a,15,18,20–21) complete the eschatological picture with the announcement of a panic from God which will befall the nations, and the future pilgrimage of the nations to Sion.

Traditio-historically ideas of the Jerusalem pre-exilic cult and themes from Ezekiel stand in the background. With Plöger and Lutz it must be held that 14, in contrast to 12.2–13.6, comes from eschatological circles which guard the heritage of the prophets. So the prophecies of Trito-Zechariah provide an important insight into the struggles of faith inside Judaism in the third century.

§ 23 Literary Types of Prophetic Speech

H. Gunkel, 'Die Propheten als Schriftsteller und Dichter', in H. Schmidt, *Die grossen Propheten*, SAT II 2, Göttingen 1923², pp. xxxiv ff.; L. Köhler, *Deuterojesaja (Jesaja 40–55) stilkritisch untersucht*, BZAW 37, 1923; J. Lindblom, *Die literarische Gattung der prophetischen Literatur*, UUÅ 1924, Teologi 1, 1924; E. Balla, *Die Droh- und Scheltworte des Amos, Leipziger Reformationsprogramm 1926*, Leipzig 1926;

H. W. Wolff, 'Die Begründung der prophetischen Heils- und Unheilssprüche', *ZAW* 52 (1934), pp. 1 ff., also in *Gesammelte Studien zum Alten Testament*, ThB 22, 1964, pp. 9 ff.; id. *Das Zitat im Prophetenspruch* [1937], ThB 22, pp. 36 ff.; J. Begrich, *Studien zu Deuterojesaja*, BWANT IV, 25, 1938, and ThB 20, 1963; R. B. Y. Scott, 'The Literary Structure of Isaiah's Oracles', in *Studies in Old Testament Prophecy*, Festschrift T. H. Robinson, Edinburgh 1950, pp. 175 ff.; G. Fohrer, 'Die Gattung der Berichte über symbolische Handlungen der Propheten', *ZAW* 64 (1952), pp. 101 ff, and in *Studien zur alttestamentlichen Prophetie*, BZAW 99, 1967, pp. 92 ff.; E. Würthwein, 'Der Ursprung der prophetischen Gerichtsrede', *ZTK* 49 (1952), pp. 1 ff.; id., 'Kultpolemik oder Kultbescheid?', in *Tradition und Situation*, Festschrift A. Weiser, Göttingen 1963, pp. 115 ff.; F. Hesse, 'Wurzelt die prophetische Gerichtsrede im israelitischen Kult?', *ZAW* 65 (1953), pp. 45 ff.; E. Pfeiffer, 'Die Disputationsworte im Buche Maleachi', *EvTh* 19 (1959), pp. 546 ff.; F. Horst, 'die Visionsschilderungen der alttestamentlichen Propheten', *EvTh* 20 (1960), pp. 193 ff.; C. Westermann, *Basic Forms of Prophetic Speech* [1960], London 1967; id., 'Das Heilswort bei Deuterojesaja', *EvTh* 24 (1964), pp. 355 ff.; id., 'Sprache und Struktur der Prophetie Deuterojesajas', in *Forschung am Alten Testament*, ThB 24, 1964, pp. 92 ff.; R. Bach, *Die Aufforderungen zur Flucht und zum Kampf im Alttestamentlichen Prophetenspruch*, WMANT 9, 1962; E. Gerstenberger, 'The Woe-Oracles of the Prophets', *JBL* 81 (1962), pp. 249 ff.; H. J. Boecker, 'Bemerkungen zur formgeschichtlichen Terminologie des Buches Maleachi', *ZAW* 78 (1966), pp. 78 ff.; R. Rendtorff, 'Botenformel und Botenspruch', *ZAW* 74 (1962), pp. 165 ff.; E. von Waldow, *Der traditionsgeschichtliche Hintergrund der prophetischen Gerichtsreden*, BZAW 85, 1963; H. J. Boecker, *Redeformen des Rechtslebens im Alten Testament*, WMANT 14, 1964; G. Wanke, "ôj und hôj', *ZAW* 78 (1966), pp. 215 ff.; J. H. Hayes, 'The Usage of Oracles against Foreign Nations in Ancient Israel', *JBL* 87 (1968), pp. 81 ff.; F. Ellermeier, *Prophetie in Mari und Israel*, TOA 1, 1968, pp. 187 ff.; W. Janzen, *Mourning Cry and Woe Oracle*, BZAW 125, 1972.

1. The task. The prophets were not originally writers. They delivered their messages as messengers of Yahweh to actual men in actual situations. It was only later that their words were written down[1]. And these written words are usually not handed down in their original form and order, but in the constantly re-edited form they have in the prophetic books, on which many

---

1. Cf. below, pp. 297 ff.

centuries have been at work, to keep alive for their own time the word once uttered. If a prophetic book is judged by modern literary standards, in spite of the arrangement by subject matter which editors have attempted to introduce, it will often seem more like accumulated chaos than a planned whole. The lack of a reliable criterion for original speech units, the minimal number of descriptions of situation (which are often in any case secondary), the lack of chronological order, and the arrangement of individual sayings, which is often only by catchwords, mean that the expositor dealing with the original unity of a speech, its authorship and date must start by freeing himself entirely from the tradition given in the book, and base his view on his own work[2].

Before he decides on the genuineness of a saying, on the basis of general historical criteria, he must establish its exact limits and its original form. Even before the considerations of syntax, metre, style and content, which he must examine, he has to deal with the criteria presented by *Gattungsforschung*, the study of literary types[3]. For however great the poetic freedom of the prophets was in a particular instance, and although we must allow for a progressive loosening of the fixed forms, they were bound by tradition and the intention of their utterances to specific literary types. For this reason a knowledge of these types is the primary means of establishing the original units.

2. *Sayings of the prophets.* From the very fact that the prophets uttered their words orally at first, it comes about that we have to look for short sayings of a few lines only at first. In contrast longer, strophically divided poems represent a later stage in the history of tradition. The start of the prophetic saying is often introduced by the messenger formula *kô 'āmar YHWH*, 'thus says Yahweh'. In the course of and at the end of a saying we often have the revelatory formula *nᵉ'um YHWH*, literally 'whisper of Yahweh'. In view of the task of the prophet to proclaim to an individual or to a community salvation or disaster, we may suppose that the many forms of speech used by the prophets in their compositions are in the end subordinated to their proclamation of salvation or disaster. In particular it should

2. Cf. above, p. 9.   3. Cf. above, p. 208.

be noticed that all the schemes proposed are auxiliary constructions used to help us notice functional relationships and grasp the
common features of prophetic speech, which is only in fact found
in a constantly changing form.

It is usual to regard 1, the threat, 2, the invective, 3, the
exhortation and 4, the word of salvation or the promise as the
four basic prophetic literary types. The threat announces
coming disaster for an individual or a community, be it a group,
the prophet's own nation, or a foreign nation. A distinction can
accordingly be made between a threat against an individual, a
group, the prophet's own nation, and a foreign nation. The
same distinctions must be made with the other types also. In its
simplest form the threat consists only of the announcement (cf.
e.g. Amos 7.11). Within this a distinction can sometimes be
made between the announcement of the intervention of Yahweh
and its consequences, and the announcement of disaster and its
consequences (cf. e.g. Amos 8.11 f. and Isa. 3.25–4.1). When it
is a threat with reason given the announcement is linked either
with a syntactically dependent reason (cf. e.g. Amos 1.3 ff.),
or with an invective or another utterance as an independent
statement of the reason (cf. e.g. Amos 3.9–11, 5.21–27 and 3.2).
Even the cry of woe, which is functionally related to the invective, but stands closer to the announcement itself, can serve as
a statement of the reason (cf. e.g. Amos 6.1 ff. and Isa. 5.8–10).
The statement of the reason can precede or follow the announcement. If it precedes it, the announcement is often introduced by
a *lāḵēn*, a 'therefore'. In this case the messenger formula too can
appear between the reason and the announcement. The invective
is found not only in connection with a threat, but also as an
independent utterance (cf. e.g. Hos. 7.3–7).

Westermann has suggested that the descriptions threat and invective
should be given up, and replaced by announcement of judgement, or
verdict, and by accusation, or justification of the announcement. A
threat leaves it open whether what is announced comes to pass, while
the word of the prophet has an unconditioned character. Invective is
an unmediated occurrence, which cannot be carried out by a messenger,
but the prophetic saying which is referred to as invective is primarily a
statement. Fohrer, arguing against this, has pointed to the possibility
of Yahweh taking back the announcement and of its non-fulfilment, as
well as to the independent occurrence of the speech of invective. This

objection to the renaming of the threat can be countered by a reference to the intention of the prophetic word, and the objection to the renaming of the invective by a reference to the possibility of calling the isolated invective saying an accusation. As long as the overriding legal and religio-historical problem is not resolved agreement on terminology can hardly be obtained.

A lively discussion has broken out in the last ten years about the cries of woe, which can be form-critically derived either from the curse, whether the cultic, the wisdom or the legal curse (so Mowinckel, Westermann, Crenshaw and Fohrer*) or by way of the dirge from clan wisdom (so Gerstenberger and Wolff). This is an argument which cannot be regarded as finished yet. The point has been made by Wanke, that a careful distinction must be made between sayings that are introduced by the interjection '*ôy* and those introduced by the interjection *hôy*; the '*ôy* sayings are found primarily as cries of distress or lamentation, e.g. 1 Sam. 4.7, Isa. 6.5 and Jer. 10.19, while the *hôy* sayings occur in the dirge (cf. 1 Kgs. 13.30 and Jer. 22.18), as well as in prophetic invectives and threats[4]. But this should be modified, with Janzen, in favour of the view that this is a secondary differentiation. Num. 21.29 and 24.23 show that the two words were then still interchangeable. Janzen has further demonstrated that *hôy* with a following description of the one addressed in a participle, noun or proper name has its original location in the cry of lamentation. Its accusing and even cursing function has its roots in the transition which took place when appropriate in the lament for the dead itself from lamentation over the dead man to accusation or even cursing of the man who has caused his death (cf. Isa. 1.21 ff.). It should be added that cries of terror and of lamentation of this sort should in principle not be restricted to one single setting in life. While the cry of *hôy* may have been used by the people in all conceivable contexts, the final literary form of the cry of woe is not to be located in popular wisdom nor yet in tribal ethics, but precisely in the lament for the dead.

The exhortation aims at an alteration in the behaviour of the man or men addressed, and demands of its hearers a decision to act in view of the possibility of God sending either salvation

---

4. Cf. S. Mowinckel, *Psalmenstudien* V, SNVAO II, 1923, 3, 1924, pp. 117 ff.; C. Westermann, *Basic Forms of Prophetic Speech*, pp. 189 ff.; E. Gerstenberger, op. cit.; H. W. Wolff, *Amos' geistige Heimat*, WMANT 18, 1964, pp. 12 ff.; G. Wanke, op. cit.; J. L. Crenshaw, 'The Influence of the Wise upon Amos', *ZAW* 79 (1967), pp. 47 f.; H.-J. Hermisson, *Studien zur israelitischen Spruchweisheit*, WMANT 28, 1968, pp. 89 f. and especially W. Janzen, op. cit.

or disaster. When the exhortation is subordinated to an announcement of judgement or of salvation, it changes into a conditional threat or a conditional promise (cf. Amos 5.4–5, 6, 14–15, Isa. 1.18–20 and Zeph. 2.3).

The words of salvation or of promise, which are in number substantially fewer than the announcements of disaster, can be divided up, with Westermann, into promise of salvation, announcement of salvation and description of salvation[5]. The promise of salvation clearly has its origin in the oracle of a favourable hearing. It occasionally refers back directly to the lament which has preceded it, and promises to the one who finds himself in distress the bestowal of salvation by God (cf. e.g. Exod. 3.7 f., and Isa. 43.1 ff.). The usual form of the prophetic promise is the announcement of salvation, which promises God's help in the future. It can occur either in connection with a promise of salvation or on its own (cf. e.g. 2 Sam. 7.8 ff.; 1 Kgs. 22.11 f.; Isa. 41.17 ff.; Jer. 28.2 ff., and also Exod. 3.7 f.). The description of salvation describes the future reality of salvation (cf. e.g. Isa. 11.1 ff. and Zech. 8.4 f.). In so far as a reason is given at all for the salvation sayings it is not the attitude of men, as in the announcements of judgement, but the will of Yahweh that is to the fore in the reason given. Finally it remains to point out that the threat sayings against foreign nations frequently amount to an announcement of salvation for the prophet's own nation.

Prophetic speech acquires colour and variety not only from the forcefulness of the language of the prophets as poets, but also from their fertility of invention in making use of literary types from other areas of life. The various literary types borrowed from the world of law, which have most recently been examined by Boecker and von Waldow, should particularly be mentioned here[6].

It is at present disputed where the real roots of prophetic lawsuit oracles (judgement speeches) are to be found. Würthwein derives them from the cultic speech of judgement, referring to a whole series of psalms which talk of Yahweh appearing for judgement, or in which a speech of God in judgement is communicated in a cultic framework[7].

5. Cf. above, pp. 263 f.   6. Cf. also above, pp. 56 ff.
7. Cf. also J. Harvey, 'Le "Rîb-pattern", réquisitoire prophétique sur la rupture de l'alliance', *Bib* 43 (1962), pp. 172 ff.

Boecker and others on the other hand have maintained the usual assumption that they were borrowed from the world of the law. Von Waldow agrees with this, but raises the question what made these borrowings possible, and proposes the legal category of the covenant of Yahweh with Israel, which is presupposed by the prophets. In view of the complicated nature of the problem, which is connected with the questions of date and cultic traditions of the psalms, of covenant and law and of prophet and cult[8], the final word has undoubtedly not been spoken yet on this subject.

A whole series of sayings of the prophets contain a condemnation by God of cultic practices. Yahweh refuses to receive sacrifices, does not hear prayers, hates feasts. While such sayings used to be regarded as a deliberate polemic against the cult by the prophets, who had left the cultic religion of the people behind them and risen to a purely ethical religion, Würthwein regards them as prophetic cultic announcements, and has cautiously left it open whether they are to be regarded as direct cultic announcements or simply as literary forms based on them (cf. e.g. Amos 5.21 ff.; Isa. 1.10 ff. and Jer. 6.19 ff.).

It would take too long to give here a list of the literary types borrowed which was even partially complete. Some examples are sufficient to give an impression of the fertility of invention of the prophets. In their announcements of judgement they made use of the love-song and of the dirge (cf. e.g. Isa. 5.1 ff.[8a]; Amos 5.1 ff.). When related to an external enemy the prophetic dirge takes on the character of a taunt song (cf. Isa. 14.4 ff.). In addition they used the taunt song itself, in fact in the form of a taunt song directed at an ageing prostitute (cf. Isa. 47; 23.16). Occasionally we come across literary types of whose existence we only know from their borrowing by the prophets or from an allusion by them, as e.g. the song of the watchman (cf. Isa. 21.11 f.[?]), or the drinking song (cf. Isa. 22.13 and 56.12, where in both cases the quotation takes over the function of the accusation). It is made clear to us yet again that the literary types and elements employed must be understood from the intention in each instance of the prophetic saying.

3. *The prophetic narrative.* As well as the prophetic saying we

8. Cf. above, pp. 62 ff.; 212 ff. and below, 343 ff.
8a. Cf. however W. Schottroff, *ZAW* 82 (1970), pp. 74 ff.

have the narrative, both as a third person narrative of the activity of the prophet and of his words, and as the first person narrative in the forms of accounts of calls, descriptions of visions and accounts of symbolic actions. The account of the call legitimates the message of the prophet (cf. e.g. Isa. 6, Jer. 1.4 ff.; Ezek. 1.1 ff.). In the account of the vision the prophet is concerned not with the private experience as such, but with the revelation of a message connected with it (cf. e.g. Amos 7.1 ff.; 8.1 ff.; 9.1 ff.; Ezek. 37.1 ff. and Zech. 1.7–6.8*)[9]. In the accounts of a symbolic action too the concern is not with a pattern of conduct by the prophet which we feel to be unusual as such, but with its prophetic significance.

If we look back over the whole range of prophetic tradition, three basic literary types can be established: 1, narratives; 2, words of prophets directed to men, and 3, words directed to God, prayers[10]. These three basic types have a very different distribution. For pre-classical prophecy we have only third person accounts of a character in saga or legend. Of the books of the writing prophets some contain no narratives at all, such as Micah, Zephaniah, Nahum, Habakkuk, Deutero-Isaiah, Trito-Isaiah, Malachi and Deutero- and Trito-Zechariah. In the exilic period, particularly noticeably in Deutero-Isaiah[11], the words of the prophet are permeated by phrases from the psalms. Mixed forms become increasingly prominent, until prophecy proper gives way to scribal proto-apocalyptic.

§ 24   From Spoken to Written Form

H. S. Nyberg, *Studien zum Hoseabuch. Zugleich ein Beitrag zur Klärung des Problems der alttestamentlichen Textkritik*, UUÅ 1935, 6, 1935; H. Birkeland, *Zum hebräischen Traditionswesen. Die Komposition der prophetischen Bücher des Alten Testaments*, ANVAO II, 1938, 1, 1939; I. Engnell, *Gamla Testamentet I: en traditionshistorisk inledning*, Stockholm 1945; id., 'Profetia och Tradition', *SEÅ* 12 (1947), pp. 110 ff.; S. Mowinckel, *Prophecy and Tradition*, ANVAO II, 1946,3, 1946; J. van der Ploeg, 'Le rôle de la tradition orale dans la transmission du

---

9. Cf. above, pp. 210 f.
10. Cf. e.g. the 'Confessions of Jeremiah', and the prophetic liturgies.
11. Cf. above, p. 264.

texte de l'Ancien Testament', *RB* 54 (1947), pp. 5 ff.; O. Eissfeldt, 'Zur Überlieferungsgeschichte der Prophetenbücher im Alten Testament' [1948], *KS* III, Tübingen 1966, pp. 55 ff.; G. Widengren, *Literary and Psychological Aspects of the Hebrew Prophets*, UUÅ 1948, 10, 1948; id., 'Oral Tradition and Written Literature among the Hebrews in the Light of Arabic Evidence, with Special Reference to Prose Narratives', *AcOr(H)* 23 (1959), pp. 201 ff.; C. R. North, 'The Place of Oral Tradition in the Growth of the Old Testament', *Expository Times* 61 (1950), pp. 292 ff.; E. Auerbach, 'Die grosse Überarbeitung der biblischen Bücher', SVT 1, 1953, pp. 1 ff.; E. Nielsen, *Oral Tradition*, SBT 11, 1954; A. H. J. Gunneweg, *Mündliche und schriftliche Tradition der vorexilischen Prophetenbücher als Problem der neueren Prophetenforschung*, FRLANT 73, 1959; O. Plöger, *Theocracy and Eschatology* [1959], Oxford 1968; G. Fohrer, 'Die Struktur der alttestamentlichen Eschatologie' [1960], in *Studien zur alttestamentlichen Prophetie*, BZAW 99, 1967, pp. 32 ff.; id., 'Entstehung, Komposition und Überlieferung von Jesaja 1–39', *ALUOS* 3 (1961–2), pp. 3 ff., and in BZAW 99, pp. 113 ff.; G. von Rad, *Old Testament Theology*, vol. 2 [1960], Edinburgh 1965, pp. 33 ff.; J. Lindblom, *Prophecy in Ancient Israel*, Oxford 1962, pp. 220 ff.; F. M. Cross, jr., 'The Contributions of the Qumrân Discoveries to the Study of the Biblical Text', *IEJ* 16 (1966), pp. 81 ff.; S. Herrmann, 'Kultreligion und Buchreligion. Kultische Funktionen in Israel und in Ägypten', in *Das Ferne und nahe Wort*, Festschrift L. Rost, BZAW 105, 1967, pp. 95 ff.; E. W. Nicholson, *Preaching to the Exiles*, Oxford 1970; W. Schottroff, 'Jeremia 2, 1–3. Erwägungen zur Methode der Prophetenexegese', *ZTK* 67 (1970), pp. 263 ff.

1. The writing down of the words of the prophets. Unlike the sayings of the wise the prophetic word is not a general truth, valid for all times, 'but an announcement of the divine will for a specific situation'[1]. On the basis of a preceding revelation the prophet speaks his word as a messenger of Yahweh to particular men at a particular point in time. It is accordingly far from self-evident that the sayings of the prophets should have been written down at all. Instead of beginning our enquiry on the basis of general observations, we do better to start from the few passages which allow us to see the beginnings of the writing down of the words of the prophets. These are Isa. 8.16 f.; 30.8; Hab. 2.2 f.; Jer. 36; 30.2; 51.59 ff.; Ezek. 2.9 f. and 43.11 f. If we confine ourselves to the most certain among the ancient witnesses, Isa. 30.8,

1. Gunneweg, op. cit., p. 42.

we encounter a motif which can be treated as paradigmatic, however limited the writing down here seem to have been:

> Now come, write it down
> and inscribe it as an inscription,
> that it may be for the days to come
> 'as a witness' for ever.

The content of the inscription may be taken with Delitzsch and Hans Schmidt to have consisted only in 30.6–7, if not simply in the 'Rahab are they?—idleness!' of verse 7. The purpose of a public inscription is clear: after the fulfilment of the message the prophetic testimony will serve as evidence that the catastrophe is not a mere accident, but was the judgement of the Lord. So the inscription challenges the survivors to take seriously Yahweh's instructions and announcements of judgement. This is how the exilic or early post-exilic editor of the words of Isaiah who speaks in 30.9–17 interprets the original writing down of the prophetic word, and that now carried out by himself[2]. The case is similar with Hab. 2.1 ff. Here too the prophet is to write out the content of his vision, which refers to a future event, in a clearly readable form, i.e. for a public. In the time between prophecy and fulfilment the writing serves to strengthen confidence and to warn[3]. Jer. 36 confirms the picture thus obtained: 36.3 underlines clearly the intention of the reading aloud, which follows on from the writing down. Even if, in view of the dubious historical value of the chapter, this may be regarded as a reflection of later usage[4], the story is in line with the indisputably pre-exilic passage in Isaiah. The intention of strengthening the impression made by the intensity of a message which has remained the same over a long period of time appears as a further theme alongside the primary proclamation. Accordingly alongside the function of witness for the future the intention of reading out the words written down in the present may have been of decisive significance for the fixing in writing. In writing down the words of Amos a part may have been played (cf. 1.1) by the intention of convincing the hearers, in view of the occurrence of the prophesied earthquake, of the seriousness of the

2. Cf. above, p. 223.
3. Cf. K. Elliger, ATD 25, Göttingen 1967[6], ad loc.
4. Cf. above, p. 241.

further prophecies which still await fulfilment, although an
intended effectiveness as a future witness is not thereby excluded.
It may be assumed, in view of Isa. 8.1 ff. and 30.8 f., that either
the prophet himself or his disciples could read and write.
Further there was the possibility of dictating the words to a
scribe, as Jer. 36 presupposes. Our estimate of the value of
Ezek. 2.9 f. and 43.11 f. as evidence depends on the view taken
of the literary problems of the Book of Ezekiel[5], but does not
affect the conclusion that words of the prophets had already
come to be put in writing in the pre-exilic period. It should
not be overlooked that the prophets also wrote things down
in the course of symbolic actions (cf. Isa. 8.1 ff. and Jer.
51.59 ff.). But it is doubtful whether, taking up the concept of the
effectiveness of the word of the prophet, we can make this the
starting point for an explanation of the writing down and
subsequent reading out of the collected words of the prophets,
both writing and reading contributing in an almost magical
sense to the heightening in effectiveness of the word once
spoken[6]. Jer. 36.23–25, 27–29 is an important witness that ideas
of this sort were known in Judaism; although admittedly the
story also shows that they were not part of the religion at its
highest.

2. *Oral and written tradition.* The thesis presented by Nyberg,
Birkeland, Engnell and others, that the fixing in writing of the
Old Testament tradition first began to a serious extent in the
exilic period runs into considerable difficulties when it is applied
to the prophets. It fails to recognize, as Widengren has pointed
out, the difference between nomadic and urban culture. It
places too great demands, in the light of the collections we
actually have, and their possible forerunners, on the memory of
the tradents, quite apart from the consideration how little we
know in concrete terms of the existence of any guilds of prophets,
in which their sayings would have had to be constantly learnt by
heart and passed on. The examples produced from the Oriental
and Islamic worlds of astonishing feats of memory are not per-
suasive, because here in almost all cases written texts stand in the
background. But there is, as again Widengren has emphasized, a

5. Cf. above, pp. 251 ff.
6. Fohrer argues for this explanation (BZAW 99, pp. 144 ff.).

difference between memorizing texts, and oral traditions. Mohammedans and Parsees do not recite orally transmitted material; they repeat by heart texts which have been learnt. A further point is that in the words of the prophets we are dealing with revelations from God, which just for that reason could lay claim to reliable preservation in a world that knew writing, so to be written down. Since there is no reason to doubt that the normal place of prophetic proclamation was the sanctuary, the assumption argued strongly by Gunneweg that the prophetic writings were preserved in the sanctuary is a reasonable one. This does not of course exclude the possibility that there were also other circles which were conscious of being responsible for the preservation of the prophetic writings. It must indeed be conceded that we know very little about the groupings which existed in pre-exilic Israel. If public effectiveness was aimed at, at least in at all normal times deposition in a sanctuary would be the best method.

In spite of these objections and qualifications it would be a mistake to throw out the baby with the bath water, and to undervalue completely the significance of oral tradition for the development of the prophetic books. If it must be agreed with Lindblom that the third person accounts in the books of the prophets were not written down by the prophet, nor at the dictation of the prophet, it is also clear that either witnesses of the work of these prophets or the hearers of these are responsible for accounts such as Amos 7.10–17, Hos. 1.2–9, Isa. 7.1–17[7] and 20. If we look at Isa. 36–39, with its obvious distortion of the figure of the prophet, and its late biases, it becomes clear that the narrative has taken hold of the prophets and itself acquired productive force. The significance of oral tradition appears probably most clearly in the Book of Jeremiah, where alongside the *ipsissima verba* of the prophet we have both sermons and narratives which have in part at least gone through a fairly lengthy oral tradition before they were joined up with the records of the words of the prophet[8]. It is a lucky accident that we have in 7 and 26 a double, and in my view in its present condition secondary, tradition of Jeremiah's announcement of the destruction of the temple. It shows how sayings of Jeremiah,

7. Here I submit for discussion my interpretation given in O. Kaiser, *Isaiah 1–12*, OTL, 1972, pp. 86 ff.   8. Cf. above, pp. 239 ff.

kept in memory for a lengthy period, have been drawn in on the one hand into exilic and early post-exilic preaching, and on the other hand into narratives, and how both have finally been added on to the record of the sayings of the prophet. This at the same time reminds us of the possibility that individual sayings of the prophet, which impressed themselves particularly strikingly on the memory, may have been added subsequently to already existing records. It can hardly be regarded as accidental that it is precisely in the Book of Jeremiah that so extensive an oral tradition is encountered; for the terrible fulfilment of his words must have had a striking effect on his contemporaries and challenged them to take up his word into the preaching of the synagogue, which was then beginning, and to tell again and again of his work and his sufferings. While there may have been similar narratives about the other pre-exilic prophets, they have not been passed down to us (apart from the preclassical prophets, and the small quantity of material mentioned above). Here we can see the sharp alteration in the general evaluation of the writing prophets after the catastrophe of 587, which found its first tangible record in Lam. 2.17:

> The LORD has done what he purposed,
> has carried out his threat;
> as he ordained long ago. . . .

3. *The origin and redaction of the books of the prophets.* Since even now there is no comprehensive investigation of the redaction history of the books of the prophets as a whole, and even the individual books still present more than enough unsolved problems, we must confine ourselves here to some remarks of principle. We must start from the result of the religio-historical investigation of prophecy, recently again argued for explicitly by Fohrer, that the change from the prophetic expectations of the future to eschatological expectations is connected with the exile[9]. The concern now is generally, and to an increasing extent, no longer (as with the pre-exilic prophets) for the future destruction or salvation of the nation, but for the fundamental

---

9. Cf. Fohrer, BZAW 99, pp. 32 ff.; also W. Cossmann, *Die Entwicklung des Gerichtsgedankens bei den alttestamentlichen Propheten*, BZAW 29, 1915, and S. Mowinckel, *He that Cometh*, Oxford 1956.

contrast between two ages, between the present age of distress and oppression, and the coming of age of salvation and the reign of God, in which Israel hopes to obtain a due share.

To the extent that the partial collections of the older prophets were not already put together in the pre-exilic period, their uniting took place in the exilic and early post-exilic period. The redactions and insertions, which are at least partly connected with the use of the books of the prophets in worship, are characteristic of the further process of transmission, and probably already of the process of redaction just mentioned[10]. Their influence must certainly be regarded as substantially stronger than has generally been supposed until now. While one might gain the impression in view of recent scholarly work on the prophets that the real literary problem consists in demonstrating what are additions, taking as a basis the principle used in Classical scholarship that it is not the authenticity of a book or passage but its inauthenticity that requires proof, in fact by reason of the redactional process, which clearly spans whole centuries, the task as posed is the opposite one. If so it gains not only in difficulty but also in significance for the history both of religion and of faith.[11] In the face of the fulfilment of the old prophecies of disaster and of their present distress the community had need of an assurance of hope. The redactors made allowance for this first by bringing up to date the old threat sayings by the insertion of small additions, which showed the connection of the older prophecies with the catastrophe which had just taken place more clearly. This process can be observed in the First-Isaiah collection. Furthermore they inserted threat sayings against their oppressors and plunderers, which at first remained entirely within the framework of the expectations of the older prophets. We can, with Fohrer, regard Deutero-Isaiah as being so far as we can tell the turning point to eschatological prophecy, for the Jerusalem cult traditions flow into this collection on a broad front. While in this book the messianic expectation appears only as re-applied to Israel, expectations of a restoration of the Davidic monarchy appear at the time of and after Deutero-Isaiah, in a historically accessible form in Haggai and Zechariah. The messianic prophecies in the books of Amos, Hosea, Isaiah,

---

10. Cf. also Schottroff, op. cit., pp. 283 f.   11. Cf. also above, pp. 208 f.

Jeremiah and Ezekiel will have been inserted into the collections between the last quarter of the sixth century and the middle of the fifth century. From now down to the Hellenistic period, we find, at least in partial contrast to the theocratic circles which can be traced from Deuteronomy through P and the Chronicler down to Jesus Sirach (Plöger), eschatological expectations directed primarily towards the coming universal judgement of the world, the gathering of the scattered of Israel connected with this, the exaltation of Zion, and the period of salvation inaugurated by this. The prophecies of disaster are now interrupted by prophecies of salvation or in some of the smaller books concluded by these, and this produces a simple or more elaborate two-element eschatological scheme, depending on the extent of the books and the intensity of their use. It can be presumed that the pre-exilic words of judgement against the prophet's own nation are intended to be understood at least as a warning against the coming judgement, in so far as they are not actually submitted to reworking in this direction. We cannot suppose a purely antiquarian interest in the handing on of the prophetic material. At the same time the speeches against foreign nations in the tradition have been partially revised in the direction of a universal expectation of judgement, so that they remain of living significance over and beyond their original occasion. The same tendency can be seen in the whole composition of the speeches against foreign nations in the book of Jeremiah. It is also responsible for the threefold division of the whole material in Isaiah 1–39, Jeremiah and Ezekiel, by which threats against the prophet's own nation are followed by oracles against foreign nations, and these by prophecies of salvation. The viewpoint implicit in the arrangement can be gathered from what has been said already: between the present time of suffering and the expected time of salvation stands the world judgement. It is clear from these examples to how great an extent deliberate theological reflection lies behind the redactional insertions. It will no doubt be the concern of scholarly work on the prophets for some decades more to examine and take further the attempts made by Fohrer and Plöger to deal with these insertions as a group.

There have however also been more or less mechanical insertions. While we cannot include the numerous glosses without further examination of them, we may probably include the collection of the Book of the Twelve Minor Prophets, and the uniting of Isaiah with Deutero-Isaiah and Trito-Isaiah into one book, as having both been determined by the length of the books of Jeremiah and Ezekiel. It must however be noticed that the collection of Isaianic writings also displays links of content, such as are clear for Deutero-Isaiah with Trito-Isaiah.

It looks as if respect for contemporary prophecy declined the more Judaism was reshaped into a religion of a book. To the extent that the prophetic books came to the fore, contemporary prophecy became anonymous and had recourse to the expansion and revision of these books. When finally the prophetic period came to be thought of as past, and carefulness about the text of the existing books increased, it became pseudonymous. While the prophets were subjected at least in part to contempt (cf. Zech. 13.2 ff.), the cultivation of the prophetic eschatological inheritance passed on to the wise men who are to be looked for among the Hasidaeans and later the eschatological sects. They threw over their own speculative expectations the mantle of a pious man of the past, in order to reach the ears of their contemporaries thereby. The limits to the redactions of the prophetic books which affect more deeply the transmitted text and make larger insertions into it lie roughly between the last quarter of the third century and the middle of the second century B.C. It is certainly connected not only with the hardening of Judaism into a book religion, but also with its rivalry with the Samaritans, and with its own internal divisions, which must increasingly have exposed expansions of the text to the suspicion of forgery. If we compare the Masoretic text with the manuscripts discovered in the Judaean desert, this will show that even then the text has not reached a completely fixed form. But anything really new is now uttered by the apocalyptists and sectarians.

§ 25   Daniel and Apocalyptic

A. Freiherr von Gall, *Die Einheitlichkeit des Buches Daniel*, Giessen 1895; H. Gunkel, *Schöpfung und Chaos in Urzeit und Endzeit*, Göttingen 1895; G. A. Barton, 'The Composition of the Book of Daniel', *JBL* 17 (1898), pp. 62 ff.; C. Julius, *Die griechischen Danielzusätze und ihre kanonische Geltung*, Biblische Studien VI 3/4, Freiburg 1901; H. Preis-werk, *Der Sprachenwechsel im Buche Daniel*, Berne 1903; P.Volz, *Jüdische Eschatologie von Daniel bis Akiba*, Tübingen and Leipzig 1903 = *Die Eschatologie der jüdischen Gemeinde im neutestamentlichen Zeitalter*, Tübingen 1934; A. Bertholet, *Daniel und die griechische Gefahr*, RV II, 17, 1907; G. Hölscher, 'Die Entstehung des Buches Daniel', *ThStKr* 92 (1919), pp. 113 ff.; W. Baumgartner, *Das Buch Daniel*, Aus der Welt der Religion, Alttestamentliche Reihe, Heft 1, Giessen 1926; id., 'Das Aramäische im Buche Daniel', *ZAW* 45 (1927), pp. 81 ff.; id., 'Ein Vierteljahrhundert Danielforschung', *ThR* NF 11 (1939), pp. 59 ff., 125 ff., 201 ff.; M. Noth, 'Zur Komposition des Buches Daniel' [1926], *Gesammelte Studien zum Alten Testament* II, ThB 39, Munich 1969, pp. 11 ff.; id., 'The Understanding of History in Old Testament Apocalyptic', in *The Laws in the Pentateuch and Other Studies*, Edinburgh and London 1966, pp. 194 ff.; 'The Holy Ones of the Most High', in *The Laws in the Pentateuch*, pp. 215 ff.; C. Kuhl, *Die drei Männer im Feuer (Daniel Kapitel 3 und seine Zusätze)*, BZAW 55, 1930; H. Junker, *Untersuchungen über literarische und exegetische Probleme des Buches Daniel*, Bonn 1932; H. H. Rowley, 'The Bilingual Problem of Daniel', *ZAW* 50 (1932), pp. 256 ff.; *Darius the Mede and the Four World Empires in the Book of Daniel*, Cardiff 1935; id., 'The Unity of the Book of Daniel' [1950], in *The Servant of the Lord*, Oxford 1965², pp. 247 ff.; id. 'The Composition of the Book of Daniel', *VT* 5 (1955), pp. 272 ff.; id., *The Relevance of Apocalyptic*, London 1963³; M. A. Beek, *Das Danielbuch. Sein historischer Hintergrund und seine literarische Entwicklung*, Diss. theol. Leiden 1935; E. Bickermann, *Der Gott der Makkabäer*, Berlin 1937; F. Zimmermann, 'The Aramaic Origin of Daniel 8–12', *JBL* 57 (1938), pp. 255 ff.; H. L. Ginsberg, *Studies in Daniel*, New York 1948; id., 'The Composition of the Book of Daniel', *VT* 4 (1954), pp. 246 ff.; T. W. Manson, 'The Son of Man in Daniel, Enoch and the Gospels' [1949], in *Studies in the Gospels and Epistles*, Manchester 1962, pp. 123 ff.; O. Eissfeldt, 'Die Menetekel-Inschrift und ihre Deutung' [1951], *KS* III, Tübingen 1966, pp. 210 ff.; id., 'Daniels und seiner drei Gefährten Laufbahn im babylonischen, medischen und persischen Dienst' [1960], *KS* III, pp. 513 ff.; S. B. Frost, *Old Testament Apocalyptic. Its Origins and Growth*, London 1952; O. Plöger, *Theocracy and Eschatology* [1959], Oxford 1968; K. Koch, 'Die Weltreiche im Danielbuch', *TLZ* 85 (1960), cols. 829 ff.; id., 'Spätisraelitisches Geschichtsdenken am Beispiel des Buches Daniel', *Historische Zeitschrift* 163 (1961), pp. 1 ff.; A. Jepsen, 'Bemerkungen zum Danielbuch', *VT* 11 (1961), pp. 386 ff.; R. Meyer, *Das Gebet des Nabonid*, SAL 107, 3, 1962; F. König, *Zarathustras Jenseitsvorstellungen und das Alte Testament*, Vienna, Freiburg and Basle 1964; W. Dommershausen, *Nabonid im Buche Daniel*, Mainz 1964; G. von Rad, *Old Testament Theology*, vol. 2, Edinburgh and London 1965; D. J. Wiseman, T. C. Mitchell and others, *Notes on Some Problems in the Book of Daniel*, London 1965; A. Caquot, 'Les quatres Bêtes et le "Fils d'homme" (Daniel, 7)', *Sémitica* 17 (1967), pp. 37 ff.; H. Hanhart, 'Die Heiligen des Höchsten', in *Hebräische Wortforschung*, Festschrift W. Baumgartner, SVT 16, 1967, pp. 90 ff.; M. Delcor, 'Les sources du chapitre VII de Daniel', *VT* 18 (1968), pp. 290 ff.; P. von der Osten-Sacken, *Die Apokalyptik in ihrem Verhältnis zu Prophetie und Weisheit*, ThEx 157, Munich 1969; J. M. Schmidt, *Die jüdische Apokalyptik. Die Geschichte ihrer Erforschung von den Anfängen bis zu den Textfunden von Qumran*, Munich 1969, pp. 35 ff.

Commentaries: HK Behrmann 1894; KHC Marti 1901; SAT Haller 1925[2]; HS Goettsberger 1928; ICC Montgomery 1936; HAT Bentzen 1952[2]; KAT[2] Plöger 1965; OTL Porteous 1965; SB Delcor 1971; SC Bevan 1892; Charles 1929.

1. The book. The Book of Daniel, consisting of twelve chapters, is placed in the Hebrew Bible not among the prophets, as in the Greek and in the translations which follow it, but in the *k͏ʿṯûḇîm* or writings, in which it is placed between Esther and Ezra. 1.1–2.4a and 8.1–12.13 are in Hebrew, 2.4b–7.28 in Aramaic. The text of the Septuagint diverges from that of the Hebrew, especially in 4–6, giving a substantially blacker picture of the heathen kings and the other opponents of Daniel. Of the additions in the Septuagint the most noteworthy are the stories of Susanna and of Bel and the dragon, placed before and after the story of Daniel, the prayer of Azariah (3.24–45), and the Song of the Three Holy Children in the fire (3.51–90). It is noteworthy that the Septuagint text of Daniel has been replaced almost completely in the manuscripts by a version which is regarded by recent studies as an early form of the text later revised by Theodotion. The original text of the Septuagint is only known from two manuscripts of the second and of the eleventh century, which show the same text as does the Syro-hexaplaric recension of Paul of Tella, and from some of the Chester Beatty papyri[1]. The book contains in chapters 1–6 the story and in 7–12

1. Cf. J. Ziegler, *Septuaginta* XVI, 2, Göttingen 1954, pp. 28 ff.; A. Schmitt, 'Stammt der sogennante "Θ"-Text bei Daniel wirklich von Theodotion?', *Nachrichten der Akademie der Wissenschaften in Göttingen* 1966, 8, Göttingen 1966, pp. 62 and 112; A. Geisen, *Der Septuagintatext*

the visions of a Jewish youth Daniel, supposedly deported by
Nebuchadnezzar to Babylonia in the third year of King Jehoiakim (608–598), who is assigned to the court by Nebuchadnezzar. Because of the fear of God and the wisdom he showed in
the reigns of the Babylonian kings Nebuchadnezzar and Belshazzar, the Median king Darius and the Persian Cyrus, he rises
to the position of one of the three governors of the kingdom,
provides proofs of his faith, interprets dreams and miraculous
writing, and himself has dreams and visions, which look beyond
the kingdoms of the world to the breaking in of the kingdom of
God.

2. Content. The Jewish youth Daniel, who has been deported to
Babylon, is selected together with his friends Hananiah, Mishael and
Azariah for court service. They are renamed Belteshazzar, Shadrach,
Meshach and Abednego (cf. chap. 3) and are nourished so successfully
under the Jewish food laws at the Babylonian court that they are
found by the king to be more handsome and cleverer than their companions (chap. 1). Daniel guesses and interprets Nebuchadnezzar's
dream of an image of gold, silver, bronze, iron and clay, which is destroyed by a stone, as referring to the succession of the four world
empires (chap. 2). The martyr legend of chap. 3 tells of the refusal of
Shadrach, Meshach and Abednego to pray to an image erected by Nebuchadnezzar, and of the vain attempt to burn them to death in the fiery
furnace. Chapter 4 (Heb. 3.31–4.34), partly presented as a letter of
Nebuchadnezzar to all nations, tells of his dream of a tree which is cut
down to its stump. Daniel interprets it as referring to the fate of Nebuchadnezzar, who then lives for a time like an animal among animals.
In 5 follows the account of Belshazzar's feast, and the Mene-Tekel
inscription, which Daniel interprets as referring to the division of the
Babylonian empire between the Medes and the Persians. An intrigue of
the satraps forces Darius the Mede to have Daniel thrown into the
lions' den. Daniel's miraculous deliverance leads to a command of the
king directed to all nations to fear the God of Daniel (chap. 6). In a
vision in chap. 7 four beasts, some winged (including lion, bear and
leopard), symbolizing four world empires, rise from the sea. The fourth
beast, which devours all around it, and has ten horns, is destroyed by
the Ancient of Days, who appears for judgement on a throne of flame,

des Buches Daniel nach dem Kölner Teil des Papyrus 967, Papyrologische
Texte und Abhandlungen 5, Bonn 1968, pp. 50 f.; and J. Schüppenhaus,
'Das Verhältnis von LXX- und Theodotion-Text in den apokryphen
Zusätzen zum Danielbuch', *ZAW* 83 (1971), pp. 49 ff.

and the other beasts are deprived of their power. Dominion over all the nations is given to the Son of Man (Israel), who appears from the clouds before the Ancient of Days. In 8 follows Daniel's vision of the fight between the ram, personifying the Median and Persian empire, and the goat which tramples down the ram, which at first had one horn, to be interpreted as Alexander the Great. After a long confession of guilt on behalf of Israel Daniel receives in 9 from the angel Gabriel an explanation of the seventy years (of exile) announced by Jeremiah (25.11; 29.10) as referring to weeks of years. An angel reveals in 10–12 the events of the end-time in the context of a presentation of the main events from the Persian period under Cyrus down to Antiochus IV Epiphanes. After a time of terrible distress everyone in Israel (which is protected by Michael the angel of the nations) whose name is written in the heavenly book is saved; many who have fallen asleep will rise to everlasting life or to everlasting contempt. A final vision seeks both to reveal and to obscure the answer to the question of the date of the coming of the miraculous end. The additions in 12.11 and 12 refer back to 8.14, and extend the time from 1,150 days to 1,296 and then to 1,355 days.

3. Literary problems. The book in its present form belongs to the period of the Maccabees. It is debated whether it originated then as a unitary product which partly incorporated older traditions, or whether it has a more complicated literary pre-history. The grounds for doubt about its literary unity are first the striking change of language in 2.4b and 8.1, and secondly the sometimes friendly attitude of the stories to the non-Jewish milieu presupposed, or the lack of impression made upon their contents by the events of the Maccabaean period. On the other hand there are such internal connections between the text of chs. 2, 7 and 8–11 in their present form, and the division of dreams and visions between King Nebuchadnezzar and the periods of Kings Belshazzar, Darius and Cyrus displays such a planned pattern that a defence of the unity can also be seen to be reasonable.

(a) THE PREHISTORY OF 1–6. It is easier to demonstrate the independent origins of the stories collected in 1–6.

Here we follow Hölscher's observations. The first striking point is that in 3 there is no mention at all of Daniel. 1 clearly prepares not only for the stories of Daniel but also for the incorporation of 3, since it identifies Shadrach, Meshach and Abednego with the three companions of Daniel, Hananiah, Mishael and Azariah. This chapter is accordingly quite indispensable as an introduction for the following narratives, which cannot have been put alongside one another in written form without chap. 1. The carelessness of the narrator of 1 emerges clearly from the fact that he has omitted to make the internal chronology of 1 and 2 agree. According to 1.5,18 the young men are supposed to appear in the service of the court only after three years. According to 2.1,14 Daniel is already in the service of the king in the king's second year. Chapters 2 and 3 are also not carefully harmonized with one another; for after the king's change of mind recounted in 2.47 his behaviour in 3 is a complete surprise. The same is true of the relationship of 3 and 4. According to 2 Nebuchadnezzar had made Daniel the chief prefect over all his wise men. So it is surprising that according to 4 he calls on his wise men, whose failure he knew from 2, at all before he turns to Daniel. The same tension exists also between 2 and 5, in which Belshazzar learns for the first time from his wise men of the existence of Daniel, when he should know him as their chief and as the vizier of the province of Babylon. Finally the relationship between the installation of Daniel as chief governor in 5 and in 6 remains obscure. It is clear therefore that the stories put together in 2–6 originally go back to independent traditions. 2 has clear links with Gen. 41 f., in the motif of the rise of the interpreter of dreams. 3 could have been occasioned by Jer. 29.22, if they do not both go back to a common tradition of the punishment of religious agitators with death by fire. 3, like 6, does not presuppose a general religious persecution, but pogroms limited in locality and time. The prehistory of chapter 4 is the clearest to us, since we have in 4QOrNab, a Prayer of Nabonidus belonging to a wisdom narrative written in Aramaic, not only a parallel, but as R. Meyer has shown, an antecedent of 4. The transfer of the residence of the Babylonian king Nabonidus to the Arabian oasis of Tema occupied the imagination not only of the Babylonians but also of the Jews settled in Arabia. The absence of the hubris motif in 4QOrNab shows that the Nabonidus story is older than our story in Daniel. This is indicated also by the anonymity of the Jewish youth who acts there as the interpreter of the dream. The narrative is transferred in Daniel also from Nabonidus to his well known predecessor Nebuchadnezzar. The Daniel story clearly did not have a place for the figure of Nabonidus, the father of Belshazzar. In 5 we have the folk-tale motif of spirit writing. 3–4 and 6 no doubt have their prehistory in the eastern, particularly the Babylonian diaspora, and 5 either in the Arabian or in the Babylonian diaspora.

There are no difficulties in explaining the transmission of these narratives, which in general belong to the type of the court story, to the Jewish homeland, in view of the lively contacts between it and the eastern diaspora. In spite of the tensions outlined and the original independence of the individual stories which this shows, there can be no doubt that 1–6 in their present form must be understood as a literary unity. The only question is whether the narrator responsible for them is identical with the author of the visions of 7–12. The problem, as recent scholarly discussion shows, cannot be separated from that of the change of language.

(b) THE PROBLEM OF THE CHANGE OF LANGUAGE. The change found in 2.4b from Hebrew to Aramaic and the corresponding change back from Aramaic into Hebrew in 8.1 have so far found no generally acceptable explanation.

If a survey is made of the attempts at a solution, they fall into the following five groups: 1. The whole book was originally written in Hebrew, but circulated also in an Aramaic translation. When the Hebrew original of 2.4b–7.28 was lost the resulting gap was filled from the Aramaic version (so e.g. Lenormant, von Gall and Barton). An argument against this however is that 2.4b–7.28 in no way give the impression of being a translation from Hebrew. It would be easier to assume with Preiswerk that 1.1–2.4a have been subsequently translated from Aramaic into Hebrew. 2. The whole book was originally written in Aramaic, but was later in part translated into Hebrew, in order to gain for it admittance into the canon (so e.g. Buhl, Marti, Charles, Zimmermann and Ginsberg). The correctness of this hypothesis is difficult to test because the differences between a Hebrew filled with Aramaisms and translation Hebrew cannot be satisfactorily established. 3. The change of language is connected with the existence of an independent Aramaic and an independent Hebrew book, which were subsequently put together. This theory occurs in two versions. On the one, which is held by Dalman, Torrey and Montgomery, a distinction is to be made between an Aramaic book of stories in 1–6 and a Hebrew book of visions in 7–12. When they were joined together the beginning of the one book was translated into Hebrew and that of the other into Aramaic in an adjustment made by the editor. This hypothesis, like the next, assumes a difference between the attitude of the narratives and that of the visions to the foreign kings and to the Gentiles. According to Hölscher[2], who is followed by Haller, Noth, Kuhl, Junker and

2. The hypothesis was originally put forward by E. Sellin[*], and worked out more fully by Hölscher.

Baumgartner, sometimes with variations, the Aramaic book included 7 too. If 7 now gives the appearance of coming from the Maccabaean period, the author of 8–12 is responsible for this as a result of having added 7.7b, 8, 11a, 20–22 and 24 f. Noth went still further in assuming later additions in 7. He attempted to show that not only 7 but also 2 in their original forms went back to the period of Alexander, and were later expanded. The difference between the visions in 2 and 7 and the learned allegorizing of 8–12 would be explained in this way. 4. The unity of the book is maintained, and psychological reasons are claimed to be responsible for the change of language. Merx regarded the Aramaic portions as intended for the general public, while the Hebrew parts were intended for a narrower circle (this hypothesis seems to have had some influence on Rowley). Behrmann and others thought that the change was connected with the speech of a foreign ruler. Furthermore the author forgot to change back at the right time from the familiar Aramaic into Hebrew. It hardly needs to be said that this explanation has found no support. Plöger has produced similar views in a more thoroughly worked out form: he too sees the change of language as determined by the content, but he starts it where the wise men begin to speak before the Babylonian king. While the foreign setting ends in 6, Aramaic was kept on into 7 because of the connection of content with 2, while the chapters directed to Israel in 8–12 were written in Hebrew. 5. A mixture of literary and traditio-historical reasons have been put forward. Rowley thinks of the publication of 2–6 preceding that of the whole book, followed later by that of 7.8–12 were written in Hebrew from the start because of their content, which was less designed for the general public. When the sections were being collected together 1 was composed, and the beginning of 2 altered. Weiser thinks of the taking over of older passages, which were left in their original Aramaic form.

This survey is not encouraging. However the discovery of 4QOrNab and of other Aramaic fragments of a pseudo-Danielic nature which have not yet been mentioned shows that the existence of such Jewish literature preceding and also following our book of Daniel must be allowed for. So it is a legitimate question whether we should not allow for Aramaic precursors of our book of Daniel, which were taken over by the author of the whole book, sometimes in an edited form. They circulated, as Kuhl suggests, separately at first, and in a form sufficiently fixed to limit the freedom of action of the collector and editor.

It remains to be seen whether further discoveries will permit a redating of the teaching about the ages of the world in 2 back into the pre-Maccabaean period. It has often been conjectured that this motif comes from Babylonia. Its diffusion from Iran as far as Greece can be demonstrated, cf. Hesiod, *Works and Days* 109 ff. The material of 7 on the one hand chooses the three most dangerous predatory animals known to the Palestinians, but on the other ascribes to the first and third what are clearly ancient Oriental mythological traits. In the rising of the four beasts from the sea there may be a recollection of the Ugaritic Yam-Leviathan complex. There is perhaps also an echo in the figure of the Ancient of Days of the mythology known from Ugarit, in which the father of the gods is known as the father of years. The origin of the idea of the Son of Man remains contested. In the ram and the he-goat of 8 we probably have echoes of Babylonian astrological geography, which assigned to each land a specific sign of the zodiac. The idea of the angels of the nations taken up in 10 also has Mesopotamian roots. It is clear that the inclusion of the hope of the resurrection in 12 attempts to solve an internal Israelite problem. It is disputed to what extent non-Israelite, and particularly Iranian, ideas have had an influence on this. With Baumgartner and against Junker we are unable to assume that the writer had particular sources for 8–12. The assumption of familiarity with individual motifs is sufficient to explain the facts. It remains to be seen whether division hypotheses, such as Ginsberg has produced not only for 1–6 but also for 7–12, will gain acceptance.

While we have the book as a whole in its original form, apart from additions in 1.20, 10.21a and 11.1 the prayer in 9.4–20 has been regarded as a later insertion, but also defended energetically as original. It is hardly possible to decide whether 12.11 f. come from the hand of the original author or not.

4. Date. It has already been repeatedly emphasized that the book in its present form comes from the period of the Maccabees. The Hebrew, which from a literary viewpoint is inferior to the Aramaic parts of the book, shows that it belongs to the latest period of the Biblical language. While it is possible to argue about the antiquity of the Akkadian and Persian loanwords, the Greek borrowings in 3.5, together with the style of the Hebrew, support an origin in the Hellenistic period. The fact that Jesus Sirach does not mention Daniel in his praise of the fathers in 44 ff. is an argument against placing the whole book before 200, as is the fact that the earliest attestations of the book are in the Sibylline Oracles III, 388 ff. (about 140 B.C.) and in 1 Macc. 2.59 f. (about 100 B.C.). Matt. 24.15 is evidence that the book was already regarded as a prophetic book in the New Testament period. Porphyry (d. 304) already recognized in his anti-Christian polemic that the book comes from the period of Antiochus IV Epiphanes (176/5–163). 8.12 f., 9.27 and 11.36 f. presuppose the prohibition of the Jewish cultus and the desecration of the temple of December 167, and 11.34 perhaps the beginnings of the Maccabaean revolt. Since no allusion is found to the dedication of the temple carried out by Judas Maccabaeus in December 164, and since 11.40 contains an unfulfilled prophecy of the death of Antiochus IV, which took place under quite different circumstances in the spring of 163, the latest possible *terminus ad quem* for the production of the book is 164. If 11.44 does not presuppose a measure of knowledge of the Parthian campaign of Antiochus, but is to be evaluated as an apocalyptic fantasy, the dating of the book would be narrowed down to the brief period between 166 and 165. With Plöger we can perhaps look for the author in the ranks of the Hasideans, who had withdrawn to the hill country in expectation of God's help (cf. 1 Macc. 1.56 and 2.29 f.). On the basis of 12.3 he could perhaps be sought among the wise, who by their apocalyptic teaching were giving courage and hope to those gathered around them in the distresses of the time. The author can hardly have been a genuine visionary, since his visions are better understood as revelatory allegories coming from a normal imagination than as real visions (Baumgartner). It remains to be mentioned that his historical ideas become extremely vague outside the Hellenistic period. In his assumption of a deportation under Jehoiakim in 1.1, he shows himself dependent on the Chronicler, as he does also in his assumption in 11.2 that between Belshazzar and Alexander only four kings reigned (cf. 2 Chr. 36.6 and Ezra 4.6 ff.). His knowledge of Babylonian history is so deficient that he makes Nabonidus' son Belshazzar son of Nebuchadnezzar and king. His insertion of a Median empire between the Babylonian and Persian ones is completely a work of imagination. Darius the Mede is supposed to have reigned before Cyrus and to have taken Babylon, according to 6.1 and 6.29. Cyrus himself is made a son of Xerxes in 9.1. On the other hand behind 5.30 f. stands the correct knowledge that Belshazzar was living in Babylon when the city fell into Persian hands. It is again clear how variable the ground of the traditions on which the author of the book had to stand was.

5. Daniel as an example of apocalyptic. Baumgartner has so well characterized the nature of apocalyptic using the example of Daniel that we quote what he says on it. In distinction from prophecy it is marked by 'pseudonymity, eschatological impatience, and an exact calculation of the end times, a widespread use of often fanciful visions, a world-historical and cosmic horizon, number symbolism and secret language, a doctrine of angels and hope of an afterlife'[3]. There is also a dualism in history. While the future was for the prophets a continuation of the present, even if they expected in it a decisive change in events through the intervention of Yahweh, for the apocalyptists it is in complete contrast to it. The apocalyptists have extended the future expectations of the prophets, and especially of the exilic and post-exilic prophets. A line of development, traceable in the editing of the prophetic books, leads from the exilic and post-exilic expectation of a change to salvation for Israel, in connection with a world-wide judgement on the nations, and from the whole complex of ideas connected with the 'day of Yahweh', to the apocalyptic expectations of the end. However, these have not reached the form in which they are found in the book of Daniel without the influence of wisdom, to which they owe at least the idea of predetermination. The extent to which wisdom traditions could become prominent in apocalyptic is shown by the Ethiopic Book of Enoch. It embeds a mass of cosmological speculations into its theory of the course of the world from creation to the dawn of the Messianic age, so that apocalyptic here seems like a universal gnosis[4]. It is nevertheless better to see the apocalyptic movement as a whole as a continuation of prophecy rather than of wisdom, although there seems to have been a convergence of the circles responsible for the transmission of the prophetic and of the wisdom traditions. We must,

3. *ThR* NF 11 (1939), pp. 136 f.
4. For this form of apocalyptic Wisd. 7.17–21 can be quoted as an example.

with Frost, distinguish between a left and a right wing of the apocalyptic movement. On the right stands our book of Daniel, on the left Enoch. Certainly Daniel, whom according to 12.3 we are to number among the wise, is also influenced by international wisdom speculation, as appears clearly in his teaching about the ages of the world.

The great history works of Israel were ultimately confessions of the God who by a wonderful providence directs the fates of his people and of the world. The prophets interpreted their own hour as the time of decision. The apocalyptist gazes fascinated at the great but wicked drama which is the world, and waits for the end of history. The author of Daniel is certainly not concerned with the penetration of the secrets of world history in themselves, although we owe to him the first interpretation of world history which goes beyond the sketch-plan of the Yahwist[5], and one which has been of inestimable significance for the whole future thought of the west[6]. His emphasis on the end time which, with Antiochus IV, is standing immediately before its goal, together with his incorporation of the older stories which are re-edited in 2–6, shows that he was concerned not to interpret history as such, but to console those attacked by persecution. He certainly thought that the time of the end could be calculated. In this he pays his tribute to a hubristic form of wisdom. And for this reason the time-limit has again and again to be postponed, since the course of world affairs had no regard for his speculations, until finally the pastorally concerned among the apocalyptists themselves warn against calculation of the end[7]. On the Rabbinic view the period of the prophets had come to an end, if not with Ezra, then at least with Alexander. 'Up to now (the time of Alexander the Great)', says the *Seder 'Olam Rabba* 30, 'the prophets prophesied in the Holy Spirit. From now onwards incline thine ear and hear the words of the wise'.[8] One who wished to prophesy at this time would have to take the course either of anonymous additions to the prophets, or of pseudonymous prediction. Perhaps there was a Babylonian

5. Cf. above, pp. 85 ff.
6. Cf. K. Löwith, *Meaning in History*, Chicago 1949.
7. Cf. W. Harnisch, *Verhängnis und Verheissung der Geschichte*, FRLANT 97, 1969.
8. Quoted after R. Meyer, *TDNT* VI, p. 818.

Jewish tradition of a wise man called Daniel who had entered
into the service of the foreign court. Perhaps the reference in
Ezek. 14.14, 20 and 28.3 to a particularly wise and just Daniel,
who is mentioned together with Noah and Job, provided the
opportunity of putting someone's own speculations on to the
lips of a man of an earlier period. In this case it would be probable that the wise king Danel of the Ras Shamra texts was
somewhere in the background as a source[9]. The fiction gives
itself away immediately, as Gunkel realized, by the fact that
the prophecy proper is preceded by a lengthy *vaticinium ex
eventu*, which has to bridge the gap in time between the supposed
standpoint of the visionary and the actual time of the writer.
In view of the catastrophes into which Judaism was dragged by
an overheated expectation of the end-time in the first and
second centuries A.D., we can understand the fact that it did not
take the apocalyptic books, with the exception of Daniel, into
the canon. Daniel had prefixed speculation about the theology
of history with a legendary testimony to the preservation of the
Jewish faith in the hour of danger, and had placed over martyr-
dom the star of hope in the resurrection, serving as a witness to
a no longer avoidable individualization of theology and of piety.
Whether it was a feeling for the special place held by the book
among the apocalypses, or only the need to provide a basis for the
regard in which it was in fact held, that gave its position to
the book, in our view the Book of Daniel deservedly stands in
the collection of Old Testament books, because it represents the
end-point of a development whose roots reach back deep into
the history of the religion of Israel. Perhaps our capacity to
listen to its witness to faith grows in proportion as we recognize
its fragmentarily mythical character, and grant to myth, over
and beyond Daniel's anti-mythical calculations of dates, its
independence as a means of interpreting the world in faith.

9. Cf. M. Noth, 'Noah, Daniel und Hiob in Ezechiel XIV', *VT* I
(1951), pp. 251 ff.

E. Israelite Poetry and Wisdom

§ 26   Basic Laws of Hebrew Poetry

K. Budde, 'Das hebräische Klagelied', *ZAW* 2 (1882), pp. 1 ff.; E. König, *Stilistik, Rhetorik, Poetik in Bezug auf die biblische Literatur*, Leipzig 1900; E. Sievers, *Metrische Studien I. Studien zur hebräischen Metrik*, Leipzig 1901; G. Hölscher, 'Elemente arabischer, syrischer und hebräischer Metrik', *Festschrift K. Budde*, BZAW 34, 1920, pp. 93 ff.; J. Begrich, 'Zur hebräischen Metrik', *ThR* NF 4 (1932), pp. 67 ff.; S. Mowinckel, 'Zum Problem der hebräischen Metrik', *Festschrift A. Bertholet*, Tübingen 1950, pp. 379 ff.; F. Horst, 'Die Kennzeichen der hebräischen Poesie', *ThR* NF 21 (1953), pp. 97 ff.; G. Fohrer, 'Über den Kurzvers' [1954], BZAW 99, 1967, pp. 59 ff.; S. Segert, 'Problems of Hebrew Prosody', SVT 7, 1960, pp. 283 ff. (further literature cited there); S. Mowinckel, *The Psalms in Israel's Worship* II, Oxford 1962, pp. 159 ff.; L. Alonso-Schökel, *Das alte Testament als literarisches Kunstwerk* [in Spanish 1963], Cologne 1971.

1. Poetry. Poetry, that which is 'made', cf. Greek *poiēsis* and Hebrew *ma'ᵃśeh* (Ps. 45.1, Heb. 45.2), is distinguished from prose by the fact that its language is controlled by a particular form. Here we must distinguish between stylistic devices and rhythmic form. Rhythmic form derives originally from the natural flow of the language. The flow of the language holds together units of meaning in normal everyday prose as well. As in prose, such units of sense must originally have been taken together in poetry too to form a line, a sentence. Rises and falls, longs and shorts are the natural linguistic means of giving emphasis to an utterance. Originally the emphasis will have allowed for the logical weight of the naturally emphasized syllable. But in poetry the pressure of the form, while starting from the natural accentuation, always wins over the natural accentuation. Otherwise no strict form could develop, such as is demanded by the musical performance which stands at the beginning of all poetry. It follows from this that almost every metrical system cannot entirely avoid doing violence to the natural rhythm of the language.

2. Terminology. A discussion of poetic forms must presuppose a basic knowledge of the terminology. For the sake of simplicity we will quote Sievers: 'The most simple rhythmical groups in verse are the feet, to which the beats in music roughly correspond. But when we have isolated the feet (beats), the formation of a rhythmical system has not yet been fully achieved. Over and above the feet (beats) there are further groups of a higher order, which are described in ascending sequence as half-line, line, period, (paragraph), strophe. But not all these levels of classification need to be present in every rhythmical formation; the paragraph occurs only occasionally as a unit in between period and strophe[1]'. We can make this clear from an example provided by Sievers. We will first give the pattern, and then set out an example of this in German poetry. The half-line is represented by H, the foot by F, and the pause by p.

Strophe

Period				Period			
Line		Line		Line		Line	
H	H	H	H	H	H	H	H
F F	F F	F F	F F	F F	F F	F F	F F

Als ich / noch ein / Knabe / war (p)	Line	
Sperrte / man mich / ein (p) / (p)	Line	Period
Und so / sass ich / manches / Jahr (p)	Line	Strophe
über mir / allein / (p)	Line	Period
wie in / Mutterleib / (p)	Line	

Lines are also sometimes called stichs, from the Greek *stichos*, or cola, from the Greek *kōlon*, a limb. The half-line is also called a hemistich or a hemicolon. The period or verse consists of two or three lines. It is more precise therefore to call it a distich or a tristich, or a bicolon or tricolon.

1. Op. cit., p. 29.

3. Structure. It may be regarded as a basic law of Hebrew poetry that the units of form and of sense are identical. It is also a rule that lines never appear on their own, but as bicola or tricola. There is no rhyme or alliteration[2]. The lines are generally held together only by their content. The acrostic or alphabetic poems are an exception to this[3]. The structure of the poems in bicola or tricola is linked to a stylistic peculiarity first described by the English scholar Lowth in his *Praelectiones de Sacra Poesi Hebraeorum* of 1753, and named by him *parallelismus membrorum.* Lowth distinguished three types of this: 1. synonymous; 2. synthetic; and 3. antithetic. Synonymous *parallelismus membrorum* means that the thought of the first line is repeated in the second with different words, which have the same meaning. We may quote as examples Ps. 2.1:

> Why do the nations conspire,
> and the peoples plot in vain?

or Ps. 5.1 (Heb. 5.2):

> Give ear to my words, O Lord;
> give heed to my groaning.

The doubling of the utterance gives it a strange air of something serenely complete and emphatic, since the one utterance supports the other.

Antithetic parallelism consists in the fact that the utterance of the first line is emphasized and explained by the second, which is in opposition to it. We may give as examples Ps. 1.6:

> For the LORD knows the way of the righteous,
> but the way of the wicked will perish.

and Ps. 40.4 (Heb. 40.5):

> Blessed is the man who makes the LORD his trust,
> who does not turn to the proud.

Antithetic parallelism may well be a later stylistic form than synonymous parallelism.

2. Cf. however Alonso-Schökel, SVT 7, 1960, p. 154, and Fohrer*, p. 49.

3. Cf. Pss. 9 f.; 25; 34; 37; 111; 112; 119; 145; Prov. 31.10–31; Nahum 1.2–8; Lam. 1–4, and Lam. 5.

Of synthetic parallelism the Swedish scholar Hylmö has justifiably said that it should really be regarded as the disintegration of parallelism. The stylistic device of connecting two lines divided from one another by a caesura is retained. But the second line continues the thought of the first line further, or adds further details. Ps. 1.3 is an example:

> He is like a tree
> planted by streams of water,
> that yields its fruit in its season,
> and its leaf does not wither.

This synthetic parallelism is found especially in the bicola of the lamentation, the *qînâ*, e.g. in Amos 5.2:

> Fallen, no more to rise,
> is the virgin Israel.

From this form of parallelism, which is certainly later again compared with the two already mentioned, the graduated and repetitive 'climactic parallelism' has evolved. The second line takes up the key word of the first again, to carry its thought through to the end. So in Ps. 29.1:

> Ascribe to the LORD, O heavenly beings,
> ascribe to the LORD glory and strength.

This graduated progression of ideas occurs particularly beautifully in the tricola. In Cant. 6.13 (Heb. 7.1) we find the schema a–b–c; a–b–d; d–c–f:

> Return, return, O Shulammite,
> return, return, that we may look upon you.
> Why should you look upon the Shulammite,
> as upon a dance before two armies?

Begrich has described two further forms of parallelism in the *qînâ*, which Horst has named 'coordinative' and 'summative'. In the coordinative the ideas run in parallel, but the elements of the sentence do not refer to one another; in the summative a basic idea is expressed in the following lines through different individual features of the same situation. Basically in both these forms we only have a more exact description of what was described above summarily as synthetic parallelism, cf. e.g. Isa. 38.5 and 52.2. Finally it should be pointed out that sequences of bicola can run in parallel in such a way that the ideas of the first and the second line regularly correspond. Further distinctions can be found in the literature on the Psalms. But so long as they have no consequences for determining the literary types and dating of the Psalms, a knowledge of them is not necessary to the student. So it will only be pointed out here that the external stylistic devices of Old Testament poetry are far from having been exhaustively described.

The distinctive character of the *parallelismus membrorum* is shared by Hebrew poetry with Egyptian, Sumero-Accadian and Canaanite-Phoenician poetry[4].

4. Metre. One of the most difficult tasks of Old Testament scholarship is the study of the metre of Hebrew poems. When we realize that a good 2,000 years lie between the origin of the oldest Old Testament poems and the fixing of their pronunciation and accentuation by the Tiberian Masoretes, the problems involved in every attempt at ascertaining the original metrical laws will be immediately realized. In this period Hebrew, like every other language, underwent numerous alterations, which led to the loss of original short final vowels, to the elision of full vowels in the middle of a word, or to their replacement by half vowels, to the insertion of transitional vowels, and to shifts of accent. The starting point for all metrical theories must be the realization that the word formed the metrical unit in the oldest Old Testament poetry. Further it is clear that the word accent falls on the last or on the penultimate syllable. It is disputed whether in Hebrew poetry we have an accentuated or an alternating metre. On the other hand a quantitative metre, counting the long and short syllables as in Greek and Latin poetry, is excluded. The accentual system starts from observations which Budde made about the Hebrew dirge, the *qînâ*. It was expanded and worked out by Ley and Sievers. Its basic presupposition is that the verse rhythm is determined by the natural rhythm of word and sentence. From the Masoretic word-accent, which falls on the last or penultimate syllable, an ascending anapaestic rhythm results, the normal form of which Sievers regards as being the trisyllabic foot, with two unaccented and one accented syllable: $+ +'$. To make this system work in every case, we must further assume that the accented syllable can be preceded by anything

4. Cf. e.g. A. L. Oppenheim, *Ancient Mesopotamia*, Chicago 1964, pp. 250 f.

between none and three unaccented syllables. If one accented
syllable occurs next to another, this is called syncope. This short
description shows how careful one must be in making textual
alterations for metrical reasons on the basis of this system; for
the variation between none and three unaccented syllables
preceding the accent allows a great deal of play. Indeed which-
ever metrical system is chosen, textual alterations for metrical
reasons are only justified if the metrical argument can be supported by further arguments from the content. Sievers distinguished between

> the two foot $++'$ $++'$,
> the three foot $++'$ $++'$ $++'$
> and the four foot $++'$ $++'$ $++'$ $++'$

as the simple line, and between the 'double three' foot or the
'double four' foot as the double line. Furthermore there are
asyndetic lines, the three-two or five foot line, which comes
from the dirge, and is therefore known as the *qînâ* metre, and
the four-three or seven foot line. Finally we must allow for
mixed metres. If when they appear no regularity can be found
among the strophes, it is better to speak of some sort of disorder,
rather than of a mixed metre. The Budde-Ley-Sievers system
has been widely accepted but has again been attacked just in
these last decades. Hölscher, starting from observations made on
Arabic and Syriac poetry, believed he could find in the alternating
system the basis of Old Testament poetry, as did Bickell in the
previous century. Robinson, Mowinckel and Horst have followed
him in this assumption. The alternating metre allows for a
simple alternation between an unaccented and an accented
syllable. While the accentuated system produces an anapaestic
rhythm, the alternating system produces an iambic rhythm. The
$+'$ is to be regarded as the basic form, and $'+$ and $++'$ as
variations on it. This system too allows for syncope. The verse
accent is usually, but not always, based on the grammatical
accent. In favour of this system it may be claimed that the tri-
literalism (the prevalence of three-consonant roots) in Hebrew
prefers two syllable words, and that in polysyllabic words the
antipenultimate also receives a subsidiary accent which the
Masoretes denoted by a *meteg*. In polysyllabic words we even
have to allow for two subsidiary accents. Word formations like

e.g. *bᵉhāḇarḇūrôṯêhem* are, as Mowinckel says[5], certainly not rushed at 'head over heels to reach the last syllable'. Finally it may be pointed out that in the *qînâ* we frequently find in the first line, which is supposedly three-accented, four words which are stressed and therefore from a metrical point of view overfill the line, and in the second, supposedly two-accented line, we find no less frequently three stressed words. If in these cases we allow for an alternating metre, we get organic structures of the pattern $+ \, ' + \, ' + \, ' + \, ' - + \, ' + \, ' + \, '$. So instead of the three-two or five accent pattern we have a four-three or seven accent pattern. We can illustrate both systems by the example of Amos 5.2:

(a) Sievers: *nāpᵉlá lō'-ṭôsîp qûm*

               bᵉṭûláṯ yiśrā'ēl.

(b) Horst: *nāpᵉlá lō'-ṭôsîp qûm*

              bᵉṭûlaṯ yiśrā'ēl.

The other metres too change correspondingly when the alternating system is used as a basis. So e.g. Sievers' double three lines become double fours in Mowinckel, and because of their frequent occurrence in wisdom poetry he calls this the *māšāl* metre[6].

We might be tempted to hope for a decision in the argument between the representatives of the two schools from ancient writers. But Josephus, who speaks of hexameters or pentameters, simply makes use of the terminology of Greek poetry, and is no more helpful with this problem than when he represents the Essenes and Pharisees to his Greek readers as schools of philosophy. Jerome does point out that there is a difference between the verses of Hebrew poetry and the Greek hexameters, but the facts he gives are too unclear to be made the starting point of an enquiry into the metre.

When we remember what has already been said about the internal changes in the Hebrew language, we must keep an open mind about the hypothesis proposed by Segert, that within the history of the language we must allow for a change in the

---

5. *ZAW* 68 (1956), p. 112.
6. An example in Horst, op. cit., p. 110.

metrical systems. On Segert's view we must make a basic distinction between ancient Hebrew poetry, the poetry of the
period of the monarchy, and that of the late period. It was only
in the middle period, on this view, that the accentuating system
was employed, while in the late period we must allow for the
use of an alternating system. This theory takes account of the
fact that in the first period the short final vowels were still
preserved, that in the middle period the short vowels in the
middle of words which were later reduced to a *shᵉwa* were still
preserved, while in the late period the auxiliary vowels introduced to avoid double consonants in segholate forms and similar
formations were not yet usual, cf. *kalb* and *keleḇ*. It can be
expected that an examination of the textual discoveries at the
Dead Sea with these problems in mind will contribute to a
decision of the disputed questions.

The result so far is that the metrical problems need in every
instance very careful treatment. In each passage we have to
examine which of the systems postulated fits the recognizable
rhythm of the language most easily. We must allow in principle
for the continued use of older systems in later passages. Textual
alterations for metrical reasons must be carefully justified, and
supported with other arguments. In poetry with several strophes,
one relatively reliable criterion is the comparison with the structure of other strophes. We must allow however for distinctive
features at the end of strophes and of the poem.

§ 27   Israelite Poetry and its Literary Types

Cf. the lists given in the preceding and following sections.

*1. The sacral roots of the lyric, and the literary types of secular
Israelite poetry.* Religio-historical and phenomenological research
make it seem probable that the original form of human song was
the sacral song. Songs for work and for entertainment are a
secondary development from this. While the magical roots of
song, which today we can explain psychologically rather than
really understand, can still be seen in this family tree, we understand immediately that the word uttered to God as the response
to the message of God given in deed or in word, is one of the

oldest utterances of faith. These utterances were originally spontaneous and entirely fitted to the situation of the moment As free prayer it was to live on in places where the community encounters the deity at a holy place and at a holy time, where it discovers and achieves a compelling interpretation of its existence in the cult, as the representation of the presence of the Holy One, and as the response to it. Since the modulation of the voice is felt in comparison with ordinary speaking to be wonderful, and particularly powerful, the sacral word was primarily sung. The song, which was experienced as effective both subjectively and objectively, demanded repetition, and became a tradition-bound instead of a situation-bound composition. Finally a stock of songs for typical occasions was kept ready at the sanctuary, so that the individual element increasingly receded behind the general and the typical. But this development can be understood from the nature of life itself, and is by no means a peculiarity of cultic composition[1].

The understanding of war as a secular, purely political enterprise is relatively recent. Remains of a sacral understanding have survived in different guises down to the present. So it can be understood that the war song generally belongs to the sacral sphere. The banner saying of Exod. 17.16, which is to be understood perhaps as both a call to the army and an 'oath of allegiance', on a widespread but not undisputed interpretation the ark sayings of Num. 10.35 f., the warcry, the battle-cry of Judg. 7.18 and 20 and the religious song for a victory dance, which perhaps preserves the original form of the hymn or song of praise (cf. Exod. 15.21 and Judg. 16.24), preserve the connection with the sacral understanding of war. So does the Song of Deborah, Judg. 5, generally described as a song of victory, but more correctly by Weiser as a liturgy intended for a victory feast; here a hymn to the God who makes himself manifest and is present in the feast (vv. 2–5), a confession of sin (vv. 6–8), a hymnic summons to the recitation of the earlier saving deeds of Yahweh (vv. 9–11), a call to procession (vv. 12–15a), a boastful listing of the participants and remembrance of the dead (vv.

1. Cf. F. Heiler, *Prayer*, New York 1932; id., *Erscheinungsformen und Wesen der Religion*, Stuttgart 1961, pp. 266 ff.; S. Mowinckel, *Religion und Kultus*, Göttingen 1953, pp. 10 ff. and 115 ff.; and C.-H. Ratschow, *Magie und Religion*, Gütersloh 1955[2].

15b–18), a description of the battle (vv. 19–22), blessing and curse (vv. 23–27), ridicule of the enemy (vv. 28–30), and a concluding prayer allied to a curse and blessing, follow in order[2]. The move away from the sacral lyric appears in the ridiculing of the enemy and the taunt song resulting from this[3] (cf. Num. 21.27–30), in the boasting song (cf. Gen. 4.23 f.), and in the profane song for a dance of victory (1 Sam. 18.7; 21.11 (Heb. 21.12); 29.5). Remains of a magical understanding of the word appear to echo more clearly in the taunt song and in the boasting song than in the song for a victory dance, which appears to be an expression of spontaneous joy and admiration, but at the same time increases the honour given to the victor.

The Song of the Well (Num. 21.17 f.) still shows clearly the connections of the work-song with the magical understanding of the world[4]. It is not the workmates who are addressed but the well itself. It was as the difference between man and world was experienced, and the magic unity broken, that the room was obtained both for the truly religious and for the profane lyric. If man has become songless in industrialized society, in earlier times he accompanied his work with song. Judg. 5.11 shows us that the Israelites, like the Beduin today or at least at the beginning of the century, sang while watering their beasts. It must have been the same for work in the fields, especially at harvest, winegathering and treading the grapes (cf. Ps. 65.13 (Heb. 65.14) and Isa. 9.2). There will also have been watchmen's songs (cf. Isa. 21.12 and Cant. 3.3 and 5.7). Neh. 4.10 (Heb. 4.4) may be quoting a song of burden-bearers.

While the magical roots of the love-song are best seen in the song of longing, the song of admiration reminds us that even dumb beasts begin to sing when in heat[5]. Isa. 22.13 and 56.12 at least (cf. 5.11 ff. and Amos 6.4 ff.) remind us of the drinking song sung at drinking bouts.

With the lament for the dead, the dirge, apart from roots in

---

2. Cf. A. Weiser, 'Das Deboralied', *ZAW* 71 (1959), pp. 67 ff.; on the problem of the Holy War cf. G. von Rad, *Der Heilige Krieg im alten Israel*, Göttingen 1965[4], and R. Smend, jr., *Yahweh War and Tribal Confederation*, Nashville and New York 1970.

3. Cf. O. Eissfeldt, *Der Maschal im Alten Testament*, BZAW 24, 1913.

4. Cf. H. Gressmann, SAT I, 2, Göttingen 1922[2], p. 107.

5. On the types of the Israelite literary love song cf. below, pp. 363 f.

the spontaneous outburst of grief, origins in ritual magic are to be suspected, with the intention of driving away the shades of the dead[6]. In accordance with the original exclusion of the realm of the dead from Israelite religion (cf. e.g. Ps. 88.5, 10 ff. (Heb. 88.6, 11 ff.); 6.5 (Heb. 6.6)) the dirge or *qînâ* in Israel is a secular literary type[7]. It was from the discovery of its metre (3 + 2) by Budde that the investigation of the rhythmic structures of Israelite poetry originated. The lament was uttered by mourning women (cf. Jer. 9.16), relatives or friends (cf. Gen. 23.2 and 50.9 f.). A lament for Saul and Jonathan (2 Sam. 1.17–27), and another one for Abner (2 Sam. 3.33 f.), are attributed to David. The dirge, like the taunt song, is taken up by the prophets, and employed for their announcements of disasters[8].

2. Older collections of Israelite songs. General considerations encourage the assumption that poetry came to be written down earlier than prose; for prose tradition, because of its less strict form, remains longer in a living process of formation than the poem with its fixed shape. Perhaps Gunkel is right in his assumption that prose composition developed out of poetry, i.e. that the freely delivered composition in prose developed in the course of time from sung and recited composition[9]. The supposed priority can in any case be attested in respect of the process of fixing in writing from the sources in the Old Testament. A *sēper milḥᵃmôṯ YHWH*, the Book of the Wars of Yahweh, is quoted in Num. 21.14 f. It can be conjectured that as well as battle and victory songs this collection also contained taunt songs and cultic, hymnic compositions like the Song of Deborah. Josh. 10.12 f. is a passage reminding us either of an incantation or of a description of a battle, from the *sēper hayyāšār*, the Book of the Upright (or, of the Valiant). According to 2 Sam. 1.18

6. Cf. H. Jahnow, *Das hebräische Leichenlied im Rahmen der Völker-dichtung*, BZAW 36, 1923.

7. Cf. W. Eichrodt, *Theology of the Old Testament*, vol. 2, London 1967, pp. 221 ff., and L. Wachter, *Der Tod im Alten Testament*, ATh II, 8, 1967; but also E. Gerstenberger, 'Der Klagender Mensch', in *Probleme biblischer Theologie*, Festschrift G. von Rad, Munich 1971, pp. 64 ff.

8. Cf. above, p. 296.

9. Cf. H. Gunkel, 'Die israelitische Literatur', in Kultur der Gegenwart I, 7, Leipzig 1925, reprinted separately Darmstadt 1963, pp. 2 f. and p. 21 above.

David's lament for Saul and Jonathan comes from the same collection. It is clear from this that the title 'the Valiant' does not refer to Yahweh as a warrior, but to human heroes. The book could certainly not have been completed before the time of David. In 1 Kgs. 8.12 f. a fragment of a song which Solomon is supposed to have uttered at the consecration of the temple is quoted. The Septuagint annotates it (3 Reg. 8.53a): 'See, is it not written in the Book of the Song?' It has been repeatedly conjectured that the Hebrew implied by the Septuagint, *sēper haššîr*, is a miswriting of an original *sēper hayyāšār*. If this is correct, we would have here a third mention of the Book of the Valiant. Since this conclusion is not however compelling, there remains the possibility that a further collection existed, the Book of Songs. If we remember how often J and E have taken up material already formed into their narratives without giving its source[10], it becomes quite clear that there were in Israel certainly already in the early monarchical period written collections of songs, and no doubt also freely circulating material too.

3. The literary types of Israelite psalm composition. Gunkel laid the foundations in the description of the literary types of Israelite psalm composition as he did for those of its narrative literature, in that he started primarily from formal considerations. It can however be noted here too that he did not carry out strictly the formal procedure for fixing categories, but in part combined it with criteria of content too[11]. While his division into hymns, individual and collective laments and songs of thanksgiving as the main categories starts from formal considerations, his separation of enthronement songs and royal psalms uses criteria of content. Although in the enthronement songs in the strict sense we have a particular group within the hymns separated off by content, all that the royal psalms have in common is that their subject is a king. Furthermore widely differing views are taken in recent scholarship about the number of psalms which came originally from the royal ritual, and were later democratized or understood in an eschatological sense[12]. Objections can be made too to the actual terminology chosen by Gunkel. Westermann has pointed out that the descriptions 'psalm of thanksgiving' and 'lamentation' refer to content, but that of 'hymn' only to the form. He has therefore suggested new names for the literary

10. Cf. above, pp. 84 f. and p. 100.
11. Cf. also above, p. 48.
12. Cf. below, pp. 343 ff.

types, bearing in mind the kinship between hymn and psalm of thanks-giving. On his view the hymn should be called 'descriptive praise' and the psalm of thanksgiving 'narrative praise', and a description of the literary types based entirely on content thereby ensured. In view of the widespread use and familiarity of the descriptions chosen by Gunkel however it remains questionable whether these new suggestions will win the day. As long as we have a correct picture of the nature of the literary types, and also make it clear which system we are using, a variation in terminology will not cause difficulty.

(a) THE HYMN, OR DESCRIPTIVE PRAISE. This consists of an intro-duction and a following main section. In the introduction we have a summons or (self-)invitation to praise Yahweh, put in the imperative second plural masculine, or in the cohortative first plural. The plural points to a setting in life of this literary type in the gathering of the congregation, or in the cult. The introduc-tion, which may be picked up again in the course of the hymn, and especially at its end, is followed by the main section with the praise of God proper in the 'predication style', in which attributes, participles, relative sentences, or causal clauses intro-duced by *kî*, 'for', are employed, which describe God's majesty and goodness as the creator or helper of his nation. The main section serves accordingly to give the motivation for the praise of God. From the frequency with which participial predication is used in this type we speak of the hymnic participle style, which is found especially in Deutero-Isaiah. As examples of the hymn we may mention Pss. 8; 19*; 29; 33; 65; 100; 136; 145–150. The songs of Zion, Pss. 46; 48; 76; 84; 87; and 122, and the enthrone-ment psalms, Pss. 47; 93; 96–99, are usually separated off as special groups[13].

In the enthronement psalms the theme of the kingship of Yahweh is sounded. These poems used to be understood in an eschatological sense. Since Mowinckel however a cult-drama understanding has predominated, although scholars have differed on whether these psalms are pre-exilic or post-exilic. While Mowinckel, Hans Schmidt and Weiser think of a celebration of the enthronement of Yahweh embedded in the pre-exilic autumn festival as the occasion for them, Kraus connects them with a

13. Cf. the introductory sections in commentaries on the psalms, Gunkel and Begrich's *Einleitung in die Psalmen*, and especially C. Wester-mann, *The Praise of God in the Psalms*, pp. 145 ff.

celebration of the entry of Yahweh the king in the post-exilic period, which also takes place at the autumn festival. Gunkel allowed for the possibility of a late pre-exilic enthronement festival, but he regarded the actual psalms preserved as post-exilic eschatological compositions. It is Westermann who argues particularly strongly for an eschatological interpretation at present. Apart from the different views taken of their relationship to the prophecies of Deutero-Isaiah, it is particularly the interpretation of the formulae *yhwh mālak* and *mālak yhwh* that is decisive for the dating and understanding of these songs. These phrases are translated by the upholders of the enthronement hypothesis 'Yahweh has become king', or 'it is king that Yahweh has become', by the opponents 'Yahweh is king', or 'king is Yahweh'[14].

(b) LAMENTATIONS form the main body of the psalter. Depending on whether it is an individual or a group who are praying, a distinction is made between individual laments and communal laments. Both types have the following constitutive elements in common: 1, the appeal; 2, the lamentation; 3, the confession of trust; 4, the petition; 5, motives that can justify divine intervention, and 6, the vow of praise. It should be noted that the sequence and number of the elements can vary. The appeal consists as a rule of an address to God and an introductory cry for help. The predication linked with the address to God has a hymnic character. It can occasionally be expanded into an introductory hymn. In the lamentation, a reference to the behaviour of the enemy can be followed by a description of the distress of the speaker, and a reference to God's attitude, often expressed in the form of a question. The prayer is often represented as a twofold wish related to the condition of the enemy, and that of the speaker. To give a motivation for it reference may be made to the respect in which God is held among the nations, to the helplessness of the speaker, and to his guilt or innocence. In the individual lament the vow of praise is often followed by a

14. Cf. below, pp. 343 f. D. Michel, 'Studien zu den sogenannten Thronbesteigungspsalmen', *VT* 6 (1956), pp. 40 ff. proposes to translate *yhwh mālak* by 'It is Yahweh who exercises royal authority', and *mālak yhwh* by 'It is as king that Yahweh reigns'. Cf. also A. S. Kapelrud, 'Nochmals Jahwä mālāk', *VT* 13 (1963), pp. 229 ff.

declaration of the 'certainty of a hearing' (confidence that the prayer has been heard), or even by a song of thanksgiving. From the confession of trust the psalm of confidence has evolved. This is seen in its purest form in Ps. 23[15].

1. We should see the setting in life of the communal laments as a public ceremony of lamentation, for which the many trials in life of the community such as external distress (wars and defeats), pestilences, threats to the harvest and hunger gave an occasion (cf. 1 Kgs. 8.33 ff.)[16]. The subject of the lament, as can be seen from the use of 'we', is the nation. When a change between 'we' and 'I' is found within a psalm, we must account for this by someone leading the intercession. So e.g. the king can appear on behalf of his people (cf. e.g. Ps. 44.4, 6, 15, Heb. 44.5, 7, 16). But usually the king is only the object of intercession. As in our own forms of confession the people was answered by either a priest or a prophet with an oracle (of salvation) (cf. e.g. Josh. 7.7 ff.; 2 Chr. 20.3 ff.; Hab. 1.12 ff.; 2.1 ff. and Dan. 9). The link between lament and oracle has been passed down to us in the prophetic liturgies (cf. e.g. Jer. 14.2– 11; 14.19–15.2, but also Lam. 4)[17]. Pss. 60, 74, 79, 80, 83, 85, 90 and 137 can be mentioned here as examples of the genre.

2. Under the influence of R. Smend sr. the character of the individual laments as individual prayers was for a long time misunderstood. In accordance with the poetic individualization of people or city it was believed that the nation could be found in the 'I' of the laments, until Balla demonstrated the genuinely individual character of the psalms[18]. A conspicuous feature of the individual laments is their formulaic language, which makes it difficult to deduce the precise nature of the distress of the person praying. To explain this situation we must remember first the history of the genre, extending back into the pre-Israelite period, secondly the democratization of laments originally written for a king to utter, and thirdly their character in part at

15. Cf. the literature listed in footnote 13, and also Westermann, op. cit. pp. 52 ff., and *ZAW* 66 (1954), pp. 44 ff.

16. Cf. in detail Gunkel and Begrich, *Einleitung in den Psalmen*, pp. 117 ff.

17. Cf. ibid., pp. 136 ff.

18. Cf. R. Smend, sr., 'Über das Ich der Psalmen', *ZAW* 8 (1888), pp. 49 ff., and E. Balla, *Das Ich der Psalmen*, FRLANT 16, 1912.

least as formularies for prayer, which were kept ready at the
sanctuaries and were designed to be appropriate to as many
situations as possible (cf. e.g. Ps. 102 superscription, Heb. Ps.
102.1). It also becomes clear from this reference that individual
laments were uttered in the sanctuary (cf. also 1 Sam. 1 f. and
1 Kgs. 8.37 f.). Matters of content too, like e.g. the change
between address to God and speech directed to the community
by God, point to their cultic use. We must allow, at least in
principle, for the possibility that private prayers which originated
outside the sanctuary were in the end taken over by the community.

Hans Schmidt wished to separate as a particular type the
prayer of the man accused, making a further distinction between
prayers of those accused (cf. e.g. Pss. 4, 7, 11, 26, 57 and 94),
and of those who were sick, and at the same time were accused
(cf. e.g. Pss. 25, 28, 35, 69 and 102). Since their innocence could
not otherwise be proved, those held in custody were to be submitted to a judgement by God in the temple (cf. 1 Kgs. 8.31 f.)[19].
On the other hand Delekat wished to connect the private psalms
of lament in respect of an enemy, with their acknowledgements
of a hearing, and actual statements that prayer has been heard,
with the right of asylum in the temple in Jerusalem and a divine
declaration of protection, and have these psalms regarded as in
origin prayer inscriptions in the sanctuary of Zion[20]. Recently
Beyerlin has connected Pss. 3–5, 7, 11, 17, 23, 26 f., 57 and 63
with cultic legal proceedings by God in the sanctuary in Jerusalem, and in connection with this has assigned Pss. 3, 5, 7, 17,
26 f. and 57 to the genre of petitionary prayer[21].

The most discussed problem of the individual laments is the
'change of mood' which can be observed at the end of quite a
number of them. In these the lament is followed abruptly by the
assurance that Yahweh has heard the prayer (cf. e.g. Pss. 6.8 f.

19. Cf. H. Schmidt, *Das Gebet der Angeklagten im Alten Testament*,
BZAW 49, 1928, and in criticism Gunkel and Begrich, *Einleitung*, p. 253,
and Eissfeldt*, p. 119, who sees a cultic legal procedure as the setting of
Pss. 7, 35, 57 and 69.

20. Cf. L. Delekat, *Asylie und Schutzorakel am Zionheiligtum*, Leiden
1967, pp. 259 ff.

21. Cf. W. Beyerlin, *Die Rettung der Bedrängten in den Feindpsalmen
der Einzelnen auf institutionelle Zusammenhänge untersucht*, FRLANT 99,
1970, pp. 139 ff.

(Heb. 6.9 ff.), 28.6 ff., 31.19 ff. (Heb. 31.20 ff.), and 56.9 ff. (Heb. 56.10 ff.)). We sometimes have a formal conjunction of lament and psalm of thanksgiving, as e.g. in Pss. 6, 28, 31, 56 and especially 22. Four theories are available to explain this problem. 1. The first, proposed by Heiler, starts from the subjective change of mood which the man praying experiences in the course of his prayer. 'The very expression of the petition awoke in the worshipper such a confidence that he thanked God in anticipation of the granting of the request'[22]. But this interpretation depends too much on the assumption that in the psalms we have religious poetry based on experience to be satisfying. 2. Following Küchler, it is assumed by Mowinckel, Gunkel, Begrich, Westermann, Kraus, Delekat and Beyerlin that the certainty of a hearing has been called forth by an oracle of hearing or salvation delivered by a priest or prophet, or by a declaration of protection or a court decision (cf. Pss. 5.3 (Heb. 5.4), 28.7, 56.9 (Heb. 56.10), 119.67 and 140.12 (Heb. 140.13), cf. also 2 Chr. 20.3 ff.)[23]. 3. The hypothesis held by Wevers connects the change of mood with the magical functioning of the invocation of the name of God. If God has been correctly invoked he is bound to hear the lament presented to him[24]. This explanation is too heavily magical, and in this ill-suited to Israel's self-understanding. It fails to recognize in particular Yahweh's judicial freedom (cf. 1 Kgs. 8.32). 4. A fourth explanation has been produced by Weiser. For him the personal hope of salvation is grounded in participation by the individual in the traditional actualization of salvation in the cult, while the conjunction of lament and psalm of thanksgiving is to be understood from a repetition of the lament on the occasion of a sacrifice of thank-offering. While the problem has not yet been discussed to a conclusion, there is much to be said for the assumption that the change in mood is evoked by an oracle of salvation. When lament and psalm of thanksgiving are conjoined, as in Ps. 22,

22. F. Heiler, *Prayer*, New York 1932, p. 271.

23. Cf. F. Küchler, 'Das priesterliche Orakel in Israel und Juda', in *Abhandlungen zur semitischen Religionskunde und Sprachwissenschaft*, Festschrift W. W. Graf von Baudissin, BZAW 33, 1918, pp. 285 ff. and J. Begrich, 'Das priesterliche Heilsorakel', *ZAW* 52 (1934), pp. 81 ff., and in *Gesammelte Studien zum Alten Testament*, ThB 21, 1964, pp. 217 ff.

24. Cf. J. W. Wevers, 'A Study in the Form Criticism of Individual Complaint Psalms', *VT* 6 (1956), pp. 80 ff.

we should explain this either from the character of the psalm as a ritual embracing both situations, or from the explanation given by Weiser.

3. With the psalm of thanksgiving, or descriptive praise, as with the laments, a distinction can be drawn between individual psalms of thanksgiving and communal psalms of thanksgiving. The latter are preserved only in Pss. 124 and 129 within the psalter, a circumstance which is probably to be attributed to the post-exilic compilation of the collection, because at that date the the time of the saving deeds of God belonged to the past.

The description 'song of thanksgiving' has been rejected by Westermann as inappropriate, since the Hebrew *hôḏâ* means properly not 'thank', but 'confess, praise'. Furthermore the Hebrew term *tôḏâ*, which Gunkel regarded as characteristic, can as Weiser says also describe the hymn. Of the various reasons given by Westermann for the title 'descriptive psalm of praise', perhaps the most convincing is that praise, unlike thanksgiving, presupposes an audience. God is praised in the community.

The difference from the hymn consists primarily in the fact that those who are praising God tell of his deeds, which have brought help either to the individual or to the community. The organic connection with the lament should at least be mentioned here. The community or the individual, having first lamented, confess after their deliverance that Yahweh has helped them, and praise him[25].

(*a*) *The communal song of thanksgiving, or descriptive praise.* Both communal songs of thanksgiving preserved in the psalter display the same structure. They are introduced by the formula 'let Israel now say', inserted as a demand into the introductory summary of the saving deeds of Yahweh. The summary is followed by a retrospect to the distress, a cry of praise, and an account of God's action. Ps. 124 ends with a confession of confidence, Ps. 129 with a prayer against the enemies of Zion.

(*b*) *The individual song of thanksgiving, or descriptive praise.* This type, as examples of which we may adduce Pss. 9–10, 18, 30, 40, 66.13 ff., shows the following elements in its structure:

25. Cf. apart from the literature mentioned in n. 13 again Westermann, *The Praise of God in the Psalms*, pp. 83 ff.

1, an announcement of the praise, in which Yahweh is regularly invoked in the vocative, or named in the accusative as the object of the praise; 2, the central section with the account of the fortunes of the one who is uttering the praise, with the four themes of (a) looking back to the distress, (b) an account of the invocation of God, (c) of the hearing which follows it, and (d) of the helping act of God. Here too it should be noticed that the pattern only gives the basic framework, and that variations appear in the individual psalms. In the cases in which the lamentation immediately precedes the song of praise, the account of the good fortune of the speaker becomes superfluous. Instead of this the theme of confession is set out more fully. The setting in life is to be seen as either the cult or the assembly of the congregation (cf. 1 Sam. 1 f. and Ps. 118). The connection of the psalm of praise with the offering is found in Ps. 66.13.

(c) *Minor literary types*. The minor literary types need only to be listed here. Wisdom and didactic psalms, which attest the connection of wisdom with the composition of psalms, may be put first. Among the wisdom psalms are Pss. 1, 49, 112 and 128, among the didactic psalms Pss. 37 and 73. Pss. 1 and 119 can also be described as Torah psalms, since here God's instruction is placed at the centre. Finally alongside the so-called historical psalms 78, 105 and 106 the cultic royal psalms, including at least Pss. 2, 18, 20, 21, 45, 72, 89, 101, 110, 132 and 144.1–11, must be mentioned. Apart from the fact that all these psalms deal with the king, they have little in common with one another in content. The royal psalms cannot therefore be described as a literary type in the strict sense at all[26]. Among the liturgies, Pss. 15 and 24 belong together as entrance liturgies, or liturgies 'for the gate'. In regard to the question whether in these and other liturgical psalms we have excerpts from rituals, or imitations of them, differing views are taken by scholars.

§ 28   The History of Psalm Study

H.-J. Kraus, *Geschichte der historisch-kritischen Erforschung des Alten Testaments von der Reformation bis zur Gegenwart*, Neukirchen 1956,

26. Cf. above, p. 330.

1969²; H. Bornkamm, *Luther and the Old Testament* [1948], Philadelphia 1969; M. Haller, 'Ein Jahrzehnt Psalmforschung', *ThR* NF 1 (1929), pp. 377 ff.; A. R. Johnson, 'The Psalms', *OTMS*, Oxford 1951, pp. 162 ff.; J. J. Stamm, 'Ein Vierteljahrhundert Psalmenforschung', *ThR* NF 23 (1955), pp. 1 ff.; A. S. Kapelrud, 'Scandinavian Research in the Psalms after Mowinckel', *Annual of the Swedish Theological Institute* 4 (1965), pp. 74 ff.; id., 'Die skandinavische Einleitungswissenschaft zu den Psalmen', *Verkündigung und Forschung* 11 (1966), pp. 62 ff.

H. Gunkel, *Ausgewählte Psalmen*, Göttingen 1904¹, 1917⁴, id., article 'Psalmen', in *RGG*¹ IV, Tübingen 1913, cols. 1927 ff.; E. Balla, *Das Ich der Psalmen*, FRLANT 16, 1912; P. Volz, *Das Neujahrsfest Jahwes* (*Laubhüttenfest*), SGV 67, 1912; S. Mowinckel, *Psalmenstudien* I Awän und die individuellen Klagepsalmen; II Das Thronbesteigungsfest Jahwäs und der Ursprung der Eschatologie; III Kultprophetie und prophetische Psalmen; IV Die technischen Termini in den Psalmenüberschriften; V Segen und Fluch in Israels Kult und Psalmdichtung; VI Die Psalmdichter, SNVAO 1921–4, repr. Amsterdam 1961; id., *The Psalms in Israel's Worship* I–II, Oxford 1962; id., *Zum israelitischen Neujahr und zur Deutung der Thronbesteigungspsalmen*, ANVAO II, 1952, 2, 1952; G. Quell, *Das kultische Problem der Psalmen*, BWANT II, 11, 1926; H. Schmidt, *Die Thronfahrt Jahves am Fest der Jahreswende im alten Israel*, SGV 122, 1927; id., *Das Gebet der Angeklagten im Alten Testament*, BZAW 49, 1928; N. Nicolsky, *Spuren magischer Formeln in den Psalmen*, BZAW 46, 1927; H. Gunkel and J. Begrich, *Einleitung in die Psalmen*, Göttingen 1933, repr. 1966; H. Birkeland, *'Anî und 'Anāw in den Psalmen*, SNVAO II, 1932, 4, 1933; id., *Die Feinde des Individuums in der israelitischen Psalmenliteratur*, Oslo 1933; id., *The Evildoers in the Book of Psalms*, ANVAO II, 2, 1955; G. Widengren, *The Accadian and Hebrew Psalms of Lamentations as Religious Documents*, Stockholm 1937; id., *Sakrales Königtum im Alten Testament und im Judentum*, F. Delitzsch Vorlesungen 1952, Stuttgart 1955; I. Engnell, *Studies in Divine Kingship in the Ancient Near East*, Uppsala 1943, Oxford 1967²; A. Lauha, *Die Geschichtsmotive in den alttestamentlichen Psalmen*, Annales Academiae Scientiarum Fennicae B 56, 1, Helsinki 1945; C. Barth, *Die Errettung vom Tode in den individuellen Klag- und Dankliedern des Alten Testaments*, Zollikon, Zurich 1947; N. H. Snaith, *The Jewish New Year Festival. Its Origin and Development*, London 1947; A. Weiser, 'Zur Frage nach den Beziehungen der Psalmen zum Kult: Die Darstellung der Theophanie in den Psalmen und im Festkult', in *Festschrift A. Bertholet*, Tübingen 1950, pp. 513 ff., and in *Glaube und Geschichte im Alten Testament und andere ausgewählte Schriften*, Göttingen 1961, pp. 303 ff.; H.-J. Kraus, *Die Königsherrschaft Gottes im Alten Testament*, BHT 13, 1951; id., *Worship* in Israel, Oxford 1966; C. Westermann, *The Praise of God in the Psalms* [1954], Richmond, Virginia 1965, London 1966; id., 'Struktur und Geschichte der Klage im Alten Testament', *ZAW* 66 (1954), pp. 44 ff., and in *Forschung am Alten Testament*, ThB 24, 1964, pp. 266 ff.; A. R. Johnson, *Sacral Kingship in Ancient Israel*, Cardiff 1955, 1967[2]; E. Kutsch, *Das Herbstfest in Israel*, Diss. ev. theol. (typewritten), Mainz 1955; D. Michel, 'Studien zu den sogenannten Thronbesteigungspsalmen', *VT* 6 (1956), pp. 40 ff.; id., *Tempora und Satzstellung in den Psalmen*, Abhandlungen zur Evangelischen Theologie I, Bonn 1960; K.-H. Bernhardt, *Das Problem der altorientalischen Königsideologie im Alten Testament*, SVT 8, 1961; *Le Psautier. Ses origines. Ses problemes littéraires. Son influence*, ed. R. de Langhe, OBL 5, 1962; G. Wanke, *Die Zionstheologie der Korachiten*, BZAW 97, 1966; L. Delekat, *Asylie und Schutzorakel am Zionheiligtum. Eine Untersuchung zu den privaten Feindpsalmen*, Leiden 1967; F. Crüsemann, *Studien zur Formgeschichte von Hymnus und Danklied in Israel*, WMANT 32, 1969; W. Beyerlin, *Die Rettung der Bedrängten in den Feindpsalmen der Einzelnen auf institutionelle Zusammenhänge untersucht*, FRLANT 99, 1970; J. C. de Moor, *New Year with Canaanites and Israelites*, I–II, Kamper Cahiers 21/22, Kampen 1972.

Commentaries: BC Delitzsch 1894[5]; KHC Duhm 1899; 1922[2]; HK Baethgen 1904[3]; ICC Briggs I 1906 II 1907; SAT[2] Stärk 1920; HK Gunkel 1926 (1968[2]); KAT[1] Kittel 1929[5-6]; HAT Schmidt 1934; HS Herkenne 1936; OTL Weiser 1962; BK Kraus 1966[3]; AB Dahood I 1966 II 1968, III 1970.

1. Because of its distinctive character as a prayer book the Psalter has at all times had a special position among the books of the Old Testament in the life of the Christian Church. As the Psalter as a whole was the prayer book of post-exilic Judaism, so it was also for the Church in services and in the life of the individual. Taking his place in the early Christian and medieval tradition, Luther found in the Psalter, as in the whole of scripture, prophecies of the passion, death and resurrection of Christ. But as well as a prophetic significance it had for him an exemplary one: The Christian can learn to pray in the psalter, for here he can hear how the saints talk with God. The number of moods which are expressed here, joy and suffering, hope and care, make it possible for every Christian to find himself in it, and to pray with the psalms[1]. While for the present-day reader and

---

1. Cf. *Luther's Works*, ed. J. T. Pelikan and H. T. Lehmann, vol. 35,

intercessor the question is posed with almost every psalm, whether as a Christian he is right to pray with them if he makes them his own words[2], the question could not arise for Luther with the same acuteness, because for him Christ stood at the centre of scripture.

2. The beginnings of historical exposition of the psalms. It was only at the moment when the grip of Trinitarian theology began to be questioned, and when under the influence of rationalism and the Enlightenment the literal sense of the Bible came to be looked at independently in each instance, that the foundations for a historical-critical study of the psalms could be laid. The revolution which occurred in the eighteenth century can hardly be described more clearly than it was by J. G. Eichhorn, who gave his readers the exhortation:

'If one studies the psalms for the sake of their content, let one not do harm to the poets of old, and torture tortured David yet more. All the poets whose songs have been gathered in the Psalms cannot bear the light of our time, and content themselves with the weak rays of their own age. Especially let one never demand Christian ethics and dogmatics, or demand that the sacred singers be superhuman saints.'[3]
And Herder could take a very similar view in his *Spirit of Hebrew Poetry*:
'No book of Scripture, except the Song of Solomon, has suffered so many misinterpretations and perversions from its original sense, as the Book of Psalms ... Every commentator, every versifier found here his own age, the wants of his own soul, his own domestic and family relations, and on this ground adapted it to the singing and reading of his own church. In that all the Psalms of David were sung, as if every member of the church had wandered upon the mountains of Judah, and been persecuted by Saul. They sung with zeal against Doeg and Ahitophel, imprecated curses upon the Edomites and the Moabites, and where they could do no more they put the imprecations in the mouth of Him, who never returned railing for railing, nor threatening for injustice. Let one read the most individualized, the most characteristically beautiful songs of David, of Asaph, and of Korah, in many

Word and Sacrament I, Philadelphia 1960, 'Preface to the Psalter', pp. 254 and 255 ff.
2. Cf. E. Hirsch, *Das alte Testament und die Predigt des Evangeliums*, Tübingen 1936, pp. 6 f.
3. *Einleitung ins Alte Testament* III, Reutlingen 1790, p. 442.

versifications of them, then turn back to the original situations and sources of the feelings which they depict, and will he find them always retaining even a shadow of their ancient form?'[4]

The history of the interpretation of the psalms will show how far Luther was right to say: 'everyone in whatever affairs he is engaged can find psalms, and a word in them, which link up with his affairs, and are to him just as if they had been placed there for his sake alone . . .'[5], and how far the reference to the original circumstances of the origins of the psalms is justified. On the one hand the historical and critical study of the psalter and of the other songs of Israel is an inescapable fact for us from which there can be no return to naiveté, on the other hand the reader who keeps at a distance cannot come near the innermost being of the Psalter. We can say with Franz Delitzsch: 'the Church, when it uses the language of the psalms in supplications, celebrates the unity of the two Testaments, and science, when expounding them, does honour to the distinction between the Old and the New. They are both in the right: the former in regarding the Psalms in the light of the one essential salvation, the latter in keeping apart the sacred eras, and the various stages through which the knowledge of salvation has passed'[6].

The first great scholarly commentary on the Psalms was published by Wilhelm Martin Leberecht de Wette in 1811, and republished four times to 1836. In the view of Delitzsch, who stood theologically in a completely different camp, de Wette's commentary opened a new epoch, in that 'it was the first to clear away the rubbish under which the exposition of the Psalms had hitherto been buried, and to introduce into it taste, after the example of Herder, and grammatical accuracy, under the influence of Gesenius'[7]. The seminal method of de Wette is displayed especially at two points: he was the first to attempt an analysis of the psalms by literary types, and made reference to the history of religion. Thus he sought to join literature and history in an

4. J. G. Herder, *The Spirit of Hebrew Poetry*, Burlington 1833, reprinted Naperville, Illinois 1971, vol. 2, pp. 225 f.; cf. also Eichhorn, op. cit., p. 439; 'Many alien ideas have long been imposed on the psalms because they can so readily be used at all times. It is better then for one to go his own way without companion or guide. . . .'

5. WA *DB* 10, 1, p. 103, 23–25.

6. *Biblical Commentary on the Psalms*, London 1887, vol. 1, p. 103.

7. Op. cit., pp. 82 f.

organic relationship. But unlike many of his predecessors and followers he was not concerned to classify and date the psalms absolutely, but only relatively.

Scholarship abandoned this restraint at once. The task suggested by some of the headings of the psalms, of explaining the psalms from specific historical situations, dominated the rest of the nineteenth century. So Hitzig, in his commentary published in 1835–6 and 1863–5, apart from fourteen psalms attributed to David, dated the whole of the material to the period of the Maccabees. This late dating can be traced from Olshausen in 1853 to Duhm in 1899 and 1922 (ed. 2). No less a man than Wellhausen supported it, in that he said in conclusion of the character of the collection as the hymnbook of the second temple: '. . . so the question is not whether there are post-exilic psalms in it but whether there are pre-exilic ones'[8]. Duhm only left Ps. 137, as exilic. Otherwise 'no single psalm . . . suggests to an unprejudiced and unbiased reader even the idea that it could be pre-exilic or indeed must be so'[9]. This scholar, whose work on literary criticism and textual criticism is so valuable, really wins the prize for late dating, by distributing the psalms across the period between Antiochus IV and A.D. 70.

Before we turn to more recent scholarship, which made Duhm's second edition obsolete before it appeared, it is appropriate to cast a side glance at the conservative commentators of the nineteenth century, of whom Hengstenberg and Delitzsch are to be regarded as the most significant. Hengstenberg came to have close sympathy with Pietism and the Revival movement, and theologically was concerned for a revival of the dogmatic position of the early Church and of early Protestantism. His four volume Psalm Commentary (1849[2]; ET 1845–48) made little contribution to historical and critical scholarship, but was nevertheless of significance in that it never allowed the theological concerns of psalm exposition to be forgotten. Delitzsch in his Commentary on the Psalms, issued five times from 1859 to 1894, often comes very close to him in his results. But it can be seen at first glance that Delitzsch is quite differently equipped theologically from Hengstenberg. Just for this reason his work on details has retained its value to the present. In a way which differs

8. Quoted in M. Haller, op. cit., p. 379.
9. KHC XIV, Tübingen 1922[2], p. xxi.

subtly in different individual cases Delitzsch attempts to renew the eschatological and messianic interpretation of the psalms, making use of a typology which is committed to an organic view of history.

3. Form-critical and cultic interpretation. Psalm study of the twentieth century stands under the dominating influence of two men, Hermann Gunkel and Sigmund Mowinckel. The former founded the form-critical school, the latter, his pupil, founded the cultic interpretation. Gunkel's realization that the collective, i.e. the literary types, is of more importance for the understanding of the Old Testament than the individual, gave new impetus to the study not only of the historical and prophetic books[10], but also of the psalms. He published the results of his methods in his *Ausgewählten Psalmen* of 1904 (1917[4]), his article 'Psalmen' in the first edition of the *RGG*, his large *Psalmenkommentar* of 1926 (reprinted 1968) and his *Einleitung in die Psalmen* (1933; reprinted 1966), completed after his death by his pupil Joachim Begrich. While, in his view, up to that time criticism and philology had been in the foreground, he wanted to bring forward religion and poetry from their place in the background. In looking at his formal achievements it is important not to miss the fact that his ultimate concern was to understand the internal religious feeling of the psalms. Without failing to recognize the primacy of the Biblical material, he consciously adduced ancient oriental, Babylonian and Egyptian lyrics in interpretation. While in this he is a member of the religio-historical school, his own achievement lies in his recognition of the formal language of the psalms, and of their original connection with the cult. The literary types point to worship as the original *Sitz im Leben* (setting in life) of psalm composition. Even when in the course of time it has moved away from this setting, its forms preserved this original connection. So it is important to be able to recognize with certainty the language of the forms of the individual categories. By means of this method the key to the puzzle of the formal character of the psalms was discovered, something which until then had insuperably defeated commentators in their concern for a historical arrangement and dating. The literary categories and the language of their forms can be recognized first of

10. Cf. above, pp. 48 ff. and 290 ff.

all by taking together all the compositions which belong to a particular form of worship or are derived from it. These will then display a common stock of ideas and attitudes, which are determined by the common setting. Attention is given first to the form of the sentences and then to the vocabulary. Within the individual categories one has then to distinguish the motifs, the small units of which the poem is composed[11]. Although, starting with these assumptions, Gunkel recognized in principle the great antiquity of Hebrew psalm composition, he still ascribed the majority of the psalms, with the exception of the royal psalms and the songs which contained a certain allusion to a reigning king, to the sixth and fifth centuries. Particularly in the individual laments he believed he could establish that although they belonged to the pre-exilic cult, they lived on as devotional songs in the post-exilic period. While he originally described the so-called enthronement psalms as post-exilic eschatological psalms, later under the influence of Mowinckel he allowed their possible pre-exilic origin.

While Duhm took no apparent notice of the works of his colleague, Stärk and Kittel were constantly influenced by him. With both however the precision of Gunkel's analysis of literary types is lacking. Kittel was concerned primarily with the religious interpretation, and this he carried through without artificialities. It is not saying too much to acknowledge that he carried out the programme proposed by Delitzsch in an exemplary way for his own time.

Gunkel had correctly recognized the connection of the psalms with the Israelite cult. Accordingly the next task for research into the psalms was the reconstruction of the cult. Mowinckel's *Psalmenstudien II. Das Thronbesteigungsfest Jahwäs und der Ursprung der Eschatologie*, published in 1922, was a pioneering work. The whole subsequent study of the psalms is determined by the degree of its assent to, modification of or rejection of the hypotheses proposed here. Like Johannes Pedersen, Mowinckel learnt not only to notice Ancient Near Eastern parallels, but also to make the spiritual attitude of the so-called primitive peoples a fertile source in the explanation of the psalms. The world disclosed itself to the Israelites, as to early men generally, through rites and myths. Starting from Pss. 47, 93, 95–100, and con-

11. On the categories cf. above, pp. 330 ff.

stantly drawing a larger circle of psalms into the inquiry, he came to assume an enthronement festival of Yahweh, which was celebrated by Israel as part of its New Year Festival, which fell in the autumn. In this New Year Festival the Israelites experienced in a cultic drama the creation of the earth after the victory over chaos or over the enemies corresponding to chaos. Then Yahweh entered his holy city in triumph, to ascend his throne and to chastise his enemies. As it came to be recognized in the course of the centuries that cult and reality were not identical, the events celebrated in the cult were projected into the future, and their fulfilment hoped for there; eschatology was born. Thus, as Haller commented, the view taken of the psalms was stood upon its head; what had hitherto been regarded as an eschatological composition was now to be regarded as a cultic poem. A direct consequence of this cultic interpretation was for Mowinckel the pre-exilic dating of the majority of the psalms. To realize the far-reaching consequences of this view one need only remember the consequences for the interpretation of the prophets: the cult attested by the psalms was detached from a historical setting after the great prophets and placed before the prophets. Completely new traditio-historical perspectives, and indeed literary-critical consequences, were bound to result from this.

Mowinckel found support for his hypotheses subsequently in the study by Volz already published in 1912, *Das Neujahrsfest Jahwes*, and in Heinrich Zimmern's discussions of the Babylonian New Year Festival. In Germany it was especially Hans Schmidt, in his little book *Die Thronfahrt Jahwes am Fest der Jahreswende im alten Israel* in 1927, who supported Mowinckel. If we concentrate on German Old Testament scholarship we must mention especially Artur Weiser and Hans-Joachim Kraus as having modified Mowinckel's position. For Weiser it is the Israelite stock of ideas in the psalms which is of central importance, more than the parallels in the history of religions and phenomenology of religion. Not attempting the reconstruction of the course of the festival in detail, he sought primarily to determine its central ideas. At the centre of a feast which, under the influence of Alt and von Rad, he calls a covenant festival, stands for him the theophany of Yahweh, his self-revelation as a proclamation of his nature and will, a recapitulation of the

saving history and the promulgation of the law. In addition the
renunciation or repudiation of foreign gods, judgement on
Israel and the foreign nations, and also the enthronement of
Yahweh, as a single element, belong to this feast. The enthronement of the earthly king, and so also the whole thought pattern
of the Zion ideology, also belong for him, as for Mowinckel and
Schmidt, within this framework. Kraus assumes a Feast of the
Renewal of the Covenant in the pre-monarchical period observed
in a seven-year cycle, which in the Southern Kingdom except in
the days of Asa, Joash and Josiah was completely replaced by a
royal festival of Zion, at the centre of which stood the election of
Zion and of the Davidic dynasty. In the enthronement psalms
on the other hand he sees a reflection of the preaching of Deutero-
Isaiah, a view in which he is returning to older lines of thought.
They had their setting in life according to him in a royal entry
of Yahweh in the post-exilic New Year Festival, in which the
ancient amphictyonic traditions of the giving of the law and
renewal of the covenant were conjoined with the contents of the
festival of Zion. The main difference between Mowinckel,
Schmidt and Weiser on one side and Kraus on the other consists
therefore in the fact that Kraus derives the covenant complex
from the pre-exilic Jerusalem cult, and disputes the existence
of an enthronement of Yahweh at all. Perlitt agrees with him to
the extent that he argues that we cannot think in terms of a pre-
exilic Covenant Festival at all[11a]. It must finally be mentioned
that Gunther Wanke has proposed a redating of the Songs of
Zion which would have extensive consequences. He regards the
theme of the battle of the nations as an exilic and post-exilic
creation, which was linked up with the Zion tradition in eschatological prophecy as well as in cultic poetry[12]. Nevertheless de
Moor seems to me to be correct in demonstrating, over against
the denials in principle of the existence of an Israelite New Year
Festival such as have been made particularly strongly by Kutsch
and Fohrer[13] for the pre-exilic period in German-speaking

11a. Cf. above, pp. 63 f.

12. Cf. also H.-M. Lutz, *Jahwe, Jerusalem und die Völker*, WMANT
27, 1968, pp. 213 ff. and F. Stolz, *Strukturen und Figuren im Kult von
Jerusalem*, BZAW 118, 1970, p. 88, n. 69, but also O. Kaiser, *Isaiah 13–39*,
OTL, 1974, p. 86, n. b.

13. Cf. G. Fohrer, *History of Israelite Religion*, London 1973, pp. 204 ff.

countries, the continuity of the Israelite New Year Festival with that of the Canaanites. The main difference then is the omission of the idea of the dying God, and of the performance of the sacred marriage, as being ideas and practices inconsistent with faith in Yahweh.

In Scandinavian work apart from Bentzen it is especially Birkeland, Widengren and Engnell who have taken over and modified Mowinckel's results. Birkeland's comparison of the enemies mentioned in the collective and in the individual laments led him to the conclusion that the enemies in both are identical, and therefore that the man praying the individual laments is the king. He had already pointed to a phenomenon which Engnell particularly emphasized, the so-called democratization of the royal psalms, i.e. the taking over of these psalms by non-royal intercessors. The cultic role of the king is emphasized by Widengren and Engnell to a degree which goes beyond Mowincke. Johnson in Britain has particularly devoted himself to the same problem; but the differences between Israelite and non-Israelite sacral kingship are emphasized by him more strongly than by Widengren and Engnell.

Work on the history of religions and history of literary types has meanwhile not been standing still. Widengren has investigated the connections between the Israelite and the Akkadian Lamentations, and has concluded that the Israelite laments are dependent on the Akkadian. The discoveries at Ras Shamra, in spite of the few cultic songs found there, have led to a clearer recognition of the connections existing between Canaanite and Israelite psalm composition, indeed even to an overvaluation of them, which has left its deposit in textual emendations which are insufficiently grounded philologically[14]. Hans Schmidt, Westermann, Delekat, Crüsemann and Beyerlin have endeavoured to suggest further qualifications and corrections of the descriptions of categories introduced by Gunkel.

In retrospect, it can be seen how fruitful the raising of the form-critical and cultic questions has basically been, and how widespread the recognition has become that in the psalms we are not dealing primarily with individual compositions but with

14. Cf. H. Donner, 'Ugaritismen in der Psalmenforschung', *ZAW* 79 (1967), pp. 322 ff. and O. Loretz, 'Psalmenstudien', *Ugarit-Forschungen* 3 (1971), pp. 104 ff.

cultic compositions. At the same time it must be said that doubts about the possibility of bringing all or even the greater part of the psalms into connection with one single feast have not been silenced. Beyond this, there is agreement neither on the character of the pre-exilic Jerusalem New Year Festival nor on the cultic role of the king[15]. Even a tendency to date a larger number of the psalms in the post-exilic period again, and to claim them in part as devotional compositions, can be noticed again[16]. It remains to hope that fundamental detailed studies will lead to our overcoming the uncertainties caused by this multiplicity of views. It should be noted that the lack of a Hebrew syntax adequately grounded in Semitic studies is painfully conspicuous in the interpretation of the psalms even more than in that of any other book[17].

§ 29   The Psalter

Bibliography: cf. the preceding paragraphs.

1. Name and position within the canon. The book, which contains 150 psalms, is called in the Hebrew Bible *sēper tᵉhillîm*, (book of praises,) or simply *tᵉhillîm* (praises). The title of the book with which we are familiar, the Book of Psalms, or the Psalter, goes back to the Septuagint, which calls it either *psalmoi*, songs for stringed instruments (cf. Luke 24.44), or *psaltērion*, collection of songs, while in Luke's writings the title *biblos psalmōn*, book of songs for stringed instruments, is found (cf. Luke 20.42, and Acts 1.20). In the Hebrew canon the book is placed in a varying position in the *kᵉtûbîm* or writings[1]. In the usual printed editions it is placed, in accordance with the Central European synagogue tradition, at the head of the writings. The usual position in

15. Cf. e.g. M. Noth, 'God, King and Nation in the Old Testament', in *The Laws in the Pentateuch and Other Studies*, Edinburgh and London 1966, pp. 145 ff., and K.-H. Bernhardt, op. cit.

16. Cf. Fohrer*, pp. 285 ff.

17. D. Michel, *Tempora und Satzstellung*, has begun the process of clarification. It is much to be hoped that O. Rössler of Marburg will soon publish the studies which he has been making over many years.

1. Cf. below, p. 406.

German (and English) Bibles, after the Book of Job, goes back to the Vulgate.

2. *The numbering of the psalms.* Different systems of numbering are found in the Hebrew Bible and in the Septuagint. Since the Septuagint treats Psalms 9 and 10 (correctly) and 114 and 115 (wrongly) as single psalms, and divides up both 116 and 147 into two psalms, the following variation in numbering, which must be remembered when the Septuagint and Vulgate are used, has resulted:

MT	G	MT	G
1–8	1–8	116.10–19	115
9/10	9	117–146	116–145
11–113	10–112	147.1–11	146
114/5	113	147.12–20	147
116.1–9	114	148–150	148–150
			151

The Septuagint also gives us one further psalm, Psalm 151, the Hebrew original of which is preserved in 11 QPs[a].

3. *The division of the psalter into five books.* The theory is attested among both Jews and Christians from the fourth century A.D. that the psalter was divided into five books analogously to the five books of Moses, and that the end of each is marked by the concluding doxologies 41.13; 72.18 f.; 89.52; 106.48 (Heb. 41.14; 72.18 f.; 89.53; 106.48), and by Ps. 150, which concludes the whole collection. Five books of David would thus correspond to the five books of Moses. The artificial nature of the theory can be seen from the highly varied lengths of the books so formed (I 1–41; II 42–72; III 73–89; IV 90–106 and V 107–150), especially when older collections can be distinguished which were made on the basis of authorship or use. Recently Gese has given reasons to think it probable that 41.13 and 72.18 f. were added to the two old collections of David psalms, which contain primarily psalms of the individual, 3–41 and 51–72 (cf. 72.20), to give them a public quality, while 106.48 (cf. 1 Chr. 16.36) is indeed derived from liturgical use, but does not indicate the end

of an older collection². In the case of Ps. 150 it must however be borne in mind that together with Pss. 146–149 it forms the so-called 'little Hallel'.

4. The origin of the Psalter. The fact that certain psalms are found twice (Ps. 14 = 53; 40.13–17 (Heb. 40.14–18) = 70; 57.7–11 (Heb. 57.8–12) + 60.5–12 (Heb. 60.7–14) = 108) suggests that our Book of Psalms has developed from originally independent collections. We may probably regard the Psalter of David contained in (2) 3–41 (only Ps. 33 lacks the heading *l'dāwîd*, 'of David') as the basic core of the Psalter. 42–83 represents another collection, the Elohistic Psalter, so called because the name Yahweh is replaced by the description Elohim, God, in the majority of instances. A comparison of Ps. 53 with Ps. 14 and of Ps. 57.7–11 (Heb. 57.8–12) and 60.5–12 (Heb. 60.7–14) with Ps. 108 shows that we have here a conscious redactional procedure. The Elohistic Psalter in its turn has developed out of a series of originally independent smaller collections. These are the psalms of Korah 42–49, the psalms of David 51–72, cf. Ps. 72.20 (without 66/67, 71, and 72, which is ascribed to Solomon), and the psalms of Asaph, 50 and 73–83. Pss. 84–89 are probably an appendix to the Elohistic Psalter, since we have in 84/85 and 87/88 further psalms of Korah, in 86 a psalm of David and in 89 a psalm of Ethan. After the uniting of the Psalter of David with the Elohistic Psalter and its appendix, Pss. 90–150 were successively added. Mention should be made among these of the Psalm of Moses (90), the Enthronement psalms (93–99*), the Halleluiah psalms (104–106; 111–117; 135; 146–150), the pilgrimage psalms (120–134), clearly an originally independent collection, and the psalms of David (101; 103; 108–110; 138–145). It is no doubt to the final redaction of the whole collection that we owe the addition of Pss. 1 and 2 as a didactic and messianic prologue, and the conclusion in the form of a doxology (Ps. 150).

5. The question of authorship. The descriptions of situation added to the psalms of David 7, 18, 34, 51, 52, 54, 56, 57, 59 and

2. Cf. H. Gese, 'Die Entstehung der Büchereinteilung des Psalters', in *Wort, Lied und Gottesspruch*, Festschrift J. Ziegler II, FzB 2, 1972, pp. 57 ff.

60 indicate that the heading *l^edāwid* was understood in the
Jewish tradition as an indication of authorship[3]. The precarious
basis of the tradition is shown by the fact that psalms like 5, 8,
63 and 69 clearly presuppose the existence of the temple in
Jerusalem, which was not built until the time of Solomon. Even
if we allow the claims of David to be an author of psalms, on the
basis of 2 Sam. 1.18 ff. and 3.33 f. (cf. also Amos 6.5), it is impossible to ascribe to him all the songs assigned to him[4]. If we
proceed from the heading of Ps. 102 (Heb. 102.1), 'A prayer
of one afflicted (*l^e'ānî*), when he is faint and pours out his complaint before the LORD', Mowinckel's suggestion that the *l^e* in
the title *l^edāwid* is to be understood not as a *l^e auctoris* but as
a *l^e ethicus* seems the most probable view. Originally this superscription would have indicated that a particular psalm belonged
to the royal ritual ('for a Davidite'). It was only later that this
liturgical indication was turned into a statement of authorship.
Scholars do indeed differ about which psalms of David originally
belonged to the royal liturgy of Jerusalem[5]. Arguments from
content and history indicate that Ps. 72 does not come from
Solomon and Ps. 90 does not come from Moses.

The Korahites according to 2 Chr. 20.19 are a guild of singers,
and according to 1 Chr. 9.19 they were among the keepers of the
threshold. While Heman (cf. Ps. 88 heading, Heb. 88.1) and
Ethan (cf. Ps. 89 heading, Heb. 89.1) are still regarded as wise
men in 1 Kgs. 4.31 (Heb. 5.11), they are regarded together with
Asaph in 1 Chr. 15.16 ff. as temple singers and musicians. The
relevant psalm headings are accordingly to be regarded at least
in part as originally classificatory notes from the library of the
second temple, which indicate that the psalms are to be performed by the group named. But here too it cannot be excluded
that the wish to have authors of standing led to secondary
headings which were understood as giving the authors. That
there were already singers both male and female in pre-exilic
Jerusalem is attested by Sennacherib's account of the tribute
imposed on Hezekiah in 701[6]. As to whether there were already

3. Yet more headings are found in the Septuagint.
4. In 11 QPs^aDav Comp, David is described as the author of 3600
psalms and of 450 songs.
5. Cf. above, pp. 343 ff.
6. Cf. *ANET*[2], p. 288, and *AOT*[2], p. 354.

guilds of singers connected with the names Asaph, Ethan and Korah in pre-exilic Jerusalem, and whether there were links between these singers and the cultic prophets, we can, in spite of 2 Chr. 20.14 ff., only conjecture[7].

6. *Technical terms in the headings.* The descriptions of the psalms chosen for the headings are in part obscure. The descriptions as *tᵉhillâ* 'praise' and *tᵉpillâ* 'prayer', *šîr* 'vocal performance' and *mizmôr* 'song accompanied instrumentally', present no problem[8]. In the combinations *šîr mizmôr* and *mizmôr šîr* we may, as Delekat suggests, have a combination of textual variants. The expressions *miktām* (perhaps from the Akkadian *katāmu* 'to cover', so psalm of propitiation), *maśkîl* (if derived from *śkl* in the hiphil, 'knowing song', so possibly 'effective song' or 'artistic song', but hardly 'didactic composition'), and *šiggāyôn* (perhaps connected with the Akkadian *šegū* 'lamentation'?) are obscure.

Among the terms used to state the occasion, the description *šîr hammaʿᵃlôt* 'pilgrimage song' and *lᵉtôdâ* 'for the confession' (or 'thanksgiving-sacrifice') are clear. *lᵉʿannôt* in Ps. 88 may be repunctuated with Mowinckel as *leʿᵉnût*, 'for (self-) humiliation'. *lᵉhazkîr*, appearing in 38 heading (Heb. 38.1) and 70 heading (Heb. 70.1), may be connected with the *ʾazkārâ* mentioned in Num. 5.26, a 'calling out of a name over the sacrifice'[9] It remains disputed whether the *yᵉdûtûn* in the headings of 39, 62 and 77 (Heb. 39.1*, 62.1 and 77.1*) is really connected with the music master of David mentioned in 1 Chr. 25.1 ff. and does not rather derive from *ydh* II hiphil, and mean a confession. The *lᵉlammēd* 'to teach' of Ps. 60 seems to have no meaning, and it may be best to connect it, with Mowinckel, with a cult oracle. Nor is agreement to be expected immediately about the sense of *lamᵉnaṣṣēᵃh*, usually translated as 'for the choir leader', but better translated with Mowinckel as 'to sound gracious', or 'in homage'. Musical directions are preserved in *binᵉgînôt*, 'with stringed accompaniment' (cf. e.g. 4 heading, Heb. 4.1), *higgāyôn* (e.g. 9.16, Heb. 9.17 and 92.3, Heb. 92.4), *ʿal-haššᵉmînît*

---

7. Cf. S. Mowinckel, *The Psalms in Israel's Worship* II, pp. 53 ff., and A. R. Johnson, *The Cultic Prophet in Ancient Israel*, Cardiff 1962², pp. 69 ff.

8. Cf. S. Mowinckel, *Psalmenstudien* IV, 1923, and now also L. Delekat, 'Probleme der Psalmenüberschriften', *ZAW* 76 (1964), pp. 280 ff. which in many respects goes its own ways; and further J. J. Glueck, 'Some Remarks on the Introductory Notes of the Psalms', in *Studies on the Psalms*, Die Ou Testamentiese Werkgemeenskap in Suid-Afrika, Potchefstroom, n.d. [1963], pp. 30 ff.

9. Cf. W. Schottroff, *'Gedenken' im Alten Orient und im Alten Testament*, WMANT 15, 1964, pp. 328 ff.

(6 and 12 headings, Heb. 6.1 and 12.1), and on the usual assumption also in the obscure *selâ*, which is translated by the Septuagint *diapsalma*, interlude. References to tunes appear to be contained in the headings to 8, 22, 45, 57, 58, 59, 60, 69, 75, 80, 81 and 84 (Heb. 8.1; 22.1; 45.1; 57.1; 58.1; 59.1; 60.1; 69.1; 75.1; 80.1; 81.1 and 84.1). So e.g. *'al yônaṭ 'ēlîm* (for *'ēlem*) *rᵉḥôqîm* is translated 'according to The Dove on Far-Off Terebinths' (cf. 56 heading, Heb. 56.1), and *'al 'ayyeleṭ haššaḥar* as 'according to The Hind of the Dawn' (cf. 22 heading, Heb. 22.1)[10].

7. *Date of the book.* It cannot be denied that the Psalter contains pre-exilic songs, in view of the royal psalms[11], nor that it contains post-exilic ones, in view of Psalms 126–137. The fact that the Odes of Solomon, written between 60 and 30 B.C., were not incorporated into the Book of Psalms, argues for the completion of the collection at the latest in the second century[12]. The songs of the first temple entered partially, no doubt not without re-editing, into the repertoire of the second temple. Out of more or less self-contained collections, such as have been indicated above, the canonical Psalter originated in a process of tradition, reworking and expansion covering centuries.

§ 30   Lamentations

M. Löhr, 'Der Sprachgebrauch des Buches der Klagelieder', *ZAW* 14 (1894), pp. 31 ff.; id., 'Threni III. und die jeremianische Autorschaft des Buches der Klagelieder', *ZAW* 24 (1904), pp. 1 ff.; H. Jahnow, *Das hebräische Leichenlied im Rahmen der Völkerdichtung*, BZAW 36, 1923, pp. 168 ff.; H. Wiesmann, 'Die literarische Art der Klagelieder des Jeremias', *ThQ* 110 (1929), pp. 381 ff.; id., 'Der geschichtliche Hintergrund des Büchleins der Klagelieder', *BZ* 23 (1935–6), pp. 20 ff.; id., 'Der Verfasser des Büchleins der Klagelieder ein Augenzeuge

10. Cf. A. Jirku, *ZAW* 65 (1953), pp. 85 f.
11. Cf. above, p. 337.
12. In the fragmentary roll of psalms published in J. A. Sanders, *The Psalms Scroll of Qumrân Cave 11*, DJD 4, Oxford 1965, which contains canonical psalms in an unusual order, and in addition eight non-canonical compositions, of which four were hitherto unknown, we probably have a liturgical work put together specially for the Qumran community.

der behandelten Ereignisse?', *Bib* 17 (1936), pp. 71 ff.; H. Gunkel and J. Begrich, *Einleitung in die Psalmen*, Göttingen 1933, repr. 1966, pp. 117 ff., 172 ff. and 400 f.; W. Rudolph, 'Der Text der Klagelieder', *ZAW* 56 (1938), pp. 101 ff.; N. K. Gottwald, *Studies in the Book of Lamentations*, SBT[1] 14, 1954; E. Janssen, *Juda in der Exilszeit*, FRLANT 69, 1956, pp. 9 ff.; B. Albrektson, *Studies in the Text and Theology of the Book of Lamentations*, Studia Theologica Lundensia 21, Lund 1963.

Commentaries: HK Löhr 1893; 1906[2]; KHC Budde 1898; HS Paffrath 1932; KAT[1] Rudolph 1939; HAT Haller 1940; BK Kraus 1956, 1968[3]; ATD Weiser 1958; KAT[2] Rudolph 1962; HAT[2] Plöger 1969; SC Wiesmann 1954; Gordis, *JQR* 58 (1967), pp. 14 ff.

1. Book and author. This book of five chapters, each of which consists of one song, is named in the Hebrew Bible after the beginning of 1.1 (cf. 2.1 and 4.1), *'êkâ*, 'ah', 'how'. According to *b. Baba bathra* 15a (cf. 2 Chr. 35.25a) it was earlier called *qînôṯ*, Lamentations, a title which has been kept in the *thrēnoi* of the Greek, and in the *threni* or *lamentationes* of the Latin Bible, and so in the more recent translations too. In the Hebrew canon the book is placed among the *keṯûḇîm* or writings, more precisely among the Megilloth or festival rolls, where its position varies in accordance with the would-be historical arrangement of the books here collected, or with their assignment to the feasts involved[1]. In the synagogue it is appointed to be read on the 9th of Ab, the day of remembrance of the fall of Jerusalem. In the Septuagint, the Vulgate and the more recent translations Lamentations is placed after the Book of Jeremiah, and called the Lamentations of Jeremiah, in accordance with the supposed authorship of the prophet.

This tradition goes back to Jewish traditions, which can be traced back through *b. Baba bathra* 15a and Josephus to 2 Chr. 35.25a. According to Chronicles Jeremiah composed lamentations over the death of Josiah, which are read 'to this day' (cf. Lam. 4.20)[2]. Repeated attempts have been made to demonstrate or refute Jeremiah's authorship of the songs by means of linguistic statistics, but because of the common store of motifs shared by the so-called confessions of Jeremiah[3] and these songs, which is derived from their literary genre, no clear results have been

1. Cf. below, p. 406.
2. Cf. also the prologue to the Septuagint translation.
3. Cf. above, p. 246.

achieved[4]. Criteria of content however exclude the assumption of Jeremianic authorship (cf. 2.9 and 4.12, 17). From this point of view 2.14, 17, 4.13 and 5.6 lose their contrary evidential value, and only show that after the catastrophe there was a change of outlook, in which the prophetic condemnation of history of a Micah or a Jeremiah nevertheless continued. While Rudolph has suggested that the unusual constructed third song should be seen as a poem fictionally put in the mouth of the prophet Jeremiah, it is sufficient to remark that the connection between Jer. 20.7b and Lam. 3.14 is not enough to bear the weight of this hypothesis, which could only be understood as being a consequence of the tradition. On the question whether the five songs come from a single author or from several, a definite answer is not possible, although it seems probable that at least the first two are to be ascribed to the same author.

2. *Form and genre.* The five songs are formally linked by the fact that the first four are acrostic, alphabetic poems, and the fifth is a pseudo-alphabetic poem.

In the first two songs each of the 22 three-line strophes begin with a letter of the alphabet in sequence. While the sequence of letters in the first song is identical with the order of Hebrew alphabet as known to us, in the second, third and fourth songs we find the unusual sequence *s–p–'* instead of *s–'–p*. The third song is the most ingeniously designed, in that here not only the first word of each line, but also that of the two following lines of each strophe begins with the appropriate letter. The fourth song on the other hand consists only of 22 strophes each of two lines, and the fifth of 22 lines. The number of lines agrees therefore with the number of letters of the alphabet, but the lines do not each begin with the corresponding letter. Much ink has been spilt over the point of the acrostic compositions[5]. It has been suggested that there was a belief in a magical power of the alphabet and of the letter, which would give especial power to the poem so formed. But we have no supporting evidence that Judaism in the sixth century knew of such an

4. Cf. M. Löhr, *ZAW* 14 (1894), pp. 31 ff., and most recently H. Wiesmann, *Die Klagelieder* (typescript), Frankfurt 1954, pp. 54 ff.

5. Cf. above, p. 321, n. 3; Löhr, 'Alphabetische und alphabetisierende Lieder im Alten Testament', *ZAW* 25 (1905), pp. 173 ff., and on the discussion N. K. Gottwald, op. cit., pp. 23 ff.

idea. The intention of providing a mnemonic aid has also been suggested. But since the compulsion of the form of the acrostic makes the sequence of ideas disconnected and discontinuous, and the form is basically noticed by the eye, but not by the ear, this explanation should also be rejected. The best route to a solution of the problem is if one remembers the proverbial 'from A to Z': i.e.

The alphabetic composition makes the claim to be a complete composition, dealing exhaustively with its subject.

Without entering into the metrical argument between the supporters of accentuating and of alternating systems of metre[6] it can be stated that the first four songs at least clearly display the form of the dirge or *qînâ*, in which as a rule a longer first hemistich is followed by a shorter second one.

Following Budde, Gunkel determined the literary type of the first, second and fourth songs as political dirge, although he did recognize that the type is not found in pure form in any of the three songs[7]. The more detailed examination of the motifs of the literary type of the dirge by Hedwig Jahnow could have given us sufficient warning against this description of the type, since she was not able to do more than demonstrate individual points of contact between Lamentations and the secular lament for the dead. The individual form of the third song too should prevent us from describing it as an individual lament, following Gunkel, since this description takes us no further than did that of dirge for the understanding of these songs. It is only in respect of the fifth song that the usual description as a collective lament[8] is appropriate. Kraus' attempt to determine the type, with the help of Sumerian parallels, as a lament for a destroyed sanctuary clearly does not do justice to the actual concern of the poems. It is therefore understandable that Weiser and Plöger, who only define chapter 5 in the sense given above, abandon completely the attempt to determine the literary type and instead are content to show the elements of forms, the sequence of ideas and purpose. When attempting to determine a literary type while at the same time recognizing a mixture of types, one must always remember that a total distinction must be made between the question of the origin of the elements of the form and the question of the literary

6. Cf. above, pp. 323 ff.

7. *RGG* III[1], Tübingen 1912, cols. 1499 ff.; cf. *RGG* III[2], 1929, cols. 1049 ff.   8. Cf. above, p. 333.

type in use on this occasion. The answer can be found, if the text is transmitted to us on its own without exact information about its setting in life, by paying attention to how the individual elements of the form function in relation to the whole. If the question of function is lost sight of, the whole question of literary types when directed to the original forms or pure types remains in the end unfruitful for the actual understanding of the text. Without going into details, what is meant can at least be illustrated by the examples of the first and the third songs.

The first song divides up into four sections: vv. 1–11, 12–16, 17 and 18–22. In 1–11 there is a lament for the overthrow of Jerusalem, portrayed as the virgin daughter of Zion, within which Jerusalem itself speaks in 9c and 11c with two heartfelt cries. In 12–16 the personified city raises its lament in the hearing of the passers-by, stressing constantly that its suffering is a consequence of Yahweh's anger and of its sin. 1.17 contains a transitional remark, which says first that no-one consoles Zion, and secondly that Yahweh himself has sent the enemies against Jacob/Jerusalem. This is followed in vv. 18–22 by a renewed lament of the virgin Zion, which now however proceeds to call on Yahweh himself. It begins with a confession of the righteousness of Yahweh, and ends with a prayer to let the day of judgement that has been announced fall upon the enemies and so punish their wickedness, as Yahweh has thought fit to punish his own people's rebellions (cf. 21c and 22). The change of voices, which has dramatic motivation, *can* be claimed to show that the poem was presented as performed by different parts, but does not need to be so interpreted. From the ending it is clear that in spite of the different elements of literary types, which have not been discussed in detail here, we are dealing with what is functionally a collective lament. With its emphasis on Zion's own guilt it pursues a parenetic intent, for confessing her own guilt Zion appears before Yahweh, whose notice is directed towards her own suffering, and whose punishment of the enemy is demanded. We may accordingly determine the type of the first song as a communal lament, or if we allow for a real change of voice in the performance, for a liturgy of lamentation in the style of a communal lament with parenetic intent. A similar result comes from the analysis of the second song (2.1–10, 11–12, probably to be taken together as 1–12, 13–17, 18–19, and 20–22) which goes further than ch. 1 to end in a prayer. The move from the lament over Yahweh's work of destruction upon Jerusalem and Judah, through the condolence, to the call to Zion to incessant lamentation before Yahweh, and to the final lament of Zion is not being over-interpreted if we ascribe to it the parenetic intention of leading the community that is present and disabled by suffering, to shared lamentation and prayer.

The third song, whose intention is at first sight puzzling, can also be interpreted with the help of this insight. In 3.1–18 we have a confession of suffering of an individual, which moves on in 3.19–24 to a confession of trust in Yahweh. It is clear that this confession has a paradigmatic intention, and presupposes the presence of the community. The correctness of this clue is shown by the continuation in 3.25–33, in which we find a didactic instruction, in the wisdom spirit, to bear the yoke laid upon them patiently and to wait for the help of Yahweh. The doubts which make it difficult for men to accept consolatory admonition are expressed in the didactic questions which follow in 3.34–39, and at the same time are refuted by the way in which they are listed. After internal opposition has been cleared away, a call to repentance and to true prayer can follow in 3.40–41, as a solemn introduction to common prayer, which follows in 3.42–47 in the form of a collective lament, without leading on to intercession. Instead there follows in 3.48–66 again a deeply felt individual lamentation. This divides up into 48–51, a lament for the misfortune of Jerusalem, 52–54 a declaration of the suffering experienced by the speaker himself, with a following confession of deliverance by Yahweh in 55–58. Accordingly in 48–54 we have a song of thanksgiving. In 59–66 on the other hand a new lament with a prayer for the destruction of the enemy breaks out. If it is assumed that the speaker in the song has both suffered the unqualified catastrophe of 587 and experienced Yahweh's help in it, and also shares in the present in the distress of his people, the apparent contradictions suggested by the facts can be resolved. If we need to find a single name for the literary type of this third song, it can best be called a liturgy of lament with parenetic intention. In the fourth song on the other hand we have a prophetic liturgy, in the sense of a prophecy of salvation[9].

9. 4.1–16 is a descriptive lamentation over the misery of the population of Jerusalem, in which it is four times emphasized that the distress is a consequence of sin, or a punishment from Yahweh. This is followed in 4.17–20 by a lamentation in the first person plural, in which an impressionistic picture of the final phase of the catastrophe is painted. In 4.21 there follows an ironic salvation saying for Edom, in 22a a salvation saying for Zion, and in 22b a threat saying for Edom. The lack of any address to Yahweh in the whole song is striking. This gives rise to the conjecture that the first two sections are intended to support the verdict passed in 22a. From the declaration contained in 22a of the blotting out of guilt we can think of an authorized speaker, from the threat against Edom in 22b of a (cultic) prophet.

3. Place and date of origin. From what has been said, it is
already clear that the songs were composed in Jerusalem and
uttered there in the course of worship. Our knowledge of the
specific circumstances of the community after the catastrophe is
too incomplete to decide the question whether they were composed for a specific ceremony of lamentation, whether unique
or repeated, or whether they were used at other occasions of
worship. Since the destruction of the temple is not explicitly
mentioned in the first song, Rudolph and Weiser connect it
with the first conquest of Jerusalem in 597. The reconstruction
of the events of the year 598/7 on the basis of the Babylonian
royal chronicle by Noth shows however that on that occasion
there was no lengthy siege of Jerusalem[10]. Jehoiachin quickly
capitulated and so saved his people from the suffering presupposed in the first song. As regards the date, in view of the
caution that is appropriate to such compositions it is best to
leave it at the statement that they originated in the years after
the disaster of 587. While a common authorship can be assumed
for the first two songs in view of their common attitude, this
remains questionable in the case of the third, fourth and fifth
songs. With Plöger, we must give up the attempt to determine
the spiritual home of the poets more exactly as belonging to a
circle of priests, of prophets or of the nobility of the court. The
poems do however give the impression throughout of having
been composed by eye-witnesses of the disaster to Judah and
Jerusalem. All five songs together give an insight into the internal
situation of the community after the disaster, which is to be
thought of not only with its distressing external accompani-
ments and consequences, but especially as a crisis of faith
caused by the prophecies of salvation which derive support
from the Zion ideology (cf. 2.14; 4.17 and 5.18–20). While the
first three songs lead the community out of its lethargy and
doubt to lamentation and intercession, the community in the
fifth and last stands again in prayer before its God. On the other
hand the thought that Zion has redeemed its guilt by its suffering
is unique to the fourth song.

10. Cf. M. Noth, 'Die Einnahme von Jerusalem im Jahre 597 v. Chr.',
ZDPV 74 (1958), pp. 133 ff.

§ 31　The Song of Songs

J. G. Wetzstein, 'Die syrische Dreschtafel. 4. Die Tafel in der Königs-woche', *Zeitschrift für Ethnologie* 5 (1873), pp. 287 ff.; K. Budde, 'Was ist das Hohe Lied?', *Preussische Jahrbücher* 78 (1894), pp. 92 ff.; T. J. Meek, 'Canticles and the Tammuz Cult', *AJSL* 39 (1922/23) pp. 1 ff.; F. Horst, 'Die Formen des althebräischen Liebesliedes' [1935], *Gottes Recht*, ThB 12, 1961, pp. 176 ff.; C. Kuhl, 'Das Hohelied und seine Deutung', *ThR* NF 9 (1937), pp. 137 ff.; H. Schmökel, 'Zur kultischen Deutung des Hohenliedes', *ZAW* 64 (1952), pp. 148 ff.; id. *Heilige Hochzeit und Hohes Lied*, Wiesbaden 1956; F. Ohly, *Hohelied-Studien. Grundzüge einer Geschichte der Hoheliedauslegung des Abendlandes bis um 1200*, Wiesbaden 1958; R. Gordis, *The Song of Songs*, New York 1954; O. Loretz, 'Zum Problem des Eros im Hohenlied', *BZ* NF 8 (1964), pp. 191 ff.; H. H. Rowley, 'The Interpretation of the Song of Songs', in *The Servant of the Lord*, Oxford 1965², pp. 197 ff.; E. Würthwein, 'Zum Verständnis des Hohenliedes', *ThR* NF 32 (1967), pp. 177 ff.

Commentaries: KHC Budde 1898 (cf. HSAT 1923⁴); HK Siegfried 1898; HS Miller 1927; HAT Haller 1940; ATD Ringgren 1958 (1962²); KAT² Rudolph 1962; BK Gerleman 1965; HAT Würthwein 1969.

1. The book. The little book of the Song of Songs (i.e. the most beautiful of songs) with its eight chapters is written according to its heading in 1.1 by Solomon. On the basis of this fiction, which depends upon a combination of 1 Kgs. 5.12 with Cant. (1.5), 3.7–11 and 8.11 (cf. 1.4, 12; 7.5, Heb. 7.6), but is put in question already by the content of the book itself, Song of Songs was, like Proverbs and Ecclesiastes, taken into the canon of the Old Testament. Rabbinic discussion shows how its entirely secular content still caused offence in the first and second centuries A.D., so that there was argument over the permissibility of reading it in a service, cf. *b. Yadaim* 3.5. In the Hebrew canon it was placed among the *kᵉtûbîm* or writings, in the *Megilloth* or festival rolls[1]. Its use as a Passover reading is first attested from the eighth century, and probably depends not so much upon the intimate connection of the poem with the spring, in which the feast falls, as upon the Jewish allegorical interpretation, according to which the whole book tells of the relationship of Yahweh to Israel, and its beginning of the exodus from Egypt.

---

1. Cf. below, p. 406.

2. The interpretations. The allegorical interpretation, which was represented in Judaism particularly vehemently by Rabbi Aqiba (d. A.D. 137), was also generally accepted in the Church. According to this the bridegroom is Christ, the bride is the Church (since Hippolytus), the individual soul (since Origen) or Mary (especially since Ambrose). The allegorical interpretation runs contrary to the clear wording of the songs. It was natural in the ancient and medieval Church, in view of its understanding of scripture[2]. Since the eighteenth century it has been increasingly on the defensive. While it still finds supporters today[3], its total disappearance can only now be a question of time, unless the sense of history and the clarity it brings themselves disappear[4].

With this point however the agreement of more recent exegetes, who are not dependent on dogmatic prejudgements, also ends. For there is no agreement whatever whether Song of Songs is to be regarded as a collection of individual songs or as an originally unitary dramatic or cult drama composition; whether its songs are popular or literary compositions; whether they refer to love within marriage or outside marriage, and whether they go back originally to a Canaanite cultic composition of the second millennium B.C. or whether we have in them compositions of the early period of the monarchy, of the pre-exilic period, or of the late post-exilic period.

The dramatic hypothesis can be traced from the beginning of the eighteenth century into the nineteenth. It starts from the observation, in itself correct, of the change of scene, and change of speaker between a woman, a man, the dialogue of the two, and we-passages. The division into individual sections has remained however very controversial. While e.g. G. W. Wachter in 1722 saw in Song of Songs an opera divided into scenes, Ewald in 1826 reached the following general interpretation, known as the 'shepherd hypothesis': 'Shulamite is brought from her home,

---

2. Cf. O. Loretz, 'Die theologische Bedeutung des Hohenliedes', *BZ* NF 10 (1966), p. 42: 'The allegorical and typological interpretation of Canticles is for us a great witness of the love for scripture and for Christ which is created in the Church by the spirit of God. It is however at the same time an unmistakable sign that it is a tribute paid by Christian thought to the circumstances of past centuries'.

3. Cf. E. Würthwein, op. cit., pp. 181 ff.

4. A happy sign of this is the unbiased discussion in Loretz, *BZ* NF 10.

where she loves a shepherd, to the royal court, to become Solomon's wife; but in the face of all the courting of Solomon and all the urging of the ladies of the court she remains firm and faithful; so the king in the end has to let her go again, and at home she marries her shepherd. For love is as strong as death[5].'
The objection to this interpretation is not so much that we have no evidence for the assumption of dramatic performances in Israel[6] as that the identification of the beloved with a shepherd is a fiction which is subsidiary in the interpretation of the whole song. We must further ask with Siegfried whether such an interpretation can be harmonized at all with what we know about the position of the wife in ancient Near Eastern and in Israelite and Jewish society. Finally and most importantly the objection must be made that this understanding has to be read from between the lines.

Similar objections finally must be made also to the cult drama and mythological interpretation, which was put forward by Meek, made the basis of his commentary by Haller among others, and elaborated by Schmökel with all the assistance possible from Oriental studies. On this hypothesis the cult of the dying and rising god of the spring, Tammuz, and his beloved, Ishtar, lies in the background. Schmökel tries to demonstrate that Canticles in its original form was a cultic composition, the parts in which are to be assigned to a choir of men and a choir of women, a priest representing Tammuz, and a priestess representing Ishtar, who consummate the sacred marriage[7]. This composition was deliberately mutilated and broken up in the post-exilic period so that the whole mythological background was concealed. It must be conceded that the Tammuz cult succeeded in penetrating Israelite popular religion, and managed to enter even the temple in Jerusalem itself (cf. Ezek. 8.14), and it may also be granted that the custom, described by J. G. Wetzstein and others, of the identification of bride and bridegroom in modern Syria and Palestine with the king and queen can be connected as a survival with originally mythical ideas related to the fertility cult. It is

5. Quoted from C. Kuhl, op. cit., p. 154.
6. A total denial of the existence of ancient Israelite cultic drama can hardly be maintained, in the light of S. Mowinckel's *Psalmenstudien* II, Kristiania 1922, pp. 35 ff.
7. Cf. his survey in *Heilige Hochzeit und Hohes Lied*, pp. 45 ff.

then possible to regard the similar identification in Canticles not as a consequence of a poetic device, a use of the figure of the king (Gerleman), but as real survivals of this marriage custom (Budde, Siegfried, Rudolph and Würthwein). But it remains incomprehensible, as Würthwein points out, that Judaism could have made a collection of love songs out of a poem dedicated to an obviously heathen cult, and included them in its holy scripture[8]. Furthermore, as Loretz points out, the comparison of Akkadian material in no way compels us to such an interpretation, which re-interprets the text to a preconceived pattern[9]. The discovery of a descriptive song about Baal, embedded in the context of a cultic drama, in the Ugaritic text Gordon 603, 5–10, which in listing the beauties of the body of Baal basically follows the same sequence as Cant. 5.10–16, points however to a possible pre-history for the literary type in ritual[9a].

In any case the view taken by J. G. Herder in 1778 in his *Lieder der Liebe*, that in Canticles we have a collection of separate poems, must stand. No trace can be found of a unified plan of composition or of a progression of ideas. The intimate union of the lovers is not first presupposed in 8.5, but already in 1.6, 16 f. The arrangement of the (roughly) thirty separate songs—the delimitation and numbering of them varies in the commentaries —is made partly on the basis of content, partly simply from association of catchwords[10]. While the songs are so live that they resist any attempt at rigid classification, we can find at least, with Horst, a song of description, corresponding to the Arabic *waṣf*, with a more or less detailed description of the beauty of the body of the beloved (cf. e.g. 4.1–7; 5.10–16 and 6.13–7.5 (Heb. 7.1–6)), the song of admiration put in the mouth of the beloved (cf. e.g. 1.15–17; 2.1–3; 4.9–11 and 7.6–10 (Heb. 7.7–11)), the song of boasting (cf. 6.8–10 and 8.11 f.), and the song of longing (cf. 5.2–8), as separate literary types. Under the influence of the description given by Wetzstein of Arab marriage customs in Hauran[11] Budde interpreted Canticles primarily as

8. Cf. Würthwein, op. cit., p. 201.
9. Cf. Loretz, *BZ* NF 8, pp. 191 ff.
9a. Cf. L. R. Fisher and F. B. Knutson, *JNES* 28 (1969), pp. 162 ff.
10. Cf. W. Rudolph, KAT², p. 100.
11. Eissfeldt*, p. 487, gives a concise summary of his observations: 'on the day before the marriage, the bride dances a sword dance to the

almost a primer for a Palestinian Israelite wedding, while not
wishing to argue for a planned composition. He later made it
clear that he did not take the view that all the songs were composed for a wedding celebration. On the basis of the modern
parallels he regarded the songs as popular compositions. While
Budde's thesis was taken up especially by Siegfried, Rudolph
has pointed out that the absence of any organic order argues
against an exclusive connection of the songs with marriage, as
do the facts that a part of the songs can only be regarded as
love songs, and that Arab songs of description are by no means
connected exclusively with marriage.

On the question whether Canticles is a popular or a literary
composition, the balance appears to be tipping in the direction
of the second assumption, as is shown by the investigations of
Schmökel, Gerleman and Würthwein. In support of its character
as a literary composition Schmökel pointed not only to the
accomplished comparisons, images and songs of description,
which presuppose a firm tradition, but also to the metre. Of the
169 verses of the book, making use of the accentuating system
he assigned 97 to the scheme 2 + 2, 46 to 3 + 2 and 25 to 3 + 3,
so that the songs appear as literary creations with a unified
stamp. Gerleman pointed especially to the connections of motif
between our songs and Ancient Egyptian love poetry, of whose
character as literary composition there can be no doubt[12].
Working from Egyptian analogies, he regards the speech of king
and queen, of shepherd and gardener not as images drawn from
wedding customs or from lovers as a class, but as 'travesties',
a playful abandonment of the roles normally played in society
by going above or below, and accordingly a further piece of evidence that the songs have been composed in a highly skilful
manner. Würthwein emphasizes especially that the great number
of songs put in the mouth of the beloved argues against describing the songs as popular composition, since it cannot be

rhythm of a song sung by one of the bystanders, a song which describes
her adornment and her bodily beauty (*wasf*). During the week which
follows on the bridal night, the young couple are fêted as king and queen;
a threshing board set up on the threshing floor serves as a throne. During
this "royal week" various songs are sung, including yet another *wasf* on
the young couple'.

12. Cf. S. Schott, *Altägyptische Liebeslieder*, Zurich 1950², and *Ä.*
Hermann, *Altägyptische Liebesdichtung*, Wiesbaden 1959.

assumed that these songs were composed by women. A glance at the dialogues between the lovers (e.g. 1.15–17 and 2.1–3), shows at once the correctness of this argument. This also establishes that in Canticles we have not poetry of experience, but poetry of roles. While Gerleman certainly goes too far in separating even songs like 3.6–11, 4.9–11 and 4.12–5.1 from their connection with marriage, it is doubtful whether it is possible, with Würthwein, to connect all the songs primarily with marriage and with married love following on from it. Songs like 2.8–14, 3.1–5 and 8.1–4 can be connected with marriage in so far as they prepare the bridal couple, and especially the bride, for the consummation of the marriage[13], but really presuppose other contexts than this. In the end the decision will no doubt have to be looked for in the middle area between the interpretations represented by Gerleman and Würthwein. Gerleman regards Canticles as a collection of literary compositions from the early period of the monarchy, which 'is only comprehensible as the achievement of a social and cultural upper class'[14]. Würthwein does not deny that the collection must come from an upper class, but ascribes it to the wise of the late post-exilic period, who intend pedagogically to show the bridal pair the way to a full future life together[15].

3. *Date.* The occurrence of the Persian loanword *pardēs* in 4.13, and of the either Greek or Iranian loanword *'appiryôn* in 3.9 as well as the Aramaisms, which on a percentage basis are the most numerous in the Old Testament after Esther and Ecclesiastes[16], make a pre-exilic origin for Canticles impossible. To interpret these, with Gerleman, as irrelevant facts which are unimportant for the dating is to ignore a part of the evidence. The fact that apart from the heading in 1.1 the relative particle *'ᵃšer* is never used, but in its stead always the relative *še*, argues unmistakably for a late post-exilic origin of the collection in the third century B.C. If the songs were used at the banqueting table, as b. Sanhedrin 101a says, this does not prove that the individual songs

13. Cf. Würthwein, HAT I 18², p. 34.
14. BK 18, Neukirchen 1965, p. 77.
15. Op. cit., pp. 211 f.
16. Cf. the statistics in M. Wagner, *Die lexikalischen und grammatikalischen Aramaismen im alttestamentlichen Hebräisch*, BZAW 96, 1966, p. 145.

were all composed for such an occasion. The fact that the songs do not display a recognizable order on this view, but have been put together secondarily and with the use of transitions (cf. 5.9 and 6.1) warns us against assuming a uniform origin. There is the further point that the comparison with the former residence of the Israelite kings in Tirzah in 6.4 is most easily explained if 6.4–7 is dated to the early monarchical period[17]. It should be assumed then that in Canticles we have a late collection of wedding and love songs from different periods.

4. *Place of origin.* The mention of the daughters of Jerusalem in 1.5, 2.7, 3.5, 10; 5.8, 16 and 8.4, of the daughters of Zion in 3.11, together with the Solomon fiction in 3.7, 9, 11 and 8.11 argue clearly for the origin and collection of the songs in Jerusalem.

The attempts to justify theologically the canonicity of the book are based entirely on the givenness of the canon. As long as they do recognize that the subject of the book from first to last verse is the love between man and woman[18], no objection can be raised to such attempts. In fact one can say that Canticles is suited to preserve or win back for Christendom the knowledge that Eros is neither something divine nor something demonic, but has its own rightful place in human life[19]. A composition which displays no kind of prudery at all perhaps attests convincingly today that a woman's love finds its fulfilment in marriage (cf. 3.4).

§ 32   Israelite Wisdom and its Literary Types

O. Eissfeldt, *Der Maschal im Alten Testament*, BZAW 24, 1913; P. Humbert, *Recherches sur les sources égyptiennes de la littérature sapientiale d'Israël*, Neuchâtel 1929; W. Baumgartner, *Israelitische und altorientalische Weisheit*, SGV 166, 1933; id., 'Die israelitische Weisheitsliteratur', *ThR* NF 5 (1933), pp. 259 ff.; id., 'The Wisdom Literature', *OTMS*, Oxford 1951, pp. 210 ff.; J. Fichtner, *Die altorientalische Weisheit in ihrer israelitisch-jüdischen Ausprägung*, BZAW 62, 1933; W. Zimmerli, 'Zur Struktur der alttestamentlichen Weisheit', *ZAW* 51 (1933), pp. 177 ff.; A. Alt, 'Die Weisheit Salomos' [1951], *KS* II,

17. Cf. R. Gordis, pp. 23 f., and Rudolph, ad loc.
18. Budde, KHC, p. X.
19. Cf. Loretz, *BZ* NF 10, p. 41

pp. 90 ff.; *Wisdom in Israel and in the Ancient Near East*, Festschrift H. H. Rowley, ed. M. Noth and D. W. Thomas, SVT 3, 1955; G. von Rad, *Old Testament Theology*, Edinburgh and London, vol. 1, 1962, pp. 418 ff.; id., *Wisdom in Israel*, London 1972; H. Gese, *Lehre und Wirklichkeit in der alten Weisheit*, Tübingen 1958; E. G. Bauckmann, 'Die Proverbien und die Sprüche des Jesus Sirach. Eine Untersuchung zum Strutkturwandel der israelitischen Weisheitslehre', *ZAW* 72 (1960), pp. 33 ff.; G. Sauer, *Die Sprüche Agurs*, BWANT V, 4, 1963; W. M. W. Roth, *Numerical Sayings in the Old Testament*, SVT 13, 1965; C. Kayatz, *Studien zu Proverbien 1–9*, WMANT 22, 1966; W. Richter, *Recht und Ethos*, SANT 15, 1966; H. H. Schmid, *Wesen und Geschichte der Weisheit*, BZAW 101, 1966; H.-J. Hermisson, *Studien zur israelitischen Spruchweisheit*, WMANT 28, 1968; W. McKane, *Proverbs. A New Approach*, OTL, 1970; R. B. Y. Scott, 'The Study of Wisdom Literature', *Interpr* 24 (1970), pp. 20 ff.; H.-P. Müller, 'Der Begriff "Rätsel" im Alten Testament', *VT* 20 (1970), pp. 465 ff.

1. In Proverbs, Job and Ecclesiastes we find within the canon of the Old Testament an intellectual concern and a form of literature which can be traced throughout the ancient world, and which in accordance with the usage of the Old Testament is usually called Wisdom. One of its characteristics which most strikes the theologian is that it is not God and his action in history that stands at the centre but man and his conduct. If wisdom could be described a few decades ago as a striving directed at human self-assurance, and its ethics as a form of eudaemonism, a change in our evaluation of it has now come in, especially under the influence of the study of Egyptian wisdom teaching[1], which allows us more clearly to grasp its religious character. 'Wisdom thinking, questioning and teaching,' H. H. Schmid summarizes, 'is directed towards locating human behaviour in an all-embracing view of the ordering of the world'[2]. Von Rad provides a similar, though more detailed, formulation. Wisdom was 'knowing that at the bottom of things an order is at work, silently and often in a scarcely noticeable way, making for a balance of

1. Cf. H. Brunner, 'Die Weisheitsliteratur', in *Ägyptologie*, HO I, I, 2, Leiden 1952, pp. 90 ff., and the references in Schmid, op. cit., pp. 1 ff. On the problem of the date of the oldest teaching cf. W. Helck, 'Zur Frage der Entstehung der ägyptischen Literatur', *WZKM* 63/64 (1972), pp. 16 ff.

2. Op. cit., p. 21.

events. . . .In such wisdom is something of the humble—it grows through having an eye for what is given, particularly through having an eye for man's limitations'[3]. It is immediately clear that its subject is right behaviour, and that the boundaries between this and mere practical wisdom are fluid, and clear too that its concern is with the place of man in the divine ordering of the world. For early mankind, and no doubt for the average man in general, right behaviour is determined by custom and usage. The upholders of these are especially the experienced elders of the community. In the period of the monarchy there appears alongside this a literary wisdom, instruction which is given by the wise to their pupils. In the late period wisdom and knowledge of the scriptures flow together, an identification is made of the instruction of Yahweh, the law, and instructions picked up from the way of the world[4].

2. *Sayings and proverbs.* Since reality places man in constantly new situations, which, being uninterpreted and unique both challenge and alarm him, he seeks to interpret the new moment, that is the fundamental prerequisite of all understanding, from his experience, and by a short saying to claim it as something which is nevertheless familiar. In this sense the short saying, which sums up an experience concisely, is the simplest means of finding one's way about the world. As the basic form of human interpretation of the world, it is like the popular proverb in connecting experience, not with other experiences, but into a unity of a religious, or even a philosophical, picture of the world. An event is laid claim to, interpreted, but not explained. Sayings of this sort are non-literary, connected with particular occasions, and as a rule also with a specific milieu[5]. By constant use the saying is consolidated into a proverb. This, unlike the saying, is not content with laying claim to a specific situation. It surveys many of them and draws as it were the quintessence from them. In its basic form the proverb merely states something (cf. e.g.

3. *Old Testament Theology,* vol. I, p. 428.
4. Characteristic of this is the wisdom of the Book of Sirach. Cf. E. G. Bauckmann, op. cit., who however overlooks the religious nature of thought about order in the older wisdom.
5. Cf. 1 Sam. 4.20; Gen. 35.17; as border cases 1 Sam. 14.12 (a challenge in saying form) and Gen. 10.9; 1 Sam. 10.12, par. 19.24 and Isa. 28.20 (on the way to becoming a proverb).

1 Sam. 24.14; Ezek. 16.44; Prov. 20.14). It leaves the practical consequences to its listeners. But even when it does not assume the form of counsel, its tendency is didactic. It contains the concentrated life experience of the nation, formed by its old and wise men, and gives the nation its moral maxims. An experienced man may have uttered a saying to those gathered around him as a fruit of his experience of life on a concrete occasion. His companions take it up, and employ it on a similar occasion, and so do parents to their children. On each repetition it gains in strength. If it goes out of use it disappears[6].

The books of the Old Testament have only one word for the most varied forms of the wisdom saying. They speak of a *māšāl*, a word which originally means likeness or similarity[7]. Eissfeldt has shown how two branches of meaning in the use of the word can be explained from this basic sense. One moves by way of popular proverbial saying to the taunt song (cf. Num. 21.27), and literary wisdom saying (cf. Prov. 26.7, 9), and to the instruction discourse (cf. Job 27.1, 29.1); the other leads from the parable (cf. Ezek. 17.2, 20.49 (Heb. 21.5) and 24.3) to the oracle, e.g. Ezek. 17 and 24[8]. However it must be recognized with Hermisson that the material contained in the Book of Proverbs, and indeed literary or didactic wisdom as a whole, cannot simply be understood as a development of popular wisdom[8a]. The man who is an expert at the discovery of these similarities is called by the Hebrews a *ḥākām*, a 'wise man', i.e. properly, as the technical use of the adjective still shows[9], an 'expert, an experienced man'.

3. Riddles and numerical proverbs. The riddle, the *ḥîḍâ*, is also part of popular wisdom. While it appears to us as a pleasant form of entertainment, fairy tales and sagas show clearly that its original intention was less harmless. So for instance the princess poses to her deliverer a series of questions in riddle form. If he

6. Cf. A. Jolles, *Einfache Formen*, Halle 1930, Tübingen 1958², pp. 150 ff.

7. Cf. A. R. Johnson, '*māšāl*', in SVT 3, pp. 162 ff. and McKane, pp. 22 ff.

8. Cf. O. Eissfeldt, op. cit., pp. 7 ff. and p. 43.

8a. Op. cit., pp. 52 ff., and especially pp. 92 ff.

9. Cf. Jer. 10.9, Isa. 40.20, Ezek. 27.8 and Exod. 31.6.

can solve them, he may release her; for he has demonstrated that
he is of equal calibre to her. If he cannot, he loses his head. So
the riddle is properly the means by which a man with knowledge
tests whether the man questioned is of equal calibre[10].

The man of inferior calibre loses, and must pay, even if only with the
mockery which is poured out upon him. The crafty man makes use of
his superiority to trap the less shrewd man. So Samson thought to play
a trick on his Philistine bodyguard by posing them the riddle:
> 'Out of the eater came something to eat.
> Out of the strong came something sweet.'

And it was only through the treachery of the (here unnamed) wife that
the Philistines were able to answer Samson, who had found bees in the
corpse of a lion:
> 'What is sweeter than honey?
> What is stronger than a lion?'

The answer can in fact be understood as an originally independent
riddle, the solution of which is 'love'[11]. The scene ends with the saying
'If you had not ploughed with my heifer, you would not have found
out my riddle' (cf. Judg. 14.10–18). The fixed form of the *māšāl* metre
(3 + 3) makes it probable that in these riddles we already have literary
creations, which come, if not from the wise, at least from real narrators.

Wisdom and riddles are very closely connected. The wise
man can make, and solve, riddles. We find the transition from
riddle to wisdom poetry in the numerical saying, which displays
both its origin in riddles and its difference from them in the fact
that the puzzling facts, recounted and characterized by their
number, are immediately followed by an actual listing of them
(cf. e.g. Prov. 30.15 ff.)[12]. The riddle is followed by the solution
of the riddle.

4. *Ancient Near Eastern and Israelite artistic wisdom.* Sauer has demonstrated the connection of the Israelite numerical saying with the North
Canaanite literature of Ugarit. This draws our attention to a phenomenon without a knowledge of which Israelite school, or literary,
wisdom cannot be evaluated, its connection with Ancient Near Eastern
wisdom. The Aramaic proverbs of Aḥikar, found in the Jewish military

10. Cf. the story of the visit of the Queen of Sheba to Solomon, 1
Kgs. 10.1 ff.; on the literary type cf. Jolles, op. cit., pp. 126 ff.
11. Cf. O. Eissfeldt, 'Die Rätsel in Jdc 14', *ZAW* 30 (1910), pp. 132 ff.
12. Cf. G. Sauer, op. cit., pp. 64 ff. and 87 ff.; but also W. M. W. Roth,
op. cit., pp. 95 ff.

colony in Elephantine in Upper Egypt, which probably go back to an Assyrian source[13], have given evidence of the connection between Israelite or Judahite and Mesopotamian wisdom. The dependence of Prov. 22.17–23.11 on the Egyptian Instruction of Amen-em-ope, which can only be interpreted as a borrowing, has provided evidence of the connections between Israelite and Egyptian wisdom[14]. Finally the Ugaritic discoveries have given evidence of the connection between Israelite and Canaanite wisdom[15]. It is clear therefore that in this area too Israel has found in Canaan a point of contact with international intellectual culture. The mediators may be on the one hand the pre-Israelite population of the land, and on the other direct contacts, especially with Egypt.

When the Davidic and Solomonic monarchy made necessary the creation of a hierarchy of civil servants, there was a need in Israel, as in the kingdoms of the Ancient Near East, for men trained to take on such tasks and offices. The necessary training could only be provided here as elsewhere by the schools of the scribes, which in the Ancient Near East were connected with the temple or with the court[16]. In these schools, apart from the art of writing itself, knowledge of the two forms of the wisdom of experience, list knowledge and practical wisdom, was transmitted. List knowledge, demonstrably first practised by the Sumerians, which gathered together 'the names . . . of everything that in any form was available or existed', and whose task it was 'to make possible a systematic ordering of the whole world of

13. Cf. e.g. A. E. Goodman, *DOTT*, pp. 270 ff.; but also H. Donner, *ZÄS* 82 (1957), pp. 16 ff. and above, p. 204, n. 14.

14. Cf. A. Erman, *Eine ägyptische Quelle der 'Sprüche Salomos'*, SAB 1924, pp. 86 ff.; H. Gressmann, 'Die neugefundene Lehre des Amen-em-ope und die vorexilische Spruchdichtung Israels', *ZAW* 42 (1924), pp. 272 ff. Most recently Irene Grumach, *Untersuchungen zur Lebenslehre des Amenopes*, Münchner Ägyptologische Studien 23, Munich and Berlin 1974, has argued for a *Vorlage* common to both, but still Egyptian.

15. Cf. e.g. W. F. Albright, 'Some Canaanite-Phoenician Sources of Hebrew Wisdom', SVT 3, pp. 1 ff.; M. Dahood, *Proverbs and Northwest Semitic Philology* (Scripta Pontificii Instituti Biblici 113), Rome 1963.

16. Cf. S. N. Kramer, 'Die sumerische Schule', *WZ M.-Luther-Universität Halle-Wittenberg* 5 (1959), pp. 695 ff.; A. Falkenstein, 'Die babylonische Schule', *Saeculum* 4 (1953), pp. 126 ff.; H. Otten in *Kulturgeschichte des Alten Orients*, ed. H. Schmökel, Stuttgart 1961, pp. 409 f.; H. Brunner, *Altägyptische Erziehung*, Wiesbaden 1957, pp. 10 ff. and H.-J. Hermisson, op. cit., pp. 103 ff.

objects and of appearances'[17], transmitted to the future priests and officials not only a knowledge how to write correctly, but also at least a basic knowledge of what the world is like. Finally the Ancient Near East also had lists in several languages, which probably served for linguistic instruction of scribes and officials as well as for a dictionary of words and of spellings[18]. Thanks to the numerous Egyptian 'instructions' which have been preserved, we can form a particularly good picture of the practical wisdom passed on to the pupils. It was certainly the wisdom of a class, in the sense that it dealt with 'table manners, behaviour towards superiors, peers and subordinates, greeting customs, patience in the waiting room of a high official', and the advantages of the scribal profession. But at the same time it educated them to 'love of truth, distinguished bearing, modesty, mercy, good manners and tact, and to the cardinal virtue of affirmation of the world and of its suffering in trust in God, what the Egyptian writer calls "the right silence" '[19]. Israel does not indeed tell us that its kings since Solomon have learnt particularly from Egyptian wisdom, although we do hear of the famous wisdom of the 'Sons of the East', the 'wisdom of Egypt' and of their neighbours, especially of the Edomites[20] (cf. 1 Kgs. 4.30 f. (Heb. 5.10 f.); Jer. 49.7, Ob. 8), and indeed individual collections of proverbs were attributed to the North Arabian or Edomite wise men (cf. Prov. 30.1 ff. and 31.1 ff.)[21]. However, in the light of recent study, there can be no doubt that in the time of the kings Israel had many connections with Egyptian wisdom, quite apart from Prov. 22.17–23.11, and not only in the area of institutions, of the king and of his officials[22]. While this collection of proverbs

17. W. von Soden, 'Leistung und Grenze sumerischer und babylonischer Wissenschaft', in B. Landsberger and W. von Soden, *Die Eigenbegrifflichkeit der babylonischen Welt*, Darmstadt 1965, pp. 32 and 36; cf. also H. Otten, op. cit., pp. 415 f. and H. Brunner, *Altägyptische Erziehung*, pp. 93 ff.

18. von Soden, op. cit., pp. 38 ff.; Meissner, op. cit., pp. 344 ff. (with examples), and A. Alt, *KS* II, pp. 95 ff.

19. H. Brunner, *Altägyptische Erziehung*, p. 119.

20. Cf. R. H. Pfeiffer, 'Edomitic Wisdom', *ZAW* 44 (1926), pp. 13 ff.

21. Cf. also what is said below, p. 387, on the origin of the material in the Book of Job.

22. Cf. the summary in O. Kaiser, 'Israel und Ägypten', *ZMH* NF 14 (1963), pp. 11 ff.

attests a connection with the Egyptian wisdom about life, 1 Kgs. 4.32 f. (Heb. 5.12 f.), as Alt has shown, attests a connection with the nature and list wisdom of Egypt[23]. According to 1 Kgs. 4.32 f. (Heb. 5.12 f.) Solomon wrote 3,000 proverbs and 1,005 songs, which spoke of 'trees, from the cedar that is in Lebanon to the hyssop that grows out of the wall', and also of 'beasts and of birds, and of reptiles, and of fish'. It can perhaps be assumed that behind the song and proverb form of nature wisdom lies a distinctively Israelite development. We come across traces of Israelite nature wisdom in any case in the speeches of God in the Book of Job and their expansions (cf. Job 38–41)[24], and probably in the lists of the nations in Genesis, although we must be cautious in forming a view in respect of Gen. 1[25].

We must picture as transmitters of this list and life wisdom in Israel not only the scribes but also the wise, who appear in Jer. 18.18 as a special class alongside the priests and prophets (cf. also Isa. 29.14 and Jer. 8.9), and who were probably also charged with the instruction of the young, although we have no direct information on this in the Old Testament. On the analogy of the Egyptian position, however, it can be conjectured that the 'son' mentioned in the proverbs includes also the pupil of the wise man. Corresponding to the use of wisdom instructions in Egyptian and Mesopotamian schooling, we can assume of the Israelite collection of proverbs and literature influenced by wisdom that these were used and developed further in school instruction[26]. The riddle too may have had its setting in life here. When the Israelite wisdom of life is compared with the Egyptian, one striking point is the absence of a class ideal in a narrower

23. Cf. A. Alt, op. cit., but also R. B. Y. Scott, 'Solomon and the Beginnings of Wisdom in Israel', SVT 3, pp. 266 ff.

24. Cf. G. von Rad, 'Job xxxviii and Ancient Egyptian Wisdom', in *The Problem of the Hexateuch and Other Essays*, Edinburgh and London 1966, pp. 281 ff., and H. Richter, 'Die Naturweisheit des Alten Testaments im Buche Hiob', *ZAW* 70 (1958), pp. 1 ff.

25. Cf. positively S. Herrmann 'Die Naturlehre des Schöpfungsberichtes. Erwägungen zur Vorgeschichte von Genesis 1', *TLZ* 86 (1961), cols. 413 ff., and with a warning to caution W. H. Schmidt, *Die Schöpfungsgeschichte der Priesterschrift*, WMANT 17, 1967², pp. 32 ff. especially pp. 45 ff.

26. Cf. Hermisson, pp. 122 ff., and B. Gemser, HAT I, 16, 1963², p. 3.

sense²⁷. We first find it represented in Sir. 38.24–39.11. The collections of proverbs and other works which belong to the category of wisdom or are influenced by it owe their origin at the first not to their use in school instruction but to the intention of offering the upper classes trained in the wisdom school suitable reading matter²⁷ᵃ.

What is the inner connection which binds together the statements of fact, counsels and reflections, with their contrasts of the wise and the foolish, of the upright and the evil-doer, or the active and the lazy, of the prudent and the imprudent, their conduct as it concerns self-mastery, enforcing justice, a man's rank in society and the esteem he holds, agriculture and trade, their images and concepts from nature and agriculture, hunting, crafts, town and house²⁸? It is a conviction of the connection between human act and consequence, between action and result, set in force by Yahweh and limited by him (cf. e.g. Prov. 16.5–7 with 16.9, 19.21, 20.24 and 21.30 f.)²⁹. The material within this framework, which appears as mere advice how to be clever, is nevertheless to be understood from 'the conviction, deep-rooted in the whole of the ancient world, that the good is always and at the same time useful'³⁰. This is not the place to trace how far and in what way the rationalistic and anthropocentric trait which is immanent in wisdom established itself over against its religious, in the last resort irrational basis, and through the dogmatic hardening of the connection between action and consequence led to a crisis of wisdom³¹. We have preserved in the Old Testament the Books of Job and of Ecclesiastes as witnesses to this crisis, and each of them overcomes it in its own way³². On the far

27. Cf. U. Skladny, *Die ältesten Spruchsammlungen in Israel*, Göttingen 1962, pp. 93 f.; H. Brunner, *Altägyptische Erziehung*, pp. 61 f. and Hermisson, pp. 94 ff.   27a. Cf. Hermisson, pp. 122 ff. and 126 f.

28. Cf. the list in Skladny, op. cit., p. 70.

29. Cf. K. Koch, 'Gibt es ein Vergeltungsdogma im Alten Testament?', *ZTK* 52 (1955), pp. 1 ff.; H. Gese, op. cit., pp. 42 ff.; U. Skladny, op. cit., pp. 89 ff.; H. H. Schmid, op. cit., pp. 146 ff. and H. D. Preuss, 'Das Gottesbild der älteren Weisheit Israels', in *Studies in the Religion of Ancient Israel*, SVT 23, 1972, pp. 117 ff.

30. G. von Rad, *Old Testament Theology*, vol. 1, p. 435.

31. Cf. e.g. E. Würthwein, *Die Weisheit Ägyptens und das Alte Testament*, Marburg 1960, pp. 11 ff., also in *Wort und Existenz*, Göttingen 1970, pp. 207 ff. and H. H. Schmidt, op. cit., pp. 155 ff.

32. Cf. below, pp. 393 ff. and 403 ff.

side of it, and outside the limits of the canon, but with the traces
of it still unmistakable, we have the collection of proverbs of
Sirach³³. It can indeed be said with H. H. Schmid that in the
process leading to this crisis we have an absolutizing of the
language used as a description of a timelessly valid truth, in
which the original purpose of wisdom, that of preserving the
word transmitted as new, recedes into the background. It would
thus be more an alteration in the understanding of the material
transmitted than an alteration in its substance that would be
responsible for this development³⁴.

5. *Literary types*³⁵. Starting from the form-critical principle that
the simple and short form unit is older than the compound and
expanded unit, we can assume that the development of the forms
of speech in literary wisdom began with the one line popular
proverb. As a result of the popular proverb, which was not
always metrically structured, being poured into a metre (with a
preference for double threes, or in the alternative system of
double fours), the literary proverb or maxim originated. By
means of antithetic (cf. e.g. Prov. 10.2 ff.), synthetic (cf. e.g.
16.17; 17.6; 27.11), synonymous (cf. e.g. 22.10, 24; 29.17) and
comparative (cf. e.g. 25.7, 24; 27.5³⁶) *parallelismus membrorum*,
the one line proverb was then expanded into the two line proverb.
There are however also proverbs of several lines, which are not
influenced by this rule of form. Among these the comparison
especially stands out (cf. e.g. 26.11, 14, 18 f.). In content we can
distinguish between the statement proverb, giving a fact, which
we can with Ellermeier call a 'truth statement'³⁷ (cf. e.g. 17.27;
18.3) and the hortatory proverb or 'counsel' (cf. e.g. 22.28; 24.1,
21). Through new combinations, especially of the 'counsel' with
other sentences, the four-, six- or more line saying results as a
further development.

33. Cf. O. Kaiser, 'Die Begründung der Sittlichkeit im Buche Jesus
Sirach', *ZTK* 55 (1958), pp. 51 ff.
34. Cf. Schmid, op. cit., pp. 196 ff.
35. On the literary types of Job and of Ecclesiastes cf. below, pp. 391
ff. and pp. 397 ff., and on the fable, parable, similitude and allegory cf.
above, pp. 150 f.
36. With Zimmerli, op. cit., pp. 192 ff. we call this form the *ṭôḇ*
proverb.
37. Cf. below, pp. 398 f.

The counsel is connected hypotactically by a consecutive clause (statement of the aim), cf. e.g. 22.24 f.; or by a causal clause (justification), cf. e.g. 23.10 f.; 23.6 f. Or an independent conditional clause (casuistic) is attached to it (cf. e.g. 22.26 f.). A combination of the counsel with the conditional clause or with the consecutive clause is also found (cf. e.g. 23.13 f. and 24.11 f.).

The numerical proverb must be mentioned again as a separate unit (cf. e.g. Prov. 6.16–19). The wisdom hortatory sermon or instruction represents a particularly accomplished literary type, which has been investigated by Christa Kayatz and McKane[38].

Apart from a section corresponding in function to a prologue (22.17–21), this is encountered typically in 1–9. Here the hortatory sermon introduced by a conditional, which states the behaviour rejected (cf. e.g. 1.10–19), can be distinguished from that introduced by an imperative, and developing the theme with further imperatives (cf. e.g. 4.1–9). The form elements found in the sermon are apart from 'counsels' statements of aims, justifications, self-declaration including cry of greeting, reflection (with scattered questions included) and promise. Kayatz has shown that Israelite wisdom in this developed form too is dependent on Egyptian wisdom. We must also regard the 'truth statement', introduced with an account of an experience (observation), and reminding us of a reflection, such as is found in 24.30–34, as a special form. A distinctive separate place is occupied finally by the speeches of personified wisdom in 1.20–33 and 8. While 1.20–33 as an invective and hortatory discourse has clear connections with the specifically prophetic forms of speech (Zimmerli, Kayatz), the derivation of 8, a self-commendation of wisdom, and of the personification of wisdom which underlies both of them, is completely in dispute[39]. The greatest probability lies with the assumption that the Egyptian goddess of the ordering of the world, of wisdom and righteousness, Maʻat, stands in the background[40], having been assimilated by the wise of Israel.

McKane has pointed out both the common features and the differences between the teachings from Egypt and the Israelite teachings preserved in Prov. 1–9 and 22.17–24.22: while the

---

38. Kayatz, op. cit., pp. 26 ff. and McKane, op. cit., pp. 1 ff.

39. For discussion cf. H. Ringgren, *Word and Wisdom*, Lund 1947, pp. 128 ff., and R. N. Whybray, *Wisdom in Proverbs*, SBT 45, 1965, pp. 80 ff.

40. Cf. H. Donner, 'Die religionsgeschichtlichen Ursprünge von Prov. Sal. 8,22 bis 31', *ZÄS* 82 (1957), pp. 16 ff.; S. Morenz, *Egyptian Religion*, London 1973, pp. 113 ff. and C. Kayatz, op. cit., pp. 86 ff. and 138 f.

Egyptian teachings are directed at an *élite* aspiring to positions of responsibility in the state, the Israelite teachings are directed to a broader stratum, especially among the young. The teaching nearest to the Egyptian teachings in the Old Testament (Prov. 31.1–9) is very noticeably ascribed to a non-Israelite, King Lemuel of Massa. While it must be maintained that in the teaching we have an international form found in Egypt, Babylonia and Assyria, nevertheless it may be assumed that it was taken over by Solomon from Egypt in connection with the erection of a bureaucracy which followed an Egyptian model, and that it is preserved for us now in the Old Testament only in these derivative applications[41].

To determine the original context and date of the individual proverbs and of the collections of proverbs we depend apart from the formal criteria on the religious and social relationships presupposed in them. Difficulties arise from the fact that the circumstances of life of the population of the land can hardly have altered decisively in the Old Testament period, and further from the dubiousness of the assumption that secular wisdom preceded theological wisdom in date.

§ 33   The Proverbs of Solomon

Cf. the references in the preceding section, and G. Boström, *Paronomasi i den äldre hebreiska Maschallitteraturen*, LUÅ NF I, 23, 8, 1928; id., *Proverbiastudien. Die Weisheit und das fremde Weib in Spr.* 1–9, LUÅ NF I, 30, 3, 1935; G. Kuhn, *Beiträge zur Erklärung des salomonischen Spruchbuches*, BWANT III, 16, 1931; P. W. Skehan, 'A Single Editor for the Whole Book of Proverbs', *CBQ* 10 (1948), pp. 115 ff.; G. Wallis, 'Zu den Spruchsammlungen Prov. 10, 1–22, 16 und 25–29', *TLZ* 85 (1960), coll. 147 f.; U. Skladny, *Die ältesten Spruchsammlungen in Israel*, Göttingen 1962; R. N. Whybray, *Wisdom in Proverbs. The Concept of Wisdom in Proverbs 1–9*, SBT 45, 1965; id., 'Some Literary Problems in Proverbs i–ix', *VT* 16 (1966), pp. 482 ff.; J. Conrad, 'Die innere Gliederung der Proverbien', *ZAW* 79 (1967), pp. 67 ff.; O. Plöger, 'Zur Auslegung der Sentenzensammlungen des Proverbienbuches', in *Probleme biblischer Theologie*, Festschrift G. von Rad, Munich 1971, pp. 402 ff.; O. Kaiser, 'Der Mensch unter dem Schicksal', *NZST* 14 (1972), pp. 1 ff.

41. Cf. McKane, op. cit., pp. 6 ff. and 407.

Commentaries: KHC Wildeboer 1897; HK Frankenberg 1898; ICC Toy 1899; HS Wiesmann 1923; ATD Ringgren 1962 (1967²); HAT Gemser 1963²; AB Scott 1965; OTL McKane 1970.

1. The book. According to its superscription in 1.1. this book of proverbs of 31 chapters has the name *mišlê šᵉlōmô*, the Proverbs of Solomon, or in abbreviated form, *mišlê*. In the Septuagint it appears under the name *paroimiai* (*Salomōntos*), and in the Vulgate as *liber proverbiorum*. While the three books attributed to Solomon, Proverbs, Ecclesiastes and Song of Songs, stand together in the Greek and Latin Bibles, in the Hebrew tradition they have been handed down separately: Proverbs after Psalms, and before or after Job, the two other books within the Megilloth[1]. Proverbs did not attain its canonical position in Judaism without a struggle, as is shown by *b. Shabbath* 30b. It must be noted when using the Septuagint that the Greek text (1) does not include some of the proverbs given in MT, (2) has a great many proverbs which are not present in MT, and in particular (3) from 24.22 follows a different order[2].

Since Solomon is not only regarded in tradition as the typically wise king, but also as himself the author of proverbs and songs (cf. 1 Kgs. 3.4 ff., 16 ff.; 4.29 ff. (Heb. 5.9 ff.) and 10.1 ff.), it can be understood that Judaism ascribed to him the authorship of the Book of Proverbs (cf. 1.1), and had previously ascribed to him individual collections within it (cf. 10.1 and 25.1). Apart from the fact that other collections expressly state another origin in their titles (cf. 22.17; 24.23; 30.1 and 31.1), form-critical arguments and arguments from content point to differing dates of origin for the collections which are the basis of the book, and so argue against the correctness of the tradition, although the possibility must be allowed for that some individual proverbs do go back to the time of Solomon.

2. Structure. If we follow the headings, we obtain the following seven collections:

I	1–9	Proverbs of Solomon
II	10.1–22.16	Proverbs of Solomon

1. Cf. below, p. 406.

2. G's order with the Massoretic numbering is as follows: 30.1–14; 24.23–34; 30.15–33; 31.1–9; 25–29 and 31.10–31.

The analysis which follows will show that the collections II, III, V, and VII each consist of two different parts.

3. Character and age of the collections

I: The collection 1–9 contains for the most part admonitory sermons. Since these display what is by a long way the form-critically most developed literary form in the whole book[3], the collection must be regarded as the latest. Its prologue 1.1–6(7) serves now as an introduction to the whole book, and was written for the final redaction of it[4]. A post-exilic date of origin might be deduced from the subject dealt with in 2.16 ff.; 5.1–23 and 6.20–7.27, the warning against the strange woman, as well as from the personification of wisdom typical of this collection. Since however the warning against the strange woman is directed not against seduction by her to the fertility cult (Boström, Ringgren) but against ordinary adultery, and since the personification of wisdom may have taken place not under Greek but under Egyptian influence, no firm date can be deduced from either point. The dependence of the preaching of repentance by wisdom in 1.20–33 on the prophetic invective and threat saying may on the other hand argue for a post-exilic date, and the lack of legalism for an origin before the end of the third century B.C.

Whybray has attempted to solve the literary problem of 1–9 by distinguishing three layers: a book with ten paternal hortatory sermons (discourses) which stands in the international and especially Egyptian wisdom tradition, and served as a handbook for school instruction, 1.1–5; 1.8–19; 2.1, 9, 16–19; 3.1–2, 3b–10; 3.21ba, 22–24, 27–31; 4.1–5*; 4.10–12, 14–18; 4.20–26; 5.1–8, 21; 6.20–22, 24–25, 32; 7.1–3, 5, 25–27, has been assimilated to Israelite thought by means of a redaction in the period of the great prophets, in that the sayings of the teacher of wisdom were equated with those of wisdom personified, 1.20–33; 2.2–4; 2.10 f.; 3.13–18; 4.5a, 6–9; 4.13; 7.4; 8.1–21, 32–36; 9.1–6, 13–18*. To this layer was appended another from the Persian period, which emphasized the origin of wisdom from Yahweh, and the identity of wisdom and the fear of Yahweh, and so bridged the gulf

---

3. Cf. above, pp. 375 f.

4. One argument for this is that in 1.6 riddles are mentioned, and these are not found until the numerical sayings of chap. 30.

between the wisdom tradition and the Israelite tradition proper, 1.7; 1.29; 2.5–8; 3.19 f.; 8.13a; 8.35b; 8.22–31. In view of the Yahweh sayings of the older collections in the Book of Proverbs, and of the connection, suggested by Christa Kayatz, between the personification of wisdom and the Egyptian goddess Maʻat, this analysis remains open to serious doubts.

II: The Solomonic collection, 10.1–22.16, can be divided on formal grounds as well as grounds of content into a) 10.1–15.33 and b) 16.1–22.16. Characteristic of a) is the 'truth statement', of two lines, marked by antithetic parallelism, which in subject centres on the contrast between the righteous (wise) and the evildoers (fools). Apart from rare attempts at grouping by sense, simple association by catchwords predominates in half the instances. Although its educational purpose is not directed to any particular group in the population or age-group, it can be described with Skladny as an instruction upon the subject matter just mentioned[5]. Characteristic of b) apart from the two line pattern is the approximately equal share of antithetic, synthetic and synonymous parallelism, as well as a growth in the number of sentences extending beyond the one line. Here too the 'truth statement' predominates absolutely in number; but it is also possible to see an increase in the number of 'counsels' and questions. If a central theme is lacking, the proverbs about the king with their generally high valuation of the monarch, respect for the word, inclusion of the theme of law, and relative distance from the world of the farmer are arguments for their localization among the upper classes in the capital, even if on formal grounds we hesitate with Skladny to see in the collection an instruction for royal officials. The city background, which appears more strongly by contrast with collection a), the inclusion of trade and of legal problems may together with the formal difference in the proverbs be seen as an argument for a date later than a), towards the end of the period of the monarchy[6]. It must be emphasized that the religious background is common to a) and b), although it appears in different forms in the two collections: while Yahweh in a) is basically the guarantor of the moral ordering of the world, in b) he is the sovereign creator and ruler of the world[7].

III: The collection with the title 'words of the wise', 22.17–24.22, shows a formally more advanced form-critical stage than the collections II a and b, because here units of more than two lines predominate. Antithetic parallelism, with one exception, disappears completely. The relationship between 22.17–23.11 and the Teaching of Amen-em-

5. Op. cit., pp. 21 ff.
6. Op. cit., pp. 40 ff. and O. Kaiser, op. cit., pp. 12 ff.
7. Cf. Skladny, op. cit., pp. 13 ff. and 25 ff.

ope[8], consisting in selection and free re-edition of the material in the Egyptian book by an Israelite 'wise man'[9] allows us here too to distinguish between a collection a) 22.17–23.11 and b) 23.12–24.22. a) is introduced in 22.17–21 by an exhortation serving as a prologue, b) is well characterized by Hamp as paternal instruction. Both instructions may well come from the monarchical period.

IV: 24.23–34 can be seen from its title to be an appendix to III. The direct exhortation and warning of the reader or hearer in vv. 27–29 and the didactic reflection in vv. 30–34 place the section nearer to the instruction which has preceded it than to the following collection with its 'truth statements' and its relatively small proportion of counsels.

V: According to the heading in 25.1, 25–29 are a collection of Solomonic proverbs, which the men of Hezekiah, King of Judah, have put together. While the mention of the 'proverbs of Solomon' may perhaps be only a description of the literary type, the report that the collection was edited by the men (i.e. no doubt the scribes or wise men) of Hezekiah, deserves credit, since no detectable bias underlies it[10]. A closer look shows that in 25–29 too we have two collections of proverbs. a) 25–27 is roughly one quarter counsels. In the 'truth statements' similes and comparisons predominate. Parallelism is found in only a half of the proverbs, and in these the comparison predominates[11]. A fifth of the proverbs have a two line structure. Finally the collection of individual proverbs into groups by sense, and a developed association by catchwords, is characteristic of this collection. In content the pictorial and conceptual material in this collection comes predominantly from nature and the country, domestic and court life, and from trade. Accordingly Skladny sees in the collection a manual for farmers and craftsmen. Hermisson however points to the separate living patterns of these two groups, and to the incorporation of themes which are typical of wisdom. Furthermore 25.1 ff. presuppose the conditions of the court[12]. b) 28–29 contains only two-line proverbs, and with the exception of 29.17, only 'truth statements'. Antithetic parallelism predominates. Formally therefore the collection is related to IIa. Whether, with Skladny, we should describe 28–29 as an ideal for rulers in the proper

8. According to H. Brunner, *Grundzüge einer Geschichte der altägyptischen Literatur*, Darmstadt 1966, p. 101, it originated probably about the beginning of the first millennium B.C. Translation in *ANET²*, pp. 421 ff. Cf. also above, pp. 288 f.

9. Cf. W. Richter, *Recht und Ethos*, SANT 15, 1966, pp. 17 ff. and 189 f., and on the literature ibid., pp. 12 f., n. 7.

10. Cf. R. B. Y. Scott, SVT 3, pp. 272 ff. H. Cazelles, SVT 3, p. 19, thinks of a North Israelite origin for the material.

11. Cf. above, p. 375.

12. Cf. Skladny, pp. 46 ff., with Hermisson, p. 77.

sense in view of its large content of political situations, and especially of the behaviour of the king, must remain doubtful[13].

VI: The collection which occupies 30, the words of Agur, son of Jakeh, apart from the verses of the framework, which show a certain similarity to the Book of Job, consists in numerical proverbs, whose connections with the Ugaritic and Canaanite world have been demonstrated by Sauer. While the names Agur and Jakeh have been found in South Arabian inscriptions, the description of his origin ascribes him to the north Arabian tribe of Massa. We must therefore assume that at least the numerical proverbs have been taken over from countries near to Israel, and probably from the Transjordan. Some scholars however regard only 30.1–4 as sayings of Agur, and treat 5 f. or 5–9 as the answer and addition of a pious Jew, while they treat the number sayings (30.15–33) as an independent collection[14].

VII: Chap. 31 contains a) in vv. 1–9 the words of Lemuel, King of Massa, with which his mother instructed him. In content we have an instruction for a king[15] in the special form of exhortation by his mother, cf. 1.8, which has been transmitted by the son. In vv. 10–31 there follows b) an acrostic praise[16] of the virtuous wife, probably added here because of the thematic connection with v. 3.

McKane proposes a fundamentally different course in the analysis of Proverbs. He distinguishes between proverbs which are intended within the framework of the old wisdom to educate the individual for a successful and harmonious life (A), those at the centre of which stands the community rather than the individual, and which primarily describe the negative consequences of anti-social behaviour (B), and those which are clearly theological in their thinking or committed to a moral pattern dependent on Yahwistic piety (C). In B the process of the adaptation of wisdom by Israel can be seen; C, beginning before the exile, does not reach its culmination until Jesus Sirach. The collections are therefore divided up by McKane into these different groups. By their percentage proportions they show to what extent the different periods contributed to them. It turns out that chs. 28–29 have the highest percentage of proverbs belonging to group C,

13. Op. cit., pp. 57 ff.

14. Cf. e.g. Toy and McKane, ad loc. Scott finds in 30.1–9 a dialogue of a pious man with a sceptic.

15. Cf. H. Brunner, 'Die Weisheitsliteratur', in *Ägyptologie*, HO I, 2, Leiden 1952, pp. 100 ff. and below, pp. 396 f.

16. Cf. above, pp. 321 and 355 f.

chs. 10–15 the next highest, ch. 16 a rather smaller percentage, and chs. 25–27 by a long way the smallest percentage. In relation to this theory the question must be raised whether we can so far separate secular pedagogical and theological wisdom in Israel and put them in a chronological sequence[17]; and it must also be discussed whether more respect does not need to be paid to the indications of structure of the individual collections found by Skladny. Even if it is granted that in instruction larger units were necessarily formed, our task is to compare the collections of proverbs not only on the basis of their content but also on that of form.

4. *The development of the book.* The analysis of the individual collections shows that they come predominantly from the pre-exilic period, cf. II, III and V[18]. IV, VI and VII give no secure point of contact for their dating. On the other hand I is in its present form post-exilic. The same is true for the book as a whole, a knowledge of which is shown by Sirach. The development of the book is perhaps to be pictured as consisting in first III and IV being linked with II, and the resulting collection with V. V either previously or subsequently drew in VI and VII. The addition of I took place probably in connection with the final redaction of the book.

§ 34   The Book of Job

K. Budde, *Beiträge zur Kritik des Buches Hiob*, Bonn 1876; K. Kautsch, *Das sogenannte Volksbuch von Hiob und der Ursprung von Hiob Cap. 1.2. 42, 7–17*, Tübingen, Freiburg and Leipzig, 1900; L. Köhler, 'Justice in the Gate' [1931], in *Hebrew Man*, London, 1956, pp. 149 ff.; F. Baumgärtel, *Der Hiobdialog*, BWANT IV, 9, 1933; A. Alt, 'Zur Vorgeschichte des Buches Hiob', *ZAW* 55 (1937), pp. 265 ff.; E.

17. Cf. also G. von Rad, *Wisdom in Israel*, pp. 61 ff., and p. 68, n. 12.

18. Whether we can deduce from the lexical Aramaisms—using M. Wagner, *Die lexikalischen und grammatikalischen Aramaismen im alttestamentlichen Hebräisch*, BZAW 96, 1966, pp. 17 ff., I count 5 in I, 6 in IIa, 5 in IIb, 4 in IIIa, 1 in IIIb, 1 in IV, 5 (6) in V—a post-exilic redaction for the collections described above as pre-exilic, must be left an open question here. We must allow for the possible addition of single proverbs at a later date.

Würthwein, 'Gott und Mensch in Dialog und Gottesreden des Buches Hiob' [1938], in *Wort und Existenz*, Göttingen 1970, pp. 217 ff.; W. B. Stevenson, *The Poem of Job*, London 1948[2]; H. W. Hertzberg, 'Der Aufbau des Buches Hiob', in *Festschrift A. Bertholet*, Tübingen 1950, pp. 233 ff.; W. Baumgartner, 'The Wisdom Literature. III. Job', *OTMS*, Oxford 1951, pp. 216 ff.; K. Kuhl, 'Neuere Literarkritik des Buches Hiob', *ThR* NF 21 (1953), pp. 163 ff., 257 ff.; id., 'Vom Hiobbuche und seinen Problemen', *ThR* NF 22 (1954), pp. 261 ff.; C. Westermann, *Der Aufbau des Buches Hiob*, BHT 23, 1956; H. Gese, *Lehre und Wirklichkeit in der alten Weisheit*, Tübingen 1958; H. H. Rowley, 'The Book of Job and its Meaning' [1958], in *From Moses to Qumran*, London 1963, pp. 141 ff.; H. Richter, *Studien zu Hiob*, ThA 11, 1959; G. Fohrer, *Studien zum Buche Hiob*, Gütersloh 1963; A. Jepsen, *Das Buch Hiob und seine Deutung*, ATh I, 14, 1963; H. H. Schmid, *Wesen und Geschichte der Weisheit*, BZAW 101, 1966, pp. 173 ff.

Commentaries: HK Budde 1896; 1913[2]; KHC Duhm 1897; ICC Driver and Gray 1921; SAT Volz 1921[2]; EH Peters 1928; HS Szczygiel 1931; HAT Hölscher 1952[2]; ATD Weiser 1963[4]; CAT Terrien 1963; KAT[2] Fohrer 1963; AB Pope 1965; BK Horst I 1968; SC Buttenwieser 1925; König 1929; Stier 1954; Torczyner (Tur Sinai) 1957; Dhorme 1967.

1. The book. The Book of Job consists of 42 chapters. In the Hebrew Canon it is placed among the $k^e \underline{t}\hat{u}\underline{b}im$ or Writings[1], where it appears in either second or third place, but always in a group with Psalms and Proverbs, with which it is linked also by a special poetic system of accentuation[2]. In Luther's Bible and other more recent translations it stands at the beginning of the poetic books. This order goes back to the Septuagint, and is probably due to the narrative framework: the book then forms a kind of transition from the historical books to the poetic books. It is named after its hero. The German form of the name, Hiob, made familiar by Luther, goes back to the Latin rendering of the initial Hebrew aleph by an h. The Hebrew name *'iyyôb* appears to go back to a name *'a(y)ya-'ab(u)* which is widely attested in the Ancient Near East[3]. In the Rabbinic period Moses was regarded as the author, no doubt because of the

1. Cf. below, pp. 406 f.
2. Cf. R. Meyer, *Hebräische Grammatik* I, SG 763/763a/763b, Berlin 1966[3], p. 74.
3. Cf. Fohrer, *Studien*, pp. 60 f., and KAT[2] 16, pp. 71 f.

patriarchal colouring of the narrative framework. Already at this period there were some who regarded the book not as an account of real events, but as a *māšāl*, a didactic composition.

2. *Structure.* The book falls into three main sections:

I	Prologue	1.1–2.13
II	Speeches	3.1–42.6
III	Epilogue	42.7–17

The sections usually described as prologue and epilogue (1.1–2.13 and 42.7–17) form a framework for the Poem of Job proper in 3.1–42.6, from which they are distinguished already at a purely formal level by their prose form. Since the literary problems of the framework and of the speeches are different, it is better to deal with them separately.

3. *The narrative framework.* The narrative framework tells in a full style, which can be called a literary prose, of the twofold testing of the pious and upright Job in suffering, and the resulting double blessing of Yahweh. It is now generally recognized that we have here an originally independent narrative. It falls into the following episodes:

1.	1.1–5	Job's piety and good fortune.
2.	1.6–22	The first test of Job's piety.
a)	1.6–12	'The first wager in heaven'. The Satan, after questioning the disinterestedness of Job's piety, receives permission to lay hands on all his property.
b)	1.13–22	The first test. Job loses his cattle and his children, but does not rebel against Yahweh, cf. 1.21.
3.	2.1–10	The second test of Job's piety.
a)	2.1–6	'The second wager in heaven'. The Satan doubts before Yahweh whether Job will persist in his piety if he is smitten with physical illness, and is given permission to smite him, but must spare his life.
b)	2.7–10	The second test. Job is smitten with ulcers. But in spite of his wife's demand that he should forswear God, he holds fast to God, cf. 2.10.
4.	2.11–13	The visit of the three friends, Eliphaz of Teman, Bildad of Zoah and Zophar of Naamah.

5.   42.7–10   Job's justification, and his intercession for the friends.

6.   42.11–17 The visit of his relatives and friends to comfort him, and the blessedness of Job's end.

The summary itself shows that the narrative framework in its present form is not without contradictions. The visit of the relatives and friends in 42.11 clashes with that of the three friends in 2.11–13. Similarly there appears to be a disagreement between 42.10 and 42.12 ff., since 42.10 anticipates what follows, if only in summary form.

The problem of the unity of the narrative framework cannot be separated from that of the unity of the whole book. Basically three solutions have been considered: 1. In the narrative framework we have an originally independent popular prose romance, which the poet of the speeches had before him in written form, and which gave him the starting point for his own composition, so e.g. Wellhausen[4], Budde and Duhm. 2. The poet of the speeches has adapted for his own purposes a story of Job current in oral form, so that he can be regarded as the actual author of the narrative framework, so e.g. Steuernagel[5], and similarly Hölscher, Weiser and Fohrer. 3. The narrative framework has been only subsequently linked with a poem which was originally independent of it, so e.g. Pfeiffer*, Stevenson[6] and Kuhl.

To reach a decision we will begin with the epilogue. An examination of this also leads to an insight into the growth of the Job story. Alt has recognized that the ending in 42.11–17 links up not with 2.10, but with 1.21 f.[7], for it knows nothing of Job's sickness. Patient Job, robbed of his cattle and of his children, is visited by his kinsmen and acquaintances who come to console and help him. When it is considered that the figure of the Satan is first attested in Judaism in the early post-exilic period, it seems probable in view of the prehistory of the Job material sketched out below, that the scene in heaven in 1.6–12 should also be excluded from the oldest version of the narrative. It is only in the post-exilic period that the single test of endurance became a double one, and the two scenes in heaven were then inserted. The problem of the prehistory of 42.7–9 is especially difficult to answer. The concluding

4. *Jahrbücher für Deutsche Theologie* 16 (1871), p. 155.
5. *HSAT* II, Tübingen 1923⁴, p. 326.
6. Stevenson, op. cit., p. 21.
7. Fohrer, *Studien*, p. 31, takes a different view.

v. 10 anticipates vv. 12 f. We have already referred to the clash between the visit of the friends in 2.11–13, and 42.11. So it is understandable that Kuhl and others have seen in 2.11 f., and especially in 42.7 ff., a relatively loose and not very skilfully inserted bridge between the framework narrative and the poem. A comparison of 1.3 with 42.12 shows that 42.10 knows the wording of 42.12[8]. There are two main possible solutions of the problem of the earlier history of 2.11 ff. and 42.7 ff. The first is that 2.11 ff. (with an allusion to 42.11) and 42.7 ff. were formed by the author of the poem of Job to link his poem with the narrative framework, which was indispensable to him. In this case we must allow for the possibility that he knew a variant of the narrative which told of the visit of the three friends. The second solution is to assume that he already had before him the narrative framework in a form expanded by 2.11 ff. and 42.7 ff., the centre of which, the temptation of Job by his friends and God's confirmation of his faithfulness, was then replaced by his own poem[9]. It is improbable that 42.7 ff. is a new completely redactional formation because (with Pope) no sign can be seen here of a preceding rejection of the doctrine of divine retribution, of a connection between action and subsequent experience.

The old narrative framework was fixed in writing in the post-exilic period (cf. 1.6 ff. and 2.1 ff. with Zech. 3.1 ff.) in circles of a piety influenced by wisdom. Unlike the poem, it has the non-Israelite Job speak freely of Yahweh, while the poet avoids the name of Yahweh except in 38.1 and 42.7 ff., and instead speaks of El Shaddai or of Eloah[10]. Its intention is to show that suffering for which men cannot be held responsible is to be regarded as a form of testing (Budde). The location of the story in the land of Uz (1.1) points to a non-Israelite prehistory for the material. While it is usual to think of Edom as the setting in view of Gen. 36.28 and 1 Chr. 1.42 (cf. also Lam. 4.21 and Jer. 25.20), Eissfeldt has attempted to show that the mention of the sons of the East in 1.3 (cf. Gen. 10.23 and 1 Chr. 1.17) is an argument for the Jebel Druze and the cultivated land to the west of it[11]. As well as the basic subject matter, the name of the hero and the

8. Cf. Fohrer, op. cit., pp. 32 ff.
9. Cf. Gese, pp. 72 f., and Pope, pp. xiv f., but also Fohrer, pp. 33 ff.
10. 12.9 is secondary.
11. O. Eissfeldt, 'Das Alte Testament im Lichte der safatenischen Inschriften' [1954], *KS* III, 1966, p. 299.

picture of life on the frontier between cultivated land and steppe
(cf. 1.3 f.) belong to this pre-Israelite stage[12]. Whether the
elaboration and duplication of the scenes took place already at
the pre-exilic stage, and instead of the confrontation of Yahweh
and Satan another controversy took place in the court of heaven,
must remain dubious. So must the attribution of the patriarchal
milieu to the period of the composition of J and E by Fohrer,
since we may have here a measure of conscious archaizing
(Hölscher). The folk story was in any case already known to the
author of Ezek. 14.12 ff.[13]. Since the author places Job alongside
Noah and Daniel, he clearly knew of him as a man whose
patience was tried and proved, not as the man who was provoked
to challenge God in argument with the friends. 42.11 shows that
the author of the framework possibly knew J and E (cf. Gen.
24.47; 33.19), and 42.17 that he did know P (cf. Gen. 25.8 and
35.29).

4. *The speeches.* (a) ANALYSIS. The main section extending from
3.1–42.6, containing the Job poem proper, can be divided up as
follows:

I	3–27 (28)	The threefold exchange of speeches between Job and his three friends Eliphaz of Teman, Bildad of Shuah and Zophar of Naamah.
II	29–31	Job's speeches challenging God.
III	32–37	The speeches of Elihu.
IV	38.1–42.6	The theophany speech of Yahweh and Job's answer.

(b) THE LITERARY-CRITICAL PROBLEM. I. The threefold exchange
of speeches in 3–27 has been subsequently expanded by chap. 28,
a didactic poem on wisdom as inaccessible to man and known
only to God, but otherwise too is not free from additions and
confusions. A glance at the arrangement will show that the third
round of speeches has been seriously disturbed:

12. Cf. however Fohrer, *Studien*, p. 62.
13. Cf. above, p. 254; but also M. Noth, *VT* 1 (1951), p. 252.

1. 3	Job	2. 12–14	Job	3. 21	Job
4–5	Eliphaz	15	Eliphaz	22	Eliphaz
6–7	Job	16–17	Job	23–24	Job
8	Bildad	18	Bildad	25	Bildad
9–10	Job	19	Job	26–27	Job
11	Zophar	20	Zophar	—[14]	

It can immediately be seen that Zophar does not speak in the third round of speeches. A comparison of the speech of Bildad in 25.2–6 with his preceding speeches in 8.2–22 and 18.2–21 arouses the suspicion that the third speech of Bildad is only partially preserved. Since the speeches of Job in 23–24 and 26–27 show discontinuities, it is quite clear that the third round has been subsequently reworked and in the course of this partly mutilated[15]. While some see in 24 at least fragments of a speech of Job, ascribe 26 in whole or part to the speech of Bildad, and find in parts of 27 remains of the lost speech of Zophar (cf. Duhm, Hölscher and Stevenson), it is better to regard 24.1–25; 26.5–14 and 27.7–10, 13–23 (with Fohrer) as being, like 28, poems later inserted[16]. This puts us on the right track for discovering the longer additions in the first round of speeches: with Fohrer we can see in 9.5–10 a secondary hymnic declaration of the creative power of God[17] and in 12.7–11 a subsequently inserted instruction on God the creator. Against Fohrer, however, 12.12–25 is to be regarded as original. In the challenge speeches in 29–31, 30.2–8 is to be excluded as secondary (with Duhm and Fohrer).

14. This division of the speeches follows that of Fohrer, who has seen that each round of speeches is opened by a speech of Job. We need do no more than refer to the hypotheses of Volz (SAT III, 2, 1921², pp. 1 f., 24) that the poem ended with ch. 31 (cf. against this Würthwein, op. cit., pp. 4 ff. and 90 ff.) and of Baumgärtel, that the dialogue originally only contained one round of speeches, preserved in the present first round. Cf. his survey, op. cit., p. 158, and in criticism Würthwein, pp. 3 f.

15. Smaller insertions and omissions must be omitted here. For these see the commentaries, e.g. the list given in Fohrer, KAT 16, pp. 57 ff.

16. On 24–27 cf. Stier, *Das Buch Ijjob*, Munich 1954, pp. 232 f., but also Westermann, op. cit., pp. 102 ff. and p. 25. Arguments have again been produced for the original character of ch. 28 by R. Laurin, 'The Theological Structure of Job', *ZAW* 84 (1972), pp. 86 ff.

17. Cf. also Duhm *ad loc.*

II. In the Elihu speeches of 32–37 scholars today, with few exceptions[18], see an insertion by a later author, who was not satisfied with the solution of the problem offered by the Book of Job. Elihu's unprepared appearance, which after 31.35 is completely out of place, shows that they can belong neither to the original Book of Job nor to an expansion undertaken by the original author himself. Their secondary nature is already shown by the fact that 42.7 ff. make no reference at all to Elihu. They criticize both Job and his friends, and attempt to outbid the wisdom of the original speech of God, in that, on the basis of the doctrine of retribution, which the friends too hold, they present an understanding of God's dealings with suffering man as taking place in several stages to warn and instruct him[19].

III. Among the simpler, though still not easy, problems of the book is the literary criticism of the speeches of God in 38–41. In their present form the first speech in 38.2–39.30 is followed by a very short second speech in 40.2, to which Job answers in 40.4–5. To the surprise of the reader a third speech of Yahweh follows in 40.7–41.34 (Heb. 41.26), which Job answers in 42.2–6. So it seems reasonable to suggest that later insertions have led to the splitting up of what was originally a single speech of God, and a single answer of Job. A direct join of 40.8–14 with 40.2, and of 42.2–6 with 40.3–5, is demanded by the subject-matter. In the course of the rearrangement 40.6–7 (cf. 38.3) and 42.1, 3 (cf. 38.2, 4) were inserted. The insertion which was responsible for splitting up the question directed to Job and its answer, is then of course to be found in the third speech of God, which treats of Behemoth and Leviathan (40.15–41.34 [Heb. 41.26])[20]. Finally the poem on the ostrich in 39.13–18 can be recognized as an insertion, since here, as in the two other secondary poems, zoological description predominates, and the fact that God is speaking is forgotten in 39.17. The original speech of God is

18. Cf. e.g. Budde and the references in Kuhl, *ThR* NF 21, pp. 261 ff.; for the contrary view especially Westermann, pp. 107 ff.

19. Cf. Fohrer, *Studien*, pp. 87 ff.

20. Cf. however Weiser *ad loc.*; Westermann, op. cit., pp. 92 ff.; Jepsen, op. cit., pp. 22 ff. and E. Ruprecht, *VT* 21 (1970), pp. 209 ff., who argues that 41.12–34 (Heb. 4–26) is an addition, and shows it is probable that Behemoth is identical with Leviathan.

accordingly contained in 38.(1)2–39.12, 19–30; 40.(1)2, 8–14, and Job's single answer in 40.(3)4–5 and 42.2, 3b, 5–6[21].

Budde, in a warning about literary-critical treatments of the Book of Job, called to mind the old cathedrals on which many ages had worked, to restore the original plans of which would be an act of barbarism[22]. If literary-critical work finds its justification in the fact that it makes it possible to discover the original intention of the author of Job, Budde's objection reminds us that the task of the exegete is not finished before he obtains an insight into the intentions of the redactor too. We must acknowledge in the man or men who were responsible for the insertion of the didactic and hymnic sections a well-intentioned purpose of pious instruction, and of evoking a meditative discursiveness.

(c) LITERARY TYPE, STRUCTURE AND PURPOSE. The Book of Job is neither a systematic treatment of the problem of innocent suffering, nor an accidental arrangement of a series of sections with no internal consistency although dealing with a common basic theme. If its structure is to be recognized and its literary type determined, both the situation presupposed and the forms of speech employed and the content must be borne in mind. Analyses based on form only or on content only lead necessarily to a one-sided view. If it is described as a didactic poem, little advance is made in understanding through this, although the book does contain instruction, albeit in a special form, and with special content. If we start from the bare fact of the changes of speaker, and then speak of a dialogue, or even of a drama, we are not much better off. The fact observed by Köhler that the book consists partly of speeches in a dispute becomes misleading when it is made an absolute by H. Richter, although a whole series of his observations are valuable[23]. With Westermann we

21. Cf. Würthwein, op. cit., pp. 278 ff.; Fohrer, op. cit., pp. 112 ff., who however in 39.13–18 only excludes vv. 15 and 17.

22. HK II, 1, 1913², p. III.

23. Cf. H. Richter, *Studien zu Hiob*, p. 17: 'The book of Job has a legal dispute as its content, which is begun, carried through and ended in the form of a legal process'. And p. 131: 'the basis which carries the whole of the drama of Job is the literary types of legal practice. Everything that is of importance for the course of the drama is expressed within these literary types.' He finds, corresponding to the three sequences

must hold firmly to the fact that the friends of Job come to him neither 'to discuss with him, nor to hold a disputation with him', but to comfort him[24]. At the beginning stands the lament of Job in 3; it is only when it becomes plain that he will not accept the grounds for consolation offered by the friends that the dialogue of comfort turns into a dispute. The fact that this gains increasingly in acerbity, and finally issues in Job's challenge to God to a legal dispute, can only be understood from the content, and so from the purpose of the author.

While the characters of the friends are clearly enough distinguished, with Eliphaz portrayed as the worthy man with experience of life, appealing to revelations of his own, giving up his reserve only in the course of the dialogue, Bildad as the Wisdom traditionalist, and Zophar as a passionate man 'full of worldly wisdom and of commonplaces'[25], they only indirectly provide a clue to the understanding of the structure, in that they allow us to observe the intensification of the dialogue which results from Job's rejection of their admonitions. A further aid of a formal nature is Westermann's observation that the friends still expect a return of Job to God in the first sequence of speeches, and encourage him to this, while exhortation ceases entirely in the second sequence, only to return in the third, where however it is felt by Job to be a form of mockery[26].

By way of Eliphaz' attempt at consolation, which is unacceptable to Job, that Job should understand his suffering as the consequence of creaturely, unconscious guilt, and so turn and repent (4–5), Job's lament in 3 grows into reproach against God in 6–7, and, by way of the rejections in 9–10 and 12–14 of the speeches of Bildad in 8 and of Zophar in 11, into an accusation against God. So the friends see no ground left for exhortation, but proceed to accuse Job, and the tone gets sharper from speech to speech, and Job's despair increases, so that he appeals to God against God (19.25 ff.). The reader is in this way prepared, after the hypothetical request in 13.18 ff., for the challenge to God to a legal contest in 31.25–37, following directly on the disputation. The fundamental questioning of the position of the friends in 21 leads to more pointed exhortation by Eliphaz and Bildad in 22 and 25, in which Eliphaz holds out before Job a list of his sins in the manner of an old-fashioned 'guide for penitents.' This strengthens Job's wish for

of speeches, a progression from the pre-trial reconciliation procedure by way of a secular trial to the process of the judgement of God.

24. Op. cit., p. 4; cf. pp. 9 ff.
25. Budde, op. cit., p. xxi.
26. Op. cit., p. 17.

a direct confrontation with God (cf. 23.3 ff.). From the great lament in which he contrasts the past and the present in 29 f., he proceeds to the oath of purification as a summary of his asseverations of innocence, at the end of which stands his challenge to God. This is necessarily followed by God's answer.

If consideration is given to the liveliness of a disputation, to the passionate nature of a lament, and finally to the fact that a distinction must be made between the original and the transferred use of forms, and between setting in life and setting in the speeches and the book (Fohrer[27]), the progression of ideas and the function of the individual passages can be recognized, without doing violence to them. It remains the particular characteristic of this book that its nature is determined by the lament, by wisdom exhortations, by dispute and law court speeches, but also by the hymn[28].

The dispute between Job and his friends derives its passionate nature on both sides from the fact that each party to it questions the self-understanding of the other[29]. In the friends we meet the representatives of a dogmatic understanding of human existence, characterized by the unshakeable conviction that there is a connection guaranteed by God between action and result, between deed and consequence (cf. 4.8 f., 8.20). While we may remember that in wisdom right action refers properly not to the self-mastery of man, but to his place in the divine order of

27. KAT, p. 52.

28. Cf. the tables in Fohrer, op. cit., pp. 51 f.

29. The following presentation owes its essentials to the work by Würthwein mentioned above, which after thirty years has still not been superseded. On the theological problem of the book cf. apart from the bibliography above, A. Weiser, 'Das Problem der sittlichen Weltordnung im Buche Hiob' [1923], in *Glaube und Geschichte im Alten Testament und andere ausgewählte Schriften*, Göttingen 1961, pp. 9 ff.; J. Pedersen, *Israel. Its Life and Culture* I–II, London and Copenhagen 1926 (rev. 1959), pp. 363 ff.; J. Hempel, 'Das theologische Problem des Hiob' [1929], *Apoxysmata*, BZAW 81, 1961, pp. 114 ff.; G. von Rad, *Old Testament Theology* I, Edinburgh and London 1962, pp. 408 ff.; H. Richter, 'Erwägungen zum Hiobproblem', *EvTh* 18 (1958), pp. 302 ff.; G. Fohrer, 'Das Hiobproblem und seine Lösung', *WZ Halle* 12 (1963), pp. 249 ff.; O. Kaiser, 'Dike und Sedaqa', *NZST* 7 (1965), pp. 251 ff. and id., 'Leid und Gott. Ein Beitrag zur Theologie des Buches Hiob', in *Sichtbare Kirche*, Festschrift H. Laag, Gütersloh 1973, pp. 13 ff.

creation[30], here in any case there is an unmistakable eudaemonistic undertone centring on men and not on God (cf. 22.2–4). When there is a gulf between action and result, there remains only the choice whether to make man or God responsible for it. Since if the latter is chosen the whole structure of teaching and life collapses, the friends deduce Job's guilt from his fate. As 29.12–20 show, Job originally lived by the same presuppositions. It was only when in the grip of suffering which is inevitably ascribed by him as an Israelite to God that the equation is broken for him, since he is conscious that he is innocent. Accordingly with the same consistency with which his friends accuse him, he must now in his turn accuse God of injustice[31]. To give in to the friends would be for him a denial of reality in favour of a theory, and so amount to false witness to God (cf. 21.5 ff.; 12.12 ff. and 13.1 ff.)[32]. God's dealings with him, as with the world generally, seem to Job not just but arbitrary. Since however he too agrees that God must be just, he on his side can only appeal to God, and so at the same time against God. An overwhelming and almighty God thus becomes the only refuge of suffering and despairing man. The speech of God does indeed refer, as Duhm and others suggest, to a secret of suffering analogous to the secret of creation. How this could be understood is shown by the narrative framework. But since the speech solves no intellectual puzzles, but only poses new ones, its questions are to be understood as intentional: they get the proportions right, and make the man who rebels against God humble. Job's assertion of the irrationality of God is confirmed, but Job is at the same time led to draw the practical consequences of his recognition of this. The man who questions God must recognize that he is always the man questioned by God[33]. It is in the encounter with God himself that this change of outlook is accomplished (42.5 f.)[34]. It is therefore understandable that in

30. Cf. Gese, op. cit., pp. 7 ff. and 33 ff.
31. Cf. Würthwein, pp. 278 f., and F. Stier, op. cit., p. 230.
32. Cf. also Westermann, op. cit., p. 73.
33. Cf. Würthwein, pp. 284 ff.
34. Cf. Stier, op. cit., p. 251: 'There may be those who have experienced this, who understand what these words mean. But one who has not this experience, will indeed ultimately, as the only scholarly procedure, have to give up searching around for words which only paraphrase it, and stop acting as if he knew how to express the inexpressible'.

view of this ending Job is nowadays described as a book of life
rather than as a book of instruction[35].

(d) ORIGIN AND DATE. After what has been said it is clear that
the author himself has undergone a schooling in wisdom, and
then, on the basis of his own experience of life, broken with it.
Since the poem with its assumption of Job's innocent suffering
and presentation of his breakthrough to a truly unselfseeking
piety[36] presupposes the narrative framework, it too cannot be
pre-exilic[37]. Vocabulary and Aramaisms point to a post-exilic
date. The *terminus ad quem* is fixed at about 200 B.C. by Sir. 49.9.
Since the composition gives no more exact indications of date,
this must be left as between the fifth and the third centuries. In
spite of its knowledge of the circumstances of life in Egypt,
Palestine is most probable place of origin.

§ 35   Ecclesiastes (Qoheleth)

K. Galling, 'Kohelet-Studien', *ZAW* 50 (1932), pp. 276 ff.; id., 'Stand
und Aufgabe der Kohelet-Forschung', *ThR* NF 6 (1934), pp. 355 ff.;
W. Zimmerli, 'Zur Struktur der alttestamentlichen Weisheit', *ZAW* 51
(1933), pp. 177 ff.; id., *Die Weisheit des Predigers Salomo*, Berlin 1936;
W. Baumgartner, 'The Wisdom Literature. IV. Ecclesiastes', *OTMS*,
Oxford 1951, pp. 221 ff.; R. Gordis, *Koheleth. The Man and His World*,
New York, 1955²; M. Dahood, 'Qoheleth and Recent Discoveries',
Bib 39 (1958), pp. 302 ff.; H. Gese, 'Die Krisis der Weisheit bei
Koheleth', in *Les sagesses du Proche-Orient Ancien*, Paris 1963, pp.
139 ff.; R. Kroeber, *Der Prediger, hebräisch und deutsch*, Schriften und
Quellen der Alten Welt 13, Berlin 1963; O. Loretz, *Qohelet und der
Alte Orient*, Freiburg, Basel and Vienna, 1964; H. H. Schmid, *Wesen
und Geschichte der Weisheit*, BZAW 101, 1966, pp. 186 ff.; F. Ellermeier,
Qohelet I, 1. Untersuchungen zum Buche Qohelet, and I, 2 Herzberg/
Harz 1967, 1970²; M. Hengel, *Judaism and Hellenism*, London 1974,
pp. 115 ff.
  Commentaries: BC Delitzsch 1875; KeH Nowack 1883; HK Sieg-
fried 1898; KHC Wildeboer 1898; ICC Barton 1908; EtBi Podechard

35. Cf. A. Weiser, ATD 13⁴, pp. 9 ff., and Terrien, op. cit., p. 48.
36. Cf. also 5.4 and 8.4.
37. Terrien's dating (op. cit., pp. 23 f.) in about 575 B.C. is scarcely
tenable.

1912; SAT Volz 1922²; HS Allgeier 1925; KAT¹ Hertzberg 1932; HAT Galling 1940, 1969²; ATD Zimmerli 1962 (1967²); KAT² Hertzberg 1963; AB Scott 1965; SC Zapletal 1911².

1. The book and its author. Ecclesiastes contains twelve chapters. In the Hebrew canon it is placed among the *kᵉṯûḇîm* or writings, more precisely among the five Megilloth or festival rolls¹, since the book was read in the Synagogue on the Feast of Tabernacles. Depending on whether the Megilloth are arranged by their supposed date or by the order of the feasts, the manuscripts and printed editions put it either in third or in fourth place. The Hebrew name of the book (*qoheleṯ*) goes back to the statement about the author in 1.1 (cf. 1.2, 12; 7.27 and 12.8 f.). It probably means 'the collector', 'the leader of the congregation', and the strange feminine form is to be understood on the analogy of *sōpereṯ* (Ezra 2.55; Neh. 7.57), 'writer', and *poḵereṯ haṣṣᵉḇāyîm* (Ezra 2.57, Neh. 7.59), 'he who has to do with gazelles' (?) as giving the title of an office². The Septuagint rendered it by *ekklēsiastēs*, which Jerome translated *concionator*. Following him Luther translated it as 'the Preacher'. The title in 1.1 ascribes the book to the preacher, the son of David, who was (or, to the) king in Jerusalem (cf. also 1.12) whom the tradition in spite of 1.16 (?) identifies with Solomon. Apart from grounds of language, style and content, 12.9 in particular shows that the assumption that Solomon was the author is wrong. Here Qoheleth is described as a wise man and an instructor of the people. His reflections show him to be a member of the upper classes, from whom his code of behaviour derives. Its quiet detachment is an argument for the conjecture that we must see in it the fruit of a long life. The identification with Solomon, which depends upon 1 Kgs. 3.16 ff.; 4.29 ff. (Heb. 5.9 ff.); 10.1 ff., was perhaps deliberately carried out in 1.12 ff. because of the fiction, influenced by the Egyptian 'royal instructions', of issuing wisdom teaching as the king's teaching³ in 1.12 ff. Then 1.12 with its 'I have been king' is explained from the Egyptian stylistic form of placing the

1. Cf. below, p. 406.
2. Cf. H. Bauer, *ZAW* 48 (1930), p. 80; but also E. Ullendorff, 'The Meaning of *qhlt*', *VT* 12 (1962), p. 215.
3. Cf. H. Brunner, 'Die Weisheitsliteratur', in *Ägyptologie*, HO I, 2, Leiden 1952, pp. 100 ff.

teaching in the mouth of the dying ruler as a sort of last testa-ment[4]. The fictitious royal authorship has had no influence upon the content beyond ch. 2. 4.13 ff., 7.19, 8.2 ff., and 10.16 ff. are clearly formulated from the point of view of the king's subject, not of the king.

2. *Composition and literary type.* Thilo was the last scholar to attempt to demonstrate a unity of theme and a continuous pattern of ideas[5], and more recent scholarship very generally agrees with Delitzsch's view: 'All attempts to show, in the whole, not only oneness of spirit, but also a genetic progress, an all-embracing plan, and an organic connection, have hitherto failed, and must fail'[6]. Various attempts have been made in disregard of the literary and conceptual character of the book to obtain an organic original form with a continuous sequence of ideas. Bickell, for instance, conjectured that the original order of the pages had been altered by mistake[7]. At the same time lacunae had developed and additions had been inserted. Siegfried on the other hand attempted to explain the facts by means of a com-plicated division into sources in which he contrasted a primary Q^1 with redactors Q^2-Q^5. He believed that it was possible to distinguish clearly the intellectual outlooks of Q^1-Q^4, while he used Q^5 to refer to a multitude of glossators building on the basis of general proverbial wisdom. The 'disorder' which had so originated was arranged by the redactor R^1 into a book, to which two appendices were subsequently added, and the final words (12.13 f.) inserted by R^2.

In contrast to these and similar attempts at a solution it has become the general view since Galling's *Kohelet-Studien* of 1932 that the book is a collection of aphoristic wisdom teaching at the basis of which is not a supposedly continuous sequence of thought, but the individual proverb of two or more lines. The

4. Cf. K. Galling, *ZAW* 50 (1932), pp. 298. H. L. Ginsberg, *Studies in Kōheleth*, New York 1950, pp. 12 ff., assumes in 1.12 an original *mōlēk*, owner, while W. F. Albright, 'Some Canaanite-Phoenician Sources of Hebrew Wisdom', in SVT 3, 1955, p. 15, note 2, thinks of a Phoenician **mallāk*, counsellor.

5. M. Thilo, *Der Prediger Salomo*, Bonn, 1923.

6. Franz Delitzsch, *Commentary on the Song of Songs and Ecclesiastes*, Edinburgh 1877, p. 188.

7. G. Bickell, *Der Prediger über den Wert des Daseins*, Innsbruck 1884.

supposed tensions in content, which gave rise to the literary-critical theories, go back, apart from a very few later additions, to the mind of the thinker Qoheleth, who in a characteristically fragmentary manner argues against the wisdom of the schools, under whose influence he stood at first, and the inadequate nature of which his own experience of the world and of life has revealed to him. Scholars hold differing views on the limits of the original units, since obviously the subjective feelings of the exegete cannot be completely excluded. Hertzberg distinguishes twelve sections basically identical with the chapters, which he further divides up into sub-sections, so that in practice he obtains thirty-four units, while Galling has twenty-seven series of sayings (thirty-seven in his first edition) and Zimmerli thirty-one[8]. Zimmerli, with the development from the single-line rule of experience of the older collections of proverbs to the broad sermon-like exhortation of the latest collection in the book of Proverbs in mind, has shown that as well as the one-line statement proverb (cf. e.g. 1.15 and 18), the comparative *ṭôḇ*-sayings ('better is A than B') (cf. e.g. 9.4b), the numerous negative exhortation sayings expanded by reasons, with direct address in the second person (cf. e.g. 10.20), the first person narrative emphasizing personal experience is frequently found (cf. e.g. 1.12 ff., 2.1 ff.). He recognized as equally characteristic of the style of Ecclesiastes the rhetorical question, usually expecting a negative answer (cf. e.g. 1.3; 2.15, 22; 6.12). These different form elements are linked up to create larger speech units, which can best be described as prose interspersed with proverbs. While it is possible to find series of sentences only held together by external associations, as in the case of 4.7–12 and 4.13–16, in other cases, as in 1.12–2.26, in spite of clearly recognizable smaller independent sections, a comprehensive pattern of ideas is not lacking. The smoothness of the transitions is responsible for the varying delimitations of the units by scholars.

Ellermeier, carrying previous work further, has attempted to achieve a more precise definition of the units of speech. In the first place he has brought more specialization to the use of the term 'maxim', which has become established since Galling, by establishing that the maxim is a generalizing single sentence of easily remembered form, which is the equivalent in literary form

8. Cf. the survey in tabular form in Ellermeier, op. cit., pp. 131 ff.

of the popular proverb. The statement proverb he calls a 'truth saying', and the proverb of exhortation, a 'counsel' (cf. e.g. 5.1–12, Heb. 4.17–5.11). He calls the larger units of speech (appropriately from the point of view of their contents) reflections, and differentiates them into 'unitary critical', 'critical broken', and 'critical reverse broken' reflections.

In the 'unitary critical reflection' the sequence of ideas starts from a negative, and is accordingly a consistent expression of criticism of an optimistic understanding of existence (cf. e.g. 3.16–22 and 6.1–6). The 'critical broken reflection', on the other hand, starts from a positive or neutral point of view, only to move on to criticism (cf. e.g. 3.1–15 and 4.13–16). In the 'critical reverse broken reflection' the thought begins with a negative, and leads on to something of relative value, without giving up the basic reservation (cf. e.g. 4.4–6 and 5.13–20, Heb. 5.12–19)[9]. There is no doubt that Ellermeier has laid the basis for a more nuanced treatment of the 'reflections', and for a more rigorous definition of them[10].

Concerning subsequent redactional work on the book, there is relatively general agreement that the superscription in 1.1 and the epilogue, at least 12.9–14, cannot come from the author of the wisdom teaching. The biographical information in 12.9 f. gives clear enough evidence of our entitlement to separate off the epilogue. In 12.12–14 the hand of a further redactor is generally recognized, in my view correctly, who both criticizes the book from an orthodox point of view, and reinterprets it.

Loretz and Ellermeier see in 1.2 f. and 12.8 a summary of the whole work by the editor, to whom in consequence 7.27 is also ascribed. While Loretz sees the original beginning of the book in 1.12, before which 1.4–8 and 1.9–11 were put by the editor, Ellermeier believes that we can only understand the present state of chapter 1 on the assumption that R[1], who is responsible for 1.2 f. and 12.8–11, still did not have a completed book roll before him, and that the arrangement of the units must be attributed to him[11]. He consequently ascribes 1.1b and 12.12–14 to R[2], who used the fiction of Solomonic authorship, and an orthodox ending, to preserve the book for use in Jewish worship.

9. Ibid., pp. 88 ff.
10. With the use of his form criteria he obtains forty-three independent units.
11. Cf. also Hertzberg, KAT[2], p. 42.

11.9b is now almost universally treated as an addition, while the verses 2.26, 3.17*, 7.26, 8.5, 8.12–13a, which are treated by all or most recent scholars as secondary, are generally regarded as a corollary of Qoheleth's own thought[12].

If we leave out of consideration the reflections and series of maxims, only the following division can confidently be established:

I   1.1   Heading
II   1.2–12.8   Wisdom instruction
III   12.9–14   Epilogue[13]

3. Language. Of all the books of the Old Testament the Book of Ecclesiastes is the one fullest of Aramaisms apart from Esther[14].

So it is at least understandable that, following Burkitt, Zimmermann and Ginsberg put forward the view that the book was originally written in Aramaic and subsequently translated into Hebrew[15]. The fact that a Hebrew fragment of a Qoheleth roll has been found in Cave 4 at Qumran, dating from about the middle of the second century B.C., is not favourable to this hypothesis[16]. It remains to be seen whether Dahood's thesis of Phoenician influence will win acceptance[17]. Particularly noticeable in the vocabulary are a whole series of abstract formations like *yiṭrôn*, profit, *kišrôn*, profit, *ḥešbôn*, reckoning, *raʿyôn*, striving,

12. Ellermeier, according to his table on pp. 131 ff., excludes as secondary 3.17aβγ, 18aα; 5.7a (Heb. 5.6a); 6.2aβ; 8.12b–13; 9.3bα; 11.9b; 11.10b and 12.1a.

13. The division proposed by H. Graetz, *Kohelet oder der salomonische Prediger*, Leipzig 1871, may be given here as a teaching aid, if accompanied by the hesitation which he himself shared: (i) 1–2 introduction, (ii) 3–9 dialectical debate, and (iii) 10–12 application.

14. Cf. M. Wagner, *Die lexikalischen und grammatikalischen Aramaismen im alttestamentlichen Hebräisch*, BZAW 96, 1966, p. 145.

15. Cf. the literature in R. Gordis, op. cit., p. 364, n. 12, and for the discussion pp. 399 and 364 f., n. 13 ff.

16. Cf. J. Muilenburg, 'A Qoheleth Scroll from Qumran', *BASOR* 135 (1954), pp. 20 ff., F. M. Cross, *The Ancient Library of Qumrân and Modern Biblical Studies*, London 1958, pp. 121 f., and M. Baillet, J. T. Milik and R. de Vaux, *Les 'petites grottes' de Qumrân*, DJD 3, Oxford 1962, pp. 75 ff., where further fragments from 2Q are published, which are ascribed to the second half of the first century B.C.

17. Cf. most recently M. Dahood, *Bib* 39 (1959), p. 302 ff., the positive reaction in Kroeber, op. cit. p. 46, and the negative one in Gordis, pp. 399 f. and 402 f.

r^e'ût, longing, *siḵlûṯ*, folly and *hôlēlôṯ*, folly, which are key words for the thought of Qoheleth. In explanation of these the influence of Greek philosophy or of Greek thought should not be assumed, but rather that of ordinary colloquial Aramaic, on the example of which these words have been formed[18]. Clearly the author of the wisdom sayings normally used Aramaic. In syntax the disappearance of the imperfect consecutive[19], the growth of participial constructions, the reduced and irregular use of the article, and the growth in use of the relative particle *še*, are striking developments.

In no other book of the Old Testament is the language so far along the road from classical to Mishnaic Hebrew as in Qoheleth[20].

4. Date. The occurrence of the Persian loan words *pardēs*, 'park', in 2.5 and *piṯgām*, 'decree', in 8.11 gives the Persian period as a *terminus non ante*. The discoveries from 4Q, with their indications of a further development, make the third century B.C. a *terminus ad quem*, even if we must be sceptical about Sirach's familiarity with Qoheleth[21]. The supposed historical allusions which have been found in 4.13 ff., 9.13 ff. and 10.16 f. are in fact stock illustrations of wisdom (Galling) and accordingly can contribute nothing towards the dating[22]. The evidence of the language and the intellectual outlook of Ecclesiastes argue for an origin in the third century B.C. In support of this we may adduce, if not a direct influence of Greek philosophy upon the thought of Ecclesiastes, at least the generally solvent effect on Judaism of the spirit of Hellenism[23], as well as the fact that

18. Cf. Kroeber, pp. 41 ff. and Gordis, pp. 59 ff.

19. Only found in 1.17 and 4.1,7.

20. Cf. R. Meyer, *Hebräische Grammatik I*, Berlin 1966[3], pp. 31 f.

21. Cf. the discussion in Gordis, pp. 46 ff.

22. K. D. Schunck, 'Drei Seleukiden im Buche Kohelet?', *VT* 9 (1959), pp. 192 ff. has given what is up to now the last historicizing interpretation. F. Dornseiff, 'Das Buch Prediger', *ZDMG* 89 (1935), pp. 243 ff. should be mentioned as a curiosity. He takes together 9.14 f. and 7.19, and connects them with Miltiades, the ten Athenian *strategoi* and even with the battle of Marathon (p. 248).

23. The thesis of Greek influence was fully worked out by H. Ranston, *Ecclesiastes and the Early Greek Wisdom Literature*, London 1925. In criticism cf. Gordis, pp. 51 ff. and especially pp. 55 f., but also O. Loretz, op. cit., pp. 45 ff., especially pp. 53 f.

Ecclesiastes itself[24] shows no connection with the legalism of Sirach or with the intellectual developments of the Maccabaean period.

5. *Place of origin.* The place of origin is more difficult to determine than the date. Three suggestions in particular have been discussed recently by scholars. According to the first, the book originated in an Egyptian (more exactly Alexandrian) milieu[25], according to the second in Jerusalem or at least in Palestine, and according to the third in Phoenicia[26]. In favour of an Egyptian or Alexandrian origin, appeal has been made to 1.12 ff.; 4.13–16; 8.2 f., 10 and 10.16 f. Since even on the historicizing interpretation of 4.13–16 and 10.16 f., which has been rejected above, we can strictly demonstrate only a knowledge of Ptolemaic history, not an origin in Egypt, there remain only 1.12 ff. and 8.2 f. and 10. These in turn can be better understood as evidence of Egyptian influence upon Ecclesiastes[27], since the book elsewhere presupposes a Palestinian situation, as Hertzberg has demonstrated at least for 11.3–12.2 and 10.8[28]. If the linguistic influences regarded as Phoenician are not to be ascribed to a late convergence of the language of Phoenicia and of Canaan[29], it could be suggested that at this period 'an origin of the book of Ecclesiastes among Jewish circles in Phoenicia practically amounted to composition of it in Palestine'[30].

Since no conclusions about the place of origin can be drawn from the fiction of the king as author in 1.12 ff., the assumption of a specifically Jerusalem origin remains a probable hypothesis but no more.

---

24. 12.12 ff. are here left out of consideration.

25. So P. Kleinert, 'Sind im Buche Kohelet ausserhebräische Einflüsse anzuerkennen?', *ThStKr* 56 (1883), pp. 779 f. and P. Humbert, *Recherches sur les sources égyptiennes de la littérature sapientiale d'Israel*, Neuchâtel 1929, p. 113.

26. So M. Dahood, 'Canaanite-Phoenician Influence in Qoheleth', *Bib* 33 (1952), p. 34; W. F. Albright, SVT 3, 1955, p. 15.

27. Loretz, pp. 57 ff., regards the assumption of Egyptian influence as unfounded even here.

28. H. W. Hertzberg, 'Palästinische Bezüge im Buche Kohelet', *ZDPV* 73 (1957), pp. 113 ff.; cf. now also E. F. F. Bishop, 'A Pessimist in Palestine (B.C.)', *PEQ* 100 (1968), pp. 33 ff.

29. So Gordis, pp. 399 f.   30. Loretz, p. 43.

6. Theology. Ecclesiastes has frequently been described as a pessimist or sceptic[31]. If the second description is taken in its literal sense it can be justified, as it is by Kroeber; for it means a mental attitude 'of wise sobriety on the basis of a steady gaze'[32]. This also brings in the new approach, found in the Old Testament for the first and only time in Ecclesiastes, of knowledge on the basis of observation, which leads to the distinctive distancing of Ecclesiastes from the traditional wisdom, which has become academically petrified, and to a strangely detached-seeming approach to the world, although Ecclesiastes' own confessions are sufficient to show that he has not fought his way through to his final insight without pain and disappointment (cf. 2.17 ff.). If we speak even in this modified sense of his scepticism, we must realize that for him the reality of God himself, however much this God is placed at a distance (cf. 5.2, Heb. 5.1), remained unshakeably firm. God is however for him not the God who is encountered in the leading of his people in history[33], but the creator (cf. 3.11; 7.29). Here he stands fully within the individualistic tradition of wisdom. Gese has correctly emphasized that ambiguity and duality can only be avoided in a theological interpretation of the book if it begins with a structural analysis of his thought[34]. As a matter of method we must start from the old wisdom, for it was within the late tradition of this that Ecclesiastes at first attempted to understand the world of men (cf. 1.13 ff.), and he did not dispute its relative value even later (cf. 2.12b ff., 7.11 f., 19 f.; 9.13 ff.), although he had to recognize

31. Cf. e.g. J. Pedersen, 'Scepticisme israélite', *RHPhR* 10 (1930), pp. 317 ff.; R. H. Pfeiffer, 'The Peculiar Scepticism of Ecclesiastes', *JBL* 53 (1934), pp. 100 ff.; A. Lauha, 'Die Krise des religiösen Glaubens bei Kohelet', in SVT 3, 1955, pp. 183 ff.   32. P. 27.

33. The avoidance of the name of Yahweh and the consistently general talk of God shows this.

34. H. Gese, op. cit., pp. 139 ff. On the theological problem cf. further K. Galling, *Die Krise der Aufklärung in Israel*, Mainzer Universitätsreden 19, Mainz 1952; id., 'Das Rätsel der Zeit im Urteil Kohelets (Koh 3,1–15)', *ZTK* 58 (1961), pp. 1 ff.; E. Würthwein, *Die Weisheit Ägyptens und das Alte Testament*, Marburg 1960; W. Zimmerli, 'Ort und Grenze der Weisheit im Rahmen der alttestamentlichen Theologie', in *Les sagesses du Proche Orient Ancien*, Paris, 1963, pp. 121 ff.; O. Kaiser, 'Dike und Sedaqa', *NZST* 7 (1965), pp. 251 ff.; id., 'Der Mensch unter dem Schicksal', *NZST* 14 (1972), pp. 1 ff., as well as the bibliography given at the head of the paragraph.

that God has given man the desire for wisdom (cf. 3.11), but not
the power to attain it (cf. 7.23 f., (7.1); 8.16 f.). Only from this
starting point, which has of course to be treated as relative and
not absolute, can it be understood that Ecclesiastes does nevertheless impart counsel. While the older Israelite wisdom also
felt a reserve in the last resort towards man's capacity to order
his fate responsibly[35], nevertheless within this framework it
presupposed the reality of the connection between the actions
and destiny of a man. This position became almost autonomous
especially in the post-exilic period, and led necessarily to a crisis
in wisdom such as we find in Ecclesiastes as well as in Job[36],
since the belief in a moral ordering of the world, based upon a
postulate of practical good sense, could not be maintained
empirically or, what in the end amounts to the same thing, as an
unshakeably valid rule (cf. 7.15; 8.10, 11 ff.)[37]. Wisdom nevertheless gives man an advantage over fools (cf. 2.12b ff.), but not
security. Like the fool, the wise man also is subject to death (cf.
2.15 f.). The fate assigned to man by God, which cannot be
comprehended by man (cf. 3.1 ff.; 2.24 ff.; 8.6–8; 9.2) evades
man's striving after security, and leads him, once it is recognized
as such, to the fear of God (cf. 3.18; 5.7 (Heb. 5.6); 7.15–18;
12.1 ff.). In the fear of God the world which stands under the
condemnation of vanity opens itself up anew for Ecclesiastes,
so that he can joyfully take the good things coming to him (cf.
8.15, 9.8 ff.) as given him by God (cf. 2.24, 7.29), but also the
ills that come his way as equally coming from the hand of God,
although the meaning of them is hidden from the sight of man
(cf. 8.16 f.)[38]. From the 'all is vanity' which runs like a theme
tune through Ecclesiastes' utterances and remains constantly in
the background, the way leads for him to the fear of God. This
latter teaches mankind not to raise itself too high (cf. 7.16–18),
and puts in place of the hubristic delusion of being able to master
one's fate by one's own powers the task of moulding it in wisdom.

---

35. Cf. H. Gese, *Lehre und Wirklichkeit in der alten Weisheit*, Tübingen
1958, pp. 38 ff. and 45 ff.; on the discussion, H. H. Schmid, op. cit., pp.
147 ff.
36. Cf. above, pp. 392 f.
37. Cf. Kaiser, *NZST* 7, pp. 251 ff.
38. Cf. Gese, *Die Krisis der Weisheit*, pp. 150 f.

F. The Old Testament

§ 36 The Canon of the Old Testament

J. Fürst, *Der Kanon des alten Testaments nach den Überlieferungen in Talmud und Midrasch*, Leipzig 1868; H. Graetz, 'Der alttestamentliche Kanon und sein Abschluss', in *Kohelet oder der salomonische Prediger*, Leipzig 1871, pp. 147 ff.; T. Zahn, *Geschichte des neutestamentlichen Kanons* II, 1, Erlangen and Leipzig 1890; F. Buhl, *Canon and Text of the Old Testament*, Edinburgh 1892; A. Kuenen, 'Über die Männer der grossen Synagoge', in *Gesammelte Abhandlungen zur biblischen Wissenschaft*, Freiburg and Leipzig 1894, pp. 125 ff.; G. Hölscher, *Kanonisch und apokryph*, Leipzig 1905; E. König, *Kanon und Apokryphen*, BFchTh 21, 6, 1917; W. Staerk, 'Der Schrift- und Kanonbegriff der jüdischen Bibel', *Zeitschrift für Systematische Theologie* 6 (1929), pp. 101 ff.; W. Beyer, article *kanōn* [1938], *TDNT* III, Grand Rapids 1966, pp. 596 ff.; R. Meyer, *TDNT* III s.v. *kryptō*, C. Supplement on the Canon and the Apocrypha, pp. 978 ff.; A. Jepsen, 'Kanon und Text des Alten Testaments', *TLZ* 74 (1949), pp. 65 ff.; id., 'Zur Kanongeschichte des Alten Testaments', *ZAW* 71 (1959), pp. 114 ff.; G. Östborn, *Cult and Canon, A Study in the Canonization of the Old Testament*, UUÅ 1950, 10, 1950; P. Katz, 'The Old Testament Canon in Palestine and Alexandria', *ZNW* 47 (1956), pp. 191 ff.; A. C. Sundberg, 'The Old Testament of the Early Church', *HTR* 51 (1958), pp. 205 ff.; J. P. Lewis, 'What Do We Mean by Jabneh?', *Journal of Bible and Religion* 32 (1964), pp. 125 ff.; J. L. Koole, 'Die Bibel des Ben-Sira', *OTS* 14, 1965, pp. 374 ff.; J. C. H. Lebram, 'Aspekte der alttestamentlichen Kanonbildung', *VT* 18 (1968), pp. 173 ff.; J. D. Purvis, *The Samaritan Pentateuch and the Origin of the Samaritan Sect*, Harvard Semitic Monographs 2, Cambridge, Mass., 1968; G. Widengren, *Religionsphänomenologie*, Berlin 1969, pp. 580 ff.

1. Name and divisions. Since the middle of the fourth century A.D. the normative collection of sacred books of the Old and New Testaments has been called the *kanōn*. This usage derives from the concept of a norm contained in the Greek word, which is first found in Early Christianity in Paul, in Gal. 6.16. The

Greek word is derived from the word *kanē*, itself a loanword from Semitic, cf. the Hebrew *qāneh*, reed, and describes first of all the straight staff, then the measuring rod, and finally in a transferred sense the norm, the completed figure, the standard measure[1]. I assume that the reader is aware that the Old Testament was originally the only sacred book of early Christianity, which took it over from Judaism[2]. This collection of sacred books is known in Rabbinic and post-Rabbinic Judaism as *miqrā'*, a book designed for reading, as *hassēper*, the book, or as *kit̲b̲ê ḥaqqôd̲eš*, holy writings. The five books of the Pentateuch are called *tôrâ*, the law, or more precisely *ḥᵃmiššâ ḥumšê hattôrâ*, 'the five fifths of the Law'. The remaining sections are known together as *qabbālâ*, 'tradition', in what is clearly a qualitative distinction. The second part, the prophetic books or *nᵉb̲î'îm*, have been divided since the eighth century A.D. into the *nᵉb̲î'îm rî'šônîm*, or former prophets, and the *nᵉb̲î'îm 'aḥᵃrônîm* or latter prophets, although it is not clear whether these descriptions are to be understood as local or temporal. The 'former prophets' include the historical books of Joshua, Judges, Samuel and Kings, and the 'latter prophets' Isaiah, Jeremiah, Ezekiel and the Book of the Twelve Prophets. The Rabbis also knew however another arrangement of this latter group, in which Isaiah was placed after Ezekiel. The last group, known as the *kᵉt̲ûb̲îm* or writings, had the following order in the Babylonian tradition (cf. *b. Baba bathra* 14b): Ruth, Psalms, Job, Proverbs, Ecclesiastes, Canticles, Lamentations, Daniel, Esther, Ezra and Chronicles. In the Palestinian tradition on the other hand the order is supposed to have been Chronicles, Psalms, Job, Proverbs, Ruth, Canticles, Ecclesiastes, Lamentations, Esther, Daniel, Ezra. In this arrangement the five Megilloth or Festival Rolls stood together, although not in their chronological order. It was German medieval manuscripts which first carried through a chronological arrangement, so that Canticles (for the eighth day of the Passover), Ruth (for the second day of the Feast of Weeks), Lamentations (for the ninth of Ab, in memory of the destruction of Jerusalem), Ecclesiastes (for the third day of the Feast of Tabernacles) and Esther (for the Feast of Purim) come

1. Cf. W. Beyer, op. cit., pp. 596 ff.
2. Cf. W. G. Kümmel, *Introduction to the New Testament*, London 1966, pp. 334 ff.

in this order, and are placed after Psalms, Proverbs and Job, and before Daniel, Ezra and Chronicles. This is the order we are familiar with in our printed editions of the Hebrew Bible.

The Septuagint manuscripts have an arrangement which in general is much less artificial. According to a convincing conjecture of Eissfeldt* the division into historical books, books of edification and instruction, and prophets, corresponds to the three dimensions of time, past, present and future[3]. It should be observed first that the sequence and the number of books in the Greek majuscule manuscripts vary. Generally Ruth comes after Judges, and Chronicles after Samuel and Kings, which are numbered as the four books of Kings (or Reigns); Lamentations usually follows Jeremiah or Baruch. Since the Septuagint was the sacred book of the early Church, and has remained so for the Eastern Church, while the Vulgate translation of Jerome had to remain dependent on the Septuagint to gain acceptance in the Church, the threefold division of books in the Greek Bible has been retained in more recent translations too. It is perhaps realized by the reader that the Septuagint (and so also the Vulgate) contains a large number of books which are lacking in the Hebrew Canon, and since the time of Jerome, and in Protestantism since the time of Carlstadt and Luther, have been known as the Apocrypha. This includes 1 Esdras[4], three Books of Maccabees, Tobit, Judith, the Prayer of Manasseh, Additions to Daniel, Additions to Esther, Baruch, the Epistle of Jeremy, Sirach and the Wisdom of Solomon. A distinction is made between this group and the Pseudepigrapha, that is, properly, books which circulate under a pseudonym. These books have been passed down especially in the Oriental Churches, but some of them are occasionally admitted to manuscripts of the Septuagint. This fact makes it clear how fluid the boundaries of the Canon originally were in the Christian Church.

2. *Early history*. The early history of the Old Testament Canon remains largely obscure. Apart from the assumption, for which we have evidence, that the books of the Old Testament were already used at an early date in worship, and that there has been a continual development from the oral instruction given by priest or prophet to the reading of individual series of

3. P. 570.   4. Cf. above, p. 177.

instructions and collections of prophetic sayings, and finally to
the books which incorporate them, we have a series of witnesses
which allow us at least to delimit the process of canonization.
These are the Samaritan Pentateuch, Sirach (c. 190 B.C.), the
prologue to the Greek translation of Sirach by his grandson (c.
130 B.C.), the manuscript discoveries in the Judaean desert, the
quotations in the New Testament, the evidence of the Jewish
historian Josephus in his *Apologia contra Apionem*, 1,38 ff. (end
of the first century A.D.), 2 Esdras 14.44 ff. (approximately the
same date), the evidence of the Mishnah (c. 200) and of the
Gemara (especially *b. Baba bathra*, f. 14b/15a), of the Septuagint
manuscripts and of the Church Fathers[5]. Taken together these
witnesses suggests a picture somewhat as follows:

Doubts have been repeatedly expressed in recent years, and
with good reason, about the traditional assumption that the final
breach between the communities of Jerusalem and of the Samaritans took place as early as the end of the fourth century B.C. It
appears that the Samaritan Pentateuch represents a separate
development, starting only in the early first century B.C., of a
text form which until then was a general Palestinian form. It is
therefore no longer possible to draw the conclusion from the
Samaritan Pentateuch as such that the Pentateuch had already
reached its present form towards the end of the fourth century
B.C.[6] At present we can do no more than draw the conclusion,
on the basis of general considerations about the earlier history of
different forms of the text and about the beginnings of the
Septuagint translation, that the Pentateuch reached its position
of special dignity at the latest in the fourth century, and that by
that date the former prophets were probably already regarded as
being sacred books[7].

5. The facts given by the Church Fathers are made conveniently
accessible in T. Zahn, op. cit., and in part also in A. Jepsen, *ZAW* 71
(1959), pp. 114 ff. For the Mishnah and Gemara cf. H. L. Strack, *Introduction to the Talmud and Midrash*, Pennsylvania 1931, pp. 3 ff.

6. Cf. F. M. Cross, 'Aspects of Samaritan and Jewish History in Late
Persian and Hellenistic Times', *HTR* 59 (1966), pp. 201 ff., and J. D.
Purvis, op. cit., pp. 86 f. and 117 f. On the origin of the Samaritan schism
cf. also H. G. Kippenberg, *Garizim und Synagoge*, Religionsgeschichtliche Versuche und Vorarbeiten, Berlin 1971, pp. 57 ff. and 92 f.

7. Cf. J. Macdonald, *The Samaritan Chronicle No. II*, BZAW 107,
1969, pp. 8 f., 35 and 223.

Sirach provides evidence that this assumption is correct in emphasizing particularly in his 'Praise of the Fathers' after Moses Joshua, Caleb, the Judges, Samuel, Nathan, David, Solomon, Elijah, Elisha, Hezekiah, Isaiah and Josiah, and clearly looks back to the Deuteronomistic history in his remark that, apart from David, Hezekiah and Josiah, all the kings of Judah acted corruptly (cf. 46.1–49.6). Among the writing prophets alongside Isaiah, Jeremiah and Ezekiel he also mentions the Twelve Prophets, and this is a sign that the collection of prophetic books was also regarded as closed c. 200 B.C. (cf. 49.7–10)[8]. While we may leave the questions whether behind the collection of historical and prophetic books there lay originally an idea of a 'prophetic succession', and whether the concentration which can be observed in Sirach on the law is to be understood as the consequence of an anti-Hellenistic movement[9], Sirach's remarks in any case show clearly that he made no distinction in principle between the Biblical books and his own writings (cf. 24.33 and 50.29). We learn from the prologue to Sirach that the later division of the Canon into three parts actually existed already at the time of Sirach; for his grandson mentions explicitly that his grandfather had studied the law, *ho nomos*, the prophets, *hoi prophētai*, and 'the other books of the Fathers', *ta alla patria biblia*. By these *alla patria biblia* are meant our hagiographa (an expression coined by the Church Fathers for the *keṯûḇîm*, or writings). The way in which the grandson explains his grandfather's intention, and places his own translation of the book alongside those which existed already of the law, of the prophets and of 'the other books', *ta loipa tōn bibliōn*, shows that the boundaries of the third group were still fluid at the end of the second century B.C.

The situation is completely different when we turn to Josephus, *Contra Apionem*, 1.38 ff. For him there are only twenty-two books, a number which clearly results from treating Judges and Ruth, and Jeremiah and Lamentations, as each single units. Apart from the Psalms and the three Solomonic writings (Proverbs, Ecclesiastes and Canticles) he appears to have included all the other books of our Canon, except for the five books

8. Cf. also above, p. 305.

9. So J. H. C. Lebram, op. cit., pp. 183 ff., who at the same time assumes Hellenistic influence upon this legalism.

of the Torah, among the prophetic books. Counting the books of the Old Testament as twenty-two is attested as being usual among the Jews also by (Melito of Sardis), Origen and Jerome. Jerome is aware that the number of books is also reckoned among the Jews as being twenty-four. This number is also found in 2 Esdras 14.44 ff. and in *b. Baba bathra* 14b/15a. This is the same as that found in our Masoretic bibles. We must allow for the possibility that this represents a Babylonian tradition. It is not however the result of a later separation of the books of Ruth and Lamentations from Judges and Jeremiah. It reflects an older tradition. Katz and Sundberg conclude from the number and delimitation of the prophetic books and of the writings proper by Josephus that at the end of the first century A.D. the line drawn between prophets and hagiographa was still different in Palestine from that attested in *b. Baba bathra* 14b. It must however be considered whether Josephus in mentioning the thirteen prophetic books is not disregarding their place in the Canon, and has in mind only the inspiration which was supposed to have lasted from Moses to Artaxerxes I. When it is remembered that in the New Testament too books other than our canonical books are quoted as being of the same dignity as these are (cf. e.g. 1 Cor. 2.9, Luke 11.49, John 7.38, Eph. 5.14, Jas. 4.5, Jude 14), and that in Qumran, Murabba'at and Masada non-canonical books have also been found, it is at any rate clear that the canon implied by Josephus only won general acceptance in Judaism when the Pharisaic movement achieved an intellectual dominance in the period between the two Jewish revolts[10].

The Church, on the other hand, at first took over the local Jewish collections of books, as is shown by the differences in arrangement and number of the books in the older manuscripts of the Septuagint. In view of the controversy about the origins of the Septuagint it is at least open to doubt whether it followed Alexandrian tradition in this[11]. In the West, in spite of Jerome's attempt to introduce the Jewish Canon which had meanwhile

10. Cf. also F. M. Cross, jr., 'The Contribution of the Qumrân Discoveries to the Study of the Biblical Text', *IEJ* 16 (1966), pp. 81 ff., especially p. 95.

11. Cf. E. Würthwein, *The Text of the Old Testament*, London 1957, pp. 43 ff., and S. Jellicoe, *The Septuagint and Modern Study*, Oxford 1968, pp. 59 ff.

become operative, the Septuagint reasserted its position down to the final decision in favour of the canonicity of the Apocrypha at the Council of Trent, while the status of the Apocrypha remained disputed in the Eastern Church[12]. In Protestantism, although no dogmatic decisions were made, the Jewish canon came to prevail in practice as a result of the return by Luther and by the reformers to the *veritas hebraica*, the principle of the authoritativeness of the Hebrew.

In the passage of Josephus referred to already the factual criteria which cannot be separated from the idea of a canon in the strict sense are also found. According to him the prophetic age, which is decisive for the canonicity of a book, is confined to the period between Moses and Artaxerxes (I). While the delimitation at the time of Ezra may reflect a certain feeling of being epigones in the late post-exilic period[13], it is in the end primarily to be understood as polemically intended and directed against pseudepigraphic, and especially apocalyptic literature, as is also the upper limit in the time of Moses. It is possible that a bias against early Christianity is also at work[14]. As factual criteria for canonicity in Josephus may be mentioned in particular (i) inspiration (the period of the prophets), (ii) a specific number of books, and (iii) holiness, cf. the expressions *hiera grammata* or *hierai bibloi* (*Ant. Jud.* XX, 261 and 264). From this the sacrosanct character of the individual letter follows in the course of time as a fourth criterion. The specific sacredness of these books is reflected in the Rabbinic equation of the *kitᵉḇê haqqôdeš*, the holy writings, with those which defile the hands, *mᵉṭammᵉ'im 'eṯ-hayyāḏaim* (cf. *b. Yadaim* III, 5) and the belief in the sacrosanctity of the letter in the ever more careful transmission of the text down to the time of the Masoretes.

It has frequently, and correctly, been emphasized that the formation of such a theoretical idea of a canon can only be understood if it has been preceded by a fairly lengthy period in which the books later regarded as canonical already enjoyed the sort of respect that is given to a canon. It can be understood why the book of Sirach, a high evaluation of which is attested in Rabbinic

12. Cf. L. Vischer, *RGG* III³, cols. 1119 ff.

13. R. Meyer, op. cit., pp. 981 f.

14. So most recently A. C. Sundberg, jr., op. cit., p. 224, and J. L. Kool, op. cit., p. 387.

writings, could not win acceptance in view of its obviously late date of composition. The same is true of 1 Maccabees, Judith and Tobit, which Origen and Jerome still found circulating among the Jews.

3. The traditional Jewish view of the origin of the canon. The critical picture of the process of canonization which has just been sketched out contrasts with the Jewish tradition, which Elias Levita (d. 1549) won acceptance for in Protestantism too. According to him the collection and division of the canonical books into three was done by Ezra and the men of the Great Synagogue. Whatever view is taken of the Biblical tradition about Ezra[15], Neh. 5.7, the main witness, cannot be adduced in favour of this hypothesis. The name of the *kᵉneseṭ haggᵉḏôlā*, the 'Great Synagogue', is not attested before the middle of the second century A.D. The inclusion of later writings such as Daniel and Esther are a decisive argument against the assumption that the canon was closed in the fifth century B.C. Finally the view is still found to the present day among critical scholars that the beginning of the canonization of the Torah can be connected with Josiah's commitment to Deuteronomy, and the conclusion of it with the promulgation of the law by Ezra (cf. 2 Kgs. 23 and Neh. 8-10). But quite apart from the fact that these passages, especially the latter one, do not speak of a canonization or of the introduction of a new law, but of an alteration in the attitude of the people to the current law, Hölscher is probably correct in maintaining that both accounts are unhistorical or reinterpreted[16]. We must remain content then here with stating that the Deuteronomic and Deuteronomistic equation of the Torah with a written book (cf. e.g. Deut. 1.5; 4.8, 44; 27.3, 8, etc.), at least favoured, if it did not introduce, the later development; and that the Samaritan schism forms the *terminus ad quem* for the completion of the Pentateuch. In spite of the location of Daniel among the prophets in the Septuagint we must be cautious about drawing the conclusion that the group of the prophetic books had still not been closed at about 200. The evidence of Sirach argues against this.

15. Cf. above, pp. 181 and 184 f.
16. On Neh. 8 cf. now K. Pohlmann, *Studien zum dritten Esra*, FRLANT 104, 1970.

Finally the hypothesis that a firm delimitation of the hagiographa[17] first took place at a synod in Jamnia about A.D. 100, at which decisions were reached in favour of the canonicity of the books of Ecclesiastes and of Canticles, continues to be asserted to the present day[18]. With Lewis, it must be maintained (a) that there was no synod at Jamnia, but only a 'school' or 'congregation'[19], and (b) that we have no accounts of a general debate about the canon held there. The only witness is *b. Yadaim* III, 5. According to this the 72 elders, on the day of the installation of R. Eleazar b. Azariah in place of R. Gamaliel II as Nasi[20], declared that both Ecclesiastes and Canticles defiled the hands. But the context shows that the discussion about both books, which was already going on at the time of Jesus between the Schools of Hillel and of Shammai, went on later too, even if it was regarded as having been decided by reference to the decision of the 72. It can indeed be deduced that the very fact that the canonicity of both books was discussed only makes sense on the presupposition that both were in practice already regarded as canonical.

4. *Conclusion.* The only certain results then are that (i) canonization was preceded by a lengthy period in which the books were treated as canonical, (ii) the limits of the *keṯûḇîm* or writings remained fluid longest, and (iii) the Pharisaic canon won general acceptance in Judaism towards the end of the first century A.D. The idea of a canon was obviously formed in the course of the last century B.C. and of the first century A.D., in the circles of the Pharisees and of their forerunners, and consolidated among the rabbis.

17. The name *keṯûḇîm* is first found in *b. Sanhedrin* 90b on the lips of Gamaliel II, who was active about 80–117 A.D. as Nasi in Jamnia.

18. Cf. e.g. A. Jepsen, *TLZ* 74 (1949), col. 70.

19. J. P. Lewis, op. cit., pp. 126 ff.; cf. already H. H. Rowley, *The Growth of the Old Testament*, London 1950, p. 170.

20. Cf. *b. Berakhoth* 27b/28a.

Introductions to the Old Testament: A Selection

Anderson, G. W., *A Critical Introduction to the Old Testament*, London 1959.

Baudissin, W. W. Graf, *Einleitung in die Bücher des Alten Testamentes*, Leipzig 1901.

Bentzen, A., *Introduction to the Old Testament I–II*, Copenhagen 1952[2].

Bertholdt, L., *Historischkritische Einleitung in sämmtliche kanonische und apokryphische Schriften des alten und neuen Testaments*, I–IV, Erlangen 1812–19.

Bewer, J. A., *The Literature of the Old Testament*, New York 1922, 1933[2] (for ed. 3 see under Kraeling below).

Bleek, F., *Eintleitung in das Alte Testament*, ed. J. F. Bleek and A. Kamphausen, rev. J. Wellhausen, Berlin 1878[4] (1893[6]).

Budde, K., *Geschichte der althebräischen Litteratur*, Leipzig 1906, 1909[2].

Cornill, C. H., *Introduction to the Canonical Books of the Old Testament* [1891], London 1907.

Driver, S. R., *An Introduction to the Literature of the Old Testament*, Edinburgh 1891, 1913[9].

Eichhorn, J. G., *Einleitung ins Alte Testament*, I–III, Leipzig 1780–3; I–V, Göttingen 1823–4[4].

Eissfeldt, O., *The Old Testament. An Introduction* [1934; 1964[3]], Oxford 1965.

Engnell, I., *Gamla Testamentet I: en traditionshistorisk inledning*, Stockholm 1945.

Fohrer, G., *Introduction to the Old Testament* [1965], Nashville, Tennessee 1968, London 1970 (rev. of Sellin).

Gottwald, N. K., *A Light to the Nations. An Introduction to the Old Testament*, New York 1959.

Gunkel, H., 'Die israelitische Literatur', in *Kultur der Gegenwart*, ed. Hinneberg, I, 7, Leipzig 1906, pp. 51 ff.; 1925[2], pp. 53 ff., reprinted separately Darmstadt 1963.

Hempel, J., *Die althebräische Literatur und ihr hellenistischjüdisches Nachleben*, Wildpark, Potsdam 1930–4; Berlin 1968[2].

Hylmö, G., *Gamla Testamentets Litteraturhistoria*, Lund 1938.

Kraeling, E. G., *The Literature of the Old Testament*, New York and London 1962[3] (rev. of Bewer).

Kuenen, A., *Historisch-critisch onderzoek naar het ontstaan en de verzameling van de boecken des Ouden Verbonds* I–III, Leiden 1861–5; 1885–93[2];

German tr. *Historisch-kritische Einleitung in die Bücher des alten Testaments, hinsichtlich ihrer Entstehung und Sammlung* I–III, Lepizig 1887–1894; ET of Pt. 1, *An Historico-critical Inquiry into the Origin and Composition of the Hexateuch,* London 1886.

Kuhl, C., *The Old Testament, Its Origins and Composition* [1953], Edinburgh 1961; *Die Entstehung des Alten Testaments,* ed. G. Fohrer, Munich 1960².

Lods, A., *Histoire de la littérature hebraïque et juive depuis les origins jusqu'à la ruine de l'état juif (135 après J.C.),* Paris 1950.

Mayer, R., *Einleitung in das Alte Testament* I–II, Munich 1965–7.

Meinhold, J., *Einführung in das Alte Testament. Geschichte, Literatur und Religion Israels,* Giessen 1919, 1932³.

Oesterley, W. O. E. and **Robinson, T. H.,** *An Introduction to the Books of the Old Testament,* London 1934.

Pfeiffer, R. H., *Introduction to the Old Testament,* New York 1941, London 1952.

Reuss, E., *Die Geschichte der Heiligen Schriften Alten Testaments,* Brunswick 1881.

Riehm, E., *Einleitung in das Alte Testament,* rev. and ed. A. Brandt I–II, Halle 1889–90.

Robert, A. and **Feuillet, A.,** *Introduction to the Old Testament* [1957] New York 1968.

Rost, L., *Einleitung in das Alte Testament,* Heidelberg 1959⁹ (rev. of Sellin).

Rowley, H. H., ed., *The Old Testament and Modern Study. A Generation of Study and Research,* Oxford 1951.

Sellin, E., *Einleitung in das Alte Testament,* Leipzig 1910, 1935⁷, ed. L. Rost, Heidelberg 1950⁸; ET of ed. 3, *Introduction to the Old Testament,* London 1923.

Steuernagel, C., *Lehrbuch der Einleitung in das Alte Testament mit einem Anhang über die Apokryphen und Pseudepigraphen,* Tübingen 1912.

Weiser, A., *Introduction to the Old Testament* [1939], London 1961.

de Wette, W. M. L., *Lehrbuch der historisch-kritischen Einleitung in die kanonischen und apokryphischen Bücher des Alten Testaments,* Berlin 1817, 1845⁶, ed. E. Schrader 1869⁸; ET of ed. 5, *A Critical and Historical Introduction to the Canonical Scriptures of the Old Testament,* 2 vols., Boston 1843.

Index

The books of the Old Testament can be found through the list of Contents, and are not included in this index.